Foundations of Bilingual Education and Bilingualism

BILINGUAL EDUCATION & BILINGUALISM

Series Editors: **Nancy H. Hornberger** *(University of Pennsylvania, USA)* and **Wayne E. Wright** *(Purdue University, USA)*

Bilingual Education and Bilingualism is an international, multidisciplinary series publishing research on the philosophy, politics, policy, provision and practice of language planning, Indigenous and minority language education, multilingualism, multiculturalism, biliteracy, bilingualism and bilingual education. The series aims to mirror current debates and discussions. New proposals for single-authored, multiple-authored, or edited books in the series are warmly welcomed, in any of the following categories or others authors may propose: overview or introductory texts; course readers or general reference texts; focus books on particular multilingual education program types; school-based case studies; national case studies; collected cases with a clear programmatic or conceptual theme; and professional education manuals.

Full details of all the books in this series and of all our other publications can be found on http://www.multilingual-matters.com, or by writing to Multilingual Matters, St Nicholas House, 31–34 High Street, Bristol BS1 2AW, UK.

BILINGUAL EDUCATION & BILINGUALISM: 106

Foundations of Bilingual Education and Bilingualism

6th Edition

Colin Baker and Wayne E. Wright

MULTILINGUAL MATTERS

Bristol • Blue Ridge Summit

Library of Congress Cataloging in Publication Data
A catalog record for this book is available from the Library of Congress.
Names: Baker, Colin – author. | Wright, Wayne E., author.
Title: Foundations of Bilingual Education and Bilingualism/Colin Baker and Wayne E. Wright.
Description: 6th edition. | Bristol: Multilingual Matters, [2017]
   | Series: Bilingual Education & Bilingualism: 106 | Previous edition: 2011.
   | Includes bibliographical references and index.
Identifiers: LCCN 2016043801| ISBN 9781783097210 (hbk : alk. paper) |
   ISBN 9781783097203 (pbk : alk. paper) | ISBN 9781783097241 (kindle)
Subjects: LCSH: Education, Bilingual. | Education, Bilingual – Great Britain.
   | Bilingualism. | Bilingualism – Great Britain.
Classification: LCC LC3715 .B35 2017 | DDC 370.117/5–dc23
LC record available at https://lccn.loc.gov/2016043801

British Library Cataloguing in Publication Data
A catalogue entry for this book is available from the British Library.

ISBN-13: 978-1-78309-721-0 (hbk)
ISBN-13: 978-1-78309-720-3 (pbk)

Multilingual Matters
UK: St Nicholas House, 31-34 High Street, Bristol BS1 2AW, UK.
USA:NBN, Blue Ridge Summit, PA, USA.

Website: www.multilingual-matters.com
Twitter: Multi_Ling_Mat
Facebook: https://www.facebook.com/multilingualmatters
Blog: www.channelviewpublications.wordpress.com

Typeset in Sabon and Frutiger by R. J. Footring Ltd, Derby
Printed and bound in the UK by Short Run Press Ltd

Contents

Acknowledgements

The first edition commenced in the early 1990s when Colin was asked by the founder of Multilingual Matters, Mike Grover, to 'consider writing THE textbook on Bilingual Education'. The Multilingual Matters team, past and present, have continually encouraged and facilitated the six editions: in particular Ken Hall, Marjukka Grover, Tommi Grover, Anna Roderick, Sarah Williams, Ellie Robertson and Laura Longworth.

Tommi Grover, as Managing Director of Multilingual Matters, was instrumental in bringing in Wayne as a co-author with Colin on this 6th edition. Tommi's enthusiastic support for this book and our collaboration has been inspirational and instrumental.

Anna Roderick, as Editorial Director and Commissioning Editor, worked closely with us in the compilation and production of this 6th edition. Completion could not have occurred without her enthusiasm for this project and her expertise.

Multilingual Matters perceptively appointed Ofelia García (The Graduate Center, City University of New York) as Academic Consultant when this project began in the early 1990s. She has consistently provided wise and judicious advice for all six editions. Much gratitude is owed to Ofelia who helped to shape this book from its beginnings to this 6th edition. *Muchas gracias.*

In the previous five editions, the following scholars were thanked for their support, advice and expertise: Panos Athanasopoulos, Hugo Baetens Beardsmore, Claudine Brohy, Jasone Cenoz, Tony Cline, Jim Crawford, Jim Cummins, Margaret Deuchar, Nancy Dorian, Viv Edwards, Peter Garrett, Tamar Gollan, Nancy Hornberger, Annick De Houwer, Meirion Prys Jones, Sylvia Prys Jones, Sharon Lapkin, Christer Laurén, Hilaire Lemoine, Gwyn Lewis, Karita Mard, Stephen May, Aneta Pavlenko, Trevor Payne, Bernard Spolsky, Merrill Swain, Terry Wiley, Cen Williams, Iolo Wyn Williams, and the person who became co-author of this 6th edition – Wayne Wright.

For the 6th edition, various scholars gave expert advice on improvements and needed developments. We wish to offer our great thanks to the following reviewers appointed by Multilingual Matters for their constructive, perceptive and expert analysis and advice on draft chapters: Sarah Compton, Jean-Marc Dewaele, Ofelia García, Alsu Gilmetdinova, Juliet Langman, Gigi Luk, Kate Mahoney, Terri McCarty, Trevor Payne, Peter Sayer, Ruth Swanwick and Terry Wiley.

Particular and special thanks go to Becky H. Huang (Bicultural-Bilingual Studies, University of Texas at San Antonio) for her excellent revision and update of Chapter 7. It has been a great pleasure to work with a young and outstanding scholar.

We also owe a debt of gratitude to former and current graduate research assistants Matthew Kraft and Yeng Yang (University of Texas at San Antonio) and Alsu Gilmetdinova, Sungae Kim and Chen Li (Purdue University) for their immense help with formatting, reformatting, proofreading, reference checking and updating, library and internet research, and assistance with the development of the glossary for this 6th edition. The department of Bicultural-Bilingual Studies at the University of Texas at San Antonio, and the Department of Curriculum and Instruction at Purdue University graciously provided funding for these outstanding students, as well as support for Wayne through a faculty development leave and course releases.

From Colin: Working on bilingualism has been inspired by my Welsh wife, Anwen, and our three bilingual children (Sara, Rhodri and Arwel). For over 30 years, they have taught me the gifts of bilingualism that go beyond language. Five greatly loved grand-children (Ioan Tomos, Joseff Rhys, Lily Enfys, Brenig Iorwerth and Steffan Tomos) allow me to observe and celebrate with them the thrilling experiences of simultaneous bilingualism from birth. *Diolch yn fawr iawn am bopeth.*

From Wayne: I had the privilege of growing up in an English-speaking home with a love for language learning. My parents studied Chinese, Hebrew, and Greek. Between myself and my five siblings are varying levels of intermediate to advanced proficiency in Spanish, Chinese, Korean, Khmer (Cambodian), Modern Yucatec Mayan, and even in Ancient Maya Hieroglyphs. My life as a bilingual continues to be inspired by my dear wife of 20+ years, Phal Mao – a native of Cambodia – and our children Jeffery Sovan, Michael Sopat, and Catherine Sophaline – as we share in our adventures of living and loving in a bilingual home. សូមអរគុណ !

From Colin & Wayne: The help and support given to us by those mentioned above has been extremely generous and received with great gratitude. However, the responsibility is ours for all that is not perfect.

Colin Baker
Wayne E. Wright

Permissions

Every attempt has been made to contact copyright holders and gain permissions where needed. If there are any omissions, we will be pleased to correct them in the next edition.

Introduction

The 6th edition of this book is intended as a comprehensive and modern introduction to bilingual education, bilingualism and multilingualism (as bilingualism often includes multilingualism). Written from a multidisciplinary perspective, the book covers a wide range of topics: individual and societal concepts in minority and majority languages; childhood developmental perspectives; general bilingual education issues; bilingual classrooms and political and ideological perspectives. Bilingualism and multilingualism relates to, for example, the use of two or more communication systems, identity and personality, globalization and assimilation, thinking and reading, education and employment, politics and culture. All of these, and more, are encapsulated in this book.

In compiling six editions, increasingly tough decisions have been made as to what to include and exclude, what to present in detail and what to summarize, what assumptions to explore and what to take 'as read'. We have been asked: 'Why don't you put Chapter X earlier?' We agree, everything should be earlier. Other frequently asked questions are 'Why don't you expand on Y?', 'Why don't you leave out Z because it is irrelevant to me?', 'Why can't we have an edition just for our region?' and 'Why isn't a chapter in an earlier edition still included?' What follows are some explanations.

An attempt is made to balance the psychological and the sociological; macro and micro education issues; the linguistic and the socio-political with discussion at individual and societal levels; and to be inclusive of major international concerns in bilingualism, multilingualism and bilingual education, based on research evidence and theory. Faced with the many social and political challenges that surround bilinguals and multilinguals, students will find in this book an attempt to analyze constructively those problems and recognize the positive values and virtues of a future multilingual world.

This book starts with definitional, sociological and psychological issues that are essential to understanding bilingual/multilingual children and bilingual education. Later discussions of bilingual education and bilingual classrooms are built on that foundation. However, the book is more than a cross-disciplinary foundation with a series of education layers built on top. Within the boundaries of clarity in writing style and structuring, explicit inter-connections are made between chapters.

In writing the book, a constant challenge has been 'From whose perspective?' There are majority language mainstream viewpoints, relatively advantaged minority language viewpoints and various disadvantaged minority language viewpoints. There are left-wing and right-wing politics, activist and constructivist ideas, debates about globalization, immigration, Europeanization, regionalism and preserving grassroots. The book attempts to represent a variety of viewpoints and beliefs. Where possible, multiple perspectives are shared. Readers and reviewers (including on YouTube) have kindly pointed out some of the hidden and implicit assumptions made, and kindly provided alternative viewpoints that we have tried to represent faithfully in the text. Where there are conclusions and dominating perspectives, we are responsible.

Another issue has concerned generalization and contextualization. The book is written for an international audience to reflect ideas that transcend national boundaries. The book attempts to locate issues of international generalizability. Unfortunately, space limits discussion of a variety of regional and national language situations. There are many other writings mentioned in the chapters that will provide necessary contextualization. Where particular situations have been discussed (e.g. US debates), it is often because of the thoroughness of documentation, plenty of research evidence, and the depth of analysis in the surrounding literature.

In an attempt to make the contents of this book relevant to a variety of contexts and regions, various chapters focus on integrating theories. From one individual research study, it is usually impossible to generalize. A study from Europe may say little about North America. Results on six year-olds may say nothing about 16 or 60-year-olds. Research on middle-class children speaking French and English in a bilingual school may say little or nothing about children from a lower social class in a bilingual environment where a second language is likely to replace the first language. From a mass of research, but occasionally despite a paucity of research, a theoretical framework will attempt to outline the crucial parameters and processes. Thus a theoretical framework on a particular area of bilingualism may attempt to do one or more of the following: attempt to explain phenomena; integrate a diversity of (apparently contradictory) findings; locate the key parameters and interactions operating; be able to predict outcomes and patterns of bilingual behavior; be capable of testing for falsification or refinement; express the various conditions that will allow the theory to be appropriate in a variety of contexts.

However, in providing a relatively comprehensive synthesis of bilingualism, multilingualism and bilingual education, the danger lies in suggesting that there is a systematic coherence to the subject. While some teachers and many students want 'recipes' and clear assertions, the current state of our knowledge and understanding rarely provides that clarity. The book therefore attempts to represent contested positions, varied viewpoints and the limitations of research and theory.

New to the 6th Edition

What are the specific changes in the 6th edition? There are many. First, to address the large number of in-text citations and a reference list that grew substantially with each new edition, we have cut over 860 citations. We focused on removing older and redundant references, while preserving citations to classic studies, seminal works, and other scholarship of historical and significant value. We also added over 350 citations to more recent scholarship on current developments in policy and practice, new theoretical constructs, and new and important research findings, most of which have been published after the 5th edition (2011). All demographic and other statistical information has been fully updated.

Second, given the book's growing length with each subsequent edition, we made a deliberate effort to shorten the text by removing some sections and condensing or re-writing others to preserve the most salient points. These cuts made space for many new sections, tables, figures and textboxes. Several chapters have been reorganized, and some have new titles to better reflect their updated content. Even with these additions, the book as a whole has been slightly shortened.

Third, and importantly, there are many new and more thoroughly covered topics including, for example: multilingualism; dynamic bilingualism; translanguaging; transliteracy; transglossia; heteroglossia; multiliteracies; superdiversity; language variation; translanguaging among Deaf students; bilingual assessment; the hybrid, constructed, complex and fluid nature of identity; coercive vs. collaborative relations of power; bilingualism and economic inequalities and advantages; digital tools for language revitalization; forces, mechanisms and counterweights in building bilingual education systems; technology-enhanced language proficiency assessments; recent developments in and limitations of brain imaging research; and bilingualism on the internet and in information technology. New or greater focus on a variety of instructional approaches and issues including: Child-friendly schools, Education For All (EFA), content and language integrated instruction (CLIL), sheltered English immersion (SEI), the Sheltered Instruction Observation Protocol (SIOP), Literacy Squared, bilingual special education, bilingual gifted and talented education, the International Baccalaureate (IB), and international schools. Important policy developments in the US context are covered, including the Common Core State Standards, ESEA Flexibility, the Every Student Succeeds Act (ESSA), the Seal of Biliteracy, response to intervention, and state consortia for shared English language proficiency standards and assessments (WIDA, ELPA21), and for alternative assessments for disabled students (National Center and State Collaborative, and Dynamic Learning Maps). Efforts have also been made to update and diversify the global examples of research, policy and practice, with a particular focus on adding examples outside of Europe and North America.

Fourth, several formatting changes have been made to improve the visual look of the text. Tables, figures, and text boxes have been re-formatted and numbered. A comprehensive glossary has been added, and **bolded terms** in each chapter have corresponding glossary entries. Fifth, end of chapter recommended readings and study activities have been updated and revised, plus discussion questions and web resources have been added (see below). All websites were accessed and checked prior to publication.

In short, the 6th edition has been thoroughly revised and updated. The textual and formatting changes provide an improved reading experience, and the updated and expanded end-of-chapter resources and activities provide a valuable resource for course instructors, professional development providers, study-group leaders and engaged individual readers.

Chapter Organization

At the beginning of the book (Chapter 1) there is a needed introduction to the language used in discussing bilingual education and bilingualism. Not only are important terms introduced, but also key concepts, distinctions and debates which underpin later chapters are presented. There are important dualisms and paradoxes throughout the study of bilingualism and multilingualism: for example, the individual bilingual person as different from groups and societies where bilinguals live; the linguistic view compared with the sociocultural and socio-political view; language skills and language competences; codeswitching and translanguaging. The opening chapters (1 to 8) present foundational issues that precede and influence discussions about bilingual education. Before we can sensibly talk about bilingual education, we need to tackle questions such as:

- Who are bilinguals and multilinguals?
- How does bilingual education fit into minority language maintenance, language decline and language revival?
- How does a child become bilingual or trilingual?
- What effect does the home and the neighborhood play in developing bilingualism and multilingualism?
- Does bilingualism have a positive or negative effect on thinking?
- What do we know about bilingualism in the brain?

Chapters 9 to 16 focus on the many aspects of bilingual and multilingual education. They commence with a broad discussion of different types of bilingual education, followed by an examination of the effectiveness of those types. After a focus on systems of bilingual education, the book proceeds to examine bilingual classrooms, multiliteracies and biliteracy, and key bilingual education strategies. The underlying questions are:

- Which forms of bilingual education are more successful?
- What are the aims and outcomes of different types of bilingual education?
- What are the essential features and approaches of a classroom fostering bilingualism?
- What are the key problems and issues of bilingual classrooms?
- Why are deaf people an important group to study both as bilinguals and in terms of bilingual education?

Chapters 17 and 18 are central to understanding bilingualism, multilingualism and bilingual education. They consider the political and cultural dimensions that surround bilingualism in society (and bilingual education in particular). Different views of the overall value and purpose of bilingualism and multilingualism join together many of the threads of the book. The finale of the book (Chapter 19) takes a look at the present and future with themes of multilingualism and the internet, employment, mass media, economy and tourism.

Thus the concluding issues of the book include:

- Why are there different viewpoints about language minorities and bilingual education?
- Why do some people prefer the assimilation of language minorities and others prefer linguistic diversity?
- How does bilingualism and multilingualism relate to particular employment, economic, technological and leisure developments in the modern world?

End-of-Chapter Resources

Recommended Readings (Updated) – Readers who wish to delve deeper into the topics covered in the chapter are referred to recent books or articles.

On the Web (New to the 6th edition) – Directs interested readers to relevant websites, videos, articles, broadcasts, images and other online resources.

Discussion Questions (New to the 6th edition) – Questions to engage students in meaningful discussions in small groups, in online forums, or for self-study on chapter topics.

Study Activities (Updated) – These are designed for students wishing to extend their learning by engaging in various practical activities. Such activities are flexible and adaptable. Instructors and students will be able to vary them according to local circumstances.

Finale

To end the beginning. Over five editions, the book became a major introduction to bilingual education and bilingualism. It has been studied by thousands of students in many countries of the world. This 6th edition provides a major and comprehensive update based on a new international partnership of two expert scholars. We hope you will read and learn, but also become interested and inspired, enthused and excited by topics that are of increasing importance in a rapidly changing world.

Bilingualism: Definitions and Distinctions

Bilingualism: Definitions and Distinctions

Introduction

Since a bicycle has two wheels and binoculars are for two eyes, it would seem that **bilingualism** is simply about two languages. **Multilingualism** is then about three or more languages. The aim of this chapter is to show that the ownership of two or more languages is not so simple as having two wheels or two eyes. Is someone bilingual if they are fluent in one language but less than fluent in their other language? Is someone bilingual if they rarely or never use one of their languages? Or if they have memorized a handful of words and phrases in another language from a tourist guidebook? Such questions need addressing before other topics in this book can be discussed.

To understand the answers to these questions, it is valuable to make an initial distinction between bilingualism and multilingualism as an individual characteristic, and bilingualism and multilingualism in a social group, community, region or country. Bilingualism and multilingualism can be examined as the possession of the individual. Various themes in this book start with bilingualism as experienced by individual people. For example, a discussion of whether or not bilingualism affects thinking requires research on individual **monolinguals**, bilinguals and multilinguals.

From sociology, **sociolinguistics**, politics, geography, education and social psychology comes a 'group' perspective. Bilinguals and multilinguals are usually found in groups. Thus linguists study how the vocabulary of bilingual groups changes across time. Geographers plot the density of bilinguals and minority language speakers in a country. Educationalists examine bilingual educational policy and provision for particular language groups. Such groups may be located in a particular region (e.g. Basques in Spain), or may be scattered across communities (e.g. the Chinese in the US).

The initial distinction is therefore between bilingualism (and multilingualism) as an individual possession and as a group possession. This is usually termed **individual bilingualism** and **societal bilingualism**. Like most distinctions, there are important links between the two parts. For example, the attitudes of individuals towards a particular minority language may affect **language maintenance**, language restoration, and downward **language shift** or **language death** in society. In order to understand the term 'bilingualism', some important further distinctions at the individual level are discussed in this chapter. (While bilingualism and multilingualism are different, where there is similarity multilingualism is – for the sake of brevity – combined under bilingualism.) An introduction to bilingualism and multilingualism as a group possession (societal bilingualism) is provided in Chapters 3 and 4.

If a person is asked whether he or she speaks two or more languages, the question is ambiguous. A person may be able to speak two languages, but tends to speak only one language in practice. Alternatively, the individual may regularly speak two languages, but competence in one language may be limited. Another person will use one language for conversation and another for writing and reading. Yet another may mix their languages in creative ways when communicating with other bilinguals. An essential distinction is therefore between language *ability* and language *use*. This is sometimes referred to as the difference between degree and function.

Terminology

Before discussing the nature of language use and abilities, a note about **terminology**. To understand bilingualism and bilingual education, an awareness of often-used terms and distinctions is needed. For example, apart from language ability there is **language achievement, language competence, language performance, language proficiency** and **language skills**. Do they all refer to the same thing, or are there subtle distinctions between the terms? To add to the problem, different authors and researchers sometimes tend to adopt their own specific meanings and distinctions.

Some Dimensions of Bilingualism

(1) **ABILITY**: Some bilinguals actively speak and write in both languages (**productive** competence), others are more **passive bilinguals** and have **receptive** ability (understanding or reading). For some, an ability in two or more languages is well developed. Others may be moving through the early stages of acquiring a second language and are **emergent bilinguals** (O. García, 2009a). Ability is thus on a dimension or continuum (Valdés, 2003) with dominance and development varied across speakers.

(2) **USE**: The **domains** (**contexts**) where each language is acquired and used are varied (e.g. home, school, street, phone, email). An individual's different languages may be used for different purposes. For example, one language is used at home and another in school.

(3) **BALANCE**: Rarely are bilinguals and multilinguals equal in their ability or use of their two or more languages. Often one language is dominant, and this can change over time.

(4) **AGE**: When children learn two languages from birth, this is often called **simultaneous bilingualism** or infant bilingualism or 'bilingual first language acquisition' (De Houwer, 2009; Valdés, 2015). If a child learns a second language after about three years of age, the terms consecutive or **sequential bilingualism** tend to be used. Chapters 5 and 6 consider age issues in detail.

(5) **DEVELOPMENT**: **Incipient bilinguals** have one well-developed language, and the other is in the early stages of development. When a second language is developing, this is **ascendant bilingualism**, compared with **recessive bilingualism** when one language is decreasing, resulting in temporary or permanent **language attrition**.

(6) **CULTURE**: Bilinguals typically become more or less **bicultural** or **multicultural**. It is possible for someone (e.g. a foreign language graduate) to have high proficiency in two languages but be relatively **monocultural**. A process of **acculturation** accompanies language learning when immigrants, for example, learn the majority

language of the host country. Bicultural competence tends to relate to knowledge of language **cultures**; feelings and attitudes towards those two cultures; behaving in culturally appropriate ways; awareness and empathy; and having the confidence to express biculturalism. Culture, however, is dynamic, and a bilingual's biculturalism is likely to be an ever shifting hybrid mix of their two cultures, into what some scholars refer to as the 'third space' (Bhabha, 2004).

(7) **CONTEXTS**: Some bilinguals live in bilingual and multilingual **endogenous communities** that use more than one language on an everyday basis. Other bilinguals live in more monolingual and monocultural regions and network with other bilinguals by vacations, phone, text messaging, email and social media, for example. Where there is an absence of a second language community, the context is exogenous (e.g. Russian bilinguals in the US). Some contexts may be subtractive, where the politics of a country favors the replacement of the home language by the majority language (e.g. Korean being replaced by Japanese in Japan). This particularly occurs among immigrant bilinguals (e.g. in the US and UK). Other contexts are additive such that a person learns a second language at no cost to their first language, as occurs in **elite** (or **prestigious**) bilinguals.

(8) **CHOICE:** Elective bilingualism is a characteristic of individuals who choose to learn a language, for example in the classroom (Valdés, 2003). Elective bilinguals typically come from majority language groups (e.g. English-speaking North Americans who learn French or Arabic; Chinese-speakers in China who learn English). They add a second language without losing their first language. **Circumstantial bilinguals** learn another language to function effectively because of their circumstances (e.g. as immigrants). Their first language is insufficient to meet their educational, political and employment requirements, and the communicative needs of the society in which they are placed. Circumstantial bilinguals are groups of individuals who must become bilingual to operate in the majority language society that surrounds them. Consequently, their first language is in danger of being replaced by the second language – a subtractive context. The difference between elective and circumstantial bilingualism is important because it immediately locates differences of prestige and status, politics and power among bilinguals.

An Individual's Use of Bilingualism

Grosjean (2012: 4) proposes a definition of bilingualism that places emphasis on the regular use of languages rather than fluency (as well as including multilinguals and those who speak a dialect): '*bilinguals are those who use two or more languages (or dialects) in their everyday lives*'. Valdés (2015: 38) offers a similar definition but with a focus on ability to function: 'Bilingual/multilingual individuals share one key characteristic: they have more than one language competence. They are able to function (i.e. speak, understand, read, or write) even to a very limited degree in more than one language'.

Language use cannot be divorced from the context in which it is used, nor from the effects of the interactions of different combinations of people in a conversation. Language is not produced in a vacuum; it is enacted in changing dramas. As props and scenery, audience, co-actors, the play and roles change, so does language. As the theatre and stage where we act changes, so does our use of two or more languages. Communication includes not only the structure of language (e.g. grammar, vocabulary) but also who is saying what, to whom, in which circumstances. One person may have limited linguistic skills but, in certain situations, be successful in communication. Another person may have relative linguistic mastery, but through undeveloped social interaction skills or in a strange circumstance, be relatively unsuccessful in communication. The social environment where the two languages function is crucial to understanding bilingual usage. Therefore, this section now considers the use and function of an individual's two languages.

An individual's use of their bilingual ability (**functional bilingualism**) moves into language production across a wide range of everyday contexts and events. Functional bilingualism concerns when, where, and with whom people use their two languages. The table below provides examples of the different targets (people) and contexts (often called domains) where functional bilingualism is enacted in different role relationships.

Table 1.1 Examples of language targets and contexts

Examples of language targets	Examples of language contexts (domains)
Nuclear family	Shopping
Extended family	Visual and auditory media (e.g. TV, radio, DVD)
Work colleagues	Printed media (e.g. newspapers, books)
Friends	Cinema, nightclubs, theater, concerts
Acquaintances	Work
Neighbors	Correspondence, telephone, email, official
Religious leaders	communication
Teachers	Clubs, society, organizations, sporting activities
Presidents, principals, other leaders	Leisure and hobbies
Bureaucrats	Religious meetings
Complete strangers	Information and communications technology
Local community	(e.g. email, texting, internet, social media)

Language Choice

Not all bilinguals have the opportunity to use both their languages on a regular basis. Where a bilingual lives in a largely monolingual community, there may be little choice about language use from day-to-day. However, in communities where two or more languages are widely spoken, bilinguals may use both their languages on a daily or frequent basis. When bilinguals use both their languages, there is often language choice. If the other person is already known to the bilingual, as a family member, friend or colleague, a relationship has usually been established through one language. If both are bilingual they have the option of changing to the other language (e.g. to include others in the conversation) or to use a mix of both languages as they communicate.

If the other person is not known, a bilingual may quickly pick up clues as to which language to use. Clues such as dress, appearance, age, accent and command of a language may suggest to the bilingual which language it would be appropriate to use. In bilingual areas of Canada and the United States for example, employees dealing with the general public may glance at a person's name on their records to help them decide which language to use. A person called Pierre Rouleau or Maria García might be addressed first in French or Spanish, rather than English.

An individual's own attitudes and preferences will influence their choice of language. In a minority/majority language situation, older people may prefer to speak the minority language. Teenagers from the 1.5 or second generation, for example, may reject the minority language in favor of the majority language because of its higher status and more fashionable image. A comment from a trilingual Chinese-Cambodian refugee high school student who arrived in the United States at a young age illustrates how perceptions about language and **identity** may affect language choice; in describing her language preference, she said, 'English has all the words to describe how I feel'.

In situations where the native language is perceived to be under threat, some bilinguals may seek to avoid speaking the majority or **dominant language** to assert and reinforce the status of the other language. For example, French-Canadians in Québec sometimes refuse to speak English in shops and offices to emphasize the status of French.

Li Wei, Milroy and Ching (1992), in a study of a Chinese community in northern England, indicate that the degree of contact with the majority language community is a factor in language choice. Chinese speakers who were employed outside the Chinese community were more likely to choose to speak English with other Chinese speakers, in contrast those with less daily contact with English speakers were more likely to use Chinese with other Chinese–English bilinguals.

Sayer's (2012) ethnographic work in Oaxaca, Mexico demonstrates the ambiguities and tensions surrounding language choice as experienced by local (Mexican) English teachers. For example, one teacher described her hesitancy to help translate for a foreigner struggling to communicate with a pharmacist out of fear of being viewed as a 'show off' by other Mexican customers. Another teacher described a conflict he had with a guy at a football pitch. During the confrontation (in Spanish), one of the guy's friends came over and said in English 'Hey, take it easy! What's the problem?' The teacher viewed the sudden interjection in English as this guy looking down on him, showing off, 'putting on airs' because he had lived in 'el norte' (The North/USA), demonstrating what he called a 'pocho attitude'. The teacher, who was well-educated and who had also spent time in the US, refused to respond to 'pocho guy' in English (despite the urging of friends) because he didn't want to 'drop down to his level'.

Some minority languages are mostly confined to a private and domestic role. This happens when a minority language has historically been disparaged and deprived of status. In western Brittany in France, for example, many Breton speakers only use their Breton in the family and with close friends. They can be offended if addressed by a stranger in Breton, believing that such a stranger is implying they are uneducated and cannot speak French.

An individual may also switch languages, either deliberately or subconsciously, to accommodate the perceived preference of the other participant in the conversation. A language switch may be made as one language is regarded as the more prestigious or as more appropriate for the other person. To gain acceptance or status, a person may deliberately and consciously use the majority language. Alternatively, a person may use a minority language as a form of affiliation or belonging to a group.

Bilingual and Multilingual Ability

The Four Language Skills

J. Edwards (2013) suggests that 'language repertoire expansion is not a particularly rare feat' and asserts 'all normally intelligent people can at least become functional in another language' (pp. 14–15). However, if we confine the question 'Are you bilingual?' to ability in two languages, the issue becomes 'what particular ability?' There are four basic language domains, abilities or skills: listening, speaking, reading and writing. As Table 1.2 illustrates, these four abilities fit into two dimensions: receptive or productive skills, and oracy or literacy.

Table 1.2 The four basic language skills

	Oracy	Literacy
Receptive skills	Listening	Reading
Productive skills	Speaking	Writing

Table 1.2 suggests avoiding a simple classification of who is, or is not, bilingual. Some speak a language, but do not read or write in the language. Some listen and read in a language with understanding (passive bilingualism) but do not speak or write that language. Some understand a spoken language but do not themselves speak that language. To classify people as either bilinguals or monolinguals is thus too simplistic. Or, to return to the opening analogy, the two wheels of bilingualism exist in different sizes and styles. O. García (2009a) suggests that a more accurate depiction of the complex and dynamic nature of bilingualism than the two wheels of a bicycle is a moon buggy with its intricate wheel system capable of moving in multiple directions across varied terrains. The four basic language skills do not exist in black and white terms. Between black and white are not only many shades of gray; there also exist a wide variety of colors. Each language skill can be more or less developed. Reading ability can range from simple and basic to fluent and accomplished. Someone may listen with understanding in one context (e.g. shops) but not in another context (e.g. an academic lecture). Many bilingual and multilingual individuals in African and Asian nations speak home languages with no writing systems, but may be literate in a standardized variety of a regional or national language.

These examples show that the four skills can be further refined into sub-scales and dimensions. There are skills within skills such as pronunciation, extent of vocabulary, correctness of grammar, the ability to convey exact meanings in different situations and variations in style. However, these skills tend to be viewed from an academic or classroom perspective. Using a language on the street and in a shop requires a greater focus on social competence with language (e.g. the idioms and 'lingo' of the street).

The range and type of sub-skills that can be measured is large and debated. Language abilities such as speaking or reading can be divided into increasingly microscopic parts. What in practice is tested and measured to portray an individual's bilingual performance is considered later in the book. What has emerged so far is that a person's ability in two languages is multidimensional and will tend to evade simple categorization.

Minimal and Maximal Bilingualism

So far, it has been suggested that deciding who is or is not bilingual or multilingual is difficult. Simple categorization is arbitrary and requires a value judgment about the minimal competence needed to achieve a label of 'bilingual'. Therefore, a classic definition of bilingualism such as 'the native-like control of two or more languages' (Bloomfield, 1933) appears too extreme and maximalist ('native-like'). The definition is also ambiguous; what is meant by 'control' and who forms the 'native' reference group?

At the other end is a minimalist definition, as in Diebold's (1964) concept of incipient bilingualism. The term incipient bilingualism allows people with minimal competence in a second language to squeeze into the bilingual category. Tourists with a few phrases and business people with a few greetings in a second language could be incipient bilinguals. Almost every adult in the world knows a few words in another language. The danger of being too exclusive is not overcome by being too inclusive. Trawling with too wide a fishing net will catch too much variety and therefore make discussion about bilinguals ambiguous and imprecise. Trawling with narrow criteria may be too insensitive and restrictive.

Valdés (2003) suggests one possibility is to view bilinguals as existing on a continuum as illustrated in Figure 1.1, where A and B are the two languages. The first letter is the stronger language, and font sizes and case suggest different proficiencies:

Language A												Language B
Monolingual	A$_b$	A$_b$	A$_b$	Ab	Ab	AB	BA	Ba	Ba	B$_a$	B$_a$	B$_a$	Monolingual

Figure 1.1 Bilingual language proficiency continuum

However, as Grosjean and Li (2013) point out:

> Bilinguals usually acquire and use their languages for different purposes, in different domains of life, with different people. Different aspects of life often require different languages. (p. 12)

They call these different uses of a bilingual's languages for different functions as the complementarity principle. Thus, a bilingual's 'stronger' language may vary depending on the context (e.g. at home, at school, at work, at church). Consider, for example, a Latina graduate student in a US university who works as a bilingual teacher and who is active in a Spanish-speaking church. She may feel more competent in English when discussing educational theories, feel competent in both languages when teaching children, and feel more competent in Spanish in discussing and practicing her religion. Thus a complex but more accurate view of a bilingual's proficiency may be shown in Figure 1.2.

	Language A												Language B
Context 1	Monolingual	A$_b$	A$_b$	Ab	Ab	Ab	AB	BA	Ba	Ba	Ba	B$_a$	B$_a$	Monolingual
Context 2	Monolingual	A$_b$	A$_b$	Ab	Ab	Ab	AB	BA	Ba	Ba	Ba	B$_a$	B$_a$	Monolingual
Context 3	Monolingual	A$_b$	A$_b$	Ab	Ab	Ab	AB	BA	Ba	Ba	Ba	B$_a$	B$_a$	Monolingual
Context 4	Monolingual	A$_b$	A$_b$	Ab	Ab	Ab	AB	BA	Ba	Ba	Ba	B$_a$	B$_a$	Monolingual
Etc...													

Figure 1.2 Complexity of bilingual language proficiency

If each of these contexts were broken down by proficiencies across each of the four basic language skills (i.e. listening, speaking, reading and writing), an even more complex, multifaceted representation of bilingualism emerges.

Who is or is not categorized as a bilingual will depend on the purpose of the categorization. At different times governments, for example, may wish to include or exclude language minorities. Where an indigenous language exists (e.g. Irish in Ireland), a government may wish to maximize its count of bilinguals. A high count may indicate government success in **language planning**. In comparison, in a suppressive, **assimilationist** approach, immigrant minority languages and bilinguals may be minimized (e.g. Asian languages in the UK in the Census – see Chapter 2).

Is there a middle ground in-between maximal and minimal definitions? The danger is in making arbitrary cut-off points about who is bilingual or not along the competence dimensions. Differences in classification will continue to exist among different authors. One alternative is to move away from the multi-colored canvas of proficiency levels to a portrait of the everyday use of the two languages by individuals.

The literature on bilingualism, however, frequently spotlights one particular group of bilinguals whose competences in both languages are well developed (i.e. those at AB or BA on the above continua). Someone who is approximately equally fluent in two languages across various contexts and domains has been termed an equilingual or ambilingual or, more commonly, a balanced bilingual. As will be considered in Chapter 7, balanced bilinguals are important when discussing the possible thinking advantages of bilingualism.

Balanced bilingualism is mostly used as an idealized concept. Rarely is anyone equally competent in two or more languages across all their domains. As the complementarity principle asserts, most bilinguals will use their languages for different purposes and with different people. Balanced bilingualism is also a problematic concept for other reasons. The balance may exist at a low level of competence in the two languages that are nevertheless approximately equal in proficiency. Or, they may have well-developed languages but in non-standard varieties that are less valued by the broader society. Or, they may equally draw upon two well-developed languages that they frequently mix in creative and effective communicative ways. While these are within the literal interpretation of 'balanced bilingual', they are not the sense employed by many researchers on bilingualism. The implicit idea of balanced bilingualism has often been of 'appropriate' competence in the standard variety of both languages, typically in academic contexts. Thus, a student who can fully understand the delivery of the curriculum in school in either language, and effectively participate in classroom activities in either language would be an example of a balanced bilingual.

Given its rarity, is 'balanced bilingualism' of use as a term? While it has limitations of definition and measurement, it has proved to be of value in research and theory (see Chapter 7). However, categorizing individuals into such groups raises the issue of comparisons. Who is judged 'normal', proficient, skilled, fluent or competent? Who judges? The danger is in using monolinguals as the point of reference, as will now be considered.

An argument advanced by several scholars (see, e.g. Grosjean & Li, 2013) is that there are two contrasting views of individual bilinguals. First, there is a **monolingual** (or fractional) view of bilinguals, which evaluates the bilingual as 'two monolinguals in one person'. There is a second, holistic (or multicompetence) view which argues that the bilingual is not the sum of two complete or incomplete monolinguals, but that he or she has a unique linguistic profile. We now consider these views in more detail.

The Monolingual View of Bilingualism

Despite the fact that between half and two-thirds of the world's population is bilingual to some degree, a monolingual (or monoglossic) view of bilingualism takes monolingualism as the norm. Thus monolingual English-speakers in countries such as the US and England may consider bilinguals to be an oddity or inferior. Valdés (2015: 39) explains:

> Embedded with the **discourse** of monolingualism are strong beliefs about (a) the dangers of early bilingualism, (b) the negative effects of 'unbalanced' bilingualism on individuals, and (c) the expectation that the 'true' or 'real' bilingualism will be identical to native speakers in both their languages.

A monolingual view leads many teachers, administrators and politicians to treat the two languages of a bilingual as separate distinct systems, as if students are two monolinguals in one. Such a view leads to overly-simplistic notions of languages simply being added or subtracted from the mind of the bilingual. The monolingual view is closely associated with the **language-as-a-problem orientation**, leading to education programs that either restrict the use of the home language or to only use it temporarily to transition students as quickly as possible to the dominant school language. Even in some stronger forms of bilingual education, a monolingual view can lead to the insistence on the strict separation of the students' languages (e.g. by time, day or subject) (Wright, 2015) (see Chapter 10).

One expectation from this fractional viewpoint is for bilinguals to show a proficiency comparable to that of a monolingual in both their languages. If that proficiency does not exist in both languages, especially in the majority language, then bilinguals may be denigrated and classified as inferior. This perceived lack of proficiency is often determined by standardized language proficiency tests in English or other languages spoken by the bilingual students in which their scores are compared to those of monolingual speakers. This results in misleading and deficit-oriented labels to describe students. One enduring label from the 1970s describes such students as '**semilinguals**' (or 'double semilinguals'), suggesting students lack vocabulary, grammar knowledge, and ability to express themselves fully in either language. MacSwan *et al.* (2002) documented a common practice in many US schools of labeling Latino immigrant children as both 'non-English speaking' and 'non-Spanish-speaking' based on the results of language proficiency tests, and referring to such students as 'non-nons'. More recently, the label 'long-term English language learners' (LTELLs) is commonly used across the US to describe students classified as '**limited English proficient**' (**LEP**) for five or more years (Menken & Kleyn, 2010; Olsen, 2010). These labels evoking the construct of 'semilingualism' from a monolingual view of bilingualism are unfair and are more politically-motivated than accurate or commonplace (N. Flores *et al.*, 2015).

A number of scholars have pointed out the major problems with 'semilingualism' and its associated terms (Edelsky *et al.*, 1983; MacSwan, 2000; MacSwan & Rolstad, 2003; MacSwan *et al.*, 2002; Menken & Kleyn, 2010; Wiley, 2005; Wiley & Rolstad, 2014). First, these terms have disparaging and belittling overtones that invoke expectations of underachievement and failure. Second, if languages are relatively undeveloped, the origins may not be in bilingualism per se, but in the economic, political and social conditions that create such under-development. Third, as noted above, most bilinguals use their two languages for different purposes in different contexts. Thus, a person may be competent in some domains but not in others. Fourth, the educational tests used to measure language proficiencies measure only standard varieties of languages and typically measure only a small, unrepresentative sample of a person's daily language behavior (see Chapter 2). Finally, these terms often serve to misrepresent and marginalize the language practices of **language minority** communities of color. For example,

N. Flores *et al.* (2015) interviewed New York high school students officially classified as LTELLs who strongly disagree with the school's classification of their language proficiency:

Candido: We already know English and all that stuff.
Claudia: For most of us, it's like our first language, I mean our main language.
Yamile: 'Cuz they think we don't know much English, but we do. Just 'cuz we know another language. (p. 129)

Flores *et al.* argue these 'are not students lacking language, but (emergent) bilinguals with a repertoire that allows them to maneuver multiple languages and contexts in ways that are complex and dynamic' (p. 130).

These criticisms do not detract from the fact that there are language abilities in which people do differ. This may not be the result of being bilingual. Economic and social factors or educational provision may, for example, be the cause. Rather than highlight an apparent 'deficit' in language development, the more equitable and positive approach is to emphasize that, under the right conditions, students are capable of developing high-levels of competence in a standardized language variety. Instead of concentrating negatively on a 'language deficit', a more proper approach is to locate the causes in, for example, the type of language tests used, material deprivation, in the type and quality of schooling, and not in language itself (see Chapters 9, 15 and 17). Second language users are not deficient communicators. They need to be seen as legitimate speakers of a language in their own right. Students in the process of developing proficiency in a new language are more accurately viewed as emergent bilinguals (O. García, 2009a). 'Emergent bilinguals' is a wide-ranging term accenting future language development towards fuller bilingualism. The term is increasingly preferred by many to labels such as '**English Language Learners**' (**ELLs**) and the deficit-oriented label 'Limited English Proficient' (LEP) students, because these labels do not acknowledge the students' other language(s). 'Emergent bilinguals' appears to include most second and third language learners, but with no obvious end-point when 'emergent' finishes. Importantly, this term suggests a more holistic view of bilinguals.

The Holistic View of Bilingualism

Those who take a holistic or **heteroglossic perspective** of bilingualism view bilingualism as the norm, and treat the languages of a bilingual as interconnected and co-existing (Wright, 2015), or, as making up a single linguistic system (O. García & Li Wei, 2014). Hopewell and Escamilla (2015: 39) explain:

Holistic understandings of bilingualism are grounded in the idea that what is known and understood in one language contributes to what is known and understood in the other, and that all languages contribute to a single and universally accessible linguistic and cognitive system.

O. García (2009a) introduced the term **dynamic bilingualism** to focus on the ways bilinguals draw on the range of features associated with socially-constructed languages within their linguistic repertoire in complex and dynamic ways as they communicate with others and engage in collaborative tasks. As explained by O. García and Li Wei (2014):

Unlike the view of two separate systems that are added (or even interdependent), a dynamic conceptualization of bilingualism goes beyond the notion of two autonomous languages, of a first language (L1) and a second language (L2), and of **additive or subtractive bilingualism**. Instead, dynamic bilingualism suggests that the language practices of bilinguals are complex and interrelated; they do not emerge in a linear way or function separately since there is only one linguistic system. (pp. 13–14)

García extends Welsh educator Cen Williams' (1994) concept of **translanguaging** to describe the natural ways bilinguals use their languages in their everyday lives as they make sense of their bilingual worlds. In contrast to 'monolingual view' practices that insist on strict separation of languages in the classroom, taking a holistic dynamic view of bilingualism, C. Williams (1994) and O. García and Li Wei (2014) argue for the use of translanguaging as a pedagogical tool for teaching and learning (see Chapter 13).

The languages of bilinguals may also be viewed positively as multicompetences (Grosjean & Li, 2013). Grosjean (2008) uses an analogy from the world of athletics, and asks whether we can fairly judge a sprinter or a high jumper against a hurdler. The sprinter and high jumper concentrate on one event and may excel in it. The hurdler concentrates on two different skills, trying to combine a high standard in both. With only a few exceptions, the hurdler will be unable to sprint as fast as the sprinter, or jump as high as the high jumper. This is not to say that the hurdler is a worse athlete than the other two. Any comparison of who is the best athlete makes little sense. This analogy suggests that comparing the language proficiency of a monolingual with a bilingual's dual language or multilingual proficiency is similarly unjust.

There is sometimes a political reality that deters the blossoming of a holistic view of the bilingual. In Australia, much of Canada, the United States and the United Kingdom, the dominant English-speaking monolingual politicians and administrators tend not to accept a different approach or standard of **assessment** (one for monolinguals, another for bilinguals). There is also the issue of preparation for the employment market. In countries like Wales, where first-language Welsh-speaking children compete in a largely English-language job market against monolingual English speakers, the dominant view is that they should be given the same English assessments at school.

Yet a bilingual is a complete linguistic entity, an integrated whole. Levels of proficiency in a language may depend on which contexts (e.g. street and home) and how often that language is used. We turn next to considerations of the language proficiency of bilinguals.

Language Proficiency

So far, this chapter has centered on the variety of language abilities and the danger of categorization using a small or biased selection of language sub-skills. One issue has been whether a wide variety of sub-skills can be reduced to a small number of important dimensions. J.W. Oller and Perkins (1980) have suggested that there exists a single factor of **global language proficiency**. This view is associated with attempts to quantitatively measure language proficiency through standardized tests. It has led to the view of a singular **'academic language' proficiency** essential for success in the classroom.

The idea of a single factor of global language proficiency is contentious as the evidence indicates that there are both global and specific aspects of language proficiencies. Most (but not all) language tests narrowly focus on language use in academic contexts (see Chapter 2). Reading and writing tests are obvious examples. Such tests leave qualitative differences between people unexplored. Out-of-school communicative profiles of people are relatively ignored.

This narrow view of a singular form of 'academic language proficiency' led to the proposal that there is a conceptually distinct category of conversational competence (Cummins, 2000b). This includes the ability to hold a simple conversation in the shop, on the street, or on the playground. This dichotomy suggests that conversational language competence may be acquired fairly quickly (e.g. two to three years), but it is not enough to cope with classroom instruction. Academically-related language competence in a second language may take from five to eight years or longer to acquire. This divide between 'conversational' and 'academic' language proficiency has been called a false dichotomy and a misrepresentation of the complex nature of language acquisition and proficiency (Valdés et al., 2015; Wiley & Rolstad, 2014). This debate is considered in detail later in the book (see Chapter 8).

Communicative Competence

The language theories of the 1960s tended to center on language skills and components. The skills comprise listening, speaking, reading and writing, and the components of knowledge comprise grammar, vocabulary, **phonology** and graphology. These earlier models did not indicate how skills and knowledge were integrated. For example, how does listening differ from speaking? How does reading differ from writing? Earlier models fail to probe the competence of 'other' people in a conversation. In a conversation, there is negotiation of meaning between two or more people. Real communication involves anticipating a listener's response, understandings and misunderstandings, sometimes clarifying one's own language to ensure joint understanding, plus the influence of different status and power between people.

Earlier models tended to be purely linguistic and ignore the social contexts where language is used. A more sociolinguistic approach examines actual content and context of communication called 'speech acts' or the 'ethnography of communication'. This approach includes looking at the rules of dual language usage among bilinguals, their shared knowledge in conversation, and the culturally, socially and politically determined language norms and values of bilingual speech events.

Various holistic models of language competence have been developed. One of the most widely accepted is **communicative competence**. This view of language proficiency was first proposed by Hymes (1972) in direct contrast to Chomsky's cognitive theory of language with its narrow focuses on the ability of native speakers to produce grammatically correct sentences. Hymes, a leading founder of sociolinguistics, argued that language proficiency considerations must include the types of knowledge speakers need to communicate competently with others in a given **speech community** (Richards & Rodgers, 2014). Canale and Swain (1980) further developed Hymes' construct by identifying and describing four dimensions of communicative competence: grammatical, discourse, sociocultural and **strategic competence**. Richards and Rodgers (2014) note that the many attempts to further refine the notion of communicative competence since it was first introduced provides evidence of its usefulness. Communicative competence provides the foundation for the **communicative language teaching (CLT)** approach prevalent today and has been influential on other widely-used communicative frameworks including the American Council on the Teaching of Foreign Languages (ACTFL) standards for foreign language learning, the Common European Framework of Reference for Languages and the Canadian Language Benchmarks (Duff, 2014). A description of the four dimensions of communicative competence by Savignon (2001, pp. 17–18) appears in Table 1.3.

Table 1.3 Communicative competence

Competences	Description
Grammatical competence	Is concerned with sentence level grammatical forms, the ability to recognize the lexical, morphological, syntactic and phonological features of a language and to make use of these features to interpret and form words and sentences.
Discourse competence	Is concerned with the interconnectedness of a series of utterances, written words, and/or phrases to form a text, a meaningful whole. Includes both bottom-up and top-down text processing and concerns with text coherence and cohesion.
Sociocultural competence	An understanding of the social context in which language is used: the roles of the participants, the information they share, and the function of the interaction.
Strategic competence	The coping strategies used in unfamiliar contexts, with constraints due to imperfect knowledge of rules or limiting factors in their application such as fatigue or distraction.

Note that this model of communicative competence is inclusive of the types of linguistic knowledge reflected in earlier models of language proficiency (i.e. grammatical and discourse competence), but here the emphasis is on the use of these skills for meaningful communication within the social context, hence the integration with sociocultural competence. This competence is sensitivity to the context where language is used, ensuring that language is appropriate to the person or the situation. This may entail sensitivity to differences in local geographical dialect, sensitivity to differences in **register** (e.g. the register of boardroom, baseball, bar and bedroom). Sociocultural competence may also refer to sensitivity to speaking in a native-like or natural way. This will include cultural variations in grammar and vocabulary (e.g. Black English). Another part of sociocultural competence is the ability to interpret cultural references and figures of speech. Sometimes, to understand a particular conversation, one needs inner cultural understanding of a specific language. A Welsh figure of speech such as 'to go round the Orme' (meaning 'to be long-winded') is only fully understandable within local northern Welsh cultural idioms. Similarly, students new to English may find western cultural idioms such as 'piece of cake' (meaning 'a simple or easy task to do') to be confusing, even when they know the meaning of each word. Sociocultural competence also includes the kind of knowledge needed in greeting people and leave-taking, in expressing feelings and persuading, matters of politeness in a particular context, the style and formality of language, and even body language (e.g. smiles, eye contact), and the use of silence.

Another important issue within the social context is how speakers cope communicatively when in less familiar contexts, when confronted with unfamiliar vocabulary or expressions, or when they need to express an idea for which they lack the precise vocabulary or structures. Strategic competence addresses strategies learners may use to compensate for gaps in their knowledge, such as requesting their interlocutors to repeat, speak more slowly, or to ask for clarification. Learners may paraphrase their own speech as needed to avoid use of unknown words and structures (e.g. substituting 'long soft chair' for unknown word 'sofa').

The holistic view of language proficiency reflected in the construct of com-municative competence has led to attempts to create language proficiency assessments that measure communicative ability (see, e.g. Bachman & Palmer, 1996; Fulcher & Davidson, 2007; Purpura, 2017). The emphasis has therefore moved over time from the linguistic to the communicative, to interactional competence and the adaptivity of a person in using two or more languages. Since competence in a language is viewed as an integral part of language performance and not abstracted from it, measuring language competence cannot just use pencil and paper tests, but also needs to investigate the language of genuine communication. Instead of tests that are artificial and stilted (e.g. language dictation tests), communicative performance **testing** involves creative, un-predictable, contextualized conversation. However, predicting 'real world' performance from such tests, and the 'one sidedness' that ignores the reality that conversations are jointly constructed and negotiated, remains problematic. This suggests that it will be difficult to measure communicative proficiency in an unbiased, comprehensive, valid and reliable way.

Discussions of language competence often move to questions about the extent to which can we measure a bilingual's performance in their two languages? How can we portray when, where and with whom people use their two languages? What are the problems and dangers in measuring bilinguals? These questions provide the themes for the next chapter.

Conclusion

Defining exactly who is or is not bilingual is essentially elusive and may ultimately be impossible. Some categorization, however, is often necessary and helpful to make sense of the world. Therefore categorizations and approximations may be required. Simple narrow definitions such as 'native-like control of two languages' (Bloomfield, 1933) offer little help as they are intrinsically arbitrary and ambiguous. Overly broad definitions that include anyone who can utter a few words or phrases in another language are also of little help.

A more helpful approach may be to locate important distinctions and dimensions surrounding the term 'bilingualism' that help to refine our thinking. The fundamental distinction is between bilingual ability and bilingual usage. Some bilinguals may be fluent in two languages but rarely use both. Others may be much less fluent but use their two languages regularly in different contexts. Bilinguals frequently translanguage, drawing from their linguistic repertoire in creative and effective ways to communicate with other bilinguals. Many other patterns are possible. Languages are not static; bilingualism is dynamic and students growing up with or learning new languages are 'emergent bilinguals' (O. García, 2009a).

Profiling a person's use of their two languages raises questions about when, where and with whom? This highlights the importance of considering domain or context. As a bilingual moves from one situation to another, so may the language being used in terms of type (e.g. Spanish, English or translanguaging), content (e.g. vocabulary) and style. Over time and place, an individual's two languages are never static but ever changing and evolving.

In terms of ability in two languages, the four basic domains are listening, speaking, reading and writing. With each of these proficiency dimensions, it is possible to fragment into more detailed dimensions (e.g. pronunciation, vocabulary, grammar, meaning and style). Those sub-dimensions can subsequently be further dissected and divided.

Creating a multidimensional, elaborate structure of bilingual proficiency may make for sensitivity and precision. However, ease of conceptualization and brevity require simplicity rather than complexity. Therefore simple categorization is the paradoxical partner of complex amplification. This chapter has considered problematic categories such as balanced bilingualism, semilingualism, long term English language learners, and monolingual (one-factor) views of language ability. These categories have received some depth of discussion and critical response in the research literature. As will be revealed in later chapters, these categories also relate to central research on bilingualism and bilingual education.

The chapter considered theories of the structure of language competence. In particular, the focus has been on linking a linguistic view of language competence with a social communicative competence view. Language can be decomposed into its linguistic constituents (e.g. grammar, vocabulary). It is also important to consider language as a means of making relationships and communicating information. This important dualism will follow us through the book: ability and use; the linguistic and the social; competence and communication.

Key Points in This Chapter

➤ There is a difference between bilingualism as an individual possession and two or more languages operating within a group, community, region or country.

➤ At an individual level, there is a distinction between a person's ability in two languages and their use of those languages.

➤ Bilinguals typically use their two languages with different people, in different contexts and for different purposes.

➤ Language domains are listening, speaking, reading and writing.

➤ Balanced bilinguals with equal and strong competence in their two languages are rare.

➤ Dynamic bilingualism focuses on the ways bilinguals draw on their linguistic repertoire in complex and dynamic ways as they communicate with others.

➤ There is a difference between a monolingual view of bilinguals and a holistic view.

➤ The monolingual view sees bilinguals as two monolinguals inside one person.

➤ The holistic view sees bilinguals as a complete linguistic entity, an integrated whole.

➤ Translanguaging describes the natural ways bilinguals use their languages in their everyday lives as they make sense of their bilingual worlds.

➤ Language competence includes not only linguistic competence (e.g. vocabulary, grammar) but also competence in different social and cultural situations with different people.

> ➤ Communicative competence considers the types of knowledge speakers need to communicate competently with others in a given speech community. A common model considers grammatical, discourse, sociocultural and strategic competence.

Suggested Further Reading

📖 Bhatia, T. K., & Ritchie, W. C. (Eds.). (2013). *The handbook of bilingualism and multilingualism* (2nd ed.). Malden, MA: Wiley-Blackwell.

📖 Grosjean, F. (2012). *Bilingual: Life and reality*. Cambridge, MA: Harvard University Press.

📖 Martin-Jones, M., Blackledge, A., & Creese, A. (Eds.). (2012). *The Routledge handbook of multilingualism*. New York, NY: Routledge.

📖 Stavans, A., & Hoffman, C. (2015). *Multilingualism*. Cambridge, UK: Cambridge University Press.

On the Web

💻 Life as a Bilingual – The Reality of Living with Two Languages (Blog)
https://www.psychologytoday.com/blog/life-bilingual

💻 International Journal of Bilingual Education and Bilingualism
http://www.tandf.co.uk/journals/1367-0050

💻 International Multilingual Research Journal
http://www.tandfonline.com/loi/hmrj20#.VYNSvlVViko

💻 Multilingual Children's Association
http://www.multilingualchildren.org/

Discussion Questions

(1) Do you consider yourself and/or people known to you as bilingual or multilingual? Would you describe yourself, or someone known to you, as 'balanced' in ability and use of two or more languages or somewhere else along the continuum represented in Figure 1.1? Which language or languages do you think in? Does this change in different contexts? In which language or languages do you dream, count numbers, pray and think aloud?

(2) What are the differences between taking a monolingual vs. a holistic view of bilingualism? Discuss some of the common beliefs or practices in your local area regarding bilingualism and which view they seem most closely aligned with.

(3) View the YouTube video *One Semester of Spanish – Love Song* (https://youtu.be/ngRq82c8Baw). Would you argue that Mike is bilingual? Discuss why or why not based on the various criteria for bilingualism described in this chapter. How would you also describe Mike's understanding/portrayal of Hispanic culture?

Study Activities

(1) This activity can be based on self-reflection or you may wish to interview someone who is bilingual or multilingual. Make a table or diagram to illustrate how one person's dual or multilingual ability and language usage has changed and developed since birth. Write down how different contexts have affected that change and development. The diagram or table should illustrate the life history of someone's languages indicating changes over time and over different contexts.

(2) In a school with which you are most familiar, find out how students are labeled and categorized in terms of their languages. Who applies what labels? Which students are seen positively and negatively? Are there consequences of labels? Is there interest in the language competences and language use of multilingual students?

(3) Explore the linguistic diversity of an area of the US using the American Fact Finder tool from the US Census Bureau (http://factfinder.census.gov). On the front page, enter your county, city, town or zip code into the Community Facts box. On the left side, click on the 'Origins and Language' tab. Report on your findings and discuss what these demographics reveal about the linguistic diversity of the community.

CHAPTER 2

The Measurement of Bilingualism

The Measurement of Bilingualism

Introduction

The topic of measuring bilinguals and multilinguals both elaborates and illuminates the previous discussion about definitions, dimensions and distinctions. Problems of defining bilinguals are illustrated by the measurement and categorization of such individuals and groups. This chapter, therefore, begins by clarifying the different reasons for measuring bilinguals and multilinguals. This occurs not only in education but also in society (e.g. censuses). Illustrations are then given of such measurement as well as ways of profiling the **language ability** and use of individuals and language groups. It is important to develop a critical awareness of language measurement, both in the internal limitations of measurement and the politics surrounding language **testing**.

It is customary to try to categorize the complexity of individual differences in **bilingualism**. We make sense of our world by continual classification. People are constantly compared and contrasted. Yet the simplification of categorization often hides the complexity of individuality. Individual differences are reduced to similarities. Yet over-complexity can be unwelcome and confusing. The measurement of bilinguals attempts to locate similarities, order and pattern.

Ambiguity of Language Assessment Terminology

The **terminology** associated with language tests and **assessments** is often confusing and ambiguous. **Language skills** tend to refer to highly specific, observable, measurable, clearly definable components such as pronunciation, spelling or handwriting. **Language competence** is a broad and general term, used particularly to describe an underlying system of an inner, mental representation of language, something latent rather than overt. **Language performance** becomes the outward evidence for language competence. By observing general language comprehension and production, language competence may be inferred. Language ability and **language proficiency** tend to be used more as 'umbrella' terms and therefore used somewhat ambiguously. For some, language ability is a general, latent disposition, a determinant of eventual language success. For others, it tends to be used as an outcome, similar to but less specific than language skills, providing an indication of current language level. Similarly, language proficiency is sometimes used synonymously with language competence; at other times as a specific, measurable outcome from language testing. However, both language proficiency and language ability are distinct from **language achievement** (attainment), which is usually seen as the outcome of formal instruction. Language proficiency and language ability are, in contrast, viewed as the product of a variety of mechanisms: formal learning, informal non-contrived language acquisition (e.g. on the street) and individual characteristics such as 'intelligence'.

The Purposes of the Measurement of Bilinguals

The measurement of bilinguals can take place for a variety of purposes (Bailey & Carroll, 2015). It is valuable to differentiate between some of these overlapping aims.

Distribution

An example of the measurement of bilinguals is census questions requesting information about ability or usage in two or more languages (e.g. in US, Canada, Ireland). Such census data estimates the size and distribution of bilinguals in a particular area. For example, the California Department of Education conducts an annual survey to determine the number of speakers of 65 specific languages among over 6 million PreK-12 students. In a recent report, however, schools reported over 13,000 speakers of other non-English languages, suggesting there could be hundreds of other languages. Linguists map the proportion and geographic location of regional and minority language groups. For examples, see the Ethnologue website: http://www.ethnologue.com/.

Selection

Bilinguals can be distinguished as a 'separate' group for selection purposes. For example, a school may wish to allocate children to classes, sets, streams, groups or tracks based on their degree of bilingual proficiency or language background. Bilinguals may be assessed for placement in bilingual, **sheltered instruction**, mainstream, or **special education** classes (see Chapter 15). A different example is measuring bilinguals at the outset of research. An investigation may require the initial formation of two or more groups (e.g. 'balanced' bilinguals, 'partial' bilinguals and **monolinguals**).

Summative and Formative Assessments

Language assessments may be used for summative or formative purposes. **Summative assessment** means 'totaling up' to indicate the destination a person has reached in their language-learning journey, for example, at the end of a semester or a school year. When measuring the current performance level of a person, a wide variety of language proficiency and achievement tests are available (e.g. reading comprehension, reading vocabulary). Such tests may be used in schools to measure the four basic language skills. In a minority language **context**, emphasis is often on measuring proficiency in both the minority language and the majority language.

A test or assessment that gives feedback (and feed-forward) during learning, and aids further development, is **formative assessment.** An example would be an assessment of a student's oral presentation or evaluation of a student's writing. The results are used to determine the student's strengths and to plan subsequent lessons focused on areas of needed improvement. MacDonald *et al.* (2015) make a distinction between *formative assessment* and *assessment for formative purposes*. Traditionally, formative assessment is understood to occur 'in the midst of instruction and compares students' ongoing progress to possible trajectories of learning' and thus 'can help identify the most productive next steps of instruction' (p. xi). In contrast, *assessment for formative purposes* 'is a much broader category of tools and processes that could be used to shape instruction over time' (p. xii). Thus any type of language assessment could be a formative assessment if the results are used to analyze and shape language instructional practices. For example, a student may be profiled on a precise breakdown of language skills to provide facilitative feedback to the teacher that directly leads to action. If the test reveals areas where a child's language needs developing, there can be immediate intervention and remedial help. A diagnosis of a problem in language may lead to the formation of a plan to effect a remedy (see Chapter 15 for more details).

Norm- and Criterion-referenced Language Tests

Measurements of bilinguals may also be used for purposes of comparison or determining level of mastery. Language proficiency tests may be classified as **norm-referenced or criterion-referenced tests.** Standardized **norm-referenced tests** essentially compare one individual with others, as IQ tests or college placement exams (e.g. SAT). A norm-referenced test of reading ability, for example, may enable the teacher to compare one student with a national or regional average (norm). The student can then be placed in an ordered list with descriptors such as 'the top 16%', '32nd percentile', 'above average' or 'bottom quartile'. However, when norm-referenced tests compare bilinguals with monolinguals, the results may misrepresent the linguistic abilities of bilingual students (Gathercole, 2013; Grosjean, 2008) (see Chapter 1).

In contrast, a **criterion-referenced test** moves away from comparing one student with another, and thus may be more fair and advantageous for bilinguals. The test results show what a student can and cannot do on a precise breakdown of language skills. Thus, rather than a score providing a comparison to other students (e.g. 16th percentile), criterion reference scores indicate the percentage of mastery (87% correct answers) and whether or not the students met or exceeded a passing cut score. Detailed score reports can indicate which test items or concepts students did well on, and which are in need of further development.

However, while criterion-referenced tests seem more fair for bilinguals in theory, in practice, they *can* be used to create comparisons between children (e.g. monolingual native speakers and bilinguals), between groups of children and between schools. Behind every criterion lurks a norm. The norm is usually the point of departure for setting criteria such as the standards the test is designed to measure and the cut scores to determine passing. Another advantage of criterion-referenced language tests is that they may facilitate feedback on student learning needs to the teacher that directly

---

Box 2.1 Criterion-referenced language tests

Criterion-referenced language tests should provide direct feedback into the following areas:

- teaching decisions (e.g. diagnosis of curriculum areas not mastered by an individual student);
- reporting to, and discussing achievement with, parents;
- recognizing children in need of special support and the type of curriculum support they need;
- identifying children for accelerated learning;
- informing about standards in the class in terms of curriculum development through a subject.

leads to intervention. Thus, they may be used as assessments for formative purposes (see Box 2.1).

Regardless of whether a test is norm- or criterion-referenced, the sub-components of language proficiency are not easily definable or measurable. Apart from language skills, there are the qualitative aspects of language that are not simply reducible for testing (e.g. the emotive, status and poetic functions of languages). There is growing recognition that a single test cannot provide an accurate measure of a bilingual's proficiency. To get an accurate picture, multiple measures are needed (Bailey & Carroll, 2015; Boals *et al.*, 2015). This may include a combination of summative and formative assessments and alternative assessments such as checklists, informal and formal observations, and portfolios of students' work (e.g. assignments, journals) (Herrera *et al.*, 2013).

Communicative Language Testing

In attempting to assess a bilingual's competence in two languages, there is a danger of using a simple paper and pencil multiple-choice test believing the test will provide a faithful estimation of everyday language life. Reducing everyday language competence to tests of specific skills is like measuring Michelangelo's art solely by its range of colors. A particular emphasis in language testing is on **communicative competence** (see Chapter 1). While tests of spelling, grammar, written comprehension and reading abound, the importance of using languages in everyday settings is reflected in current testing preferences. Communicative competence assessment is based on genuine communication with various participants. Sometimes such conversation moves in unpredictable directions and only makes sense within a particular social context. An alternative is seeing how bilinguals perform in both languages in a range of real communicative situations: in a shop, at home, at work and during leisure activity. This idea is time-consuming and may be biased by the presence of the researcher. Thus, a test that measures purposeful communication across sufficient contexts without tester effects is improbable. For some, the answer is simply not to test. For others, a best approximation is accepted. Communicative language tests therefore tend to measure the more limited notion of performance rather than the wider idea of competence.

Two major language proficiency tests – the Test of English as a Foreign Language (TOEFL) and the International English Language Testing System (IELTS) – are designed to determine if students have sufficient English language proficiency across the four basic language skills to communicate competently in the context of an English-medium university classroom. Most universities in Australia, Canada, New Zealand, the United Kingdom, and the United States accept one or both of these tests. While minimum acceptable scores vary by university or degree programs, a common admissions requirement is that international students from non-English dominant countries obtain a score 6.5 or higher on the IELTS, or 79 or higher on the internet-based version of the TOEFL (iBT).

Table 2.1 outlines each of the four sections of the TOEFL (iBT). Note that the tasks attempt to replicate the ways students may need to use and understand English in the classroom. For example, on the listening section the student may listen to a short excerpt of a lecture on the greenhouse effect; for the speaking section, the student may be asked to describe some places in their country they would recommend to a friend from another country to visit.

Table 2.1 TOEFL iBT Test sections

Section	Time Limit	Questions	Tasks
Reading	60–80 min	36–56 questions	Read 3 or 4 passages from academic texts and answer questions.
Listening	60–90 min	34–51 questions	Listen to lectures, classroom discussions and conversations, then answer questions.
Speaking	20 min	6 tasks	Express an opinion on a familiar topic; speak based on reading and listening tasks.
Writing	50 min	2 tasks	Write essay responses based on reading and listening tasks; support an opinion in writing.

Source: http://www.ets.org/toefl/ibt/about/content/

The IELTS includes similar questions and tasks, but also includes an oral interview in the speaking section. A candidate answers basic questions for 11 to 14 minutes about topics such as: where you live, clothes, travel, family, free time and shopping. Questions on shopping might ask:

- Do you like shopping? Why or why not?
- What kind of things do you like to buy?
- When do people in your area usually do their shopping?
- What are some of the advantages and disadvantages of large shops?

Candidates receive scores on a band scale from one to nine, with allocation based on a rigorous and detailed system of performance descriptors, as shown in Box 2.2.

Such interview procedures like those used on the IELTS may not reflect authentic everyday situations and use. Does genuine communication take place between strangers in a contrived, artificial context? Is the language repertoire of a person truly elicited? Is 'interview language' representative of a person's everyday language? Can we generalize from oral communicative tests based on a single type of test, given on a single occasion, based on a test interview which is not a typical daily event? To what extent are language abilities comprehensively sampled in an interview? There are doubts about whether such interview procedures can validly imitate and investigate real communicative competence. In addition, the tester is an influence on the outcome and not neutral. The conversation is constructed by both tester and tested (assessor and student). Performance and achievement are the result of a social event and not just an individual's competence. It is a joint performance. Thus the issue of 'whose performance' suggests that the result is about the assessor as well as the assessed. At the same time, these types of interviews are a compromise between artificial pencil and paper tests and the impracticality of the detailed observation of individuals across many **domains**.

Another, more holistic communicative competence framework for language assessment is the Council of Europe's (1992) Common European Framework of Reference (CEFR). The Framework defines levels of proficiency that allow assessment of learners' progress irrespective of age, language or region. This CEFR identifies three levels of language users – (A) basic, (B) independent, and (C) proficient – with two levels of proficiency for each (i.e. A1, A2, B1, B2, C1, C2). Descriptions of each level are shown in Table 2.2. The CEFR was designed to 'provide a common basis for the elaboration of language syllabuses, curriculum guidelines, examinations, textbooks, etc. across

Box 2.2 International English Language Testing System (IELTS) Score Bands

Band 9 Expert User
Has fully operational command of the language: appropriate, accurate and fluent with complete understanding.

Band 8 Very Good User
Has fully operational command of the language with only occasional unsystematic inaccuracies and inappropriacies. Misunderstandings may occur in unfamiliar situations. Handles complex detailed argumentation well.

Band 7 Good User
Has operational command of the language, though with occasional inaccuracies, inappropriacies and misunderstandings in some situations. Generally handles complex language well and understands detailed reasoning.

Band 6 Competent User
Has generally effective command of the language despite some inaccuracies, inappropriacies and misunderstandings. Can use and understand fairly complex language, particularly in familiar situations.

Band 5 Modest User
Has partial command of the language, coping with overall meaning in most situations, though is likely to make many mistakes. Should be able to handle basic communication in own field.

Band 4 Limited User
Basic competence is limited to familiar situations. Has frequent problems in understanding and expression. Is not able to use complex language.

Band 3 Extremely Limited User
Conveys and understands only general meaning in very familiar situations. Frequent breakdowns in communication occur.

Band 2 Intermittent User
No real communication is possible except for the most basic information using isolated words or short formulae in familiar situations and to meet immediate needs. Has great difficulty understanding spoken and written English.

Band 1 Non User
Essentially has no ability to use the language beyond possibly a few isolated words.

Source: http://www.ielts.org/institutions/test_format_and_results/ielts_band_scores.aspx

---

Europe' (p. 1). However the CEFR has moved beyond Europe and is used in language programs in countries such as Argentina, China, Colombia, Japan, New Zealand, Taiwan and the United States (Byram & Parmenter, 2012).

A great danger lies in only viewing languages inside an academic context. The classroom is one language domain where **language minority** students from different cultural contexts may not reveal their wealth of language talents. Thus, academic testing is often more suited to elective bilinguals (see Chapter 1) whereas **circumstantial bilinguals** require their language abilities and uses to be portrayed across out-of-school domains so as to be fully representative.

To collect *realistic and representative* communicative competence data, we need to know how situations (domains) relate to one another. We also need to know the sample of language performance that relates adequately to all round language competence (see Chapter 1).

Table 2.2 Common European Framework of Reference

Proficient User	C2	Can understand with ease virtually everything heard or read. Can summarise information from different spoken and written sources, reconstructing arguments and accounts in a coherent presentation. Can express him/herself spontaneously, very fluently and precisely, differentiating finer shades of meaning even in more complex situations.
	C1	Can understand a wide range of demanding, longer texts, and recognise implicit meaning. Can express him/herself fluently and spontaneously without much obvious searching for expressions. Can use language flexibly and effectively for social, academic and professional purposes. Can produce clear, well-structured, detailed text on complex subjects, showing controlled use of organisational patterns, connectors and cohesive devices.
Independent User	B2	Can understand the main ideas of complex text on both concrete and abstract topics, including technical discussions in his/her field of specialisation. Can interact with a degree of fluency and spontaneity that makes regular interaction with native speakers quite possible without strain for either party. Can produce clear, detailed text on a wide range of subjects and explain a viewpoint on a topical issue giving the advantages and disadvantages of various options.
	B1	Can understand the main points of clear standard input on familiar matters regularly encountered in work, school, leisure, etc. Can deal with most situations likely to arise whilst travelling in an area where the language is spoken. Can produce simple connected text on topics which are familiar or of personal interest. Can describe experiences and events, dreams, hopes and ambitions and briefly give reasons and explanations for opinions and plans.
Basic User	A2	Can understand sentences and frequently used expressions related to areas of most immediate relevance (e.g. very basic personal and family information, shopping, local geography, employment). Can communicate in simple and routine tasks requiring a simple and direct exchange of information on familiar and routine matters. Can describe in simple terms aspects of his/her background, immediate environment and matters in areas of immediate need.
	A1	Can understand and use familiar everyday expressions and very basic phrases aimed at the satisfaction of needs of a concrete type. Can introduce him/herself and others and can ask and answer questions about personal details such as where he/she lives, people he/she knows and things he/she has. Can interact in a simple way provided the other person talks slowly and clearly and is prepared to help.

Source: www.coe.int/t/dg4/linguistic/Source/Framework_EN.pdf

Examples of the Measurement of Bilinguals in Research

A full inventory of bilingual measurement devices would be immense and is not provided (see Li Wei & Moyer, 2009 for a comprehensive survey of this area). The examples given below help to make some essential points and tend to exemplify some of the styles most often used in research on bilinguals.

Language Background Scales

Language background or **functional bilingualism** scales are self-rating scales. They endeavor to measure actual use of two languages as opposed to proficiency. An example for bilingual Spanish-English schoolchildren is presented in Figure 2.1 (adapted from C. Baker, 1992).

This scale has limitations besides the problems of ambiguity and 'social desirability' considered later. It is not exhaustive of targets (people) or of domains (contexts). Language activity with uncles and aunts, dance clubs, correspondence, organizations,

Here are some questions about the language in which you talk to different people, and the language in which certain people speak to you. There are no right or wrong answers. Leave an empty space if a question is inappropriate.

	Almost always in Spanish	In Spanish more than English	In Spanish and English about equally	In English more often than Spanish	Almost always in English
In which language do YOU speak to the following people?					
Father					
Mother					
Brothers/sisters					
Friends in the classroom					
Friends on the playground					
Friends outside school					
Teachers					
Neighbors					
Grandparents					
Other relatives					
In which language do the following people speak TO YOU?					
Father					
Mother					
Brothers/sisters					
Friends in the classroom					
Friends on the playground					
Friends outside school					
Teachers					
Neighbors					
Grandparents					
Other relatives					
Which language do YOU use for the following?					
Speaking on the telephone					
Text messaging					
Using the computer/internet					
Watching TV/DVDs/videos					
Listening to radio					
Listening to music					
Reading newspapers/ comics/magazines					
Reading books					
Shopping					
Playing sports					
Participating in clubs/ societies					
Working/earning money					
Attending religious services					
Other leisure activities					

Figure 2.1 Language background scale

Box 2.3 Language use surveys

The language background of a language group needs to include many different contextual dimensions. Listed below are some of the contexts that need to be included in such a language use or language census survey. The examples are from the European Commission (2006)

- Geographical (areal) extent of the language; number and density of users.
- Legal status of language; use of the language in bureaucracy; effect of local and central government on the language.
- Recent and past immigration and emigration affecting the language.
- Use of the language by parents with their children and between siblings; use of the language in new and existing marriages.
- Use of language in elementary and secondary education, vocational, technical, adult, continuing and higher education; language learning classes.
- Literacy and biliteracy of the language group.
- Unemployment in the language group. Types of employment in the language group (e.g. socio-economic status).
- Amount of language activism among the language group, especially in younger age groups.
- Cultural vitality of the language group; institutions dedicated to supporting the language and **culture**.
- Attitudes of speakers and non-speakers to the language. Optimism or pessimism surrounding the language.

---

social media, hobbies and travel are not included, for example. The choice of items included in such a scale is somewhere between an all-inclusive scale and a more narrow sample of major domains. At first glance, it may appear that the more inclusive a scale is the better. There is a problem, illustrated by the following example. A person who says she speaks Spanish to her father (mostly working abroad), her grandparents (seen twice a year), her friends (but tends to be a loner), reads Spanish books and magazines (only occasionally), attends church services in Spanish (marriages and funerals only), but spends most of her time with an English speaking mother and in an English speaking school, might gain a fairly high 'Spanish' score.

The example above suggests that the 'to whom' question is insufficient. Frequency of usage in such contexts and with certain targets needs adding. To accompany 'to whom and where', a 'how often' and 'why' question are necessary. Also, such scales do not indicate networking or status and power in relationships which are important in **language shift** and language attitudes.

Language Balance and Dominance Measures

Various tests have been devised to gauge the relative dominance or balance of a bilingual's two languages (Grosjean & Li, 2013). While such measures have been used in research, they have also been important in US education. Because instruction for US language-minority children may take place in the child's **dominant language**, some measure of language dominance is needed. This may be through, for example, English language and Spanish language proficiency tests. Some examples of the types of tasks and test items used to determine language dominance are given below. A discussion of neurological measures is given in Chapter 7.

- *Vocabulary knowledge.* A simple picture identification is used to determine the extent of known vocabulary of the bilingual in both languages. The language with the highest number of correct responses is assumed to be dominant.

- *Speed of reaction in a word association task.* This seeks to measure whether a bilingual can give an association to stimulus words more quickly in one language than the other. The language with the fastest responses is assumed to be dominant.
- *Quantity of reactions to a word association task.* Bilinguals are measured for the number of associations given within one minute when a stimulus word (e.g. 'color') is presented. The language with the highest number of associations is assumed to be dominant.
- *Detection of words using both languages.* Words in both languages are extracted from a nonsense word such as DANSONODEND. This requires languages that use the same alphabet, and it can be difficult to create as the letters must be equally representative of both languages. The language with the largest number of extracted words is assumed to be dominant.
- *Time taken to read.* The language a bilingual can read the fastest is assumed to be dominant.

In seeking to determine the dominant language, it must be remembered that dominance is different from competence. A person may be competent in two or more languages while being dominant in one. Also, some cultures do not value speed of reaction, preferring accuracy. Thus there may be a cultural **bias** in the use of such tests. Another major problem with such balance and dominance tests lies in the representativeness of the measure of language proficiency and performance. In this respect, such tests would appear to tap only a small part of a much larger and more complex whole (language ability or language use). The tests cover a small sample of language sub-skills that might be tested. Dominance will vary by domain and across time, being a constantly changing personal characteristic. It is possible to be approximately equally proficient in two languages, yet one may be dominant. Speed of processing may provide evidence about balance but not about dominance in actual language use, either in different sociocultural contexts or over time.

Self-rating on Proficiency

A simple means of determining language balance and dominance is to ask students to assess their own language strengths and weaknesses. An example to illustrate self-rating on language proficiency appears in Figure 2.2.

Can You Understand:	English?	Spanish?	Can You Speak:	English?	Spanish?
Yes – fluently	☐	☐	Yes – fluently	☐	☐
Yes – fairly well	☐	☐	Yes – fairly well	☐	☐
Yes – some	☐	☐	Yes – some	☐	☐
Yes – just a little	☐	☐	Yes – just a little	☐	☐
No – not now	☐	☐	No – not now	☐	☐
Can You Read:			**Can You Write:**		
Yes – fluently	☐	☐	Yes – fluently	☐	☐
Yes – fairly well	☐	☐	Yes – fairly well	☐	☐
Yes – some	☐	☐	Yes – some	☐	☐
Yes – just a little	☐	☐	Yes – just a little	☐	☐
No – not now	☐	☐	No – not now	☐	☐

Figure 2.2 Self-rating of bilingual language proficiency (English/Spanish)

Limitations in Measurement

Self-assessments, such as the example in Figure 2.2, may cover the basic four language abilities across two languages (e.g. Spanish and English). The answers are possibly too broad (e.g. there are many gradations possible in between each of the answers). Apart from this problem of scaling, there are other problems frequently encountered when measuring language competence. These may be listed as:

(1) **AMBIGUITY**. Words such as 'speak', 'understand', 'read' and 'write' include a wide variety of levels of proficiency. The range is from an absolute beginner to Bloomfield's (1933) maximum notion of 'native-like control of two languages'. Tests also often contain only a small unrepresentative sample of the totality of language proficiencies.
(2) **CONTEXT**. A bilingual may be able to understand a language in one context (e.g. a shop) and not in another context (e.g. an academic lecture). Proficiency and usage will vary with changing environments.
(3) **SOCIAL DESIRABILITY/SUBJECTIVITY**. Respondents may consciously or sub-consciously give a 'halo' version of themselves. Self-ratings are vulnerable to exaggeration or understatement. People may say they are fluent in a second language (when in reality they are not) for **identity**, self-esteem or status reasons. Others may indicate they do not speak a language when they actually can. This may occur, for example, in a low prestige minority language environment where the introduction of the second language may replace the first language. Questions about proficiency can be interpreted as about personal attitudes and identity and not just language.
(4) **ACQUIESCENT RESPONSE**. There is a slight tendency for respondents to answer 'Yes' rather than 'No' in self-rating questions. It appears preferable to be positive rather than negative. This also tends to hold with a slight preference for 'Agree' rather than 'Disagree'.
(5) **SELF-AWARENESS**. A self-rating depends on accuracy of knowledge about oneself. For one person, the frame of reference may be other neighborhood children who are not so fluent. When compared to children in another community, apparent fluency may be less. What is competent in one environment may seem less competent in another. The age, nature and location of the reference group may cause self-assessment not to be strictly comparable across a representative sample of people.
(6) **POINT OF REFERENCE**. There is a danger in using monolingual proficiency and performance as the point of comparison (see Chapter 1).
(7) **TEST AURA**. Another danger is raising language measurement to the level of scientific measurement with an accompanying exaggerated mystique. More 'natural' forms of language sampling may be given lower status (e.g. recording natural conversation) as they rarely carry the mystique of educational and psychological (psychometric) measurement, but they may provide more authentic samples of language.
(8) **NARROW SAMPLING OF DIMENSIONS OF LANGUAGE**. Language measurement may unwittingly be perceived as something tangible and concrete (as when measuring height and weight). Rather, language tests mostly contain a specification of language skills that is open to interpretation.

(9) **INSENSITIVITY TO CHANGE.** It is seen as good practice to produce measurement that is reliable over time and across occasions (give consistent scores for the same individual over weeks or months). However, the paradox is that such measurement may be insensitive to change within individuals. Test scores need an expiry date (e.g. not valid after one year).

(10) **LABELING.** Test scores are apt to create labels for individuals (e.g. someone is seen as being an underperformer) which create expectations (e.g. of further underachievement) that may lead to a self-fulfilling prophecy.

A Political View of Language Testing

Language testing is not a neutral activity. For example, language tests are sometimes introduced to achieve curriculum change. Indeed, there is almost no more powerful route to educational policy control or curriculum change than tests that virtually force the teacher to 'teach to the test'.

Centrally or locally imposed language tests define what skills are to be accented (e.g. communicative competence or literacy) and what languages are to be promoted (e.g. the majority language at the expense of minority languages). Language tests can include or exclude, marginalize or motivate, stagnate or innovate. Behind language tests are often agendas, motives, **ideology** and politics. A language testing policy is typically an operationalized language policy (Shohamy & Menken, 2015).

Language testing relates to cultural, social, political, educational and ideological agendas that shape the lives of all students and teachers. Such language tests are deeply embedded in cultural, educational and political debates where different ideologies are in contest. Shohamy (2006) therefore proposes a perspective she terms 'critical language testing' that views test-takers as political subjects in a political context. An example is high-stakes language assessment in the US (see Chapter 9).

Critical language testing asks questions about whose formal and hidden agendas tests relate to, and what sort of political and educational policies are delivered through tests. Critical language testing argues that language testers must ask themselves what sort of vision of society language tests create, and for what vision of society tests are used. For example, are language tests intended to fulfill pre-defined curricular or proficiency objectives, or are there other hidden aims, maneuvers or manipulations?

Critical language testing asks questions about whose knowledge the tests are based on. What is the intended or assumed status of that knowledge (e.g. 'truth' or something that can be negotiated and challenged)? What is the meaning and use of language test scores, and to what degree are they prescriptive, final and absolute, or to what extent are they open to discussion and interpretation?

Critical language testing thus widens the field of language testing by relating it to political and social debates. As Shohamy and Menken (2015) argue:

> In most societies tests have been constructed as symbols of success, achievement and mobility, and reinforced by dominant social and educational institutions as major criteria of worth, quality, and value. Tests, then, have been associated with standards and merit, and, in the context of immigration, are markers of productivity in the workplace, citizenship, and academic achievement in school. Tests are accepted as objective measures, which serve to enforce conformity and ensure the continuity of various declared agendas of policy makers. Governments and other central authorities

use tests to impose their policies and agendas, knowing that those who are affected by such tests will change their behavior, given their fear of failure and its associated high stakes consequences; accordingly, they are eager to succeed. (pp. 254–255)

Shohamy and Menken also note the power of language tests to privilege certain language practices, raise the status of tested (usually dominant) languages, and suppress non-tested languages in school and society.

Bilingual Assessment and Testing

A major limitation of monolingual tests is they fail to capture the full linguistic repertoire of bilinguals, nor do they allow bilinguals to draw on this repertoire to fully demonstrate their knowledge and skills. As Valdés and Figueroa (1994) argue:

> When a bilingual individual confronts a monolingual test, developed by monolingual individuals, and standardized and normed on a monolingual population, both the test taker and the test are asked to do something they cannot. The bilingual test taker cannot perform like a monolingual. The monolingual test can't 'measure' in the other language.

Monolingual forms of testing and assessment treat bilinguals as two monolinguals in one, as if their two languages are isolated and disconnected. However, as we saw in Chapter 1, bilinguals actually use their languages in complex, dynamic and flexible ways. Thus, there is a need for bilingual assessment policies and practices that enable students to show what they know and can do (Shohamy & Menken, 2015). Shohamy (2011) has proposed such policies and practices. For example, a selected response test could display questions and answers in both of a student's languages, allowing the student to answer either one, or consult one while determining the answer in the other. Open-ended constructed response items could allow students to respond in one or both languages. She provides an example of a bilingual student who accurately used both English and Hebrew to complete a recipe writing task. She provides other empirical evidence suggesting the potential of such multilingual assessment practices to provide a more valid measure of bilingual student knowledge and skills. However, Shohamy and Menken (2015) acknowledge that very little research had been conducted, and that there are many questions to answer and issues to resolve. Nonetheless, by accepting **multilingualism** as the norm, researchers and assessment experts are now beginning to explore dynamic assessments that allow bilinguals to demonstrate their knowledge and skills using their entire linguistic repertoire.

Language Censuses

The Belgian census of 1846 was one of the first national censuses to ask language questions. Other countries were soon to follow Belgium's lead: Switzerland in 1850, Ireland in 1851, Hungary in 1857, Italy in 1861, Canada in 1871, Austria and Finland in 1880, India and Scotland in 1881, the United States in 1890, Wales in 1891 and Russia in 1897 (Ó Gliasáin, 1996). Other countries such as Venezuela, Bolivia and Australia have more recently asked language questions in a census. Such censuses are often perceived by governments as providing relatively accurate measures of the number of language speakers in local communities, regions and countries.

Languages in the United States Census and the American Community Survey

The United States Census was instituted at the beginning of the United States political system in Article 1 Section 2, which stated that political representation in the House of Representatives was to be based on a population census. The census has been taken every 10 years since 1790, when Secretary of State Thomas Jefferson supervised the first census. A question on race was included in that first census. Questions on race and ethnicity were revised in subsequent censuses to reflect changing demographics, understandings and views. A question on Hispanic origin was introduced in 1970 and 'ancestry' in 1980 (see Macías, 2000). Further changes to race and ethnicity questions are anticipated for the 2020 Census to better capture 'multiethnic America' (The Leadership Conference Education Fund, 2014). The first time a question was asked about 'languages spoken at home' was in 1890. Increasingly, census data helps states and localities 'benchmark' and measure progress in meeting their objectives and legislatively mandated targets. Thus a census does not just provide information. It also can assist or invoke political action (e.g. the 1910 US Census spurring the Americanization campaign). In 2005 the US Census Bureau began administering the annual American Community Survey (ACS) in addition to the decennial census to collect population data on a more frequent basis, including language data.

Three examples are given below of language questions from the US, the first from the 1910 Census, the second from the 2000 Census, and the third from the 2013 ACS. These examples illustrate how census questions are constructed in a way that does not always give accurate and comprehensive information about use of languages, and also reveals implicit official attitudes towards the use and maintenance of minority languages.

The United States Census of 1910

In the 1910 United States Census, advice was given to enumerators when asking respondents about the **mother tongue** of members of the household. The extracts in Box 2.4 illustrate notions from a bygone era.

Note that:

- The question of mother tongue excluded those born in the United States. This indicates an assumption that all those born in the United States would be able to speak English, and that the maintenance of minority languages or bilingualism in English and a minority language was not considered.
- A person's ability in languages other than English was ignored if they were able to speak English.

Box 2.4 Extracts from Advice to Enumerators in the United States 1910 Census

'127. The question of mother tongue should not be asked of any person born in the United States'

'133. Column 17. Whether able to speak English; or, if not, give language spoken. This question applies to all persons age 10 and over. If such a person is able to speak English, write English [on the form]. If he is not able to speak English – and in such cases only – write the language which he does speak, as French, German, Italian.'

- Ability in a **heritage language** was counted only if a person was unable to speak English.
- The language of under-10-year-olds was ignored.

The United States Census of 2000

In 2000, a census of the population was taken throughout the United States. Starting in January 2000 with visits to very remote areas and in March 2000 with postal delivery, Census 2000 questionnaires were made available in six languages – English, Spanish, Chinese, Tagalog, Vietnamese and Korean. Language Assistance Guides were produced in 49 languages apart from English. Two questionnaires or forms were used. A short form was sent to about five in six of every household in the US requesting information on individual household members (e.g. gender, race, Hispanic origin, home ownership and age). The long form was sent to about one in six of all US households. The longer form includes the same questions as the short form, with additional questions about ancestry, residence five years ago (migration), income, education, and home languages. Thus, the language data is based on a sample of one in six households. Statistical procedures are used to generalize to the entire US population. The language question on the 2000 Census long form was phrased as shown in Box 2.5.

Box 2.5 Language question on the 2000 US Census

(a) Does this person speak a language other than English at home?
  ☐ Yes
  ☐ No *Skip to 12*

(b) What is this language? *(For example: Korean, Italian, Spanish, Vietnamese)*

(c) How well does this person speak English?
  ☐ Very well
  ☐ Well
  ☐ Not well
  ☐ Not at all

This question is more comprehensive than the 1910 language question. It asks about the use of a minority language in the home irrespective of command of English. It also asks a more searching question about the level of ability in English, which is the dominant question.

The 2013 American Community Survey (ACS)

In 2005 the US Census Bureau moved the language questions from the decennial census long form to the annual American Community Survey (ACS). The wording of the language question remains the same (US Census Bureau, 2015a). The ACS is sent to about one in 38 households (US Census Bureau, 2015b). Thus, the annual administration of the ACS provides much more timely data about language, however the smaller sample size means estimates are less accurate, particularly for smaller language minority populations.

The 2013 ACS estimated that out of the total US population ages 5 and older (291.5 million), there are 60.3 million (20.7%) people who speak a language other than English as home. Of these 37.5 million (62.1%) speak Spanish, 10.7 million (17.8%) speak another Indo-European language, 9.5 million (15.8%) speak an Asian or Pacific Island language, and 2.6 million (4.4%) speak other languages. Over 25% of the population speak a language other than English in the home in Arizona, Florida, Hawai'i and Nevada, and over 30% in California, New Jersey, New Mexico, New York and Texas.

The US Census Bureau identified 381 languages spoken in the US (Ryan, 2013). The 2013 ACS reports the 10 languages other than English with the higher number of speakers are: Spanish (37,458,624), Chinese (2,896,766), Tagalog (1,613,346), Vietnamese (1,399,936), French (including Patois, Cajun) (1,307,742), Korean (1,117,343), German (1,063,773), Arabic (924,374), Russian (879,434), and Italian (708,966). Of indigenous languages, Navajo had 166,826 speakers, and there were 197,505 speakers of other Native North American languages.

The 2000 US Census and the 2013 ACS showed a substantial increase since the 1980 US Census in the number and percentage of residents five years old and over speaking a language other than English at home (see Table 2.3).

Table 2.3 Number of US speakers of languages other than English

Year	Number Speaking a Language Other than English	Percentage of US Population
US Census 1980	23.1 million	11.0%
US Census 1990	31.8 million	13.8%
US Census 2000	46.9 million	17.9%
America Community Survey 2013	60.3 million	20.7%

Limitations of Language Censuses

Language census data contain limitations, even when there is a long tradition of census compilation.

- Census questions about home language, mother tongue and first language are often ambiguous. In the 2011 Canadian Census, one of the four language questions was 'Can this person speak English or French well enough to conduct a conversation?' The term 'speak well enough' may be interpreted in different ways. What one person considers 'well enough' may be at a different level of fluency to another. Another Canadian Census question asks 'What is the language this person first learned at home in childhood and still understands?' The terms 'first learned' and 'still understands' are also subject to interpretation. This question also poses challenges for simultaneous bilinguals who learned two languages at home in childhood at the same time. The census question suggests there can only be one that was learned 'first.'
- Sometimes census questions do not distinguish between language use and language ability (see Chapter 1). Thus a question, 'Do you speak English?' does not specify whether the question is about everyday language use, ability to speak the language irrespective of regular use, or both use and ability.
- Questions on census forms do not usually include the four basic language skills: listening, speaking, reading and writing. Thus typically only oracy is measured, not literacy.
- Questions about contexts or domains of language use (e.g. home, school, religion, street, shopping) are rarely asked. Therefore, a response is very generalized across many domains and insensitive to where languages are used.

- Census data may rapidly become out of date when factors such as migration, social upheaval, war or a high birth rate mean that the language situation is rapidly changing.
- Language questions can be politically inflammatory. For example, in the 1846 Belgian census the language question simply asked what language is usually spoken by respondents. Subsequent censuses restricted choices to knowledge of official languages only. This provoked contention and controversy. Combined with other political controversies, in 1961, the majority of parliamentarians in Belgium decided to suspend the language censuses to avoid further dispute.
- Not all censuses include questions on language. Some censuses ask about ethnic groups, which may not correspond to language groups. This occurred in the 2001 Census in England where there was no language census question and only a question on ethnic origins. The later 2011 Census in England included questions on ethnic group, 'main language' and English proficiency so as to respond to such criticism.
- Conversely, a language question in a census may be treated by respondents as referring to identity. For example, in Ireland, a non-Irish speaker may wish to be seen as Irish and therefore positively answer the Irish language question. Thus a census language question may be interpreted as an attitude question. People from a particular ethnic group may feel they ought to say that they speak the indigenous or heritage language even if they do not. Alternatively, if a minority language is disparaged and of low status, a speaker of that language may claim not to speak the language.
- Censuses do not usually cover all of the population of a country despite considerable efforts to be inclusive. Some of the population may refuse to respond through the mail system, or to answer census personnel calling at their dwelling. Some recent immigrants may be fearful of the census. For example, the 1980 US Census is suspected to have substantially undercounted the Cambodian refugee population. When native Cambodian American census takers made home visits to those who failed to return the census form (sent in English), many were accused of collecting information to send to the oppressive political regimes back in Cambodia. Other people are out of reach or difficult to track down. Itinerants, illegal immigrants and the homeless, for example, may be missed by the census.

Conclusion

Just as dimensions and categorizations can never capture the full nature of bilingualism, so measurement usually fails to capture fully various conceptual dimensions and categorizations. Just as the statistics of a football or an ice hockey game do not convey the richness of the event, so language tests and measurements are unlikely to fully represent an idea or theoretical concept. Complex and rich descriptions are the indispensable partner of measurement and testing. The stark statistics of the football or ice hockey game and the colorful commentary are complementary, not incompatible.

There are many language background scales to measure language usage and even more tests to measure language proficiency. The latter includes norm-referenced and criterion-referenced language tests, self-rating scales and language dominance tests. Particular attention in this chapter has been given to criterion-referenced tests measuring mastery of specific language objectives. Suitable for both first and second languages, sometimes based on theoretical principles, sometimes eclectic, such tests tend to relate directly to the process of teaching and learning. Bilingual assessments hold the potential to provide more valid measures of bilinguals' knowledge and skills. The assessment and testing of bilinguals in school will be addressed more fully in Chapter 15.

Key Points in This Chapter

➤ Bilinguals are measured both for their proficiency and use of their languages.

➤ Examples include census surveys of languages in a population, selection for different classes in school according to language ability, assessment of competency following second language learning.

➤ Language background scales measure a person's use of their languages in different domains and in different relationships.

➤ Language balance and dominance measures seek to gauge the relative strength of each language of a bilingual.

➤ Communicative language testing attempts to measure a person's use of language in authentic situations.

➤ Criterion-referenced language tests seek to provide a profile of language sub-skills, whereas norm- referenced tests compare a person with other people.

➤ 'Critical language testing' examines whose knowledge the tests are based on, and for what political purposes the tests will be used. It regards test-takers as political subjects in a political context.

➤ Bilingual assessments have the potential to enable bilinguals to demonstrate their knowledge and skills by drawing on the full range of their linguistic repertoires.

➤ Language censuses are used in many countries to measure the extent and density of speakers of different languages. There are problems with terms used, validity of the questions and reliability of the answers.

Suggested Further Reading

📖 Byram, M. & Parmenter L. (Eds.) (2012). *The Common European Framework of Reference: The globalisation of language education policy*. Bristol, UK: Multilingual Matters.

📖 Gathercole, V.C.M. (Ed.). (2013). *Issues in the assessment of bilinguals*. Bristol, UK: Multilingual Matters.

📖 King, K. & Lai, Y-J. (2017). *Research methods in language and education* (Vol. 10 of the *Encyclopedia of Language and Education*, 3rd ed., Stephen May, Editor). New York, NY: Springer.

📖 MacDonald, R., Boals, T., Castro, M., Cook, H. G., Lundberg, T., & White, P. A. (2015). *Formative language assessment for English learners: A four-step process*. Portsmouth, NH: Heinemann.

On the Web

⌨ Modern Language Association Language Map
https://www.mla.org/map_main

⌨ American Fact Finder (access to US Census and ACS data)
http://factfinder.census.gov/faces/nav/jsf/pages/index.xhtml

⌨ Ethnologue – Languages of the World
https://www.ethnologue.com/

⌨ European Commission – Languages
http://ec.europa.eu/languages/index_en.htm

⌨ European Charter for Regional or Minority Languages
http://www.coe.int/t/dg4/education/minlang/default_en.asp

Discussion Questions

(1) Why is the measurement of bilinguals so challenging? Describe any experiences you have had with language proficiency tests or assessments. What was challenging about these measures, and how accurately did they reflect your perceived level of proficiency?

(2) Complete the Language Background Scale (Figure 2.1) and/or the Self-Rating of Bilingual Language Proficiency (Figure 2.2). Compare and discuss your background and ratings with other members in the class. Specify the criteria you used to determine your responses.

(3) Listen to the sample listening task item for the TOEFL available here – *http://www.ets.org/toefl/ibt/about/content/*. How realistic and representative do you feel this task is in terms of the communicative competence needed for success in university classrooms?

Study Activities

(1) Using a local school(s), find out what tests are used to measure language achievement in the classroom. These may be listening, speaking, reading, writing or language development tests. Find out whether these are norm-referenced or criterion-referenced tests and if they are used for summative or formative purposes. How fair are these to bilingual children?

(2) Gather detailed information about one country's language census (e.g. US, Canada, East Africa, Wales, Ireland, Scotland (Gaelic), Australia, India, Bolivia, Venezuela, Caucasus Region). What were the major findings? What problems are there in the wording of the question(s)? What other limitations do you find in the survey?

(3) Obtain and analyze a standardized language proficiency test or sample test (e.g. TOEFL, IELTS, Pearson Test of English, BEST Plus, BEST Literacy, WMLS-R, IPT, Access 2.0, ELPA21, CELDT, TELPAS, Peabody Picture Vocabulary Test, etc.). Assess strengths and weaknesses of the test when used with bilingual students in the classroom (e.g. selection, placement, formative and summative judgments, etc.).

Endangered Languages: Planning and Revitalization

CHAPTER 3

Endangered Languages:
Planning and Revitalization

Introduction

How would you feel if you were the last speaker of your language? Chief Marie Smith Jones, the last speaker of the Alaskan Eyak language, gave her answer (Nettle & Romaine, 2000: 14): 'I don't know why it's me, why I'm the one. I tell you, it hurts. It really hurts.' Richard Littlebear (1999), a Native American Cheyenne citizen, tells of his meeting with Chief Marie Smith Jones. 'I felt that I was sitting in the presence of a whole universe of knowledge that could be gone in one last breath. That's how fragile that linguistic universe seemed.' She died, age 89, on January 21, 2008, at her home in Anchorage. Her name in Eyak was *Udach' Kuqax*a'a'ch'* meaning 'a sound that calls people from afar'.

To be told that a loved one is dying or dead is one of the most unpleasant experiences in life. To talk about a dead language or a dying language sounds academic and without much sentiment. Yet languages have no existence without people. A language typically dies with the last speaker of that language, or lies dormant awaiting future revival, if possible (Hermes *et al.*, 2012). For humanity, that is a great loss. It is like an encyclopedia formed from that language and **culture** being buried. Three further examples will illustrate.

- In Cameroon in 1994/95, a researcher, Bruce Connell, visited the last speaker of a language called Kasabe (or Luo). In 1996, he returned to research that moribund language. He was too late. The last speaker of Kasabe had died on November 5, 1995, taking the language and culture with him (Crystal, 2014). Simply stated, on November 4, 1995, Kasabe existed. On November 5, it was dead.
- In June of 2013, Grizelda Kristina, the last speaker of the ancient Baltic language of Livonian, died at the age of 103. Born and raised in a fishing village along the northern coast of Latvia, Grizelda's village and dozens of other Livonian villages were devastated by Nazis, and later by the Soviets. She fled Latvia in 1944 to escape the war, and settled in Canada where she remained until her death (Berlin, 2013).
- On February 4, 2014, Hazel M. Sampson died at the age of 103 in Port Angeles, Washington. She was the last native speaker of Klallam, a language targeted for elimination by the US Government along with all other Native American languages since the 1800s. A reversal in federal policy under the Native American Languages Act of 1990/1992 provided funding for Klallam (Kaminksy, 2014), but this support was too little too late to save the language from extinction. However, revitalization

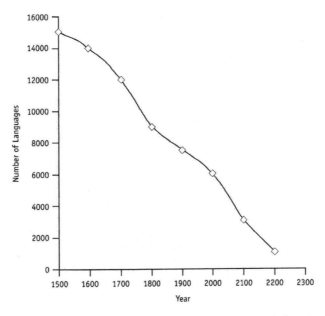

Figure 3.1 Approximate number of languages in the world, 1500–2200 (After Graddol, 2006: 60)

efforts using recordings of Sampson and other deceased tribal elders are being used for Klallam as a second language in a few local schools.

Figure 3.1 illustrates the historical trends in the number of languages in the world since 1500, and leads to a consideration of how many will survive in the future.

Endangered Languages

Language shift, endangerment, and death are phenomena that have existed as long as languages themselves have existed. Well-known historical examples of major language decline include Latin and Ancient Greek. However scholarly attention to issues of language endangerment began in earnest in the 20th century. There is no exact agreement as to the number of living languages in the world today. Many estimates have placed the number between 6,000–7,000 languages (Austin & Sallabank, 2015). The 18th edition of SIL International's *Ethnologue* lists a total of 7,102 living languages, distributed across the globe as shown in Table 3.1 (M.P. Lewis *et al.*, 2015).

Table 3.1 Distribution of living languages in the world

Area	# of languages	Percent
Africa	2,138	30%
Americas	1,064	15%
Asia	2,301	32%
Europe	286	4%
Pacific	1,313	19%

Source: M.P. Lewis *et al.* (2015)

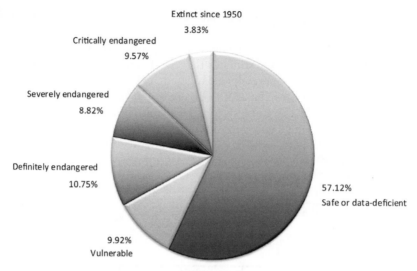

Figure 3.2 Overview of the vitality of the world's languages. Source: Moseley (2010)

There is also a lack of agreement about the exact number of languages that will die, though most experts acknowledge many languages are in trouble. UNESCO's *Atlas of the World's Languages in Danger* (Moseley, 2010) claimed 43% of the world languages are at various stages of endangerment (see Figure 3.2). Thomason (2015) suggests most experts agree about half of the world's languages will be extinct by the end of the 21st century.

The estimates in Figure 3.2 are based on UNESCO's **Language Vitality** and Endangerment Framework of six categories (Moseley, 2010) defined as follows:

- *Safe:* Language is spoken by all generations; **intergenerational transmission** is uninterrupted.
- *Vulnerable:* Most children speak the language, but it may be restricted to certain **domains** (e.g. home).
- *Definitely endangered:* Children no longer learn the language as **mother tongue** in the home.
- *Severely endangered:* Language is spoken by grandparents and older generation; while the parents' generation may understand it, they do not speak it to children or among themselves.
- *Critically endangered:* The youngest speakers are grandparents and older, and they speak the language partially and infrequently.
- *Extinct:* There are no speakers left.

Variations in estimates are due to the fact that languages are dynamic, variable, and constantly changing (M.P. Lewis *et al.*, 2015). It is difficult to identify separate, distinct languages given that languages are constructed socially and often are politically rather than linguistically defined (Makoni & Pennycook, 2007). Boundaries between languages and their different varieties and dialects are blurred and overlapping. There are also problems of gathering reliable, valid and comprehensive information about languages in large expanses such as Africa, South America and parts of Asia. R.E. Moore *et al.* (2010) outline the challenges and pitfalls of linguistic enumeration, and argue for an 'alternative vision that centres not on distinct, named, countable languages, but on speakers and repertoires, and on the actual resources that speakers deploy in actual contexts' (p. 1).

Of the approximately 7,000 languages in the world today, it is predicted that most will not survive. UNESCO estimates that 596 languages are vulnerable, 695 are definitely endangered, 529 are severely endangered, 574 are critically endangered, and 230 have become extinct (Moseley, 2010). Thomason (2015) suggests a language dies (becomes 'dormant') every three months or so. She notes variations in estimates of the demise of current living languages with optimists arguing that 50% of languages will become extinct by 2100, while pessimists suggest a figure closer to 90%. Thus, as few as 700 languages (10%) may survive. There are consequently enthusiastic conservation measures in progress. If approximately 90% of the world's languages are vulnerable, **language planning** measures to maintain linguistic and cultural diversity are urgently required, as is an **ecology of languages** (Vandenbusschem *et al.*, 2014) as will be discussed later in this chapter.

Thomason (2015: 19–35) identifies six causes of language endangerment:

- *Conquest* – The conquerors' language replaces the language(s) of the conquered.
- *Economic pressures* – Employment (or perception that employment) requires proficiency in the majority language.
- *Melting pots* – A nation state with a strong **ideology** towards linguistic and cultural **assimilation** places pressure on immigrants and indigenous groups to abandon their native languages and cultures.
- *Language politics* – Nation states establish (formal and informal) language policies designed to restrict or suppress uses of minority languages.
- *Attitudes* – The way minority speakers feel about their language, its value and its usefulness (due to internal and external societal pressures).
- *Loss of linguistic diversity via standardization* – Most endangered languages have no standardized form. Selection of a single variety for standardization for use in written communication and in schools may lead to further endangerment and ultimate loss of other varieties of the language.

These causes are not necessarily independent of another. They often overlap in complicit ways that lead to **language loss**, particularly of smaller languages associated with less powerful groups.

Crystal (2014) suggests that there are five basic arguments why retaining language diversity is essential and why language planning is needed:

(1) **Diversity is essential.** The concept of an ecosystem is that all living organisms, plants, animals, bacteria and humans survive and prosper through a network of complex and delicate relationships. Damaging one of the elements in the ecosystem will result in unforeseen consequences for the whole of the system. Cultural diversity and biological diversity may be inseparable. For example, where forests are decimated, so are the homelands of the linguistic minority groups living there. Where biodiversity and rich ecosystems exist, so do linguistic and cultural diversity.

Evolution has been aided by genetic diversity, with species genetically adapting in order to survive in different environments. Diversity contains the potential for adaptation. Uniformity holds dangers for the long-term survival of the species. Uniformity can endanger a species by providing inflexibility and inadaptability. The range of cross-fertilization becomes less as languages and cultures die and the testimony of human intellectual achievement is lessened. In the language of ecology, the strongest ecosystems are those that are the most diverse. That is, diversity is directly related to stability; variety is important for long-term survival. Our success on this planet has been due to an ability to adapt to different kinds of environment (atmospheric as well as cultural) over thousands of years.

(2) *Languages express identity*. Identity concerns the shared characteristics of members of a group, community or region. **Identity** helps provide the security and status of a shared existence. Sometimes identity is via dress, religious beliefs, rituals, but language is almost always present in identity formation and identity display. Language is an index, symbol and marker of identity (see Chapter 18).

(3) *Languages are repositories of history*. Languages provide a link to the past, a means to reach an archive of knowledge, ideas and beliefs from our heritage. 'Every language is a living museum, a monument to every culture it has been vehicle to' (Nettle & Romaine, 2000: 14). The range, richness and wealth of cultures, homelands and histories are lost when a language dies. This limits the choice of 'pasts' to preserve, and the value of life past and present. It is analogous to humanity losing one of its whole libraries built over years. The Sicilian poet, Ignazio Buttitta (1972), expressed it thus:

> Shackle a people, strip them bare, cover their mouths: they are still free. Deprive them of work, their passports, food and sleep: they are still rich. A people are poor and enslaved when they are robbed of the language inherited from their parents: it is lost forever.

Batibo (2005), in discussing the potential demise of many of Africa's 2,000 languages, provides the example of medicine. If African languages die, so will centuries of knowledge of the powers of natural medicines: 'some of the traditional medicines used by some of these communities have proved to be effective in treating complex diseases such as cancer, asthma, leprosy and tuberculosis, as well as chronic cases of STD, bilharzia and anaemia' (p. 41). The stored knowledge and understandings in oral languages (without literacies) may die with the death of that language. Written text may store accumulated meanings after **language death**, although translations will often lose a degree of stored insight and nuance.

(4) *Languages contribute to the sum of present human knowledge*. Inside each language is a vision of the past, present and future. When a language dies, its vision of the world dies with it. Language not only transmits visions of the past but also expressions of social relationships, individual friendships as well as community knowledge, a wealth of organizing experiences, rules about social relationships plus ideas about art, craft, science, poetry, song, life, death and language itself. A language contains a way of thinking and being, acting and doing. Different languages contain different understandings of people as individuals and communities, different values and ways of expressing the purpose of life, different visions of past humanity, present priorities and our future existence.

Language lies at the heart of education, culture and identity. When a language dies, so does a considerable amount of the culture, identity and knowledge that has been passed down from generation to generation through and within that language. Knowledge about local land management, lake and sea technology, plant cultivation and animal husbandry may die with language death. Each language contains a view of

---

Box 3.1 Avoiding language death

Crystal (2014) suggests that there are a number of solutions to avoid language death. While the solutions will be different for languages at different stages of survival and revitalization, he suggests that an endangered language will progress if its speakers:

- increase their prestige within the dominant community;
- increase their wealth relative to the dominant community;
- have access to a stable economic base;
- increase their legitimate power in the eyes of the dominant community;
- increase the number of domains in which their language is used;
- have a critical mass in communities and regions;
- have a strong presence in the educational system;
- have a literacy in that language;
- make use of electronic technology;
- have a strong sense of ethnic identity;
- have internal and external recognition as a group with unique unity;
- resist the influence of the dominant culture or are protected and formally recognized by that dominant culture.

---

the universe, a particular understanding of the world. If there are approximately 7,000 living languages, then there are at least 7,000 overlapping ways to describe the world. That variety provides a rich mosaic.

(5) *Languages are interesting in themselves*. Language itself is important, each language having different sounds, grammar and vocabulary that reveal something different about linguistic organization and structure. The more languages there are to study, the more our understanding about the beauty of language grows.

Language Policies

The solution to avoiding language death involves language policy, with interventions to stop or reverse the decline of a language. This is also termed minority **language revitalization**. Some majority languages, particularly English, have expanded considerably during the last century. Many minority languages are in danger of extinction and therefore need extra care and protection. Intervention by language planning is essential to avoid such trends.

In contrast, a language policy-maker who is concerned only for majority languages will regard protecting rare languages as expensive and unnecessary, and will wish to standardize the variety of language in the country. In the US, for example, many politicians prefer monolingualism to **bilingualism**. The preference is for the assimilation of minority language communities into a more standardized, monochrome language world. Many policy makers may have an evolutionist attitude towards languages. That is, following Darwin's idea of the survival of the fittest, if a weaker language fails to adapt to the modern world, it deserves to die. A different way of expressing this is in terms of a free, *laissez-faire* language economy. Languages must survive on their own merits without the support of language planning.

There are criticisms of this evolutionary or laissez-faire viewpoint:

(1) Survival of the fittest is too simplistic a view of evolution. It only accents the negative side of evolution: killing, exploitation and suppression.

> **Box 3.2** The ecology of language
>
> Hornberger (2006) succinctly expresses three themes of an ecology of language perspective: 'The first theme is that languages, like living species, evolve, grow, change, live, and die in relation to other languages – a language evolution theme. Second, languages interact with the environment (socio-political, economic, cultural, educational, historical, demographic, etc.) – the language environment theme. A third theme is the notion that some languages, like some species and environments, may be endangered and that the ecology movement is about not only studying and describing those potential losses, but also counteracting them; this I call the language endangerment theme.' Hult (2013: 1) explains 'the ecology of language is a conceptual orientation to critical thinking about multilingualism that calls upon researchers to focus on relationships among languages, on relationships among social contexts of language, on relationships among individual speakers and their languages, and on inter-relationships among these three dimensions'.

(2) There are human-made reasons why languages die due to political and economic policies. It is possible to analyze and determine what causes language shift rather than simply believing language shift occurs by accident. Social and political factors, and not just 'evolution', are at work in language loss. Power, prejudice, discrimination, marginalization and subordination are some of the causes of language decline and death (e.g. Native American languages in the US). Language loss is thus not 'evolutionary' but determined by politicians, policy-makers and peoples (May, 2011).

(3) Evolutionists who argue for an economic, cost–benefit approach to languages, with the **domination** of a few majority languages for international communication, hold a narrow view of the function of languages. Languages are not purely for economic communication. They are also concerned with human culture, human heritage, identity and social relationships, and the value of a garden full of different languages rather than the one variety.

(4) Those who advocate monolingualism often feel that their particular culture and perspectives are the only legitimate or modern varieties – others are inferior and less worth preserving. Rather than constant competition, a more positive and accurate view of evolution is interdependence, that is, cooperation for mutually beneficial outcomes.

Language Planning

If the world's languages are to be retained, then immediate policy interventions and impactful strategies are needed. Language planning, sometimes called language management or language engineering, refers to 'deliberate efforts to influence the behavior of others with respect to the acquisition, structure, or functional allocation of their language codes' (Cooper, 1989: 45). Wiley (2015) notes that Cooper's definition helped move language planning away from a narrow view of solving language 'problems'. Wiley adds that Cooper's use of the word *influence* 'suggests that planning is not always official or even explicit as influence often functions as a dimension of ideological control, wherein compliance can be obtained through the "manufacture of consent" rather than by coercion' (2015: 166).

Traditionally, language planning involves three inter-dependent and integrated processes (Wiley, 2015): (a) **acquisition planning** (creating **language spread** by increasing the number of speakers and uses), (b) **status planning** (e.g. raising the status of a language within society across as many institutions as possible), and (c) **corpus planning** (e.g. modernizing terminology, standardization of grammar and spelling). We consider each below in more detail.

(1) **Acquisition planning** is the bedrock of language planning. In the past acquisition planning focused mainly on the acquisition of a language in school. It is now also particularly concerned with language reproduction in the family. The intergenerational transmission of a language – parents passing their language(s) onto their children – and language learning in bilingual education is an essential but insufficient foundation for language survival and maintenance. In all minority languages, there are families who use the majority language (e.g. English) with their children, perhaps under the belief that this will lead to economic, employment or educational advantages. Or that the majority language has such high prestige in the neighborhood that parents feel the minority language has associations of poverty or powerlessness. Such attitudes can have an immediate effect on the fate of a language. This lack of family language reproduction is a principal and direct cause of language shift. In this scenario, a minority language can die within two or three generations unless bilingual education can produce language speakers who then find everyday purposes (e.g. economic, social, religious) for that language.

Language acquisition planning is therefore partly about encouraging parents to raise their children bilingually. Morris and Jones (2008) note grass-roots interventions to persuade parents to use a minority language with their very young children in the Basque country, Wales, Ireland and Sweden. They portray a scheme whereby midwives, nurses and health workers provide expectant mothers and new parents with information about the many benefits of bilingualism. This intervention attempts to lead new parents to make a deliberate and rational choice about the languages of the home, choice in pre-school education and later bilingual education. They also indicate the strong influence of the mass media in a child's socialization process. Barron-Hauwaert (2011) reveals the powerful effect of siblings on the development of a minority language in the home. Where there is a shortfall in **language maintenance** in families, education becomes the principal means of producing more language speakers. L. Hinton (2015) identifies a number of school-based language revitalization approaches, such as language classes, bilingual education programs (including immersion programs, small immersion schools and language nests), and adult education programs.

(2) **Status planning** is political by nature, attempting to gain more recognition, functions and capacity for a language. By maintaining use in particular domains (contexts), and sometimes spreading into new language domains, a language may hopefully be secured and revitalized (e.g. official use of that language in courts of law, local (regional) and central government, education, mass media and as many public, private and voluntary institutions as possible). Through laws, rights (see Chapter 17) and constitutions, but also by persuasion and precedent, status planning attempts to conserve, revitalize or spread a language. For example, there are well-established bilingual or multilingual parliaments (legislatures) in the Basque Country, Canada, Catalonia, Ireland, Scotland, Singapore, South Africa, Switzerland and Wales. Such parliaments give the minority language(s) prestige and value. Special attention is often given to modernization to ensure that the language is used in modern, influential spheres such as on television, radio, movies, advertising, newspapers and magazines, computers, smartphones and

other mobile devices, the internet, and in popular culture domains such as rap, reggae and hip hop music (Moriarty, 2015).

Status planning is found in a variety of policies: political movements seeking recognition or official status for a language (both minority languages like Māori and Welsh, and majority languages like English in the United States), as well as religious and nationalist movements seeking revitalization of a language, such as Hebrew in Israel. However, while individuals may be influenced by such changes in status of a language, such actions are not guaranteed to maintain a language. To influence language change, status planning has to affect everyday usage in the home and street, family and work relationships, and not just official usage. Thus opportunity planning for daily use of the minority language is essential. Demand has to precede and follow supply. Also people's choices about language may be governed by their perceptions of the 'market', and be neither easily influenced nor rational (as is supposed by rational interventions in language planning).

(3) **Corpus planning** is a typical part of language planning both where languages are precarious and where they are resurgent. Many endangered languages are spoken but lack writing systems, and/or their use has traditionally been almost entirely in oral domains. Thus, corpus planning may be deemed necessary to undertake orthographic development to provide an endangered language with a writing system (Lüpke, 2015). However, such efforts to provide a standardized writing system for use in bilingual education and other language revitalization education programs may actually result in an artificial idealized form based on just one variety of the language, and may further endanger authentic traditional varieties of the language. Weber and Horner (2012) argue this was the case with efforts surrounding the Breton language in France. In Cambodia, attempts to address the concern of privileging one variety over the other in the creation of an orthography for the indigenous Tampuen language are handled in part through a Tampuen Language Committee consisting of speakers representing different varieties. This committee reviews and approves books and other materials created for use in bilingual education programs.

A common process for all languages, majority and minority, is to modernize vocabulary. Science and information communications technology (ICT) are just two examples where standardized terminology is created and spread. An alternative is the increasing use of 'loan words'. Schools, books and magazines, television, movies, radio, the internet and social media all help to standardize a language, and hence new concepts need an agreed term. The Catalans, Basques, Welsh and Irish are examples of language groups that formally engage in corpus planning through centrally-funded initiatives. Another example is France, which, since the establishment of the Académie Française, has tried to maintain the purity of French and halt the influence of English. When corpus planning is about purity and normalization there is a danger that power and status will go to those who claim to speak a purer language and a lower status will be ascribed to those who speak non-standard varieties and dialects.

In Wales, it has been found useful to also consider a fourth category: usage or opportunity language planning (see Box 3.3). This refers to top-down and bottom-up language planning interventions that directly seek to increase the integrative use of the Welsh language and its attendant culture in areas such as leisure, sport and technology, to foster social networking through Welsh, and to increase the instrumental use of the Welsh language in the economy, for example in the workplace, employment

Box 3.3 Language planning: the strategy in Wales

ACQUISITION
1. Family Language Reproduction
2. Bilingual Education – pre-school to university
3. Adult Language Learning

STATUS – SOCIETAL
1. Institutionalization (e.g. use in local and national government and organizations)
2. Modernity (e.g. use on television, internet)

CORPUS
1. Linguistic Standardization (e.g. by dictionaries, school, TV)
2. Public Vernacular (Clear or Plain Welsh)

USAGE / OPPORTUNITY – INDIVIDUAL
1. Economic, workplace (instrumental)
2. Culture, leisure, sports, social, religious, social networks (integrative)

and education (C. Baker, 2008). McCarty (2013) shows that efforts to revitalize Native American Indigenous languages in the United States can successfully include grass-roots language planning, through community involvement, parent-community links, asserting the link between language and ancestral land, 'master speakers' mentoring apprentice language learners, and **heritage language** schooling.

However, such planning is inter-connected. What happens inside the family is affected by government policies, and vice versa. The spreading of a language into more high status domains is both a cause and an effect of increased intergenerational transmission of a language (e.g. the use of a minority language for employment).

It is possible to plan for the status, corpus and acquisition of a language and yet not affect the daily language usage of ordinary people. To be effective in achieving its goals, language planning has to impact on individual language life. Languages decline when speakers drop in number and their daily usage diminishes. Therefore, language planning has to relate to everyday language life as enacted in homes, streets, schools, communities, workplaces and leisure activities. In Wales, such planning involves interventions in the economy so that minority language speakers can function in Welsh in employment (C.H. Williams, 2014). A Welsh saying declares 'No local economy, no community; no community, no language.' Such planning also involves targeting key local cultural, leisure, social and community institutions where minority languages speakers will use their language, and form relationships and networks using that language. Planning also needs to empower local communities directly, enabling everyday language life to be enacted through a minority language. Opportunities for 'teenagers and twenties' to use their minority language is particularly crucial as they are the next generation of parents, and hence the fate of a minority language partly rests on these shoulders.

However, even the most advanced and dynamic language planning may not be enough to save a threatened minority language (see Box 3.4). Such planning can attempt to persuade parents and speakers; it cannot control. It is nearly impossible to plan for a less dominant role for English or control its spread across domains and dominions. Language planning also has to be part of wider economic, social and political processes and policy-making, sensitive to regional and area differences and traditions.

Cooper (1989: 98) provides a classic scheme for understanding language planning by asking a series of key questions:

- **which actors** (e.g. elites, influential people, counter-elites, non-elite policy implementers)
- **attempt to influence which behaviors** (e.g. the purposes or functions for which the language is to be used)
- **of which people** (e.g. of which individuals or organizations)
- **for what ends** (e.g. overt (language-related behaviors) or latent (non-language-related behaviors, the satisfaction of interests))
- **under what conditions** (e.g. political, economic, social, demographic, ecological, cultural)
- **by what means** (e.g. authority, force, promotion, persuasion)
- **through what decision-making processes and means**
- **with what effect or outcome?**

This relatively comprehensive set of questions indicates that language planning may be generated by different groups. For example, poets, linguists, lexicographers, missionaries, soldiers as well as administrators, legislators and politicians may become involved in language planning. Cooper argues, however, that language planning is more likely to succeed when it is embraced or promoted by elite groups or counter-elites. Such elites tend to work primarily from their own self-interests. Language planning is thus often motivated by efforts to secure or reinforce the interests of particular people. Makoni and Makoni (2015), reflecting on many tensions and conflicts that have arisen between different language institutions in South Africa operating in the policy sphere, concluded that sometimes 'too many cooks spoil the broth' (p. 552). However, language planning may positively affect the masses by adding to their self-identity, self-esteem and social connectedness and giving increased economic and employment opportunities.

A consideration of language planning runs the danger of over-emphasizing its importance in overall political planning. Language planning is rarely high priority for governments. First, there is often piecemeal political pragmatism rather than planning. The revival of Hebrew is often quoted as one triumphant and successful example of language planning. Yet the rapid advance of Hebrew in Israel appears to have occurred by improvisation and diverse ventures rather than by carefully structured, systematic and sequenced language planning (Weber & Horner, 2012).

Second, political and economic decisions usually govern language decisions. Language decisions are typically relatively minor concerns of governments, whose pervading interests are more frequently about power and purse. Language is usually an outcome from other decisions rather than a determinant of social, political or economic policies. Yet, as the European Commission has increasingly stressed, the need for bilingualism and **multilingualism** in Europe relates to European cultural and economic development, and to stability and equality in society. Bilingualism is one part of inter-connected politics anywhere in the world. Third, language planning depends on winning hearts and minds (e.g. of parents). Top-down government language planning cannot control, it merely attempts to influence. Therefore, bottom-up language planning is also needed. As C.H. Williams (2014) reflects on many years of Welsh language revitalization efforts:

> If the Welsh example of language revitalization teaches us anything, it is that stubborn collective action by the community must be stimulated before government language

Box 3.4 Littlebear's litany on failed language planning for Native American languages

Language planning has tended to proceed by trial and error and not by well-conceived prioritization. Richard Littlebear's (1996: 1) litany on failed language planning measures with Native American languages tells of that history:

Probably because of [a] tradition of failure, we latch onto anything that looks as though it will preserve our languages. As a result, we now have a litany of what we have viewed as the one item that will save our languages. This one item is usually quickly replaced by another.
    For instance, some of us said, 'Let's get our languages into written form' and we did,
      and still our Native American languages kept on dying.
Then we said, 'Let's make dictionaries for our languages' and we did,
      and still the languages kept on dying.
Then we said, 'Let's get linguists trained in our own languages' and we did,
      and still the languages kept on dying.
Then we said, 'Let's train our own people who speak our languages to become linguists' and we did,
      and still our languages kept on dying.
Then we said, 'Let's apply for a federal bilingual education grant' and we did and got a grant,
      and still our languages kept on dying.
Then we said, 'Let's let the schools teach the languages' and we did,
      and still the languages kept on dying.
Then we said, 'Let's develop culturally-relevant materials' and we did,
      and still our languages kept on dying.
Then we said, 'Let's use language masters to teach our languages' and we did,
      and still our languages kept on dying.
Then we said, 'Let's tape-record the elders speaking our languages' and we did,
      and still our languages kept on dying.
Then we said, 'Let's video-tape our elders speaking and doing cultural activities' and we did,
      and still our languages kept on dying.
Then we said, 'Let's put our native language speakers on CD-ROM' and we did,
      and still the languages kept on dying.
In this litany, we have viewed each item as the one that will save our languages,
    – and they haven't.

policy responds in a reactive manner, but having so responded, that community engagement must also be maintained, for fear of losing direction and long-term momentum. (p. 268)

Menken and García (2010) argue that teachers play a major role as language policy makers and planners in their classrooms and schools. Teachers are authoritative role models who can influence both language assimilation (e.g. when they only use one majority language in the classroom) or language sustainability (e.g. when they use the minority language in the classroom). When top-down language policy and planning enters the classroom door, it is up to the teacher to understand, negotiate and implement the policy. Thus, teachers often control language norms, what constitutes educated speech, and thereby allow bilingualism or monolingualism to flourish.

Status, corpus, acquisition and usage language planning cannot focus exclusively on the minority language, but must also address bilingualism. Minority language monolingualism is usually impracticable and unfavorable to individuals (e.g. for employment). Where minority languages exist, there is usually the need to be bilingual if not multilingual. A 'monolingualism' approach to a minority language and culture may be tantamount to language death. Thus, language planning centered on bilingualism may be key to a minority language's survival.

Language Revitalization

According to C.H. Williams (2014), language revitalization is an attempt to counter the factors and trends that lead to the decline in the learning and use of a language. He describes language revitalization as a 'sometimes mysterious, often idiosyncratic process which always involves struggle, sacrifice, and tension,' and ultimately is 'a conscious effort to change ideas, values, attitudes, and behaviors' (p. 242). UNESCO identifies nine factors that may affect language revitalization (see Box 3.5).

We need a historical and sociological perspective to help explain patterns of interaction that relate to language revitalization. C.H. Williams (2000) suggests there are often five historical stages in minority language revitalization: (a) idealism (e.g. to construct a vision of language revival); (b) protest (e.g. to mobilize people to change the use or status of a minority language); (c) legitimacy (e.g. to attain language rights for the minority language, in order to secure its survival and enhance its status); (d) institutionalization (e.g. to secure the presence of the language in key agencies of the state, such as public administration, law, education, employment and commercial activity); and (e) parallelism (e.g. to extend the minority language to as many social domains as possible, such as sport, media, entertainment, public services, private industry). C.H. Williams (2014) also identified four pillars of language revitalization: (a) language policy and socio-legal developments; (b) formal education; (c) the family; and (d) community life.

Language revitalization is possible even for so called 'dead' or 'extinct' languages that have not been spoken for generations (Hinton & Hale, 2001). Examples of such language 'regenesis', 'resurrection' and 'reclamation' among Indigenous languages in North America include Wôpanâak and Miami/Myaamia (Leonard, 2008; McCarty, 2013; see Chapter 4 for the example of Manx Gaelic in the United Kingdom). Due to the potential for revival, many scholars and revivalists prefer to speak of dormant or 'sleeping languages,' or what Ghil'ad Zuckerman calls 'sleeping beauties' (Zuckerman & Monaghan, 2012).

We must also recognize that within a language ecology, the revival of one language can lead to the decline of other languages within the same area. For example, Weber and Horner (2012) note that revitalization efforts for Hebrew in Israel were harmful to other languages such as Arabic and Jewish languages such as Yiddish and Ladino. Shohamy (2008) analyzed historical documents from the Hebrew revitalization period,

---

Box 3.5 UNESCO's nine factors affecting language revitalization

1. Intergenerational language transmission
2. Absolute number of speakers
3. Proportion of speakers within the total population
4. Shifts in domains of language use
5. Response to new domains and media
6. Availability of materials for language education and literacy
7. Governmental and institutional language attitudes and policies, including official status and use
8. Community members' attitudes towards their own language
9. Amount and quality of documentation

Source: http://www.unesco.org/new/en/culture/themes/endangered-languages/faq-on-endangered-languages/

finding that not only were the policies often subtractive of linguistic diversity, but also violated the basic human rights of many individuals. As she describes it, 'The goal of reviving Hebrew was so important that all means were justified, no questions asked' (2008: 215). In Canada, Europe, Cambodia, and other countries, efforts to revitalize many of the indigenous languages have not been matched by an interest in the languages of immigrants.

A Theory of Language Reversal

In the early 1990s, Joshua Fishman (2001) began refining his major theories grounded in his many years of research and reflection regarding the reversal of language shift (see O. García, Peltz & Schiffman, 2006; Hornberger & Pütz, 2006 for collections of Fishman's writings). Fishman sought to answer the question 'what are the priorities in planning language shift?' For example, what is the point of pouring money into minority language mass media and bilingual bureaucracy when home, family, neighborhood and face-to-face community use of the minority language is lacking? It is like blowing air into a punctured balloon.

Fishman's underlying philosophy is to achieve social justice and to support **cultural pluralism** and cultural self-determination. The destruction of minority languages is the destruction of intimacy, family and community, often involving oppression of the weak by the strong, subjugating the unique and traditional by the uniform and central. Thus, Fishman argues for greater sociocultural self-sufficiency, self-help, self-regulation and initiative among linguistic communities.

Fishman also argues that language reversal derives not just from a societal philosophy but also from personal motivations. There are those who believe that reversing a language shift is purely about the accumulation of power and money by a minority language group. This view is simplistic and misguided. Fishman argues that human values, feelings, loyalties and basic life-philosophies are present in the complex reasons for language change. Language activists often have ideals, commitments, even altruism, that make their motives more than just power and money. Minority languages and cultures, in their desire for a healthy existence, may be sometimes irrational or superrational. This is similar to religion, love, art and music where there are personal elements that transcend conscious rationality, and go beyond self-interest in power and money.

Steps in Reversing Language Shift

Fishman first began systematically publishing on his Graded Intergenerational Dislocation Scale (GIDS) in the early 1990s as an aid to understanding language planning and attempted language reversal from an international perspective across all minority languages. Table 3.2 provides the most current version which appeared in Fishman (2001), and has subsequently been reprinted, including in Fishman (2013). Thus it remains an influential scale. Just as the Richter scale measures intensity of earthquakes, so Fishman's scale gives a guide to how far a minority language is threatened and disrupted in international terms. The higher the number on the scale, the more a language (referred to as 'Xish') is threatened by a dominant majority language (referred to as 'Yish'). The idea of stages is that it is little good attempting later stages if earlier stages are not at least partly achieved. Various foundations are needed before building the upper levels. The value of the scale is that it prioritizes major actions for reversing languages in decline. The eight stages are briefly summarized below.

Table 3.2 Toward a theory of reversing language shift: stages of Reversing Language Shift and severity of intergenerational dislocation (read from the bottom up)

1	Educational, work sphere, mass media, and (quasi-)governmental operations in Xish at the highest (nationwide) levels.
2	Local/regional mass media and (quasi-)governmental services in Xish.
3	Local/regional (i.e. supra-neighborhood) work sphere, both among Xmen and among Ymen.
4b	Public schools for Xish children, offering some instruction via Xish, but substantially under Yish curricular and staffing control.
4a	School in lieu of compulsory education and substantially under Xish curricular and staffing control.
B	*RLS efforts to transcend **diglossia**, subsequent to its attainment?*
5	Schools for Xish literacy acquisition, for the old and/or for the young, and not in lieu of compulsory education.
6	The organization of intergenerational and demographically concentrated home-family-neighborhood efforts: The basis of Xish mother-tongue transmission.
7	Cultural interaction in Xish primarily involving the community-based older generation (beyond the age of giving birth).
8	Reconstructing Xish and adult acquisition of XSL.
A	*RLS to attain diglossia (assuming prior ideological clarification)?*

Source: (Fishman, 2013)

Limits and Critics

While Fishman is careful to point out that one stage is not necessarily dependent on a previous stage, there are priorities. The more advanced stages cannot usually be secured unless the fundamental stages are either first built or repaired. The danger is in advancing on all fronts. Attempting to win individual battles without having a strategy for the whole war does not champion success. There is also a danger in working solely for tangible, newsworthy, easily recognized victories. Changing the language of road signs and tax forms and gaining minority language presence on television are battles that have been fought and won in some minority language regions. It is more difficult, but more important, to support and encourage the minority language for communication in daily family and community life. For Fishman, it is the informal and intimate spoken language reproduced across generations that is the ultimate pivot of language shift.

Fishman (2013) is particularly guarded about how much bilingual education can achieve in reversing language shift. There is sometimes the belief that, where families do not transmit the minority language, the school is there to do it instead. Where parents do not bring up their children in the minority language, the school is expected to be the substitute minority language parent. A school can initiate second language acquisition in the minority language. However, not all students will continue to use the school-learnt language throughout life, including in parenting their children. Even when a child successfully learns minority language oracy and literacy skills in school, unless there is considerable support in the community and the economy outside school, that language may wither. A classroom-learnt second language may become a school-only language.

For that language to survive inside the individual, a person needs to become bonded in **language minority** social networks while at school, and particularly after leaving school. There needs to be pre-school, out-of-school and after-school support and reward systems for using the minority language. The minority language needs to be embedded in the family–neighborhood–community experience and in the economics of the family. Unless this happens, it is much less likely that bilingually-educated children will pass on the minority language to the next generation. Thus, for Fishman, each stage needs examining for how it can be used to feed into Stage 6 – the inter-generational transmission of the minority language.

Fishman's eight stages must be seen as overlapping and interacting. In language revival, it is not the case of going one step or stage at a time. The myriad factors in language reversal link together in complex patterns. A language at Stage 2 may still be securing elements of previous stages. A language at Stage 6 may be engaged in long-term planning to secure higher stages.

Language settings vary so much that the scale cannot be indiscriminately applied to each. For example, different communities and different geographical areas may be at different stages within the same nation. Also, the use of the minority language in business and the local economy may vary considerably from rural to urban areas, social class to social class, and according to closeness of access to airports, roads, railways and sea links. Some minority language groups may just aspire to an oral rather than a literate transmission of language to succeeding generations. For other minority language groups, reaching the highest GIDS point may be difficult to achieve and more of a long-term aim, for example the language being used in higher education. There may not be the financial basis for developing mass media or any political will for minority language higher education.

Spolsky (2004: 215) suggests that the danger of Fishman's scale is that it 'puts too much emphasis on language and language management, and so distracts attention from the social and economic factors which are likely to be the major sources of changes in language shift'. Hornberger and King (2001) also argue that Reversing Language Shift does not indicate the economic processes and interventions that are so important for language revival. For parents to raise their children in the minority language, for schools to have a strong reason for content teaching through the minority language, economic and employment incentives and rewards are crucial to language revival, but not sufficient in themselves. Economic prescriptions are needed to provide a strong rationale for intergenerational transmission. Integrative motives and cultural sentiment may not be enough to persuade parents, educators and students to use the minority language. The economic base of the language community can be a vital safeguard to the maintenance of a threatened language. The state, and not just the local language community, is thus important (e.g. in economic regeneration of a language minority area). Material dimensions of success (individual and societal) and economic advancement have grown in importance in a consumerist society. Because these areas are often controlled by majority language groups, a power struggle becomes vital.

Digital Tools for Language Revitalization

The promise of internet technology and other digital tools for language revitalization efforts were mentioned briefly in the discussion above, but require deeper consideration. Thomason (2015) notes that modern efforts are heavily dependent on the internet. Revitalization websites exist for many endangered languages. Social networking, video streaming, Twitter, Facebook, blogs, wikis, smartphones, tablets and other mobile devices, talking digital dictionaries, and machine translation hold great promise for opening up new domains for the use of endangered languages, especially among the 'digital native' youth who rely on digital tools for much of their verbal and textual communications. However, Thomason also outlines several concerns and other issues that need to be considered in language revitalization efforts in the digital age:

(1) Informed consent – The ease of making language data widely available online raises complications with treating members of the **speech community** with respect and obtaining their informed consent. Some in the community may object to having their voices, or the voices of their deceased ancestors, online and available to the general public.

(2) Intellectual property rights – Should language communities have the right to decide if their languages are included for use in software packages such as Microsoft products or Google Translate?

(3) Digital divide – The majority of endangered languages are unlikely to cross the digital divide because most speakers do not have access to expensive digital tools or the Internet. Those who do have access may lack the requisite knowledge to create websites or use their languages on existing sites, and thus resort to using a dominant societal language.

(4) Forms of writing – While official webpages established for endangered languages may attempt to establish use of a standardized (and perhaps artificial) variety of the language, the use of written language in social media, especially by the youth, tends be to very informal. However, such informal use may in fact foster language use among the youth.

Nonetheless, Thomason notes there have been many successful initiatives to establish a digital presence for endangered languages. For example, revitalization efforts for the Native American language Northern Pomo – spoken in northern California for thousands of years – include a website (http://northernpomolanguagetools.com/) featuring a range of digital language tools, and mobile apps for both iOS and Android devices. Perhaps as the cost for digital tools comes down, as free or affordable access to the internet expands around the world, and as social media sites become ever more accommodating of linguistic diversity, language revitalization activists and digital native youth will find it increasingly easier and quite natural to use their languages online for fun, meaningful and authentic communication purposes.

Conclusion

This chapter commenced with the current concerns about the future of over 7,000 languages, many of which are dying. Forecasts of wide-scale language decline and death are met with calls to retain language diversity. Such retention of the world's languages requires intervention: language planning. Such language planning requires a reproduction and production line among the young, via families and schools. For parents and schools to be motivated to pass on minority languages, there must be reasons: instrumental and integrative, economic, employment, social and cultural, sometimes religious. The fate of minority languages requires an understanding of how two or more languages interact in society.

Language planning is aided by conceptual frameworks regarding language vitality, revitalization and language reversal. Language reversal sometimes means that such language groups shift to insignificance, even death. At other times, they attempt to spread and not just survive. One argument for the survival of languages has been that as languages die, so does part of the totality of human history and culture. However, language revival efforts may be undertaken to awaken dormant or 'sleeping' languages. A theory of language revitalization is also about the realities of everyday futures for children.

Key Points in This Chapter

➤ The languages of the world are rapidly declining in number with predictions of 50–90% of the world's languages dying or near death in the next century. The world's language and cultural diversity is thus endangered.

➤ Language planning is needed for language maintenance, revitalization and reversing language shift. Language planning includes acquisition planning (e.g. home and education), status planning (e.g. in key institutions) and corpus planning (e.g. standardization and modernization).

➤ Language revitalization efforts are affected by a range of factors, including intergenerational language transmission, number and proportion of speakers, shifts in domains of language use, attitudes towards the language, and availability of and responses to materials, new domains and media.

➤ Fishman's model of Reversing Language Shift has eight stages that reflect different conditions in the health of a language and steps needed to revive a language.

➤ The transmission of a minority language in the family is an essential foundation for the re-building of that language.

➤ So called 'dead' languages may be better thought of as dormant or 'sleeping beauties' that can be revived or 'awakened'.

➤ Digital technology holds great promise but also introduces new challenges in language revitalization.

Suggested Further Reading

📖 Austin, P. K., & Sallabank, J. (Eds.). (2015). *The Cambridge handbook of endangered languages.* Cambridge, UK: Cambridge University Prssssess.

📖 Coronel-Molina, S. M., & McCarty, T. L. (Eds.). (2016). *Indigenous language revitalization in the Americas.* New York, NY: Routledge.

📖 Hirsch, D. (2014). *Endangered languages, knowledge systems and belief systems.* New York, NY: Peter Lang.

📖 Jones, M. C. (Ed.) (2015). *Policy and planning for endangered languages.* Cambridge, UK: Cambridge University Press.

📖 Thomason, S. G. (2015). *Endangered languages: An introduction.* Cambridge, UK: Cambridge University Press.

On the Web

🖥 Ethnologue, Languages of the World
http://www.ethnologue.com/

🖥 Terralingua: Unity in Bicultural Diversity
http://www.terralingua.org/

🖥 Foundation for Endangered Languages
http://www.ogmios.org/home.htm

🖥 UNESCO Atlas of the World's Languages in Danger
http://www.unesco.org/languages-atlas/en/atlasmap.html

Discussion Questions

(1) Why should we care when a language dies? Of the arguments for language diversity offered by Crystal, which do you find the most compelling?
(2) What are the three major types of language planning? How are they interlinked, and why is each needed to preserve or revitalize a threatened language?
(3) View the following video about Eliezer Ben-Yehuda, a key activist in the revitalization of Hebrew: https://youtu.be/pgjq8uqQ79E. Discuss the issues of language planning and language revitalization described in this chapter that are evident in Ben-Yehuda's efforts.

Study Activities

(1) Using the Ethnologue website (http://www.ethnologue.com/) identify and map an endangered language within your local region or country. Drawing on library, internet, and/or original source materials (i.e. interviews with local speakers), create a multimedia presentation about the language, its stage on the GIDS scale (Table 3.2), and what revitalization efforts are currently taking place, or could be taking place to preserve the language.
(2) Search on the internet for information on one revived language (e.g. Manx Gaelic in the Isle of Man, Hebrew, Basque, Catalan, Welsh). What is the recent history of the language in numbers and use across domains? What revival efforts have been made? What interventions have been particularly successful?
(3) Choose an immigrant language in your community. Using Thomason's (2015) framework of 6 factors leading to language endangerment, and Crystal's solutions for avoiding language death (Box 3.1), interview some youths from the community to evaluate the degree to which their immigrant language may be endangered.

CHAPTER 4

Languages in Society

CHAPTER 4

Languages in Society

Introduction

Bilinguals are present in every country of the world, in every social class and in all age groups. Numerically, bilinguals and multilinguals are in the majority in the world: it is estimated that they constitute between half and two thirds of the world's population (Grosjean, 2012). As Romaine (2013) observes:

> The concentration of the world's 6,900 languages into about 200 countries means that there are over 30 times as many languages as there are countries, or in other words, that bilingualism and multilingualism is present in practically every country in the world, whether officially recognized or not. (p. 448)

The bilingual population of the world is growing as internationalism is spreading in trade and travel, communications and mass media, immigration and an interlinked global economy. Globalization and interculturalism are both the cause and an effect of bilingualism and multilingualism.

Bilingual individuals do not exist as separated islands. Rather, people who speak two or more languages usually exist in networks, communities and sometimes in regions. People who speak a minority language within a majority language **context** may be said to form a **speech community** or language community.

Bilingualism at the individual level is half the story. The other essential half is to analyze how groups of language speakers behave and change. Such an examination particularly focuses on the movement and development in language use across decades. Such change in a minority language is often downwards. A **language minority** is rarely stable in its size, strength or safety. Therefore, examining the politics and power situation in which minority languages are situated becomes important (see Chapters 17 and 18).

This chapter focuses on the idea that there is no language without a language community. Since language communities do not usually exist in isolation from other communities, it becomes important to examine the contact between different language communities. The rapid growth of access to information (e.g. across the internet) and international travel has meant that language communities are rarely if ever stable. Some languages become stronger (e.g. English); other languages decline, even die. Some languages thought to be dead may occasionally be revived (e.g. Manx Gaelic in the Isle of Man). This chapter therefore seeks to examine language communities, language contact, language change and language conflict. This will reveal that decisions about bilingual education are part of a much wider whole. That is, bilingual education can only be properly understood by examining the circumstances of language communities in which such education occurs.

This chapter takes a sociolinguistic perspective. **Sociolinguistics** is the study of language in relation to social groups, social class, ethnicity and other interpersonal factors in communication. The chapter examines central sociolinguistic concepts such as **diglossia, transglossia, language shift, language maintenance, language death** and **language spread** (including the rise of global English in bilingualism and multilingualism).

Diglossia and Transglossia

The term bilingualism is typically used to describe the two languages of an individual. When the focus changes to two languages in society, the term often used is **diglossia** (C.A. Ferguson, 1959). Terms such as **triglossia**, multiglossia or polyglossia are used to describe societal contexts with three or more languages (Batibo, 2005; Kemp, 2009). While the term diglossia has become broadened and refined, it was originally derived from the Greek word for having two languages. In practice, a language community may use one language in certain situations and for certain functions, the other language in different circumstances and for different functions. For example, a language community may use a minority language in the home, for religious purposes and in social activity, but use the majority language at work, in education and with mass media. This is not universal, and some language communities use two or more languages for the same purpose (e.g. in bilingual education).

C.A. Ferguson (1959) first described diglossia in terms of two varieties of the same language (dialects). Fishman (1980) extended the idea of diglossia to two languages existing side-by-side within a geographical area. Ferguson's original description distinguishes between a higher status language (called H) and a lower status one (called L). This distinction can reflect the difference between a majority (H) and minority (L) language within a country. In both situations, different languages or varieties may be used for different purposes as illustrated in Table 4.1.

Table 4.1 Diglossia

Context	Majority Language (H)	Minority Language (L)
1 The home and family		✓
2 Schooling	✓	
3 Mass media, internet sites	✓	
4 Business and commerce	✓	
5 Social and cultural activity in the community		✓
6 Email, texting, social media		✓
7 Correspondence with government departments	✓	
8 Religious activity		✓

Table 4.1 illustrates how the minority language is more likely to be used in informal personal situations and the majority language used more in formal official communication contexts. It is sometimes embarrassing or belittling for a speaker to use the 'low' variety of language in a situation where the 'high' variety is the norm. For example, at a graduation ceremony at a rural high school deep in southern Thailand, students

giggled and teachers squirmed with embarrassment as the student speaker slipped from Standard Thai (H) into the local southern dialect (L).

The distinction between majority and minority languages is possibly more about the status and power of languages than about the languages as language varieties. Table 4.1 suggests that different language situations usually make one language more prestigious than the other. The majority language will often be perceived as the more eminent, elegant and educative language. It is usually seen as the door to both educational and economic success. With concern that labels such as H and L suggest that L languages and varieties are inferior, Fishman (1991) updated his diglossia model to describe X*ish* and Y*ish* functions, where X represents a threatened (minority) language and Y represents an unthreatened or less threatened (majority) language.

The concept of diglossia has been examined alongside the concept of **individual bilingualism.** Fishman (1980) combines the terms bilingualism and diglossia to portray four language situations where bilingualism and diglossia may exist with or without each other, as shown in Table 4.2.

Table 4.2 Diglossia and bilingualism

		Diglossia	
		+	−
Individual bilingualism	+	1. Both diglossia and bilingualism	3. Bilingualism without diglossia
	−	2. Diglossia without bilingualism	4. Neither bilingualism nor diglossia

The first situation is a language community containing both diglossia and bilingualism. In such a community, almost everyone will be able to use both the majority and minority language. The majority language is used for one set of functions, the minority language for a (more or less) separate set of functions. In Paraguay, for example, most people speak both Spanish and Guaraní, but mainly use Spanish for official purposes and Guaraní for more **identity** functions (O. García, 2009a).

The second situation is diglossia without bilingualism. In such a context there will be two languages within a particular geographical area. One group of inhabitants will speak one language, another group a different language. This tends to be a theoretical case with few strong examples. Historically, in a colonial situation, a ruling power group might speak the 'high' language, with the larger less powerful group speaking only the 'low' language. For example, English (e.g. in India) or French (e.g. in Haiti and Vietnam) spoken by the ruling elite, with the local language(s) spoken by the masses.

The third situation is bilingualism without diglossia. In this situation, most people will be bilingual and will not restrict one language to a specific set of purposes. Either language may be used for almost any function. Or, as in the case of the US, many people are bilingual due to immigration, but there are few societal supports to develop, maintain, promote, or protect immigrant languages (O. García, 2009a). Fishman regards such communities as unstable and likely to change. Where bilingualism exists without diglossia, the prediction is that the majority language will become even more powerful and extend its use. The other language may decrease in its functions and decay in status and usage. Fishman (2013) laments the historical track record of the US in squandering, destroying and neglecting non-English languages.

The fourth situation is where there is neither bilingualism nor diglossia. One example is where a linguistically diverse society has been forcibly changed to a relatively

monolingual society. In Cuba and the Dominican Republic, the native languages have been exterminated. In Japan, efforts by the Meiji Government to create a common Japanese language resulted in the near extinction of the languages of indigenous Ainu and Ryukyu people (Tomozawa & Majima, 2015). A different example would be a small speech community using its minority language for all functions and insisting on having no relationship with the neighboring majority language.

Fishman believes that keeping up with the prestige and power of a worldwide language such as English is impossible and impractical. If a minority language attempts to take over (or share) the functions of the majority language, it is doomed to fail as the majority language will be too powerful, too high status, and impossible to defeat. He argues that minority language survival requires each language having its own separate set of functions and space, without threatening the other. Otherwise, minority language shift and death may occur. Fishman in particular argues that trying to reclaim all functions for the minority language sets the wrong goal for that language. Instead, **intergenerational transmission** of the minority language must be safeguarded in the home and community through primarily self-supporting operations, rather than relying completely on public or other outside sources. As Fishman (2013) argues:

> Without such self-supported, self-protected and self-initiated islands of demographic-ally concentrated local non-English language-and-culture transmission, particularly given the social mobility, modernization, and urban interaction so typical of American life, non-English mother tongues lack 'safe houses' or 'safe harbors' wherein the young can be socialized according to the languages, values, and traditions of sidestream cultures. They also increasingly lack a protected intimate space for adults and old folks during their after-work and out-of-work lives. (p. 475)

However, family language reproduction does not exist in a vacuum. Parents and children are influenced by the status and prestige of a language in society (e.g. its use in institutions and government). If high status functions operate in the majority language, the message to parents and children is about the power of the majority rather than the minority language. Thus, increasing the functions of a minority language is also about sending the right signals to parents and teachers.

Fishman's model of diglossia and bilingualism has helped (and continues to help) guide many valuable studies of **societal bilingualism**. Yet scholars are finding that linguistic realities in many countries often do not neatly conform to the model. For example, bilingualism without diglossia is predicted to lead to the decay of the minority language. In Wales, however, Welsh has been increasingly available in hitherto English language **domains** (e.g. in education, television and pop music), thus giving bilinguals a choice of language. It is believed in Wales that allowing separate functions for Welsh will relegate the language to low status and subordinate uses only. For the Indian community in Singapore, Vaish (2007) found that language shift and main-tenance varied by domain and even varied within some domains depending on different sites and situations, role-relationships and topics of conversation. Stable diglossia in a globalized language world is becoming less likely as the discussion of World Englishes later in this chapter will illustrate. O. García (2009a) notes other concerns: diglossia accepts situations of **domination** as normal, takes language arrangements to be consensual, and fails to consider underlying conflicts. Furthermore, rather than compartmentalization of languages as suggested in diglossic situations, the reality is an overlapping and intermeshing use of languages. Some scholars have called such situ-ations 'leaky diglossia'.

Given this co-existence and interplay between languages, O. García (2009a) suggests 'transglossia might be a better term to describe societal bilingualism in a globalized world: a stable, and yet dynamic, communicative network with many languages in functional interrelationship, instead of being assigned separate functions' (p. 79). For example, the Puerto Rican community of East Harlem in the US where Spanish and English are used concurrently within the same domains reveals a more fluid use of two or more languages. Individuals translanguage in a way that maximizes efficiency of communication and reflects multiple identities.

Diglossia with and without bilingualism tends to provide a relatively stable, enduring language arrangement. Yet such stability may be increasingly rare. With the growing ease of travel and communication, increased social and vocational mobility, a more global economy and more urbanization, there tends to be more contact between language communities, thus leading to greater transglossia. Changes in the fate and fortune of a minority language occur because the purposes of the two languages tend to change across generations. Neither a minority language community, nor the uses that community makes of its minority language, can be permanently compartmentalized. The geographical and personal boundaries that separate one language from another are never permanent. These boundaries are conceptualized as territorial and personality principles.

The territorial principle occurs when language rights or laws apply to a specific region. Keeping boundaries between the languages and compartmentalizing their use in society is regarded by many language planners as important for the minority language to survive. For example, in Belgium there are three designated regions where Flemish, French and German speakers have language rights inside their regions, but not outside those regions. Switzerland is another example. In contrast, the personality principle applies when status to the language is given to individuals or groups wherever they travel in a country (C.H. Williams, 2013). For example, in Canada francophones have the theoretical right to use French wherever they travel across Canada (although most areas outside Québec do not have French language service provision).

An attempted merging of the territorial and personality principles when applied to language rights has been termed the 'asymmetrical principle' or 'asymmetrical bilingualism'. As conceived by its Canadian advocates (e.g. in Québec), the principle gives full rights to minority language speakers and fewer rights to the speakers of a majority language. This is a form of positive discrimination, seeking to discriminate in favor of those who are usually discriminated against. The argument is that the minority language can only survive if it is given protection and preferential treatment. Some of the functions of a minority language will be regulated, so as to preserve that language. This may result in enforcement and 'language policing' rather than (or as well as) winning hearts and minds through education and persuasion. We return to the underlying question of individual and minority group language rights in Chapter 17.

An argument for the maintenance and revitalization of **indigenous languages** is often based on their historic existence within a defined geographical boundary, for example, Basque in the Basque Country (Spain), Quechua in the Andes (South America), or Dong in Guizhou (China). Language rights for indigenous languages may be enshrined in national laws. But what status do immigrant languages have when they cannot claim either territorial or personality rights? Geographical arguments for an indigenous language can have unfortunate implications for immigrant language minorities. Do languages belong to regions and territories and not to the speakers of those languages wherever they may be found? Do immigrant languages in countries such as Australia, Canada, Germany, Korea, Thailand, the United Kingdom and the United States not 'belong' as they are not indigenous languages? Do such immigrant languages only belong in the home country (e.g. Korean in Korea, Turkish in Turkey, or Somali in Somalia)? Should immigrant language minorities either speak the language of the territory or return to their home country or region? In Europe, there are many national (or autochthonous) languages that are seeking preservation status in the European Community, but almost no status is accorded to the immigrant languages of Europe (e.g. the various Asian languages such as Panjabi, Urdu, Bengali, Vietnamese, Korean, Hindi and Gujarati).

In language communities, the functions and boundaries of the two languages will both affect and be reflected in bilingual education policy and practice. In diglossic and transglossic situations, how are the majority and minority languages used in the different stages of schooling, from kindergarten to university? If the minority language is used in the school, in which curriculum areas does it function? Is the minority language just used for oral communication or is biliteracy a goal of the curriculum? Are science, technology and computing taught in the majority or minority language? Is the minority language just allowed for a year or two in the elementary school with the majority language taking over thereafter? Are the minority and majority languages rigidly separated in the curriculum, or is **translanguaging** allowed and used as a pedagogical tool? Or does the school deliberately exclude the minority language as a medium for classroom learning? The purposes and functions of each language in diglossic or transglossic situations are both symbolized and enacted in the school situation (see Chapter 10).

From Additive and Subtractive to Recursive and Dynamic Bilingualism

This chapter has indicated the potential importance of different functions for the minority and majority language. Various models attempt to describe the functions and relationships between languages in a bilingual context. In the 20th century, bilingualism was viewed as being either additive or subtractive (Lambert, 1974). In the 21st century new models describe bilingualism as recursive or dynamic (O. García, 2009a).

In an **additive bilingualism** context, the addition of a second language and culture is unlikely to replace or displace the first language and culture. For example, students in China and Korea learning English will remain proficient in Chinese and Korean respectively. They do not lose their native language, but gain another language and some of its attendant culture. The 'value added' benefits may not only be linguistic and cultural, but social, economic and cognitive as well.

When the second language and culture are acquired with pressure to replace or demote the first language, **subtractive bilingualism** may occur. Students who immigrate to countries such as Australia, England and the United States, are required to learn English and conform to the dominant culture, just as immigrants in Japan are under immense pressure to learn Japanese and assimilate to Japanese culture as quickly as possible. This may relate to a less positive self-concept, loss of cultural or ethnic identity, with possible alienation or marginalization. For example, an immigrant may experience pressure to use the **dominant language** and feel embarrassment in using the home language. When the second language is prestigious and powerful, used in mainstream education and in the job market, and when the minority language is perceived as of low status and value, minority languages may be threatened.

In the 21st century, the constructs of additive and subtractive bilingualism remain helpful, but new understandings of bilingualism require additional constructs. For example, in cases of **language revitalization** efforts to reverse the effects of linguistic discrimination and suppression (e.g. Māori in Aotearoa/New Zealand, Hawaiian in Hawaii, Navajo in the four corners region of the US), or in programs targeting heritage speakers (e.g. Vietnamese for Vietnamese-Americans) who are dominant English-speakers due primarily to English-medium schooling, students are not starting from

Figure 4.1 A Facebook example of dynamic bilingualism in social media

the beginning of the language acquisition process to simply 'add a new language'. Such students have some knowledge and proficiency of these languages due to exposure in the home and in their communities. O. García (2009a) introduced the term **recursive bilingualism** to describe the ways 'it reaches back to the bits and pieces of an ancestral language as it is reconstituted for new functions and as it gains momentum to thrust itself forward towards the future' (p. 53).

García also introduced the construct of **dynamic bilingualism** to reflect the complex bilingual competence often needed to communicate in the 21st century due to increasing migration, transnationalism and globalization. Rejecting the simple linear nature of additive and subtractive bilingual models above, she argues:

> With language interaction taking place on different planes including multimodalities, that is, different modes of language (visuals as well as print, sound as well as text, and so on) as well as multilingualism, it is possible for individuals to engage in multiple complex communicative acts that do not in any way respond to the linear models of bilingualism. (2009a: 54)

The dynamic, simultaneous existence of different languages in communication makes for a close interrelationship between languages, which is more than being additive. Dynamic bilingualism reflects the translanguaging practices of bilinguals as they draw on all of their linguistic resources to communicate and learn (O. García & Li Wei, 2014). Such dynamic use of linguistic resources and multimodalities is evident in the way many Cambodians in Cambodia interact with each other and with Cambodians living in countries around the world via social media. A typical Facebook post, for example (see Figure 4.1), may include a text in either Khmer or English, or a mixture of both. The post may be accompanied by a photo, a video, an article, or an image combined with text, that may be in one or a mixture of the two languages. Likewise, comments on the post from friends may be in Khmer, English, or both, may incorporate emojis, and may also include images, photos, videos, memes or links across the two languages. Some Cambodians will even use the English alphabet to write Khmer phonetically (as in Oun's comment in Figure 4.1), because they do not have access to Khmer fonts, because they do not know how to write using the Khmer script, or simply because they find it faster to write it that way. This dynamic use of translanguaging and multimodalities is used by many other bilinguals in various languages across social media for meaningful and effective communication. The dynamic, hybrid, overlapping and simultaneous use of different languages and modalities reflects transcultural identities and multilingualism in an increasingly globalized world of communication. O. García and Li Wei (2015) argue that a dynamic bilingualism lens has the potential to transform structures and practices of bilingual education (see Chapters 10 and 11).

Language Shift and Language Maintenance

With changes of season and weather come growth and death, blossoming and weakening. Minority language communities are similarly in a constant state of change. Such language shift may be fast or slow, upwards or downwards, but never absent.

Language shift refers to a reduction in the number of speakers of a language, a decreasing saturation of language speakers in the population, a loss in **language proficiency,** or a decreasing use of that language in different domains. The ultimate outcome of language shift is language death, although a language could be revived from recordings (oral and written). Language maintenance usually refers to relative language stability in the number and distribution of its speakers, its proficient usage by children and adults, and its retention in specific domains (e.g. home, school, religion). **Language spread** concerns an increase – numerically, geographically or functionally – in language users, networks and use.

However, there is a danger in the ways these terms are used because they are ambiguous and may refer to the numerical size of the language minority, their saturation in a region, their proficiency in the language or the use of the language in different domains. In addition, terms such as 'language death' and 'extinct languages' suggest a negative, pessimistic and irreversible situation. Instead, McCarty (2013) prefers to talk about sleeping or dormant languages, because if there is a record of that language and a community is motivated to resurrect it, then language reversal is possible. Such is the case with Klallam, a dormant language being learned by some Native American students in Washington through recordings of deceased ancestors (Kaminksy, 2014). Zuckerman and Monaghan (2012) refer to such extinct languages as 'sleeping beauties'.

A variety of factors create language shift. For example, out-migration from a region may be vital to secure employment, a higher salary or promotion. In-migration can be forced (e.g. the capture of slaves) or voluntary (e.g. guest workers). Sometimes this movement of minority language groups occurs within a particular geographical area. Within a country, marriage may also cause a shift in bilingualism. For example, a bilingual person from a minority language community may marry a majority language monolingual. The result may be majority language monolingual children. Increasing industrialization, urbanization and globalization has led to increased movement of labor. With the growth of mass communications, information technology, tourism, road, sea and air links, minority languages seem more at risk. Bilingual education, or its absence, will also be a factor in the ebb and flow of minority and majority languages.

Table 4.3 provides a relatively comprehensive list of factors that may encourage language maintenance or loss. This list essentially refers to immigrants rather than indigenous minorities, but many factors are common to both groups. What is missing from this list is the power dimension.

This initial consideration of important factors in language shift has shown that such shifts are particularly related to economic and social change, to politics and power, to the availability of local social communication networks between minority language speakers, and to the legislative and institutional support supplied for the conservation of a minority language. While such factors help clarify what affects language shift, the relative importance of these factors is debated and still unclear.

There are various approaches to establishing the causes of language shift, levels such as the political, the economic, the psychological (e.g. at the individual or home level) and the sociolinguistic. A list of the relative importance of these factors is simplistic because the factors interact and intermingle in a complicated equation. Such a list does not distinguish the more important factors in language shift. Nor does it reveal the processes and mechanisms of language shift. It is thus difficult to predict which minority languages are more or less likely to decline, and which languages are more or less likely to be revived.

A frequent, if generalized, scenario for immigrants observed in the US is a three-generation shift to English. The first generation (grandparents) maintains their native language even if they gain some proficiency in English. The second generation (children) – born in the US but raised in a home where the non-English language is

Table 4.3 Language maintenance and language loss

Factors encouraging language maintenance	Factors encouraging language loss
A. Political, social and demographic factors	
1. Large number of speakers living closely together.	1. Small numbers of speakers well dispersed.
2. Recent and/or continuing in-migration.	2. Long and stable residence.
3. Close proximity to the homeland and ease of travel to homeland.	3. Homeland remote or inaccessible.
4. Preference to return to homeland with many actually returning.	4. Low rate of return to homeland and/or little intention to return and/or impossible to return.
5. Homeland language community intact.	5. Homeland language community decaying in vitality.
6. Stability in occupation.	6. Occupational shift, especially from rural to urban areas.
7. Employment available where home language is spoken daily.	7. Employment requires use of the majority language.
8. Low social and economic mobility in main occupations.	8. High social economic mobility in main occupations.
9. Low level of education to restrict social and economic mobility, but educated and articulate community leaders loyal to their language community.	9. High levels of education giving social and economic mobility. Potential community leaders are alienated from their language community by education.
10. Ethnic group identity rather than identity with majority language community via nativism, racism and ethnic discrimination.	10. Ethnic identity is denied to achieve social and vocational mobility; this is forced by nativism, racism and ethnic discrimination.
B. Cultural factors	
1. Mother-tongue institutions (e.g. schools, community organizations, mass media, leisure activities).	1. Lack of mother-tongue institutions.
2. Cultural and religious ceremonies in the home language.	2. Cultural and religious activity in the majority language.
3. Ethnic identity strongly tied to home language.	3. Ethnic identity defined by factors other than language.
4. Nationalistic aspirations as a language group.	4. Few nationalistic aspirations.
5. Mother tongue is the homeland national language.	5. Mother tongue not the only homeland national language, or mother tongue spans several nations.
6. Emotional attachment to mother tongue giving self-identity and ethnicity.	6. Self-identity derived from factors other than shared home language.
7. Emphasis on family ties and community cohesion.	7. Low emphasis on family and community ties. High emphasis on individual achievement.
8. Emphasis on education in mother tongue schools to enhance ethnic awareness.	8. Emphasis on education in majority language.
9. Low emphasis on education if in majority language.	9. Acceptance of majority language.
10. Culture unlike majority language.	10. Culture and religion similar to that of the majority language.
C. Linguistic factors	
1. Mother tongue is standardized and exists in a written form.	1. Mother tongue is non-standard and/or not in written form.
2. Use of an alphabet which makes printing and literacy relatively easy.	2. Use of writing system which is expensive to reproduce and relatively difficult to learn.
3. Home language has international status.	3. Home language of little or no international importance.
4. Home language literacy used in community and with homeland.	4. Illiteracy (or aliteracy) in the home language.
5. Flexibility in the development of the home language (e.g. limited use of new of new terms from the majority language).	5. No tolerance of new terms from majority language; or too much tolerance of loan words leading to mixing and eventual language loss.

Source: Adapted from Conklin and Lourie (1983)

spoken – typically become bilingual, though most often are more dominant in English. The third generation (grandchildren) are typically monolingual English speakers.

However, this 'three generation shift' is not the only possible pattern. Some groups, such as the Pennsylvania Dutch (Amish), historically avoided a three or four generation shift by retaining boundaries between them and the outside world. Other examples of language maintenance beyond the 3rd generation include Yiddish-speaking Ultra-Orthodox Jews; French speakers in northern Vermont, New Hampshire and Maine; and Spanish-speakers in small rural communities in Arizona, New Mexico, and Texas along the US–Mexico border (Fishman, 2013). In recent immigrant groups, however, language shift may occur by the second generation, especially in cases where younger members of the first generation – the 1.5 generation – start school at a young age with few opportunities to develop or maintain their native language (Wright, 2014a).

Among Panjabi, Italian, Gaelic and Welsh communities in Britain, there are occasional fourth generation individuals who sometimes wish to revive the language of their ethnic origins. For some, **assimilation** into the majority language and culture does not give self-fulfillment. Rather, such revivalists seek a return to their roots by recovering the language and culture of their ethnic heritage. In Europe, with increasing pressure towards a European identity, language minority members seem increasingly aware of the benefits of a more distinctive and intimate local identity. The pressure to become part of a larger whole seems to result in a counter-balancing need to have secure roots within a smaller and more domestic community. A local language is valuable in this more particular identity. Bilingualism provides the means to be both international and local.

Language Decline and Death

Another way of identifying the causes of language shift is to examine a dying language within a particular region. In a classic study, Gal (1979) studied the replacement of Hungarian by German in the town of Oberwart in eastern Austria. After 400 years of relatively stable Hungarian–German bilingualism, economic, social and family life became more German-language based. By focusing on intervening processes, Gal showed how social changes such as industrialization and urbanization change social networks, relationships between people, and patterns in language use in communities. As new environments arise with new speakers, languages take on new forms, new meanings and create new patterns of social interaction. This suggests that social networks may play a more important role than communities in language shift.

Another celebrated study is a detailed case study by Dorian (1981) on the decline of Gaelic in east Sutherland, a region in the northeast highlands of Scotland. Historically, English and Gaelic co-existed, with English generally perceived as the high status 'civilized' language and Gaelic the 'savage' language of lower prestige. The last two groups in the region to speak Gaelic were the 'crofters' (small land farmers) and the fishing community. Surrounded by English speaking communities, these fisher-people originally spoke only Gaelic and later became bilingual in English and Gaelic. When the fishing industry began to decline, the boundaries between the Gaelic speakers and the English speakers began to crumble. The fisher-folk began to find other jobs, inter-marriage replaced in-group marriage, and 'outsiders' migrated to the east Sutherland area. Over time, the community gave up its fishing identity and the Gaelic language tended to decline with it. In the 20th century, a three-generation shift from monolingual Gaelic grandparents to monolingual English grandchildren was apparent.

Violent metaphoric labels such as 'language murder', 'language suicide' and 'linguicide' (linguistic genocide) are often used to draw attention to ways dominant languages oppress minority languages, or that some linguistic groups purposely abandon their native languages. Thomason (2015), however, urges caution:

> It seems to me that these terms are overblown. ... The death of any language is a sad event for a speech community. ... But using labels of violence tends to distract attention from the real and complex sociolinguistic issues surrounding language death. A term like 'suicide' appears to blame the victim, the speech community that is losing its heritage language; the term 'murder' suggests that dominant-language speakers are actively killing the language as opposed to creating – often without intending any such result – conditions under which a minority speech community finds it impossible to maintain its own language. (p. 68)

While Thomason's point is well taken, the histories of the Native American languages of Canada and the US, and particularly the histories of the African languages of those who were enslaved, provide strong evidence of extreme linguistic oppression deliberately designed to eradicate native tongues. In many cases actual physical violence was used on individuals to enforce oppressive anti-native-language policies (Wiley & Wright, 2004).

When minority language speakers become bilingual and prefer the majority language, the outcome for the minority language may be decline, even death. Yet, where people are determined to keep a language alive, it may be impossible to destroy a language. Language activists, pressure groups, affirmative action and language conservationists may fight for the survival of the threatened language. In Puerto Rico, failed English-only instruction policies were followed by instruction policies aimed at the bilingualization of the island. Nonetheless, factors such as nationalism, political uncertainty and the relationship between language and identity has led to resistance, keeping the majority of the island's population functionally monolingual in Spanish.

For J. Edwards (2012), language shift often reflects a pragmatic desire for social and vocational mobility, an improved standard of living, and a personal cost–benefit analysis. However, there may be a gap between the rhetoric of language preservation and harsh reality. This is illustrated in a story from Spolsky's (1989) early work among Native Americans:

> A Navajo student of mine once put the problem quite starkly: if I have to choose, she said, between living in a hogan a mile from the nearest water where my son will grow up speaking Navajo or moving to a house in the city with indoor plumbing where he will speak English with the neighbors, I'll pick English and a bathroom! (p. 451)

However, where there are oppressed language minorities who are forced to live in segregated societies, there is often little choice of where to live and work. In the quote, the Navajo mother may have had the choice. In actuality, many language minorities have little or no real choice.

Language shift and the erosion of minority languages have been related to the growth of a few powerful majority languages such as English, Spanish, Arabic, Mandarin and Hindi/Urdu. For some, bilingualism is threatened by such growth. However, the chapter continues with the more positive and optimistic possibilities of language resurrection, using the example of Manx Gaelic. This example particularly reveals the major part that education can play in the fast decline of a minority language and in its slow resurrection.

Language Resurrection

Manx Gaelic is a Celtic language, closely related to the Gaelic spoken in Scotland and Irish in Ireland. It is spoken on the Isle of Man, a small island set between Ireland and England. In a survey in 1874, close to 50% of the island's population were found to speak Manx Gaelic, numbering around 12,350 speakers. However, the 1872 Education Act banned Manx Gaelic in schools. If Manx was spoken by a child in school, a whipping could result. While not the only cause of language decline, banishment from schools triggered a fast shift to English. A language expelled from education sends a message to parents: the language is becoming obsolete with no employment or economic value. The language transmission of Manx Gaelic in the home no longer prepared children for school, employment or a social life.

By 1931, the Isle of Man Census showed only 531 speakers of Manx remaining. In 1974, Edward (Ted) Maddrell died, regarded as the last native speaker of Manx Gaelic (Abley, 2005). Thereafter, the word among international linguists was that Manx was dead. In the 1981 Decennial Census on the Isle of Man, a language question was symbolically eradicated.

However, there remained a few second language speakers of Manx. Even at the lowest point (the 1961 Census), there were 165 recorded second language speakers (0.3% of the population), thus making revival possible. By the 1991 Census, an increase to 643 speakers had occurred, and the 2011 Census counted 1,823 speakers out of population of 84,497 (2.2%) (Economic Affiars Division, 2012). Remarkably, new native speakers began to appear in 2001, having been spoken to in Manx Gaelic by their fluent second language parents from birth. Manx Gaelic is being slowly resurrected.

The Manx Gaelic revival continues, inspired by the dedication of a number of language revival enthusiasts. This revival is particularly driven by the desire for an Isle of Man identity that is separate and different from only having a general British identity. A Manx language immersion education program is successfully operating and called '*Bunscoill Ghaelgagh*'. There are second language Manx Gaelic classes in Isle of Man elementary and high schools (Ó hIfearnáin, 2015).

The main point of this illustration is that a language can be very rapidly massacred by its ban from all schools and its non-transmission in the home. The revival of a language via schooling is very slow. A language can be cut down within a few decades, but takes much time to grow from small seedlings, and even longer to spread. The revival in education does not only start with young children; it needs *a priori* the training and availability of teachers who can operate in the revived language. Teachers thus join crusading parents, language activists and language planners as the human foundation of language salvage and salvation.

Apart from the societal and speech community levels of analysis of language change, there is the individual person level in revival. Teachers and their students are important individuals in such revitalization efforts. This point is strongly made by McCarty (2013: xx): 'When we speak of language loss and revitalization, we should be ever mindful of the living, breathing children, families and communities those abstractions reference'.

Language Conflict

Contact between ethnic groups with differing languages does not always occur in a peaceful and harmonious fashion. There are sometimes tensions, rivalries and disputes. Such disputes do not always lead to conflict, although, as in the cases of Indonesia, Ethiopia, Rwanda, Bosnia, Serbia and the Middle East, ethnic conflicts do develop. As an extreme, there can be 'linguistic cleansing'. When there is extreme inter-ethnic conflict and civil war, an attempt to enforce the language of the ascendant group may be attempted.

Thus as one instrument of social control, languages can be a component in social conflict. For example, a monolingual and centralized bureaucracy may believe that multilingualism is like Babel: when there is linguistic diversity, there is a state of chaos, with resulting effects on law and order, economy and efficiency. Monolingualism is seen as a stable condition, multilingualism as linguistic imperfection leading to problems and conflicts (see Chapter 17).

When languages (e.g. official, national, ethnic, indigenous, immigrant languages) enter such conflicts between groups, language tends to become a marker or a symbol of the conflict, rather than the real source of the conflict, which is often racial, ethnic, religious, economic or cultural. When there are struggles for power and dominance between groups in society, language is often the surface feature or focal point of the deeper-seated conflicts underneath. For example, in the United States conflicts about the place accorded to immigrant languages in bilingual education hide deeper concerns about political dominance, status, defense of economic and social position, as well as concerns about cultural integration, nationalism and an American identity. Thus language minorities may, on the surface, appear as a threat to national unity, with language acting as a symbol of the threat. Underneath, the conflict is more about economic and political advantage, political power, and ethnic or national solidarity, and not least about identity (see Chapter 18).

The source of a conflict is often rooted in political power struggles, economic tensions and issues about rights and privileges. Social and economic disadvantages often tend to underlie language conflicts. Language is a usually a secondary sign of the primary or fundamental causes of conflict. Nevertheless, politicians and administrators often seize upon language as if it were the cause, and sometimes as if it were the remedy. Underlying causes are thus ignored or avoided. In essence, conflicts cannot occur between languages, they only occur between the speakers of those languages. Thus, the idea of language conflict can be a misnomer.

Language and Nationalism

Nationalism concerns a consciousness of belonging to a perceived separate people, located in a defined territory, bound by a belief in having a common culture and history, with common institutions and the desire to achieve or maintain political autonomy. Language helps create that consciousness and has been an important symbol of national identity. Nationalism is often said to have emerged after the French Revolution and became a major determinant of political policy and change throughout much of the 19th and 20th centuries.

Yet, particularly in the latter half of the 20th century, many minority ethnic groups became concerned about their own identity, including the desire to maintain their languages and cultures and to achieve a measure of political self-determination. The maintenance of regional ethnic identities, however, is often seen by many as contrary to the unity of the nation. Thus, attempts have been made by governments to eradicate minority languages and emphasize the majority language by means of education and compulsory use of the majority language in public and official life. In recent decades the rise of cosmopolitan multilingual cities has posed a challenge to this view of nationalism. Cities such as Brussels, London, Montréal, New York and Phnom Penh contain multinational and transitional peoples, with a multitude of languages, identities and cultures.

The concept of a supra-ethnic nation state has been perceived as a necessity in many African and Asian countries in the post-colonial era. For example, countries such as Indonesia, Kenya, Nigeria, Papua New Guinea and Tanzania consist of many local ethnic groups. Hence, the maintenance of supra-ethnic unity has been regarded as vital for economic and technological development. One practical outcome of this is the need for a majority language for international relations, official life and education, with local **vernaculars** being used in the home and neighborhood. This shows that the concept of a nation does not inevitably mean cultural assimilation and the eradication of local languages.

Nationalism often has negative connotations due to its association with 20th century fascism in Germany, Italy and Spain. Extreme nationalistic views overlap with forms of racism and language imperialism. Racist nationalism maintains that some 'races' and languages are superior to others. Afrikaner nationalism in South Africa was traditionally based on the myth of the white man's superiority. The racist **ideology** of Nazis and neo-Nazis represents an extreme form of nationalism based on the myth of racial purity. This is also evident in contemporary British nationalism where, for example, some extreme right wing groups express their nationalism with explicit racism and hatred of languages other than English.

The basis of United States nationalism also relates to recent support for the increased dominance of English over immigrant languages. US nationalism cannot be based on historical territory given the massive immigration into the country. There is no long, shared history, and no overall religious dimension that unites people into nationhood. While political feeling, for example against communism and terrorism, has been used as a means of trying to create nationalist unity, US nationalism is instead based around dimensions such as political freedom, emancipation, social and economic mobility, individual freedoms and liberties, individual enterprise, economic advantage and military advantage, the English language and the superiority of US military, political and economic power in the world. United States nationalism is thus based in modernity rather than history, on a shared economic and political aspiration rather than on long ownership of territory, and is based on self-determination and strong patriotism. Such a basis for US nationalism has strong implications for language policy, including policies favoring the replacement of immigrant languages by English.

Language is often viewed as the pre-eminent badge of loyalty that expresses a sense of belonging to a national group (e.g. English in the US). Language becomes a symbol of the independence of a separate nation and of a separate people. The Basques define their boundaries and separatism by who speaks, and who does not speak, the Basque language. Language comes to represent an attitude to independence and separation. Thus the Québécois in Canada make French a symbol of their drive for more independence from Canada.

Nevertheless, language is not essential to either nationalism or ethnicity. Concerns about loyalty, self-determination and political independence do not necessarily require a separate language. African nationalism is not based on language. Given the many different languages and dialects in Africa, language is clearly not a common denominator in African self-determination, membership or loyalty, nor in the desire for self-determination and political independence from Europe. In countries such as Pakistan, it is religion that tends to be the cement and symbol of loyalty rather than language. Thus language is a valuable but not essential condition for nationalism to survive and thrive.

Bilingualism is often seen as an obstacle to nationalism. Given that a minority language is always in danger of being swamped by a majority language, bilingualism can also be seen as an unstable state, a halfway house for people who are moving from the minority language to the majority language. However, bilingualism can be supported by nationalism, particularly in areas where there are a variety of ethnic groups, and where a group is in a numerical minority but uses a majority language as its mother tongue.

Political changes throughout the world are changing the concept of nationhood. In China, with 55 officially recognized indigenous minority groups, Feng and Adamson (2015) note 'the promotion of English into the classrooms dominated by minority groups has further amplified the complexity' of the nation's linguistic situation (p. 488). There are tensions in the desire to promote trilingualism in regional languages and English while upholding Mandarin as a national language. As one concerned policymaker urged, 'we must put Chinese at the center and focus our attention on promoting Chinese national consciousness and identity' (p. 489).

In Europe, with the growth of the European Union and the drive towards Europeanization, a sense of a more European identity rather than a purely national identity has begun (e.g. Irish, Slovenian). In the world of the internet, the global economy and ease of transport between countries, the growth of economic and political interdependence in the world, new forms of loyalty and identity are beginning to occur. Thus supra-nationalism is beginning to have effects on language.

In the 21st century new demographic patterns of immigration have altered the nature of language minority communities in European nations and beyond. Traditional patterns involved large influxes from a relatively small number of countries (e.g. former colonies, bordering countries, impoverished countries, sites of armed conflict). Today, however, rapidly growing diversity in these nations is often made up of smaller groups from a much wider variety of countries. The term superdiversity has been refined by sociologist Steven Vertovec (2007) to describe these new patterns. Using Britain as an example, Vertovec describes the country's superdiversity as 'distinguished by a dynamic interplay of variables among an increased number of new, small and scattered, multiple-origin, transnationally connected, socio-economically differentiated and legally stratified immigrants who have arrived over the last decade' (p. 1024). Superdiversity also describes diversity within individual immigrant and ethnic minority groups (diversity within diversity). Blommaert (2013) credits two connected forces in the development of superdiversity – the end of the Cold War opening up new migration possibilities, and the internet, particularly Web 2.0 technologies in the late 1990s which offer 'a vast and unparalleled expansion of the means for exchanging long-distance information and for developing and maintaining translocal ties' (p. 5). Sociolinguistics are beginning to explore the ways this new diversity 'becomes the site of negotiations over linguistic resources,' not just among the newly arrived, but also among established ethnic minority communities (Creese & Blackledge, 2010a: 550), and how it is changing the linguistic landscape (Blommaert, 2013).

An embracing of superdiversity, and the move towards supra-nationalism may have a positive effect on bilingualism. The drive to share a wider identity (e.g. to be European or part of the global village) may lead to a reaction among individuals. To belong to a supranational group may initially require local loyalty, a rootedness in local group cohesion, a sense of belonging to a community first of all, and before being able psychologically to identify with large supranational groups. Thus bilingualism in the majority and the minority language may become important in gaining a feeling of rootedness locally, as well as belonging to an increasingly larger identity.

Language Variation

In addition to a variety of different languages in a society, there is also variation within a given language. Speakers of a language can often pinpoint another speaker's country of origin, or even a particular region within a specific country, based on how they talk. The study of language variation considers the different varieties or dialects of language, and the ways a standard variety of a language is often privileged over non-standard varieties. In the US for example, controversy erupted when the Oakland Unified School District proposed an Ebonics program designed to recognize and value the variety of English spoken by many African American students while helping them master Standard American English (D.J. Ramirez et al., 2005). Immigrant students lumped together as 'Arabic speakers' speak many different varieties of Arabic, some of which are not even mutually intelligible. Many 'mother-tongue' bilingual programs in the US and around the world focus on developing a standard variety of a language which may in fact be very different from the varieties students actually speak at home (Sayer, 2013; Weber, 2014). Puerto Rican students, for example, may find their variety of Spanish marginalized in bilingual programs where the teacher and other students are predominantly from Mexico. Some well-meaning school districts recruit bilingual teachers from Spain who end up teaching standard Castilian Spanish that is quite foreign to their students born in the US, Mexico and Central America. These issues speak to the need for educators to develop critical language awareness (Alim, 2010; Fairclough, 2013) or critical dialect awareness, that is, the ability to analyze language differences critically, be aware of how varieties and dialects are valued differently, under-stand aspects of language and power, and plan appropriate programs and instruction accordingly. Curricular programs can also be provided to help students develop critical language awareness (Alim, 2005). Language variation is central to considerations of the use and spread of English around the world.

English as a Global Language

The spread of English throughout the world is sometimes viewed favorably as a homogenizing, positive characteristic of globalization. Others see such spread unfavorably as leading to the loss of small minority languages, colonization and **linguistic imperialism**. These are ideological positions to which need adding the perspectives of individuals who speak different forms of native and international English, plus a recognition of the increasing varieties of World Englishes. As this term reveals, English is more than one language. Standardized forms of English such as Standard American English, Standard British English and Standard Australia English are just three of many standard and non-standard varieties of English. Englishes have local and international dimensions, are ever-changing and complex. They interact with cultural heritage and popular culture, technology and travel, identity and belonging to imagined communities. Englishes are powerful and pervasive, yet many varieties are related to inequality of access and assimilation of immigrants, empowering some and disempowering others (Kirkpatrick, 2010).

World Englishes reveal that the situation of English and its relation to bilingualism is not uniform throughout the world but varies according to a multitude of factors, including the local political situation, other languages spoken in the country, inter-ethnic relations and cultural attitudes (Coupland, 2013). Tupas (2015) uses the term unequal Englishes to emphasize that non-standard varieties of English are rarely treated equally within society. In the last decade, there has been a growing emphasis on the inclusion of a standardized variety of English in the curriculum in many countries of the world. This is partly based on English-dominant economic, financial and political associations with the language. However, there can also be the paradoxical resurgence of localism and the vernacular language as a subtle resistance to English (Tollefson & Tsui, 2014; Tupas & Rani, 2015).

Kachru (2005) conceptualized World Englishes as three concentric circles: the inner circle, the outer circle, and the expanding circle (see Dewey & Leung, 2010 for a critique). In the inner circle are countries where English is the first language of the majority of the population. In the outer circle are countries where English is spoken widely as a second language and enjoys official status. In the expanding circle are countries where English has no official status but may be used, for example, in business, and multinational communications. Kachru's circles largely correspond to respectively ENL (English as a Native Language), **ESL (English as a Second Language)**, and EFL (English as a Foreign Language). The world pre-eminence of English lies in that it is a first, second and foreign language and is found across the globe in all three categories. These three categories will now be considered more fully in turn.

(1) Inner-circle countries: English is the first language and often the only language of the majority of the population. In the United States, Australia, Canada, the UK, Ireland and New Zealand, the majority of the population are monolingual English speakers. Historically, however, the spread of English in the wake of political and economic expansion has led to the decline and sometimes death of indigenous languages in all these countries. In Ireland, English gradually superseded Irish in the 19th century. Despite the status of Irish as the official language of Ireland and its great symbolic significance to the citizens, it is spoken on an everyday basis by only a small minority of the population. In the US, indigenous Native American languages and immigrant languages have been dwarfed by English, which became a symbol of national cohesion and the common language. In many countries, people such as the Maori in New Zealand and Irish speakers in Ireland struggle to preserve their national languages in the face of English domination.

(2) Outer-circle countries: English co-exists as a second language in bilingual or multi-lingual contexts. In former British colonies English has often remained the official language or at least one of the official languages. English is still used widely in official contexts and education (e.g. South Africa, India). English is not spoken as a first or home language by the majority of the population. It may be spoken only by

an exclusive social elite, and only used in certain contexts (e.g. official and formal contexts).

(3) ***Expanding circle countries:*** English is a foreign language, may have no official status, and may not be spoken at all by the majority of the population (e.g. Cambodia, China, Japan, Mozambique, Thailand, Malaysia). In these countries, however, English is acknowledged as an important and prestigious language, and people may be exposed to it in particular domains. There may be considerable emphasis on the teaching of English as a foreign language in schools and also in business and industry. English language films may be shown with subtitles on television and in the cinema, and English language pop songs may be widespread. Many English words may have been adopted by the indigenous language, and English may be used widely in advertising to suggest power, popularity and prestige. In the former Soviet republics, for example, bilinguals used to speak their local language plus Russian. Now they tend to be moving to the local language plus English (Dilāns & Zepa, 2015). In other Eastern Europe countries (e.g. Slovenia), English has no official status but is increasingly spoken by younger people.

Attempting to force countries into one of these circles or categories, however, is increasingly difficult and may be insensitive to a variety of differences (Kirkpatrick, 2010). Tupas and Rani (2015) express concern that the concentric circles model makes an ideological claim about the ownership of English:

> No one has the exclusive rights to the language; anyone who speaks it has the right to own it. The norms of use are multilingual norms and the strategies to teach English are also multilingual in nature. The English language is deeply embedded in the multilingual and multicultural lives of its speakers – so who are the native speakers of English today? To insist that those who can be called native speakers are only those who come from Inner Circle countries, especially the United States and the United Kingdom (where users of English are typically described as 'native speakers'), is to disenfranchise the majority of English speakers today. (p. 1)

Furthermore, the concentric circles model suggests a one-way flow from inner-circle to the outer and expanding circles. However, as Pennycook (2013) argues, the global cultural flows of culture and knowledge, including language, are complex and 'new technologies and communications are enabling immense and complex flows of people, signs, sounds, images across multiple borders in multiple directions' (p. 593). For example, the global hip hop movement may have roots in African American rap music, but flows through many countries and is influenced by, and hybridized with local languages and cultures (see, e.g. Lin, 2015).

The Spread of English

The spread of English, like that of other prestigious languages throughout time, has come about in a variety of ways, including political domination, the subordination of vernacular languages, trade, colonization, emigration, education, religion, mass media, technology and social media. Through such channels, the English language has penetrated to the furthest reaches of the globe. However, the influence of each of these factors, and the level of intent in domination or market-led change, is much contested (see, e.g. Phillipson & Skutnabb Kangas, 2013; Vaish, 2008).

According to SIL International's Ethnologue (www.ethnologue.com), approximately 335 million people in the world speak English as a first language and an even greater number, 505 million, speak it as a second language (M.P. Lewis *et al.*, 2015). However, these and other estimates are often contentious. Variations are due to guesses or estimates being required in many countries, and to the criteria for inclusion as a second language speaker (see Chapter 1) being highly variable (see Crystal, 2012). The numbers who have learned English as a foreign language also varies very widely with estimates ranging from 100 million to 1,100 million depending on how much 'learning' has occurred. Graddol (2006) suggests that the number of people learning English will soon reach a peak of around 2 billion people. Crystal's (2012) 'middle of the road' estimate is of a grand total of 1,200 to 1,500 million English speakers in the world.

Numbers of speakers is less important when considering the spread of English than the prestigious domains and functions into which English has spread and often dominates. The international prestige of English and English-speaking nations and the popularity of Anglo-American culture has given the English language associations of status, power and wealth. Access to English means access to valued forms of knowledge and access to affluent and prestigious social and vocational positions.

As a global language, English has dominated many prestigious domains and functions: international communication, science, technology, medicine, computers, research, books, periodicals, transnational business, tourism, trade, shipping, aviation, advertising, diplomacy, international organizations, mass media, entertainment, news agencies, the internet, politics, youth culture and sport.

At the end of the 1990s it was estimated that 80% of the information on the internet was stored in English, though in hindsight, that estimate was likely exaggerated (Crystal, 2006). While English remains the single most commonly used language online, a 12-year study by UNESCO estimated that the amount of English content decreased to about 45% by 2005 (Pimienta *et al.*, 2009). UNESCO found large increases in the number of web pages in languages such as Russian, German, Spanish, Japanese, French, and Chinese, among many other languages. Even less commonly used languages are flourishing online (Graddol, 2006). And while social media sites such as YouTube and Facebook may have English platforms, the multimodal content generated by users around the world is truly multilingual. Nonetheless UNESCO also found that English speakers (native and 2nd language speakers) make up over half (55%) of internet users, and English content remains substantial.

Such a widespread use of English has ensured that Anglo culture, Anglo institutions and Anglo ways of thinking and communicating are spreading. English has displaced some of the functions of other languages and even displaced the languages themselves.

The Future of English

Figure 4.2 provides estimates from Graddol (2006) on the number of past and future native (L1) speakers of English and other major languages. While acknowledging that estimating these figures is 'surprisingly difficult', Graddol nonetheless concludes that the second rank of English in native-speaker rankings is declining with emergence of similar numbers of native speakers of Spanish, Hindi/Urdu and Arabic.

Recent data from *Ethnologue* suggests Graddol's prediction was right. As shown in Table 4.4, Spanish has already claimed the second position for L1 users. However, when the number of second language (L2) users is considered, the rank of English as the second most commonly spoken language in the world remains strong. Note also

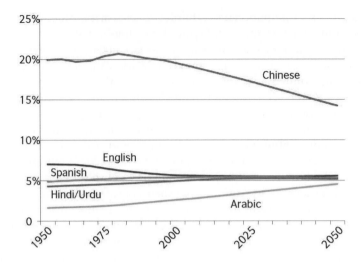

Figure 4.2 Trends in native-speaker numbers for the world's largest languages, expressed as the proportion of the global population. Source: Graddol (2006: 60)

that accounting for L2 speakers substantially narrows the gap between the number of Mandarin and English speakers.

Table 4.4 Number of L1, L2 and total number of users of major world languages

Language	L1 Users*	L2 Users**	Total Users
Mandarin	847,808,270	178,000,000	1,025,808,270
English	335,491,748	505,000,000	840,491,748
Spanish	398,931,840	89,500,000	488,431,840
Hindi	260,333,620	120,000,000	380,333,620
Arabic	242,391,860	n/a	242,391,860
Bengali	189,261,200	19,200,000	208,461,200
Portuguese	203,352,100	n/a	203,352,100
Russian	166,167,860	n/a	166,167,860
French	75,916,150	87,000,000	162,916,150
Urdu	64,035,800	94,000,000	158,035,800

Notes: Data from Ethnologue (M.P. Lewis *et al.*, 2015).
*L1 users are world wide.
**L2 Users are world wide except for Mandarin, Hindi, Bengali, and Urdu.

The advantages and disadvantages of English are much debated by scholars (e.g. Crystal, 2012; Phillipson & Skutnabb Kangas, 2013; Vaish, 2008). On one side there are those who regard English as, for example, valuable for international and inter-cultural communication, *de facto* the global language, a relatively neutral vehicle for communication, and giving access to quality higher education. A developing country that encourages the learning and use of English in trade and business may facilitate economic and employment opportunities. However, English is not alone in this scenario, with Spanish, Mandarin Chinese and Arabic, for example, also having growing prestigious economic and employment associations. Since 2004, China has been actively promoting Chinese language learning around the world by establishing over 400 non-profit Confucius Institutes in over 110 countries (see http://confuciusinstitute.unl.edu/institutes.shtml).

Many people on all continents have been willing to learn and accept English as a universal utilitarian language. Such learners have been willing to embrace English, not for Anglo-American **enculturation**, but as an international language that facilitates trade and commerce, and international and multinational communication. English is regarded by such learners as a means of communication to an economic or political (rather than a cultural or social) end. In such situations, the stigma of a colonializing English is being replaced by a positive attitude about the multinational functionality of English amidst globalization (Bhatia & Ritchie, 2013). However, 'long shadows' of inequality and divisiveness, class divides and subordination remain (Tupas, 2015).

The growth of English in China is an example of the rapid spread of English as a universal language (Feng, 2011). Feng and Adamson (2015) attribute this growth to China's open-door policy which views English as key to modernization, along with other important factors such as membership in the World Trade Organization in 2001, the 2008 Olympic Games in Beijing, and the 2010 World Expo in Shanghai, all of which have led to high levels of enthusiasm for English competence. There are estimates of 440 to 650 million people in China learning English – a number far greater than the total US population (Hong & Pawan, 2014). Since 2001, English has been a compulsory subject in grades 3 and higher in Chinese schools, and universities are expected to provide 5% to 10% of undergraduate instruction in English or another foreign language.

On the other side there is a critical perspective that sees English as part of linguistic imperialism, dominance by the US and other English-speaking countries, a means of reproducing structural, cultural, educational and economic inequalities, maintaining capitalist economic advantages and control, and oppressing weak minority languages and their peoples (Phillipson & Skutnabb Kangas, 2013). Gandhi (1927), for example, accused English of being an intoxicating language, denationalizing a country such as India, and encouraging mental slavery to Anglo forms of thinking and culture. He argued that English has been used in some multilingual societies to internally colonize, and to preserve the power of ruling elites. English has imposed linguistic uniformity that is culturally, intellectually, spiritually and emotionally restricting. Other languages are then portrayed as confining, ethnocentric, divisive, alienating and anti-nationalistic. Asserting the dominance of English can become a means by which power elites justify exclusion and sustain inequality.

The relationship between Islam and English is a topic of ongoing concern as a result of issues such as 9/11 and the Global War on Terrorism (Karmani & Pennycook, 2005). Rahman (2005) claims that there are three Islamic responses to English: acceptance of English and assimilation into Anglophone culture; rejection and resistance based on religion and preferred identity and values; and pragmatic utilization so as to share power and knowledge, raise wealth and social status, and 'learn the language of your enemy'. While there may sometimes be a clash of cultural values and a polarizing conflict between Islam and Western, Anglophone culture, this is not necessarily the preferred position of Islam. Mohd-Asraf (2005) suggests that the Qur'an invokes many Muslims proselytizing by the learning of other languages, and the gaining of wisdom from other cultures through their languages. She argues the learning of English is not in conflict with Islamic values; so long as a child is socialized thoroughly into Islamic religion, identity, culture and the Muslim way of life, then bilingualism and biculturalism have additive effects that are enabling rather than conflicting.

Yet it is not the language that is dominating but the people who use it. A language such as English is not intrinsically dominating. No language is more suited to oppression, domination, westernization, secularization or imperialism than another. It is the speakers of that language who are the oppressors and dominators. Whether English is empowering or divisive, it is those who, for example, impose, teach, learn and use it that make it so. The danger is that language is made the symbolic scapegoat for political and economic domination, which are, in fact, the consequences of people and politics.

There are major concerns over English as a language of former colonial powers and the need for efforts to promote national and regional languages (Phillipson & Skutnabb Kangas, 2013). Others stress this should not prevent us from acknowledging that English gives access to personal status, modernization (e.g. technology, science), global economy and international communication. Dörnyei, Csizér and Németh (2006), for example, suggest that English provides the *lingua franca* in a world that is getting smaller, providing the means of direct communication (e.g. face-to-face, phone, texting, email, video conferencing, social media) between people of different languages, cultures and economies. Thus students are often very motivated to learn English. Nevertheless, the advantages for individuals in the globalization of English need to be understood against the elitism and hegemony that has often been attached to English (Pennycook, 2013). For example, Bhatia and Ritchie (2013) cite a 1835 colonial education document by Lord Macaulay in India providing his vision of elite English education to create 'a class of persons, Indian in blood and colour, but English in taste, in opinions, in morals and intellect'.

For some, the spread of English has been connected to the decline and death of many indigenous languages (e.g. Phillipson & Skutnabb Kangas, 2013). The dissemination of Anglo-American culture is claimed to have caused the weakening and eradication of local, indigenous cultures. Such a widespread use of English means that Anglo culture, Anglo institutions and Anglo ways of thinking and communicating are spread. English then tends to displace the functions of other languages and even displace the languages themselves. For example, in technology, communications and entertainment, English has sometimes become the dominant language in a country. It can take over some of the internal functions of other languages in a country (e.g. in business, mass media) and become the means of the external link in, for example, politics, commerce, science, tourism and entertainment.

Where English has rapidly spread, the danger is that it does not encourage bilingualism but rather a shift towards English as the preferred language, especially in schools. English has sometimes become an official language or a national language (e.g. Singapore, India, Kenya) and local vernaculars may be viewed as substandard. Advanced schooling, for example in Kenya, has often required English to be the principal medium of language in the classroom. The use of vernaculars in the classroom will then be seen as of lower status, for the poor or less socially and economically mobile peoples.

There are exceptions to the growth of English in various countries of the world. Where a country has a 'great tradition', the place of English may be restricted to particular modern and separate functions. For example, in Arabic and Islamic countries, and in some Asian countries such as Malaysia, the strong promotion of religion or nationalism may help restrain English from infiltrating a variety of domains. Yet in other countries such as Singapore and India, English has been adopted as a unifier between different regions and as a common language. In India, there are 15 languages that have constitutionally guaranteed status, with English and Hindi being the main languages of intercommunication between different regions.

When there are reactions against English as a colonizing language, the arguments tend to take on different dimensions: that English creates anti-nationalism and is likely to destroy native cultures; that English will introduce materialism and values that may destroy the religion of the people (e.g. Islam, Hinduism, Buddhism); that a people learning English will be rootless, in a state of flux and transition; that decadent Western values such as sexual permissiveness, drug use and lack of respect for elders will be transmitted by the language; that English will bring divisions both in the country, in the community and in families, separating those who speak the native languages and those who prefer to move towards English; that there will be alienation from traditional culture, heritage values and beliefs, plus a lack of individual and unique identity.

The predictions in Figure 4.2 suggest the rise of English globally may have peaked and may fade in the future. With current changes in internationalism, the global economy, global companies, technology, telecommunications and religion, the international information and knowledge economy may move the world away from monolingual English operations to one where languages such as Spanish, Arabic and Mandarin Chinese may grow in use. The rising major economies of India, China, Brazil and Russia are already indicating that varieties of World Englishes rather than the standardized varieties of 'Native' English will be the prestigious varieties of the future. In this world, bilinguals and multilinguals will be of more economic value than monolinguals.

Conclusion

This chapter has focused on languages at the group, social and community level. Majority and minority languages are frequently in contact, sometimes in conflict. The relationship between the two languages tends to shift constantly as a consequence of a variety of changeable cultural, economic, linguistic, social, demographic and political factors.

Indigenous languages are located in a defined territory and will claim the territorial principle for their preservation. Immigrant language minorities may lay claim to the personality principle: their language group having unifying ethnic characteristics and identity. But the future of languages goes wider and deeper. The history of nationalism and the modern role of global English suggest that the fate of languages relates to wider social, economic and political issues. The future of the world's languages, and the future of English as the international language, is not only about the behavior of individuals but also about the economic, social and symbolic values attached to different languages, about institutional support, and not least about regional and global politics.

Key Points in This Chapter

➢ Diglossia has traditionally been used to describe and analyze two languages existing together in a society in a relatively stable arrangement through different uses attached to each language.

➢ Transglossia considers the co-existence and interplay between languages as bilinguals translanguage in ways that challenge traditional views of diglossia.

➢ The territorial principle is a claim to the right to a language within a geographical area, while the personality principle is a claim to the right to use a language based on an individual's ownership of a language that belongs to them wherever they travel within their country.

➢ There are a variety of factors that may contribute to language maintenance or language loss.

➢ Minority languages may decline by a three-generation shift: L1 monolingual grandparents, bilingual children, to L2 monolingual grandchildren. Languages may decline more rapidly in some recent immigrant communities.

➢ Language resurrection is slow and challenging, but possible, and often starts with a few enthusiasts.

➢ Language has been a key symbol of national identity and seen as a badge of loyalty.

➢ There is not a single language called English, but rather, a wide variety of World Englishes.

➢ The English language has spread rapidly, mostly as a second and foreign language.

➢ There are more second language speakers of English than native speakers.

➢ The advantages and disadvantages of English as an international language are much contested, as are its effects on the future of indigenous and minority languages.

➢ Bilingualism and multilingualism in English and another language or languages is globally increasing.

Suggested Further Reading

📖 Blommaert, J. (2013). *Ethnography, superdiversity and linguistic landscape: Chronicles of complexity*. Bristol, UK: Multilingual Matters.

📖 Coupland, N. (2013). *The handbook of language and globalization*. Malden, MA: Wiley-Blackwell.

📖 Weber, J.-J., & Horner, K. (2012). *Introducing multilingualism: A social approach*. New York, NY: Routledge.

📖 McCarty, T. (Ed.). (2017). *Language policy and political issues in education* (Vol. 1 of the *Encyclopedia of Language and Education*, 3rd ed., S. May, Editor). New York, NY: Springer.

On the Web

A day in the life of the Bunscoill Ghaelgagh (Video of Manx language revitalization school)
https://youtu.be/6rUEZ8A-678

25 Maps that Explain the English Language
http://www.vox.com/2015/3/3/8053521/25-maps-that-explain-english

David Crystal – World Englishes (Video)
https://youtu.be/2_q9b9YqGRY

Discussion Questions

(1) Using Table 4.2, discuss which label best describes the relationship between individual bilingualism and diglossia in your community or within your larger society. Would transglossia be a more accurate description? Why or why not?

(2) Read and listen to the audio clips from the National Public Radio story 'Living in two worlds, but with just one language': http://tinyurl.com/o74s9rt. How does O'Brien's experience relate to the three-generation shift? What factors contributed to this shift? How has this shift impacted O'Brien?

(3) What do you see as the future of English as a global language? Do you agree with the predictions shown in Figure 4.2? Why is it important to think of English in the plural, Englishes, particularly now that second language speakers outnumber native speakers of English?

Study Activities

(1) Using the list of factors in Table 4.3, conduct a study on a minority language in your community to determine if there is likely to be maintenance or loss of the language over the next 10 years.

(2) Explore online social media platforms (e.g. Facebook, YouTube, Instagram, etc.) to find and analyze examples of dynamic bilingualism.

(3) Interview individuals from immigrant language minority families in your community. Is the 'three generation shift' pattern evident in some or most of those families? What have been the changes in language use and status since immigration in those families? What reasons do the families give for language change? What factors seem to aid language preservation?

CHAPTER 5

The Early Development of Bilingualism

The Early Development of Bilingualism

Introduction

This chapter looks at the various ways in which young children become bilingual and multilingual. There are various routes to **bilingualism** and **multilingualism**, some from birth, others much later (see Chapter 6). Such bilingual routes include: acquiring two languages early on in the home; acquiring a second language in the street, in the wider community, in the nursery school, elementary or high school; and, after childhood, learning a second or foreign language in adult language classes and courses or by informal interaction with others. This chapter outlines different major routes to becoming bilingual early in childhood and examines some of the central issues involved in this more informal aspect of language development.

As the previous chapters of this book have illustrated, a discussion of bilingualism and multilingualism has to include psychological, linguistic, social and educational factors. Later in the book, it will be shown that political factors are also crucial in understanding bilingualism and bilingual education. While psychologists and linguists have studied the development of children's two languages, it is valuable to examine simultaneously the social and political **context** in which children acquire their languages. Early bilingual development in the home, for example, does not take place in isolation. It occurs within a community, country and **culture**, which means that the home is surrounded by expectations, pressures and politics.

For example, being a member of an immigrant community, an elite group, a majority or a minority language group are important societal or 'macro' influences in the acquisition of bilingualism. Consider the different life experiences of middle- and upper-class privileged bilinguals (e.g. children of diplomats, expatriates learning two prestigious languages), majority language children living in minority language communities, and minority language children living in majority language communities (e.g. immigrants, Native Americans). In each of these groups, societal pressures and family language planning may be supportive or conflicting, affecting choices, access and language outcomes. There are also 'micro' environments such as the street, crèche, nursery, school, local community and the extended family that similarly foster bilingualism. Such contexts tend to make dual language use by a child a constantly shifting rather than a stable phenomenon.

The variety of individual differences and social contexts makes simple generalizations about the development of bilingualism difficult and risky. The chapter therefore commences with a basic typology of the development of childhood bilingualism.

Childhood Bilingualism

More children worldwide grow up to become bilinguals or multilinguals rather than **monolinguals**. Some children become bilinguals almost effortlessly from birth. Others learn a language in school or later as adults. An initial distinction is between simultaneous and sequential childhood bilingualism. Simultaneous childhood bilingualism refers to a child acquiring two languages at the same time from birth, sometimes called infant bilingualism, bilingual acquisition and bilingual first language acquisition (De Houwer, 2009). For example, where one parent speaks one language to the child, and the other parent speaks a different language, the child may learn both languages simultaneously. This is called the one parent-one language (OPOL) approach (Barron-Hauwaert, 2004). An example of sequential childhood bilingualism is when a child learns one language in the home, then goes to a nursery or elementary school and learns a second language. For these **emergent bilinguals** (see Chapter 1), there are no exact boundaries between **simultaneous** and **sequential bilingualism**, although the age of acquisition is often used as a marker.

In contrast, second language classes for children and adults usually foster bilingualism through direct instruction (see Chapter 6). This leads to a distinction between informal language acquisition and more formal language learning. However, the boundary between acquisition and learning is not distinct. Informal language acquisition can occur, for example, in a second language classroom. Thus, the distinction between naturally becoming bilingual and being taught to become bilingual has imprecise borders. Serratrice (2013) notes that the profile of bilinguals constantly changes as their need for and use of each of their languages can vary greatly over time, depending on such factors as context, purpose, the formality of the situation, and who they wish or need to interact with. The term **dynamic bilingualism** captures this ever-changing nature of language use by emergent bilinguals (O. García, 2009a).

The Simultaneous Acquisition of Bilingualism and Multilingualism

Parents, members of the public and politicians sometimes buy into the false belief that acquiring two languages from birth is detrimental to a child's language growth. On the contrary, babies appear biologically ready to acquire, store and differentiate two or more languages from birth onwards (Serratrice, 2013). Infant bilingualism is normal and natural, with evidence that it is typically beneficial in many ways: cognitively (see Chapter 7), culturally (see Chapter 18), communicatively (see Chapter 1), for higher curriculum achievement (see Chapters 11 and 12), and to increase the chances of employment and promotion (see Chapter 19).

To acquire successfully two languages from birth, babies need to be able to: (a) differentiate between the two languages, and (b) effectively store the two languages for both understanding (input) and speaking (output). Research suggests infants have these capacities, making infant bilingualism very viable (De Houwer, 2009; Serratrice, 2013).

As early as eight months, but more often around a bilingual child's first birthday, they may utter their first words in both languages. While the growth in each language may be uneven due to differential experience in each language, the vocabulary of such bilingual children tends to show a similar number of meanings. Studies of early bilinguals 'that compare the total number of meanings (or conceptual vocabulary) that bilingual children expressed with monolingual children's total number of meanings found no differences between the two groups' (De Houwer, 2009: 229). Early bilinguals may even have an advantage compared with monolinguals in that they learn new words and labels for concepts at a faster pace (De Houwer, 2009). This may be due to their need to understand people referring to the same thing in two languages.

Differentiation Between Two Languages in the Infant

Infants show discrimination between the two languages very early. Memory for language sounds even operates in the fetal stage, such that the processes of bilingual acquisition appear to start before birth. Upon birth, newborns immediately prefer their mother's voice to that of any other mother, but not if the mother's recorded voice is played backwards. Also, newborns respond more to prose passages read to them regularly before birth than to new prose, even when not read by the mother. Thus an infant is not just recognizing the mother's voice. There is also immediate sound discrimination: the beginning of 'breaking the code'. There appears to be an immediate **receptive language** differentiation in the newborn particularly in intonation (De Houwer, 2009). Moon *et al.* (2013), in a study of newborn infants in Sweden and the US, found evidence that soon after birth, babies respond to the familiar native language they heard in the womb differently than to unfamiliar non-native languages. In a study by Byers-Heinlein *et al.* (2010) newborn babies born to bilingual Tagalog-English mothers could discriminate between, and showed preferences for, the two languages equally. This was in contrast to the control group of babies born to English monolingual mothers who showed a strong preference for English. Maneva and Genesee (2002) found that infants in the babbling stage (around 10–12 months of age) exposed to two languages from birth have a tendency to babble in their stronger language and demonstrate language-specific babbling features of each language. Garcia-Sierra *et al.* (2011) found that the brains of infants raised in bilingual Spanish-English homes demonstrate a longer period of being open and flexible to different languages in comparison with infants raised in monolingual households whose brains typically narrowed to their sole language by the end of their first year.

Research has shown that by age two bilingual children know which language to speak 'to whom' and in 'what situation' (De Houwer, 2009; Serratrice, 2013). They are able to use 'appropriate language matching' when talking to others, and can even rapidly and accurately accommodate the monolingualism or bilingualism of a stranger and talk in the appropriate language (Deuchar & Quay, 2000; Genesee, Boivin & Nicoladis, 1996). Bilingual children tend to mix languages less when addressing monolinguals, but translanguage more when addressing bilinguals (see below) (Comeau *et al.*, 2003). Thus, the ability to use the appropriate language with a particular person occurs very early. A variety of factors affect a child's language choice: exposure to two languages in different social contexts, the attitudes of parents to the two languages and to mixing the languages, the **language competences** and metalinguistic abilities of the child, personality, peer interaction, exposure to different forms of language education, as well as sociolinguistic influences such as the norms, values and beliefs of the community.

Language Choices of Parents

When parents can potentially use more than one language with their children, there is language choice in raising their children. This choice has been referred to as 'private language planning' (Piller, 2001) and more recently as 'family language policy' (Schwartz & Verschik, 2013). Where parents have the ability to speak both languages to their children, there may be a latent understanding or sometimes a conscious strategy about which language to use with the child from birth upwards. However, Piller (2002) found that many couples do not make a conscious decision about which language(s) to use in the home. Such language choice may derive from a habit formed from the first interaction between the couple, compensation (e.g. using one's native language in return for not living in the homeland) and **identity** (projecting a desired self-image). Parents' attitudes to languages, their preferred identity, and an overall cost benefit analysis are also influential in their choices. Other influences include the extended family and friends. Language choice may change depending on where a family currently resides. For example, a transnational bilingual Japanese-English family is more likely to use more Japanese at home while living in Japan but more English while living in Australia. Similarly, a bilingual Spanish-English family living in Nogales along the Mexican border in southern Arizona may find their use of Spanish at home decline if they move further north to Phoenix or Flagstaff.

Children's own preferences can be highly influential. As Fogle (2013) argues, 'Family language policy is not simply the result of parental ideologies and strategies, but rather a dynamic process in which children play an active role of influencing code choice and shaping family language ideologies' (pp. 196–197). Sibling interactions are also a major determinant of language choice (Barron-Hauwaert, 2011). Older and younger brothers and sisters play their part in shaping language interactions in the family. Multilingual extended families may have increased choices of language, particularly if coming from 'elite' circumstances. Grandparents, aunts and uncles, cousins and caregivers can all affect which language a child speaks with whom, when and where. Other families may not always have the luxury of options (e.g. less educated or disadvantaged minority language parents in a majority language community).

Some bilingual parents choose to use just one of their languages with the child. For varied reasons, a mother and father, for example, may use just Arabic or only English with the child. A different approach, as noted earlier, is the one-parent one-language approach (Barron-Hauwaert, 2004). For example, the mother may speak Arabic to the child and the father may speak English. Very few families obtain an equal balance between the two languages (e.g. as parents may speak to each other in one language). A third circumstance is when bilingual parents both speak the minority language to their children, leaving the child to learn the majority language outside the home.

Parents make language choices by conscious, subconscious and spontaneous decisions that are both general and local/specific (Lanza, 2007; Pavlenko, 2004). Piller (2002) found that parental choice of family languages relates to desired language, cultural and gender identity. Fogle and King (2013) found that child agency and language use patterns also have an impact on a parent's language behaviors. Thus, the societal contexts in which the family is placed affect language choices. Such choices may be relatively stable across time, but there are also choices that reflect a local, particular event (e.g. when a stranger enters the house everyone changes to the majority language). Thus, strategies and choices are often pragmatically flexible in family language situations, as visitors and contexts change.

Emotions affect language choice and strategies. Different languages may be used by parents to convey the emotions of praise and discipline, love and instructions, such that parents are often multilingual and not monolingual in language interactions with their children (Pavlenko, 2004). Pavlenko (2004) observed, 'Many [parents] draw on multiple linguistic repertoires, uttering "I love you" in one language, endearments in another, and "Go clean your room!" in yet another' (p. 200).

Bilingualism in childhood is also influenced by factors outside of parents and the home. With recent immigrants, the parents may speak the **heritage language**, but the children (especially teenagers) speak to each other in the language of the street, school and television. Playing with neighborhood children, making friends in and out of school with majority language speakers and use of the mass media may help create bilingualism in the child. An alternative scenario is when the grandparents and other relations use a different language with the child than the home language. For example, Chinese-American children may speak English at school and at home with their parents and siblings, but acquire at least a passive understanding of Chinese through regular visits to extended family members (Rampton & Charalambous, 2012).

Types of Early Childhood Bilingualism

Broad types or categories of early childhood bilingualism may be considered based on the language or languages spoken by the parents to the children and the language of the community. Not all children fit neatly into such categories. For example, De Houwer (2009) suggests that the most typical input pattern a bilingual child experiences is a combination of hearing some people only speaking one language plus hearing other people speaking both languages on a regular basis. Some families also are exceptions (e.g. one of the parents always addresses the child in a language that is not his/her native language). Parents who have learnt Basque as a second language sometimes speak Basque to their children so that it becomes their first language. There will also be an uneven distribution in the use of two or more languages, and that tends to change over time as family, social and educational circumstances, and language use opportunities vary. A bilingual child rarely or never has an equal balance in two-language experience. Hence, **balanced bilingualism** (see Chapter 1) is more of a myth than a reality.

(1) One Parent – One Language

The one-parent one-language (OPOL) approach, as described earlier, is commonly viewed as a highly successful strategy (Example: mother speaks English; father speaks Dutch – the community language). However, it tends to imply incorrectly that it is only the parents that influence language acquisition. Community influences are also important (e.g. pre-school, extended family, mass media). A particular example is when children are raised in multilingual cities (e.g. Brussels, New York, Sydney), and the diverse language experience may add much variation to this strategy. As De Houwer (2007) found in research on 1,899 families in Flanders, Belgium, the OPOL strategy does not provide a necessary nor a sufficient context for the growth of bilingualism in children. The success rate in her families was 75%. Also, the OPOL approach is much more difficult than it sounds, and can be physically and emotionally taxing on families (Barron-Hauwaert, 2004; Okita, 2002). It assumes the child interacts equally with both parents – an unlikely scenario if one parent works outside the home and the other is the primary caregiver. Furthermore, the fact that it requires such constant conscious effort suggests that it grinds against the dynamic nature of bilingualism and the natural ways bilinguals actually use their languages in daily life (O. García, 2009a).

(2) Home Language is Different from the Language Outside the Home

There is much variation within this category (e.g. in terms of parental first language, neighborhood and language of schooling). What is central is that the child acquires one language in the home, and a different language outside the home. Both parents will use the same language in the home, and the child will acquire another language formally or informally outside the home. One parent may be using their second language. (Example: father is a native English speaker but uses fluent Korean with his child; mother speaks Korean; the community language is English.) The parents' language may be the same as that of the local neighborhood, or it may be different. If it is different, then the child may, for example, acquire the second language at school. One further variation can produce multilingualism. If each parent speaks a different language to the child from birth, the child may gain a third language outside the home. This often results in trilingualism. (Example: mother speaks German; father speaks Italian; the community language is English.)

(3) Mixed Language

The parents speak both languages to the child. Translanguaging (see later) is acceptable in the home and the neighborhood. The child will typically translanguage with other bilinguals but not with monolinguals. However, some **domains** (e.g. school) may expect separation of language code. The community may have a **dominant language** or not. (Example: mother and father speak Maltese and English; the community language is Maltese and English.)

(4) Delayed Introduction of the Second Language

Where the neighborhood, community and school language is a higher status and dominant language, parents may delay exposure to that dominant language. For example, parents may exclusively speak Farsi in the home until the child is two or three years of age, then add English. The tactic is to ensure a strong foundation in a heritage language before the dominant language outside the home becomes pervasive.

Limitations

One main limitation of this category system is that most types are concerned with 'prestigious bilingualism', where there is a relatively stable additive bilingual environment and a family commitment to bilingualism. In communities where **subtractive bilingualism** operates, and **assimilation** (see Chapter 18) is politically dominant, childhood bilingualism can be much less stable. Piller (2001) also suggests that, of the four types listed above, types one and two have come to be regarded as successful strategies, and that types three and four are more negatively evaluated. However, this masks a social class difference. Type one is associated particularly with 'elite' and middle class families. Types three and four are often found among relatively economically disadvantaged heritage language groups, immigrants and working-class families.

Note that the above types do not account for languages spoken by siblings or others who may be living in the home, or other major linguistic influences in the home such as books, mass media, the internet and social media. Also, there are agencies other than the family that can play a major role in early childhood bilingualism. Before the age of three, the language experience with neighbors, friends, crèche and the nursery school may be a particularly important part of becoming bilingual. This chapter continues by focusing on the relatively well-documented routes to childhood bilingualism.

Case Studies of Early Bilingualism

Some of the earliest research on bilingualism concerns detailed case studies of children becoming bilingual. For example, Ronjat and Escudé (1913) described a case of the mother speaking German and the father speaking French in a French community. This case study introduced the OPOL concept. While there have been a number of case studies of children growing up bilingually since then, one of the most detailed of case studies is by Leopold (1970). In his classic study of his daughter Hildegard from 1930 to 1949, Leopold spoke only German and his wife spoke only English to Hildegard at home. Leopold was a phonetician by training and made a comprehensive record of the development of Hildegard's speech, which he published in four books.

One important aspect of Leopold's studies is the shifting balance of the two languages in childhood. When Hildegard went to Germany, her German became stronger. When back in the US and attending school, Hildegard's English became the dominant language. Many bilingual situations are changeable, where, at an individual level (and not just at a societal level), the languages shift in dominance. Hildegard, for example was reluctant to speak German during her mid-teens, with German becoming the weaker language. Leopold's second daughter, Karla, understood German but spoke very little German to her father. In childhood, Karla was a passive bilingual. Yet at the age of 19, Karla visited Germany where she was able to change from receptive German to productive German, managing to converse relatively fluently in German.

A more recent longitudinal study of bilingual first language acquisition is by Taura and Taura (2012) who documented the linguistic and narrative development of a Japanese-English bilingual girl for 14 years from early childhood (age 4;09) to late adolescence (19;01). The girl, referred to as 'M', grew up in Japan with an English-speaking mother and a Japanese-speaking father. She received most of her education in Japan except for Kindergarten and grade 6 which she received during extended stays in Australia. M attended a bilingual secondary school in Japan for grades 7–12 where half the subjects were taught in English and half were taught in Japanese. Despite the typological distance between English and Japanese, and despite far less exposure to English than Japanese during her lifespan, Taura and Taura found that with just a few exceptions, M's English language development was 'similar or identical to that of a monolingual [English speaker] in core linguistic areas' (p. 475). However, they acknowledge that it is difficult to tell if M's English proficiency would have been the same without the time she spent living and attending school in Australia. Nonetheless, like Hildegard in Leopold's study, M experienced some notable shifts in her language balance at various points during her childhood and adolescent years.

Other examples of shifting bilingualism in childhood are also found in shorter-term case studies by Fantini (1985) who details a child's shift between English, Italian and Spanish, and Yukawa (1997) who examines three cases of first language Japanese loss and re-acquisition. Yamamoto (2002) found in Japan that 'many parents testify, however, that in spite of their full-fledged care, their children have not developed active bilingual abilities' (p. 545). De Houwer (2003) found that among some 2,500 bilingual families, 1 in 5 children reared bilingually do not later use one of those languages. But as Quay (2001) concludes with regard to trilinguals: 'passive competence is valuable as the potential exists for his two weaker languages to be activated and used more actively later on … The status of strong and weak languages can change over the course of the child's life' (p. 194). De Houwer (2006) suggests that passive competence can rapidly change to **productive** competence by a major increase in input and a need to speak that language (e.g. visiting monolingual grandparents, a vacation).

Apart from the OPOL approach of raising children bilingually, there are other case studies showing different approaches. Two of these approaches have already been mentioned: each parent speaking a different language to the child; and parents speaking a minority language to the child who acquires a second language in the community or extended family. A third approach, which may be more common, occurs where both parents (and the community) are bilingual and use both their languages with the children. For example, this is quite common across Spanish bilingual communities in the US and other English-speaking countries (Fuller, 2013; Potowski & Rothman, 2011). Parental mixing of languages can still lead to a child communicating effectively in two languages, especially as the child learns that the two languages have relatively distinct forms and uses.

An example of parents using both languages with their first-born is by Deuchar and Quay (2000). A simplified profile of such dual language use with Deuchar's daughter (from 0;10 to 2;3) follows:

- *Mother:* Born in UK, native speaker of English, learnt fluent Spanish in adulthood.
- *Father:* Born in Cuba, later lived in Panama and then UK, native speaker of Spanish, began learning English at high school and became fluent in English.
- *Language spoken to daughter by mother:* English up to age 1, then Spanish. Spanish used by the mother when talking to the father; English when in the company of English speakers (e.g. crèche) or in a specific context (e.g. university campus).
- *Language spoken to daughter by father:* Spanish except when English speaker present, then he used English.
- *Language spoken to daughter by maternal grandmother/caregivers/crèche:* English.
- *Community:* English.
- *Trips abroad:* Spanish.

What is significant in this case study is that the daughter experienced her parents speaking both languages, with the context providing the rule-bound behavior. Both parents were fluent and effective role models in both languages, although each parent was a native speaker of one language and a learner of a second language. The switching between English and Spanish was not random but governed by the situation. This illustrates a danger of the OPOL model in that it can restrict discussion to the home, as if the parents are almost the only language influence. In contrast, siblings, extended families, caregivers, crèche, pre-schooling, friends of the family and many varying contexts (e.g. religious, geographical mobility) often have an additional language effect (Barron-Hauwaert, 2011). Parents may be able to plan language use when together as a nuclear family, however, once other people enter the house, and especially in the child's language experience outside the home, parental control is limited.

The development of a child's bilingualism is affected by both local (e.g. street, school) and regional contexts. For example, Chang (2004) found in Taiwan that children can find themselves in an awkward language context. The pressure is to gain perfect English, but if they become too Americanized, for example in emotional expression, they can be rejected for not being Chinese enough.

One-Parent Families and Bilingualism

Most case studies of bilingual children have been based on two-parent families. Books dealing with raising children bilingually tend to assume the presence of two parents in the family home. By accident rather than design, this implies that a one-parent family has little or no chance of raising a child bilingually. This is not true. Two examples will illustrate this.

(1) A second language is often acquired outside the home. In parts of Africa, children acquire one language at home or in the neighborhood and another language (or even two or three) at school or in inter-ethnic communication in urban areas (see, e.g. Chimbutane, 2011). Children of immigrant United States communities may acquire Spanish, for example, in the home and neighborhood, and learn English at school. A single parent who speaks French but resides in the US may decide to make French the family language so that the children may have the opportunity of bilingualism. In cases like these, the absence of a father or mother does not necessarily hinder a child's bilingual development.

(2) In some cases, the maintenance of a family's bilingualism may be challenged by the absence of a parent. In cases such as those in (1) above, where one parent speaks the dominant language of the community to the children, and the other parent uses a minority language with them, the death or departure of the second parent may mean that the family becomes monolingual. However, if the remaining parent is committed to the maintenance of the family's bilingualism, it can be accomplished in various ways.

The disruption of a family by death or divorce is typically traumatic for both parents and children. At times of great mental and emotional stress, when many practical difficulties and changes have to be faced, bilingualism may seem low on the list of priorities. However, single-parent families are often adept at meeting challenges and may look for ways of maintaining a child's bilingualism without causing further disruption to the child's life. In addition, where a child has undergone such stress, it may be wise, if possible, to avoid the added trauma of losing a language, a culture and an intrinsic part of the child's identity.

Trilingualism/Multilingualism

Many people are multilingual and not just bilingual. For example, some Swedish people are fluent in Swedish, German and English. Many individuals in the African and Indian continents speak a local, regional and national or international language. In the Republic of Zaire, children may learn a local **vernacular** at home, a regional language such as Lingala or Kikongo in the community or at school, and French as they proceed through schooling. Early trilingualism, when a child is exposed to three languages from birth, is rarer than trilingualism achieved through schooling (e.g. two languages learnt at school).

Particular examples of trilingual schooling are found in the Basque Country (Basque, Spanish, English) (see Cenoz, 2009), Catalonia (Catalan, Spanish, English) (see Muñoz, 2000), Finland (Finnish, Swedish, English) (see Bjorklund & Suni, 2000), Friesland (Frisian, Dutch, English) (Ytsma, 2000), and Romania (Romanian, Hungarian, English) (see Iatcu, 2000). **Trilingual education** is common throughout South Asia (Panda & Mohanty, 2015) and China (Feng & Adamson, 2015) with instruction in a regional and national language, plus English as an international language. A particular challenge in these settings, however is maintaining an appropriate balance between powerful international and national languages and the local and regional languages. Trilingual education is returned to in Chapter 11.

One route to multilingualism is parents speaking two different languages to their children at home. The children then take their education through a third language. Alternatively, the children pick up a third language from their grandparents, caregivers, visitors, playmates or the mass media. The majority language of the community is likely to influence the relative strengths of the three languages. The relative proficiency in each of the three languages may also change over time. Stable trilingualism seems less likely than stable bilingualism. Three languages can be acquired simultaneously or consecutively with a wealth of individual and societal variables interacting with such acquisition. Hence, simple conclusions about the development of trilingualism become difficult. However, metalinguistic awareness (see Chapter 7) seems to be a typical outcome of trilingualism (Jessner, 2006).

There are very few case studies of the development of multilingual children (see Quay, 2011 for a review). Wang (2008, 2011, 2015) provides a most comprehensive, detailed and thorough study as both an academic and as a mother. Her 11-year observation of her two sons acquiring French (their father's language), Chinese (Putonghua – their mother's language) and English (in the context of the United States) involved careful observation on a daily basis, videotaping and audiotaping. This remarkable study is refreshingly holistic, including linguistic and sociolinguistic perspectives, while at the same time revealing considerable parental insight and wisdom. Wang details the complexities, challenges and achievements of a decade of development, not only of three languages but also of related identity, personality and literacy.

Quay (2001) researched a child raised in German (spoken by the father to the child and the language used between mother and father) and English (used by the mother when addressing the child). Both parents were fluent in Japanese, which was the language of the local community (e.g. where their son attended daycare that operated in Japanese). There was a change in language exposure over the first two years, for example due to visits abroad and changes in the father's work schedule (see Table 5.1). Such changes are quite common for early trilinguals and bilinguals.

The table shows that this child was less exposed to German than English. At 1;3 it was not apparent that the child understood much German. Yet after two weeks in Germany at 1;3 the mother reports that he 'shocked us with how much he understood in German when spoken to by the extended family' (Quay, 2001: 174). This is also a common experience for families: understanding (and speaking) a second or third language quickly grows once there is sufficient exposure and incentive. However, Quay also shows that the child was a developing trilingual rather than an active trilingual. This child preferred to speak Japanese to his parents as he had more lexical resources in

Table 5.1 Language exposure of a trilingual child

Age of child	% English heard	% German heard	% Japanese heard
Birth to 11 months	70%	30%	0%
11 months to 1:0 year	50%	20%	30%
1:0 to 1:5 years	43%	23%	34%
1:5 to 1:6 years	45%	10%	45%

Note: Adapted from Quay (2001)

Japanese, and his parents understood and accepted his Japanese utterances. He tended to be a passive trilingual, understanding English and German, but speaking Japanese.

A case study by Dewaele (2000) follows Livia, who was raised in Dutch by her mother, in French by her father, with English acquired in her London neighborhood. The mother and father use Dutch when speaking together, making Dutch the dominant language of the family. English quickly became her 'default language' when meeting new children in London. From 0;5 to 2;6 Livia learnt Urdu from a childminder, thus becoming quadralingual at an early age. By 1;2 she had a passive knowledge of some 150 French, Dutch, Urdu and English words. Multiword utterances in Dutch and French appeared at 2;2. Awareness of her languages (metalinguistic awareness – see Chapter 7) came before her second birthday. The value of multilingualism was also understood at a very early age: 'If she doesn't get the cookie she ordered in one language, she codeswitches to the other, just to make sure we understand her request' (p. 5).

However, by five years of age, status and acceptance by peers had become important. Her father reports that she 'does not want me to speak French to her at school and addresses me …. in English, or whispers French in my ear' (Dewaele, 2002: 547). She wanted to avoid standing out from her peers, even in multiethnic London. In later childhood, Livia remained fluent in three languages but because 'she goes to an English school, is surrounded by English-speaking friends, watches English films, reads English books, hence the logical and inevitable dominance of English. It is her social language and also her 'inner' language' (Dewaele, 2007: 69). Livia was also allowed to respond in English when her parents talked to her in another language. 'By insisting too much on using our languages, we feared we could create the opposite effect, namely a complete refusal to use the languages at all' (p. 70). Dewaele concludes that, by the age of 10, becoming trilingual from birth was not hard to achieve, but the difficulty predominately exists in the maintenance and development of all three languages.

In a review of research on trilingualism, Cenoz and Genesee (1998) conclude that 'bilingualism does not hinder the acquisition of an additional language and, to the contrary, in most cases bilingualism favors the acquisition of a third language' (p. 20). Cenoz (2003) also suggests that 'studies on the effect of bilingualism on third language acquisition tend to confirm the advantages of bilinguals over monolinguals in language learning' (p. 82). The cognitive advantages of bilingualism such as a wider linguistic repertoire, enhanced learning strategies, cognitive flexibility and metalinguistic awareness (see Chapter 7) and the development of enhanced linguistic processing strategies may help explain this positive effect of bilingualism on acquiring a third language (Cenoz, 2003, 2009). The linguistic interdependence hypothesis (see Chapter 8) also suggests that positive influences may occur from bilingualism to tri-lingualism (Cenoz, 2003, 2009).

Clyne *et al.* (2004) found multiple positive social, cultural and cognitive advantages of multilingualism. Such multilinguals were found to be effective and enduring language learners, whose bilingualism is a language apprenticeship for further language learning. They conclude that 'acquiring a third language at school boosts students' confidence in their bilingualism and makes them appreciate their home language more, in some cases even leading to a desire to maintain their heritage language in the future and pass it on to the next generation' (p. 49). Clyne *et al.* also found that acquisition of a third language awakens and deepens interest in other languages, cultures and countries, creating more **multicultural** and global citizens.

Codeswitching and Translanguaging

One issue frequently raised by parents and teachers of bilingual children of differing ages is about one language being mixed with another. Terms such as Hinglish, Spanglish, Tex-Mex and Wenglish (respectively for Hindi-English, Spanish-English, Texan Mexican-Spanish and Welsh-English) are used – sometimes in a derogatory fashion – to describe what may have become natural practices within a bilingual community.

Codeswitching

Various terms have been used to describe switches between languages in conversation, and **terminology** remains a vexed issues (Gardner-Chloros, 2009). The terms **codemixing** and **codeswitching** were often used interchangeably, though some scholars make subtle distinctions between them based on where the switches occur. Here we will simply use the term codeswitching to refer to any switches between languages that occur within or across sentences during the same conversation or **discourse**.

Very few bilinguals keep their two languages completely separate, and the ways in which they mix them are complex and varied. Grosjean and Li (2013) distinguish between the 'monolingual mode' when bilinguals use one of their languages with monolingual speakers of that language, and the 'bilingual mode' when bilinguals are in the company of other bilinguals and have the option of switching languages. Even in the 'monolingual mode', bilinguals occasionally switch their languages intersentententially. Here are a few examples of types of codeswitches:

- Switching a single word within an utterance or sentence (Spanish/English):
  Leo un magazine [I read a magazine]

- Switching within a sentence (English/Spanish):
  Please go to the mercado and buy some leche y queso. [Please go the store and buy some milk and cheese]

- Switching from one sentence to the next (English/Welsh)
  Come to the table. Bwyd yn barod. [Food is ready]

Many scholars study codeswitching from a linguistic perspective (e.g. 'where in a sentence can a speaker change languages?'). Some seminal and recent examples include Myers-Scotton (1997), Poplack and Meechan (1998), Muysken (2000), Toribio (2004), and MacSwan (2013, 2014). One main language (called the matrix language) provides the grammatical rules that govern how something is said when there is codeswitching (Myers-Scotton, 2002). Codeswitching thus involves a rule-bound (e.g. word order, verb endings) use of the 'other' language, as such language insertions will fit those matrix language rules.

In contrast, **language interference** was a term that was once used to refer to when people acquiring two languages mixed their languages. Many bilinguals regard this as a negative and pejorative term, revealing a monolingual perspective and suggesting that there is a problem when a bilingual speaks. For the child, moving between languages may occur to convey thoughts and ideas in the most personally efficient manner. The child may also realize that the listener understands such switching. As Toribio (2004) suggests: intra-sentential [within sentence] codeswitching 'is not a random mixture of two flawed systems; rather, it is rule-governed and systematic, demonstrating the operation of underlying grammatical restrictions. Proficient bilinguals may be shown to exhibit a shared knowledge of what constitutes appropriate intra-sentential codeswitching' (p. 137).

Translanguaging

The term **translanguaging** has recently been introduced and has become highly popular in usage across different disciplines. However, since it is new, its meaning and use are still developing. For many scholars, translanguaging goes well beyond the relatively more linguistic idea of codeswitching. Thus codeswitching and translanguaging are not two discrete terms and have overlaps. In listening to a conversation in a classroom, to differentiate between codeswitching and translanguaging is often difficult. For O. García (2009a), codeswitching is a component inside translanguaging, with translanguaging incorporating codeswitching. However, there is a relatively long and solid tradition in linguistics research on codeswitching such that using both terms is currently important.

Translanguaging recognizes that the languages we use integrate, change and adapt to new learning and new situations, with effects on identity and experiences. We combine all our language resources to unlock meaning and share our understandings with others. Our use of two or more languages changes across people, time, place and need. Translanguaging in bi/multilingual communication is thus fluid and dynamic, sometimes messy and inventive, making and conveying meaning as best as possible (O. García, 2009a). 'Trans' suggests continual movement across and between languages, but also suggests that such translanguaging is transformative in thinking and speaking, in identity and interpersonal relationships, for example.

Thus, translanguaging has recently been used in a different way to codeswitching by focusing on how bilinguals actually use their two languages in daily life as they draw upon all of their linguistic resources to make sense of their world and meaningfully communicate with others (O. García, 2009a). In other words, codeswitching tends to focus relatively more on the 'code' (i.e. the language itself), whereas translanguaging focuses relatively more on bilingual speakers and the ways in which they use their various linguistic resources (O. García & Li Wei, 2014). García acknowledges that from an external social perspective, the behavior of codeswitching and translanguaging may look the same, 'but seen from the internal perspective of the bilingual speaker, translanguaging behavior is clearly different' because it 'legitimizes the fluid language practices with which bilinguals operate' and also 'posits that bilinguals have

---

Box 5.1 Language borrowing

Language borrowing refers to foreign loan words or phrases that have become an integral and permanent part of the recipient language. Examples are *le weekend* from English into the French language and *der computer* from English into the German language. All languages borrow words or phrases from other languages with which they come into contact. Words commonly used by English speakers such as *patio*, *croissant* and *jaguar* are loan words from Spanish, French and Portuguese respectively. Loan words may start out as frequently occurring codeswitches, though it is often difficult to distinguish between them. It may be more accurate to think of them as forming a continuum.

---

a much more complex and expanded repertoire than monolinguals' (Grosjean, 2016: 1). Our discussion in this section will consider the natural ways bilinguals make use of codeswitching in their translanguaging practices (see Chapter 13 for further discussions on translanguaging).

The Context of Codeswitching and Translanguaging

Children's codeswitching and translanguaging is influenced by the language model provided by parents and significant others in the family, school and community. If parents use both languages regularly, then their children may imitate. If, on the other hand, parents discourage mixing languages (e.g. by clear language separation), then less codeswitching may occur. What is culturally appropriate, the norm of the community, and what is valued by parents and others will have an important influence, as may the extent of the child's repertoire in each language.

Codeswitching and translanguaging may also be less acceptable for political, social or cultural reasons. If a power conflict exists between different ethnic groups, then language may be perceived as a prime marker of a separate identity, and codeswitching may seem disloyal. Some monolinguals have negative attitudes to codeswitching and translanguaging, believing that it shows a communication deficit, or a lack of mastery of both languages. Some monolinguals and bilinguals are language purists who strongly believe that codeswitching is a corruption of both languages. When scholar Ilan Stavans (2003) published a Spanglish dictionary, translated a portion of Don Quixote into Spanglish, taught a university course about Spanglish, and undertook other activities in defense of Spanglish, he reported receiving hostile messages and even death threats from individuals in the United States, Spain, Mexico, Colombia and Argentina (Stavans, 2014). But Stavans noted he has was also 'showered with great applause' and held up by many as a 'folk hero' and 'a subversive intellectual undermining the status quo' (p. 2). Codeswitching is thus not always acceptable, and that includes to bilingual speakers themselves. Some bilinguals adopt a relatively more monolingual approach and attempt to keep their languages separate. Bilinguals themselves may be defensive or apologetic about their codeswitching and attribute it to laziness or sloppy language.

Some bilingual education programs (e.g. dual language education, see Chapter 11) attempt to insist on a relatively strict separation of the languages. However, translanguaging can be a valuable thinking tool, including in the classroom. It does not happen at random. There is typically purpose and logic in changing languages, as will be shown below. It is using the full language resources that are available to a bilingual, usually knowing that the listener fully understands the dual language or multilingual communication.

If codeswitching is highly prevalent in a language group, it is sometimes regarded as a sign that the minority language is about to disappear. Such codeswitching may be seen by some as a halfway house in a societal shift from the minority language to the dominant majority language. Identifying the matrix (main, dominant) language that provides the rules from codeswitching becomes a key indicator of the health of a minority language. For example, if the matrix language is Navajo and there are English insertions, this indicator for the future of Navajo will be positive. However, if the grammatical frame is English, this indicator for Navajo may be negative.

Familiarity, projected status, the ethos of the context and the perceived linguistic skills of the listeners affect the nature and process of codeswitching and translanguaging (Martin-Jones, 2000). Thus, codeswitching and translanguaging are not just linguistic; they indicate important social and power relationships. A variety of factors may affect the extent to which children and adults switch between their languages. The perceived status of the listeners, familiarity with those persons, atmosphere of the setting and perceived linguistic skills of the listeners are examples of variables that may foster or prevent codeswitching and translanguaging. Such factors operate as young as two years of age.

The Purposes and Uses of Codeswitching

The following text mostly derives from the history of writings on codeswitching. However, given the overlap between codeswitching and translanguaging, much of the text also appears to relate to translanguaging. Codeswitches and translanguaging have a variety of purposes and aims. Translanguaging will vary according to who is in the conversation, what the topic is, and in what kind of context the conversation occurs. The languages used may be negotiated and may change with the topic of conversation. Also, social, economic, political, identity and symbolic factors can influence translanguaging. For example, competition between language groups, the relationships between the language majority and **language minority**, the norms of the community and inter-group relations in a community may have a major effect on the use of translanguaging.

Fourteen overlapping purposes of codeswitching and translanguaging will now be considered:

(1) *Emphasis.* Codeswitches may be used to emphasize a particular point in a conversation. If one word needs stressing or is central in a sentence, a switch may be made (e.g. English/Welsh: 'get out of the mud, *hogyn drwg*! [bad boy]).

(2) *Substitution.* If a person does not know a word or a phrase in a language, that person may substitute a word in another language. As Genesee (2006) suggests, 'bilingual children might be compelled to draw on the resources of their more proficient language in order to express themselves fully when using their less well-developed language' (p. 53). This lexical gap often happens because bilinguals use different languages in different domains of their lives. A young person may, for instance, switch from the home language to the language used in school to talk about a subject such as mathematics or computers. Similarly, an adult may codeswitch when talking about work, because the technical terms associated with work are only known in that language.

(3) *Concepts without equivalences.* Words or phrases in two languages may not correspond exactly and the bilingual may switch to one language to express a concept that has no equivalent in the culture of the other language. This is part of the recent conceptualization of translanguaging. For example, a French–English bilingual living in Britain may use words like 'pub' or 'bingo hall' when speaking French, because there are no exact French equivalents for these words. Likewise, in Cambodian university courses on education policy, words and phrases such as 'child-centered instruction', 'active learning' and even 'codeswitching' may be used in English during lectures presented in Khmer, as standardized equivalents of these terms in Khmer have not yet been coined and widely adopted.

(4) *Problem solving.* Children sometimes move between their languages to help think through a problem. Having tried a problem in one language, they may use their other language(s) to re-phrase and re-think. For example, different associations of words in another language, moving to or from the pedagogic language by teachers, or using the counting system in another language, may help problem solve. This is part of the origins of the term 'translanguaging'.

(5) *Reinforcement.* Codeswitching may be used to reinforce a request. For example, a French language teacher may repeat a command to accent and underline it (e.g. '*Taisez-vous les enfants*! Be quiet, children!'). An Arabic-speaking mother in New York may use English with her children for short commands like 'Stop it! Don't do that!' and then switch back to Arabic.

(6) *Clarification.* Repetition of a phrase or passage in another language may also be used to clarify a point. Some teachers in classrooms introduce a concept in one language, and then explain or clarify it in another language, believing it adds reinforcement and completeness of understanding.

(7) *Identity.* Codeswitching and translanguaging may be used to express identity, shorten social distance, and communicate friendship or family bonding. For example, moving from the common majority language to the minority language which both the listener and speaker understand well may communicate friendship and common identity. Similarly, a person may deliberately use codeswitching to indicate the need to be accepted by a peer group. Someone with a rudimentary knowledge of a language may inject words of that new language into sentences to indicate a desire to identify and affiliate. The use of the listener's stronger language in part of the conversation may indicate deference, wanting to belong or to be accepted.

(8) *Reported speech.* In relating a conversation held previously, the person may report the conversation in the language or languages used. For example, two people may be speaking Spanish together. When one reports a previous conversation with an English monolingual, that conversation is reported authentically – for example, in English – as it occurred. For example a son might say to his mother, 'Mi maestro me dijo, [My teacher told me] "you can't go to the fieldtrip until your parents sign the form."'

(9) *Interjections.* Codeswitching is sometimes used as a way of interjecting into a conversation. A person attempting to break into a conversation may introduce a different language. Interrupting a conversation may be signaled by changing language.

(10) *Ease tension and/or inject humor.* Codeswitching and translanguaging may be used to ease tension and inject humor into a conversation. If discussions are becoming tense in a committee, the use of a second language may signal a change

in the 'tune being played'. Just as in an orchestra, different instruments may be brought in during a composition to signal a change of mood and pace, so a switch in language may indicate a need to change mood within the conversation. A professor in Cambodia who mostly taught his courses in English described using codeswitching as a way of 'waking up' students who were drifting off.

(11) *Change of attitude or relationship*. Codeswitching and translanguaging often relate to a change of attitude or relationship. For example, when two people meet, they may use the common majority language (e.g. Swahili or English in Kenya). As the conversation proceeds and roles, status and ethnic identity are revealed, a change to a regional language may indicate that boundaries are being broken down. A switch signals that there is less social distance, with expressions of solidarity and growing rapport indicated by the switch. Conversely, a change from a minority language or dialect to a majority language may indicate the speaker's wish to elevate their own status, create a distance between themselves and the listener, or establish a more formal, business relationship. For example, a Vietnamese American customer at a department store might notice the cashier is also Vietnamese and strike up a friendly conversation in Vietnamese, then ask for a discount. The cashier may switch the conversation back to English to indicate, 'Sorry, can't do that'.

(12) *Exclusion*. Codeswitching can also be used to exclude people from a conversation. For example, when traveling on the metro (subway, underground), two people speaking English may switch to their minority language to talk about private matters, thus preventing other passengers from eavesdropping. Bilingual parents may use one language together to exclude their monolingual children from a private discussion. A doctor at a hospital may make a brief aside to a colleague in a language not understood by the patient. However, monolinguals sometimes feel threatened and excluded by codeswitching, even when that is usually not the intention of the speakers.

(13) *Change in topic*. In some bilingual situations, translanguaging occurs regularly when certain topics are introduced. For example, English might be used to discuss the local sports team (e.g. 'Go Spurs Go!') while Spanish is used to discuss a recent episode of a popular *telenovela* (Spanish soap opera). Bilinguals may use English when discussing financial matters with American currency, but the home language when discussing currency used in the home country (e.g. 'Mi abuela en Guatemala wants me to send her 100 quetzales' [My grandmother in Guatemala wants me to send her 100 quetzals]. However, use of 'Spanglish' terms for American coins and currency are commonly used in the Southwest United States such as *daime* (dime), *cuara* (quarter), and *dolar* (dollar). Thus, codeswitching does not just involve clean switches between two languages, but also involves the creation of new terms in the mixing.

(14) *Imitation*. In some contexts, children are simply copying the codeswitching and translanguaging practices of the peers and adults around them. If a daughter in England frequently hears her French-speaking father say 'Let's go to le boulangerie' [the bakery], chances are she'll start saying it that way too. When children are emulating adults, they may be identifying with higher status and more powerful people in their lives.

The chapter concludes by examining a topic related to translanguaging: children acting as interpreters for their parents and others.

Children as Language Interpreters and Brokers

In language minority families, children sometimes act as interpreters (or **language brokers**) for their parents and others (Guo, 2014; N. Hall & Sham, 2007). In first- and second-generation immigrant families, parents may have little or no competency in the majority language. Therefore, their children act as interpreters in a variety of contexts (as do 'hearing' children with deaf parents). Language brokering goes beyond translation. Rather than just transmit information, children act as cultural mediators, often ensuring the messages are 'socially and culturally translated' as in the following example:

Father to daughter: (in Italian): *Digli che è un imbecille*! [Tell him he is an idiot!]
Daughter to trader: My father won't accept your offer.

Valdés (2003) argues that young immigrant's ability to use their bilingual skills to mediate for their families both linguistically and culturally in this manner is evidence of 'giftedness' that is rarely recognized by schools. This is extended by Orellana (2009) who researched immigrant children in Los Angeles and Chicago to explore how children translate and act as language and culture brokers at home and school, but also in the community and across institutions. Using two or more languages, children 'work' to shoulder the responsibility for some quite complicated verbal exchanges for non-English speaking adults. Orellana expands the definition of child labor by portraying children as working as unpaid translators. She also shows how such children's sociocultural learning and development is shaped by acting as translators.

Language minority students can be important language brokers between the home and the school. Also, when there are visitors to the house, such as sellers and traders, religious persuasionists and local officials, a parent may call a child to the door to help translate what is being said. Similarly, at stores, hospitals, medical and dentist offices, motor vehicle and social security offices, schools and many other places where parents visit, the child may be taken to help interpret and mediate interculturally. Interpretation may be needed in more informal places: on the street, when a parent is phoned, watching the television or listening to the radio, reading a note from school, reading a local newspaper, or working on the computer.

Pressure is placed on children in language brokering: linguistic, emotional, social and attitudinal pressure. First, children may find an exact translation difficult to achieve as their language is still developing. Words often have multiple meanings making interpretation far from a simple or straightforward process. Second, children may be hearing information (e.g. medical troubles, financial problems, marital issues, arguments and conflicts) that is the preserve of adults rather than children. Third, children may be expected to be adult-like when interpreting and child-like at all other times; to mix with adults when interpreting and 'be seen and not heard' with adults on other occasions. Fourth, there can be stress, fear and uncertainty for the child in providing an accurate and diplomatic interpretation. Fifth, seeing their parents in an inferior position may lead to children despising their minority language. Children may quickly realize when language brokering that the language of power, prestige and purse is the majority language. Negative attitudes to the minority language may result. Sixth, bilinguals are not necessarily good interpreters. Interpretation assumes an identical vocabulary in both languages. Since bilinguals tend to use their two languages in different places with different people, an identical **lexicon** may not be present. Also, proficiency in two or more languages is not enough. Some reflection on language such as an awareness of the linguistic nature of the message may also be required (i.e. meta-linguistic awareness).

Despite these pressures, language brokering may also result in positive outcomes for children and their families, such as the following:

(1) *Self-esteem*. Children earn parental praise and status within the family, leading to gains in self-esteem.
(2) *Maturity*. Children quickly learn adult information, learn to act with authority and trust, and take on great responsibility, leading to greater maturity.
(3) *Unity*. Children and parents learn to trust and rely on each other, leading to greater feelings of family unity.
(4) *Empowerment*. Children learn to take initiative such as answering questions on their own rather than relaying the question to their parents, leading to a greater sense of personal **empowerment**. But this can also lead to a shift of power from parents to children, and may cause parent feelings of inadequacy, frustration or resentment.
(5) *Metalinguistic awareness*. Children learn to address the problems and possibilities of translation of words, figures of speech and ideas, leading to greater gains in metalinguistic awareness.
(6) *Empathy*. Children learn to negotiate between two different social and cultural worlds while trying to understand both, and leading to greater feelings of empathy.

Conclusion

This chapter has discussed bilingual development in early childhood through themes of differentiating between languages. Parental influence starts at the fetal stage with language difference being apparent at babbling stage. Children of two and three raised in two languages form birth will know 'what language to speak to whom'.

One parent – one language is a well-documented and successful route to bilingual-ism in early childhood, but there are many other successful pathways. Some parents use two languages with their children. Some bilingual children are raised in one language but become bilingual early via influences outside the home. One-parent families can be as successful as nuclear and extended families. However, **language loss** can occur when political contexts are particularly unfavorable to minority **language maintenance**. Other families succeed in raising trilingual children, although it is not usual to become equally proficient in all three languages.

Codeswitching and translanguaging are frequent behaviors among bilinguals, with a variety of valuable purposes and benefits. Interpreting is a similarly frequent expectation of bilinguals – including young children in immigrant families.

Suggested Further Reading

📖 Anderson, K. J. (2015). *Language, identity, and choice: Raising bilingual children in a global society*. Lanham, MD: Lexington Books.

📖 De Houwer, A. (2009). *Bilingual first language acquisition*. Bristol, UK: Multilingual Matters.

Key Points in This Chapter

➢ Children are born ready to become bilinguals, trilinguals, multilinguals.

➢ There is a difference between simultaneous (acquire two languages together) and sequential (acquire one language later than the other) childhood bilingualism.

➢ Dual language acquisition starts at the fetal stage, extends into babbling and can be operating successfully at two and three years of age.

➢ Young children learn to differentiate between two languages.

➢ Early studies of bilingual children revealed that if each parent speaks a different language to the child, dual language competence can occur, although the balance shifts throughout an individual's language history.

➢ The 'one person – one language' parental approach in a family is a well-documented and often successful route to bilingualism. Many other routes are equally successful, including when both parents speak both languages to the child.

➢ Trilingualism and multilingualism can also be successfully achieved in young children, although the languages may not become equally strong.

➢ Bilinguals tend to have an advantage in learning a new language.

➢ Codeswitching and translanguaging are typical in bilinguals and have many valuable purposes in relationships and relaying messages, as well as expressing roles, norms and values.

➢ Codeswitching and translanguaging vary according to who is in the conversation, what the topic is, and in what kind of context the conversation occurs.

➢ Children may act as language and culture brokers for parents when their proficiency in the majority language is ahead of their parents'. This has many advantages and disadvantages for the child.

📖 Jernigan, C. (2015). *Family language learning: Learn another language, raise bilingual children.* Bristol, UK: Multilingual Matters.

📖 Schwartz, M., & Verschik, A. (Eds.). (2013). *Successful family language policy: Parents, children and educators in interaction.* Dordrecht, Netherlands: Springer.

On the Web

🖥 8 Year Old Polyglot Mabou Loiseau (Video)
https://youtu.be/j5oPimuyFUE

🖥 Bilingual Monkeys: Ideas and Inspiration for Raising Bilingual Kids (without going bananas)
http://bilingualmonkeys.com/

🖥 Public Radio International (PRI) – A Hidden History of Spanglish in California
http://www.pri.org/stories/2015-02–11/hidden-history-spanglish-california

Discussion Questions

(1) How easy or difficult do you think it would be to raise children bilingually? If you were to raise a bilingual child, which approach or approaches mentioned in this chapter would you use? If you were raised bilingually, or have or are currently raising a bilingual child, share what strategies seem to be effective.

(2) If you are bilingual, consider your own use of translanguaging. How frequently do you translanguage? For what purposes? In which contexts? If you are not bilingual, what translanguaging practices have you observed among bilingual school children or other bilinguals around you?

(3) What are the pros and cons of using bilingual children as interpreters? What are some situations where the use of children to interpret may be more or less appropriate?

Study Activities

(1) Conduct a case study of a child's bilingual (or trilingual) development. Using this chapter and specific research studies of children's bilingual development, prepare a list of questions appropriate to ask the child and her or his parents during an interview to identify if there were particular stages of their development. Share the findings in a written report and/or class presentation.

(2) Observe and record samples of codeswitching and translanguaging. Try to determine the different purposes of the codeswitching. Ask the people in your sample how conscious they are of codeswitching. What are their explanations for codeswitching? What particular purposes for codeswitching did they give? How regular was codeswitching in the conversation? What is the personal history of those you observed or recorded that may help explain such codeswitching?

(3) Visit the website Bilingual Zoo (http://bilingualzoo.com/), which features a discussion board for parents raising their children bilingually. Review the kinds of questions being asked and the advice being given. Choose one of these topics or questions and analyze the answers. Write your own response to this question, using research to support your answer.

The Later Development of Bilingualism

CHAPTER 6

The Later Development of Bilingualism

Introduction

Sequential acquisition of **bilingualism** refers to the situation where a child or adult acquires a first language, and later becomes proficient in the second language and sometimes further languages. The sequential acquisition of bilingualism takes us into the field of second language acquisition. Such acquisition may be through formal or informal means; informally through street, nursery school and community, or formally through school, adult classes and language courses. There is no single 'best' route by which learners, young or old, become competent in a second language. There are a variety of informal and formal educational means of acquiring proficiency in a second language.

Many children become competent bilinguals through the process of **simultaneous bilingualism**. The track record of bilingualism achieved through sequential routes (e.g. foreign language learning) is not always so positive (see Box 6.1). In the US and UK, despite extensive foreign language learning in school (and extensive research on second language acquisition), only a small proportion of children learning a foreign language become functionally and fluently bilingual. Even among US college students who major in common foreign languages, the average student only reaches a limited working proficiency in the language (Brown & Brown, 2015). There are various popular reasons for such failure: the emphasis on grammar, reading and writing rather than on authentic communication; having a low aptitude to learn a second language; a lack of motivation and interest, and a lack of opportunity to practice second language skills. Another popular explanation is attempting to learn a language too late; that is, believing that it is easier to learn a language when someone is younger rather than older. The issue of age in learning a language is considered later.

In certain European countries (e.g. the Netherlands, Luxembourg, Slovenia, Sweden, Belgium) and eastern countries (e.g. Israel, Singapore), foreign language learning has been relatively more successful. Such international comparisons highlight the need to bring political, social, cultural and economic factors into second language learning discussions (Atkinson, 2011). No language learner or language instruction is an island. Surrounding the shores of the individual psychology of effective second language acquisition lie the seas of social, cultural and political **context**. Any map of **sequential bilingualism** needs to include all these features.

Box 6.1 America's foreign language deficit

In 2012 *Forbes* magazine (Skorton & Altschuler, 2012) decried 'America's Foreign Language Deficit', in response to reports about decreasing numbers of elementary and middle schools offering students opportunities to learn another language (from 24% to 15% in public elementary schools, and from 75% to 58% in middle schools between 1997 and 2008). *Forbes* declared:

> We should care – a lot – about our foreign language deficit. We need diplomats, intelligence and foreign policy experts, politicians, military leaders, business leaders, scientists, physicians, entrepreneurs, managers, technicians, historians, artists, and writers who are proficient in languages other than English. And we need them to read and speak less commonly taught languages (for which funding has recently been cut by the federal government) that are essential to our strategic and economic interests, such as Farsi, Bengali, Vietnamese, Burmese and Indonesian....
>   The message is simple: in 1957, after the Russians launched Sputnik, Congress passed and President Eisenhower signed the National Defense Education Act, which provided federal support for foreign language instruction as well as science education. We may not be quite as frightened as we were during the height of the Cold War, but we must be just as resolute in designing a comprehensive approach to foreign language acquisition that will prepare the next generation of Americans for success in a highly competitive, tightly interconnected world.

In 2015 *The Atlantic* magazine also decried 'America's lacking language skills', declaring, 'Budget cuts, low enrollments, and teacher shortages means the country is falling behind the rest of the world' (A. Friedman, 2015). Noting that 'only 7% of college students in America are enrolled in a language course' and that 'less than 1% of American adults today are proficient in a foreign language that they studied in a U.S. classroom,' *The Atlantic* also expressed concerned about a mismatch between the languages studied vs. global realities:

> Another challenge emerges when looking at the languages these students are learning, too. In 2013, roughly 198,000 U.S. college students were taking a French course; just 64, on the other hand, were studying Bengali. Yet, globally, 193 million people speak Bengali, while 75 million speak French. In fact, Arne Duncan, the U.S. education secretary, noted back in 2010 that the vast majority – 95 percent – of all language enrollments were in a European language. This is just one indicator demonstrating the shortcomings and inequalities in language education today. (Friedman, 2015: 1)

Reasons for Second Language Learning

The various overlapping reasons why second or third languages are taught can be clustered under two headings: societal and individual. Such purposes may clash. For example, national politics may insist on the teaching of a national language for unity and social cohesion, while individuals may prefer instruction through the regional language. Basque separatists in Spain, and Eastern Europeans rejecting Russian as the language of Communism, are two examples of difference between societal and individual wishes. Some reasons are for learning a language, others for teaching a language, and there may be variance between the two.

Societal Reasons

For language minority children, the aim of second language instruction may be **assimilationist** and subtractive. For example, the teaching of **English as a second language** in the US and the UK often aims at rapidly assimilating minority language groups into mainstream society. Assimilationist **ideology** (see Chapter 18) tends to work for the dominance of the second language, even the repression of the home, minority language. In contrast, children are sometimes taught minority languages in order to preserve or restore a language that is being or has been lost (see Chapter 3). A different societal reason for second language acquisition is to reduce conflict and obtain increased harmony between language groups through bilingualism. In Canada, French-speaking children learning English and English-speaking children learning French may help parents and politicians produce a more integrated Canadian society.

The assimilationist, preservationist and harmony viewpoints all argue for the importance of a second language for careers, access to further and higher education, access to information and communications technology and for travel. However, it is important to distinguish whether the second language is intended to replace the first language or to be added to that first language.

While teachers may be relatively powerless to change the basic societal aims and reasons in second language teaching, understanding the role they play in such teaching is important. Second language teaching does not exist in a political vacuum. Nor is language teaching a neutral, value-free activity. Even within an assimilationist system, teachers have some degree of influence and power as policymakers within their own classrooms and schools (Menken & García, 2010) and can help create an environment that values and encourages bilingualism (de Jong, 2011; Wright, 2015).

Second and third language learning is often encouraged for economic and trade reasons. In tourist areas, learning additional languages such English, Chinese, French and Japanese is valuable for those working in hotels, shops, cafes and restaurants, and other tourist attractions. Given notions such as globalization, common markets, open access to trade, the free market economy and the importance of international trade to developing nations, then facility with languages is seen as opening doors to economic activity. Selling to the Japanese, for example, may be quite difficult through English or German. Speaking Japanese and having a sympathetic understanding of Japanese **culture**, manners, values and thinking may be the essential foundation for success-ful economic activity (see Chapter 19). There is a growing realization that speaking foreign languages is important in increasingly competitive international trade, even as a matter of long-range economic self-interest. Translation jobs in the US tend to be filled by foreign-born individuals because there are relatively few US students and adults – including heritage speakers – who are proficient enough in the second languages required for such posts.

Second and third language learning is also encouraged for its potential value in interaction across continents. For many mainland Europeans, for example, to speak two, three or four languages is not uncommon. Such language facility enables time to be spent in neighboring European countries or in North, Central or South America. In the attempted unification of Europe, traveling across frontiers is becoming more common, encouraging a person to acquire a repertoire of languages. However, English is growing as a 'common denominator' language, not only in Europe but internation-ally. Therefore, the learning of English as a second or foreign language has grown considerably (see Chapter 4).

Languages provide access to information and hence power. Whether the informa-tion is in academic journals, on the internet, on satellite television or in international new media, a repertoire of languages gives wider access to social, cultural, political, economic and educational information. For the business person and the bureaucrat, for the scholar and the sports person, access to multilingual international information opens doors to new knowledge, new skills and new understanding.

Language learning is also ideally a means of promoting intercultural understanding and peace. Such ideals have become more focused following a new wave of terrorism across the world, but interact uncomfortably with defense and intelligence needs. For example, following the September 11, 2001 terrorist attacks in New York, the lack of foreign **language proficiency** in US intelligence was much criticized (Brecht & Ingold, 2002). Since 9/11, it is more apparent that English cannot be the only language of international diplomacy or the lens to view the world. Languages identify, symbolize and embody their cultures. Ideally, to create coalitions, foster friendships, and to produce peace, requires the use of languages other than English. To heal longstanding wounds from the past requires bridges built through the languages of old opponents and recent rivals. Yet, in contrast, the more basic need is often to search out intelligence, which requires ground operatives, interpreters and translators. A supply line of both operatives and translators is possible not only via language learning in school and at college, but also via heritage language speakers (e.g. Arabic, Farsi, Pashto). In contrast, however, current US ideology tends to prefer the **assimilation** of heritage language speakers by the sole use of English at school (Gandara & Hopkins, 2010). As Brecht and Ingold (2002) suggest:

> The United States has an unprecedented need for individuals with highly developed language competencies not only in English, our societal language, but also in many other languages. In fact, the need for individuals with proficiency in languages other than English for use in social, economic, diplomatic, and geopolitical arenas has never been higher. Even before the events of September 11, 2001, Congressional hearings had begun to document a shortage of professionals with the language proficiencies required to carry out a wide range of federal government activities. More than 70 government agencies reported a need for individuals with foreign language expertise. (p. 1)

Such shortages of staff with foreign language expertise hinder US military, law enforcement, intelligence, counter-terrorism, and diplomatic efforts. Brecht and Ingold (2002) indicate that there is a reservoir of language talent currently being ignored:

> There exists, however, a largely untapped reservoir of linguistic competence in this country, namely heritage language speakers – the millions of indigenous, immigrant, and refugee individuals who are proficient in English and also have skills in other languages that are developed at home, in schools, in their countries of origin, or in language programs provided by their communities in the United States.

Unfortunately, in the US there is a great divide between national language needs and federal education policies which seek to assimilate **language minority students** and squander their linguistic skills which are critically needed by the country (Wright, 2010). Some initiatives in the US to address shortages in the areas of critical needs languages include the National Security Education Program, STARTALK, and the National Heritage Language Resource Center.

Individual Reasons

There are many reasons why the individual child or adult can benefit from being taught a second or third language. Gallagher-Brett (2005) identified 700 reasons within the academic literature for learning a second language, and has made these available in a searchable database (see www.idiomas.idph.com.br/textos/700_reasons.pdf).

One reason is for cultural awareness. To break down national, ethnic and language stereotypes, second language learning may help lead to intercultural sensitivity and awareness. This is seen as important as the world becomes more of a global village, with more sharing of experience and mutual understanding. Cultural awareness in the classroom may be achieved at one level by discussing ethnic variations in eating and drinking, rituals of birth, death and marriage, and religious practices. Such activity widens human understanding and attempts to encourage sensitivity towards other cultures and creeds. While cultural awareness may be conveyed in the first language, the inseparability of culture and language means that such awareness may best be achieved through simultaneous language learning.

A second 'individual' reason for second language teaching has traditionally been for cognitive development. The learning of foreign languages has been of general educational and academic value. Just as history and geography, physics and chemistry, mathematics and music have traditionally been taught to increase intellectual fitness and stamina, so modern language learning has been defended as a way of sharpening the mind and developing the intellect. Given the memorization, analysis (e.g. of grammar and sentence structure) and the need to negotiate in communication, language learning has been regarded as a valuable academic activity in itself.

A third reason for an individual to acquire a language is for social, emotional and moral development, self-awareness, self-confidence and social and ethical values. Such affective goals include the possibility of **incipient bilinguals** being able to create more effective relationships with target language speakers. Bilinguals can potentially build social bridges with those who speak the second language.

Self-confidence and enhanced self-esteem may result from being able to operate socially or vocationally with those who speak the second or third language. The

---

Box 6.2 Eurobarometer language survey

The European Commission (2012) Eurobarometer language survey of 28,751 people in 27 countries of Europe includes the following selected findings:

- The most widely spoken mother tongue is German (16%), followed by Italian and English (13% each), French (12%), then Spanish and Polish (8% each). The five most widely spoken foreign languages are English (38%), French (12%), German (11%), Spanish (7%) and Russian (5%).
- Just over half of Europeans (54%) are able to hold a conversation in at least one additional language, a quarter (25%) are able to speak at least two additional languages and one in ten (10%) are conversant in at least three.
- Almost all respondents in Luxembourg (98%), Latvia (95%), the Netherlands (94%), Malta (93%), Slovenia and Lithuania (92% each), and Sweden (91%) say that they are able to speak at least one language in addition to their mother tongue
- Countries where respondents are least likely to be able to speak any foreign language are Hungary (65%), Italy (62%), the UK and Portugal (61% in each), and Ireland (60%).
- 44% of Europeans say that they are able to understand at least one foreign language well enough to be able to follow the news on radio or television.
- 88% of Europeans think that knowing languages other than their mother tongue is very useful.
- 67% of Europeans consider English as one of the two most useful languages for themselves, followed by German (17%), French (16%), Spanish (14%) and Chinese (6%).
- 98% of Europeans consider mastering other foreign languages as useful for the future of their children
- The most widespread method used to learn a foreign language is through lessons at school. Just over two thirds of Europeans (68%) have learnt a foreign language in this way.
- The majority of Europeans (81%) agree that all languages spoken within the EU should be treated equally.

addition of a second language skill can boost an individual's self-confidence as a learner, a linguist and a cultural broker. An old Czech saying is 'learn a new language and get a new soul'.

A fourth 'individual' reason for acquiring a language is for careers and employment. For language minority and language majority children, being able to speak a second or third or fourth language may mean avoiding unemployment, opening up possibilities of a wider variety of careers or gaining promotion in a career (see Chapter 19). Potential individual careers include becoming translators and interpreters, working in tourism, buying and selling goods and services, exchanging information with local, regional, national and international organizations, migrating across national frontiers to find work, gaining promotion in neighboring countries, and becoming part of an international team or company, as well as working from home or from the local village and using multilingual telecommunications to spread a product (e.g. US and UK call centers that are located in India).

Bourdieu (1991) argued that language learning takes place in the competitive and political dynamics of society. Inequality, dominance and social hierarchicization shape language learning, in that the individual engaged in such learning is also negotiating their social worth and wealth. Languages operate in a marketplace, since languages have different currency values. The ability to 'command the listener' is unequal for different speakers, owing to the power relations between them (e.g. a minority language person learning English). Norton (2013) has applied this perspective to language learning, suggesting that such learners invest in additional languages to enrich their social, cultural and economic capital, and their symbolic and material resources. It is an investment that may yield a return (e.g. US immigrant learning English; employment and promotion for being a multilingual, evolving a multiple **identity**) or not (e.g. marginalization by the target language community).

Formal Second Language Learning

Where a second language is not acquired in the community, the school has been the major institution expected to produce second language learning (for both elective and **circumstantial bilinguals** but for different reasons – see Chapter 1). Through second language and foreign language lessons, via language laboratories and computer-assisted language learning, drill and practice routines, immersion classes, drama and dance, the initial stages of moving from monolingualism to bilingualism may occur.

The routes to bilingualism are not solely in early childhood and in formal education. Voluntary heritage language classes, complementary schools and supplementary schools sometimes exist for school-age children. When the school does not support immigrant languages, reproduction of those languages in the family may not be enough for **language maintenance**. Therefore, local community groups have developed extra schooling for their children. In England, Canada and the US for example, evening classes, vacation classes, Saturday schools and Sunday schools are organized by various communities for children to learn the heritage language of their parents and grandparents. Children of second, third or fourth generation immigrants may have learnt English as their first or **dominant language**. If parents have chosen to speak English to their children, even if their own first language is not English, the heritage language may be learnt in voluntary classes. Where English is the dominant language of the community and the only language of the school, such voluntary heritage language classes may be important in attaining bilingualism rather than moving children towards majority language monolingualism (Creese & Martin, 2008; Wiley *et al.*, 2014).

Such voluntary provision may be for religious, cultural, social, integrative and ethnic minority vitality reasons. Thus the providers are often religious institutions such as synagogues, mosques, temples and Orthodox churches. Jewish families attending a local synagogue are often enthusiastic for Hebrew to be taught to their children to maintain a Jewish identity and for religious observance. Muslims have often been keen for Qur'anic Arabic to be transmitted for worship in the mosque, just as gurdwaras have been instrumental in the acquisition of Panjabi. The Roman Catholic Church has also promoted the community language teaching of Polish, Ukrainian and Lithuanian.

In the United States and the United Kingdom there are thousands of heritage and community language classes (or complementary schools) in at least 60 languages, including Spanish, French, German, Japanese, Czech, Chinese (Mandarin and Cantonese), Arabic, Hebrew, Khmer, Vietnamese, Finnish, Italian, Portuguese, Greek, Turkish, Urdu, Hindi, Gujarati, Panjabi and Bengali, just to name a few. In the case of some European languages, High Commissions and embassies in London have often lent support. In other communities across the US and UK, particularly among Asians, the providers are groups of enthusiastic parents and local community organizations who rent premises such as schools and halls to teach a heritage language. Foreign governments sometimes provide financial or material assistance to promote the teaching of their national languages to heritage speakers (and others), such as promoted by the Goethe Institute, Académie Française and the support provided by China through the Confucius Institutes. Such schools also have broad educational, literacy and identity outcomes for their children, and also play an important role in community cohesion and heralding bilingualism as an advantage rather than as a deficit (Creese *et al.*, 2006; Creese & Martin, 2008). Parents are often volunteer teachers. There is typically a focus on literacy, a large age range of students in the same class, and some use of English as well as the heritage language (Chao-Jung, 2006; Ghuman, 2011; Li Wei, 2006). Community-based heritage language schools also typically face a wide range of challenges in providing quality and consistent language education and in keeping students motivated to come and reach high levels of proficiency (J.S. Lee & Wright, 2014).

Apart from voluntary classes for children, another well-traveled route to developing bilingualism and **multilingualism** is adult provision. Such provision takes varying forms in different geographical areas:

- *Evening classes.* Sometimes called night schools or classes, a second or foreign language is taught on a once or twice weekly basis for several weeks to several years. Such classes have often traditionally aimed at securing formal qualifications in the language (e.g. passing exams in a second majority language) or at gaining proficiency in the majority language. One example is 'English as a Second Language' classes established for immigrants in the US and UK. Recently, the growth has also been in acquiring **communicative competence** in a heritage language (e.g. Hebrew, Basque, Welsh).
- *Ulpan courses.* Perhaps the most notable example of a mass movement of adult language learning has been the case of Hebrew in Israel. After the establishment of the State of Israel in 1948, the steady flow of immigration became a flood. Emergency measures were needed to teach Hebrew in a short time to large numbers of people as a living, spoken language. The idea of creating an intensive Hebrew language course was born and called an *Ulpan* (Raijman, 2012). The word '*Ulpan*' is derived

from an Aramaic root meaning 'custom, training, instruction, law'. There were originally about 25 students in a class, and they met for six hours each day apart from the Sabbath. From the beginning, the emphasis was on equipping the learners for everyday communication in the spoken language. Cultural activities such as singing and field trips were part of the course. Over the years different kinds of *Ulpanim* have been established in Israel. Like Israel, the Basque and Welsh *Ulpanim* vary in intensity from five days a week courses to two mornings or two evenings a week (C. Baker & Jones, 1998; Newcombe, 2007). Some vocational courses are held for teachers, hospital workers, administrators and workers in industry. Other courses have a bias towards the needs of particular groups such as parents. As in Israel, the emphasis is on developing competence in the spoken language.

- *Distance learning and online methods.* A variety of media-based courses for learning a second language are often available to adults. Radio and television series, books, DVDs, CDs, computer programs (computer-assisted language learning) correspondence courses, podcasts, websites, YouTube videos, social media and paid and free online courses including MOOCs (Massive online organized courses) are all well-tried or emerging approaches in second language acquisition. Evaluation studies of the relative effectiveness of these different approaches tend to be lacking.

In early childhood, becoming bilingual is often a subconscious event, as natural as learning to walk or to ride a bicycle. In a school situation, a child is not usually the one who has made a decision about the language(s) of the classroom. Second language acquisition at school is often required by teachers and a local or national educational policy. For migrant workers, refugees and immigrants, adult language learning also may be essential for work and adaptation to new institutions and bureaucracy. However, for other adults, second language acquisition sometimes becomes more voluntary, more open to choice. This raises the issue of whether it is preferable to learn a new language as a child or as an adult.

Apart from formal language learning, bilingualism is often achieved through the informal acquisition processes of the street and screen, friends and siblings. A child sometimes acquires a second or third language rapidly in addition to that of the home without planning or intent by parents. Peers in the playgroup or street, cartoons and shows on television or the internet are two examples of language influences that may informally lead to bilingualism in the child. Little researched, the almost incidental addition of a second or third language via the street and screen may be as influential as formal education, and sometimes more potent than language classes. This particularly tends to be the case with acquiring the majority language of the neighborhood (see the discussion of circumstantial bilinguals in Chapter 1).

The Age Factor

A much-debated theme in second language acquisition is the relationship of age in learning a second language and success in gaining language proficiency. One argument is that the lower the age at which a second language is learnt, the greater the long-term proficiency in that language. This is the basis of the **critical period hypothesis**, which suggests younger children have biological cognitive advantages for language learning that close as they enter adolescence and adulthood. Others tend to argue that older children and young adults have some advantages that may help them learn a language more efficiently and quickly than young children. For example, a 14-year-old learning Spanish as a second language has superior intellectual processing skills to the five-year-old learning Spanish. Therefore, it is thought that less time is required in the teenage years to learn a second language than in the younger years owing to older children's cognitive superiority. However, the use of two or more languages changes across the years, so exact comparability is difficult.

Reviews of this area are provided by Marinova-Todd *et al.* (2000), Singleton and Ryan (2004), Cenoz (2009) and Birdsong (2006). Their analyses may be briefly summarized as follows:

(1) Younger second language learners are neither globally more nor less efficient and successful than older learners in second language acquisition. There are many factors that intervene. Simple statements about age and language learning are simplistic and untenable.

(2) Children who learn a second language in childhood do tend to achieve higher levels of proficiency than those who begin after childhood. This difference found between younger and older learners reflects typical outcomes rather than potential. Thus, a finding favoring the young does not contradict the idea that someone can become proficient in learning a second language after childhood. This may be related to social contexts in which language is acquired and maintained or lost (e.g. kindergarten), as well as to the psychology of individual learning (e.g. motivation, opportunity). As Marinova-Todd *et al.* (2000) suggest, older learners tend in practice not to master a second language as well as young learners, but 'age differences reflect differences in the situation of learning rather than in the capacity to learn' (p. 9).

(3) In a formal classroom language learning situation, older learners tend initially to learn quicker than younger learners. However, the length of exposure (e.g. the number of years of second language instruction) is an important factor in second language success. Those children who begin to learn a second language in the elementary school and continue throughout schooling, tend to show higher proficiency than those who start to learn the second language later in their schooling. In absolute rather than comparative terms, this still includes the possibility of late learners becoming highly proficient, particularly when they are strongly motivated or have strong needs (e.g. immigrants, missionaries) or excellent opportunities (e.g. extensive immersion across many months). Adults can learn to a native-like level of competence in a second language.

(4) There is some research and much public discussion about the large numbers of high school students and adults who fail to learn a second language (Marinova-Todd *et al.*, 2000). In comparison, there is a lack of research on adults who are successful learners of second and third languages. Research itself is in danger or perpetuating a 'younger is better' belief about age and language learning.

(5) In the United States, federal and state education policies place immense pressure on schools and teachers to help immigrant children to learn English as soon as possible (see Chapter 9).

Proponents of the critical period hypothesis claim that the optimal time to learn a language is from age three to seven, and because of supposed biological constraints, such learning should occur before the onset of puberty. In a review of this area, Kenji Hakuta (2001) argues that:

> The evidence for a critical period for second language acquisition is scanty, especially when analyzed in terms of its key assumptions. There is no empirically definable end point, there are no qualitative differences between child and adult learners, and there are large environmental effects on the outcomes. ... The view of a biologically constrained and specialized language acquisition device that is turned off at puberty is not correct. (p. 11–12)

A more recent review by Singleton and Muñoz (2011) likewise found little support for a critical period:

> Postulating a critical period for language acquisition is fraught with problems.... There is no consensus regarding the duration and scope of such a critical period, and the evidence presented in support of the notion of a critical period is far from conclusive. (p. 419)

Singleton and Muñoz provide a musical comparison to illustrate: 'The fact that children who start to play the violin early tend to reach higher levels of attainment than adult beginners does not lead us to conclude that there is a "critical period" for violin playing' (p. 419). Similarly, Marinova-Todd *et al*. (2000) conclude that 'age does influence language learning, but primarily because it is associated with social, psychological, educational and other factors that can affect L2 proficiency, not because of any critical period that limits the possibility of language learning by adults' (p. 28).

A 'weaker' version of the critical period hypothesis suggests that there may be an age-related advantage for younger learners in the area of **phonology**. In other words, older learners, including those who are highly successful in attaining proficiency in a second language, may nonetheless retain a slight foreign-sounding accent, whereas younger learners are more likely to gain a second language with no discernable accent.

Huang (2014) suggests that the larger debate over the critical period hypothesis is drawing attention away from needed scholarship to better understand age effects in second language learning. She argues for a framework of multiple critical/sensitive periods given that different **domains** of linguistic dimensions such as grammar, morphosyntax, phonology (including prosody), and spatial **semantics** may have different timelines in terms of age advantages. Her own research with Mandarin-speaking immigrants to the US, for example, found the age of learning variable had a stronger impact on speech production than on grammar. Furthermore, her recent synthesis on the age effect in formal instruction contexts (i.e. foreign language learning contexts) reveals potential limited benefits in the phonology dimension, but not other dimensions (Huang, 2015). Taken together, the new research findings suggest that the strength of the age effect varies across linguistic domains and interacts with language input and exposure.

Debates over the critical periods of language learning aside, there are clearly advantageous periods. Early childhood and elementary and secondary school days seem to be two advantageous periods. How successful are adults in becoming bilingual? There is a distinction between answering this question in an absolute and a relative manner. The 'absolute' answer simply is that adults do learn a second language to varying degrees of fluency including incomplete acquisition. Some fall by the wayside; others reach a basic, simple level of communication, yet others become operationally bilingual. In Israel, Wales and the Basque country, the adult route to bilingualism has many success stories.

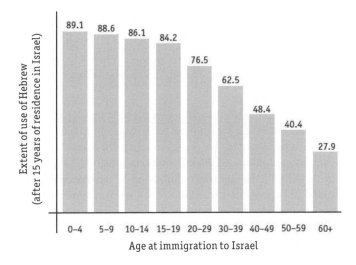

Figure 6.1 Extent of use of Hebrew (after 15 years of residence in Israel) by age of immigration. Adapted from Bachi (1955)

The 'relative' answer involves comparing children and adults of varying ages. In this sense, the question becomes 'Who is more likely to become proficient in a second language, children or adults?' Chiswick and Miller (2008) plot immigration into the United States against English speaking proficiency using data from the 2000 US Census. Their graphs suggest that children before the age of 11 have a much better chance of becoming fluent in English than those who immigrate at high school age. After the age of 16, the probability of becoming proficient in English declines fairly linearly over the next 40 years (i.e. age 16 to 55+).

From 1950s Israeli census data, it is possible to examine whether older or younger adults become functional in Hebrew. For example, do young immigrants become more or less functional in Hebrew as a second language compared with older immigrants? The results follow a clear pattern (Bachi, 1955). As Figure 6.1 illustrates, the extent of the everyday use of Hebrew varies with age of immigration. The younger the child, the more likely he or she will be to use Hebrew. Between 30 and 40 years of age, a notable drop occurs. Is this due to a loss of learning ability, less exposure to Hebrew, less motivation or decreasing social pressure? From age 40 onwards, the likelihood of being functional in Hebrew falls again. Birdsong (2006) provides a more complex graph that shows a fairly linear decline in language attainment among US immigrants from age 5 to 50 according to age of arrival.

Language Loss in Children

Apart from children learning a second or third language, it is important to mention that **language loss** occurs in bilingual and multilingual children and adults. Children and adults from language minorities (indigenous and particularly immigrant children) are sometimes at risk of losing their minority language, even when very young. Immigrant adults may also lose, mostly or partly, their first language(s) particularly in an assimilationist context (e.g. US – see Chapters 17 & 18). With a higher status majority language ever-present on the screen, in the street, at school and in shops, children and adults quickly learn which language has prestige, power and preference. They soon understand that there are differences in language, behavior, ethnicity and culture, and some children, and particularly teenagers, may come to perceive their minority language and culture as undesirable. Students quickly perceive what helps them belong in mainstream society.

Among adults, Birdsong (2006) has reviewed the considerable research on the typical decline in second language attainment with increasing age, and the less native-likeness found in the later learner. He suggests that there are complex biological, cognitive, experiential, linguistic, and affective dimensions of L2 learning and processing all involved. For example, associative memory and 'incremental learning elements of language learning' decline with age, as does the working memory and processing speed. Other variables include the amount of time spent in second language speaker contact, the relative use of the first and second language in everyday activities, the amount of formal education in the second language, motivation to lean a language, integration with the second language culture, language aptitude, imitative **language ability**, metalinguistic awareness, and learning styles and strategies.

Language loss in children is a particular reality in the United States. Research by Hakuta and d'Andrea (1992), Fillmore (1991), Wright (2004) and Valdés (2004) indicates that the strength of the dominance of English in US society places considerable pressure on language minority students not only to acquire English at a young age, but also to replace their minority language with English. In such subtractive situations, the ideal of early bilingualism meets a challenge owing to a societal ethos that frequently does not favor bilingualism. Hakuta and d'Andrea (1992) found in the United States that early exposure to English (e.g. in the home) can lead to a shift from Spanish to English and the potential loss of Spanish. Such early exposure to English in the US may also decrease the chances of placement in a dual education program where Spanish is used.

This is not to warn against early bilingualism, but rather to suggest that the minority language needs care and attention, status and much usage in the young child. This is not a limitation of early bilingualism, but rather a caution that minority language development needs particular nurturing in political situations where another language is ever dominant. For example, when English is introduced very early and dominantly into a US language minority child's life, the minority language may be insufficiently stable and developed, and may therefore be replaced by the majority language. A loss of the minority language may have social, emotional, cognitive and educational consequences for the child, as later chapters (e.g. Chapter 17) will examine. As Fillmore (1991) argued in her classic article, 'When Learning a Second Language Mean Losing the First':

> What is lost is no less than the means by which parents socialize their children: When parents are unable to talk to their children, they cannot easily convey to them their values, beliefs, understandings, or wisdom about how to cope with their experiences (p. 343).

These and other consequences of losing one's language are listed in Box 6.3.

The immigrant, refugee and asylum seeker context and its affect on family language patterns is under-researched, with most of the studies on early childhood bilingualism being located in middle class, majority language and geographically stable families.

Box 6.3 Consequences of first language loss

- Children are unable to communicate effectively with parents.
- Parents have difficulty passing on their values, beliefs, understandings, and wisdom.
- Breakdown in communication can lead to conflicts between children and their parents.
- Children may lose respect for their parents.
- Children experience difficulty, embarrassment, and shame when trying to communicate with older relatives and community members.
- Children may face humiliation and shame if they return to their (or their parents') home country and cannot effectively communicate.
- Children may become ashamed of their home language and culture and struggle with identity issues.
- Losing proficiency in the home language before attaining proficiency in standard English often leads to academic difficulties.
- Learning to read in English is more difficult if students cannot read in their home language.
- Students may have fewer job opportunities than they would have otherwise had they maintained their home language.
- The society as a whole loses needed linguistic resources to fulfill the language demands of national and international institutions, organizations, and agencies.

Source: Wright (2015: 22)

Tannenbaum and Howie (2002) argue that immigration often potentially means loss of the extended family and significant people, a loss of familiarity, family cohesion, family 'atmosphere' and secure attachment. Uprooting may affect not only the act of parenting but also the cultural and linguistic development of young children and the language patterns of the immigrant family. Tannenbaum and Howie's research on Chinese immigrant families in Australia suggests that family relations affect language maintenance or loss. Families that are more cohesive, more positive in relationships and with secure attachment patterns tend to foster language maintenance in young immigrant children.

The dialogue that takes place between parents and children is an important contributor to the child's cognitive development. As children interact with parents, they are introduced to new features of language. When the child loses the home language, the parent can no longer offer this language education to the child in that language. Important cognitive **scaffolding** is dismantled. Thus minority language loss is an issue not just of geographical regions and language communities but also for individual children. Family **language planning** is needed to initiate, establish and maintain childhood bilingualism (Schwartz & Verschik, 2013).

Individual Differences: Attitudes and Motivation

A popular explanation for success or failure to learn a second language (or for success in learning) is attitudes and motivation (C. Baker, 1992; Cenoz, 2009; Dörnyei, MacIntrye & Henry, 2015; R.C. Gardner, 2010; Garrett, 2010). As Dörnyei (1998) suggests:

Motivation provides the primary impetus to initiate learning in the L2 and later the driving force to sustain the long and often tedious learning process. ... Without sufficient motivation, even individuals with the most remarkable abilities cannot accomplish long-term goals, and neither are appropriate curricula and good teaching enough on their own to ensure student achievement. (Dörnyei, 1998: 117)

What are the motives for learning a second language? Are the motives economic, cultural, social, vocational, integrative or for self-esteem and self-actualization? Reasons for learning a second (minority or majority) language tend to fall into two major groups or types of motivation:

Group 1: A wish to identify with or join another language group (**Integrative Motivation**)
Learners sometimes want to affiliate with a different language community. Such learners wish to join in and identify with the minority or majority language's cultural activities, and consequently find their roots or form friendships.

Group 2: Learning a language for useful purposes (**Instrumental Motivation**)
The second reason is utilitarian in nature. Learners may acquire a second language to find a job and earn money, further career prospects, pass exams, help fulfill the demands of their job, or assist their children in bilingual schooling.

Considerable research on this area was conducted by R.C. Gardner and associates (see R.C. Gardner, 2008 for a review). Gardner argued that integrative and instrumental attitudes are independent of 'intelligence' and aptitude. Integrative motivation may be particularly strong in an additive bilingual environment. R.C. Gardner (2010) has proposed a socio-educational model of motivation and language acquisition that sees motivation impacted by the education and cultural context, and impacting language use in formal and informal contexts with a range of linguistic and non-linguistic outcomes. These usages and outcomes are simultaneously impacted by and interact with students' actual ability in the language. Dörnyei *et al.* (2006) suggest integrative motivation is rather an ambiguous and enigmatic concept that has recently been expanded to include integration with the global community among some of those learning English as an international language. Furthermore, Dörnyei *et al.* (2015) have argued that principles of complex dynamic systems may be needed to better understand the shifting nature of motivation in individual learners and classrooms.

Much of the research in this area, but not all, links integrative motivation rather than instrumental motivation with the greater likelihood of achieving proficiency in the second language. R.C. Gardner and Lambert (1972) originally considered that integrative motivation was more powerful in language learning than instrumental motivation. The reason was that integrative motivation concerns personal relationships that may be long lasting. On the other hand, instrumental motivation may be purely self-oriented and short term. When employment has been obtained or financial gain has accrued, instrumental motivation may wane. An integrative motive was thought to be a more sustained motive than an instrumental motive owing to the relative endurance of personal relationships.

A problem with integrative motivation is: with whom does the language learner wish to integrate? If an adult is learning Navajo, then the target community is obvious. But what if a student is learning English? Is the target group English speakers in the US, England, New Zealand or Kenya? Given that English has become the predominant international language, then with whom do those learning 'international English' wish to integrate? Is it the global English-speaking community? Can integrative motivation be towards a global community? Or is this really instrumental motivation? Dörnyei *et al.* (2006) suggest that such integrative motivation can be explained by the 'ideal self concept' rather than the need for integration with a target reference group. That is, the motivation to learn international English may be the attraction of becoming (and being seen as) a second language speaker of global English, even having mutual intelligibility of a global or world citizen.

Pavlenko (2002) provides a critique of these socio-psychological studies. In a post-structuralist approach, language attitudes are partly replaced by language ideologies that are seen as more socially and culturally derived, ever-developing and not static, and capable of being criticized and changed. For example, saying that someone has an integrative attitude to Irish may imply a relatively stable trait that is individually derived and owned. Instead, it is possible to depict that person's language identity as related to political, cultural, social and economic ideologies surrounding Irish that are ever-changing and fluid but open to challenge and conflict. Language attitudes thus become part of larger societal processes and ideologies that can be examined for bias, racism, discrimination and oppression. The psychological is merged into the political. A relatively stable and separate variable (attitude) is a part of a multiple and dynamic scenario (identity construction) that allows second language acquisition to have individual, group and societal dimensions.

Pavlenko (2002) suggests that such research tends to be: reductionist and static in its approach; not offering insight into the social and political origins of attitudes; assuming that cause–effect is stable and in one direction whereas social contexts and attitudes/motivation constantly shape and influence each other; individual differences are socially constructed with variations across communities and cultures; and a tendency of such research to relate to wholesome, agreeable contexts whereas 'In reality, no amount of motivation can counteract racism and discrimination, just as no amount of positive attitude can substitute for access to linguistic resources such as educational establishments' (Pavlenko, 2002: 281).

Teachers are still left with the question: 'How can I motivate learners?' What interventions and strategies are possible to motivate language learners? Box 6.4 provides a few suggestions.

Box 6.4 Strategies for motivating students

Research has suggested many overlapping and interacting strategies teachers can use to motivate students in the language learning classroom. The following are just a few suggestions from Dörnyei (1994):

1. Include a sociocultural component in the syllabus (e.g. television programs, inviting native speakers).
2. Promote student contact with second language speakers (e.g. exchange programs, pen pals, trips).
3. Promote favorable self-perceptions of competence in the second language (e.g. highlighting what students can do rather than what they cannot do, students not worrying about making mistakes).
4. Encourage students to set attainable sub-goals for themselves (e.g. by a personal learning plan).
5. Make the syllabus of the course relevant (e.g. based on a student 'needs analysis').
6. Increase the attractiveness of course content (e.g. use of more authentic materials, audio-visual aids, multimedia technology).
7. Match the difficulty of the students' language learning tasks with students' abilities.
8. Use motivating feedback, give feedback that is informative, and not over-react to errors.
9. Minimize any detrimental effects of **assessment** on intrinsic motivation by focusing on improvement and progress, avoiding comparison of one student with another.
10. Use cooperative learning techniques by plenty of group work where the evaluation of success is appropriate to the group rather than a focus on individual success.

Identity and Second Language Acquisition

All the world's a stage,
And all the men and women merely players. They have their exits and their entrances;
And one man in his time plays many parts.
(William Shakespeare from 'As You Like It', Act 2, Scene 7)

This drama metaphor suggests that we are like actors. We play different roles that vary according to the scenery, the audience, our fellow actors and the expected lines of the play. As scenery, co-actors, audience and the play change, so do our many identities in life's drama. We construct our identities yet they are also created and confined by other players, situations and the unfolding play. Second language acquisition is such a play and it relates to identity formation (Pavlenko, 2003b).

Social Identity and Second Language Learning

While psychometric tests attempt to profile us as individuals (e.g. extrovert, creative, 110 IQ), we are also simultaneously members of different groups (e.g. woman, young parent, teacher, Muslim, Democrat, Californian, bilingual). Such membership helps form our social identity. Our multiple social identities are thus created dynamically by us, by our interactions and negotiations with other group actors, the expectations of each group, and the varying social environments in which we play. Second language acquisition is affected by, and affects our membership of groups (e.g. majority and minority language networks and groups). Acquiring a second language is not just about gaining vocabulary, grammar and pronunciation. When we use a second language, it is a social event with particular others. It is also often about joining a social group (e.g. a target language community or networks) and finding an accepted voice. Bourdieu (1991) argued that finding such an accepted voice is about the value given to people who are speaking (e.g. a newly learnt language). A speaker wants to be understood but there is also a social dimension to this: being believed, respected and valued as a speaker.

This has been extended by Norton (2013) with her concept of 'investment'. Language learners may be aware of the social, political, economic, power and status value (or not) of investing in second language learning. If successful, they may acquire more symbolic, social, identity and material resources, which can increase their cultural capital and social power. For example, learners might not be very motivated to learn a language, but may invest in that language if they are then seen as historically more employable or politically as of higher social status.

Language learning is partly about becoming socialized through interaction with other language speakers in particular social contexts (Pavlenko, 2002). Classrooms, in this perspective, have major limitations. They tend not to provide spontaneous interaction. Outside the classroom, target language speakers may be reluctant or refuse to interact with learners (e.g. too low level of conversation, or because of gender, race, ethnicity, heritage language, social class, age, sexuality or creed). Opportunities for participation in the second language may be rare – a limitation of bilingual education that often produces competent bilinguals who only use one language outside the school. Authentic language situations may be restricted by target language speakers 'gate-keeping', or suitable opportunities not being available for new speakers to internalize the 'voices' of target language speakers. A sense of vulnerability and powerlessness may decrease a learner's investment in language learning (Norton, 2013).

Second language learners become socialized by and through language into new areas of knowledge, understandings and cultural practices. The learner of Chinese as a second language acquires not only new vocabulary but also new ideas, expectations, relationships, knowledge, values and ideologies. That is, when a second language is acquired, there is a parallel inculcation into a culture, a possible change in identify, and a socialization into the life that surrounds that second language (Bayley & Langman, 2011; Duff, 2010).

Constructing Meaning in Second Language Learning

While language has shared sounds, signs and symbols, there are often different and sometimes contested meanings and values attached to such language. 'When I use a word,' Humpty Dumpty said, in rather a scornful tone, 'it means just what I choose it to mean – neither more nor less' (Carroll, 1872). Words don't have fixed or ideal meanings.

Humpty Dumpty apart, words are constructed by people in dialogue with others to find shared or contested meanings. Such **discourse** takes place in changing situations (contexts) with differences of power and status between people affecting whose meaning is ascendant or dominant, and with such meanings being open to change, even conflict. For example, there is no correct or true definition of a 'bilingual' or of 'bilingual education'. Meanings of these terms vary across people, time and place, with dominance at any one time being about who has status, prestige and power. Meaning and the importance of an utterance is thus determined in part by the status and value attributed to the second language speaker.

Language and Power

Interacting in a second language both uses and shapes our identity, and this relationship needs to be understood in terms of differential power and prestige between people and language groups. In this post-structuralist tradition, learning a second language is not just about language. It is also about who we are, what we want to become, and what we are allowed (e.g. by first language speakers) to become.

In all language contexts, there are underlying dimensions of control and influence, **domination** and subordination (see Chapter 18). Gaining belief, respect and social value from dialogue with others is not straightforward as there is unequal dominance, status and power in relationships. There may be sensitive listeners, empathic conversationalists in the target language community, and much faith in second language learning. However, many immigrants have experiences of obstruction, ridicule or rejection when using the majority language. Thus power relationships and social structures in the target language community are an important component in the extent to which a second language learner (including those exiting from bilingual education) will be accepted as a speaker of that language. Opportunities for practicing and participating in that new language, access to the usual utterances of native speakers, acceptance of errors when using that language, and acceptance as 'nonnative speakers' by the target community will affect a learner's acceptance, identity and language life.

Multiple Identities and Second Language Acquisition

The identity of second language learners has hitherto sometimes been seen as relatively stable, essential to a coherent 'core' in an individual's psyche. Just like IQ and personality traits, identity was seen as fairly fixed. A contemporary view is that identity is multiple, complex, context contingent, varied, overlapping, sometimes fragmented and even contradictory across different contexts. Our identities constantly develop and change, across time and across situations. We are made and remade in our conversations across time, place and person. Acquiring a second language may, for example, change our identity from an 'immigrant' to a 'Californian' (Pavlenko, 2003b).

Since not all languages are equal in power and status, learning a prestigious language may (or may not) lead to employment, social mobility, new friends, and access to good quality education. Learning a minority language may also affect identity, for example increasing the chances of acceptance into a local community. Acquiring a language affects individual identity, but this interacts with other dimensions (e.g. gender, socioeconomic class, race, ethnicity, creed) that mediate the outcomes of such acquisition (Pavlenko, 2002). The success of language learning may be affected by the wealth or restriction of opportunities for identity development in new networks (e.g. acceptance, rejection). Identity conflict may sometimes occur, for example, when our preferred self-identity (e.g. as a Latino) is different from other people's attempts to label us (e.g. as an American). This is sometimes found in the case of immigrants where second language learners of a majority language are regarded as incompetent workers or uneducated parents or social oddities. They may find resistance from majority language speakers to their having a new identity via second language acquisition, with subsequent effects on the extent of second language acquisition and reconstruction of identities. Surrounding ideologies may work against the best of language acquisition intentions. Or language minority speakers may resist the symbolic domination of them as a people that is attempted by majority language power and politics.

M. Kim (2016) documented the case of a North Korean defector to South Korea who went through a dramatic identity-transformation process while learning English. Having grown up in North Korea and taught that English was the language of the enemy, the defector was appalled by the amount of English present in South Korea (including in the signage of the linguistic landscape). She originally resisted learning English as it challenged the core of her identity. However, she eventually yielded to the need for English learning, and over time, she became 'an active learner who found English learning valuable and meaningful' and finally, she became 'a visionary who aimed to care about those in need, particularly English-learning needs' (p. 3). Thus, 'During the identity-transformation process, the defector constantly negotiated her identities in response to multiple social factors' (p. 3).

Language learning may change how we think of ourselves, how others see us, and importantly (in turn) how we then confirm their expectations in our behavior. Acquiring a second language goes beyond linguistic competence to having the potential to be heard in that language, the means to address an audience in that language on chosen stages, and to mix with other actors using that language. Language learning is not just a cognitive activity operating in the mind, but is also about becoming part of a new language community and developing multiple identities (see Chapter 18).

An important component in being accepted as a speaker is our other identities (e.g. gender, race, religion), which interact with being a second language learner. A second language learner's identity is multiple and goes well beyond language to gender, social class, ethnicity, sexuality, age, creed, lifestyle, networks and many other constantly changing scenarios. Sometimes, despite achieving linguistic proficiency in a second language, access to a language community is difficult, as other dimensions of identity bar easy (or any) access.

Imagined Communities

Language learning, negotiating meanings and identity also come together in the recent concept of 'imagined communities'. As described by Kanno and Norton (2003), 'imagined communities refers to groups of people, not immediately tangible and accessible, with whom we connect through the power of imagination' (p. 241). For example, when students in second language classrooms are learning French in the US, they commence as beginners. The teacher is introducing them to the language practices of a community of French speakers. What language practices? What is the 'imagined community' for such learners? Or are such communities 'imagined' for them in a controlled manner? Desirable imaginings may motivate learners; less desirable and low status imaginings may de-motivate learners; hidden or controlled imaginings from outside may remove understanding and alienate. For example, a second language learner imagines obtaining well-paid employment; another imagines returning to the land of her ancestors and extended family.

Some further examples from research demonstrate the powerfulness of 'imagined communities'. Dagenais (2003) found that parents with Asian background children attending **immersion bilingual education** in Canada were investing in such education to prepare their children for imagined multilingual, transnational, multiple communities of the future. In Japan, Kanno (2003) found that schools have visions of 'imagined communities' for which they are preparing their students: the least privileged children for impoverished bilingual communities; the most privileged children for elite international bilingualism. Pavlenko (2003a) found that teaching TESOL students about bilingualism and second language acquisition opened up new imagined communities for them, as bilingual or multilingual multi-competent speakers. The low expectation of becoming two competent **monolinguals** in one person and belonging to two separate imagined communities was replaced by feeling part of an imagined community of worthy multilingual speakers.

Conclusion

There are both societal and individual reasons for a person learning a second language later in life. This mirrors the opening chapters of this book that portrayed bilinguals as individuals and as groups, and communities. Once societal reasons are present, then politics is not far away. Such reasons are varied, even paradoxical: assimilation but also harmony between different language communities; trade and profit but also intercultural understanding; security and defense yet also diplomacy. Individual reasons for language learning are not separate from societal reasons. Languages for career enhancement and employment have become more important motives as international trade and globalism have risen. Schools and communities influence language learning, in that societal and individual reasons interconnect and merge.

Sequential bilingualism occurs through a variety of routes, with school a major source of formal learning. Such schools may be state-funded and mainstream with long histories of language teaching. But also there are many schools run by religious organizations, language communities and embassies that teach new languages after school or on the weekends, for example. For adults, language learning can be by classes at work and for leisure, self-study or an intensive Ulpan experience. The vehicles of voluntary classes and adult courses provide the opportunity for a second or foreign language to be learnt and developed. Also, playing in the street and using mass media and internet technology can be informal means to bilingualism and multilingualism.

Such 'later' routes to bilingualism and multilingualism allow individuals of all ages to become bilingual and multilingual. While younger learners tend to achieve higher levels of proficiency in practice, older learners tend to learn faster. While there may be no critical periods for language learning, there are times when there will be greater opportunities (e.g. in school) and varying levels and types of motivation. Surrounding societal ideologies (e.g. for immigrants) and individual differences may interact to make language learning more or less successful.

There are outcomes from language learning that go further than bilingualism and multilingualism. For immigrants, this may relate to assimilation or integration into the host society. For students, this may mean employment and career progression. For adults, it may mean moving closer to desired imagined communities. For all these groups, language learning affects identity. Such learners are socialized into new meanings and values as well as new language. They enter into new relationships that involve different status and power, acceptance or rejection. Learning a language means changes to our multiple identities. Language learning is so much more than learning a language.

Key Points in This Chapter

➤ Reasons for second language learning include ideological (e.g. assimilation), international (e.g. trade, peace) and individual (e.g. cultural awareness, employment) reasons.

➤ Formal foreign language instruction, voluntary language learning classes, community classes, Saturday schools, classes in the mosque, synagogue, temple or church and Ulpan adult language learning schemes are routes to sequential bilingualism and minority language maintenance in individuals.

➤ While there are no critical periods of language learning, there are advantageous periods. Early childhood and school days are two advantageous periods. Many successful adult second language learners show that increasing age is not a disadvantage.

➤ Individuals differ in their language learning histories because of societal and personal factors.

➤ Among immigrants, language loss is often present as assimilation can be a dominant influence. Among individuals, differences in integrative and instrumental motives are regarded as influencing success.

➤ Second language learning affects social identity. Language learning is partly about socialization into a new group. We learn the meaning, values and power relationships of a new group, and change our multiple identities.

Suggested Further Reading

📖 Dörnyei, Z., MacIntrye, P. D., & Henry, A. (Eds.). (2015). *Motivational dynamics in language learning.* Bristol, UK: Multilingual Matters.

📖 Ellis, R. R. (2012). *Language teaching research and language pedagogy.* Malden, MA: Wiley-Blackwell.

📖 Hinkel, E. (Ed.) (2011). *Handbook of research in second language teaching and learning* (Vol. II). New York, NY: Routledge.

📖 Nicoladis, E., & Montanari, S. (Eds.). (2016). *Bilingualism across the lifespan: Factors moderating language proficiency.* Washington, DC: American Psychological Association.

📖 Norton, B. (2013). *Identity and language learning: Extending the conversation* (2nd ed.). Bristol, UK: Multilingual Matters.

On the Web

💻 American Council on the Teaching of Foreign Languages
http://www.actfl.org/

💻 Confucius Institutes
http://english.hanban.org/

💻 National Heritage Language Resource Center
http://www.nhlrc.ucla.edu/nhlrc

💻 National Security Education Program
http://www.nsep.gov/

💻 STARTALK
https://startalk.umd.edu/public/

Discussion Questions

(1) Consider your own or others' successes and failures with learning a new language. What role did motivation play, and what was the nature of this motivation? How can motivation and investment change over time?

(2) Explore the Centre for Languages, Linguistics & Area Studies database of 700 reasons to study a foreign language (www.idiomas.idph.com.br/textos/700_reasons.pdf). Choose two or three reasons to discuss with your group.

(3) While there may not be a critical period for language learning, there are advantageous periods. What are some advantages for younger learners? What are some advantages for older learners?

Study Activities

(1) Visit a school where students are learning a new language. By interviewing the teachers and observing classroom sessions, describe the overt and latent reasons for second (or third) language acquisition. Ask the teachers and the students their purposes in learning the language. If there are differences in aim between teachers and students, examine whether you think these can be made compatible or are in conflict.

(2) Visit the webpages for the National Security Education Program (http://www.nsep.gov) and the STARTALK program (https://startalk.umd.edu/public). What organizations are behind these efforts? Explore the various programs and activities of these initiatives to increase the number of Americans with high levels of proficiency in critical need languages. Who seems to be the primary target of these programs? What programs, if any, target heritage speakers? Review the most recent annual reports and analyze the level of success of the various programs.

(3) Listen to the Freakonomics Radio (podcast) program 'Is learning a foreign language really worth it?' (http://freakonomics.com/2014/03/05/is-learning-a-foreign-language-really-worth-it-full-transcript/). What is the economic value of learning a foreign language, according to these economists? What language or language(s) seemed to have the highest return on investment (ROI)? In what ways is ROI too narrow of a view on the 'value' of learning a new language?

Bilingualism, Cognition and the Brain

Updated by Becky H. Huang

Bilingualism, Cognition and the Brain

Introduction

There is one piece of advice that parents sometimes receive from well-meaning teachers, doctors, speech therapists, school psychologists and other professionals: *Don't raise your child bilingually or problems will result.* Predicted problems range from **bilingualism** as a burden on the brain, mental confusion, slowing down of the acquisition of the majority language, **identity** conflicts, split loyalties, alienation, and even schizophrenia. The population of the world is estimated as approximately 7.3 billion, and if approximately half are bilingual (Grosjean, 2012), then do 3.7 billion bilinguals in the world share these problems? Clearly not. Yet prejudice about the problems of bilingualism has been widespread particularly in English-speaking regions.

Parents and teachers are sometimes still advised by professionals to use only one language with individual children. However, in the last decade or so, such prejudiced and unfounded advice has decreased. Better advice based on a wealth of research is slowly spreading. Yet historically, anti-bilingualism advice has frequently predominated. For example, when Welsh children persisted in speaking two languages in school, having their mouths washed with soap and water and being beaten with a cane for speaking Welsh were once common.

A quotation from a professor at Cambridge University in 1890 portrays this historical (and hysterical) deficit viewpoint:

> If it were possible for a child to live in two languages at once equally well, so much the worse. His intellectual and spiritual growth would not thereby be doubled, but halved. Unity of mind and character would have great difficulty in asserting itself in such circumstances. (Laurie, 1890: 15)

Such anxieties about bilingualism and thinking remain among some members of the public. The anxiety that two languages may have a negative effect on an individual's thinking skills tends to be expressed in two different ways. First, some tend to believe that the more someone learns and uses a second language, the less skill a person will have in their first language. Rather like weighing scales or a balance, the more one increases, the more the other decreases. Second, concern is sometimes expressed that the ability to speak two languages may be at the cost of efficiency in thinking. The intuitive belief is sometimes that two languages residing inside the thinking quarters will mean less room to store other areas of learning. By comparison, the monolingual is pictured as having one language in residence and therefore maximal storage space for other information.

Does the ownership of two languages interfere with efficient thinking? Do monolinguals have more effective thinking quarters? Is a bilingual less intelligent than a monolingual because of a **dual language** system? This chapter examines these typically negatively phrased questions and evaluates the evidence on bilingualism and **cognition**. Cognition is defined as the internal processing involved in language, memory, perception, and thought (Eysenck *et al.*, 1994). The specific topics covered in this chapter, which include **intelligence, Intelligence quotient (IQ), metalinguistic awareness, executive function, communicative sensitivity,** and **divergent/creative thinking,** have been the focus of bilingualism research.

We start by considering the relationship between intelligence and bilingualism. 'Intelligence' has been a major concept in psychology and sometimes related to bilingualism. It is also a term often used by members of the public in phrasing questions about bilingualism. We also provide an overview of the historical timeline of bilingual research, discussing the shift of perspectives and attitudes toward bilingualism. The chapter then moves on to consider recent research that focuses on a wider sample of products and processes of a bilingual's cognition. Do bilinguals and monolinguals differ in thinking styles? Are there differences in the processing of information? Does owning two languages create differences in thinking about language? These types of question are examined in this chapter.

Bilingualism and 'Intelligence'

The Period of Detrimental Effects

From the early 19th century to approximately the 1960s, the dominant belief amongst academics was that bilingualism had a detrimental effect on thinking. The early research on bilingualism and cognition tended to confirm this negative viewpoint, finding that monolinguals were superior to bilinguals on mental tests. Research up to the 1960s looked at this issue through one concept – 'intelligence'. A typical piece of research gave bilinguals and monolinguals an 'intelligence test'. When bilinguals and monolinguals were compared on their **Intelligence Quotient (IQ)** scores, particularly on verbal IQ, the usual result was that bilinguals were behind monolinguals. An example of this early research is by a Welsh researcher, Saer (1923). He gathered a sample of 1,400 children aged 7 to 14 from bilingual and monolingual backgrounds. A 10–point difference in IQ was found between bilinguals and monolingual English speakers from the rural areas of Wales. Saer concluded that bilinguals were mentally confused and at a disadvantage in thinking compared with monolinguals. Further research by Saer (1924) suggested that university student monolinguals were superior to bilinguals: 'The difference in mental ability as revealed by intelligence tests is of a permanent nature since it persists in students throughout their university career' (p. 53).

While it is possible that situations exist where bilinguals may perform on such tests at a lower level than monolinguals, the early research that pointed to detrimental effects has a series of weaknesses that tend to invalidate the research in terms of individual studies and cumulatively across studies. These limitations are considered as follows.

Defining and Measuring Intelligence

The construct of 'intelligence' and the use of intelligence tests are controversial and hotly debated (H. Gardner, 2011). One part of the controversy lies in the problems of defining and measuring intelligence. The underlying questions are: What is intelligence and who is intelligent? A thief who cracks a bank vault? A famous football coach? Someone poor who becomes a billionaire? Don Juan? Is there social intelligence, musical intelligence, military intelligence, marketing intelligence, monitoring intelligence, political intelligence? Are all or indeed any of these forms of intelligence measurable by a simple IQ test that requires a single, acceptable, correct solution to each question? IQ tests tend to relate to a middle class, white, Western view of intelligence (Valdés & Figueroa, 1994).

A challenge to the construct of a single intelligence quotient is H. Gardner's (2011) **multiple intelligences** theory, which includes eight distinct types of intelligence – logical-mathematical, verbal-linguistic, visual-spatial, musical-rhythmical, bodily-kinesthetic, naturalist, interpersonal, and intrapersonal – in addition to one speculated type (existentialist). A further recent interest is in emotional intelligence both as a personality trait and as a component in performance (Goleman, 2006). Emotional intelligence may have facets related to bilingualism and multiculturalism such as adaptability, perception and communication of feelings, relationship skills, self-esteem, social competence and empathy (Pavlenko, 2014). A study of university students in China learning English found moderate to strong associations between emotional intelligence, foreign language anxiety and the students' English achievement and self-rated English proficiency (Shao *et al.*, 2013).

A subjective value judgment is required about what constitutes intelligent behavior, as well as about the kind of person regarded as of more worth. This stance may affect how language minorities are seen. A simple view of intelligence can enable language majorities to justify social inequalities impacting ethnic or linguistic minorities as a natural consequence of their 'lack of intelligence'. In a challenge to these simplistic views of IQ, Sternberg (2002) reminds that so called 'intelligent' individuals often do incredibly stupid and foolish things.

More recent work by Dweck (2002, 2006) sidesteps issues of defining intelligence, and instead focuses on how an individual's behavior may be impacted by their own implicit theories – or 'mindsets' – about intelligence. Dweck contrasts students who believe intelligence cannot be changed (the **'fixed' mindset**) vs. those who believe intelligence can increase with hard work and persistence (a **'growth' mindset**). She argues that when parents, teachers, and others praise students for their intelligence (e.g. 'You got an A on your vocabulary quiz. *You are so smart!*'), students may internalize a **fixed mindset** that may actually impede their academic growth. Alternatively, students can be praised on their effort and progress in ways that help them develop a **growth mindset** (e.g. 'You studied hard and got an A on your vocabulary quiz. *Great work!*').

Language of Testing

Another problem is the language of the IQ test. Standards established by the American Education Research Association, American Psychological Association, and National Council on Measurement in Education (2014) call for bilinguals to be tested in their stronger language or in both languages. In the early research, however, many verbal IQ tests were administered in English only (Hakuta, 1986). This tended to be to the disadvantage of bilinguals in that they were tested in their weaker language and thus under-performed on the IQ test. Even **testing** bilinguals in their stronger language may be less than fair. Tests that cater holistically and sensitively for the dual language capabilities of bilinguals may be preferable (Sanchez *et al.*, 2013; Shohamy & Menken, 2015) (Also see Chapter 2 for issues related to bilingual assessments).

Analysis

The early research tended to use simple averages when comparing monolingual and bilingual groups. Statistical tests were often not performed to see whether the differences between the average scores were real or due to chance factors. Thus, for example, when W.R. Jones (1966) re-analyzed Saer's (1923) research, he found that there was no statistically significant difference between the monolingual and bilingual groups.

Classification

As has been shown in Chapter 1, the classification of people into bilingual and monolingual groups is fraught with difficulty. It is too simplistic to place people into a monolingual or a bilingual group. We need to ask what **language competences** are being used for classification (Grosjean, 2012). Are all four basic language abilities being used? What is the degree of fluency in each language? Were bilinguals classified by their use of languages (**functional bilingualism**) or by their ability in language? As Chapter 1 revealed, who is or is not bilingual is a complex issue. The earlier research on bilingualism and cognition tended to regard classification as non-problematic. This means that the research results are simplistic and ambiguous, having classified bilinguals in an imprecise manner.

Generalizability

Another problem concerns sampling and the generalizability of research results to the population of bilinguals. With all research, the findings should be restricted to the population that the sample exactly represents. In particular, research using a non-random sample of a population, merely a convenience sample, should theoretically have no generalization beyond that sample. Much of the research on bilingualism and cognition is based on convenience samples. Thus research on 11-year-olds cannot be generalized to other age groups. Findings in the US cannot be generalized to bilinguals in the rest of the world. In much of the early research on bilingualism and cognition, the sampling is both small and inadequate, making generalization dangerous.

Context

The language and cultural environment of the research sample needs to be considered. This relates to the notion of subtractive and additive environments (see Chapter 4). Negative, detrimental cognitive findings may be more associated with minority language groups in subtractive environments. Subtractive environments are where the child's first language is in danger of being replaced by a more prestigious second language. Where bilingualism has high prestige in an additive environment, a different pattern of results may be more likely. Also, IQ and similar tests are presented as context-free circumstances. In reality, 'intelligent' responses will be affected by the particular context in which a task is completed (Gordon, 1997). 'Intelligent' responses are relative to situations (e.g. car driving, money-making, musical composition, classroom learning).

Matched Groups

The final problem is particularly important. To compare a group of bilingual children with monolinguals on IQ, or on any other measure of cognitive ability, requires that the two groups be equal in all other respects. The only difference between the two groups should be in their bilingualism and monolingualism. If such control does not occur, then the results of the research may be due to the other factor(s) on which the groups differ, rather than their language backgrounds. Take the example of a monolingual group being mostly of higher socioeconomic status, and the bilingual group being mostly of a lower socioeconomic status. A result (e.g. showing monolinguals to be ahead of bilinguals) may be due to social class rather than, or as well as, bilingualism. The great majority of research on bilingualism and 'intelligence' failed to match the groups on other factors that might explain the results. It is necessary to match the groups on variables such as socioeconomic and cultural class, gender, age, type of school attended and urban/rural and subtractive/additive environments.

However, as Bialystok (2001a) notes, exact equivalency of groups is impossible. Bilingual children are never exactly the same as monolinguals. They may differ socially (e.g. mixing in varying language communities), in family dynamics (e.g. learning a language from the extended family), in their travels (e.g. to the 'homeland'), and in their attendance of after-school or weekend **heritage language** classes. Therefore, cognitive differences between bilinguals and monolinguals may have explanations other than language.

Summary

The period when research accented detrimental effects lasted from approximately the 1920s to the 1960s. While the dominant conclusion was that bilinguals were inferior to monolinguals, particularly on verbal IQ, these early studies share many serious methodological weaknesses. Singly and cumulatively, the early research on bilingualism and IQ has so many limitations and methodological flaws that its conclusion of detrimental effects cannot be accepted.

Modern research suggests that bilinguals have a few potential cognitive disadvantages when compared with monolinguals. There are studies that identified differences favoring monolinguals in language-specific processing. For example, Bialystok, Craik, and Luk (2008) show that a monolingual's semantic fluency is a little faster than a bilingual's semantic fluency, as bilinguals need to ensure the correct word is chosen from their two languages. Bilinguals also appear slower in picture naming (Kaushanskaya & Marian, 2007) and less able to identify a word through noise (Rogers *et al.*, 2006). They are more likely to report a 'tip of the tongue' state, that is, being unable to immediately retrieve a word (Gollan & Acenas, 2004). This is possibly because they use some words in each language less often (Michael & Gollan, 2005), and there is interference from words from the other language (Costa, 2005), particularly when those words are false **cognates** (share the same sound but have different meaning in the two languages. For example, Welsh *glas* means blue but sounds the same as the English word *glass*.) Also, bilingual children initially possess a smaller vocabulary in each of their languages than their monolingual peers (Bialystok & Feng, 2011). However, research comparing bilingual children's 'conceptual vocabulary' (i.e. the combined vocabulary size in both of their languages minus the overlapping words) with that of monolinguals show no reliable differences between the two groups (Bedore *et al.*, 2005).

However, none of these studies suggests that bilinguals have a mental overload, process inefficiently or have weaknesses compared with monolinguals in everyday thinking. In areas such as speed of reaction in retrieving words, the milliseconds differ-ence is of little or no importance in everyday functioning. In any case, word frequency (i.e. how often words are used in everyday language production) rather than bilingual-ism per se seems to be the important factor in how quickly humans are able to access and retrieve words. According to Gollan *et al.* (2008), bilinguals by definition use each language less often than monolinguals. By implication, bilinguals use words in each language less frequently than monolinguals, and decreased use may lead to slightly weaker lexical access.

The Period of Neutral Effects

There are a series of studies that reported no difference between bilinguals and monolinguals in IQ. For example, early research in the United States by Pintner and Arsenian (1937) found a zero correlation (no relationship) between verbal (and non-verbal) IQ and Yiddish–English bilingualism/monolingualism. While the number of studies with a 'no difference' conclusion is small in number, the period of neutral effects is important because it highlighted the inadequacies of the early detrimental effect research. An example is the research by W.R. Jones (1959) in Wales. Using 2,500 children aged 10 and 11, Jones initially found that bilinguals were inferior to mono-linguals on IQ. A re-analysis showed that this conclusion was invalid. After taking into account the varying socioeconomic class of bilinguals and monolinguals, Jones concluded that monolinguals and bilinguals did not differ significantly in non-verbal IQ so long as parental occupation was taken into account. He also concluded that socioeconomic class largely accounted for previous research that had reported the inferiority of bilinguals on non-verbal IQ. Therefore, his conclusion was that bilingual-ism is not necessarily a source of intellectual disadvantage.

While the period of neutral effects overlaps chronologically with the detrimental and additive periods, there was a period when (in Wales, for example) such neutral effects were taught and publicized. Such a 'neutral' conclusion was historically important as it gave a boost to parents who wished to support bilingualism in the home and in the school. As a transitional period, it both helped to question a fashionable belief of bilingualism as a source of cerebral confusion, and became a herald for the modern and current additive effects period.

The Period of Additive Effects

A major turning point in the history of the relationship between bilingualism and cognition was reached in Canadian research by Peal and Lambert (1962). This research broke new territory in three respects, each setting the pattern for future research.

First, the research overcame many of the methodological deficiencies of the period of detrimental effects. Second, the research found evidence that bilingualism need not have detrimental or even neutral consequences. Rather, there is the possibility that bilingualism leads to cognitive advantages over monolingualism. Peal and Lambert's (1962) finding has been widely quoted to support bilingual policies in various educa-tional contexts. The political implication of the study was that bilingualism within a country was not a source of national intellectual inferiority. Third, the research by Peal and Lambert, while using IQ tests, moved research towards a broader look at cognition (e.g. thinking styles and strategies). Other areas of mental activity apart from IQ were placed firmly on the agenda for research into bilingualism and cognitive functioning.

Peal and Lambert (1962) commenced with a sample of 364 children aged 10 years drawn from middle-class French schools in Montréal, Canada. The original sample was reduced to 110 children for two reasons. First, to create a group of balanced bilinguals and a group of monolinguals. Second, to ensure that the bilingual and monolingual groups were matched on socioeconomic class. Bilinguals performed significantly higher on 15 out of the 18 IQ measures, and there was no difference between balanced bilinguals and monolinguals on the other three measures. Peal and Lambert concluded that bilingualism provides: greater mental flexibility; the ability to think more abstractly, and more independently of words, providing superiority in concept formation; that a more enriched bilingual and **bicultural** environment benefits the development of IQ; and that there is a positive transfer between a bilingual's two languages, facilitating the development of verbal IQ. These results provided the stimulus for further research and debate.

The study by Peal and Lambert (1962), while being pivotal in research on bilingualism and cognitive functioning, has four basic methodological weaknesses that need to be briefly considered before accepting the research at its face value. First, the results concern 110 children 10 years of age and of middle-class, Montréal extraction. This is not a sample that can be generalized to the population of bilinguals either in Canada or throughout the world. This is particularly true since the 110 children were selected from an original sample of 364. It remains unknown how the other 254 children performed across the broad range of tests.

Second, children in the bilingual group were 'balanced' bilinguals (see Chapter 1). While the term 'bilingual' includes balanced bilinguals, there are many other groups of children 'less balanced'. We cannot assume that the results from this study apply to such 'less balanced' bilinguals.

The third problem with Peal and Lambert's (1962) research is the chicken and egg problem. Which comes first? Is it bilingualism that enhances IQ? Or does a higher IQ increase the chances of becoming bilingual? When research suggests that IQ and bilingualism are positively related, we cannot conclude the order of cause and effect. The relationship may also be such that one is both the cause and the effect of the other. Research by Diaz (1985) suggests that, if there is a particular direction in the relationship, it is more likely to be bilingualism positively affecting 'intelligence', rather than 'intelligence' affecting bilingualism.

The fourth problem concerns socioeconomic status. While Peal and Lambert (1962) tried to equate their bilingual and monolingual groups for socioeconomic class, they did not control for all the differences in a child's home environment. Socioeconomic class is only a simple and very partial measure of a child's home and environmental background. This is true of monolingual children. It is even more so with children who are bilingual/bicultural; there may be an even more complicated home and family background with regard to sociocultural factors.

In the following example, notice how the sociocultural element is very different, yet the socioeconomic class is the same. Take two Latino children of the same age and gender living on the same street in New York. Their fathers both have the same job – taxi drivers. One family regularly attends church services in Spanish and belongs to a Latino/Latina organization with cultural activities in Spanish. This taxi driver and his wife send their children to a Spanish–English dual language school. The child is bilingual. In the second family, the child speaks English only. There is no interest in sending their children to a dual language school. Neither does the family attend a church or another organization where Spanish is spoken and valued. Their

Latin-American roots are neither discussed nor appreciated. While the families are matched on socioeconomic status, the sociocultural differences between them are considerable. In this example, the first child is bilingual and the second child is monolingual, with the bilingual child having a higher IQ. The child's bilingualism may not be the only explanation of a higher IQ. Rather the alternative or additional explanation may be in the different social and cultural environment of these children. Thus, with Peal and Lambert's (1962) study, socioeconomic class may have been controlled, but not sociocultural class.

This completes the examination of Peal and Lambert's (1962) historically important and pivotal study. Since their research, the dominant approach to bilingualism and cognitive functioning has moved away from IQ testing to a range of thinking styles, strategies and skills. As an overview, studies since the 1960s mostly confirm Peal and Lambert's positive findings.

A related area of research concerns the mental representation of a bilingual's two languages and the processing emanating from such representation (Fabbro, 2015; Kroll & Bialystok, 2013). A principal issue has been the extent to which a bilingual's two languages function independently or interdependently. The early research attempted to show that early bilinguals (compound bilinguals) were more likely to show interconnections and inter-relatedness in their two languages than late (coordinate) bilinguals. In the 1960s, Kolers (1963) re-defined the issue in terms of memory storage. A **separate storage hypothesis** stated that bilinguals have two independent language storage and retrieval systems, with the only channel of communication being a translation process between the two separate systems. A **shared storage hypothesis** stated that the two languages are kept in a single memory store with two different language input channels and two different language output channels. Evidence exists for both independence and interdependence (Heredia & Brown, 2013; Ng & Wicha, 2013). Recent theories and research have therefore emphasized both the separate and connected aspects of bilinguals' mental representations by integrating the topic with general cognitive processing theories. For example, Kroll and Bialystok (2013) suggest that the lexical representations for each language are separately stored by a bilingual, while the conceptual representations are shared. This is further considered in the next chapter. However, there is general agreement that (a) both languages are active when just one of them is being used, and (b) that even if there are shared conceptual representations and both languages are active in bilinguals, functionally the languages are independent (e.g. when speaking, reading, writing).

Bilingualism and the Brain

Just as members of the public ask basic questions about 'intelligence' and bilingualism, so questions often arise about bilinguals' brains. Neuroscientific/neurolinguistics research on bilingualism frequently asks interrelated questions such as: How are multiple languages represented and controlled in the brain? And what are the consequences and implications of experience with multiple languages? (Buchweitz & Prat, 2013). The expectation has been that images of relevant areas of the brain would help us answer these questions. Advances in neuroimaging have led to bilinguals being studied by (a) event-related brain potentials (ERP), (b) positron emission tomography (PET), and (c) functional magnetic resonance imaging (fMRI). Basically, each approach tries to take a snapshot of which part of the brain is doing what when we are thinking. ERP is a technique used to tell us precisely *when* things are happening in the brain during thinking or perceiving external stimuli. We know, for example, that it takes about 400 milliseconds for the brain to register the semantic anomaly in the sentence 'I like my coffee with cream and dog'. fMRI and PET techniques generally tell us *where* things are happening in the brain by measuring changes in blood flow in certain areas of the brain while performing a task (when an area of the brain is working hard, more blood flows into that area). The past two decades has witnessed an explosion in bilingual-ism research that utilizes neuroimaging techniques (Buchweitz & Prat, 2013; Kroll & Bialystok, 2013), in particular the fMRI technique (B.T. Gold *et al.*, 2013).

To understand how multiple languages are represented and organized in the brain, neurolinguistics researchers examine lateralization (M. Paradis, 2004). In the majority of right-handed adults, the left hemisphere of the brain is dominant for language processing (Vaid, 2002). The question has naturally arisen as to whether bilinguals are different from monolinguals in this left lateralization. Using a quantitative procedure called meta-analysis to review previous research in this area, Hull and Vaid (2007) found that the left hemisphere dominated language processing for monolinguals while bilateral involvement was pronounced in early fluent bilinguals compared with late fluent bilinguals. Thus bilinguals appear to be less left lateralized than monolinguals, and the degree of lateralization among bilinguals vary as a function of their age of exposure to the second language (Fava *et al.*, 2011; Peng & Wang, 2011).

Another recent area of such research on bilinguals is how their two languages are stored and used in the brain. For example, if someone learns two languages from birth, are the two languages stored differently in the brain from someone who learns a second language at school or in adult life? The effect of age of learning on language and cognition outcomes, commonly known as the **Critical Period Hypothesis**, has been a topic of heated debate in psycholinguistics/neurolinguistics research communities (DeKeyser & Larson-Hall, 2009; Huang, 2014). One much publicized piece of neuro-linguistics research by Mechelli *et al.* (2004) suggested that learning a second language increases the density of gray matter. When comparing 25 monolinguals, 25 early bilinguals and 33 late bilinguals, gray matter density was greater in bilinguals than monolinguals, with early bilinguals having increased density compared with late bi-linguals. Thus such density of gray matter 'increases with second language proficiency but decreases as the age of acquisition increases' (p. 757) such that 'the structure of the brain is altered by the experience of acquiring a second language' (p. 757). Moreover, the region of the brain where this increase in gray matter has been observed is activated during vocabulary acquisition in both monolinguals and bilinguals, but yields enlarge-ments in slightly different areas, depending on the specific languages of the bilingual (Green *et al.*, 2007). However, the implications of such early findings for everyday thinking and performance are not clear.

K.H. Kim *et al.* (1997) appeared to show a difference between early bilinguals (e.g. both languages learnt before three years of age) and late bilinguals. Using fMRI technique, the authors found that the two languages were both represented in frontal cortical areas in early bilinguals, but were spatially separated in late bilinguals. The results suggested that age of language acquisition may contribute to the functional organization of the human brain. Although the study received much attention in the press, there were a few major limitations, in particular the lack of objective measures of bilinguals' language proficiency (Li, 2013).

In a more recent fMRI study, Wartenburger *et al.* (2003) included three groups of Italian-German bilinguals who varied on age of learning and second language (L2) proficiency: early bilinguals with high proficiency, late bilinguals with high proficiency, and late bilinguals with low proficiency. All participants judged the well-formedness and semantic contents of sentences with and without syntactic or semantic violations. The results showed that the processing of the L2 was more effortful than that of L1 for all three bilingual groups. However, the patterns of brain activity differed by bilinguals' age of learning and L2 proficiency, as well as the specific language domain (**syntax** vs. **semantics**).

Further evidence from neuroimaging studies shows that frontal regions of the brain are activated when bilinguals are switching or selecting languages (see Rodriguez-Fornells *et al.*, 2005). Several recent fMRI studies also provide the first direct neural evidence for cognitive control advantages among bilinguals (B.T. Gold *et al.*, 2013). However, as argued by Li (2013), we are only just beginning to understand the neural architecture underlying language and cognitive processing in bilinguals. There is a danger of believing that brain images represent thought. Such snapshot brain images are a visible consequence of thinking but do not reveal the complex operation of the mind. The correspondence between these images of the brain and thought processes is not yet known. De Bot (2008) offers a critical overview of the added value of neuroimaging techniques, concluding that neuroimaging has failed so far to provide any real breakthrough in our understanding of the multilingual brain. The reasons for this are many. The main one seems to be that the majority of studies are carried out by neuroscientists who have only recently developed an interest in **multilingualism** research.

As such, these researchers tend to ignore or not measure adequately several important variables that have been shown to affect multilingual processing, and that multi-lingualism specialists routinely take into account. These variables include age of second language acquisition, level of proficiency, language contact and use, motivation to learn the language, language aptitude, and attitudes towards the L1 and L2, among others. As a result, it is not possible to draw any firm conclusions regarding the functional organiz-ation of the multilingual's languages in the brain. In addition, multilinguals typically exhibit larger individual variation in their patterns of brain activity than monolinguals, by virtue of the fact that they may still be in the process of learning. Some neuroimaging studies tend to treat this variation as unwanted noise and ignore it, whereas in many cases it is in this variation that the real information about language processing in the brain may lie (see De Bot, 2008 for specific examples). Several researchers have argued recently (Bialystok, 2015; García-Pentón *et al.*, 2015; Kroll & Bialystok, 2013) that many neurolinguistics of bilingualism questions remain unanswered (e.g. differences in brain organization depending on how many languages are known). Nevertheless, neuroimaging techniques have opened up new research possibilities with the potential to better understand the multilingual brain. Some researchers are beginning to use more sophisticated research methodologies such as collecting longitudinal imaging data and combining neuroimaging techniques with behavioral data such as language proficiency in advanced statistical models (see, e.g. Andrews *et al.*, 2013).

Bilingualism and Divergent/Creative Thinking

One problem with IQ tests is that they restrict children to finding the one correct answer to each question. This is often termed convergent thinking. Children have to converge onto the sole acceptable answer. An alternative style is called **divergent**

thinking. A child regarded as a diverger is more creative, imaginative, elastic, open-ended and free in thinking. Instead of finding the one correct answer, divergent thinkers prefer to provide a variety of answers, all of which can be valid.

Divergent (or creative) thinking is investigated by asking questions such as: 'How many uses can you think of for a brick?' 'How many interesting and unusual uses can you think of for tin cans?' On this kind of question, the student has to diverge and find as many answers as possible. For example, on the 'uses of a brick' question, a convergent thinker would tend to produce a few rather obvious answers to the question: to build a house, to build a barbecue, to build a wall. The divergent thinker will tend to produce not only many different answers, but also some that may be fairly original: for blocking up a rabbit hole, for propping up a wobbly table, as a foot wiper, breaking a window, making a bird bath.

In the North American tradition, it is more usual to talk about creative thinking (see Simonton, 2008 for a review). Torrance (1974) analyzes answers to the 'uses of an object' test (e.g. unusual uses of cardboard boxes or tin cans) by four categories. This test may be adapted into any language, with a culturally appropriate use of objects. Also, there are figural tests where a person is given a sheet of 40 circles or 40 squares and asked to draw pictures using these individual circles or squares, and subsequently place a label underneath. A person's fluency score in creative thinking is the number of different acceptable answers that are given. A flexibility score is the number of different categories (listed in the test manual) into which answers can be placed. Originality is measured by reference to the test manual that gives scores of 0, 1, or 2 for the originality (statistical infrequency) of each response. Elaboration refers to the extent of the extra detail that a person gives beyond the basic use of an object.

The underlying hypothesis concerning creative thinking and bilingualism is that the ownership of two or more languages may increase fluency, flexibility, originality and elaboration in thinking. Bilinguals will have two or more words for a single object or idea. For example, in Welsh, the word *ysgol* not only means a school but also a ladder. Thus having the word *ysgol* in Welsh and *school* in English may provide the bilingual with added associations – the idea of the school as a ladder (e.g. the steps as going through the grades). Similarly, having words for *folk dancing* or *square dancing* in different languages may give a wider variety of associations than having a label in just one language.

Research has compared bilinguals and monolinguals on a variety of measures of divergent thinking (Adesope *et al.*, 2010; Kharkhurin, 2015; Leikin, 2012; Onysko, 2015). The research is international and cross-cultural: from Ireland, Malaysia, Russia and elsewhere in Eastern Europe, Canada, Singapore, Mexico, New Zealand and the US, sampling bilinguals using English plus Chinese, Bahasa Melayu, Tamil, Polish, German, Greek, Hebrew, Māori, Russian, Spanish, French, Ukrainian, Yorubo, Welsh, Italian or Kannada. The research findings largely suggest that bilinguals are superior to monolinguals on divergent thinking tests.

Jim Cummins (1977) found that relatively balanced bilinguals were superior to 'matched' non-balanced bilinguals on the fluency and flexibility scales of verbal divergence, and marginally on originality. The 'matched' monolingual group obtained similar scores to the balanced bilingual group on verbal fluency and flexibility but scored substantially higher than the non-balanced group. On originality, monolinguals scored at a similar level to the non-balanced bilinguals and substantially lower than the balanced group. Probably because of the small numbers involved, the results did not quite attain customary levels of statistical significance. The differences found between matched groups of balanced bilinguals and non-balanced bilinguals suggests that bilingualism and superior divergent thinking skills are not simply related. Thus Cummins proposed that the difference between balanced and non-balanced bilinguals can be explained by a threshold. Once children have obtained a certain level of competence in their second language, positive cognitive consequences can result. However, competence in a second language below a certain threshold level may fail to give any cognitive benefits. This is the basic notion of the **Threshold Theory** that is examined further in Chapter 8.

The evidence suggests that balanced bilinguals have superior divergent thinking skills compared with other less balanced bilinguals and monolinguals. In a review of 24 studies, Ricciardelli (1992) found that in 20 of these studies, bilinguals performed higher than monolinguals. Studies not supporting bilingual superiority sampled less proficient bilinguals, a result consistent with the Threshold Theory. A study by Kharkhurin (2008) using the methods of Torrance described above revealed that superior divergent thinking was facilitated by bilinguals' proficiency in the two languages, the age of acquisition of these languages and the length of exposure to a new cultural environment.

However, some care must be taken in reaching too firm a conclusion. For example, U. Laurén (1991) found that linguistic creativity differences were found in Grades 3, 6 and 9. Older bilinguals were ahead on only one of the four measures (use of compound nouns). Kharkhurin (2009) showed that bilingualism enhances the ability to *activate* a multitude of unrelated concepts, but not the ability to *generate* novel ideas, suggesting that even if bilinguals are more divergent thinkers than monolinguals, this does not necessarily mean that they are also more creative. Nonetheless, Kharkhurin (2015) asserts that 'altogether, the empirical findings suggest that bilingual development may facilitate an individual's creative thinking' (p. 44). The term 'creativity' is defined in different ways. As U. Laurén (1991) reveals, there are different interpretations by psychologists (e.g. cognitive flexibility, fluency, originality and elaboration; tolerance of ambiguity); by linguists (e.g. the ability to create new meanings in different contexts); child development researchers (e.g. transforming the language input of parents and teachers); and creative writing proponents.

Bilingualism and Metalinguistic Awareness: Initial Research

The research on bilingualism and divergent thinking suggests that bilinguals may have some advantage over matched monolinguals. For many bilingual children, the size of their total vocabulary across both languages, including the overlapping words, is likely to be greater than that of a monolingual child in a single language (Bedore *et al.*, 2005). Does a larger overall vocabulary allow a bilingual to be more free and open, more flexible and original particularly in meanings attached to words? Is a bilingual person therefore less bound by words, more elastic in thinking owing to owning two languages?

Leopold's (1970) famous case study (see Chapter 5) of the German–English development of his daughter, Hildegard from 1939–1949 noted the looseness of the link between word and meaning – an effect apparently due to bilingualism. Favorite stories were not repeated with stereotyped wording; vocabulary substitutions were made freely in memorized songs and rhymes. Word sound and word meaning were separated. Hildegard is a single case. What has research revealed about samples of bilinguals?

Ianco-Worrall (1972) tested the sound and meaning separation idea on 30 Afrikaans–English bilinguals aged four to nine. The bilingual group was matched with monolinguals on IQ, age, sex, school grade and social class. In the first experiment, a typical question was: 'I have three words: CAP, CAN and HAT. Which is more like CAP: CAN or HAT?' A child who says that CAN is more like CAP would appear to be making a choice determined by the *sound* of the word. That is, CAP and CAN have two out of three letters in common. A child who chooses HAT would appear to be making a choice based on the *meaning* of the word. That is, HAT and CAP refer to similar objects. Ianco-Worrall showed that four- to six-year-old bilinguals tended to respond to word meaning whereas monolinguals more to the sound of the word. However, by seven years of age, both groups' answers were governed by the meaning of the word. Ianco-Worrall concluded that bilinguals 'reach a stage of semantic development, as measured by our test, some two – three years earlier than their monolingual peers' (p. 1398).

In a further experiment, Ianco-Worrall (1972) asked the following type of question: 'Suppose you were making up names for things, could you call a cow 'dog' and a dog 'cow'?' Bilinguals mostly felt that names could be interchangeable. Monolinguals, in comparison, more often said that names for objects such as cow and dog could not be interchanged. Another way of describing this is to say that monolinguals tend to be bound by words and bilinguals tend to believe that language is more arbitrary. For bilinguals, names and objects are separate. This seems to be a result of owning two languages, giving the bilingual child awareness of the free, non-fixed relationship between objects and their labels.

Other early research in this area, for example, by Ben-Zeev (1977b) suggested that the ability of bilinguals to analyze and inspect their languages stems from the necessity of avoiding 'interference' between the two languages. That is, the process of separating two languages and avoiding **codemixing** may give bilinguals superiority over monolinguals through an increased analytical orientation to language. One of Ben-Zeev's tests, called the Symbol Substitution Test, asked children to substitute one word for another in a sentence. For example, they had to use the word 'macaroni' instead of 'I' in a sentence. Thus, 'I am warm' becomes 'Macaroni am warm'. Respondents have to ignore word meaning, avoid framing a correct sentence and evade the interference of word substitution in order to respond to the task correctly. Bilinguals in Ben-Zeev's study were superior on this kind of test, not only with regard to meaning, but also with regard to sentence construction. Therefore bilinguals appear to be more flexible and analytical in **language skills**.

Bilingualism and Metalinguistic Awareness: Recent Research

Much of the older research on bilingualism and cognitive functioning has concentrated on cognitive style (e.g. divergent and creative thinking). The focus of research tended to be on the person and on the product. It attempted to locate dimensions of thinking where bilinguals perform better than monolinguals. The recent trend has been to look at the *process* of thinking rather than the *products* of thinking, working within the information processing, memorization and language processing approaches in psychology (e.g. Bialystok, 2001a, 2009). In particular, much of the recent research effort has been devoted to investigating the effect of bilingualism on two cognitive domains: nonverbal executive functioning (Bialystok & Martin, 2004; Bialystok & Viswanathan, 2009) and metalinguistic awareness (Bialystok, Peets & Moreno, 2014; Hermanto et al., 2012).

Nonverbal executive functioning refers to a set of interrelated processes in the brain, particularly the frontal lobe (Bialystok & Viswanathan, 2009; Miyake et al., 2000). The executive control system is generally believed to consist of three components: inhibition, updating (a.k.a. working memory) and shifting (a.k.a. cognitive flexibility).

However, there is still debate over the specific number and nature of these components. On the other hand, metalinguistic awareness may loosely be defined as thinking about and reflecting upon the nature and functions of language (see Bialystok, 2001a for more precise definitions and differences). Metalinguistic awareness includes a collection of abilities, such as print awareness, morphological awareness, grammatical awareness and phonological awareness. They are distinct from language proficiency, but are crucial to academic achievement and the acquisition of literacy (Bialystok, Craik, Binns, Ossher & Freedman, 2014). An example of metalinguistic knowledge is second language learners who do not have to relearn the fundamentals of language structure. They already have that metalinguistic knowledge from first language acquisition.

Not all such studies are 'favorable to bilinguals' (Adesope et al., 2010; Bialystok, 2009; Paap et al., 2015b). For example, bilinguals were found to be slower in their access and retrieval of vocabulary (Bialystok, 2009). However, despite these potential disadvantages, bilinguals may be equally as good at problem solving and getting correct mathematical solutions (Bialystok, 2001a). McLeay (2003) found advantages for adult 'balanced' bilinguals in dealing with complex mathematical spatial problems, while Kessler and Quinn (1982) found bilinguals were superior on scientific problem solving. Research also shows that bilingual children are able to solve problems that contain misleading cues earlier than monolingual children. Bialystok and Martin (2004) asked children to group a set of stimuli by one common feature (e.g. color) and then to re-group them by another common feature (e.g. their shape). In order to complete the task successfully in the second round, children needed to be able to attend to the new relevant feature while ignoring the previously relevant feature. The study showed that bilingual children were able to complete the task successfully at an earlier age than monolingual children.

There is another limitation to research on bilinguals and cognition. Is the research about bilingualism, or is it really about cognition (or both)? Research on memorization, language recall, reaction times and processing times tends to use bilinguals to help describe and explain the larger issues surrounding cognitive processing and language processing. Comparisons with monolinguals aim to aid psychological understanding of cognitive processes rather than explain the nature of bilinguals per se. Pavlenko (2000) provides a review that is critical of research in this area, but places understanding the bilingual at the forefront.

As mentioned earlier, research that has focused on bilinguals has particularly studied the **metalinguistic awareness** of bilingual children (Bialystok, Craik et al., 2014). Early research suggested a relationship favoring bilinguals in terms of increased metalinguistic awareness (see Bialystok, Craik et al., 2014 for a review). It appeared that bilingual children develop a more analytical orientation to language through organizing their two language systems. To illustrate, in research that directly examines bilingualism and metalinguistic awareness, Bialystok and colleagues (Bialystok, 2001a, 2001c; Bialystok,

Craik *et al.*, 2014) found that bilingual children were superior to monolingual children on measures of the cognitive control of linguistic processes. Bialystok (1987a) conducted three studies each involving children aged five to nine. In the experiments, children were asked to judge or correct sentences for their syntactic acceptability irrespective of meaningfulness. Sentences could be meaningfully grammatical (e.g. Why is the dog barking so loudly?); meaningful but not grammatical (e.g. Why the dog is barking so loudly?); anomalous and grammatical (e.g. Why is the cat barking so loudly?); or anomalous and ungrammatical (e.g. Why the cat is barking so loudly?). The instructions requested that the children focus on whether a given sentence was grammatically correct or not. It did not matter that the sentence was silly or anomalous. Bialystok found that bilingual children in all three studies consistently judged grammaticality more accurately than did monolingual children at all the ages tested.

Bialystok (1987b) also examined the difference between bilinguals and monolinguals in their processing of words and the development of the concept of a word. She found in three studies that bilingual children showed more advanced understanding of some aspects of the idea of words than did monolingual children. A procedure for testing children's awareness of 'what is a word?' is to ask children to determine the number of words in a sentence. It can be surprisingly difficult for young children to count how many words there are in a sentence. Until children are about six to seven years of age and learning to read, they do not appear to have this processing ability.

To be able to count how many words there are in a sentence depends on two things: (a) knowledge of the boundaries of words; (b) a knowledge of the relationship between word meaning and sentence meaning. At around seven years of age, children learn that words can be isolated from the sentences in which they are contained, having their own individual meaning. Bialystok (1987b) found that bilingual children were ahead of monolingual children on counting words in sentences because (a) they were more clear about the criteria that determined the identity of words; and (b) they were more capable of attending to the units of speech they considered relevant.

A conclusion based on an overview of research can be summarized as follows. A bilingual does not have across-the-board metalinguistic advantages or universally superior metalinguistic abilities. Relatively balanced bilinguals have increased metalinguistic abilities particularly in those tasks that require selective attention to information (e.g. when there is competing or misleading information). Such selective attention relates to two components: (a) bilinguals' enhanced analyzing of their knowledge of language, and (b) their greater control of attention in internal language processing.

Implications and Explanations

Bilinguals appear to understand the symbolic representation of words in print earlier than monolinguals as they see words printed in two separate ways. In turn, this may facilitate earlier acquisition of reading. Such metalinguistic awareness is regarded by Bialystok (2001c) as a key factor in the development of reading in young children. This hints that bilinguals may be ready slightly earlier than monolinguals to learn to read. In a review of this area, Bialystok (2007) analyzes the effects that early bilingualism has on children's early literacy development but urges caution. Three areas of early literacy development are analyzed: experience with stories and book reading, concepts of print, and phonological awareness. These three areas cover the social, cognitive and linguistic aspects of literacy learning. Bialystok argues that each of these three areas of competence will have a different link to bilingualism.

However, there are many intervening variables that make simple statements currently impossible. The child's experience and level of proficiency in each language, the relationship between the two languages, and the type of writing systems employed by each language are examples of intervening factors that alter the nature of the bilingual experience. For example, the L1–L2 pairings of bilinguals play a role in determining the metalinguistic advantage. For bilinguals to develop a specific type of metalinguistic skill, it may be necessary for both of the bilinguals' two languages to include that same language feature or share the same writing system (Adesope et al., 2010). Crosslinguistic studies that compared children's development of phonological awareness have revealed an important role of a shared writing script and phonological system (Bialystok, Luk, & Kwan, 2005; McBride-Chang et al., 2004). Bialystok, Luk et al. (2005) compared the early literacy skills of four groups of first graders: a monolingual English-speaking group, and three groups of bilinguals from different L1–L2 pairings (Hebrew–English, Chinese–English and Spanish–English). All children were learning to read in English, and the bilinguals were also learning to read in another language. The results showed a bilingual advantage in phonological awareness for Spanish–English and Hebrew–English bilinguals whose L1 and L2 are both alphabetic writing systems, but not for Chinese–English bilinguals whose L1 uses a logographic writing system. However, a bilingual advantage in non-word decoding tasks was observed for all three bilingual groups relative to the monolingual group.

Apart from literacy, Bialystok and Codd (1997) found that four and five year-old bilinguals were ahead of monolinguals in developing concepts of number (cardinality of number) owing to their higher levels of attentional control. Bilingual children need to be attentive to which language is being spoken, by whom, where and when. This attentiveness appears to give advantages in early number work, when attention to the symbolic nature of number is needed.

The research of Galambos and Hakuta (1988) provides further refinement of the reasons for differences between bilinguals and monolinguals on cognitive processes. In two studies with low income Spanish–English bilingual children in the US, Galambos and Hakuta used a series of tests that examined children's ability to spot various errors in Spanish sentences. Such errors might be in terms of gender, word order, singular and plural, verb tense and time. For example, on a grammatically-oriented test item, a child had to correct the following: 'La perro es grande'. The correction would be 'El perro es grande'. In a content-oriented test item, 'La perro es grande' would become 'El perro es pequeño'. In the experiment, children were read the sentences, asked to judge whether they had been said in the right way, and then correct the error. The effect of bilingualism on the processing of the test items was found to vary depending on the level of bilingualism and the difficulty level of the items. The more bilingual the child was (i.e. where both languages were relatively well developed), the better he or she performed on the test items. Galambos and Hakuta concluded that metalinguistic awareness is most developed when a child's two languages are developed to their highest level.

Carlisle et al. (1999) also found that the degree of bilingualism constrains or enhances metalinguistic performance. Those in the early stages of bilingualism do not share the benefits until sufficient vocabulary development, in both languages, has occurred. However, crosslinguistic studies on bilingual advantage (Bialystok, Luk et al., 2005) showed that metalinguistic benefits are more apparent in bilinguals whose languages have similar sound structures or writing systems (e.g. Spanish–English bilinguals) than in bilinguals whose languages use distinctly different sound structures or writing systems (e.g. Chinese–English bilinguals), suggesting that enhanced metalinguistic awareness may not necessarily be a product of bilingualism per se, but rather of speaking specific combinations of languages with similar features.

Age Effects

Are these metalinguistic advantages of balanced bilinguals temporary and located with certain younger children (e.g. those already embarked on the initial stages of reading)? Do they give a child an initial advantage that soon disappears with growing cognitive competence? Are the effects in any way permanent? Are these early benefits for bilinguals cumulative and additive?

Older bilingual adults may have some advantages. Bialystok and her colleagues provide evidence across a series of studies, which shows that bilingualism helps lessen some of the negative cognitive effects of aging in adults (Bialystok *et al.*, 2008; Bialystok, Craik *et al.*, 2005; Bialystok, Craik, Klein & Viswanathan, 2004). Bialystok *et al.* (2004) used the Simon Task to compare groups of younger and older bilinguals and monolinguals. In the Simon Task colored stimuli are presented on either the left or the right side of a computer screen. Each of two colors (or two pairs of colors) is associated with a response key on the two sides of the keyboard underneath the stimuli. Participants in the experiment press the key on the correct side. For example, a correct 'congruent' response occurs when the participant presses the left key when red is presented on the left side of the screen. A correct 'incongruent' response is when the subject presses the left key when red is presented on the right side of the screen. An incorrect response is when red is presented on the right side and the person presses the right key. The time taken to respond is an important measurement (i.e. 'incongruent' trials have longer reaction times and this is termed the Simon effect). Longer reaction times tend to occur with aging. Across a series of experiments, Bialystok *et al.* (2004) found that performance on the Simon task was superior in bilinguals than in monolinguals and that this result was evident in younger and older bilinguals. Balanced bilinguals tended to perform the Simon Task quicker than 'matched' monolinguals, irrespective of age, and showed less interference in the 'incongruent' trials, and bilingualism also significantly reduced the age-related lower performance. This implies that 'the lifelong experience of managing two languages attenuates the age-related decline in the efficiency of inhibitory processing' (Bialystok *et al.*, 2004: 301). The results have been replicated in a later study (Hilchey & Klein, 2011).

Bialystok *et al.* (2008) used another measure of inhibitory control called the Stroop Task with younger and older bilingual and monolingual individuals. Participants have to name the color of the ink that a color word is written in (e.g. name the ink that the word 'green' is written in). In congruent trials, the color of the ink is the same as the color word (e.g. the word 'green' written in green ink), but in incongruent trials the color of the ink conflicts with the color word (e.g. the word 'green' written in red ink). Typically, participants are slower to respond in the incongruent condition than in the congruent condition. Bialystok *et al.* found that this switching cost between the congruent and incongruent trials was smaller in both younger and older bilinguals than in their age-matched monolingual counterparts.

The Simon and Stroop effects are similar to advantages found in bilingual children (discussed previously) and young adults, who appear to be superior in selective attention to problems, inhibition of attention to misleading information, and switching quickly between competing alternatives. From these experiments, such inhibitory control appears to last a lifetime (Bialystok *et al.*, 2004). This advantage may be due to bilinguals using one language while both their languages are constantly active. Bialystok *et al.* (2004) concluded that metalinguistic advantages for bilinguals appear to be sustained into adulthood with some lessening of cognitive processing decline with aging. The bilingual advantage appears to be in complex cognitive processing that requires executive control. In a follow-up study, Bialystok, Craik *et al.* (2005) used magnetoencephalography (MEG) to identify the neural correlates of executive control in the bilingual and monolingual brain. Results from monolingual and bilingual young adults performing the Simon task showed that bilinguals used more areas of the brain than monolinguals, suggesting that bilinguals have more brain resources at their disposal when performing tasks based on non-verbal conflict.

Since abilities that depend on executive cognitive control show a decline in efficiency with aging, bilingualism may also provide a partial defense against the normal decline in cognitive control associated with aging. Indeed, research demonstrated that older bilingual adults (e.g. age 60 and above in these experiments) fare better than their monolingual peers in preserving memory (Bialystok, Craik *et al.*, 2014; Schroeder & Marian, 2012). Research also has shown delays in the signs of dementia (Bialystok, Craik & Freedman, 2007) or in reported onset of symptoms for Alzheimer disease in older bilingual adults (Bialystok, Craik & Luk, 2012; Bialystok, Poarch, Luo & Craik, 2014; Craik, Bialystok & Freedman, 2010) four years later than their monolingual peers.

Bilingualism and Communicative Sensitivity

Social preferences based on primary categories such as gender, race and age have long been documented in the literature for both adults (Stangor *et al.*, 1992) and children (Kowalski & Lo, 2001). Since spoken language provides information about individuals' ethnicity, regional membership and social class, researchers have argued that spoken language may also function as an additional social category that guides individual preferences (Kinzler *et al.*, 2007). In particular, research on bilingualism have shown that bilinguals appear to have increased sensitivity to the social nature and communicative functions of language, i.e. *communicative sensitivity*. In Ben-Zeev's seminal research (1977a) on the comparative performance of bilingual and mono-lingual children on Piagetian tests, she found that bilinguals were more responsive to hints and clues given in the experimental situation. That is, bilinguals seemed more sensitive in an experimental situation, and corrected their errors faster compared to monolinguals. Ben-Zeev's research gave the first clue that bilinguals may have cognitive advantages regarding communicative sensitivity. Because bilinguals need to be aware of which language to speak in which situation, they need to constantly monitor the appropriate language in which to respond or in which to initiate a conversation (e.g. on the telephone, in a shop, speaking to a superior). Not only do bilinguals often attempt to avoid interference between their two languages, they also have to pick up clues and cues as to when to switch languages. The literature suggests that this may lead to bi-linguals' advantage in communicative sensitivity.

Genesee, Tucker and Lambert (1975) compared children in bilingual and mono-lingual education on their performance on a game. Five to eight year old children were asked to explain a board and dice game to two listeners, one blindfolded and the other not. It was found that, compared with children in the monolingual education group, the bilingual education children were more sensitive to the needs of listeners and gave more information to the blindfolded listener than to the sighted listener. The authors concluded that children in bilingual education 'may have been better able than the control children to take the role of others experiencing communicational difficulties, to perceive their needs, and consequently to respond appropriately to these needs' (p. 1013).

Recent researchers have also found a similar advantage among bilingual children in perspective-taking (Fan *et al.*, 2015) and in integrating multiple cues to understand speakers' intent (Comeau *et al.*, 2003; Yow & Markman, 2011, 2015). Researchers have also discovered that bilingual infants, compared to their monolingual peers, were better able to exploit the audiovisual speech cues because of the need to process two languages and to keep them apart (Lewkowicz & Hansen-Tift, 2012; Pons *et al.*, 2015; Sebastián-Gallés *et al.*, 2012). This implies that bilingual children may be more sensitive than monolingual children in a social situation that requires careful communication. This links with sociolinguistic and **communicative competence** (see Chapter 1) and suggests a heightened social awareness among bilinguals of verbal and non-verbal message cues and clues in communication.

More research is needed to define precisely the characteristics and the extent of the sensitivity to communication that bilinguals may share. Research in this area is important because it connects cognition with interpersonal relationships. It moves from questions about bilinguals' cognitive skills to their social skills.

Thinking Implications of Speaking Specific Languages

Is it the case that different languages, or combinations of languages, influence the thinking of individuals? The Whorf Hypothesis (Whorf, 1956) holds that speakers of different languages perceive the world through the lens of their native language, and speakers' perceptions and information processing may vary as a function of the differences in the linguistic features across languages (Gleitman & Papafragou, 2005). Recent research has focused on individuals who view the world through the lens of more than one language. This new line of research focuses on the thinking *processes* rather than the thinking *abilities* of the bilingual. The targeted thinking processes include both perceptual (e.g. color and objects) and conceptual domains (e.g. numbers, spatial frames of reference), and the predictors of differences in those processes between L1 and L2 speakers include age of L2 acquisition (Kersten *et al.*, 2010), and L2 use and proficiency (Bylund & Athanasopoulos, 2014a), and L2 proficiency (Pavlenko & Malt, 2011) (for a detailed overview see Bylund & Athanasopoulos, 2014b).

To illustrate, Athanasopoulos and colleagues have focused on categorization of objects and substances in noun class and classifier languages (see Athanasopoulos, 2011). Noun class languages like English distinguish between count and mass nouns grammatically. Count nouns refer to discrete entities that are marked for number (e.g. candle – candles). In classifier languages like Japanese or Chinese, there is no count/mass distinction. Nouns in these languages refer to substances and are accompanied by numeral classifiers (e.g. one long thin wax [=candle]). Speakers of the two types of languages were shown to perform differently on a similarity judgment task that required participants to match objects based on their common shape or material. Speakers of English favored shape and speakers of Japanese favored material, presumably because noun-class languages draw speakers' attention to discreteness of entities and classifier languages to material (Imai & Gentner, 1997; Lucy & Gaskins, 2001). Japanese–English bilinguals were influenced by the level of proficiency in the

L2 and their length of stay in the UK when making their judgments (Athanasopoulos, 2007). Those bilinguals with advanced-level proficiency and/or longer length of stay were beginning to resemble speakers of their L2 English in favoring shape over material in similarity judgments.

Other studies have also shown shifts in mental representation of bilinguals in different perceptual domains such as time (Boroditsky, 2001), motion events (Bylund & Athanasopoulos, 2015), and grammatical gender (Bassetti, 2007). What is particularly interesting is that different factors appear to affect the degree of cognitive restructuring observed. So for domains like grammatical number and gender, it seems that proficiency achieved in the L2 is the most important factor, while factors such as length of stay and frequency of language use appear to affect color cognition. Boroditsky (2001) found that the degree to which time representations changed in Chinese–English bilinguals depended on the age at which they had started to acquire English, while the study by Boroditsky *et al.* (2002) found that bilinguals shifted their behavioral responses towards the language in which they received task instructions. The application of the Whorfian hypothesis to bilingualism has the potential to reveal invaluable information about how the bilingual mind views the world as a result of speaking specific languages; yet research is still at a very early stage, and the precise role of specific linguistic and socio-cultural factors, as well as the extent of the effects in different perceptual domains, remains elusive for the time being (see Bylund & Athanasopoulos, 2014a; Pavlenko, 2014 for detailed discussions).

Crosslinguistic differences have also been identified in how languages employ grammatical devices to encode emotions (Martinovic & Altarriba, 2013). For example, in English, emotions are relayed through adjectives as emotional states, while in Russian the tendency is to convey emotions more via verbs as actions and processes, with for example, more attention to body language. Pavlenko and Driagina (2007) found that advanced American learners of Russian use the copula verbs '*byt*' ('be') and '*stanovit'sia*' ('become') with emotion adjectives in contexts where Russian monolinguals use emotion verbs. These patterns suggest that in discussing emotions in Russian, these learners transfer the L1 concept of emotions as states into their L2, and have not yet internalized the representation of emotions as processes. Evidence of internalization comes from a study by Panayiotou (2007) who found that Greek–English bilinguals internalized the notion of 'frustration' from English and codeswitched to refer to it when speaking Greek. For example: '*Imoun polla* frustrated *me tin katastasi*' ('I was very *frustrated* with the situation') (Panayiotou, 2006: 8). Using a sorting task, Stepanova Sachs and Coley (2006) found that Russian–English bilinguals grouped situations eliciting jealousy and ones eliciting envy together as similar, whereas Russian monolinguals sorted the two types of situations separately. This suggests a certain degree of restructuring of emotion perception in bilinguals. Pavlenko (2011) further discusses similar research that shows that bilinguals may have access to different conceptual representations, experience different imagery and index more varied **discourses** and identities than monolinguals.

Limitations of the Findings

In a recent meta-analysis of the cognitive advantages of bilingualism, Adesope *et al.* (2010) reviewed 63 empirical studies, and found that bilingualism is associated with several cognitive benefits. Those include increased working memory (cf. Bialystok,

2009), attentional control, metalinguistic awareness, and abstract and symbolic representations. The research reviewed in this chapter converged with the meta-analysis and suggested cognitive advantages of bilinguals. However, the research on bilingual advantages mostly focuses on balanced bilinguals, who are a subgroup of all bilinguals. MacNab (1979) argued that (balanced) bilinguals are a special, idiosyncratic group in society. Because they have learned a second language and are often bicultural, bilinguals are different in major ways from monolinguals. For example, parents who want their children to be bicultural/bilingual may encourage creative thinking in their children and foster metalinguistic skills. They may also want to accelerate their children's language skills, and thus give higher priority to the development of languages within their children than monolingual parents do. While this does not detract from the possibility that bilinguals do share some cognitive advantages, it does suggest a need to consider non-language factors (e.g. the immigrant experience, political pressures, subtractive and additive contexts) before attributing the cognitive advantages to bilingualism.

We also need to ask which types of children share the benefits of bilingualism? This concerns whether children of all socioeconomic backgrounds and cognitive skills share the cognitive advantages of bilingualism (Paap et al., 2015b; Valian, 2015). Many bilingualism studies either did not report socioeconomic information, or included bilingual children from middle or higher socioeconomic status relative to the monolingual group (Adesope et al., 2010). Those that controlled for socioeconomic backgrounds of the monolingual and bilingual groups (Dunabeitia et al., 2014; Gathercole et al., 2014) or included children from lower socioeconomic backgrounds (Ladas et al., 2015) yielded mixed results, suggesting an important gap in the area for future research. On the other hand, Cheatham et al. (2012) reviewed comparison studies that investigated the impact of bilingualism for bilingual students with disabilities. The researchers concluded that a bilingual cognitive advantage may be shared by bilingual children with below average cognitive skills (or with cognitive impairments) and not limited to bilingual children with average and above average cognitive skills.

In addition, researchers have found that levels of education, exercise, music training, among other cognitively enriching activities, can also improve cognitive functioning, and these factors should have been controlled in studies that compared monolinguals and bilinguals to examine bilingual cognitive advantages (Valian, 2015). When reviewing all research we also need to consider the hopes and the ideologies of the researcher (confirmation bias) as well as the bias of journal editors to publish only positive results (publication bias) (de Bruin et al., 2015). Rosenthal (2009) has shown that experimenters' expectations can affect the outcomes and results of human and animal studies. As Hakuta (1986: 43) suggests: 'a full account of the relationship between bilingualism and intelligence, of why negative effects suddenly turn in to positive effects, will have to examine the motivations of the researcher as well as more traditional considerations at the level of methodology'. Have the assumptions and political preferences of authors crept unintentionally into their research and affected both the results and the interpretations of the results? Has there recently been a built-in bias towards finding and publishing positive over null or negative results on bilingualism and cognitive functioning?

As Pavlenko (2005) argues, the dominant research on bilingualism and cognition is about the implications of bilingualism for individual cognition. This assumes that such cognitive effects of bilingualism are universal.However, neither behavioral nor neuroscience data have provided unequivocal evidence for a universal bilingual advantage in cognition (Paap et al., 2015a, 2015b). The current consensus in the research community is that a bilingual cognitive advantage exists for selective components of cognitive functioning, and may be restricted to specific circumstances of bilingualism (Valian, 2015). To specify and determine the mechanism, future research that addresses the above-mentioned methodological issues are clearly needed.

Conclusion

This chapter has reviewed the view from the 1920s to the 1960s that bilingualism leads to lower intelligence. Recent research has shown this to be a misconception. The narrow view of intelligence contained in IQ tests and severe flaws in the design of early research cast doubts on this negative link.

Rather, the need is to specify the **language ability** levels of bilinguals (see Chapter 1) and to ensure like is compared with like. Since 1960, the indication has been that a more positive relationship between bilingualism and cognitive functioning can be expected, particularly in 'balanced' bilinguals.

A review of research on cognitive functioning and bilingualism suggests that two extreme conclusions may both be untenable. To conclude that bilingualism gives undoubted cognitive advantage fails to consider the various failures of replication studies and limitations of research in this area (Paap *et al.*, 2015a, 2015b). It also fails to recognize the potential disadvantages of bilinguals compared to monolinguals. However, to conclude that all the research is invalid fails to acknowledge that the judgment of the clear majority of researchers tends to be that there are many positive links between bilingualism and cognitive functioning (Valian, 2015), with bilinguals having some distinct cognitive as well as social-communicative advantages over monolinguals. Such advantages are not just individual, but societal and global: 'those who envision a future world speaking only one tongue … hold a misguided ideal and would do the evolution of the human mind the greatest disservice' (Whorf, 1956: 244).

Key Points in This Chapter

➢ Historically, bilinguals were regarded as having a relatively lower IQ than monolinguals.

➢ The idea of 'intelligence' as a singular fixed construct has been challenged by more recent theories of multiple intelligences, emotional intelligence and mindsets.

➢ Research on the relationship between intelligence and bilingualism has moved from a period of investigating 'detrimental effects' to a current focus on the additive effects given by bilingualism.

➢ The ownership of two languages does not interfere with efficient thinking. On the contrary bilinguals who have two well-developed languages tend to share cognitive advantages.

> ➤ Bilinguals have advantages on certain thinking dimensions, particularly in divergent thinking, creativity, early metalinguistic awareness and communicative sensitivity. There are likely to be many other cognitive skills on which there are no real differences between bilinguals and monolinguals.

> ➤ Research on the metalinguistic advantages of bilinguals is strong, and suggests bilinguals are aware of their languages at an early age, separating form from meaning, and having reading readiness earlier than monolinguals.

> ➤ Research on language-specific cognitive consequences of bilingualism shows that bilinguals may have a unique perspective of the world, dissimilar to that of monolinguals of either language.

> ➤ Recent neurological studies suggest that bilingualism may help fend off the decline of cognitive function in late adulthood, and delays the onset of aging and diseases such as dementia and Alzheimer's disease.

Suggested Further Reading

📖 Grojean, F., & Li, P. (2013). *The psycholinguistics of bilingualism*. Malden, MA: John Wiley & Sons.

📖 Kroll, J. F., & De Groot, A. M. (Eds.) (2005). *Handbook of bilingualism: Psycholinguistic approaches*. Oxford, UK: Oxford University Press.

📖 Paradis, M., (2004). *A neurolinguistic theory of bilingualism*. Philadelphia, PA: John Benjamins.

📖 Pavlenko, A. (Ed.) (2011). *Thinking and speaking in two languages*. Bristol, UK: Multilingual Matters.

📖 Pavelenko, A. (2014). *The bilingual mind and what it tells us about language and thought*. Cambridge, UK: Cambridge University Press.

On The Web

💻 François Grosjean's Bilingualism website
http://www.francoisgrosjean.ch/index.html

💻 Howard Gardner's Multiple Intelligence website
http://multipleintelligencesoasis.org/

💻 Ellen Bialystok's Lifespan Cognition and Development Laboratory website
http://lcad.lab.yorku.ca/research-projects/

💻 Max Planck Institute for Psycholinguistics
http://www.mpi.nl/

💻 Does learning language make kids smarter? (Video featuring Ellen Bialystok and Laura-Ann Petitto)
https://www.youtube.com/watch?v=UfNXtUFUbxE

💻 How bilingualism helps your brain (Video featuring Ellen Bialystok)
https://www.youtube.com/watch?v=6sDYx77hCmI

Discussion Questions

(1) Why is it difficult to measure intelligence in general, and for bilinguals in particular? As the majority of IQ tests include a verbal intelligence component, how can

we make sure that the test results are not confounded with bilinguals' language proficiency? Describe any experience you have had with IQ tests, and discuss ways to improve their validity.

(2) If you speak more than one language, compare your languages in terms of (a) the expressions of time, (b) grammatical gender, (c) emotional terms, and (d) other significant differences. Do these crosslinguistic differences affect your thinking when you switch from one language to another? Compare and discuss these cross-linguistic differences and their role in thinking.

(3) Reflect on your experience interacting with monolinguals and bilinguals, or observations of interactions between monolinguals and bilinguals. Do bilinguals appear to be more communicatively sensitive than monolingual, as the research suggests? If so, in what ways? If not, why do you think your experiences do not reflect the research results?

Study Activities

(1) Find one or more examples of an IQ test (e.g. Wechsler Adult Intelligence Scale for adults, Wechsler Intelligence Scale for Children, Woodcock-Johnson Tests of Cognitive Abilities). Examine the content of the test, and locate any items that you think may be unfair to bilinguals in your region. Examine both the language and the cultural content of the IQ test.

(2) Find a student or a teacher whom you consider to be bilingual. Ask them to talk about the relationship between their bilingualism and thinking. Ask them if they feel it gives them any advantages and any disadvantages. Collect from them examples and illustrations.

(3) Using one of the tests or experiments mentioned in this chapter, select a student (or a group of students) and give them that test. For example, ask them how many uses they can think of for a brick or for a cardboard box. Compare the answers of those who are more and less bilingual and see if there are differences in quality and quantity of answers.

Theories of Bilingualism and the Curriculum

CHAPTER 8

Theories of Bilingualism and the Curriculum

Introduction

This chapter considers the historical development of ideas about **bilingualism**, particularly about how languages may operate in the brain. These theories led to curriculum implications not only for teaching strategy and learning activities, but also for **assessment**. However, these theories have also led to misunderstandings about language and have contributed to the oversimplification of the complex nature of bilingualism and the multifaceted processes of second language learning. The chapter concludes with more recent theories and understandings of these issues and the ways that they are leading to newer instructional and assessment strategies.

The Balance Theory

The previous chapter noted that initial research into bilingualism and cognitive functioning often found bilinguals to be inferior to **monolinguals**. This connects with an outdated and naïve theory of bilingualism that represents the two languages as existing together in balance like on a balance scale; as proficiency in one language increases on one side of the scale, the proficiency of the language on the other side of the scale decreases. Since this 'balance' idea is still current among sections of the population and not least among some politicians, (e.g. in the US and UK), it is important to portray it, and its criticisms. A similar negative picture portrays the monolingual as having one well-filled balloon, while the bilingual is pictured as having two less filled or half filled balloons. As the second language balloon is pumped higher (e.g. English in the US), the first language balloon (e.g. Spanish) diminishes in size, leading to confusion, frustration and failure. These depictions falsely suggest the brain only has room for one fully developed language.

Cummins (1981) referred to this false view as the **Separate Underlying Proficiency** (**SUP**) model of bilingualism. The SUP model conceives of the two languages operating separately without transfer and with a restricted amount of 'room' for languages. As Bialystok (2001a) argues: 'nothing we know about memory substantiates these fears. Indeed, the fact that millions of children routinely grow up with more than one language in their environment and appear to suffer no obvious trauma should allay the concerns of most parents' (p. 59).

What appears logical is not always psychologically valid. While both the balance and balloon ideas seem plausible, neither fits the evidence. As the previous chapter indicated, there are cognitive advantages rather than disadvantages from being bilingual. Similarly, Chapters 11 and 12 will show that strong forms of bilingual education appear to result in performance advantages (e.g. in two languages and in general curriculum performance) compared with **submersion** in a monolingual education. Research has also suggested that it is wrong to assume that the brain has only a limited amount of room for **language skills** (see Chapters 5 and 7). There are substantial cerebral living quarters not only for two languages, but multiple languages as well.

There is another fallacy with the balance or balloon theory. The assumption of this theory is that the first and second language are kept apart inside the head. The evidence suggests the opposite – that language attributes are not separated in the cognitive system, but transfer readily and are interactive. For example, when school lessons are through the medium of Spanish, they do not solely feed a Spanish part of the brain. Or when other lessons are in English, they do not only feed the English part of the brain. Rather concepts learnt in one language can readily transfer into the other language. Teaching a child to multiply numbers in Spanish or use a dictionary in English easily transfers to multiplication or dictionary use in the other language. A child does not have to be re-taught to multiply numbers in English. A mathematical concept can be easily and immediately used in English or Spanish if those languages are sufficiently well developed.

Common Underlying Proficiency Model

To counter the Separate Underlying Proficiency Model, Cummins (1981) proposed the **Common Underlying Proficiency (CUP)** model of bilingualism. The CUP model can be pictorially represented in the form of two icebergs (see Figure 8.1). The two icebergs are separate above the surface. That is, two languages are visibly different in outward production. Underneath the surface, the two icebergs are fused so that the two languages do not function separately. Both languages operate through the same central processing system.

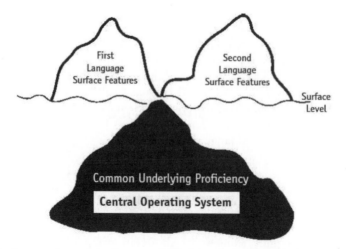

Figure 8.1 Iceberg analogy of the Common Underlying Proficiency (CUP) model of bilingualism

The CUP model may be summarized as follows:

(1) Irrespective of the language in which a person is operating, the thoughts that accompany talking, reading, writing and listening come from the same central engine. When a person owns two or more languages, there is one integrated source of thought.

(2) Bilingualism and **multilingualism** are possible because people have the capacity to store two or more languages. Many people function in two or more languages with ease.

(3) Information processing skills and educational attainment may be developed through two languages as well as through one language. Cognitive functioning and school achievement may be fed through one monolingual channel or equally successfully through two language channels. Both channels feed the same central processor.

(4) The language the child is using in the classroom needs to be sufficiently well developed to be able to process the cognitive challenges of the classroom.

(5) Speaking, listening, reading or writing in the first or the second language helps the whole cognitive system to develop. However, if children are made to operate in an insufficiently developed second language, the system will not function at its best. If children are made to operate in the classroom in a poorly developed second language, the quality and quantity of what they learn from complex curriculum materials and produce in oral and written form may be relatively weak.

While helpful, the distinction between the SUP and CUP models does not sum up the findings from research on cognitive functioning and bilingualism, nor does it reflect recent research on the brain and bilingualism (see Chapter 7). The continuing debate on the Sapir-Whorf hypothesis (e.g. that different languages intrinsically lead to different views of the world) may challenge the idea that bilinguals have one integrated source of thought (Pavlenko, 2014). Language influences both the content and process of thinking. Thus, varied languages can influence thought differently through their structure and particularly through their customary **discourse**, concepts and meanings. If this is so, second language learning may augment and enhance a person's understandings, views and ideas. It may offer alternative and extra meanings. The extent to which bilinguals change their thinking when changing languages is complex without a simple 'black or white' answer. Translation of meaning can occur across languages, yet some enduring relativity within a language seems also to occur. Thus, while the CUP model does not fully illustrate the complexities of the bilingual brain, it provides a more accurate picture than SUP.

The Thresholds Theory

Many studies have suggested that the further the child moves towards **balanced bilingualism**, the greater the likelihood of cognitive advantages (for a review see Chapter 7 and Bialystok *et al.*, 2012; Grosjean & Li, 2013; Li, 2013). These studies raised the question, 'Under what conditions does bilingualism have positive, neutral and negative effects on cognition?' How far does someone have to travel up the two language ladders to obtain cognitive advantages from bilingualism?

One theory that partially summarizes the relationship between cognition and degree of bilingualism is called the Thresholds Theory, first postulated in the mid-1970s by Cummins (1976) and Toukomaa and Skutnabb Kangas (1977). It became a powerful expression of the thinking advantages of bilingualism to counteract any 'balance' and 'balloon' ideas among public and students. They suggested that the research on cognition and bilingualism is best explained by the idea of two thresholds. Each threshold is a level of language competence that has consequences for a child. The first threshold is a level for a child to reach to avoid the negative consequences of bilingualism. The second threshold is a level required to experience the possible positive benefits of bilingualism. Thus, according to the theory, when a child has age-appropriate ability in both their languages, they may have cognitive advantages over monolinguals. Some research appears to support the Thresholds Theory (see Cummins, 2000b for a review).

The Thresholds Theory relates not only to cognition but also to education. With children in bilingual immersion education (see Chapters 11 and 12), there is usually a temporary lag in achievement when the curriculum is taught through the second language. Until the second language (e.g. French) has developed well enough to cope with curriculum material, a temporary delay may be expected. Once French has developed sufficiently to cope with the conceptual tasks of the classroom, Immersion Education is unlikely to have detrimental achievement consequences for children.

Proponents of the Thresholds Theory believed it helps explain why minority language children taught through a second language (e.g. immigrants in the US) sometimes fail to develop sufficient competency in their second language (e.g. English) and fail to benefit from 'weak' forms of bilingual education (see Chapter 10). Their low level of proficiency in English, for example, limits their ability to cope with the curriculum. Therefore, **dual language programs** that allow a child to operate in their more developed home language can result in superior performance compared with submersion and **transitional bilingual education** (see Chapter 10).

A problem with the Thresholds Theory is in precisely defining the level and nature of **language proficiency** a child must obtain in order, first to avoid the negative effects of bilingualism, and second, to obtain the positive advantages of bilingualism. What language skills need to be developed to what point so as to reach a higher threshold level? Indeed, the danger may be in constructing artificial 'critical stages' or levels, when transition is gradual and smooth. Furthermore, the thresholds theory is related to the discredited construct of semilingualism (see Chapter 1), and does not account for the dynamic nature of bilingualism. It also tends to suggest that language needs to be developed to a high level before high levels of cognition can be activated. It thus fails to understand the more complex, interactive nature of language and thinking (see Chapter 7).

The Evolution of the Thresholds Theory

From out of the Thresholds Theory Cummins developed a succession of more refined theories of bilingualism. The first considered the relationship between a bilingual's two languages. To this end, Cummins (2000a) outlined the linguistic Developmental Interdependence hypothesis. This hypothesis suggests that a child's second language competence is partly dependent on the level of competence already achieved in the first language. The more developed the first language, the easier it will be to develop the second language. Proctor's (2003) sophisticated analysis of Spanish/English 4th Grade data from Boston, Chicago and El Paso showed that students with well-developed Spanish and English vocabularies outperformed their less bilingual (e.g. Spanish dominant, English dominant) counterparts in English reading achievement. Such findings also appear to hold for learning a third language (Cenoz, 2003; Errasti, 2003).

Alongside this, a distinction developed between surface fluency and the more evolved language skills required to benefit from the education process (Cummins, 1984). Cummins (1979) found that everyday 'conversational language' could be acquired in two years while the more complex language abilities needed to cope with the curriculum could take five to seven or more years to develop. In California, Hakuta *et al.* (2000) found that English oral proficiency takes three to five years to develop, while English proficiency needed for academic success can take four to seven years. More recent studies in the US on the number of years it typically takes students classified as **English language learners (ELLs)** to attain sufficient proficiency in English to be redesignated as **fluent English proficient (FEP)** support earlier findings that it may take more than a few years (A. Burke *et al.*, 2016; Conger *et al.*, 2012; Umansky & Reardon, 2014). However, these studies also found that the length of time to **redesignation** as FEP can vary based on a range of factors including age of arrival, prior education and language learning experiences, ethnicity, socioeconomic status, program model, and quality of instruction. These consistent findings make it clear that calls for just one-year of English immersion schooling for immigrant children to acquire English are unrealistic and damaging.

Simple communication skills (e.g. a conversation with a friend) may hide a child's relative inadequacy in the language proficiency necessary to meet the academic demands of the classroom. The language used when playing with a ball on the school playground is very different from 'calculate, using a protractor, the obtuse angle of the parallelogram and then construct a diagonal line between the two obtuse angles and investigate if this creates congruent triangles'. Teaching mathematics, for example, in multilingual classrooms requires particular care with language (Barwell, 2009; Hansen-Thomas & Langman, 2017; Moschkovich, 2007). The mathematical use of words such as chord, column, figure, mean, odd, point, table, and value all differ from everyday usage. Mathematics problems are often word problems and not just about numbers. The **syntax** of mathematical discourse is often complex and very different from other content-area subjects (Wright, 2015).

In the late 1970s, Cummins (1979) first expressed this distinction between language use for simple conversations vs. more academic purposes as *basic interpersonal communicative skills* (BICS) and *cognitive academic language proficiency* (CALP). It was typically explained to teachers and others that BICS refers to highly contextualized conversational skills, such as the language children spoke out on the playground ('playground language'). In contrast, as teachers were told, CALP refers to language use in context-reduced academic subjects of the classroom, including reading and writing ('classroom language' or 'academic language').

The BICS/CALP distinction has been historically highly influential in guiding policy, programs and instruction for bilingual students for over three decades. It has helped teachers develop some sensitivity about students' language proficiency and the need to provide linguistic support. The distinction also helped educators recognize why bilingual students who 'sounded' proficient in English nonetheless struggled with the literacy and academic demands of English language instruction in mainstream classrooms.

However, the BICS/CALP distinction has been criticized by other scholars as an oversimplification of the complex and dynamic nature of second language learning (Valdés *et al.*, 2015). Thus before leaving this BICS/CALP distinction, it is important to declare some of its boundaries and limitations as outlined by it critics (see, e.g. MacSwan & Rolstad, 2003; Martin-Jones & Romaine, 1986; Valdés *et al.*, 2015; Wiley, 2005) and as clarified by Cummins in its defense (see, e.g. Cummins, 2017a):

(1) The BICS/CALP distinction may be intuitive, however, a bilingual's language competences are evolving, dynamic, interacting and intricate. They are not simple dichotomies, easily compartmentalized and static (see Chapter 1).
(2) The relationship between language development and cognitive development is not unequivocal or simple. It is not simply a case of one growing as a direct result of the other. Cognitive and linguistic acquisition exist in a relationship that is influenced by various other factors (e.g. politics, power relationships, social practices, **culture**, **context**, motivation, school, home and community effects). Language proficiency relates to an individual's total environment, not just to cognitive skills.
(3) The assumed sequential nature was BICS first followed by CALP. However, the order is not absolute. For example, older newcomer students who studied English as a foreign language in their home country often could read and write well in English but initially struggled with oral communication skills. This challenges the underlying theoretical underpinnings of the distinction.
(4) Oral language and interpersonal communication are not necessarily less cognitively demanding than so called 'academic language'. Careful logic, metaphor and other abstract aspects of language occur in face-to-face communication and not just in written language. Consider, for example, the cognitive differences (if any) between having an oral discussion about the results of a science experiment and writing a journal entry about the favorite part of a story read. Also consider the number of 'higher-order thinking processes' typically associated with CALP that students may use out on the playground as they organize a soccer match (e.g. analyzing, synthesizing, comparing, evaluating, etc.).
(5) School-based 'academic language' does not represent universal higher-order cognitive skills nor all forms of literacy practice. Different sociocultural contexts have different expectations and perceived patterns of appropriateness in language and thinking such that a school is only one specific context for 'higher order' language production.

To elaborate the distinction, Cummins (1981) proposed a model of two intersecting continua – context and cognitive demand – forming four quadrants, as shown in Figure 8.2.

Context refers to the amount of contextual support available to a student (e.g. body language, gestures, pointing, visual support, intonation, facial expressions, etc.). In context reduced communication there will be fewer cues to the meaning that is being transmitted. The cognitive continuum refers to the level of the cognitive demand required in the communication. Cognitively demanding communication may occur in a classroom where much information at a challenging level needs processing quickly. Cognitively undemanding communication is where a person has the language skills sufficient to enable easy communication.

Different types of communicative and academic activities or tasks would be located in different quadrants depending on the level of context and cognitive demand. For example, playing catch with a friend out on the playground would be in the 1st quadrant given it is highly contextualized but of low cognitive demand. Talking on the telephone with a friend could be in the 2nd quadrant – only hearing the voice reduces

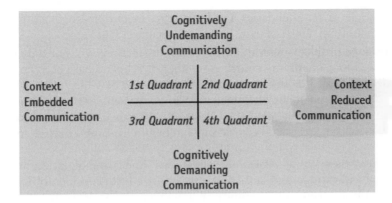

Figure 8.2 Cummins' four quadrants

the context, but the topic of the conversation may not be cognitively demanding. A task such as using math manipulatives to demonstrate fractions could be located in the 3rd quadrant given that the task is cognitively demanding, but the visual and tactile support of the manipulatives provide context. But then a task such as taking a test on fractions would be in the 4th quadrant; the cognitive demand remains, but the context has been reduced to words and numbers on the printed page.

Curriculum Relevance

Many teachers found the four quadrants (see Figure 8.2) to be a helpful tool in 'creating instructional and learning environments that maximize the language and literacy development of socially marginalized students' (Cummins, 2017a: 81). A teacher takes into account students' linguistic development and experience, as well as their background knowledge and understanding of the topic. Then the teacher can create activities or experiences that are cognitively challenging and contextually supported as needed. Thus, teachers aimed to provide the types of instruction and learning experiences in the 3rd quadrant that would ultimately help students to accomplish the types of activities that take place in the 4th quadrant. In other words, the four quadrants helped teachers consider the linguistic and cognitive demand of various classroom tasks and learning experiences and the kinds of **scaffolding** that would be needed to help students successfully participate and complete these tasks.

In practice, however, placement of instructional activities within the four quadrants was problematic and never straightforward. The idea of 'context embedded/reduced' is misleading, because everything a student does at school is embedded in some sort of context – the context of the school, of the classroom, of the unit or lesson, of what was taught/practiced the day before, of the particular activity or task at hand, etc. Even the written math test is embedded in the context of the classroom, of a math test, and of prior instruction, while illustrations, known words, known numbers, and known symbols on the printed page, provide 'context cues' that can help students determine the meaning. Thus, there is always a context. Also, what is cognitively demanding and the amount of scaffolding needed can vary widely from student to student, and can vary depending on the topic or nature of the learning activity.

Criticisms

The original problems with the BICS/CALP distinction were not fully resolved in the elaborated four quadrants model. A number of scholars have been critical of the work (Edelsky, 2006; Edelsky *et al.*, 1983; Frederickson & Cline, 2015; MacSwan & Rolstad, 2003; Martin-Jones & Romaine, 1986; C. Rivera, 1984; Valdés *et al.*, 2015; Wiley, 2005; Wiley & Rolstad, 2014). Detailed rebuttals can be found in Cummins (2000a, 2000b, 2003, 2017a). The criticisms can be briefly summarized as follows:

(1) The early theory was essentially individual and psychological. Bilingualism, bilingual education, and academic success need to consider other variables: social, cultural, economic, political, community, teacher expectations and home factors. Each and all of these variables help explain bilingualism as an individual and societal phenomenon. Cummins (2000a, 2017a) has addressed these issues in further theoretical formulations.
(2) The criterion of educational success tended to center on dominant, middle-class indices of achievement. Alternative outcomes of schooling such as self-esteem, social and emotional development, divergent and creative thinking, long-term attitude to learning, employment and moral development were not initially considered.
(3) The dichotomy between de-contextualized and contextualized communication is misleading as all communication appears in some kind of context. Thus, in practice it is difficult if not impossible to separate the 'cognitive' from the 'contextual,' given that all teaching and learning takes place within some kind of context.
(4) The theory needs to sit alongside an individual child's cognitive strategies and style in learning.
(5) Finally, as the previous chapter has considered, there is a new wave of research on bilinguals' brains and developing research on bilingualism and cognition. This will in turn be related to the curriculum with implications for teaching and learning by bilinguals. For example, such research points to the value of bilingualism from an early age, suggesting that bilingual education should begin earlier rather than later.

However, credit must be given to Jim Cummins, whose ideas and theories have helped guide bilingual education policies and programs, and have helped ESL, bilingual, and other classroom teachers pay closer attention to students' language proficiency and to think about ways to modify and scaffold their instruction.

New Understandings and Directions

After 30 years of influence on research and practice in the education field, researchers and educators are beginning to move away from oversimplified and problematic concepts and constructs such as thresholds, BICS/CALP, and the four quadrants model, and on to more sophisticated ways of viewing the dynamic nature of bilingualism and the language development of bilingual students. Issues, however, remain. For example, while the term 'CALP' may be used less frequently, the construct lives on as many educators, policymakers and researchers now focus on 'academic language' or 'academic English' as if there really is a singular type of English proficiency that is a pre-requisite for academic success in all content areas. The problematic construct of 'academic language' is even moving outside the realm of **language minority** education and into the realm of language majority education and even teacher education. For example, in the US the Common Core State Standards have established language standards designed to ensure all students learn and use 'academic language' (Wiley & Rolstad, 2014). Teacher certification in the US through EdTPA assessments require all teacher candidates to both use and demonstrate their ability to teach 'academic language'. As the term has moved into the mainstream, some scholars are declaring, 'there are no native speakers of academic language', suggesting that even native English speakers must learn 'academic English' to be successful in school (Filmore, 2013). Despite its broadening and widespread usage, there is no clear and agreed-upon definition of what exactly 'academic language' is (Valdés *et al.*, 2015). Wiley and Rolstad (2014) reject the idea that 'the ability to use academic English is a prerequisite for understanding academic content' (p. 51). They argue:

> One sees the persistence of the idea that language itself is the gateway to greater cognitive development, and that the language of the literate somehow contributes special qualities which permit access and insight into academic disciplines which other forms of language do not allow. … Proficiency in academic language cannot be associated with universal cognitive thresholds; rather, literacy and academic success is associated with one's ability to accept the norms, practices, and expectations of school. It is simply not the case that literacy and academic language involve higher order cognition, while other domains in which we use specialized language do not. (p. 51)

Wiley and Rolstad (2014) emphasize that instead, the focus must be to 'engage students in interesting, challenging work which can then lead to the expansion of students' linguistic repertoires and their development of literacy, rather than the other way around' (p. 51). MacSwan and Rolstad (2003) introduced the term second language instructional competence (SLIC), suggesting that the amount of SLIC needed to complete an academic task depends on the linguistic demand of that task. Thus, for example, an academic task such as discussing and giving examples of the five senses would have a lower linguistic demand than the academic task of reading a science text about how the five senses are interrelated and then writing a summary.

The English language proficiency standards established by Teachers of English to Speakers of Other Languages (TESOL, 2006) moved away from the idea that conversational language is non-academic and reserved for the playground and that all language use in the classroom is academic. Furthermore, the TESOL standards moved away from the idea of a singular type of English language proficiency (e.g. CALP) that students either have or don't, that they must possess to achieve academically. Rather, the TESOL standards recognized that students communicate for social, intercultural, and instructional purposes in a variety of contexts within the school setting. In addition, the TESOL Standards recognize that language use to 'communicate information, ideas, and concepts' is different across various content areas. Thus, TESOL has separate standards for the language of (a) language arts, (b) mathematics, (c) science, and (d) social studies.

In the US, the majority of states have joined the WIDA Consortium (2012) to share common English language proficiency standards, which are nearly identical to the TESOL standards. A smaller group of states have joined the English Language Proficiency Assessment for the 21st Century (ELPA21) Consortium. Rather than taking a deficit view of what students *can't do* because of limited skills in English, the WIDA and ELPA21 standards focus on describing what students *can do* at each level of English proficiency. Through 'Model Performance Indicators' or 'Achievement Level Indicators' teachers are given specific examples of academic tasks that students are capable of accomplishing across five levels of English language proficiency, with proper scaffolding and support. Thus, the standards show that even beginning-level students are capable of 'academic' work. More importantly, teachers learn how to write their own performance indicators by thinking about the linguistic demands of a particular academic task (e.g. describe the life cycle of a plant), determining what might be reasonable to expect of students at each level of English proficiency, and identify the scaffolding and support that students would need to meet these expectations.

As an example, Figure 8.3 shows the performance indicators in connection with a high school English language arts lesson in the domain of reading focused on the topic of cause and effect relationships. The particular context for language use in this lesson is students read (as a group, with a partner, independently, or read-aloud to them) a short contract, and then analyze the text to identify the cause-and-effect relationships.

COGNITIVE FUNCTION: Students at all levels of English proficiency ANALYZE cause-and-effect relationships in informational texts

DOMAIN: Reading	Level 1 Entering	Level 2 Emerging	Level 3 Developing	Level 4 Expanding	Level 5 Bridging	Level 6 – Reaching
	Match illustrated cause-and-effect cards on a graphic-organizer template in a small group.	Match cause-and-effect cards on a graphic-organizer template with a partner.	Complete a cause-and-effect graphic organizer using a highlighted version of the text with a partner.	Highlight cause-and-effect statements in the text and complete a cause-and-effect graphic organizer with a partner.	Highlight cause-and-effect statements in the text and complete a cause-and-effect graphic organizer.	

Figure 8.3 Example of Model Performance Indicators used in conjunction with WIDA ELP standards

Note that the task and expectations are modified based on students' English language proficiency. Note also the types of scaffolding and support provided students such as illustrated cause-and-effect cards, graphic organizers, highlighted versions of the text, and opportunities to work in small groups or with a partner. Observe how the level of scaffolding decreases as the difficulty – and language demand – of the task increases at each level of proficiency. Nonetheless, as indicated in the 'Cognitive Function' section, all students are engaged in the academic tasks of analyzing cause-and-effect relationships.

Along with this new direction is a growing recognition that students can do highly 'academic' work in 'less than perfect English', including through **translanguaging** (O. García & Li Wei, 2015; Sayer, 2013). In a study of a middle school social studies classroom made up of linguistically diverse students, Bunch (2014) made an important observation as he focused on how students drew on a wide range of their linguistic resources as they engaged in academic tasks. As students worked in small groups to discuss and generate their ideas, their English was less than perfect, and would fall into what teachers typically call 'conversational' or 'informal' language. However, as students prepared their presentation materials and presented their work to the class, their language use was more formal. Bunch calls this difference the *language of ideas* versus *the language of display*. He also found that the students were aware of the different **registers** and made strategic use of them for different purposes and audiences.

These new standards and ways of understanding students' language development and ability to use their emerging English proficiency to engage in academic work have moved the field forward in a new and positive direction. Rather than taking a deficit view of what an individual student *can't do* because 'he only has BICS,' the focus now shifts to 'What are the linguistic demands of this academic task, and what modifications and types of scaffolding would be needed to help students at different levels of English proficiency accomplish this task'? The performance indicators also form the basis for effective classroom assessments, providing teachers with a clear road map of where a student is at and what types of instruction can push them up to the 'next level' of English proficiency.

However, these standards are nonetheless limited. Note that they only focus on the English language development of an **emergent bilingual** student. Also, they create the impression that language development is linear as student progress up through neatly defined stages. The WIDA Consortium has also developed Spanish language proficiency standards and tools to guide practice and assessment in bilingual classrooms. This is certainly very important, and as indicated above, space has opened up for translanguaging as students draw upon all of their linguistic resources. However, the existence of separate English and Spanish standards (and the absence of similar standards for other languages) demonstrates we still need models to better understand bilingual development. One recent development in this area is the state of New York's Bilingual Common Core Initiative (EngageNY, 2014). Rather than ESL standards and Spanish language arts standards, the initiative features New Language Arts progressions and Home Language Arts Progressions (applicable to different home languages). These progressions show how emergent bilinguals can access academic content at five levels of language proficiency in both their home and new languages. These progressions emphasize the dynamic nature of bilingualism, and the use of multiple languages and translanguaging practices to teach and access academic content. Another recent development is Literacy Squared – a model that emphasizes the simultaneous development of literacy in two languages (Escamilla *et al.*, 2013). It also provides tools for planning and observing bilingual instruction and for evaluating the writing development of emergent bilinguals across their two languages (see Chapter 14).

Conclusion

Early and now discredited ideas of two languages within an individual are represented by two pictures. First, two languages as a balance; second, two languages operating as two separate balloons in the head. Such misconceptions can be replaced by pictures such as the dual iceberg illustrating a common underlying proficiency with easy transfer of concepts and knowledge between languages. Early theories made a distinction between basic interpersonal communication skills (BICS) and cognitive academic language proficiency (CALP), later elaborated into four quadrants emphasizing levels of context and cognitive demand. These early theories guided much policy and practice for bilingual students and drew attention to the needs to consider students' language proficiency and provide appropriate scaffolding. Other scholars were highly critical of these theories arguing they were oversimplified and misleading. New understandings of language, the dynamic nature of bilingualism, and language learning are moving the field towards standards and practices that recognize external factors that impact students' language learning. The focus is now on what students *can do* – even at beginning levels of English proficiency – to engage in academic tasks. We now recognize that language use varies across different content-areas, and recognize that students have a wide range of linguistic resources upon which to draw to engage in academic work. New curricular and pedagogical models are developing that better reflect these newer understandings.

Key Points in This Chapter

➤ The concept of the two languages acting like a balance in the brains of a bilingual is incorrect.

➤ The Common Underlying Proficiency model suggests that languages operate from the same central operating system.

➤ On average, English oral proficiency takes three to five years to develop, while English proficiency needed for academic success can take four to seven years. A variety of factors impact the amount of time it takes for students to reach 'fluency' in English.

➤ The Thresholds Theory suggested that bilinguals who have age-appropriate competence in both languages share cognitive advantages over monolinguals.

➤ Early theories made a distinction between everyday context-embedded conversational language and decontextualized academic language, and argued that cognitive academic language proficiency is a prerequisite for academic success in school.

➤ These early theories have been highly criticized by a number of scholars as misleading and an oversimplification of the nature of language, the dynamic nature of bilingualism, and language learning. Nonetheless, they continue to be influential.

➤ Newer understandings of language emphasize that there is no singular 'academic language' that students must attain in order to achieve academic success.

➤ English language proficiency standards now recognize that students use language for social, intercultural and academic purposes in school settings, and that the language use differs across various content areas.

➤ With proper scaffolding and support, there is much that students *can do* at each level of English proficiency to engage in academic tasks.

➤ Students are aware of different registers and make strategic use of their linguistic repertoires as they engage in the language of ideas and the language display.

Suggested Further Reading

📖 Bunch, G. C. (2014). The language of ideas and the language of display: Reconceptualizing 'academic language' in linguistically diverse classrooms. *International Multilingual Research Journal, 8*, 70–86.

📖 Cummins, J. (2008). BICS and CALP: Empirical and theoretical status of the distinction. In B. Street & N. H. Hornberger (Eds.), *Encyclopedia of language and education* (Vol. 2: Literacy, pp. 71–83). New York: Springer Science + Business Media LLC.

📖 Wiley, T. G., & Rolstad, K. (2014). The Common Core State Standards and the great divide. *International Multilingual Research Journal, 8*(1), 35. doi:10.1080/19313152.2014.852428

📖 MacSwan, J., & Rolstad, K. (2003). Linguistic diversity, schooling, and social class: Rethinking our conception of language proficiency in language minority education. In C. B. Paulston & R. Tucker (Eds.), *Sociolinguistics: Essential reading* (pp. 329–341). Oxford, England: Blackwell.

📖 Valdés, G., Poza, L., & Brooks, M. D. (2015). Language acquisition in bilingual education. In W. E. Wright, S. Boun, & O. García (Eds.), *Handbook of bilingual and multilingual education* (pp. 56–74). Malden, MA: Wiley-Blackwell.

On the Web

💻 New York State Bilingual Common Core Initiative
https://www.engageny.org/resource/new-york-state-bilingual-common-core-initiative

💻 TESOL PreK-12 English Language Proficiency Standards
https://www.tesol.org/advance-the-field/standards/prek-12-english-language-proficiency-standards

💻 WIDA Spanish Language Development Standards
https://www.wida.us/standards/sld.aspx

💻 English Proficiency Assessment for the 21st Century (ELPA21)
www.elpa21.org

Discussion Questions

(1) Why do you think the balance and balloon picture theories of bilingualism and cognition were held so intuitively by many people? Discuss how these theories, along with the contrasting dual iceberg theory, compare with the findings of cognitive research about bilingualism and the brain as presented in Chapter 7.

(2) Why is the construct of 'academic language' problematic? In what ways have you seen students use less than perfect English to accomplish academic tasks?

(3) Some have argued that teachers only need simple theories of language such as the BICS/CALP distinction and the four quadrants model, because sophisticated and competing language, bilingualism, and language learning theories are too complex to inform practice. How does such an argument view teachers? And how are newer understandings of language, bilingualism, and language learning moving the field forward with more effective instructional practices?

Study Activities

(1) Observe a classroom with bilingual children. Make a 10-minute audio recording of the discourse between the teacher and various students, and/or between students themselves. Use the concepts and ideas of this chapter to describe and discuss the language used.

(2) Download and review some of the *Can Do Descriptors* from the WIDA website (https://www.wida.us/standards/CAN_DOs/). Describe how these descriptors provide evidence that students do not need so called 'academic language' as a prerequisite to effectively engage in academic tasks.

(3) Choose a grade-level academic task that would want students to complete as part of lesson plan. Using Figure 8.3 as a guide, create your own model performance indicators for each level of English proficiency, including the scaffolds or supports students would need to complete the task.

Historical Introduction to Bilingual Education: The United States

CHAPTER 9

Historical Introduction to Bilingual Education: The United States

Introduction

One of the illusions about bilingual education is that it is a recent phenomenon. The 20th century saw bilingual education blossom in publications and practice. The first books on bilingual education were by Sissons (1917) on Canada and Aucamp (1926) on South Africa. In the US it may appear that bilingual education was born in the 1960s. The US dual language school approach is dated from 1963 (see Chapter 11). The Canadian bilingual education movement is often charted from an experimental kindergarten class set up in St Lambert, Montréal, in 1965. Earlier than that, bilingual education in Ireland is sometimes presented as a child of the Irish Free State of 1922. The story of bilingual education in Wales often starts in 1939 with the establishment of the first Welsh-medium elementary school. Coyle (2007) suggests that bilingual education was established in Europe in the 19th century, for example in Luxembourg in 1843 with **trilingual education** in 1913. But bilingual education started well before the 20th century.

The illusion of bilingual education as a modern phenomenon is dangerous on two counts. First, it fails to recognize that bilingual education has existed in one form or another for 5,000 years or more (Mackey, 1978; Ostler, 2005). **Bilingualism** and **multilingualism** are 'a very early characteristic of human societies, and monolingualism a limitation induced by some forms of social change, cultural and ethnocentric developments' (E.G. Lewis, 1977: 22). Second, there is a danger in isolating current bilingual education from its historical roots. In many countries (e.g. the US, Canada, England and Sweden), bilingual education must be linked to the historical **context** of immigration as well as political movements such as civil rights, equality of educational opportunity, affirmative action and melting pot (integrationist, **assimilationist**) policies.

Bilingual education relates to debates about the fundamental purposes and aims of education in general: for individuals, communities, regions and nations. Bilingual education, while isolated as a concept in this chapter, is one component inside a wider social, economic, educational, cultural and political framework. The political context of bilingual education is considered in Chapters 17 and 18. The history of bilingual education in the United States is now considered, with a particular emphasis on the dynamic and ever developing nature of bilingual education policy.

A Short History of Bilingual Education in the United States

In the United States, bilingual education has been determined partly by federal government, partly by state government, partly by litigation, partly by local initiatives, and partly by individuals (e.g. **Proposition 227** in California – see below). There has been neither total centralization nor full devolution to states in bilingual education. While states engage in much planning and policy-making, the federal government has exerted a powerful influence through funding, legislation and law. Bilingual education in the United States has moved through constant changes in the perspectives of politicians, administrators and educationalists that indicate underlying shifts in **ideology**, preference and practice

Pre 20th Century

Long before European immigrants arrived in the United States, the land contained many native (indigenous) languages. When the Italian, German, Dutch, French, Polish, Czech, Irish, Welsh and other immigrant groups arrived, there were already more than 300 separate (Native Indian) languages in the United States. The indigenous languages were not immediately colonized. Often led by Jesuits and Franciscans, the Catholic Church sometimes taught through Spanish (also French and English) but often through a native language. Other missionaries (e.g. Dutch Reform, German Moravian) also instrumentally used indigenous languages to secure conversion to Christianity and for teaching (McCarty, 2004).

Immigrants brought with them a wide variety of languages and initially there was linguistic tolerance (McCarty, 2004). In the 18th and 19th centuries in the United States, up until World War I, linguistic diversity was often accepted and the presence of different languages was frequently encouraged through religion, newspapers in different languages, and in both private and public schools.

There were exceptions to the acceptance of language diversity in this early period, such as Benjamin Franklin's anti-German stance in the 1750s, the Californian legislature mandating English-only instruction in 1855 and the ruthless language suppression policies of the Bureau of Indian Affairs in the 1880s (Crawford, 2004). The concepts of 'bilingualism' and 'language minorities' were not part of a major national consciousness about language in the 18th and 19th centuries. A high profile and much-debated US language policy has not been present until recent years.

However, there were early, pioneering public and private examples of bilingual education in the United States as in the German-English schools in the mid 19th century (Wiley, 1998). Set up by German communities in Ohio, Pennsylvania, Missouri, Minnesota, North and South Dakota, Wisconsin and Texas, bilingual as well as **monolingual** German education was accepted. This was not just a 19th century phenomenon as German-speaking Americans started schools using their **mother tongue** as early as 1694 in Philadelphia (Crawford, 2004). Also, Dutch, Danish, Norwegian, Swedish, Hungarian, Italian, Polish, Spanish, French, Russian and Czech were among the languages of instruction within ethnic-based and other schools in the 1800s or early 1900s (Kloss, 1998).

This openness to immigrant languages in the latter half of the 19th century was partly motivated by competition for students between public and private schools.

Other factors such as benevolent (or uninterested) school administrators, the isolation of schools in rural areas, and ethnic homogeneity within an area also enabled a permissive attitude to mother tongue and bilingual education before World War I.

In most large cities in the latter half of the 19th century, English monolingual education was the dominant pattern. However, in cities such as Cincinnati, Baltimore, Denver and San Francisco, **dual language bilingual education** was present. In some schools in Cincinnati, for example, half the day was spent learning through German and in the other half the curriculum was delivered through English.

Earlier 20th Century

At the turn of the 20th century, Italian and Jewish immigrants were mostly placed in English medium mainstream schools. However, examples of bilingual education existed and were permitted. For example, some Polish immigrants in Chicago attended Catholic schools where a small amount of teaching was through the mother tongue. So long as policy was within the jurisdiction of local towns and districts, the language of instruction did not become an issue in educational provision.

In the first two decades of the 20th century, a change in attitude to bilingualism and bilingual education occurred in the United States. A variety of factors are linked to this change and a subsequent restriction of bilingual education.

- The number of immigrants increased dramatically around the turn of the 20th century. Classrooms in many public schools were filled with immigrants. This gave rise to fear of new foreigners, and a call for the integration, harmonization and **assimilation** of immigrants. Immigrants' lack of English language and English literacy was a source of social, political and economic concern. A demand for Americanization was made, with competence in English becoming associated with loyalty to the United States. The Nationality Act (1906) required immigrants to speak English to become naturalized Americans. The call for child literacy in English rather than child labor, socialization into a unified America rather than ethnic separation, along with increased centralized control, led to a belief in a common language for compulsory schooling.
- In 1919, the Americanization Department of the United States Bureau of Education adopted a resolution recommending all private and public schools in each state be conducted in the English language. By 1923, 34 states had decreed that English must be the sole language of instruction in all elementary schools, public and private.
- A major influence on bilingual education in the United States came with the entry of the United States into World War I in 1917. Anti-German feelings in the United States spread, with a consequent extra pressure for English monolingualism and a melting pot policy achieved through monolingual education (Wiley, 1998). The German language was portrayed as a threat to the unity of Americanization. Linguistic diversity was replaced by linguistic intolerance. Schools became the tool for the socialization, assimilation and integration of diverse languages and **cultures**. Becoming an American meant the elimination of languages and cultures other than English from schools. An interest in learning foreign languages declined.

This period was not totally restrictive (Wiley, 2013a). In 1923, the US Supreme Court declared that a Nebraska state law prohibiting the teaching of foreign languages to children in private language classes was unconstitutional under the Fourteenth

Amendment. This case, known as *Meyer v. Nebraska* concerned a case against a teacher at a private elementary school for teaching a Bible story in German to 10-year-old children outside of regular school hours. The original Nebraska ruling was that such mother-tongue teaching cultivated ideas and attachments that were foreign to the best interests of the country. The Supreme Court, in overturning the Nebraska ruling, found that proficiency in a foreign language was 'not injurious to the health, morals, or understanding of the ordinary child'. A similar case, *Farrington v. Tokushige,* reached the US Supreme Court a few years later in 1927, wherein the court ruled that attempts by Hawai'ian education authorities to put restrictions on after-school community-based Japanese and Chinese **heritage language** programs was unconstitutional (Del Valle, 2003).

These Supreme Court findings did not, in essence, support bilingualism or bilingual education. Rather, the court upheld the right of state governments to dictate the language of instruction in schools, but declared that states cannot prevent private language instruction outside of the regular school system. The Court observed that the desire of a state legislature to foster a homogeneous people was 'easy to appreciate'.

Later 20th Century

In 1957, the Russians launched their Sputnik satellite into space. For US politicians and the public, a period of soul-searching led to debates about the quality of education, scientific creativity and competence to compete in an increasingly international world. Doubts arose about the hitherto over-riding concern with English as the melting-pot language, and a new consciousness was aroused about the need for foreign language instruction. In 1958, the National Defense Education Act was passed, promoting foreign language learning in elementary schools, high schools and universities. This, in turn, helped to create a slightly more soul-searching attitude to languages other than English spoken among ethnic groups in the US.

In the US in the 1960s, various other factors allowed a few opportunities to bring back bilingual education, albeit in a disparate, semi-isolated manner. This needs to be understood in the wider perspective of the Civil Rights movement, the struggle for the rights of African-Americans, and the call to establish general equality of opportunity (and equality of educational opportunity) for all people, irrespective of race, color or creed. The 1964 Civil Rights Act prohibited discrimination on the basis of color, race or national origin, and led to the establishment of the Office of Civil Rights. This Act symbolized a less negative attitude to ethnic groups, and possibilities for increased tolerance of ethnic languages, at least at the Federal level.

The restoration of bilingual education in the US in the second half of the 20th century is often regarded as starting in 1963, in one school in Florida. In 1963, Cuban exiles established the first modern dual language school (Coral Way Elementary School) in Dade County in South Florida. Believing they were only in exile for a short period, the educated, middle-class Cubans set up this Spanish-English bilingual school. The need to maintain their mother tongue of Spanish was aided by (a) highly trained professional teachers being ready to work in such schools, (b) the Cubans' plight as victims of a harsh Communist state, and (c) their expected temporary stay in the United States. Their unquestioned loyalty to United States' policies and democratic politics gained sympathy for the Cubans. Bilingual education in Dade County received both political support and funding. While Coral Way gained the most attention, there were a few other bilingual programs in the US during this same period. In the mid-1960s the National Education Association (1966) held a meeting and issued a subsequent report on the dire educational needs of Mexican-American students, and called for legislation supporting bilingual education. To make their case, the NEA conducted a survey documenting innovative school programs making use of Spanish in Texas (El Paso and Laredo), New Mexico (Albuquerque and Pecos), California (Merced), Colorado (Pueblo), and Arizona (Tucson). While the re-establishment of bilingual schools in the US has benefited from the example and success of Coral Way and other schools, an understanding of bilingual education in the United States requires a grasp of legislation and lawsuits.

Legislation and Lawsuits

In 1967, one year after the NEA report, Texas Senator Ralph Yarborough introduced a **Bilingual Education Act** as an amendment of the 1965 Elementary and Secondary Education Act (ESEA). The legislation was originally conceptualized to help mother tongue Spanish speakers who were seen as failing in the school system, but ultimately was expanded to include all students for whom English was not their native language. Enacted in 1968 as Title VII of the ESEA, the Bilingual Education Act (BEA) indicated that bilingual education programs were to be seen as part of federal educational policy (Wiese & Garcia, 2001). It authorized the use of federal funds for the education of speakers of languages other than English. It also undermined the English-only legislation still lawful in many states. The 1968 BEA allocated funds for such minority language speakers while they shifted to working through English in the classroom. Since 1968, the BEA was re-authorized as part of the ESEA in 1974, 1978, 1984, 1988 and 1994 (see San Miguel, 2004 for details).

A landmark in US bilingual education was the *Lau v. Nichols* lawsuit. A court case was brought on behalf of Chinese students against the San Francisco School District in 1970. The case concerned whether or not non-English speaking students received equal educational opportunities when instructed in a language they could not understand (Wiley, 2013a). The failure to provide a program that adequately addressed the students' linguistic needs was alleged to violate both the equal protection clause of the 14th Amendment and Title VI of the Civil Rights Act of 1964. The case was rejected by the federal district court and a court of appeals, but was accepted by the Supreme Court in 1974. The verdict outlawed English mainstreaming (often called '**submersion**') programs for students who are not yet proficient in English. The Supreme Court ruled that 'There is no equality of treatment merely by providing students with the same facilities, textbooks, teachers and curriculum; for students who do not understand English are effectively foreclosed from any meaningful education.'

Following the ruling, the Office of Civil Rights issued a set of guidelines for school districts called the Lau Remedies. These remedies acknowledged that students not proficient in English need help. Such remedies included classes in **English as a Second Language**, English tutoring and some form of bilingual education. The Lau remedies created some expansion in the use of minority languages in schools. However, the accent nationally was still on a temporary, transitional use of the home language for **English language learners**.

The Lau case is symbolic of the dynamic and continuing contest to establish language rights in the US particularly through testing the law in the courtroom. However, the kind of bilingual education needed to achieve equality of educational opportunity for **language minority** children was not defined. Although the right to equal opportunity for language minorities was asserted, the means of achieving that right was not declared. Nevertheless, during this era, there was a modest growth in developmental maintenance bilingual education and ethnic community mother tongue schools (Fishman, 2006).

From the 1980s, there were moves against an emergence of a strong version of bilingual education in the US, particularly found in the rise of pressure groups such as English First and US English that sought to establish English monolingualism and cultural assimilation (consideration of such political movements is found in Chapter 18). In recent decades in the US, bilingual education has become contentious, as will now be illustrated by examining recent legislative changes.

Title VII Bilingual Education Act

We return to the 1968 Title VII Bilingual Education Act. This provided a compensatory 'poverty program' for the educationally disadvantaged among language minorities. The original version lacked a definition of bilingual education and did not necessarily require schools to use a child's home language other than English. However, it did allow a few educators to bring 'home languages' into the classroom rather than exclude them. In the 1974 reauthorization of the ESEA Title VII provided clearer definitions of bilingual education and required schools receiving grants to include teaching in a student's home language so as to allow the child to progress effectively through the educational system (Wiese & Garcia, 2001). Effective progress in student achievement could occur via the home language or via English. However, this gave rise to fierce debates about how much a student's native language should be used in school. Some argued that it was essential to develop a child's speaking and literacy skills in their native language before English was introduced in a major way. Others argued that educational equality of opportunity could best be realized by teaching English as early as possible and assimilating language minority children into mainstream culture. The 1974 reauthorization stressed **transitional bilingual education** over maintenance bilingual education programs, and did not allow **dual language programs**.

In 1978, the US Congress again reauthorized the ESEA. The 1978 version lifted the restrictions on dual language programs under Title VII, but the political climate still favored transitional bilingual education in which the native language was to be used only to the extent necessary for a child to achieve competence in the English language. The 1984 and 1988 reauthorizations of ESEA allowed support for more developmental and maintenance program models under Title VII, but also increasing percentages of Title VII funds were made available specifically for programs where a student's first language was not used (Wiese & Garcia, 2001).

The Reagan administration was generally hostile to bilingual education. In the *New York Times* on March 3, 1981, President Reagan is quoted as saying that 'It is absolutely wrong and against the American concept to have a bilingual education program that is now openly, admittedly, dedicated to preserving their native language and never getting them adequate in English so they can go out into the job market'. Reagan believed that preservation of the native language meant neglect of English language acquisition. Bilingual education programs were seen as serving to neglect English **language competence** in students. Reagan dismissed bilingual education in favor of mainstreaming/submersion and transitional programs.

The Lau remedies were weakened by the Reagan administration and no longer had the force of law. The federal government left local politicians to create their own policies. Further changes in the rights to bilingual education in the US are given in Table 9.1 (p. 188). This reveals that legislation and litigation mostly led to 'weak' forms of bilingual education (e.g. transitional bilingual education). During the Reagan and George H.W. Bush Presidencies in the United States, the accent was more on mainstreaming/submersion and transitional bilingual education. The right to early education through a minority language failed to blossom in those years (Crawford, 2004).

In the early 1990s, the election of Bill Clinton as President brought some hope as he 'had campaigned in support of bilingual education and promised to strengthen it' (San Miguel, 2004: 79). In 1994, the 103rd Congress undertook a major reform of education through legislation entitled Goals 2000: Educate America Act. Also, the ESEA was reauthorized in 1994 as the Improving America's Schools Act (IASA). This extensive reform included an acknowledgement that students for whom English was a second language ('limited English proficient' students) should be expected to achieve high academic standards. Such legislation aimed to provide children with an enriched educational program, improving instructional strategies and making the curriculum more challenging. Title VII strengthened the state role by requiring state educational authorities to review Title VII appropriations and provide additional funds for specific groups such as immigrants (Wiese & Garcia, 2001). Thus, the 1994 reauthorization continued limited federal support for bilingual education programs. The issue about bilingual education moved partly from being narrowly focused on the language of in-struction to a broader range of questions being asked about the quality and standards of education for **language minority students**. The Clinton administration tended to a more 'language as a resource' (see Chapter 18) stance but also tended to lessen federal influence on bilingual education (Crawford, 2004).

Opponents of bilingual education in the US do not generally oppose foreign language programs for English speakers. Such programs are regarded as important in educating students for the global economy. Some forms of bilingualism (e.g. English–Japanese, English–French) are seen to be of value for US economic prosperity. One of the goals of the National Education Goals Panel (1999) was that the percentage of students who are competent in more than one language should substantially increase. The 1994 revisions to the Bilingual Education Act meant that proficient bilingualism became a desirable goal when it brought economic benefits to individuals and particu-larly to the nation. Hence the revisions resulted in funding for a larger number of dual language programs.

However, the 1994 reauthorization of Title VII came under attack both by politi-cians and the US press. Congress considered legislation to repeal the law and eliminate its funding. While this did not succeed, it nevertheless pointed to many politicians and much of the mass media being against bilingual education. Title VII appropriations were reduced by 38% between 1994 and 1996 leading to cuts in bilingual programs and in teacher training, and reducing the budgets for research, evaluation and support.

'English for the Children' State Voter Initiatives

Between 1978 and 2000, the number of English language learners (ELLs) in Cali-fornia rose from approximately 250,000 to 1.4 million, with significant populations of Vietnamese, Hmong, Cantonese, Tagalog, Khmer, Korean, Armenian, Mandarin, Russian, Ukrainian, Serbo-Croatian, Urdu, Hindi and Punjabi students, for example.

With a multilingual population, California had become a state where both experimentation and experience with bilingual education had blossomed.

In early 1996, the *Los Angeles Times* gave extensive coverage to the political activism of a small group of Spanish-speaking parents pulling their children out of the Ninth Street Elementary School. Ron Unz, a Silicon Valley businessman saw this as his political opportunity after his failed attempts to get elected to political office in years prior. Based on a personal philosophy of assimilation, he criticized bilingual education and made claims about the supposed educational ineffectiveness of bilingual schools in California (Ovando, 2003). The press were delighted to add heat to the debate with mostly one-sided, personality-based, controversy-cultivating reports (Crawford, 2004).

California's Proposition 227 – the 'English for the Children' Initiative – was presented as an effort to improve English language instruction for children who needed to learn English for economic and employment opportunities. It aimed at outlawing bilingual education in that state. 'Therefore' says the text of Proposition 227 'it is resolved that: all children in California public schools shall be taught English as rapidly and effectively as possible' and such children 'shall be taught English by being taught in English'. Bilingual education programs were greatly restricted and required meeting ambiguous waiver provisions of the law; sheltered (or structured) English-immersion programs were put in their place (Crawford, 2004; Quezada *et al.*, 1999/2000).

Proposition 227 was approved by voters on June 2, 1998 by a margin of 61% to 39%. Analysis of the voting and subsequent surveys found that many Latinos were clearly against the proposition, but nevertheless, bilingual education had become virtually illegal. With the sweet scent of victory in California, Unz proceeded elsewhere across the United States with successful **English for the Children initiatives** in Arizona (**Proposition 203** passed by a 63% vote in 2000) and Massachusetts (**Question 2** passed by a 68% vote in 2002). In these two states the waiver provisions were more stringent, parental choices were more severely limited, and penalties for non-compliance increased, including the threat of personal lawsuits. However, Unz was soundly defeated in Colorado (44% vote) in 2002 thanks to a politically savvy campaign with support of billionaire businesswoman Pat Stryker whose daughter was in a dual language program (Escamilla, Shannon, Carlos & Garcia, 2003) (see Crawford, 2004 for a critical view of the campaign).

Those teachers or administrators who willfully and repeatedly violate the mandates of the English for the Children initiative are left open to being sued by parents and are personally liable for financial damages and legal fees. However, there is a provision for parental waivers and exceptions. The student numbers in California bilingual education programs fell from 498,879 in 1997 to 167,163 in 2000 (Valdés, Fishman, Chavez & Perez, 2006) and to around 141,000 students (9% of LEPs) in 2002 (Crawford, 2004). There were also substantial reductions in bilingual programs in Arizona and Massachusetts (de Jong, Gort & Cobb, 2005; Wright & Choi, 2006). The waiver provisions have preserved some bilingual programs in school districts where there is strong parental support and a history of effective bilingual education. Wiley and Wright (2004) indicate variations in the extent to which parents were informed of their right to waivers from English-only programs, and the continuation of some quality bilingual programs.

Since its passage, there is little evidence that Proposition 227 has led to faster English language learning or higher rates of academic achievement (Bali, 2001; Crawford, 2004; Gándara *et al.*, 2000; Parrish *et al.*, 2002; Rumberger *et al.*, 2003; Thompson *et al.*, 2002; Valdés, 2006; Wiley & Wright, 2004; Wright, 2004). A five-year evaluation of the effects of the implementation of Proposition 227, commissioned by the state of California, concluded that there is no evidence to support the argument that the English-only programs mandated by Proposition 227 are superior to bilingual education models (American Institutes for Research & WestEd, 2006). Research in Arizona similarly found that there is no evidence that Proposition 203 resulted in higher academic achievement (Wright & Pu, 2005) or greater increases in English proficiency among ELL students (Mahoney *et al.*, 2005).

Since the passage of the first 'English for the Children' initiative in 1998 and the attempts to eliminate bilingual education, bilingual programs are alive and well in California, Arizona and Massachusetts and other states throughout the US. Loopholes, waiver provisions and various degrees of interpretations and implementation of the law by different state superintendents of public instruction have enabled many existing bilingual programs to survive or expand, and many new ones to be established. Bilingual education survived because, when properly implemented, it works, and because many parents want their children to be bilingual. It is important to note that many of the surviving and new programs have been dual language immersion programs, which are particularly popular among language majority parents and thus attract greater political support.

In 2014 California Senator Ricardo Lara drafted Senate Bill 1174 to give Californians the opportunity to repeal Proposition 227. The approved bill was placed on the November 2016 ballot as Proposition 58 under the title of 'English proficiency. Multilingual Education'. The official voter guide indicated that the proposition 'Preserves

---

Box 9.1 Defending and promoting bilingual education

The attempted outlawing of bilingual education in California, Arizona and Massachusetts, and the current effort to reject and repeal such legislation, indicate important considerations in its defense and promotion:

- The need to disseminate research findings on bilingual education, not just to teachers but also to parents and the public. The public image of bilingual education needs to be based on fact rather than fiction, on evidence rather than on prejudice.
- Bilingual education is not simply about provision, practice and pedagogy but is unavoidably about politics. To survive and thrive, bilingual education needs to demonstrate it works for the national interest in helping students attain proficiency in English and in producing the bilingual citizens the country needs.
- Secure evidence is needed, not just from individual case studies, studies of outstanding schools or examples of effective practice. In a culture of high-stakes testing, standards and accountability, raising the achievement of all students in all schools is needed. Bilingual education needs to provide evidence for high standards, high achievements and those outputs and outcomes of schooling that parents, public and politicians regard as important. This includes helping children acquire a thorough competence in English. Such outcomes go beyond language to other curriculum areas (e.g. mathematics, science), affective outcomes (e.g. self-esteem) and employment and vocational success.
- Evidence is not enough. There is a propaganda battle that goes beyond the dissemination of research. The media (e.g. newspapers, magazines, television, online news sites) are influential and can be utilized to support bilingual education. McQuillan and Tse (1996) found that in the period 1984 to 1994, 82% of research studies reported favorably on the effectiveness of bilingual education. However, only 45% of newspaper articles in the US took a similarly favorable position on bilingual education. Less than half of all newspaper articles made any mention of research findings, while nearly a third of such articles relied on personal or anecdotal accounts. This implies that research may need to become more accessible as well as being disseminated through influential mass media channels. Promotion and marketing of research and reviews may be necessary in such a politicized climate, targeted at policy-makers and politicians, parents and the press. The alternative is that prejudice and ignorance will be dominant.

the requirement that public schools ensure students be proficient in English', but also 'authorizes schools districts to establish dual-language immersion programs for both native and non-native English speakers'. Other points indicated parental and community input on language acquisition programs, and the rights of parents to 'select an available language acquisition program that best suits their child'. Proposition 58 passed on November 8, 2016 by a wide margin, with 72% voter approval. The result will likely have a national impact. California tends to be a trendsetter for the nation, and thus could potentially lead to repeals of anti-bilingual laws in Arizona and Massachusetts, and lead to legislation in other states supportive of bilingual and multilingual education.

No Child Left Behind

No Child Left Behind (NCLB) was approved on December 13, 2001 by an overwhelming vote of 381 to 41 in the House of Congress. President George W. Bush signed it into law on January 8, 2002. It reauthorized the ESEA and remained in effect several years past its expected reauthorization due date. NCLB was radical in its requirements for the treatment of English language learners (ELLs). Symbolically demonstrating a break with the past, the Title VII Bilingual Education Act was eliminated; ELL issues were addressed under Title III 'Language Instruction for **Limited English Proficient** and Immigrant Students'.

NCLB's use of the term 'limited English proficient' (LEP) brought back a deficit view of students, focusing on what they lack (English) rather than on focusing on who they are (emergent bilinguals) what they are actively doing (learning English and other languages). 'Bilingual' as a term was silenced. For examples, the Office of Bilingual Education and Language Minority Affairs was renamed the 'Office of English Language Acquisition'. NCLB had a narrow focus on **English language development** and little focus on developing bilingualism.

States were required to ensure students are taught by 'highly qualified teachers'; however, no criteria were outlined for teachers of ELLs. Also, NCLB eliminated the direct encouragement of and specific funding for bilingual education (with the exception of some program support for Indian, native Hawai'ian and native Alaskan education). Bilingual programs were still allowed, but it was up to each state to determine what program models would be eligible for federal funding. NCLB only required that supported approaches be 'scientifically based' on research. However, as Wiley and Wright (2004) found in the case of Arizona, the superintendent of public instruction at the time touted a single study by Guzman (2002) – which experts in the field found to be highly flawed – as 'scientific' evidence that bilingual education is ineffective. The following chapters examine previous 'scientific' research. Suffice to add at this point that the research evidence tends to support 'strong' forms of bilingual education. These forms appear, paradoxically, to have been discouraged by NCLB.

NCLB held states, districts, schools and teachers accountable for the academic performance and English language development of 'LEP' students. The requirements included the following: (a) Establish academic standards for content areas and English language development; (b) Assess LEP students annually on their progress in learning English (based on the standards) and attaining proficiency; (c) Test all students annually in Grades 3 to 8 and high school on their attainment of reading and mathematics standards (plus science at selected grade levels); (d) Ensure that students in different subgroups (race/ethnicity, **special education** and LEP) make adequate yearly progress

(AYP) towards the ultimate goal of 100% of student passing state standards-based tests by 2014; (e) Ensure that LEP students make adequate yearly progress (AYP) in learning English and attaining English proficiency; and (f) Implement a system of increasingly severe sanctions for schools and/or districts with subgroups of students who fail to make AYP two or more years in a row.

Originally NCLB did not allow any exclusion of newcomer ELL students from state tests, but after much protest from states two allowances were subsequently added for students in the country less than one year: (a) Students may be excluded from the state reading test, and (b) Students must take the state math test, but their scores could be excluded from school-wide AYP calculations (Wright, 2005a). NCLB also called for ELLs to be tested in a valid and reliable manner using 'reasonable' accommodations. Unfortunately, these are not specified in the law, and research on **testing accommodations** for ELL students remains sparse and insufficient to inform practice (Francis *et al.*, 2006; Rivera & Collum, 2006; Wright, 2015).

While bilingual education programs still qualified for funding if states allowed it, the federal legislation functioned in a manner that encouraged English-only instruction. The rule of law was joined by the heavy influence of high-stakes **assessment**. There is almost no more powerful way to transform a curriculum than via compulsory and focused assessment. Despite limited allowances for testing in languages other than English for the first few years if 'practicable', most states only provided exams in English, and even in states with non-English tests, the vast majority of ELLs took state exams in English.

Such testing placed pressure on teachers to ensure the rapid learning of test-driven content-area and English language skills and to avoid sanctions. Each state was required to establish a timeline with gradually increasing annual goals (passing rates) to ensure adequate yearly progress (AYP) towards the mandate of 100% passing rates by 2014. Schools that did not meet test annual performance targets for each subgroup were labeled as 'failing schools'. Such subgroups include major ethnic groups and 'LEP' students.

Where there is assessment failure, then the blame is likely to be placed (often unfairly) on the school and on the teacher (and not the system, e.g. lack of support for a child's bilingualism). Underachievement on tests is therefore seen as an education management problem, not a societal issue (see Chapter 16). **High-stakes testing** may improve assessment results; this is different from improving the quality of learning. Wiley and Wright (2004) noted potential negative outcomes: drop-out rates increase, less time for curriculum areas other than mathematics and English, failure to rectify human and material resource inequalities between schools, measurement of an instable and inconsistently defined LEP subgroup producing inaccurate results, and the loss of fluent bilingual teachers and native-speaker aides as insufficiently qualified.

The ESEA was due for reauthorization in 2007. However, the US Congress failed to take any actions on the federal education law until 2015 (see below). This left the requirements of NCLB in place for an additional eight years, despite growing dissatisfaction and wide bi-partisan recognition of the law's flaws, unrealistic expectations and failures.

Race to the Top

President Barack Obama was elected 44th President of the United States in November 2008. During the presidential campaign, education took a backseat in the debate over other major national issues. Nonetheless, Obama occasionally acknowledged problems with NCLB and its heavy emphasis on testing, and the need for more effective education reform. He also spoke in favor of bilingual education. Given the failure of Congress to reauthorize the ESEA, Obama began his own initiatives for major educational reform through his American Recovery and Reinvestment Act (ARRA) of 2009, designed to help the country recover from economic crisis. The Recovery Act included over $44 billion in stimulus funding for education, as Obama believed that improving education is central to rebuilding the American economy. Over $10 billion was reserved for Title 1 schools, and funds were used to raise standards, improve teacher quality, and turn around struggling schools.

In addition, in July 2009 President Obama announced a new program as part of the Recovery Act called 'Race to the Top' (RTTT), with $4.3 billion in competitive grants for states to pursue education reform activities. The administration outlined four general requirements for states to qualify for stimulus funding and Race to the Top grants: (a) Adopt internationally benchmarked standards that prepare students for success in college and the workplace ('college and career readiness standards'), and high-quality assessments that are valid and reliable for all students, including English language learners and students with disabilities; (b) Recruit, develop, reward and retain effective teachers and principals; (c) Increase transparency by building data systems that measure student success and inform teachers and principals how they can improve their practices; and (d) Support effective intervention strategies to turn around the lowest-performing schools. Advocates for ELLs were disheartened that these reforms still centered on high-stakes testing, and were especially alarmed at requirements that teacher evaluation be tied directly to student test performance. Ultimately, 11 states plus the District of Columbia were awarded RTTT Grants. More importantly, RTTT set the agenda for further reforms that impacted the entire country, as will be seen below.

Common Core State Standards

Soon after the Obama Administration began its education reform efforts, a major state-led initiative emerged to develop college and career readiness standards in English language arts and math that would be shared across participating states. The development of the Common Core State Standards (CCSS) was completed in 2010 through the leadership of the National Governors Association, and the Council of Chief State School Officers (CCSSO). By 2016 a total of 42 states, the District of Columbia, four territories, and the Department of Defense Education Activity (DoDEA) had adopted the standards. Two state consortia were formed to develop 'next generation' computer-based exams to the measure the CCSS – the Partnership for Assessment of Readiness for College and Careers (PARCC), and the Smarter Balanced Assessment Consortium. Common Core States were free to join one of these testing consortia, or develop their own state assessments to measure the CCSS. These new Common Core standards and assessments still met the mandates for NCLB, but also made states eligible for RTTT and other federal initiatives (see below).

The period of rapid and widespread adoption of the Common Core was followed by substantial political backlash. Many educators and ELL advocates were concerned about the continuing focus on accountability through high-stakes testing. Neither PARCC nor Smarter Balanced developed exams in Spanish or other languages, raising concerns that teachers would be under pressure to prepare ELL students for

English-only exams, further discouraging bilingual education programs. However, most of the backlash against the Common Core has come from conservatives. They viewed the Common Core as pseudo national standards and testing and thus an intrusion on state rights. While the Common Core was technically a voluntary 'state-led' initiative, it was neatly aligned with the Obama Administration's reform agenda. The US Department of Education provided grants to PARCC and Smarter Balanced to develop its assessments, and other Administration reform efforts encouraged the adoption of the Common Core (see below). Some critics took to calling the Common Core, 'Obama Core'. While only a few states have officially withdrawn from the Common Core, others have attempted to avoid controversy by simply renaming the standards to something more local sounding (e.g. 'Utah Core Standards'). However, membership of the two testing consortia have declined substantially with less than half of the original participating states remaining in PARCC or Smarter Balanced by early 2016.

ESEA Flexibility

The Obama Administration made an unprecedented move in 2011 to offer states waivers from some of the accountability mandates of NCLB under a program called ESEA Flexibility. This move stemmed from (a) the continuing failure of Congress to reauthorize the ESEA, (b) a growing number of states, districts and schools failing to meet increasingly unrealistic AYP targets, (c) an unattainable mandate for 100% test passing rates just a few years away, and (d) few defenders of NCLB remaining. To qualify, states were required to create their own alternative testing and accountability plans aligned with key principles reflective of the administration's RTTT program: (a) Adopt college and career readiness standards for all students, (b) adopt English **language proficiency** (ELP) standards that correspond to the college- and career-readiness standards, (c) adopt 'next generation' assessments to measure these standards, and (d) develop a rigorous administrator and teacher evaluation system, including the requirement to consider student test scores as part of the evaluation (US Department of Education, 2012). ESEA Flexibility proved to be very popular, and by 2015 nearly all states had approved plans.

To meet these principles, states had the option of adopting the Common Core State Standards or developing their own college and career readiness standards. Those that adopted the Common Core had the option of joining the PARCC or Smarter Balanced assessment consortiums, or developing their own assessments. States also had the option of developing their own ELP standards and assessments, or join WIDA, a state consortium with shared ELP standards and assessments that met the federal criteria (see http://wida.us). As of 2016, 35 states plus the District of Columbia, the US Virgin Islands, and the Northern Mariana Islands had joined WIDA. Ten states belong to smaller state consortia called English Proficiency Assessment for the 21st Century (ELPA21) (see http://www.elpa21.org/).

A major concern was that many state plans eliminated tracking the achievement of ELLs as a separate subgroup, and simply lumped them along with other 'at-risk' students into one large 'super-subgroup.' States would then require schools to focus on students within the lowest quartile of performance on state achievement tests. Morita-Mullaney *et al.* (forthcoming) call the ESEA flexibility waivers a 'language blind' policy, given that the unique linguistic and academic needs of ELLs would be buried within the super-subgroup. Also, the language needs of ELLs in the other three quartiles would also potentially be ignored. However, ESEA Flexibility did not waive Title III requirements that held districts and states accountable for increases in and attainment of English proficiency.

Seal of Biliteracy

A concurrent but separate initiative from the above education reform efforts began in California in 2011. Under the leadership of the nonprofit ELL advocacy group Californians Together, legislation was passed to recognize the bilingual skills of graduating high school seniors with a Seal of Biliteracy attached to their high school diploma. By 2015 nearly 32,000 California students had earned the Seal. The Seal of Biliteracy quickly went national, including support from the National Association for Bilingual Education (NABE) and the American Council of Teachers of Foreign Languages (ACTFL). As described on the initiative's website:

> The Seal of Biliteracy is an award given by a school, school district, county office of education or state in recognition of students who have studied and attained proficiency in two or more languages by high school graduation. Our vision is to help students recognize the value of their academic success and see the tangible benefits of being bilingual. (http://sealofbiliteracy.org/)

It is also believed that the Seal will have an economic advantage and be valued by employers seeking to hire bilingual employees (see Chapter 19). As of 2016, 23 states had approved a State Seal, and in 7 states the Seal was in various stages of consideration or adoption.

While requirements and types of Seals may vary slightly across states, districts and schools, in general (former) ELL students can demonstrate their bilingual skills by reaching the proficiency level on state English language proficiency exams, and by passing their state's English language arts exam. Native English speakers and heritage language speakers can demonstrate their proficiency through completion of advanced levels of heritage language and foreign languages courses and/or by pre-determined scores on language proficiency tests, such as Advanced Placement (AP) exams in world languages.

The Seal of Biliteracy marks an important move away from the restrictions on bilingual education under the 'English for the Children' initiatives, the elimination of the Title VII Bilingual Education Act, and the lack of recognition and value of bilingualism under NCLB. However, there is some concern moving forward as the Seal of Biliteracy gains in popularity (Mitchell, 2015). Some fear that the Seals will overwhelmingly be awarded to and benefit affluent native English speakers rather than lower-income current and former ELLs who arguably have higher levels of bilingualism and far greater use of two or more languages in their daily lives. Another concern is to what degree the Seals will be taken seriously beyond being a simple symbolic gesture. Finally, and most important, is what will states actually do to help students develop and/or maintain bilingualism and biliteracy? This is a particularly important concern for ELLs as most school programs are subtractive in nature. ELL students enter school as emergent bilinguals, but typically graduate as dominant English speakers with weakened oral language skills and little to no literacy skills in their home languages (Fillmore, 1991; Wright, 2004; Wright & Boun, 2011).

Every Student Succeeds Act

Eight years after the ESEA was due for reauthorization in 2007, the US Congress finally approved bipartisan legislation for a new version of the federal education law. The Every Student Succeeds Act (ESSA) was signed into law by President Barack Obama on December 10, 2015, thus bringing NCLB to an end. This new version of the ESEA reflects some recognition of the failures of NCLB including its unrealistic achievement expectations and overreliance on high-stakes standardized tests as the sole measure of student achievement. The testing regimen outlined in Title I remains the same – annual testing of English language arts and mathematics in grades 3–8 and high school. However, reflective of the ESEA Flexibility program, states are given greater flexibility for goal setting and how they will intervene in low performing schools. States are also expected to consider factors other than test scores in their school account-ability program. This could open the way for a student's level of English proficiency to be considered when setting achievement targets and in interpreting their test scores, or for other measures of students' opportunities to learn to be considered. There may be more opportunities to consider a student's growth over time, rather than just meeting set passing scores.

States are required, however, to track the progress of separate subgroups of students – including ELLs – rather than lump students together in a single super-subgroup. This addressed a major concern of the ESEA Flexibility program, as noted above, and should help ensure that the unique language and academic needs of ELLs are not overlooked. ELL students will be required to take state ELA and math exams regardless of how long they have been in the US. However, states are given some flexi-bility in how ELL test scores are included in school accountability ratings (see Box 9.2).

The requirements for English language proficiency standards and assessments, and the expectations for ELLs to make progress in learning and ultimately attaining English proficiency remains the same. However, these requirements were moved from Title III to be included alongside the academic achievement testing and accountability require-ments of Title I. This change marks a further departure from a separate section of the law focused on ELL students; but inclusion under the accountability requirements of

---

Box 9.2 Inclusion of ELLs in state testing and accountability programs under ESSA

ELLs are required to take state Reading/English Language Arts (ELA) and Math tests, regardless of how long they have been in the US. States have two options for including ELL test scores in school accountability ratings.

OPTION A
- ELL test scores count towards a school's rating only after they have been in the US for one year

OPTION B
1st Year in the United States
- Test scores must be reported to the public
- Test scores won't count towards a school's rating

2nd Year in the United States
- States must incorporate ELL scores for both Reading/ELA and Math, using some measure of growth

3rd Year in the United States
- ELL scores incorporated just like any other students

Title I may elevate the focus on the language needs of ELL students. As in NCLB, there will be some allowances for testing ELLs in their home language.

In a major step back from a key policy priority of the Obama Administration, the ESSA removed requirements that teacher evaluations be tied to student test scores. This change may help relieve pressure on teachers who were being held accountable for ELL test scores of questionable **validity**. And in another direct challenge to the perceived Obama Administration's ties to the Common Core, ESSA explicitly forbids the US Secretary of Education from forcing or encouraging states to adopt any set of standards. While some conservative legislators have boasted their new education law is a repeal of federal mandates for the Common Core, in reality there were never any federal mandates or presidential executive orders to repeal. States' option to adopt the Common Core standards or join one of the assessment consortia remain unchanged. The option to join English language proficiency standards or assessment consortia (e.g. WIDA, ELPA21) also remains unaffected.

The implementation of ESSA is just beginning. The Office of English Language Acquisition of the US Department of Education is engaged in the process of negotiated rule making, formulating and issuing guidelines for states and districts on how to implement these new requirements. Education reform through accountability based on the results of large scale standardized tests remains as the centerpiece of the federal education law, and ELLs are still required to take and ultimately pass these exams. A two-year exclusion of ELL test scores from school accountability ratings is likely to be insufficient. However, the greater flexibility afforded to states to design their own accountability systems opens up the possibility for more realistic expectations for ELL students, more attention to their linguistic needs, and potential for greater support for bilingual education programs. It remains to be seen how ESSA will work in practice, and the degree to which individual states will develop accountability programs that are fair and beneficial for ELLs and which value and promote bilingualism.

Table 9.1 provides a timeline and overview of important legislation, acts of litigation, and initiatives that impact or have implications for bilingual education.

Current Statistics

The estimated number of English language learners (ELLs) in the United States is over 4.4 million, making up 9% of all Pre-Kindergarten to Grade 12 students in 2012 (National Clearinghouse for English Language Acquisition, 2015d). These latest figures mark a slight decrease from a high in 2010 when 5.2 million ELLs made up over 10% of the total student population. Nonetheless there has been a 40% increase from 1994 when there were 3.2 million ELL students. The growth of the ELL population in the United States is given in Table 9.2.

In 2012 ELLs made up over 10% of the total student population in eight states (Alaska, California, Colorado, Hawaii, Nevada, New Mexico, Oregon and Texas) and between 5% to 9% in 22 states (Arizona, Arkansas, Connecticut, Delaware, Florida, Idaho, Illinois, Kansas, Maryland, Massachusetts, Minnesota, Nebraska, New York, North Carolina, Oklahoma, Rhode Island, South Carolina, Utah, Virginia, Washington, Washington, DC and Wisconsin). Between 2004 and 2012 ELLs increased by over 100% in seven states (Kansas, Louisiana, Massachusetts, Maryland, Michigan, South Carolina and West Virginia). All but 13 states also saw increases in their ELL student populations over this same period (National Clearinghouse for English Language

Table 9.1 US legislation, litigation and initiatives impacting bilingual education

Year	Legislation, litigation or initiatives impacting bilingual education	Implication
1906	Nationality Act passed	First legislation requiring immigrants to speak English to become naturalized.
1923	*Meyer v Nebraska* ruling by the US Supreme Court	The ruling outlawed, as an unconstitutional infringement of individual liberties, arbitrary restrictions on the teaching of languages other than English outside of regular school hours.
1950	Amendments to the Nationality Act	English literacy required for naturalization.
1954	*Brown v Board of Education*	Segregated education based on race made unconstitutional.
1958	National Defense Education Act	The first federal legislation to promote foreign language learning.
1965	Immigration and Naturalization Act	The Act eliminated racial criteria for admission, expanding immigration especially from Asia and Latin America. The Act also emphasized the goal of 'family unification' over occupational skills. This encouraged increased immigration by Mexicans in particular.
1965	Elementary and Secondary Education Act (ESEA)	First federal K-12 education law. An outgrowth of the Civil Rights movement, federal funds specifically granted to meet the needs of 'educationally deprived children'.
1968	Title VII Bilingual Education Act, an amendment to Elementary and Secondary Education Act (ESEA)	Provided competitive grants to establish bilingual programs for students who did not speak English and who were economically poor.
1974	*Lau v. Nichols* ruling by the US Supreme Court	Established that language programs for language minorities not proficient in English were necessary to provide equal educational opportunities.
1974	Reauthorization of ESEA and the Title VII Bilingual Education Act	Native-language instruction was required for the first time as a condition for receiving bilingual education grants. Bilingual education was defined as transitional (TBE). Grant could support native-language instruction only to the extent necessary to allow a child to achieve competence in the English language. Funding was thus restricted to TBE; maintenance and dual language programs were ineligible for funding.
1975	Lau Remedies	Issued by the Office of Civil Rights following the *Lau v. Nichols* decision. Provided guidelines on schools' obligations toward LEP students. This required the provision of bilingual education in districts where the civil rights of such students had been violated.
1976	*Keyes v. School District no. 1, Denver, Colorado*	Established bilingual education as compatible with desegregation.
1978	Reauthorization of ESEA and the Title VII Bilingual Education Act	Restriction of dual language programs lifted; The term 'Limited English Proficient' (LEP) introduced, replacing LES (Limited English Speaking).
1980	Lau Regulations	The Carter Administration attempted to formalize the Lau Remedies, requiring bilingual instruction for LEP students where feasible. The Reagan Administration subsequently withdrew the proposal, leaving uncertainty about schools' obligation in this area.
1983	US English movement	An organization advocating for English to be declared as the official language of the US, and opposing the use of languages other than English in government and education. Sparked national debates about the dominant place of English in law, society and education.
1984	Reauthorization of ESEA and the Title VII Bilingual Education Act	While most funding was reserved for TBE, monies for maintenance programs were once again permitted. However, for the first time funds were made available for 'Special Alternative' Instructional (English-only) Programs.

1988	Reauthorization of ESEA and the Title VII Bilingual Education Act	Same as in 1984, but an increase up to 25% of funding given for English-only Special Alternative Instructional (SAIP) programs.
1994	Improving America's Schools Act (IASA) – Reauthorization of ESEA and the Title VII Bilingual Education Act	Full bilingual proficiency recognized as a lawful educational goal. Funded dual language programs that included English speakers and programs to support Native American languages. The quota for funding SAIP programs was lifted. The new law sought to bring LEP students into mainstream school reform efforts, making it more difficult for their particular needs to be ignored in policymaking.
1998	Proposition 227 passed in California	The 'English for the Children initiative' imposed severe restrictions on bilingual education for English learners in California and mandated structured English immersion. Most bilingual programs dismantled.
2000	Proposition 203 passed in Arizona	The 'English for the Children initiative' imposed severe restrictions on bilingual education for English learners in Arizona and mandated structured English immersion. Criterion for waivers made more stringent and penalties for noncompliance added. Most bilingual programs dismantled.
2002	Question 2 passed in Massachusetts	The 'English for the Children initiative' imposed severe restrictions on bilingual education for English learners in Massachusetts and mandated structured English immersion. Many bilingual programs were dismantled, but blanket waivers were subsequently given by the state to dual language programs.
2002	Amendment 31 defeated in Colorado	The 'English for the Children initiative' is rejected by Colorado's votes. Unz abandons efforts to take the initiative to other states.
2002	No Child Left Behind (NCLB) Act – Reauthorization of the ESEA; the Title VII Bilingual Education Act is repealed and replaced by Title III	Approved by Congress on December 8, 2001 and signed into law by President George W. Bush in January 2002, NCLB replaced IASA. The Bilingual Education Act is eliminated and replaced by Title III, 'Language Instruction for Limited English Proficient and Immigrant Students.' Bilingual education allowed but not valued or encouraged. Mandates for accountability through high-stakes testing in content areas and English proficiency, and the threat of sanctions associated with failures to make adequate yearly progress encourage a move towards more English-only programs.
2009	Race To The Top	An initiative of President Barack Obama to provide $4.3 billion in competitive grants for states to pursue education reform activities. Includes a focus on the development of college and career readiness standards.
2010	Common Core State Standards (CCSS) Initiative	A state-led initiative to develop shared college and career readiness standards in English language arts and math. States also had the option of joining one of two consortia developing tests to measure the CCSS – PARCC and Smarter Balanced.
2011	Seal of Biliteracy	California becomes the first state to offer bilingual students an opportunity to earn a Seal of Biliteracy on their high school diploma. Many states have since adopted the Seal.
2011	ESEA Flexibility	An initiative of the Obama Administration to offer states waivers from key accountability provisions of NCLB and to propose their own accountability system meeting the Administration's guidelines. This included the requirement to develop or adopt college and readiness standards and assessments and corresponding English language proficiency standards and assessments.
2015	Every Student Succeeds Act (ESSA) – Reauthorization of the ESEA	Signed into law by President Barack Obama on December 10, 2015, ESSA replaced NCLB. Accountability through testing of content and English language proficiency is still in place, but states are afforded greater flexibility to set achievement goals and to use multiple measures to assess students.
2016	Proposition 58	The 'English Proficiency. Multilingual Education' ballot initiative repealed Proposition 227 in California.

Table 9.2 US ELL student population enrollment trends

Year	Total Pre-K to Grade 12 Enrollment	ELL Enrollment	Percentage of ELL	Percentage Growth Since 1994–95
94–95	47,745,853	3,184,696	6.67%	
95–96	47,582,665	3,228,799	6.79%	1.38%
96–97	46,714,980	3,452,073	7.39%	8.40%
97–98	46,023,969	3,470,268	7.54%	8.97%
98–99	46,153,266	3,540,673	7.67%	11.18%
99–00	47,356,089	4,416,580	9.33%	38.68%
00–01	47,665,483	4,584,947	9.62%	43.97%
01–02	48,296,777	4,750,920	9.84%	49.18%
02–03	49,478,583	5,044,361	10.20%	58.39%
03–04	49,618,529	5,013,539	10.10%	57.43%
04–05	48,982,898	5,119,561	10.45%	60.76%
05–06	49,324,849	5,074,572	10.29%	59.34%
06–07	49,792,462	5,218,800	10.48%	63.87%
07–08	49,914,453	5,297,935	10.61%	66.36%
08–09	49,487,174	5,346,673	10.80%	67.89%
09–10	49,866,700	5,208,247	10.44%	63.54%
11–12	49,427,331	4,472,563	9.05%	40.44%

Sources: National Clearinghouse for English Language Acquisition (2011, 2015d).

Note: Data for 2010–2011 was not available.

Table 9.3 Top 20 languages spoken by ELLs in the US

Languages	Reported number of ELL Speakers
Spanish	3,562,860
Chinese	88,798
Vietnamese	79,021
Arabic	64,487
Hmong	40,445
Haitian, Haitian Creole	38,227
Tagalog	23,192
Somali	19,514
Navajo	9,372
Russian	8,687
Urdu	8,614
Portuguese	8,416
Bengali	8,385
Yupik Languages	7,072
Korean	5,868
Polish	5,302
Creoles and pidgins	3,785
Karen languages	3,589
Iloko (Ilocano)	3,347
Marshallese	3,257

Source: National Clearinghouse for English Language Acquisition (2015b)

Acquisition, 2015d). Table 9.3 shows the top 20 languages spoken by ELLs in the US. Note how these are languages spoken in North, Central and South America, Europe, Asia, Africa, the Middle East and the Pacific Islands, thus demonstrating the great diversity of the US ELL population.

Explanations of Underachievement in Bilinguals

In the US (and in other countries with high immigration) language minorities are frequently found to underachieve or have high drop-out rates. On the 2013 National Assessment of Educational Progress (NAEP), ELLs scored significantly lower than non-ELLs. For reading, the gap in 'scores between ELs and non-ELs widened by grade, from 39 points in grade 4, to 45 points in grade 8, and to 53 points in grade 12' and for math 'from 25 points in grade 4, to 41 points in grade 8, and to 46 points in grade 12' (National Clearinghouse for English Language Acquisition, 2015a: 1). And in 2014, the graduation rate for ELLs was 62.6% compared to the national average of 82.3%. Also graduating at lower rates than the national average were American Indian/Alaskan Native (69.6%), Black (72.5%) and Hispanic (76.3%) students (National Clearinghouse for English Language Acquisition, 2015c).

Why do many language minority children appear to exhibit underachievement in the classroom? Explanations are likely to be multiple, complex, about associations that are not necessarily causal, and may include the following: majority language competence, socioeconomic background, poverty and material home conditions, racism, gender, school attendance, parental encouragement and assistance (e.g. with homework), peer influence, and the quality of teachers and school. Eight of the most typical explanations are now considered.

(1) *Bilingualism.* Bilingualism itself is sometimes viewed as a cause of cognitive confusion. The explanation given is a picture of the bilingual brain with two engines working at half throttle, while the monolingual has one well-tuned engine at full throttle. As detailed in Chapter 8, such explanations are based on mis-understandings of how languages are stored and work in the brain, and ignore the cognitive advantages that may be related to bilingualism.

(2) *Insufficient exposure to English.* Obviously, the less proficient students are in the language of a test, the less likely they are going to do well on it, even if they know a great deal about the tested content. 'Insufficient exposure to English' is often used as an excuse to eliminate bilingual education programs under the view that students should receive instruction in the same language as the test. This explanation falsely equates English language exposure with English language proficiency, and also fails to note the advantages of bilingual education for English language learning and academic achievement. Bilingual education, when effectively implemented, is not the cause of lack of English proficiency and underachievement; rather it is the cure (C. Baker & Lewis, 2015). The research support for bilingual education is detailed in Chapter 12.

(3) *Mismatch between home and school.* The language, literacy practices and culture of most classrooms in the US more closely match those of monolingual English speakers from the middle and upper class. Thus, linguistic minorities are placed at a disadvantage. While this mismatch explanation for underachievement is widely recognized, a common 'solution' is an expectation that the child, family and home

adjust to a uniform mainstream language and culture to ensure their child's success in school. As an extreme, this reflects a majority viewpoint that is assimilationist, imperialist and even oppressive. For example, some teachers, educational psychologists and speech therapists may advise language minority parents to only speak to their children in English at home. Parent education programs may attempt to train language minority parents how to talk, read and interact with their children like middle-class White parents. The alternative view is that the school system should be flexible enough to value and incorporate home languages and cultures. A mismatch between home and school can be positively addressed by 'strong' forms of bilingual education (see Chapter 11). Parent engagement programs can involve parents in the operation of the school as partners and participants in their child's education (Arias, 2015), recognizing and building upon rather than attempting to replace parents' **funds of knowledge** (N. González *et al.*, 2005). The mismatch can become a merger. Instead of assimilation, an additive outcome is then probable: bilingualism, biliteracy and biculturalism.

(4) *Socioeconomic factors.* The correlations between students' socioeconomic status and academic achievement are consistently strong. However, correlation does not equal causation. Socioeconomic status does not explain *why* different language minorities of similar socioeconomic status may perform differently at school. Some have attempted to attribute student underachievement to a 'culture of poverty', however, such explanations are grounded in a deficit view that 'blames the victim'. Also, underachievement cannot be simply related to one cause. Rather the focus should be on seeking to understand the causes and impact of structural inequalities, economic deprivation, material circumstances and living conditions, as well as psychological and social features such as **identity**, self-esteem, racial prejudice and discrimination. Solutions can then focus on ways schools can help address these inequalities. For example, if underemployment means parents can not afford to buy books, and if good public libraries are not accessible to students in their local neighborhoods, then schools can focus on developing well-stocked school and classroom libraries, and increase students' opportunities to check out books for use at home. Thus, instead of socioeconomic factors being static explanations or political criticism, actions must result to change and enhance. After the elucidation of cause must come transformation.

(5) *Type of instructional model.* Academic achievement may depend on the types of program models that exist in the schools students attend. Does the school offer ESL, sheltered content-area instruction or bilingual education programs? Or are bilingual students thrown into submersion mainstream classrooms and left to 'sink or swim?' There are often different outcomes for language minority children in 'strong' compared with 'weak' and 'non' forms of bilingual education (see Chapter 10 and 11). The same child will tend to attain more if placed in programs that use the home language as a medium of instruction rather than in programs that seek to replace the home language as quickly as possible. Therefore, when underachievement occurs, the system of schooling needs scrutiny. A system that suppresses the home language is likely to be part of the explanation of individual and ethnic group underachievement where such problems exist.

(6) *Quality of education.* Even if a school offers 'strong' forms of bilingual education, the models themselves may not make a difference if they are not implemented correctly. Also, the language of instruction is just one of many factors that need to be considered in the quality of education. Chapter 13 considers some of the

attributes that need examining to establish the quality of education for language minority children (e.g. the supply, ethnic origins and bilingualism of teachers, the commitment of teachers to bilingual education, the balance of language minority and **language majority students** in the classroom, the use and sequencing of the two languages across the curriculum over different grades, reward systems for enriching the minority language and culture, appropriate curriculum resources and the engagement of parents).

(7) *Interrupted schooling.* Many immigrant and refugee bilingual students experience interruptions in their formal education (Lukes, 2015). Access to schools in the home country may have been limited, or they may be been prevented from attending school for long periods of time due to war, civil unrest or oppression. Schools are often unavailable in refugee camps and refugee students seldom have access to schools in temporary host countries. Transnational students frequently travel back and forth between their current and their 'home' countries (e.g. US and Mexico) during the school year. Economic necessities sometimes require older students to leave school temporarily to work one or more jobs to help support the family. Complicated enrollment procedures (forms, immunizations, testing) can sometimes lead to months of delays for newcomer students to start school. Such interruptions lead to missed opportunities to learn, further compound challenges of learning and learning through a new language, and make it even more difficult for catch up with grade-level peers.

(8) *Real learning difficulties.* Bilingual children are susceptible to the same types of disabilities and cognitive deficit disorders that can impact any children, and may require some form of special education. However, it is critical to make a distinction between real and apparent learning difficulties. Too often, bilingual children are labeled as having learning difficulties that are attributed to their bilingualism. Language and learning challenges that are a normal part of second language development may be misinterpreted as speech impediments or cognitive difficulties. Other perceptions of apparent learning problems may be much less in the child and much more in the school or in the education system. In the 'sink or swim' mainstreaming approach, 'sinking' can be attributed to an unsympathetic system and to insensitive teaching methods rather than individual learning problems. Tests, assessments and procedures used to identify students for special education must distinguish between real, genuine individual learning difficulties and problems that are language learning related or caused by factors outside the individual. These issues will be addressed in Chapter 15.

Conclusion

Three conclusions. First, there is sometimes a perception that educational policy is fairly static, conservative and slow to change. The history of bilingual education in the United States tends to falsify and contradict such beliefs. Such history shows that there is constant change, a constant movement in ideas and ideology. One conclusion is that change will always occur in bilingual education policy and provision. Nothing is static. While there will be periods when bilingual education is criticized, forbidden and rejected, there will be reactions, with the possibility of more positive, accepting periods ahead. Uncertainty and constant change provide occasional opportunities for bilingual education to progress.

Second, the conclusion must not be that bilingual education only moves in one direction: from more positive 'golden' times to being dismissed and rejected. The history of bilingual education in the Basque Country and Wales follows a different sequence from the US. In these countries, bilingual education has moved from being dismissed and suppressed to a period of considerable expansion. From a time when Basque and Welsh were banned in the classroom, there is currently a widespread acceptance and provision of bilingual education in these countries.

Third, a current international issue is the underachievement of many language minority students. The blame for this is easily but wrongly attributed to bilingualism or to insufficient experience in learning a majority language. Instead, the achievement gap is often related to failing to use a child's ability and achievements that are available

Key Points in This Chapter

> Bilingual education has a history spanning 5,000 or more years.

> Bilingual education in the United States has a rapidly changing history, impacted directly or indirectly by a wide range of legislation, litigation and state and federal initiatives.

> 'English for the Children' voter initiatives in California, Arizona and Massachusetts have not lived up to their promise of faster English language learning and higher academic achievement. They have reduced, but failed to fully eliminate bilingual education programs.

> The Seal of Biliteracy affords graduating high school seniors recognition and value of their bilingual skills.

> The shift of federal education policy from NCLB to ESSA continues a focus on education reform through testing and accountability, but states are afforded more flexibility with potential for more reasonable expectations for ELLs and a greater focus on their language and academic needs. But it is too early to tell the extent to which students may benefit from these changes.

> Underachievement in school is typically unfairly blamed on bilingualism. Lack of exposure to the majority language and a mismatch between the languages of home and school are often cited as causes of underachievement.

> The real causes of underachievement tend to lie in relative social and economic deprivation and exclusion, a school which rejects the home language and culture of the child, and occasionally real learning difficulties.

in their home language. Sometimes the achievement gap is blamed on language, when the real roots are situated in the relatively impoverished economic, social and educational environments that immigrants, for example, experience. For such students, bilingual education utilizing the home language becomes the cure and not the cause of underachievement.

Suggested Further Reading

📖 Arias, M. B. & Faltis, C. (2012). *Implementing educational language policy in Arizona: Legal, historical and current practices in SEI*. Bristol, UK: Multilingual Matters.

📖 Gandara. P. & Hopkins, M. (2010). *Forbidden language: English learners and restrictive language policies*. New York, NY: Teachers College Press.

📖 Hamayan, E., & Field, R. F. (Eds.). (2012). *English language learners at school: A guide for administrators* (2nd ed.). Philadelphia, PA: Caslon Publishing.

📖 McField, G. (Ed.) (2014). *The miseducation of English learners: A tale of three states and lessons to be learned*. Charlotte, NC: Information Age Publishing

📖 Moore, S. C. (2014). *Language policy processes and consequences: Arizona case studies*. Bristol, UK: Multilingual Matters.

Discussion Questions

(1) Choose three of the items from the historical timeline in Table 9.1 and discuss why and how these impacted bilingual education.

(2) There have been direct attempts to eliminate bilingual education (e.g. the 'English for the Children' initiatives), the Title VII Bilingual Education Act was eliminated in 2002, and under NCLB there was a lack of federal funding and encouragement for bilingual education. Nevertheless, bilingual education remains alive and well in the US. Why do you think bilingual education has been able to survive?

(3) What recent policy changes and initiatives may further support or restrict bilingual education going into the future?

Study Activities

(1) Visit one or more schools and ask about the history of the bilingual education program or other language programs within that school. What have been the aims of the school with regard to languages? Have these aims changed over the last 10 or 20 years? How do the teachers perceive the first and second language of children being ignored or used over the last decade or more? Are there issues about the 'achievement gap' in the school? If so, what explanations do teachers give for underachievement?

(2) Choose one of the more recent initiatives or policies discussed in the chapter to further explore. Conduct an internet search to find news articles, reports, videos, social media postings and research articles to learn of the historical and more recent developments and how they are impacting language minority students and bilingual education.

(3) Visit the website of the National Clearinghouse for English Language Acquisition. Select one or more of the Fast Facts publications (http://www.ncela.us/fast-facts). Prepare a short presentation based on these Fast Facts, and discuss the implications for Bilingual Education.

CHAPTER 10

Types of Bilingual Education

Types of Bilingual Education

Introduction

So far in this book, the term 'bilingual education' has been used as if its meaning is unambiguous and self-evident. The opposite is the case. Bilingual education is a simplistic label for a complex phenomenon. At the outset, a distinction is needed between education that uses and promotes two languages versus relatively **monolingual** education in a second language, typically for **language minority** children. This is a difference between (a) a classroom where formal instruction fosters **bilingualism** and (b) a classroom where bilingual children are present, but bilingualism is not promoted in the curriculum. The umbrella term 'bilingual education' has been used to refer to both situations leaving the term ambiguous and unclear. This chapter aids understanding of 'bilingual education' by specifying the major types of bilingual education. To commence, one distinction in the aims of bilingual education is that between transitional and maintenance types.

Transitional bilingual education aims to shift the child from the home, minority language to the dominant, majority language. Social and cultural assimilation into the language majority is the underlying aim. Maintenance bilingual education attempts to foster the minority language in the child, and the associated **culture** and **identity** (e.g. Irish language education). This is sometimes referred to as **enrichment bilingual education** for language minority children. (The term is also used for language majority

---

Box 10.1 Ten examples of the varying aims of bilingual education

- To assimilate individuals or groups into the mainstream of society; to socialize people for full participation in the community.
- To unify a multilingual society; to bring unity to a multi-ethnic, multi-tribal, or multi-national linguistically diverse state.
- To enable people to communicate with the outside world.
- To provide language skills which are marketable, aiding employment and status.
- To preserve ethnic and religious identity.
- To reconcile and mediate between different linguistic and political communities.
- To spread the use of a colonial language, socializing an entire population to a colonial existence.
- To strengthen elite groups and preserve their privileged position in society.
- To give equal status in law to languages of unequal status in daily life.
- To deepen an understanding of language and culture.

Source: C.A. Ferguson *et al.* (1977)

---

children who are adding a second language in school). Enrichment bilingual education aims to extend the individual and group use of minority languages, leading to **cultural pluralism** and linguistic diversity.

The aims of different forms of bilingual education can vary greatly (Wright & Baker, 2017). In the late 1970s C.A. Ferguson *et al.* (1977) provided 10 examples of the varying aims of bilingual education; these remain relevant today (see Box 10.1). This list shows that different types of bilingual education have varying and conflicting philosophies and politics surrounding the aims of bilingual education. C. Baker (2010a) suggests that bilingual education has four major contemporary perspectives: (a) as part of language planning (see Chapter 3), (b) as politics (see Chapter 17), (c) as economics and cost-efficiency (see Chapters 18–19), and (d) as pedagogy (see Chapter 13). Bilingual education is not just about education. There are sociocultural, political and economic issues ever present in the debate over the provision of bilingual education, particularly politics.

A Typology of Bilingual Education

A typology of bilingual education helps illustrate the varying and different aims of 'bilingual education' and is presented in Table 10.1. Eleven types of language education are portrayed. Many international examples of these different types of can be found in O. García (2009b), Skutnabb Kangas and Heugh (2013) and Wright *et al.* (2015). The 11 different types of program have multitudinous sub-varieties, as Mackey's (1970) 90 varieties of bilingual education indicate. Even more variety is achieved by including multilingual education (Cenoz, 2009).

However, one of the intrinsic limitations of typologies is that not all real-life examples will fit easily into the classification. For example, elite 'finishing schools' in Switzerland, and classrooms in Wales where first language Welsh speakers are taught alongside 'immersion' English first language speakers make classification overly simplistic, although necessary for discussion and understanding (de Mejía, 2002). This is well illustrated by Bartlett and García (2011) in their case study of Gregorio Luperón High School in New York. The school is a hybrid of maintenance (heritage) bilingual education and transitional bilingual education. It also moves away from a focus on individual second language learners of English to a social process involving the identity of an entire **speech community** of Dominican students. Spanish is given a high status and bilingualism is the norm. At the same time, there is a rigorous academic preparation in English. Such a school does not fit easily into a typology.

The whole notion of a 'program model' is now being challenged as problematic out of concern that models represent a **monolingual/monoglossic perspective** in which the languages of bilingual students are treated as two separate distinct systems, as if students are two monolinguals in one and placed in programs where languages are simply subtracted or added (N. Flores & Baetens Beardsmore, 2015; O. García, 2009a). In contrast, a multilingual/hetereoglossic perspective views the languages of bilinguals as dynamic and co-existing. Such a perspective opens up space to engage with optimal classroom translanguaging practices that maximize growth and gains for individual students, as well as positive outcomes for schools in an accountability era (O. García & Li Wei, 2014; G. Lewis *et al.*, 2012). We thus may be witnessing a shift from effective *models* to effective *practices*, although the latter is built upon the former, and space can be made within existing program models for multilingual/hetereoglossic perspectives

Table 10.1 Typology of program models for bilingual students

MONOLINGUAL FORMS OF EDUCATION

Type of Program	Typical Type of Child	Language of the Classroom	Societal and Educational Aim	Aim in Language Outcome
MAINSTREAMING/ SUBMERSION	Language Minority	Majority Language	Assimilation	Monolingualism
MAINSTREAMING/ SUBMERSION with Pull-Out Majority Language Instruction Support	Language Minority	Majority Language	Assimilation	Monolingualism
SHELTERED (STRUCTURED) IMMERSION	Language Minority	Majority Language	Assimilation	Monolingualism
SEGREATIONIST	Language Minority	Minority Language (forced, no choice)	Apartheid	Monolingualism

WEAK FORMS OF BILINGUAL EDUCATION

Type of Program	Typical Type of Child	Language of the Classroom	Societal and Educational Aim	Aim in Language Outcome
TRANSITIONAL	Language Minority	Moves from Minority to Majority Language	Assimilation/ Subtractive	Relative Monolingualism
MAINSTREAMING with World (Foreign) Language Teaching	Language Majority	Majority Language with with L2/ FL lessons	Limited Enrichment	Limited Bilingualism
SEPARATIST	Language Minority	Minority Language (out of choice)	Detachment/ Autonomy	Limited Bilingualism

STRONG FORMS OF BILINGUAL EDUCATION

Type of Program	Typical Type of Child	Language of the Classroom	Societal and Educational Aim	Aim in Language Outcome
IMMERSION	Language Majority	Bilingual with initial emphasis on L2	Pluralism and Enrichment	Bilingualism & Biliteracy
MAINTENANCE/ HERITAGE LANGUAGE	Language Minority	Bilingual with emphasis on L1	Maintenance, Pluralism and Enrichment	Bilingualism & Biliteracy
TWO WAY/DUAL LANGUAGE	Mixed Language Minority & Majority	Minority and Majority	Maintenance, Pluralism and Enrichment	Bilingualism & Biliteracy
MAINSTREAM BILINGUAL	Language Majority	Two Majority Languages	Maintenance, & Biliteracy and Enrichment	Bilingualism

Notes: L2 = Second Language, L1 = First Language, FL = Foreign Language; This table is based on discussions with Ofelia García. She also has provided an in-depth discussion of models in O. García (2009a).

and effective translanguaging practices. Some effective practices may be similar across models, making pedagogic decisions more universally informed rather than just from within a model.

While the typology is about programs in K-12 schools, bilingual education can be cradle to grave, including preschool education, further education, higher education and lifelong learning. A growing interest is in bilingual education at university level (van der Walt, 2015). This is particularly concerned with including minority languages as a medium for teaching, dual language approaches to lectures (e.g. use of translation, translanguaging), the identity of multilingual students at university, and progression from bilingual schooling to university (Hibbert & van der Walt, 2014; van der Walt, 2013).

Typologies have value for conceptual clarity, and for comparisons across countries and **contexts**, but they have limitations: (a) models suggest static systems whereas bilingual schools and classrooms constantly develop and evolve; (b) there are wide and numerous variations within a model; (c) models address 'inputs' and 'outputs' of the education system, but rarely address the classroom process; (d) models do not explain the successes or failures or the relative effectiveness of different types of bilingual education; (e) models are non-theoretical, reductionalist, essentialist and, compared to complex individual schools, tend to simplify unsympathetically; (f) models are often relevant to one context (e.g. Canada) and cannot be exported or imported without the traditions and ideologies of a new context being considered; (g) the models derive from Northern Hemisphere countries, particularly North America and Europe, with Southern Hemisphere traditions weakly represented (Benson, 2009; Heugh & Skutnabb-Kangas, 2010); (h) models are not typically part of the way that policymakers, administrators, and particularly teachers talk about bilingual education.

C. Baker (2008) suggests that it is increasingly more valuable to profile the key dimensions and issues along which bilingual schools vary, such as the language profile of children and balance of languages, use and allocation of languages in the classroom, the language profile of staff in the school, learning resources, staff development and parental inclusion. Cenoz (2009) proposes a 'continua of multilingual education', which draws on insights from Hornberger's (2008) continua of biliteracy (see Chapter 14). The continua of multilingual education considers the sociolinguistic context including the school context, teacher, language of instruction, the school subject, and the linguistic distance between the home and school language. It also considers macro factors such as the speakers, their status, the media, and linguistic landscape, as well as micro factors such as the students' parents, siblings, peers, and their neighborhood. Each of these dimensions interact in dynamic ways. Cenoz's model illustrates the complex realities that challenge simplistic typologies. To assist educators in decision making within the complex realities of multilingual schools, de Jong (2011) outlines four principles to be considered when designing programs and instruction:

(1) Striving for educational equity – Engage in practices that reflect respect, non-discrimination, and fairness for all students.
(2) Affirming identities – Respect students' linguistic and cultural identities, and validate their cultural experiences in school policies and classroom practices.
(3) Promoting **additive bilingualism** – Build on students' existing linguistic repertoires and create opportunities for using, developing, displaying, and engaging in multiple languages.
(4) Structuring for integration – Look at how a school's various components (students, parents, teachers, as well as programs and activities) connect, relate, and interact with each other and how these relations reflect equal status among those involved. (pp. 170, 178)

Having acknowledged these challenges and complexities, we now briefly consider each of the broad types of program models in this chapter and the next.

Mainstreaming/Submersion Education

Submersion education is a label to describe education for language minority children who are placed in mainstream education. However, no school calls itself a submersion school. 'Mainstreaming' is the more common label. Submersion contains the idea of a language minority student thrown into the deep end and expected to learn to swim as quickly as possible without the help of floats or special swimming lessons. The language of the pool will be the majority language (e.g. English in the US) and not the home language of the child (e.g. Arabic, Chinese, Spanish, etc.). The language minority student will be taught all day in the majority language, often alongside fluent speakers of the majority language. Both teachers and students will be expected to use only the majority language in the classroom, not the home language. There is no provision of specialized instruction in the majority language (e.g. **English as a second language**) or attempt to modify the curriculum and instruction to make it more comprehensible (e.g. **sheltered instruction**). The teacher does not have any specialized training or certifications for providing such instruction or support. Thus, **language minority students** will sink, struggle or swim.

The basic aim of such mainstreaming is the **assimilation** of language minority speakers, particularly where there has been immigration (e.g. US, UK, Japan, Korea). Also, where indigenous language minorities are perceived as 'outside' the common good, mainstreaming becomes a tool of integration (Crawford, 2008). Considerable variations in student **language ability** in a mainstream classroom can create challenges in teaching and class management for the teacher. If the classroom contains students who range from fluent majority language speakers to those who can understand little classroom talk, the task of the teacher may be onerous. It is unreasonable to assume that children will quickly and effortlessly acquire the majority language necessary to cope in the curriculum (see Chapter 8).

Alongside problems of language, there may be problems of social and emotional adjustment for mainstreamed language minority children. Wright (2004) documented the experiences of former students who began school in the US as newcomer refugees with little to no proficiency in English, and were placed in submersion classrooms:

> Many had difficulty initially just understanding what was being said in class. Bo, describing his first year, laughed and said, 'I just sat there'. Ken remembers being very bored in 2nd and 3rd grade because he simply could not understand what was being said. Many described her frustration of wanting to participate in class discussions, but was afraid that she might say something wrong, or that the other students would laugh at her English. Ken never raised his hand for the same reason. Even if the teacher called on him, he would not respond. ... Ken recalls his kindergarten class: 'I could tell the difference between an apple and an orange, but I couldn't say the words right. Some of those kids, they could spell it too. They just spelled the word apple, but I couldn't. I just struggled to say the word. I guess they were just smarter than me.' (p. 14)

It is not just the child's home language that is deprecated. The identity of the child, the parents, grandparents, the home, community, religion and culture appear to be deprecated, discredited and disparaged. It is not only the students' language that is denied. It also denies or denounces what they hold most sacred: self-esteem, identity, relationships, roots, religion and sometimes race. One of the former refugee students in Wright's study recalled denying his ability to read and write in his native Khmer language to a paraprofessional at his school:

By now, I was very ashamed, because people would say 'go back to your country' and all this. I didn't want anything to do with that. I want to fit in. I was embarrassed about being Khmer, by knowing how to read and write. That's when I said, I'm not going to write anymore, people will see me writing that stuff. You get a lot of these kinds of pressures. (p. 16)

Learning through an undeveloped language in mainstreaming is stressful. Listening to a new language demands high concentration. It is tiring, with a constant pressure to think about the form of the language and less time to think about curriculum content. A child has to take in information from different curriculum areas and learn a language at the same time. Stress, lack of self-confidence, 'opting-out', disaffection and alienation may occur.

Submersion mainstream education was declared illegal by the US Supreme Court in the landmark 1974 case *Lau v. Nichols* (see Chapter 9). In writing the court's opinion, Justice William Douglass declared 'There is no equality of treatment merely by providing students with the same facilities, textbooks, teachers, and curriculum; for students are who do not understand English are effectively foreclosed from any meaningful education.' Thus, US schools are required to do *something* to address the language and content-area learning needs of **English language learners** (ELLs), as will be reflected in the other types of programs discussed below and in Chapter 11.

Mainstreaming With Pull-out Classes

Mainstream education may take a step beyond submersion with the provision for 'withdrawal' or 'pull-out' classes to teach the majority language. Language minority children in mainstream schools may be withdrawn for 'compensatory' lessons in the majority language (e.g. English as a second language [ESL] or English as an additional language [EAL] pull-out programs in the US and UK). Most ESL programs aim to develop English language skills (grammar, vocabulary and communication) for communication and academic purposes. Some programs may also teach '**content-based ESL**,' focusing on the vocabulary and language structures students will encounter during actual content-area instruction in their mainstream classrooms. Others may go as far as substituting for and 'sheltering' the English language arts instruction students would ordinarily receive in their regular classroom. The hope is that such pull-out programs provide a way to help language minority children cope in their mainstream classrooms. The more English they learn from their **pull-out ESL** teacher, the more they can understand and participate in their regular mainstream classroom. This is preferable to giving no English language support. In the US such ESL support is therefore valuable, giving students not only English language learning provision, but also the chance to build self-esteem and acquire the sole language of instruction. In short, pull-out ESL is far better than nothing (Wright, 2008).

However, 'withdrawn' children may fall behind on curriculum content delivered to others while they are out of the classroom. There may also be a stigma for absence and extraction, and feelings of alienation. A student may be seen by peers as 'remedial', 'disabled' or 'backward in English' (Ovando & Combs, 2017). Wright (2015) documented the feelings of one such former student reflecting on what it was like being pulled out of her mainstream classroom for ESL instruction: 'The other kids wouldn't say anything, but I would feel lost. Here I go again. Why do I have to do this? I felt so dumb. I felt like I'm dumb' (p. 107).

Pull-out ESL classes tend to be frequent in the US, but as Wright (2015) notes, the model has been highly criticized as the least effective model:

> The problems are many. First and perhaps most important, students miss out on instruction in their regular classrooms when they are pulled out. Second, pull out ESL may lead some mainstream classroom teachers to view that the ELLs are mainly the responsibility of the ESL teacher. Third, many students feel stigmatized about being pulled out day after day in front of their English-only peers. ... And finally, ESL instruction provided by the pull-out teacher typically is not coordinated with what the students are learning in their regular classrooms, largely because ESL teachers generally pull out students from several different classrooms, making it very difficult to coordinate with every teacher. Furthermore, pull-out teachers sometimes find mainstream teachers are unwilling to collaborate. (p. 107)

Wright also notes pull-out ESL is more expensive because it requires the hiring of additional teachers beyond the regular classroom teachers, and also creates challenges finding appropriate space for the pull-out teacher in typically overcrowded schools. Thus students may receive their ESL instruction in the hallway, the cafeteria, the basement, the auditorium stage, or even in converted broom closets or storage rooms in the back of other teachers' classrooms. Such accommodations can send students implicit messages about the value of ESL instruction, and how the school values them (and their ESL teacher). One alternative is 'push-in' ESL, where the ESL teacher comes into the mainstream classroom to provide ESL instruction (e.g. in the back of the room), and/or to provide instructional support during the regular teacher's instruction. In the best-case scenario, there is co-teaching (or complementary teaching), where the ESL and classroom teacher plan and deliver linguistically appropriate classrooms lessons together. However, when such planning does not take place, ESL teachers can become 'overpaid pointers' who simply lurk around the desks of ELL students quietly pointing to things in the students' books or on their worksheets while the classroom teacher lectures on and on.

Sheltered (Structured) Immersion

A better alternative to submersion with pull-out is when classroom teachers are trained and licensed to provide majority language instruction and to modify their curriculum and content-area instruction for students who are not yet proficient in the majority language. In the US, such classrooms are called structured or **sheltered English immersion (SEI)** programs (Brisk, 2006). In California and other states, sheltered instruction is called 'specially designed academic instruction in English' (SDAIE). Thus, rather than students being pulled out of their regular classroom, the students receive ESL and sheltered content-area instruction directly from their regular classroom teacher.

The argument for an SEI program instead of a bilingual program is often pragmatic. In a class of 20 or more children, there may be many different home languages. For example, in London, there are over 300 immigrant languages. In many US school districts with high ELL enrollments, over 100 different languages are spoken. With such linguistic diversity, many schools claim that bilingual education is impossible, and SEI is the most practical approach. However, in many such diverse schools, there may still be a sufficient number of speakers of the same language to offer a bilingual program.

In Texas and a few other states, bilingual education is required when there are at least 20 ELLs who speak the same language.

In **sheltered English** content-area instruction, content is taught in English, but the academic instruction is specially designed to make it comprehensible for English language learners, commensurate with their level of English proficiency (Echevarría & Graves, 2011; Faltis, 2005). The teaching is also designed to facilitate students' **English language development** and thus helps supplement (but should not supplant) the teacher's ESL instruction (Wright, 2015). Sheltered instruction may feature simplified vocabulary, purpose-made materials, and a variety of instructional strategies to make input comprehensible and language use interactive (e.g. cooperative learning, use of non-verbal communication, visual aids, demonstrations, hands-on experience, and frequent checks for understanding). Echevarría *et al.* (2016) present a model of 30 specific components and strategies for effective sheltered instruction called the **Sheltered Instruction Observation Protocol** (SIOP). The SIOP Model provides a tool for planning, observing and evaluating a teacher's implementation of sheltered instruction that teaches content material to ELLs. In immersion, dual immersion and other bilingual programs geared towards native English speakers learning a minority language such as Spanish, then sheltered Spanish content-area instruction is provide. For example, the Center for Applied Linguistics has extended the SIOP model to TWIOP (Two Way Immersion Observation Protocol) that adds cultural objectives to a well-defined and elaborate instructional approach (Howard, Sugarman & Coburn, 2006).

SEI programs are designed for English language learners, though in practice many SEI classrooms contain a mix of ELL and English-proficient students. While some **primary language support** can and should be used in an SEI classroom, such use is quick and temporary; students' home languages are not developed or used for instruction (Wright, 2015). In the US and the UK, bilingual paraprofessionals or 'English as an additional language' (EAL) support staff are found in some primary (elementary) and secondary schools to aid the transition (F.S. Baker, 2012). Such bilingual support staff provide individual support, translate where needed, team-teach with the class teacher, and may occasionally manage the whole class for bilingual storytelling sessions. However, some classroom teachers may feel use of a language other than English is inappropriate or embarrassing, or may feel uncomfortable not knowing everything that is being said, and therefore mostly use English. Regardless of such bilingual support, SEI has a linguistic aim of monolingualism in the majority language.

In both majority language and minority language contexts, there are sometimes transitional 'newcomer centers' using an SEI type model. For example, in the US recent immigrants and refugees may be placed in a newcomer program, particularly if they arrive in the US as older secondary school students (Short & Boyson, 2012). In Welsh language regions in Wales, English speakers will often be placed in 'latecomer (newcomer) centers' so as to learn Welsh rapidly before moving to bilingual elementary or high mainstream schools (Brentnall *et al.*, 2009). Such centers offer a 'shock-absorber' transitional experience, culturally, educationally and linguistically. In a sheltered, welcoming and supportive environment, newcomers can adjust to a new language, receive an orientation to the new society, adapt to a new culture over one or two semesters, or one to two years. A student with low-level literacy skills may stay in such a center for longer.

SEI may involve temporary segregation from first language English speakers for one or more years until students reach sufficient proficiency for placement in a mainstream classroom. Faltis (1993: 146) notes that there can nonetheless be some positive features to temporary segregation: (a) Greater opportunity for participation among students (they may be less inhibited because of no competition or comparisons with first language speakers of English); (b) greater sensitivity among teachers to the linguistic, cultural and educational needs of a homogeneous group of students; and (c) a collective identity among students in a similar situation. However, such language segregation removes first language role models; may produce social isolation with overtones of stigmatization and reinforce negative stereotypes; may encourage the labeling of segregated students as linguistically and educationally inferior, deprived and in need of remedial attention; and may generate inequality in treatment (e.g. in curriculum materials and the lack of relevant training of teachers).

On the other hand, when SEI classrooms contain a mix of both language majority and language minority students, teachers may focus more attention on the native speakers and those with higher levels of English proficiency. Many teachers do not understand the differences and the relationship between ESL and **sheltered content instruction**, and mistakenly believe the latter is sufficient for both. A particular challenge in the US is that many teachers believe that SEI is 'just good teaching', and thus modifications specific to ELLs are not really needed (de Jong & Harper, 2005). This means in practice, SEI classrooms may actually be no different from mainstream submersion. In Arizona, following the passage of **Proposition 203** mandating SEI instruction (see Chapter 9), Wright (2014b) found that the state's initial enforcement of SEI simply meant making sure ELLs were only taught in English. When such ill-defined SEI instruction proved to be insufficient, the state established a rigid 4-hour SEI model that focused on isolated grammar and vocabulary instruction devoid of academic content (Lillie & Moore, 2014). This model was widely criticized by ELL experts and advocates as lacking any grounding in second language acquisition research and what we know about effective second language teaching and learning (Lillie & Markos, 2014). The model also prevented ELLs full access to the academic curriculum, and even prevented high school ELLs from obtaining the credits they needed to graduate. The Arizona case illustrates how SEI can vary widely in terms of program design and effectiveness (S.C.K. Moore, 2014).

SEI – when implemented properly – will potentially provide students with much greater opportunities for majority language development and academic content learning than submersion with pull-out and submersion alone. However, all three are forms of monolingual education for bilinguals and are **assimilationist**. These forms neglect students' bilingual development and fail to build on students' strengths of existing and emergent linguistic repertoires. A classic intensive two-year study by Valdés (2001) focused on Latino students in US schools. Her findings provide an exemplification of the paradox of English language learning policies enacted in such US schools that can deny access to the language and knowledge that could empower immigrant children. She shows that, separately and cumulatively, there are complex interacting classroom factors that frequently work against a student's English language development, achievement, employment, citizen rights and opportunities and self-esteem. Such factors include: impoverished second language interactions owing to a teacher–student ratio of over 1:30, passive learning and 'tight discipline' strategies, mixed **language competence** classes working to a low common denominator, subject matter kept simplistic as the second language is insufficiently developed, and teachers' concerns with 'flawed language' forms rather than communication. Valdés engages multi-level explanations: 'Placing blame is not simple. Structures of dominance in society interact with educational structures and educational ideologies as well as with teachers' expectations and with students' perspectives about options and opportunities' (Valdés, 2001: 4).

In other research in New York, Menken *et al.* (2012) found that English language learners, even after seven years of elementary education through the medium of English, arrive in high school orally bilingual for social purposes, yet have limited academic literacy skills in English. Thus, their English is insufficiently developed to cope with the high school curriculum. Also, their native language literacy skills are often insufficiently developed to read in that language at the high school level or for such skills to transfer to English literacy. Since performance at high school depends greatly on literacy, they are impeded in developing to their potential.

Segregationist Education

Another form of monolingual education for bilinguals is segregationist language education (Skutnabb Kangas, 2000). This is quite rare. Segregationist education occurs where minority language speakers are denied access to those programs or schools attended by majority language speakers. Such separation can be through law (*de jure*) or practice (*de facto*). Monolingual education through the medium of the minority language can be for apartheid (e.g. educating a colonial people only in their native language). The ruling elite prescribes education solely in the minority language to maintain subservience and segregation. Such language minorities 'do not learn enough of the power language to be able to influence the society or, especially, to acquire a common language with the other subordinated groups, a shared medium of communication and analysis' (Skutnabb Kangas, 1981: 128). Segregationist education forces a monolingual language policy on the relatively powerless.

Transitional Bilingual Education

Far preferable over monolingual forms of education are programs that provide at least some instruction through students' home languages. In the US and other parts of the world, the most common form of bilingual education is transitional bilingual education (TBE). In the US this was the most frequently supported model under the Title VII **Bilingual Education Act** (see Chapter 9). The aim of transitional bilingual education is, nonetheless, assimilationist. It differs from monolingual forms of education in that language minority students are temporarily allowed to use their home language. Such students are taught through their home language for just a few years or until they are thought to be proficient enough in the majority language to cope in mainstream education. Thus, transitional education is a brief, temporary swim in one pool until the child is perceived as capable of moving to the mainstream pool. The aim is to increase use of the majority language in the classroom while proportionately decreasing the use of the home language in the classroom.

An educational rationale is based on perceived language, social and economic priorities: children need to function in the majority language in society. The argument used is that if competency in the majority language is not quickly established, such children may fall behind their majority language peers. Thus, arguments about equality of opportunity and maximizing student performance are used to justify such transitional programs. The extent to which such justifications are valid or invalid is considered in Chapter 12.

Transitional bilingual education can be split into two major types: early exit and late exit. Early-exit TBE has been predominant. In the US early-exit TBE programs typically begin in kindergarten and seek to fully transition students to all English instruction by the end of 3rd grade. In many schools, however, TBE programs may only last for one to two years. Late-exit TBE allows around 50% of classroom teaching in the **mother tongue** until the 6th grade. Late-exit programs designed to help students develop and maintain their bilingualism are stronger forms more accurately described as maintenance bilingual programs (see Chapter 11). Some TBE programs are for older students (e.g. middle and high schools) who have received education through their native language, immigrated, and require a transition to mainstream classes.

Ovando and Combs (2017) criticize the early-exit TBE model for being remedial, compensatory and segregated, perpetuating the status quo by separating language minority students from the mainstream and thus reproducing differences in power and progress for those with lower class status.

While majority language monolingualism is the aim of transitional bilingual education, teachers or their assistants need to be bilingual. The temporary home language swim requires, for example, a Spanish-speaking teacher who may be more sensitive and successful in teaching English to Spanish speaking children than English-only teachers. The former can switch from one language to another and be more sympathetic to the language of the children. Nonetheless, a bilingual teacher can become the unwitting promoter of transition from one language to another, and of assimilation into the majority culture. However, bilingual teachers – especially native-speakers who share the same cultural background as their students – may alternatively recognize the needs and wishes of their own communities. Thus they may continue to push the rapid transition to English in transitional bilingual education, but also try to preserve Spanish in the children, becoming allies of the community and not just allies of politicians and bureaucrats.

Similarly, in schools with transitional programs, there can be a hidden message in the staffing. People with power and prestige – the principals, assistant principals, counselors, and the majority of the school's teachers – are often English monolinguals (Menken & Solarza, 2015). The people with the least power and status are cooks, lunch monitors, custodians, office staff and paraprofessionals, who, for example, speak a minority language such as Spanish. The language of formal announcements is English; the language used by those who serve may be Spanish.

The transitional model is not just found in the United States. Where there is a majority language and much immigration, education is often expected to provide a linguistic and cultural transition (Wright et al., 2015). Also, in developing countries such as Cambodia, transitional models have been successful in extending educational opportunities to indigenous ethnic minorities who do not speak the national languages (Wright & Boun, 2015). In such cases as the latter, the notion of TBE as a 'weak form' may be called somewhat into question. In this case of Cambodia, Wright and Boun (2015) described several empowering features of the establishment of so called 'weak' TBE programs, including: (a) the development of orthographies of previously oral-only languages, (b) the recognition and valuing of their language by the national government as a medium of instruction in state schools, (c) access to education in villages where previously schools were linguistically or physically inaccessible, (d) the status-raising of the language through the publication of high-quality books and instructional materials, (e) opportunities for village leaders and members to oversee the school through community school boards, (f) employment opportunities for community members as bilingual teachers, (g) a 'foot-in-the-door' strategy of establishing a transitional bilingual model that can later be extended to a stronger developmental model, and (h) an increase in ethnic minorities attending and graduating from high school, thus leading to an educated class that can better advocate for their communities.

Mainstream Education with World Language Teaching

In the US, Australia, Canada and parts of Europe, most language majority school children receive their education through their home language. For example, children whose parents are English speaking monolinguals attend school where English is the sole teaching medium. However, there is often some learning of other languages. Traditionally the term 'foreign language' is used. However, in a growing number of schools, the term 'world languages' is preferred to emphasize that in our inter-connected global world, other languages are not so 'foreign' and may even be spoken widely locally and nationally (e.g. French in Canada, Spanish in the US).

In Wales and elsewhere, world languages are sometimes informally called a 'drip-feed' language program. The term 'drip-feed' highlights the kind of language element in mainstream schooling. Second (foreign) language lessons of around half an hour per day may constitute the sole 'other' language diet. Drip-feeding Arabic, French, German, Chinese Mandarin (Putonghua), Japanese or Spanish makes the language a subject in the curriculum similar to science and mathematics. This is distinct from teaching through the medium of a second language where curriculum content is the main focus rather than language learning (the latter is sometimes called embedding or content instruction).

The American Council on the Teaching of Foreign Languages (ACTFL) (2011) periodically conducts a surveys of foreign language instruction in the United States. Wright and Ricento (2017) provide a summary of key findings for K-12 public schools:

> In the 2007–2008 school year only 18.5% of students (8.9 million) were enrolled in foreign language courses – a slight increase from 18% (8.6 million) in 2004–2005. However, students in just five states (CA, TX, NY, FL, and PA) account for 40% of foreign language enrollment. Enrollments have decreased in 17 states since 2005. The majority of students study Spanish (72.6%), followed distantly by French (14.8%) and German (4.43%). The other most commonly studied languages are Latin (2.3%), Japanese (0.82%), Chinese (0.67%) and Russian (0.14%). Despite these low numbers, some have seen sharp increases in enrollment since 2004, including Chinese (194.99%), Japanese (35.01%) and German (8.21%) while there were decreases for Latin (-8.97%) and French (-3.24%).

There was also a sharp increase (35.01%) in the study of other languages such as Arabic, Korean, Portuguese, Swahili, Turkish, Vietnamese and Native American languages. This may be indicative of increasing demands by **heritage language** students for opportunities to further develop their languages at school (Wiley *et al.*, 2014). **Heritage language education** will be discussed further in Chapter 11. However, in our increasing globalized world, the distinctions between bilingual education, foreign/ world language, and heritage language are harder to discern. For example, as O. García (2008b) noted there is growing interaction 'between Spanish as a global language on the one hand, and Spanish as the minoritized language of US Latinos' (p. 31). In the US, Spanish can now be taught as a foreign/world language, a heritage language, in **dual language bilingual education**, and as part of global language teaching.

In England and the US, world language study is minimal. In the US for example, most students only take two years of world language courses in high school. Thus, relatively few world language students become competent in that second language. Where children receive a short second language lesson per day for between 5 and 12 years, few students become functionally fluent in the second language.

The Canadians found that after 12 years of French drip-feed language teaching, many English background students were not fluent enough to communicate in French with French Canadians. Similarly in the UK, five years of French or German or Spanish in secondary school (age 11 to 16) results in only a few sufficiently competent to use that second language. For the great majority, the second language quickly shrivels and dies. Mainstream education rarely produces functionally bilingual children. A very limited knowledge of a foreign language tends to be the typical outcome for the mass of the language majority.

This is not the only outcome of second and foreign language teaching. The learning of English in, for example, Scandinavia and Slovenia, many countries in Asia and Africa, does not fit this pattern, with many learners becoming fluent in, for example, English as a second or third language. When personal motivation and the status of a language is high, and when economic and vocational circumstances encourage the acquisition of a trading language, then foreign language teaching may be more successful. Learning a foreign language in the elementary school has become increasingly favored in mainland Europe. The learning of English as an international language has increased in schools throughout the world.

Separatist Education

A narrower view of language minority education would be to choose to foster monolingualism in the minority language in an area where another language is dominant. The aims are minority language monolingualism and monoculturalism in a context where such choice is possible. Such 'minority language only' education is relatively rare. The language minority group aims to detach itself from the language majority to pursue an independent existence. As a way of trying to protect a minority language from being over-run by the language majority, or for political, religious or cultural reasons, separatist minority language education may be promoted. This type of education may be organized by the language community for its survival and for self-protection. It is unlikely that a school would formally state its aims in a linguistic separatist fashion. Rather, in the implicit functioning of isolationist religious schools and the political rhetoric of extreme language activists, the 'separatist' idea of such schools exists. Small in number, the importance of this category is that it highlights that language minority education is capable of moving from the goal of pluralism to separatism. In times of globalization, such separatism disconnects and withdraws children from the wider world.

Exclusion and Interruptions

Before concluding, it must be acknowledged that many language minority students are excluded – in part or in whole – from a meaningful education. In Cambodia, for example, prior to policies promoting multilingual mother-tongue based education programs, thousands of indigenous ethnic minority children in remote areas of the northeastern provinces had little to no access to even a basic education. In many cases, there simply were no schools in the village or surrounding area for children to attend. In some villages, schools were available, but students did not attend because they could not understand the teacher or the curriculum taught only in the national language (Wright & Boun, 2015, 2016). Many oppressed ethnic minority groups are denied access to national schools in their home countries. Wars and refugee crises may prevent children from attending school for several months or years. Civil unrest, drug violence, and government corruption (e.g. demanding bribes for 'free' public education) may also prevent some children from attending school. In the United States, immigrant and refugee students who have experience such exclusions are officially referred to as 'students with interrupted formal education' (SIFE) (Wright, 2015). Lukes (2015) provides a detailed account of the interruptions in schooling experienced by many Latino youth in the US.

Even within the US and other 'developed' countries, there are extreme cases where language minorities have been completely denied access to schooling. In 2016 the Associated Press reported:

> In at least 35 districts in 14 states hundreds of unaccompanied minors from El Salvador, Guatemala, and Honduras have been discouraged from enrolling in schools, or pressured into what advocates and attorneys argue are separate but unequal alternative programs – essentially an academic dead end, and one that can violate federal law'. (G. Burke & Sainz, 2016: 1)

More often, it is subtle forms of exclusion that prevent full access to education. In the context of immigration debates in the US, Wiley (2013b) describes the process of constructing 'illegal children' (even in cases where children of immigrants are US born citizens), and how this dehumanizing discourse is an assault on the educational rights of language minority children. Lillie (2016) describes the experiences of high school English language learner students in Arizona who were prevented from taking core academic courses needed to graduate because of the state's mandated 4-hour English Language Development (ELD) model. Ramanathan (2013) refers to these and other practices that prevent immigrants from fully participating in society as citizens of their adopted nation as a form a (dis)citizenship.

Excluding linguistic minority students from schooling is clearly a violation of the basic rights of children (Skutnabb Kangas, 2015), and against the law in most countries (or individual states of the US) where constitutions guarantee children's access to education. Educational practices that prevent students from obtaining credits needed to graduate from high school must also be challenged. For immigrant students with limited or interrupted formal education, the traditional program models described above – including the strong forms of bilingual education – alone may not be sufficient to fully address the students' linguistic and academic needs, and may require creative solutions tailored to the needs of individual students.

Conclusion

The typology of bilingual education introduced in this chapter reveal important differences between monolingual, weak and strong forms of education for bilingual students. Monolingual forms are clearly assimilationist-oriented and most often result in students who can only speak one language. However, this chapter has also revealed that weak forms of bilingual education are also often assimilationist, and at best lead to limited levels of bilingualism.

Having considered some of the history of bilingual education and 'weak' types of such education, the next chapter moves onto 'strong' forms of bilingual education where bilingualism and biliteracy are part of the aims. What can then be examined (in Chapter 12) is the relative success and effectiveness of these different forms of 'weak' and 'strong' bilingual education.

Key Points in This Chapter

➢ Monolingual forms of education for bilinguals promote assimilation and aim for monolingualism in the majority language.

➢ Submersion mainstream education programs provide no linguistic or academic support for language minority students. In the US such instruction was declared illegal by the US Supreme Court in *Lau v. Nichols*.

➢ Some support can be provided for language minority students in mainstream classrooms through pull-out instruction designed to help students gain proficiency in the majority language.

➢ In sheltered (structured) English immersion (SEI) programs the classroom teacher provides ESL and sheltered content-area instruction in English. Primary language support may also be provided.

➢ The basic aim of 'weak' forms of bilingual education is assimilation of language minorities rather than maintenance of their home languages and cultural pluralism.

➢ Transitional bilingual education allows a student temporary use of their home language for content learning. The basic aim remains assimilation and not bilingualism or biliteracy.

➢ Some students are completely or partially excluded from access to education. This is a violation of children's rights in most places.

➢ Immigrant students with interrupted formal education (SIFE) may require additional assistance tailored to their linguistic and academic needs, beyond placement in a traditional (bilingual) program model.

➢ World (foreign) language programs for majority language students rarely result in students becoming proficient bilinguals.

Suggested Further Reading

📖 de Jong, E. J. (2011). *Foundations for multilingualism in education: From principles to practice.* Philadelphia, PA: Caslon Publishing.

📖 Garcia, O. & Lin, A. (Eds.) (2017). *Bilingual education* (Vol. 5 of the *Encyclopedia of Language and Education* (3rd ed.), edited by Stephen May). New York, NY: Springer.

📖 Ovando, C., & Combs, M. C. (2017). *Bilingual and ESL classrooms: Teaching in multicultural contexts* (6th ed.). Lanham, MD: Rowman & Littlefield.

📖 Mehisto, P. (2012). *Excellence in bilingual education: A guide for school principals.* Cambridge, UK: Cambridge University Press.

📖 Mohan, B., Leung, C., & Davison, C. (Eds.). (2013). *English as a second language in the mainstream: Teaching, learning, and identity.* New York, NY: Routledge/Taylor & Francis.

On the Web

💻 Video – Sheltered English Immersion classroom (El Paso, TX)
https://youtu.be/fHgSnEOOvro

💻 Video – Multilingual Education in Cambodia: A bridge for ethnic children at school
https://youtu.be/-bX0Y-Zn8JE

💻 National Association for Bilingual Education
http://www.nabe.org/

💻 American Council of Teachers of Foreign Languages
http://www.actfl.org/

Discussion Questions

(1) Share your experiences participating in or observing any of the program types described in this chapter. How effective did you find this program to be in helping (or not helping) you become bilingual?

(2) The presence of many different languages in a school is often used as an excuse for not providing a bilingual program, even when there are large numbers of speakers of the same language (e.g. Spanish). The argument may be 'we can't do a bilingual program for our Chinese, Burmese, Somali and Arabic speakers, so we shouldn't do one for our Spanish speakers'. How would you respond to such an argument?

(3) In the US and other countries, many language minority students start school bilingual but end school monolingual or with very limited bilingual skills. At the same time, students are expected to study a world language in high school for a couple of years. What are the problems with such a system that fails to produce bilingual students?

Study Activities

(1) Observe and report on a transitional bilingual education classroom. Note the nature and amount of use of the two languages in the program for different content areas or different parts of the day.

(2) Teachers of sheltered (structured) English immersion (SEI) are supposed to provide their own ESL and sheltered content-area instruction within their own classroom.

However, some programs are SEI in name only, and differ little from mainstream submersion. Observe and report on an SEI classroom, noting what specific ways, if any, differentiate the classroom from a mainstream classroom in ways that are beneficial to the language and academic development of the students.

(3) Interview a teacher of one of the program types described in this chapter. Ask about the educational, societal and linguistic aims of the program. How does that compare to those listed in Table 10.1?

Education for Bilingualism and Biliteracy

Education for Bilingualism and Biliteracy

Introduction

The two previous chapters provided a historical background to bilingual education and an introduction to 'weak' forms of bilingual education. This chapter examines the 'strong' forms of bilingual education introduced in the typology outlined in Chapter 10. Both US and international models are examined.

Strong forms of bilingual education have **bilingualism**, biliteracy and biculturalism as intended outcomes. Some schools aim for **multilingualism**, multiliteracies and multi-culturalism. This chapter particularly examines (a) dual language bilingual education, (b) **heritage language** bilingual education, (c) **immersion bilingual education**, and (d) mainstream bilingual education through two or more majority languages. Each of these models is well established, favorably evaluated and flourishing.

Dual Language Bilingual Education

In traditional **dual language** (or **two way**) **bilingual education** in the United States, approximately equal numbers of **language minority** and **language majority students** are in the same classroom and both languages are used for instruction. For example, approximately half the children may be from Spanish speaking homes, the other half from English **monolingual** homes, and they work together in the classroom. Since both languages are used for learning, the aim is to produce relatively balanced bilinguals. Biliteracy is as much an aim as full bilingualism (see Chapter 14).

There have been a variety of terms used to describe such programs, including: Two way immersion, two way bilingual education, **developmental bilingual education** (a term also used to describe late-exit bilingual education), dual language education and dual language immersion.

The growth of these programs has been considerable, with the oldest dating back to 1963 in Dade County, Florida, developed by a US Cuban community (O. García & Otheguy, 1988). The Center for Applied Linguistics (CAL) maintains a national database of two-way bilingual immersion schools with over 450 programs listed in 2016 (see http://www.cal.org/twi/directory/index.html). The list is incomplete. For example, the Dual Language Training Institute associated with the Gómez and Gómez Dual Language Enrichment Model claimed in 2016 that over 700 schools across 10 states had adopted this particular model alone (see http://dlti.us/3.html). However, according to Palmer (2014) this model does not meet CAL's criterion for inclusion because some English-speaking students in PreK to grade 1 receive less than 50% of instruction through Spanish. The National Association for Bilingual Education estimates over 2,000 **dual language programs** across the country (D.M. Wilson, 2011).

Traditional US dual language programs tend to share the following features:

(1) A non-English language (i.e. a minority language) is used for at least 50% of instruction that lasts for up to six years.
(2) In each period of instruction, only one language is normally used. Instruction must be adjusted to the student's language level, but must also be challenging, empowering and enabling. Language is learned primarily through content.
(3) Both English and non-English speakers are present in approximately balanced numbers and integrated for most content instruction. The English and non-English speakers are integrated in all lessons.

A language balance among students close to 50%–50% is attempted because if one language becomes dominant the aim of bilingualism and biliteracy may be at risk. The reality of such schools is often different, with an imbalance towards larger numbers of **language minority students** being more common.

Where there is a serious imbalance in the two languages among students, one language may become dominant (e.g. Spanish speaking children having to switch to English to work cooperatively). Alternatively, one language group may become marginalized (e.g. Spanish-speakers become excluded from English speaking groups). Segregation rather than integration may occur. In the creation of a dual language school or classroom, careful student selection decisions have to be made to ensure a social language balance that goes beyond a balance of numbers. Differences in minority and majority language status, and power relations between English and other languages, make language balance decisions crucial in such a school. Thus, numerical balance and attempts to designate specific times, subjects or spaces for one language or the other do not necessarily lead to language balance.

A study of third grade two-way dual immersion classrooms in Texas by Henderson and Palmer (2015) found that much English was spoken by the students and even the teacher during times and in spaces specified for Spanish. There was also some Spanish use by students during English-designated instructional time. While they found students had some agency in their hybrid language practices, Henderson and Palmer found that an 'overarching dominant language ideology of English superiority was present and powerful' (p. 75).

When an imbalance does exist, it may thus be preferable to have more language minority children. Where there is a preponderance of language majority children, the tendency is for language minority children to switch to the higher status, majority language. In most language **contexts**, the majority language is well represented outside school (e.g. in the media and for employment). Therefore, the dominance of the majority language outside school can be complemented by a corresponding weighting towards the minority language in school (among student enrollment and in curriculum delivery). However, if the school enrolls a particularly high number of language minority children, the prestige of the school can sometimes suffer (both among language majority and language minority parents). Also, dual language schools aim to develop both languages fully and fluently, so both languages need growth to all individuals' optimal potential.

In dual language magnet schools in the US, students may be drawn from a wide geographical area. Attracting language majority students to a dual language bilingual school is sometimes difficult. Hence, a good reputation and perceived effectiveness of the program is crucial. Language minority parents may be supportive of such a program. Majority language parents may need more persuading. Community backing and community involvement in the school may also be important in initial and long-term success. The development of dual language bilingual schools may preferably start with the creation of a dual language kindergarten class. As the kindergarten students move through the grades, a new dual language class is created each year.

Apart from elementary dual language bilingual schools, there is also dual language secondary education in the US and, with different names, in many other countries of the world (e.g. Wales, Spain, India). A dual language bilingual school may be a whole school in itself. Also, there may be a dual language strand within a 'mainstream' school, with one dual language classroom in each grade.

The following are major goals of dual language programs:

- High levels of proficiency in students' first language and a second language.
- Reading and writing at grade level in both languages.
- Academic achievement at, or above, grade level (e.g. mathematics, science, social studies).
- Positive intercultural (multicultural) attitudes and behaviors.
- Communities and society to benefit from having citizens who are bilingual and biliterate, who are positive towards people of different cultural backgrounds, and who can meet national needs for language competence and a more peaceful co-existence with peoples of other nations.

The aim of dual language bilingual schools is thus not simply to produce bilingual and biliterate children. Such schools enhance inter-group **communicative competence** and cultural awareness. The integration of native speakers of two different languages (e.g. Spanish and English) provides authentic, meaningful communication between children from the two different language groups, both of whom are native-speakers. Such schools produce children who, in terms of inter-group relations, are likely to be more tolerant, respectful, sensitive and equalized in status. Genuine cross-cultural friendships may develop, and issues of stereotyping and discrimination may be diminished.

To gain status and to flourish, dual language schools need to aim to show success throughout the curriculum (Lindholm-Leary & Genesee, 2014). On high-stakes state **testing,** on attainment compared with other schools in the locality, and in specialisms (e.g. music, sport, science), dual language bilingual schools will strive to show relative success. A narrow focus on proficiency in two languages will be insufficient.

Dual language schools also aim to promote the competencies students will need to enter the global job market. Students graduating in Spanish and English, for example, should be well placed to operate in international markets, transnational businesses and global operations (e.g. national defense), as these two languages are spoken across different continents and in many countries outside the US (see Chapter 19). However, this has drawn some criticism. For example, it may be that native English speakers becoming fluent in Spanish may benefit most. It may be that this reduces Latinos' natural advantage as bilinguals in such employment and promotion competitive op-portunities (Valdés, 1997).

The mission of dual language bilingual schools may also be couched in terms such as 'equality of educational opportunity for children from different language backgrounds', 'child-centered education building on the child's existing language competence', 'a positive self-image for each child', 'a community dedicated to the integration of all its children', 'enrichment not compensatory education', 'a family-like experience to produce multicultural children' and 'supporting bilingual proficiency not limited English proficiency'. The mission of all dual language schools (compared with mainstreaming) is to produce bilingual, biliterate and multicultural children. Language minority students are expected to become literate in their native language as well as in the majority language. At the same time, majority language students should make 'age-relevant' progress in their first language and in all content areas of the curriculum. To achieve these aims, a variety of practices are implemented in dual language bilingual schools:

(1) The two languages of the school (e.g. Spanish-English, Japanese-English) are given equal status in the school. Both languages will be used as a medium of instruction, with an integration of language and content learning. Math, science and social studies, for example, may be taught in both languages. However, care has to be taken not to be repetitive, and not to teach the same content in both languages.

(2) The school ethos will be bilingual. Such an ethos is created by classroom and corridor displays, notice boards, curriculum resources, cultural events, lunchtime and extra-curricular activity using both languages in a relatively balanced way. Announcements across the school address system will be bilingual. Letters to parents will also be in two languages. While playground conversations and student-to-student talk in the classroom are difficult to influence or manipulate, the school environment aims to be transparently bilingual.

(3) Language arts instruction is provided in both languages. Here, aspects of spelling, grammar, metaphors and communicative skills may be directly taught. Biliteracy is as much an aim as full bilingualism. Literacy will be acquired in both languages either simultaneously or with an initial emphasis on native language literacy (see Chapter 14).

(4) Most staff in dual language classrooms are bilingual. The exception is some co-teaching models that pair a bilingual teacher with a monolingual (English) teacher. Some teachers use both languages on different occasions with their students. In school-wide programs, bilingual paraprofessionals, secretaries, custodial staff, and/or parents volunteers complement classroom instruction. Language minority parents can be valuable 'teacher auxiliaries' in the classroom. For example, when a wide variety of Spanish **cultures** from many regions are brought to the classroom, parents and grandparents may describe and provide the most authentic stories, dances, recipes, folklore and festivals (see Chapter 14). This underlines the importance of the culture of language minorities being shared in the classroom to create an additive bilingual and multicultural environment.

(5) The length of the dual language bilingual program needs to be longer rather than shorter. Such a program for two or three grades is insufficient. A minimum of four or five years, or extending as far as possible through the grades is more effective (see Chapter 8). A relatively longer experience of a dual language bilingual program is important to ensure a fuller and deeper development of **language skills**, and biliteracy in particular. Where a US dual language bilingual program exists across more years, there is a tendency for the curriculum to be increasingly taught in English.

A longstanding practice in dual language bilingual schools is language separation and compartmentalization. In each period of instruction, only one language is used. Language boundaries are established in terms of time, curriculum content and teaching. This practice is beginning to be questioned, as will be discussed below.

A decision is made about when to teach through each language. One frequent preference is for each language to be used on alternate days. On the door of the classroom may be a message about which language is to be used that day. For example, Spanish is used one day, English the next, in a strict sequence. Alternatively, different lessons may use different languages with a regular change over to ensure both languages are used in all curricula areas. For example, Spanish may be used to teach mathematics on Monday and Wednesday and Friday; English to teach mathematics on Tuesday and Thursday. During the next week, the languages are reversed, with mathematics taught in Spanish on Tuesday and Thursday. There are other possibilities. The division of time may be in half days, alternate weeks, alternate half semesters. The essential element is a careful distribution of time to achieve bilingual and biliterate students.

The model used, the names such models are called, the composition of language minority and majority students, and the amount of time spent learning through each language varies greatly across states and schools (Boyle *et al.*, 2015). The two main models in the US are 50:50 and 90:10. In the 90:10 model, 90% of instruction is in the minority language in the kindergarten and 1st grade, with 10% to develop English oral **language proficiency** and pre-literacy skills (see Figure 11.1). Variations are possible where the minority language will be given more time than the majority language (80:20, 75:25, 60:40), especially in the first two or three years. Over the remaining elementary grades this ratio changes to 50:50 (e.g. by the 4th to 6th grade).

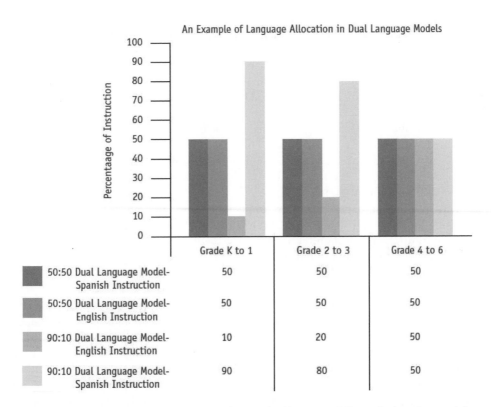

Figure 11.1 Language allocation in 50:50 and 90:10 dual language bilingual education models

The Gómez and Gómez Dual Language Enrichment Model (Gómez *et al.*, 2005) is unique in that in that allocates different languages for different content areas. That is, it divides languages by subject and not time (although overall, English and Spanish are approximately equally used). Mathematics is taught through the English language, science and social studies through Spanish. This model also does not require a balance of dominant English and Spanish-speakers, and thus is particularly popular in schools with high Latino populations such as those along the Texas–Mexico border where it was first developed. Usage of this model has expanded to hundreds of schools across 10 states, but is restricted to schools that have agreements with the Dual Language Training Institute (http://dlti.us/3.html), and requires strict fidelity to the model. However, in a study of the implementation of the model in a central Texas school district, Palmer *et al.* (2015) found that 'the primarily top-down implementation appears to have mixed results when confronted with the realities of different school contexts and educator language ideologies' (p. 453).

Whatever the division of time or subject, instruction in most dual language bilingual programs attempts to keep boundaries between the languages. However, both languages will, in reality, sometimes be mixed in the classroom (e.g. in private conversations, in further explanations by a teacher, and internal use of the dominant language). Use of languages by children, especially when young, is not usually consciously controlled. Switching and translanguaging often have both communication value (see Chapter 5) and pedagogic value (see Chapter 13). Translanguaging can be as natural as smiling. Thus, in practice, however, the degree to which strict separation is practiced or enforced can vary widely (Henderson & Palmer, 2015). For example, when a student did not understand curriculum content or instructions, a teacher might naturally move into the child's stronger language to explain. However, the danger is that students learn that they do not need to understand the second language because the teacher or peers will translate for them.

One danger in language separation is when the allocation of languages is by content (e.g. the majority language is used for science and technology and the minority language is used for social studies). In this example, the majority language becomes aligned with modern technology and science, while the minority language becomes associated with tradition and culture. This may affect the status of the language in the eyes of the child, parents and society. The relationship of each school language to employment prospects, economic advantage and power also needs to be considered. Valdés (1997) cautions that power relations between, for example, Spanish and English speakers in dual language schools are important, especially where programs contain white middle-class English speakers and low income Spanish speakers. Opportunities for both groups to reach high levels of achievement are important. Otherwise native Spanish speakers may be exploited as a language resource, and English speakers become the bilinguals with high achievement and the economic/employment advantages of bilingualism and biliteracy.

Other issues about dual language bilingual education programs need to be considered. First, will both language groups gain high competence in a second language? Or, for example, will the teacher need to spend much time on developing Spanish in English-language speakers, with consequent effects on the language development of Spanish speakers in both Spanish and English? The opposite could also occur. Will the English language receive preferential treatment in instruction as English is the status language in society and legislation? For example, Palmer and Lynch (2008) observed that the language of high stakes tests became the dominant language of instruction, despite program models being officially 50:50. Thus, for students taking the tests in Spanish, instruction was predominantly in Spanish, while for students taking the tests in English, instruction was predominantly in English. The pressure associated with raising test scores transformed the dual language program in more of a monolingual education program. K.A. Hinton (2015) also observed this phenomenon in a high poverty overwhelmingly majority Latino (over 90%) school district, where many programs for ELLs were what he called 'bilingual-in-name-only classrooms' (p. 265).

Second, O. García and Li Wei (2015) argue that translanguaging occurs naturally in a bilingual classroom where children move between their languages spontaneously and pragmatically. For most bilingual children, and some bilingual teachers, it is cognitively, linguistically and operationally sensible to use both languages. It maximizes both linguistic and cognitive resources, and helps achievement and progress. Thus, dual language education that insists on strict boundaries and compartmentalization between languages may now be dated, difficult and unreasonable. Third, dual language bilingual education is not just about a more or less desirable form of education with educational and dual language effectiveness as its *raison d'être*. The underlying politics of dual language education need also to be understood. Salaberry (2009a) shows that such schools are instruments of social engineering, 'aiming to develop a more coherent and demographically representative new mainstream civic identity' (p. 193). Such dual language education is the antithesis of **assimilation**. Instead it may provide children with a cosmopolitan, integrated, multilingual, pluralistic **ideology**. It relates to what R. Schmidt (2009) regards as:

the adoption of linguistic pluralism as a 'common sense' good for *all* Americans, both privately and publicly. ... if linguistic pluralism were to *replace* assimilation to English as the dominant discursive formation in relation to language policy in the US, the probability that Latinos and other language minorities would retain and develop their native-language fluency will be greatly improved. (pp. 147–148)

Origins and Development

Dual language bilingual education programs in the US date from 1963 in Dade County, Florida, and were developed by the US Cuban community in that area (O. García & Otheguy, 1988). In September 1963, the Coral Way Elementary School started a bilingual program that embraced both Spanish and English speaking students. During the 1960s, another 14 such bilingual schools were set up in Dade County. This is related to the fact that many Cubans expected to return to Cuba, believing the Castro regime would not survive. Local people supported the maintenance of Spanish among the 'soon-to-leave' Cubans.

Local English-speaking children from middle class families were enrolled in the school. This reflected a wish among majority language parents for more foreign language instruction following Russia's initial triumph over the US in the space race following the launch of Sputnik in 1958. Since that era, there has been a steady rise in the number of dual language bilingual education programs (Palmer *et al.*, 2015). The languages of instruction in US dual language bilingual programs are predominantly Spanish/English – 95% of the programs in CAL's Directory of Two-Way Immersion Programs (http://www.cal.org/twi/directory/). However, the following non-English languages are also represented in the directory: French, German, Italian, Chinese (Cantonese and Mandarin), Japanese and Korean. There are likely programs using other languages that are not listed in the directory. However, their future under both federal and state policies and politics is not assured. While dual language school philosophy favors an equal balance between two languages, the current US political preference is tilted very strongly towards English.

One early example of a dual language bilingual school – documented in an ethnographic account by R.D. Freeman (1998) – is the James F. Oyster Bilingual Elementary School in Washington, DC. The school's two way Spanish/English program commenced in 1971. The initiative was taken by the local community (by parents and local politicians) to produce a school that crossed language, cultural, ethnic and social class lines. Parents are active in the running of the school. In 1998, Freeman reported an ethnic mix of students (from kindergarten to 6th grade) of around 60% Hispanic, 20% White; 15% Black and 5% Asian and other language minorities. Approximately two in every five children came from low-income families (e.g. they were eligible for the free-lunch program under federal guidelines). In 2002, when 30 new enrollment slots became available in the kindergarten, many English-speaking parents camped out in the snow for up to five days hoping to gain a place for their child (Crawford, 2004).

The Oyster program has been distinctive because it has two teachers in each classroom: one teacher speaks only Spanish to the students; the other teacher speaks only English (a relatively expensive approach). The students experience Spanish and English medium instruction for approximately equal amounts of time. Strong equality dimensions pervade the curriculum (ethnic, multicultural, linguistic, social class), with the contributions of different children encouraged and respected. The notion of language equality permeates the ethos of the school (R.D. Freeman, 1998, 2004) which is reflected in the school's mission statement:

> Oyster Bilingual School's focus is on the development of bilingualism, biliteracy, and biculturalism for every student through the mastery of academic skills, the acquisition of language and communicative fluency, the appreciation of differences in racial and ethnic backgrounds, and the building of a positive self-concept and pride in one's heritage.

R.D. Freeman (2004) summarizes the delivery of the mission:

> It is considered successful because Spanish-speaking students maintain and develop expertise in their native language, English-speaking students acquire Spanish as a second language, all students achieve academically through two languages, and everyone develops positive intergroup understanding and relations. (p. 67)

As Dicker (2003) notes about English language children learning through Spanish, Oyster students learn that the gift of bilingualism is not reserved for Latinos. Oyster students graduate from the school fluent in two world languages such that they can communicate proficiently in many countries on different continents.

Dual Language Schools and Peace

In several countries around the world dual language bilingual education attempts to effect social, cultural, economic or political change, particularly in strengthening the weak, empowering the powerless, and working for peace and humanity in the midst of conflict and terror. As Lo Bianco (2016) explains, 'the term *peacebuilding* is generally understood to involve a range of measures to reduce the risk of lapse or relapse into conflict by addressing causes and consequences of conflict' (p. 1). In his own research and peacebuilding efforts in Malaysia, Myanmar and Thailand, Lo Bianco (2016) found that 'some aspects of language are present in many conflicts, some kinds of conflict involves many aspects of language, and some conflicts are only about language' (p. 2). Two particular examples – Macedonia and Israel – demonstrate the potential of dual language schools as a measure for addressing such language aspects in peacebuilding efforts.

The role of dual language schools in bringing peace in Macedonia is well illustrated by Tankersley (2001) in her article aptly entitled 'Bombs or Bilingual Programmes?' Contextualized within the recent ethnic conflict in the Balkans, she examines a Macedonian/Albanian dual language program. The program demonstrated success in aiding community re-building after the war and the growth of cross-ethnic friendships. The research shows the potential for bilingual education programs to develop students' respect for different languages and cultures, and help to resolve ethnic conflict. However, since the Macedonian language was connected with greater power and prestige, obtaining an equal balance of languages in the classroom was complex.

Dual language Arabic/Hebrew (Palestinian-Jewish) bilingual programs in Israel that aim to break down barriers of mistrust and build peace are portrayed by Bekerman (2016), who has studied such bilingual schools since 1998. She explains:

> The schools … aspire to offer a new educational option to two groups of Israelis – Palestinian Arabs and Jews – who have been in conflict with each other for the past 100 years. The goal of this initiative is to create egalitarian bilingual multicultural environments that will facilitate the growth of Israeli youth who can acknowledge and respect 'others' while maintaining loyalty to their respective cultural traditions. The hope is that Hebrew and Arabic will be used equally in these environments and that the historical narrative and heritage of each group will be recognized. (p. ix)

Each of the dual language bilingual schools has Arab and Jewish co-principals and each classroom is co-taught by Jewish and Arab teachers. Schools attempt to keep equal numbers of Arab and Jewish pupils in each class, although some have a narrow majority. Students are instructed in and through both Hebrew and Arabic. They learn to cherish both languages and cultures and build mutual understanding, tolerance and respect. Such schools provide a showcase to reveal that Jews and Arabs can study, work and seek to live together in peace, forgiveness and reconciliation (Amara *et al.*, 2009).

Peace schools are inevitably part of a wider society, such that equality of languages and resoluteness of purpose and mission can be difficult to maintain (Amara *et al.*, 2009). Arabic has less power and cultural capital than Hebrew in Israel. Many Arabs speak Hebrew, while most Israeli Jews do not know much Arabic. As Cummins (2000a) has argued, bilingual education cannot reconstruct power and status differences in society. Such schools cannot be islands, and 'bottom-up' rather than 'top-down' initiatives are not always easy to sustain in such contexts. Parents also have other dreams, such as English language fluency, high educational achievement and social mobility for their children. That makes language and political ideology just one component in a complex whole. Yet such initiatives symbolize that bilingual education can include a vision that goes beyond languages, beyond a troubled past, and work towards a better present and future. Through dialogue and reconciliation, social change may be achieved.

Heritage Language Bilingual Education

Heritage language education refers to a wide variety of in-school and out-of-school programs that give students an opportunity to develop higher levels of proficiency in their home or heritage languages. Some programs provide only a few hours of language instruction as an add-on to the regular curriculum. Such programs are weak forms of bilingual education because they are unlikely to lead to high levels of proficiency in the heritage language. However, heritage language programs may be considered a 'strong form' of bilingual education when the home or heritage language of language minority children is used as a medium of instruction with the goal of full bilingualism. In addition a strong form of heritage language bilingual education requires adequate resources, sufficient instructional time focused on developing the heritage language, and proper training and professional development for the teachers. The *Handbook of Heritage, Community, and Native American Languages in the United States* (Wiley *et al.*, 2014) provides examples of education through, or more often partly through, the medium of: American Sign Language, Arabic, Chinese, Filipino, French, German, Hindi, Italian, Japanese, Khmer, Korean, Portuguese, Russian, Spanish and Yiddish, in addition to Native American languages including Navajo, Pueblo languages, Miami, Hawaiian and Warm Springs languages. Heritage language programs are also found for indigenous speakers in many countries including Mexico, Canada, Australia, Japan, the United Kingdom, Peru, India and South American, African, European, Middle Eastern and post-Soviet countries (see Wright *et al.*, 2015). The native language is protected and cultivated alongside development in the majority language.

In New Zealand, the Māori language has been promoted in schools with indications of positive outcomes in achievement and expansion (Hill & May, 2014). The full immersion pre-school programs (called Te Kohanga Reo – language nests) were first established in 1982 and have become internationally famous for their early language success with Māori speakers. An early start to bilingual education can create a 'domino effect', producing a demand for bilingual education beyond pre-school to elementary, secondary and higher education, helping to legitimize the language minority, and transforming its power and status. A similar promotion of Aboriginal languages occurs in heritage language education in Australia (Nicholls, 2005).

In Ireland, Irish medium education is sometimes available for children from Irish language backgrounds (Harris & Cummins, 2013). Children become fluent in English and Irish and possibly other European languages. In China there are 55 ethnic minority groups plus the Han who are in a majority (92% of the 1.2 billion population). Since 1979, minority language education has been provided for over 20 minority groups, partly as a way of improving ethnic minority relationships with the central government (Feng & Adamson, 2015). Similar movements are reported in Papua New Guinea and elsewhere across Oceania (Lo Bianco, 2015) and for Native Americans (McCarty, 2013).

In its more inclusive usage, heritage language education is found (a) in schools and classes for established and recent *immigrant* language groups and (b) in community-based language initiatives (Wiley, 2014a, 2014b). For example, in the early 1980s in the US, Joshua Fishman located 6,553 heritage language schools (mostly private), with an impression that there were 1,000 more he had not located (Fishman, 2014). These schools were using 145 different **mother tongues** of various communities. Focused on students who appeared to have lost or were losing their 'native' language, the schools mostly taught that native language and used it as a medium of instruction. Such schools may receive some support from community organizations, foreign governments or

religious institutions (churches, mosques, temples, synagogues). Some community-based organizations foster afterschool programs, Saturday schools, weekend schools and religion-based programs. These supplemental schools have grown, especially among the Chinese and Korean communities (J.S. Lee, 2014; McGinnis, 2008). Such efforts are grassroots-based and therefore often have much vibrancy and an enthusiasm to succeed. Currently, heritage language schools are poorly documented. There is no recent national or local survey.

Day schools are typically fee-paying, private establishments. Hence the students tend to come from middle-class or relatively more affluent working-class backgrounds. For example, there are over 350 Jewish day schools in New York alone, most of which provide some instruction in Hebrew or Yiddish (Avni & Menken, 2013; Peltz & Kliger, 2013). In contrast, non-religious day schools organized by ethnic groups have tended to become more English-focused. For example, many Greek schools in New York are now teaching in English, with Greek taught as a second language class each day of the week. Hantzopoulos (2013) identified just 11 Greek Orthodox parochial day schools (operating under the Direct Archdiocesan District), with 39 Modern Greek language teachers. However, Hantzopoulos notes that most Greek children learn Greek language (and culture) at church-sponsored afternoon or Saturday-school schools.

While US bilingual education has received decreasing federal or state support, there are positive signs of hope for indigenous languages. For example, Hawaiian now shares official language status with English in Hawai'i and is used in some schools for content teaching (W.H. Wilson, 2014). Also, when the US Heritage Language Initiative commenced in 1998, it provided the opportunity for heritage **language planning** on a nation-wide basis (Peyton *et al.*, 2001).

In Canada, heritage language education refers to language education programs in languages other than the official languages of English and French (Duff, 2008). The Canadian Multicultural Education Act (1988) encourages – but does not provide any federal funding support for – ethnic groups to preserve their languages and cultures through heritage language instruction (Ricento, 2015). Some support is available from the provinces and territories, but as Ricento (2015) notes, there is considerable variability in 'the amount of funding they provide for heritage-language teaching, the languages offered, and the grades in which classes are offered' (p. 467). For example, in Alberta, British Columbia, Saskatchewan, and Manitoba there are bilingual programs where heritage language instruction is provided for at least 50% of the instructional time in languages such as Arabic, Chinese (Mandarin and Cantonese), Filipino, German, Greek, Hebrew, Italian, Japanese, Polish, Portuguese, Spanish, Ukrainian and Yiddish (see also Babaee, 2012; Duff, 2008). However, in Ontario, Ricento notes that heritage language instruction takes place outside of regular school hours.

While the term 'heritage language' is used for indigenous peoples as a language minority, it can also include 'foreign born', colonial (e.g. German in Pennsylvania) and African-American Vernacular English in the US (D.J. Ramirez *et al.*, 2005). Wiley (2014b) and Valdés (2014) examine the definitional issues of 'heritage language' in terms of educational programs, community and the language itself. In the US, the term encompasses those raised in a non-English language home who understand and may speak a language other than English. However, heritage language education programs will teach (and typically teach through) a heritage language, and not just include heritage language children. Such a program may include other native language children as well.

The term 'heritage language' may also be called 'native language', 'ethnic language', 'minority language', 'ancestral language', 'aboriginal language' or, in French, *'langues d'origine'*. A danger of the term 'heritage' is that it points to the past and not to the future, to traditions rather than the contemporary (Wiley, 2014b). Partly for this reason, the UK and Australian term tends to be 'community language'. The term 'international languages' is increasingly used in Canada (Ricento, 2015). Thus, the heritage language may or may not be an indigenous language. Both Navajo and Spanish can be perceived as heritage languages in the US depending on an *individual's* perception of what constitutes his or her heritage language.

Heritage language programs in the US and elsewhere vary in structure and content. The strongest forms are similar to **bilingual immersion programs**, or may resemble a 90:10 model of dual language education. In weaker forms the heritage language is simply taught as a subject. For example at the primary school level instruction in the HL may just be provided for a few hours a week as a separate subject. At the secondary level HL classes often take the form of traditional world language courses, but carry designations such as Spanish-for-Spanish speakers or Arabic for Heritage Speakers. Heritage language students may take these courses to fulfill world language credits needed for graduation and college admissions. In many cases HL classes are school-sponsored informal after-school classes that do not carry any credits. However, such courses can lay the foundation for a HL course that can later be incorporated as an official credit-bearing class – a strategy that can be effective for less commonly taught languages (see Chik & Wright, 2017). Most HL programs, however, are community-based programs that vary widely in terms of size, organization, support, consistency, and effectiveness (J.S. Lee & Wright, 2014).

Some of the likely features of strong school-based heritage language programs are as follows:

(1) Most, but not necessarily all of the children will come from language minority homes. At the same time, the minority language may be the majority language of a local community. In certain areas of the US, ethnic minority groups (e.g. Chin, Chinese, Cubans, Hmong, Karen, Mexicans, Puerto Ricans, Somalians, Vietnamese, etc.) are in a majority in their neighborhood or community. In Gwynedd (Wales, UK) where the minority language (Welsh) is sometimes the majority language of the community, heritage language programs are prevalent (I.W. Williams, 2003). The children are frequently joined in these programs by a smaller number of majority language children.

(2) Parents will often have the choice of sending their children to mainstream schools or to heritage language programs. Ukrainian, Jewish and Mohawkian heritage language programs in Canada, and Hmong charter schools in Minnesota and California, for example, have given parents freedom of choice in selecting schools.

(3) The language minority student's home language will often be used for approximately half or more of the curriculum time. The Ukrainian programs in Manitoba have allotted half the time to Ukrainian, half to English. Mathematics and science, for example, have been taught in English; music, art and social studies in Ukrainian. There is a tendency to teach technological, scientific studies through the majority language. Other models use the student's home language for between 50% to almost 100% of curriculum time. Changes across grades usually move from much early use of the student's home language to approximately equal use of the two languages (e.g. by Grade 6).

(4) In the later stages of elementary schooling, increasing attention may be given to majority language development, ensuring that full bilingualism occurs. Heritage

language programs will quickly be seen to fail if students do not become fully competent in the majority language.

(5) Heritage language schools are mostly elementary schools. This need not be the case. In Wales, for example, such schools are available to the end of secondary education and the heritage language can be used as a medium of vocational and academic study at college and university (C. Baker & Jones, 2000). Another example is a Hawaiian heritage language program that operates from kindergarten through to Grade 12, with additional opportunities for Hawaiian medium instruction through graduate school (W.H. Wilson, 2014).

Dual language bilingual schools differ from heritage language (developmental maintenance) schools in aiming for more of a balance of majority and minority language children. Heritage language education is comparatively more concerned with preservation of the ethnic language, ethnic culture and, in many cases, has a large preponderance of language minority children. The type of school possible in a neighborhood is often determined by the demographic and sociolinguistic character of the school population (e.g. the size of one or more language minority groups, the presence of recent or more established immigrants, the numbers of majority language speakers).

Box 11.1 Ten certainties about multilingual education policy and practice

From a wealth of experiences in indigenous forms of bilingual and multilingual education, Hornberger (2009: 197) has expressed a 'deep conviction that multilingual education constitutes a wide and welcoming educational doorway toward peaceful coexistence of peoples and especially restoration and empowerment of those who have been historically oppressed.' This is expressed in terms of 10 certainties about multilingual education policy and practice:

- National multilingual language education policy opens up ideological and implementational spaces for multilingual education.
- Local actors may open up – or close down – opportunities for multilingual education as they implement, interpret and perhaps resist policy initiatives.
- Ecological language policies take into account the power relations among languages and promote multilingual uses in all societal domains.
- Models of multilingual education establish linguistic and sociocultural histories and goals in a particular context.
- Language status planning and language corpus planning go hand in hand.
- Communicative modalities encompass more than written and spoken language.
- Classroom practices can foster transfer of language and literacy development along receptive productive, oral-written and L1–L2 dimensions and across modalities.
- Multilingual education activates voices for reclaiming the local.
- Multilingual education affords choices for reaffirming our own.
- Multilingual education opens spaces for revitalizing the indigenous.

Indigenous Education in the United States

An important example of heritage language bilingual education is provision for indigenous American Indians, Alaskan Natives and Native Hawaiians. T.S. Lee and McCarty (2015) note that in 2012 there were 556 federally-recognized tribes and 617 reservations and Alaska Native villages. Approximately 300 or more American Indian languages were once spoken in the US (McCarty, 2017). The number is quickly declining. According to McCarty (2014), recent counts place the number of Native American languages at 169, with approximately 397,000 speakers among 6.7 million self-identified American Indian, Alaska Native, Native Hawaiian and other Pacific Islander peoples. As few as 20 of those languages are likely to survive (e.g. Navajo, Ojibwa, Dakota, Choctaw, Apache, Cherokee, Tohono O'odham, Yup'ik), because only about 20 are spoken in the home by younger generations. Such language transmission in the family is highly important for language survival (Fishman, 2001). All of California's 50+ Native American Indian languages may be dying as they are only spoken by small numbers of elders.

A history of American Indian education is a record of attempts to eradicate their heritage languages and cultures (Reyhner & Eder, 2004). Forced assimilation has been prevalent for over 100 years, symbolized in phrases from the Commissioner of Indian Affairs, John D.C. Atkins (1887), in his 1887 annual report to the Bureau of Indian Affairs: 'Teaching an Indian youth in his own barbarous dialect is a positive detriment to him' and 'the first step toward civilization, toward teaching the Indians the mischief and folly of … their barbarous practices, is to teach them the English language' (p. 23).

One technique was to remove children from their tribes and send them to distant boarding schools. Stories abound of children being kidnapped from their homes and taken on horseback to boarding schools, many of which were located at former military forts. Such children were given an English-only curriculum, military-style discipline with resulting physical and psychological scars (Spring, 2013). There was severe punishment (e.g. use of belts and hoses) for speaking their native language and a manual labor system that required them to work half days in kitchens and boiler rooms to minimize school costs.

In the 1970s, Congress approved the Indian Education Act (1972) and the Indian Self-Determination and Educational Assistance Act (1975). In 1990, with the passage of the Native American Languages Act (authorized for funding in 1992), and in 2006 the Native American Languages Preservation Act (with additional funding provided in 2008) further efforts have been made to preserve, protect and promote the rights and freedoms of Native Americans to use and develop their own indigenous languages. However the amount of funding is far from sufficient.

An example of a Native American **language maintenance** program is the Rock Point Community School in Arizona, which was established in the mid-1930s, and has been famous since the early 1970s for its role in maintaining the Navajo language (Holm & Holm, 1990). Rock Point is a reservation-interior community on the middle reaches of Chinle Wash in northern Arizona. Enrolling 99% Navajo children, the languages used in this kindergarten to Grade 12 bilingual education program are Navajo and English. The three program aims are defined as: (a) students to become proficient speakers, readers and writers of the Navajo and English languages; (b) students to acquire cultural knowledge of at least two cultures: Navajo and Anglo-American; (c) students to develop critical thinking skills in Navajo and English. In Kindergarten to Grade 5, Navajo is used for 50% of class time; in Grade 6 for 25%, and in Grades 7 to 12 for 15% of total class time. In Kindergarten to Grade 5, reading, language arts, math, science, social studies and health are taught through both Navajo and English, with separation of languages by differing blocks of time.

In Grades 6 to 12, teaching through Navajo occurs for literacy, social science, electives and science (one semester in Grade 6) with teaching in English for reading, language arts, math, science, social studies, health, home economics and physical education. The language of initial reading in instruction for Navajo speakers is Navajo and for English speakers it is English. All program teachers are proficient in both languages. Over 90% of the teaching staff are members of the Navajo ethnic group and provide bilingual role models. A similar Navajo case study of Rough Rock is effectively portrayed in words and pictures by McCarty (2002) and of Fort Defiance by Arviso and Holm (2001). T.S. Lee and McCarty (2015) note however, that despite these successes, 'by the mid-1980s, a shift to English was becoming more apparent across the Navajo Nation' and thus 'the goals of Navajo education have increasingly turned to revitalization' (p. 413; see Chapter 3).

Master-Apprentice Language Learning Programs have been developed by the Advocates for Indigenous California Language Survival (AICLS) organization (Hinton, 2017). They pair someone fluent in a native and threatened Californian language with someone who is often of child-bearing age with a commitment to learn that language and transmit it to others. The apprentice is expected to avoid using English and use just the native language (and gestures) for communication (immersion). Authentic, everyday situations are used so that the language learned relates to real-life contexts such as housework, preparing food and family life. The master and apprentice typically spend between 10 and 20 hours per week together over a three-year program. At the end, the apprentice typically emerges with full conversational fluency. Such apprentices then go on to teach the language to others in a cascade fashion, some becoming teachers in schools who can pass on the native language in an educational setting (Hinton, 2017). T.S. Lee and McCarty (2015) describe efforts among the Pueblo communities of New Mexico to establish language nest immersion programs, summer language programs for children and youth, and language activities in Head Start and local elementary schools. In 2012 the Keres Children's Learning Center opened for pre-school children ages three to six with Cochiti Keres medium instruction designed to 'educate the whole Pueblo child' (p. 415).

These interventions show that bilingual education can be successful in raising language awareness, raising standards of education, and preserving the indigenous languages of the United States. Such bilingual education gives a sense of identity and pride in their origins to American Indian children, preserving not just their languages but also their rich cultures. This reflects the growing US awareness of historical, brutal assimilation and the current need to preserve the deep repository of history, customs, values, religions and oral traditions that belong to Native Americans but which can be valuably shared far beyond the reservations to enrich all people.

Yet language rights and bilingual education programs do not guarantee language maintenance for American Indians. Parents have sometimes made choices against language maintenance, often based on their own indoctrination that 'white and English is best' (McCarty, 2002). Also, it is dangerous to expect too much from heritage language education in saving a language and culture (see Chapter 3). This form of education can produce new speakers and ensure deeper language and cultural roots for native speakers. Without these kinds of initiatives, a minority language can quickly die. When schools do nothing, it is not only the minority language that is not being produced in children. Such a policy also signals the low value, economic worthlessness and stigmatization of a language, affecting the decisions of both parents and students, and not least the fate of the language.

Heritage language schooling is a language and cultural supply line that creates potential. But supply is dependent on demand. Also, potential has to be turned into everyday language usage, outside the school and for the life span. Parents and students expect bilingual education to have purpose and value beyond schooling. It needs to lead to economic and employment, social and cultural opportunities, or heritage language education can create a fine product without much future use.

Immersion Bilingual Education

When applied to language, 'immersion' was first used to describe intensive language programs for US troops about to go abroad in World War II. In the 1960s, 'immersion education' was coined in Canada to describe a new form of bilingual education. Genesee (2015) provides a thorough overview of the factors, forces, mechanisms and counterweights that shaped the development of immersion education in Canada. Immersion bilingual education derives from a Canadian educational experiment in the 1960s in the Montréal suburb of St. Lambert in 1965 (Lambert & Tucker, 1972) although Rebuffot (1993) suggests that École Cedar Park in West Island Québec (started in 1958) and the Toronto French school (dating from 1962) were already in existence. A few English speaking, middle-class parents persuaded school district administrators to set up a French immersion kindergarten class of 26 children. The stated aims were for students (a) to become competent to speak, read and write in French; (b) to reach normal achievement levels throughout the curriculum including the English language; (c) to appreciate the traditions and culture of French-speaking Canadians as well as English-speaking Canadians. In short, the aims were for children to become bilingual and **bicultural** without loss of achievement. The economic and employment advantages to be gained from bilingualism, biliteracy and biculturalism may also have been motivations (see Chapter 19).

It is important to clarify upfront that the bilingual immersion model originating from Canada is a strong form of bilingual education that differs substantially from the monolingual form of education called structured English immersion in the United States (see Chapter 10). Table 11.1 contrasts these two models, and makes clear that bilingual immersion programs are designed to help majority language speakers become bilingual and biliterate.

Table 11.1 Differences between Canadian immersion and US structured immersion approaches

	Structured English immersion (US)	Bilingual immersion (Canada)
Use of first (home) language in classroom	No	Yes
Bilingualism as an outcome	No	Yes
Biliteracy as an outcome	No	Yes
Cultural diversity promoted	Unlikley	Yes
Teacher operates bilingually	No	Likely
Bilingual (certified) teacher	No	Likely
Home language of the student	Minority	Majority
Underlying Ideology	Assimilation	Pluralism

Types of Immersion Bilingual Education

Immersion education is an umbrella term. Within the concept of immersion experience are various programs (in Canada and countries such as Finland, Spain, Ireland and the US) differing in terms of the following aspects:

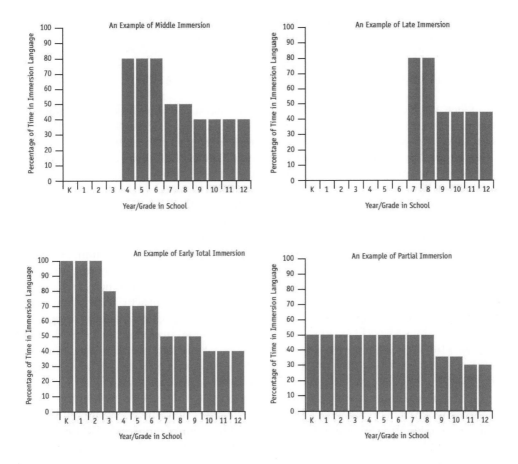

Figure 11.2 Examples of bilingual immersion programs

- Age at which a child commences the experience. This may be at the kindergarten or infant stage (early immersion); at nine to 10 years old (delayed or middle immersion), or at secondary level (late immersion);
- Amount of time spent in immersion. Total immersion usually commences with 100% immersion in the second language, reducing after two or three years to 80% per week for the next three or four years, finishing junior schooling with approximately 50% immersion in the second language per week. Partial immersion provides close to 50% immersion in the second language throughout infant and junior schooling.

Early total immersion has been the most popular entry-level program in Canada, followed by late and then middle immersion. Figure 11.2 illustrates several possibilities, with many other variations around these.

The St. Lambert experiment was a success. Evaluations suggested that the educational aims were met. Attitudes and achievement were not hindered by the immersion experience. Tucker and d'Anglejan (1972) summarized the outcomes as follows:

the experimental students appear to be able to read, write, speak, understand, and use English as well as youngsters instructed in English in the conventional manner. In addition and at no cost they can also read, write, speak and understand French in a way that English students who follow a traditional program of French as a second language never do. (p. 19)

Since 1965, immersion bilingual education has spread rapidly in Canada and in parts of Europe. In 2014 there were 392,430 Canadian children (7.8% of the total school population) enrolled in French immersion schools – an increase of 47% from 1992 (Statistics Canada, 2013, 2015). According to the 2011 Canadian Census, 21.5 million Canadians reported English as the language spoken most often at home, with 6.8 million reporting French, and 3.7 million reporting other (non-official) languages as the language most often spoken at home. Only 17.5% of the total Canadian population reported being able to conduct a conversation in both English and French, however French-English bilingualism is much higher in Quebec where 42.6% reported they could converse in both languages (Statistics Canada, 2013). Immersion education, as well as language reproduction in the home, is a key to maintaining Canada's bilingualism.

From one school started in 1965, immersion education spread rapidly in Canada. What are the essential features of this swift educational growth? First, immersion in Canada aims at bilingualism in two prestigious and official majority languages (French and English). This relates to an additive bilingual situation. Such a situation is different from 'structured or sheltered immersion' of children from language minority backgrounds in the majority language (e.g. Spanish speakers in the US 'immersed' in English). Use of the term 'immersion' in a subtractive, **assimilationist** situation is best avoided. **Submersion** is a more appropriate term.

Second, immersion bilingual education has been optional, not compulsory. Parents choose to send their children to these schools. The cultural and economic convictions of parents plus the commitment of the teachers may aid the motivation of students. Immersion thrives on conviction, not on conformity. Third, children in early immersion are often allowed to use their home language for up to one and a half years for classroom communication. There is no compulsion to speak the second (school) language in the playground or dining hall. The child's home language is appreciated and not belittled. Fourth, the teachers are competent bilinguals. They initially appear to the children as able to speak French but only understand (and not speak) English.

Fifth, classroom language communication aims to be meaningful, authentic and relevant to the child's needs; not contrived, tightly controlled or repetitive. The content of the curriculum becomes the focus for the language. Perpetual insistence on correct communication is avoided. Learning a second language in early immersion becomes incidental and subconscious, similar to the way a first language is acquired. Emphasis is placed on understanding before speaking. Later on, formal instruction (e.g. French grammar) may occur. Sixth, the students start immersion education with a similar lack of experience of the second language. Most are monolingual. Students commencing schooling with relatively homogeneous language skills not only simplifies the teacher's task, it also means that students' self-esteem and classroom motivation are not at risk because other students are linguistically more expert. Seventh, students in immersion education experience the same curriculum as mainstream 'core' students.

Eighth, immersion is not simply an educational initiative. There is also a societal, political and sometimes economic rationale that will differ from country to country. In Canada, immersion matches a French/English dual language history and differentiates

Canada from its larger neighbor, the US. In the US some bilingual immersion programs focus on helping revive or preserve threatened indigenous languages (e.g. Navajo, Hawaiian, Yup'ik), however most immersion programs tend to be advocated more from a foreign language perspective serving language majority (English-speaking) middle and upper-class parents who wish for their children to become bilingual in languages such as Spanish, Japanese and Chinese. In Wales and Ireland, bilingual immersion is partly about establishing a Celtic identity separate from England (D.V. Jones & Martin-Jones, 2004). Unification of a country with varying languages, economic advantage in global trade, international communications and increasing peace, harmony and integration may also be elements of a wider rationale than education.

As with all forms of bilingual education, there are challenges, issues and questions with bilingual immersion (Tedick *et al.*, 2011). For example: (a) Many language majority students do not achieve native-like language proficiency in speaking and writing the second language, even after 12 or 13 years of immersion schooling. (b) What kinds of students do not share in the achievement advantages of immersion education? There are a variety of language and learning difficulties (see Chapter 15 on **special education** needs). What are the outcomes for children who are dyslexic, have autism, Asperger's syndrome or Down's syndrome, for example? What about ethnically diverse students who are long-term or recent immigrants? (c) What are the social and cultural benefits, possibly long-term, for immersion students (e.g. increased tolerance of diversity and difference)? (d) What is the optimal initial training for immersion teachers, and continued professional development, as teachers are such an important part of the equation in immersion education? (e) What are the economic and financial advantages of immersion education, both at an individual and societal level?

Immersion schooling occurs internationally: Australia, the Basque Country, Catalonia, Colombia, Finland, Hungary, Hong Kong, Ireland, Japan, New Zealand, Scotland, Singapore, South Africa, Switzerland and Wales, for example. With over 1,000 research studies, immersion bilingual education has a track record of unusual success and growth (see Johnstone, 2002, for an overview of the international research; see also Chapter 12). It has influenced bilingual education throughout the world with variations to suit regional and national contexts. For example, the Finnish implementation of immersion derived not from parents but from a politically active women's group at Vaasa (Finland), which quickly gained political credibility for integrating Swedish and Finnish-speaking children. It also gained high academic credibility from the research of Laurén and his team at the University of Vaasa (de Mejía, 2002; C. Laurén, 1994). The Finnish implementation is also noted for (a) evolving into incorporating third and fourth languages (e.g. English and German) to produce fluent multilinguals, and (b) providing high quality teacher preparation courses (including by distance learning) that include immersion teaching methodology.

In Catalonia, research indicates that Spanish speaking children who follow an immersion program not only become fluent in Catalan, but also their Spanish does not suffer. Throughout the curriculum, Catalan immersion children 'perform as well and sometimes better than their Hispanophone peers who do not [follow an immersion program]' (Artigal, 1993: 40–41). Similarly, research studies in the Basque Country show that their Model B immersion program (50% Basque and 50% Spanish) has successful outcomes in bilingual proficiency (Cenoz, 2009).

Immersion bilingual education differs from dual language schools in the language backgrounds of the students. Immersion schools usually contain only language majority children learning much or part of the curriculum through a second language

---

Box 11.2 Core and variable features of bilingual immersion programs

Swain and Johnson (1997) and Swain and Lapkin (2005) provide a list of the core features and variable features of bilingual immersion programs, to include contexts where children are learning through French as their third language (e.g. immigrants).

Core Features
- The immersion language is the medium of instruction.
- The immersion curriculum is the same as the local first language curriculum.
- The school supports development in all the child's languages.
- Additive bilingualism occurs.
- Exposure to the immersion language is largely confined to the classroom.
- Students enter with similar (limited or nonexistent) levels of proficiency in the immersion language.
- All the teachers are bilingual.
- The classroom culture needs to recognize the cultures of the diverse language communities to which the students belong, including immigrant communities.

Variable Features
- The grade level at which immersion is introduced.
- The extent of immersion, full or partial.
- The ratio given to the first and second language in content-based teaching at different grade levels.
- Whether there is continuity from elementary to secondary education, and occasionally from secondary to further and higher education (e.g. University of the Basque Country (Cenoz & Etxague, 2013), University of Barcelona, University of Ottawa, University of Helsinki, University of Fribourg, Aberystwyth and Bangor Universities in Wales; Stellenbosch University (see van der Walt, 2013)).
- The amount of language support given to students moving from their first to their second language, including the training that teachers need so as to give bridging support.
- The amount of resources that are available in the first and second language and the teacher training to use these. The commitment of teachers and students, administrators and politicians to immersion.
- The attitudes of students particularly towards the second language culture.
- The status of the second language.
- What counts as success in an immersion program.

(e.g. English speaking children learning through the medium of French in Canadian schools). Dual language bilingual schools aim to contain a balanced mixture of children from two (or more) different language backgrounds (e.g. from Spanish speaking and English speaking homes in the US).

Bilingual Education in Majority Languages

Bilingual education in majority languages (mainstream bilingual education) comprises the joint use of two (or more) majority languages in a school. The aims of these schools usually include bilingualism or multilingualism, biliteracy and **cultural pluralism** (de Mejía, 2002). Such schools exist in societies where much of the population is already bilingual or multilingual (e.g. Singapore, Luxembourg) or where there are significant numbers of natives or expatriates wanting to become bilingual (e.g. learning through English and Japanese in Japan). Asian examples of bilingual education in majority languages include Arabic–English, Bahasa Melayu–English, Mandarin Chinese (Putonghua)–English and Japanese–English. In Africa and India there are also schools where a 'majority' regional language and an international language coexist as teaching media in a school. Bilingualism in that regional language and an international language (e.g. French, English) is the aim and outcome of formal education. Generally, these schools will contain majority language children, with variations in the language heterogeneity or language homogeneity of the classes.

In the Asian examples, a country (e.g. Brunei, Taiwan) or a region may have one dominant indigenous language with a desire to introduce a second international language (especially English) into the school. The international language will be used as a medium of instruction alongside the native language. The aim is for fully bilingual and biliterate students through an **enrichment bilingual education** program. For example, the *Dwibahasa* (two language) school system in Brunei operates through Standard Malay and English (G.M. Jones, 2012). However, many students in Brunei speak indigenous languages, and even Malay speakers in Brunei speak a national variety – Brunei Malay – that differs from the Standard Malay taught in the schools. Thus, as G.M. Jones (2015) has observed, 'children starting school in Brunei have never had the benefit of studying in their mother tongue' (pp. 536–537). In Nigeria, bilingual education is present in English and one of the national languages of Nigeria (Hausa, Ibo or Yoruba,) particularly at the secondary school level, though implementation varies widely in different regions of the country (Igboanusi & Peter, 2015). In Singapore, English plus Mandarin, Malay or Tamil (the four official languages of the country) create bilingual education (Silver & Bokhorst-Heng, 2016).

Content and Language Integrated Learning (CLIL)

Bilingual education in majority languages means that some curriculum content is learnt through a student's second language. In Europe, this is increasingly called **content and language integrated learning** (CLIL). CLIL has blossomed in many European countries, building partly on the evidence-based success of Canadian immersion and US dual language bilingual education (Mehisto, 2012). Launched in 1995/1996, CLIL is a generic term and 'was originally introduced to bind together diverse dual-focused educational practices with explicit attention given to both content and language' (Marsh, 2008: 243). While definitions vary, Coyle *et al.* (2010) describe it as 'a dual-focused educational approach in which an additional language is used for the learning and teaching of both content and language' (p. 1). Cenoz *et al.* (2014) argue that CLIL is better understood as an umbrella term, and cite a need for a taxonomy of different forms of CLIL to bring about greater conceptual clarity that may better guide research and practice.

For example, CLIL may involve Dutch-speaking secondary school students in the Netherlands learning content areas such as sciences, humanities and/or arts through the medium of English (or occasionally German), while at the same time developing proficiency in Dutch (De Graff & van Wilgenburg, 2015). Some 10% to 50% of the curriculum may be taught through another language. While there are many variations in CLIL, the additional language is typically taught as a subject in itself and not just as a vehicle for transmitting content. Yet the emphasis is very much on education and not just on language: 'the major concern is about *education*, not about becoming bilingual or multilingual, and that multiple language proficiency is the "added value" which can be obtained at no cost to other skills and knowledge, if properly designed' (Baetens Beardsmore in O. García, 2009a: 211).

CLIL has some similarities with **content-based instruction** (CBI) in the United States including sheltered content-area instruction, in that the focus is on learning a new language through the medium of content area instruction in that language. However, CBI and **sheltered content instruction** in the US are forms of monolingual and assimilationist education focused on helping language minority students attain proficiency in English (see Chapter 10). In contrast, CLIL is a form of bilingual education focused on helping language majority students attain proficiency in an additional language. Nevertheless, CLIL could benefit from using similar strategies and techniques as used in sheltered content instruction to help make content-area instruction in a second language more comprehensible.

Educators and advocates provide a strong rationale for CLIL (Ball *et al.*, 2016). First, learning a language may be quicker when it is via an integration of language and content, and much slower if just learnt as a language. Second, CLIL ensures a student gains language competence in academic domains and not just in social communication. Third, such an integration of language and content is efficient. Two outcomes can be achieved at the same time: learning a language and subject matter learning. Fourth, CLIL provides a communicative approach to second language teaching that emphasizes meaningful and authentic communication. The purpose of using language is to interpret, express and negotiate meaning. Thus integrating second language and content provides a purpose for using that second language reflecting real curriculum needs and purposeful learning for success in the curriculum. Constructivist theory also stresses that learning best takes place in a holistic sense with the parts making a unified whole in a meaningful way.

CLIL is present in over 30 European countries with considerable variations in terms of, for example intensity, starting age, duration and amount of explicit language teaching (Cenoz *et al.*, 2014). As yet, CLIL practice has advanced without the same research evidence as is present with Canadian immersion and US dual language schools. Cenoz *et al.* (2014) note that 'there are challenges to carrying out research on CLIL because of the diversity of CLIL program formats and the lack of a standardized CLIL framework' (p. 257). Nonetheless, the growing research attention to various forms of CLIL attests to its growing success, strength and sustainability.

CLIL cannot be understood from a purely linguistic or educational perspective. As with all forms of bilingual education, there is a political ideology underneath. CLIL has a strong political basis in the European Union's vision of a multilingual Europe in which people can function in two or three or more languages. With growing communication and trade between European countries, there is an increased demand for multilingual employees (e.g. speaking English and other European national languages). CLIL is about helping to create Europeanisation, a multilingual and global economy, and transnational workers.

International Schools

There are over 8,000 English-medium international schools across nearly every country of the world (http://www.iscresearch.com/). Mainly for affluent expatriates, parents pay fees for mostly private, selective, independent education but there are also scholarships and bursaries. Children in these schools often have parents in the diplomatic service, multinational organizations, or in international businesses and who are geographically and vocationally mobile. Other children in an international school come from the locality, with typically affluent parents who want their children to have an English-medium education in a school meeting international standards. The schools tend to follow a US or British curriculum, with some inclusion of the local tradition. The teachers are from various countries, usually with a plentiful supply of American, Australian, British and Canadian trained staff. Many international schools have an International Baccalaureate (IB) program, which focuses on preparing children for US or British IP examinations and for future attendance in universities in Europe and North America. The official language policy of the International Baccalaureate Organization (2014) declares that is it 'committed to supporting multilingualism as fundamental to increasing intercultural understanding and international-mindedness, and is equally committed to extending access to an IB education for students from a variety of cultural and linguistic backgrounds' (p. 1). Each IB program is encouraged to establish its own local language policy, though a review of language policies and programs at selected IB programs by the Center for Applied Linguistics found that practice varies widely (Fee *et al.*, 2014).

International schools that have English as the sole medium of transmitting the curriculum cannot be included under the heading of Bilingual Education in Majority Languages. Such schools may become bilingual when a national or international language is incorporated in the curriculum (Carder, 2007). The degree to which a school is bilingual may vary by students. An English-medium school is a monolingual form of education for native English speakers, but may serve as a form of English immersion education for international and local students from other language backgrounds. Thus a key question is the extent to which the school provides opportunities to (a) help students develop and maintain proficiency and literacy in their native languages, and (b) develop proficiency and literacy in additional languages. For example, does the school provide instruction for international students in the national language(s) of the country where the school is located?

Carder (2013) argues that international schools provide an ideal setting for developing bilingualism, biliteracy and cultural pluralism:

> International students are living in an 'international space'. Much of their life will be lived in an 'international' arena: the parents(s) probably work in an international organization where English is likely to be the medium. Their friends will be international school students, and they may be viewed by those not in this milieu as being an elite; elite children, however, may well require as much understanding and attention to their linguistic, emotional and related profiles as any other children. In fact the model most applicable for such students is that of pluralism and multiculturalism; in international schools an assimilationist model is not appropriate as there are no political pressures for assimilation; there is no nation-state to assimilate to, nor political measures to treat immigrants circumspectly. Therefore, a model can be provided that promotes enrichment in each student's mother tongue while encouraging students to gain biliteracy with English; international schools provide a unique opportunity for a truly multicultural and multilingual teaching program. (p. 276)

While many international schools provide some instruction in languages other than English, practices vary widely. Sometimes second language instruction (for up to 12 years) is only as a language and not to transmit curriculum content. In other schools, the second language is used as a medium to teach part of the curriculum. Some schools enable their students to acquire third and fourth languages. Generally, the languages of International Schools are majority languages with international prestige. Minority languages are rarely taught in these schools. In some cases, international schools may even be subtractive. For example, in Cambodia some local children of the affluent attend English-only international schools where they have no opportunities to learn how to read and write or develop their oral language skills in Khmer – the national language. Despite the high-status and growing use of English in Cambodia, this nonetheless places these students at a considerable disadvantage. The government now requires most private English-medium (and other foreign-language medium) schools in the country to also provide the Khmer curriculum for Cambodian students.

European Schools Movement

Another European example of bilingual education in majority languages is the European Schools movement. The first school opened in Luxembourg in 1953. Today the European Schools are a network of 14 schools serving about 26,000 students across seven countries – Belgium, Netherlands, Germany, Italy, the United Kingdom, Spain and Luxembourg (http://www.eursc.eu/). Most students (mainly the children of elite European civil servants) begin primary school in their first language, a second European language is added as a subject towards the end of primary school and then used as a medium of instruction in secondary school, and then a third language is added as a subject and potential language of instruction (Cenoz & Gorter, 2015). Students are linguistically mixed to avoid stereotypes and prejudices, and to build a supranational European identity.

The outcome of such schooling tends to be functionally bilingual and often multilingual students with a sense of European multiculturalism and European identity. Integration and harmonization of students from different nationalities is facilitated in part through collaborative group project lessons called 'European Hours'. These lessons provide students and teachers with opportunities to communicate in different languages while exploring cultural subjects through fun and creative activities.

A major difference between the European schools movement and bilingual immersion programs is that the second language is taught as a subject before being used as a medium of instruction. The second language also continues to be taught as a subject (language learning), leading to a high level of grammatical accuracy. Research by Housen (2002) suggests multiple positive program outcomes from the European Schools model. He found that L2 proficiency is close to native speaker levels by the end of secondary schooling at no cost to either L1 proficiency or academic achievement. Pupils also gain high levels of proficiency in a third, and sometimes fourth language, becoming multilinguals. However, bilingualism, biliteracy and multiculturalism are not only due to the effects of schooling. The parents may also be bilingual or multilingual, and the children are more likely to come from literacy-oriented, middle class bureaucrat homes, with a positive view of bilingualism.

Other European Examples

In Europe, there are many other schools that use two or more prestigious languages in the curriculum (Cenoz & Gorter, 2015). In the Basque Country, bilingual schools have effectively provided content teaching in Basque and Spanish. Increasing interest by parents in English language learning led to English instruction starting at kindergarten or in Grade 3 for about three hours per week (Zalbide & Cenoz, 2008). **Trilingual education** is now being evaluated with positive outcomes in terms of multilingualism and educational achievement (Jessner, 2008). The European Commission promotes a policy of 'Mother tongue plus two' languages through early second and foreign language instruction. However, as Cenoz and Gorter (2015) have observed, 'it is often the case that students acquire very limited competence in languages other than English unless they are speakers of minority languages who also learn the state language' (p. 474).

In Luxembourg, children who speak Luxembourgish (Lëtzebuergesch) after birth become trilingual (Luxembourgish, French and German) through schooling. As explained by Horner (2014)

> Luxembourgish has increasingly become the main language used in preschool education. Then, in the first years of primary school, all children go through a German-language literacy programme. ... French is introduced in the second year of primary school and becomes a full subject from the third year onwards. Most other subjects continue to be taught through the medium of German throughout primary school (with the exception of sports, music, and arts where Luxembourgish is specified as the medium of instruction). (p. 149)

Most students have a working knowledge of three languages by the conclusion of schooling. However, Horner notes the rigidity of this model assumes Luxembourgish is the 'mother tongue' of students, fails to recognize the varieties of German and French spoken by the students at home, and fails to address the linguistic needs of immigrant students who speak other mother tongues and languages.

In Switzerland, there are four national languages (German, French, Italian and Romansh) although, contrary to popular expectation, 'the majority of Swiss citizens are not multilingual' (Grin, Hexel & Schwob, 2003: 86). Each of the 26 Swiss cantons has control over language, culture and education without central rule. English is on the increase as a student-favored language, and central guidelines favor children becoming trilingual. Brohy (2005) portrays the many and varied optional and compulsory models of bilingual and trilingual education in Switzerland. She finds that the optional or compulsory component of such bilingual education has political rather than pedagogic justifications.

Conclusion

Support for bilingual education tends to circle around eight interacting advantages of bilingual education that are claimed for students:

(1) Bilingual education typically enables a student's two languages to attain higher levels of competency. This potentially enables children to engage in wider communication across generations, regions and cultural groups.
(2) Bilingual education ideally develops a broader **enculturation**, a more sensitive view of different creeds and cultures. Bilingual education will usually deepen an engagement with the cultures associated with the languages, fostering a sympathetic understanding of differences.
(3) 'Strong' forms of bilingual education frequently lead to biliteracy (see Chapter 14). Accessing literacy practices in two or more languages adds more functions to a language (e.g. using it in employment), widening the choice of literature for enjoyment, giving more opportunities for understanding different perspectives and viewpoints, and leading to a deeper understanding of history and heritage, traditions and territory.
(4) Research on dual language schools, Canadian bilingual immersion education and heritage language education suggests that classroom achievement is increased through content learning occurring via dual language curriculum strategies. This is considered later in the next chapter.

(5) Plentiful research suggests that children with two well-developed languages share cognitive benefits (see Chapter 7).
(6) Children's self-esteem may be raised in bilingual education for minority language students. The opposite occurs when a child's home language is replaced by the majority language. Then, the child, the parents and relatives, and not least the child's community may appear as inadequate and disparaged by the school system. When the home language is used in school, children may feel themselves, their home, family and community to be accepted, thus maintaining or elevating their self-esteem.
(7) Bilingual education can aid the establishment of a more secure identity at a local, regional and national level. Sharing Welsh, Māori or Native American identities may be enhanced by the heritage language and culture being celebrated and honored in the classroom. Developing a Korean-American, Bengali-British or Greek-Australian identity can be much aided by 'strong' forms of bilingual education, and challenged or even negated by 'weak' forms.
(8) In an increasing number of regions (e.g. Catalonia, Scandinavia) there are economic advantages for having experienced bilingual (or trilingual) education. Being bilingual can be important to secure employment in many public services (see Chapter 19), particularly when there is a customer interface requiring switching effortlessly between two or more languages. To secure a job as a teacher, to work in the mass media, to work in local government and increasingly in the civil service in countries such as Canada, Wales and the Basque Country, bilingualism has become important. Thus, bilingual education is increasingly seen as delivering relatively more marketable employees than monolingual education.

To this list may be added the potential societal, ethnic group or community benefits of bilingual education such as: continuity of heritage, cultural transmission, cultural vitality, empowered and informed citizenship, raising school and state achievement standards, social and economic inclusion, socialization, social relationships and net-working, ethnic identity, ethnic group self-determination and distinctiveness. There are also societal benefits that have already been alluded to and will be considered in Chapter 17.

At the same time, bilingual education does not guarantee effective learning. The language policy, provision and practices of the school are but one component alongside many that enables children to succeed. There are many other components that also need to be effective for 'strong' forms of bilingual education to prosper, for example: high-quality and well-trained teachers, good quality learning resources especially available in the minority language, and support by stakeholders be they politicians, policymakers, practitioners or parents and the local community. 'Strong' forms of bilingual education raise the probability of higher learning achievement by children. They do not assure it. This will be considered in the next chapter.

Having summarized various types of bilingual education in this and the previous chapter, the natural question to ask is whether one type is more effective than another. For Spanish speaking children in the US, is it better for them to be placed in main-stream, transitional, developmental maintenance or dual language schooling? For a monolingual English speaker, is it detrimental to enter immersion schooling compared with mainstream schooling? Such questions will be examined in the next chapter by 'effectiveness' research.

Key Points in This Chapter

➢ Varieties of bilingual education include different forms of 'strong' bilingual education where the use of both languages in the curriculum is fostered.

➢ 'Strong' forms of bilingual education aim for students to become bilingual, biliterate and bicultural, and sometimes multilingual, multicultural and with multiliteracies.

➢ Immersion, heritage language and dual language education are the most well known forms of strong bilingual education.

➢ Dual language bilingual education is growing in popularity in the United States mixing majority and minority language students.

➢ In heritage language programs, the revitalization of home (or ancestral) languages and cultures is a key aim.

➢ Immersion bilingual education started in Canada and has spread to many countries of the world.

➢ Immersion bilingual education caters to majority language children learning through a second language.

➢ Content and language integrated learning (CLIL) is a European form of bilingual education and refers to a variety of approaches in which an additional language is used for the learning and teaching of both content and language.

➢ Content teaching can occur through two or more majority languages as in the European Schools movement.

➢ The varieties of 'strong' bilingual education differ in the amount of time given to the minority and majority languages in the classroom but full bilingualism and biliteracy are expected as outcomes.

Suggested Further Reading

📖 Abello-Contesse, C., Chandler, P. M., López-Jiménez, M. D., & Chacón-Beltrán, R. (Eds.). (2013). *Bilingual and multilingual education in the 21st Century: Building on experience*. Bristol, UK: Multilingual Matters.

📖 Ball, P., Kelly, K., & Clegg, J. (2016). *Putting CLIL into practice*. Oxford, UK: Oxford University Press.

📖 Bekerman, Z. (2016). *The promise of integrated multicultural and bilingual education: Inclusive Palestinian-Arab and Jewish schools in Israel*. Oxford, UK: Oxford University Press.

📖 Gorter, D., Zenotz, V., & Cenoz, J. (Eds.). (2014). *Minority languages and multilingual education: Bridging the local and the global*. New York, NY: Springer.

📖 Hamayan, E., Genesee, F., & Cloud, N. (2013). *Dual language instruction from A to Z: Practical guidance for teachers and administrators*. Portsmouth, NH: Heinemann.

📖 Wiley, T. G., Peyton, J. K., Christian, D., Moore, S. K. C., & Liu, N. (Eds.). (2014). *Handbook of heritage and community languages in the United States: Research, educational practice, and policy*. Washington DC & New York: Center for Applied Linguistics & Routledge.

On the Web

⬛ Video – Making Dual Immersion Work (Claremont Immersion School in the US)
https://youtu.be/j1UlcByWXNQ

⬛ European Schools Website
http://www.eursc.eu/

⬛ Video – Content and Language Integrated Learning (CLIL) examples from primary schools and vocational colleges
https://youtu.be/dFuCrxRobh0

⬛ Video – International School in the US with immersion programs in Chinese, Japanese and Spanish
https://youtu.be/Juz3bQyMqBw

Discussion Questions

(1) Share your experiences participating in or observing any of the strong forms of bilingual education described in this chapter. How successful was this program in producing bilingual, biliterate and bicultural students? To what do you attribute this success (or lack thereof)?

(2) Dual language bilingual education is growing in popularity, particularly among language majority parents who want their children to become bilingual. The presence of language majority students and the strong support of their parents have helped to move bilingual education away from remedial to enrichment forms of education. However there is a concern that language majority students, their language (e.g. English) and their parents are more empowered than the language minority students, their language and their families. Why might this be? What can be done to help ensure a true balance in dual language programs?

(3) There is often confusion between Canadian (bilingual) immersion and US structured (English) immersion, and about the differences between content-based instruction (CBI) or **sheltered instruction (SI)** in the US and content and language integrated learning (CLIL) in Europe. What are the differences? Why are these strong forms of bilingual education in Canada and Europe, but monolingual (English) forms of education in the US? How can these approaches be transformed into bilingual models for the US?

Study Activities

(1) Observe and report on a dual language bilingual education classroom. Note the nature and amount of use of the two languages in the program for different content areas or different parts of the day. How much mixing or translanguaging is allowed?

(2) Interview a teacher of one of the strong forms of bilingual education described in this chapter. Ask about the educational, societal and linguistic aims of the program. How does that compare to the program as listed in Table 10.1?

(3) Conduct an internet search to identify schools within your region that implement one or more of the strong forms of bilingual education described in this chapter. Prepare a report on the number of these schools and their respective programs. What do the presence of these schools reveal about bilingualism in your region?

The Effectiveness of Bilingual Education

The Effectiveness of Bilingual Education

Introduction

Having considered various types of bilingual education in the last two chapters, this chapter turns to considering research on the major types of bilingual education. Is there a 'best model'? How effective are these major models for different types of children? What are the successes and limitations of different models? From very early research in the 1920s in Wales (Saer, 1923) and Malherbe's (1946) evaluation of bilingual education in South Africa, there have been many evaluations of bilingual projects, programs and interventions. While the research has been international, the research tends to be about one or two models of bilingual education within a particular country.

In the history of research on bilingual education, it is possible to find research support for most of the different forms of bilingual education by selecting and emphasizing a particular study. For example, Dannoff *et al.* (1978) found mainstreaming to be superior to **transitional bilingual education** with a large US sample of almost 9,000 children. In contrast, McConnell (1980) found US transitional bilingual education to be better than mainstreaming, while Matthews (1979), also in the US, found no difference between these two forms of bilingual education. This chapter attempts to provide both an overview of research, and the varying results that relate to particular political and educational contexts.

Key Themes in School and Classroom Effectiveness

The effectiveness of bilingual education can be addressed from different perspectives. First, there is the effectiveness at the level of the individual child. Within the same bilingual classroom, children may respond and perform differently. Second, there is effectiveness at the classroom level. Within the same school and type of bilingual education program, classrooms may vary considerably, for example because of the teacher and instructional style. Third, effectiveness is often analyzed at the school level. What makes some schools more effective than others even within the same type of bilingual education program and with similar student characteristics? Fourth, beyond the school level there can be aggregations of schools into different types of program (e.g. transitional compared with **heritage language** programs) or into different geographical regions.

It is possible to look at effective bilingual education at each and all of these levels, and at the inter-relationship between these four levels. For example, at the individual level we need to know how bilingual education can best be effective for children of different levels of ability, background and learning needs. How do children with specific language learning needs (e.g. dyslexia, language delay) fare in bilingual education? At the classroom level, we need to know what teaching methods and classroom characteristics create optimally effective bilingual education. At the school level, the characteristics of staffing, the range of language abilities and the language composition of the school all affect 'whether, where, when and how' bilingual education is successful. At all these levels, there are frequently issues about human, material and physical resources. The demands are for an adequate supply of well-trained bilingual teachers, curriculum materials in all content areas, buildings and facilities in order for success to be maximized.

Apart from individual classroom and school characteristics, the effectiveness of bilingual education is influenced by the social, economic, political and cultural context of such education. For example, the differences between being in a subtractive or additive context (see Chapter 4) may affect the outcomes of bilingual education. Chapters 17 and 18 explore how political and ideological differences impact on bilingual education. The willingness of teachers to involve parents, and good relationships between the school and its community, may be important in effective bilingual education. Also, the local economics of schooling play an important part. Where the funding of schools is based on a local tax, then 'per student' expenditure in more affluent areas will be considerably greater than in the less affluent areas. In the US for example, **language minority students** from an economically poor district will typically have considerably less expenditure on them (per student) than those in more wealthy suburbs. It is more difficult to advance the effectiveness of bilingual education with very limited financial and material resources.

It is also important in bilingual education effectiveness research to examine a wide variety of outcomes from such education. Such outcomes may derive from **high-stakes testing**, measures of basic skills (e.g. oracy, literacy, numeracy, information and computer literacy), or the broadest range of curriculum areas (e.g. science and technology, humanities, mathematics, languages, arts, physical, practical and theoretical pursuits, skills as well as knowledge). Non-cognitive outcomes are also important to include in an assessment of effectiveness (Rolstad *et al.*, 2005b). Such non-cognitive outcomes may include: attendance at school, attitudes, self-concept and self-esteem, tolerance, social and emotional adjustment, employment and moral development.

For example, (Crawford & Krashen, 2007) showed that bilingual education is not the cause of dropping-out in United States schools – but it may be the cure. While methods for calculating drop-out rates can vary widely, Latino students are consistently found to have among the highest drop-out rates – an issue of great concern (Lukes, 2015). However, Crawford and Krashen note that less than half of Latino students are classified as English language learners, and even before California passed **Proposition 227**, only about 17% of Latino ELLs were even enrolled in bilingual education programs. Thus, high drop-out rates cannot be attributed to bilingual education. They also note that evidence suggests that those who had experienced bilingual education were significantly less likely to drop out. Factors such as poverty, having both parents in the home, and length of time in the US all attribute to the drop-out rate. When these factors are controlled statistically, the drop-out rate among Latinos is the same (or virtually the same) as for other groups. Since 'strong' forms of bilingual schooling tend to produce higher standards of academic English and performance across the curriculum, then such schools become part of the cure.

Effective bilingual education is not a simple or automatic consequence of using a child's home language in school (as in **heritage language education**) or a second language (as in immersion education). Various home and parental, community, teacher, school, stakeholder and society effects may act and interact to make bilingual education more or less effective. Any effectiveness equation is complex, variable across region and politics, multivariate, and often contested.

The Effectiveness of Bilingual Education: The United States Debate

This section centers on the United States debate about the effectiveness of bilingual education. After a substantial number of individual research studies on bilingual education had accumulated in the US, various reviews and overviews appeared. A reviewer will assemble as many individual studies as possible and attempt to find a systematic pattern and an orderliness in the findings. Is there a consensus in the findings? Is it possible to make some generalizations about the effectiveness of different forms of bilingual education? Rarely, if ever, will all the individual researches agree. Therefore, the reviewer's task is to detect reasons for variations. For example, different age groups, different socioeconomic class backgrounds, varying types of measurement device, different experimental designs and varying research methodologies may explain variations in results.

Early Research

The initial reviews of bilingual education effectiveness were published in the late 1970s. Zappert and Cruz (1977), Troike (1978) and Dulay and Burt (1978, 1979) each concluded that bilingual education in the US effectively promoted **bilingualism** with language minority children and was preferable to **monolingual** English programs. From the late 1970s to the end of the 20th century, many more individual studies and reviews emerged (e.g. August & Hakuta, 1997; Dutcher & Tucker, 1996).

While in the 1960s and 1970s bilingual education slowly evolved in the US, from the late 1970s to the present, politicians have not tended to favor such evolution (see Chapter 9). One branch of political opinion in the US sees bilingual education as failing to foster integration and producing underachievement. Such opinion regards bilingual education as leading to both a lack of proficiency in English and to social and economic divisions in society along language lines. Minority language groups are sometimes portrayed as using bilingual education for political and economic self-interest, even separatism. In this kind of political context, the federal government commissioned a major review of bilingual education in the early 1980s.

K.A. Baker and de Kanter (1983) posed two narrow questions to focus their review. These two questions were: (a) Does transitional bilingual education lead to better performance in English? (b) Does transitional bilingual education lead to better performance in non-language subject areas? Only English language and non-language subject areas were regarded as the desirable outcome of schooling. Other outcomes such as self-esteem, employment, preservation of minority languages, the value of different **cultures**, moral development, **identity**, social adjustment and personality development were not considered.

K.A. Baker and de Kanter (1983) located 300 pieces of bilingual education research from North America and the rest of the bilingual world, rejected 261 studies as irrelevant or poor quality and contentiously used 39 studies. Canadian French immersion (a bilingual program majority language speakers) was incorrectly classified as the same as US Structured English Immersion (a non-bilingual program for minority language speakers). The conclusion of their review is that no particular education program should be legislated for or preferred by the US Federal Government. The review therefore came out in support of English-only and transitional bilingual education. **Assimilation** and integration appeared as the social and political preference behind the conclusions.

There was considerable criticism of the K. A. Baker and de Kanter (1983) review (e.g. American Psychological Association, 1982; Rolstad *et al.*, 2005a; Willig, 1981). The main criticisms may be summarized as follows: a narrow range of outcome measures was considered, although this is often the fault of the original research rather than the review; focusing on transitional bilingual education implicitly valued assimilation and integration and devalued aims such as the preservation of a child's home language and culture; and the criteria used for selecting only 39 out of 300 studies were narrow and rigid.

The approach of K.A. Baker and de Kanter (1983) is narrative integration. This is essentially a subjective and unsystematic process, and the methods of procedure tend to be variable from reviewer to reviewer. A comparison of the reviews of Baker and de Kanter with the earlier reviews by Zappert and Cruz (1977), Troike (1978) and Dulay and Burt (1978, 1979), shows that reviews of almost the same studies can result in differing conclusions. That is, different reviewers use the same research reports to support contrary conclusions.

An alternative and more rule-bound strategy is to use meta-analysis (Rolstad *et al.*, 2005a). The technique mathematically examines the amount of effect of differences in the research studies. For example, how much difference is there in outcome between transitional and **immersion bilingual education**? There is no need to exclude studies from the meta-analysis that the reviewer finds marginal or doubtful in terms of methodology. The quality of the evaluations can be allowed for statistically.

Willig (1985) adopted a statistical meta-analysis approach to reviewing bilingual education. She selected 23 studies from the K.A. Baker and de Kanter (1983) review. All of her 23 studies concerned United States bilingual education evaluations and excluded Canadian immersion education evaluations. As a result of the meta-analysis, Willig (1985) concluded that bilingual education programs that supported the minority language were consistently superior in various outcomes. Small to moderate advantages were found for bilingual education students in reading, **language skills**, mathematics and overall achievement when the tests were in the students' second language (English). Similar advantages were found for these curriculum areas and for writing, listening, social studies and self-concept when non-English language tests were used. A criticism of Willig's (1985) meta-analysis is that she only included 23 studies. An international review of the bilingual educational effectiveness studies could have included many more studies and provided more generalizable conclusions. Further criticisms of Willig are given by August and Hakuta (1997) and K.A. Baker (1987).

An eight-year, congressionally mandated, 4.5 million dollar longitudinal study of bilingual education in the US compared structured English 'immersion', early exit and late exit bilingual education programs (J.D. Ramirez, 1992; J.D. Ramirez *et al.*, 1991).

The term 'immersion' is not used in the original Canadian sense – English **submersion** or mainstreaming is more accurate. Over 2,300 Spanish-speaking students from 554 Kindergarten to 6th grade classrooms in New York, New Jersey, Florida, Texas and California were studied.

As a generalization, the outcomes were different for the three types of bilingual education. By the end of the 3rd grade, mathematics, language and English reading skills were not particularly different between the three programs. By the 6th grade, late exit transitional bilingual education students were performing higher at mathematics, English language and English reading than students on other programs. Parental involvement appeared to be greatest in the late exit transitional programs. One conclusion reached by J.D. Ramirez *et al.* (1991) was that Spanish-speaking students 'can be provided with substantial amounts of primary language instruction without impeding their acquisition of English language and reading skills' (p. 39). When language minority students are given instruction in their home language, this does not interfere with or delay their acquisition of English language skills, but helps them to 'catch-up' to their English speaking peers in English language arts, English reading and math. In contrast, providing ELL students with instruction almost exclusively in English does not accelerate their acquisition of English language arts, reading or math, that is, they do not appear to be 'catching-up'. The data suggest that by Grade 6, students provided with English-only instruction may actually fall further behind their English-speaking peers. Data also document that learning a second language will take six or more years.

The results also showed little difference between early exit and the English immersion (submersion) students. Opponents of bilingual education have used this result to argue for the relative administrative ease and less expensive mainstreaming (submersion) of language minority students (e.g. K.A. Baker, 1992).

A series of reviews and criticisms of the J.D. Ramirez *et al.* (1991) research followed (e.g. K.A. Baker, 1992; Cazden, 1992; Dolson & Mayer, 1992; Meyer & Fienberg, 1992; Rossell, 1992; Thomas, 1992; United States Department of Education, 1992). These critiques included a particular emphasis on the following:

- The benefits of 'strong' forms of bilingual education programs are not considered (e.g. Two-way bilingual education; heritage language education). This makes statements about bilingual education based on an incomplete range of possibilities. Mainstream classrooms with English second language (ESL) pull-out (withdrawal) classes – widely implemented in the US – were also not included in the study.
- The range of variables used to measure 'success' is narrow. For example, language minority parents may expect attitudinal, self-esteem, cultural and ethnic heritage goals to be examined as a measure of successful outcomes.
- The considerable differences that exist within bilingual education programs (let alone differing types of bilingual education programs) make comparisons and conclusions most difficult. Also, the complexity of organization within a school, its ethos and varying classroom practices make watertight categorization of schools into bilingual education programs formidable (Willig & Ramirez, 1993).
- The design of the study was ill-suited to answer key policy questions. More clarity in the aims and goals of bilingual education in the US is needed before research can be appropriately focused. The goals for bilingual education in the US are typically more implicit than explicit.
- The lack of data to support the long-term benefits of late-exit transitional programs over other programs.

Rossell and K.A. Baker (1996) reviewed 75 studies they regarded as methodologically acceptable. They concluded that there was no evidence to show that bilingual programs were superior to English-only options. Greene (1998) re-analyzed the Rossell and Baker (1996) studies using meta-analysis (echoing the Willig (1985) re-analysis of K.A. Baker and de Kanter (1983)). Greene (1998) indicates that classification of 'weak' forms of bilingual education into transitional bilingual education (TBE), ESL and developmental maintenance is fraught with difficulty. What is called TBE in one district could be ESL in the next. Crucially, Greene controlled for background characteristics between 'treatment' and control groups (e.g. socioeconomic class, parents' level of education); thus a third of the 75 research studies were ruled out of analysis. Other studies were excluded because of the need for legitimate control groups, some studies were unpublished or unavailable, duplicated reporting of the same program, and not being an evaluation study of bilingual education. From the 11 remaining studies, it was found that the use of native language instruction helps achievement in English. That is, use of the home language in school tends to relate to higher achievement than English-only instruction. The numerical 'effect size' of home language programs on English reading, mathematics and a non-English language were almost an exact mirror of Willig's (1985) findings, although only four studies were in common.

21st Century Research

Research on the effectiveness of bilingual education in the US continues in the 21st century with renewed interest, especially given the debates surrounding the political restrictions on bilingual programs through state voter initiatives (e.g. **Proposition 227, Proposition 203** and **Question 2**) and the de-emphasis of bilingual education in federal education policy (e.g. NCLB – see Chapter 9). A meta-analysis by Rolstad *et al.* (2005a) included 17 studies conducted after Willig's (1985) study, also found that 'bilingual education is consistently superior to all-English approaches' (p. 572). Rolstad *et al.* (2005b) also conducted a separate meta-analysis with four post-Willig evaluation studies focused on Arizona, and once again found a positive effective for bilingual education over English-only instruction. They conclude that 'the evaluation literature has been remarkably clear in demonstrating that bilingual education is not only as effective as English-only alternatives, but that it tends to be *more effective*' (p. 62). Another meta-analysis by Slavin and Cheung (2005) included 17 studies that focused narrowly on the language of reading instruction for ELLs. They found that 'existing evidence favors bilingual approaches, especially paired bilingual strategies that teach reading in the native language and English at different times each day' (p. 247).

One of the most recent studies is by McField and McField (2014) who conducted a 'meta-analysis of meta-analyses,' including the major studies discussed above. Taking an innovative approach, McField and McField pulled from the studies included in the previous meta-analyses, but with attention to not just *research* quality (as done in the previous meta-analyses), but also *program* quality (e.g. weak, strong, or undefined bilingual education programs). Consistent with the prior meta-analyses, McField and McField found bilingual education to have positive outcomes when compared to English-only programs. However, by considering both research and program quality, McField and McField found an even higher effect for strong forms of bilingual education that were nearly double the size of weak forms of bilingual education.

Public Opinion and the Effectiveness of Bilingual Education

Apart from effectiveness studies, research on bilingual education research includes public opinion surveys. The amount of parental and public support that exists for different forms of bilingual education is important in participative democratic societies as bilingual education is both an educational and political key topic (Crawford, 2004). The opinion of teachers is also important to survey, particularly when there is a difference from parents' viewpoints. Krashen (1999) provides a wide-ranging review of US public opinion polls regarding bilingual education. In polls that attempted to ask a representative sample of people, approximately two thirds of the public are in favor of bilingual education. However, considerable differences in public opinion polls occur because questions differ considerably. How bilingual education is defined differs widely. Leading questions that hint at the preferred or desirable answer, and the ambiguity of what respondents perceive as bilingual education, clearly have an effect on results.

Certainly there is little support in the US for a separatist form of bilingual education in which only the home language is used. There is a high degree of support for English **language proficiency** for all children. When questions are phrased so that bilingual education includes proficiency in both languages, then generally there is a consensus support for bilingual education.

Expert Overviews of the Effectiveness of Bilingual Education

While public opinion surveys are infrequent, expert opinion is more likely to be privately or publicly sought. The United States Committee on Education and Labor asked the General Accounting Office (1987) – now called the Government Accountability Office (GAO) – to conduct a study on whether or not the research evidence on bilingual education supported the current government preference for assimilationist, transitional bilingual education. The GAO therefore decided to conduct a survey of experts on bilingual education. Ten experts were assembled, mostly professors of education, selected from prestigious institutions throughout the US.

In terms of learning English, eight out of 10 experts favored using the native or heritage language in the classroom. They believed that progress in the native language aided children in learning English because it strengthened literacy skills that easily transferred to operating in the second language. On the learning of other subjects in the curriculum, six experts supported the use of heritage languages in such teaching. However, it was suggested that learning English is important in making academic progress.

Another high profile review was by an expert panel of the US National Research Council – The Committee on Developing a Research Agenda on the Education of **Limited English Proficient** and Bilingual Students. It declared that (a) all children in the US should be educated to be become fully functional in the English language; (b) the expectations of, and academic opportunities given to, such students must equal those of other students; and (c) 'in an increasingly global economic and political world, proficiency in language other than English and an understanding of different cultures are valuable in their own right, and should be among the major goals for schools' (August & Hakuta, 1997: 17).

This expert panel concluded that use of a child's native language in school does not impede the acquisition of English, but there is 'little value in conducting evaluations to determine which type of program is best. First, the key issue is not finding a program that works for all children and all localities, but rather finding a set of program components that works for the children in the community of interest, given the goals, demographics, and resources of that community' (August & Hakuta, 1997: 147). That is, a bilingual developmental maintenance program or a structured English immersion program can both be successful in particular local contexts.

Also, many ELL children come from materially poor and disadvantaged homes, schools and communities. While bilingual programs academically benefit such children, the effect of these programs does not close the gap between disadvantaged and middle-class populations. These bilingual students face many issues beyond language, at home and at school, which affect their achievement. Simply introducing bilingual programs will not by itself solve all the educational problems such children face – although they are one important part of the package.

The conclusion from the expert panel of the US National Research Council was that the effectiveness debate was too simple and polarized (August & Hakuta, 1997). All programs could be effective (e.g. transitional, mainstreaming, dual language, developmental maintenance) depending on the subtle chemistry of interacting ingredients, environments and processes. Attempts to prove the superiority of a particular model are pointless and unproductive. Theory-based research and interventions which predicted the effects of components on the 'growth' of children in different environments were needed.

As Crawford (2004) notes, being even-handed, wanting to depoliticize the issue and injecting scientific detachment into research is an academic vision that has little or no impact on journalists and politicians. The 487-page expert review was seized on by both opponents and proponents of bilingual education as justification of their quite different positions. The report thus became a tool used by opposing political groups to support their position

In 2006 there were major reviews conducted by two groups of experts of the scientific research literature on language and literacy instruction for ELLs. One review was conducted by the Center for Research on Education, Diversity, and Excellence (CREDE) (Genesee, Lindholm-Leary, Saunders & Christian, 2006), and the other by the National Literacy Panel (NLP) on Language Minority Children and Youth (August & Shanahan, 2006). Both studies received support from the US Department of Education's Institute for Education Science. The findings outlined in the CREDE and NLP reports highlight what is currently known – and what isn't known – about language and literacy development for ELLs. While these panels of experts were not charged with nor attempted to compare program models, both reports include conclusions in strong support of bilingual education. One of the major conclusions of the CREDE report is that 'use of home language for beginning-level ELLs contributes to academic development'. Major findings in the NLP report include the following:

- Home language literacy skills plus good English oral language skills are strongly associated with good English reading comprehension skills.
- Oral proficiency and literacy in the first language is an advantage for literacy development in English.
- Home language experiences can have a positive impact on literacy achievement.
- Students with literacy skills in their home language can transfer many of these skills to English writing.

Bilingual education programs are designed to facilitate this kind of oral language, literacy, and academic development in the home languages of ELLs, and help students transfer their knowledge and skills from the home language to English.

This chapter now examines recent reviews and major research on dual language, immersion education and heritage language education. Each of these three models has a relatively large collection of literature allowing some overview of findings. In comparison, there are relatively few sufficiently rigorous evaluations of other types of bilingual education (e.g. CLIL), preventing consideration here.

The Effectiveness of Dual Language Education

Many evaluations of the effectiveness of dual language (or two-way immersion) schools and recent overviews indicate relative success (Cazabon *et al.*, 1993; Howard, Christian & Genesee, 2004; Krashen, 2004a; Lindholm, 1991; Lindholm & Aclan, 1991; Lindholm-Leary, 1994, 2001; Lindholm-Leary & Borsato, 2006; Lindholm-Leary & Genesee, 2010, 2014; Thomas & Collier, 1995, 2002b; Thomas *et al.*, 1993). As Lindholm-Leary and Genesee (2014) summarize:

> Over three decades of research in the U.S. indicates that minority language students in two-way [dual language] and DBE [**developmental bilingual education**] programs acquire English speaking, listening, reading and writing skills as well and as quickly as their minority language peers in mainstream programs. ... Minority language students in TWI [two-way immersion] programs achieve at similar or higher levels than their peers in mainstream English-only programs; this includes achievement in mathematics, science, social studies, and other content areas. (p. 172)

Many individual studies have small sample sizes, are short-term rather than longitudinal, inadequately control variables such as social class and initial language differences, and ignore variations in design and program (Krashen, 2004a). Students in dual language education are not a random selection of the population of students. They are self-selecting. Hence, it is difficult to know if the successes of dual language schools are due to the program, the characteristics of the students, or both these, or other factors such as the quality of the teachers.

One of the most rigorous and comprehensive evaluations of dual language schools is by Lindholm-Leary (2001). With wide-ranging and well-documented data from 18 schools, she analyzed teacher attitudes and characteristics, teacher talk, parental involvement and satisfaction, as well as student outcomes (using 4,854 students) in different program types. These programs included transitional bilingual education, English-only, the 90:10 dual language model and the 50:50 dual language model. The measured outcomes included Spanish and English language proficiency, academic achievement and attitudes of the students. Socioeconomic background and other student characteristics were taken into account in reporting results. Among a wealth of findings, Lindholm-Leary found the following:

- Students who had 10% or 20% of their instruction in English scored as well on English proficiency as those in English-only programs and as well as those in 50:50 dual language (DL) programs.
- Spanish proficiency was higher in 90:10 than 50:50 DL programs. Students tended to develop higher levels of bilingual proficiency in the 90:10 than the 50:50 DL program.
- For Spanish-speaking students, no difference in English language proficiency was found between the 90:10 and 50:50 DL programs. However, DL students

outperformed transitional bilingual education (TBE) students in English by Grade 6.

- Students in both the 90:10 and 50:50 DL programs were performing about 10 points higher in reading achievement than the Californian state average for English-speaking students educated in English-only programs.
- Higher levels of bilingual proficiency were associated with higher levels of reading achievement.
- On mathematics tests, DL students performed on average 10 points higher on Californian norms for English-speaking students educated only in English. There was a lack of difference in the scores of 90:10 and 50:50 DL students.
- DL students tended to reveal very positive attitudes towards their DL programs, teachers, classroom environment and the learning process.

Lindholm-Leary (2001) concludes that DL programs are effective in promoting high levels of language proficiency, academic achievement and positive attitudes to learning in students. In contrast, English language learners educated in mainstream classes tend to lack the English academic language skills needed to understand content well even after 10 years of English instruction (Lindholm-Leary & Genesee, 2010). Also, parents and teachers involved in such DL programs are both enthusiastic and recommend the expansion of such programs to raise the achievements of other majority and minority language children.

Thomas and Collier (2002b) compared the performance of dual language students with those in other programs. Their data spans from 1982 to 2001 and includes around 700,000 language minority students from school districts around the US. Their conclusion is that two-way bilingual education at the elementary school level is the optimal program for the long-term academic success of language minority students. Such students maintain their first language skills and cognitive/academic development while developing in a second language. In such a model, students develop deep academic proficiency and cognitive understanding through their first language to compete successfully with native speakers of the second language.

> 90–10 and 50–50 one-way and two-way developmental bilingual education (DBE) programs (or dual language, bilingual immersion) are the only programs we have found to date that assist students to fully reach the 50th percentile in both L1 and L2 in all subjects and to maintain that level of high achievement, or reach even higher levels through the end of schooling. The fewest drop-outs come from these programs. (Thomas & Collier, 2002b: 333)

Thomas and Collier (1995, 1997, 2002a, 2002b) produce a growth pattern of language minority English **language achievement** in different types of bilingual education programs. Major findings include the following:

- In Kindergarten through to Grade 2, there is little difference between language minority children in ESL 'pull-out', transitional and two-way (dual language) programs in the United States. On an 'English language achievement' scale of 0–100 (with 50 as the average performance of native English language speakers), language minority children score around the 20 mark.
- ESL 'pull-out' children initially (Grades 1 and 2) progress faster in English language achievement than children in transitional and **dual language programs**. This might be expected as they have more intensive English-medium activity.

- By Grade 6, students in dual language programs and late-exit transitional programs are ahead on English **language performance** compared with early-exit and ESL pull-out students. Dual language and late-exit transitional students' achievements in English language tests are close to those of native English speakers (i.e. around the 50th percentile). Early-exit and ESL pull-out students tend to perform around the 30th percentile on such tests.
  By Grade 11, the order of performance in the English language is:
  (1) Two-way bilingual education (*highest performance*)
  (2) Late-exit transitional bilingual education
  (3) Early-exit transitional bilingual education
  (4) ESL pull-out programs (*lowest performance*).
- By Grade 11, two-way bilingual education students are performing above the average levels of native English speakers on English language tests. On an 'English language achievement' scale of 0–100, two-way bilingual education students average around 60, late-exit students about the same as native English speakers (around 50), early-exit students around 30 to 40, and ESL pull-out students around 20.

More recent work by Thomas and Collier has extended and corroborated these earlier findings (Collier & Thomas, 2009; Thomas & Collier, 2012). This includes extensive work in collaboration with the North Carolina Department of Education to research the effectiveness of the state's dual language programs. While longitudinal studies of North Carolina students have not yet been completed, Thomas and Collier (2012) describe their findings from studies that compared current students in DL programs with students not in DL programs, across Grades 3 to 8 in 2009. In each grade level DL students scored higher on end-of-grade exams in reading and math than non-DL students. These findings held true in separate analyses of different types of DL and Non-DL students: Whites, African Americans, ELLs, language minority students fluent in English (mostly Latinos), and low socio-economic students. Advantages were also found for **special education** students also in DL programs. Thomas and Collier note that 'by the middle school years and sometimes sooner, two-way dual language students, regardless of subgroup, are often at least one grade level ahead of their comparison group' (p. 72).

Criticisms of Thomas and Collier's methodology and growth trajectories of language minority English language achievement in different types of bilingual education programs include the following:

- Their aggregation is based on selective individual research studies and well-implemented and mature programs.
- Little information is presented on how the growth trajectories were determined.
- The effects of student geographical mobility (e.g. leaving a district) are not clear and may produce biased results (e.g. when such students are excluded from longitudinal data).
- Few details are provided about the hundreds of thousands of language minority students on which the growth trajectories are based and which date from early 1980s to the early 2000s.

More recently, Umansky and Reardon (2014) and Umansky *et al.* (2016) analyzed 12 years of data (2000–2012) from a large urban California school district with four types of ELL programs: English immersion, transitional bilingual education, maintenance bilingual education, and **dual language bilingual education**. In this diverse school district, the bilingual programs served speakers of Spanish, Cantonese, Mandarin, Filipino, and Korean. Only ELLs who began schooling in the district in kindergarten during the time frame of the study – about 40,000 students – were eligible for inclusion. Students in the four programs were compared on three outcomes: attainment of English proficiency, reclassification (from ELL to **fluent English proficient**), and academic performance and growth. The 2014 study focused only on the ELLs in the Spanish-speaking Latino population, while the 2016 study included all ELL students. The findings of both studies are roughly similar. Thus, we will focus here on the findings from the more inclusive 2016 study.

In terms of English acquisition, Umansky *et al.* (2016) found that regardless of program type, over 90% were proficient by 7th grade. However, ELLs in the two-language programs (e.g. transitional, maintenance and dual language) took slightly longer to become proficient in English. While rates were nearly identical by 5th grade (about 80%) there were slight differences in 7th grade with more students in maintenance bilingual (95%) and dual immersion (94%) reaching proficiency in comparison with students in English immersion and transitional bilingual (both at 92%). Reclassification rates were also very similar across program models by Grade 7, however rates were highest for students in transitional bilingual (92%), followed by English immersion (88%), maintenance bilingual (87%) and dual immersion (86%). These results are illustrated in Figure 12.1.

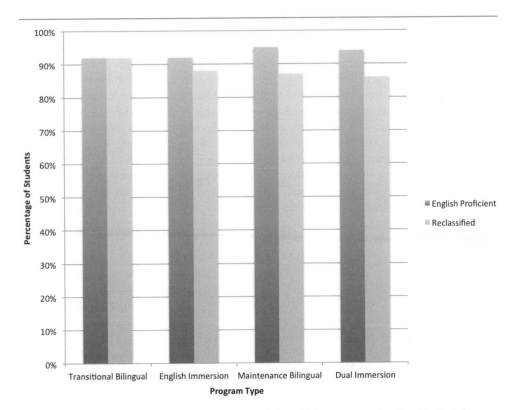

Figure 12.1 Percentage of students attaining English proficiency and reclassification by 7th grade, by program type. Adapted from Umansky *et al.* (2016).

There were also variations in terms of academic achievement and growth across the four program types. Taking a short view, by 2nd grade, students in transitional bilingual had the highest English language arts (ELA) and math scores, while students in dual language had the lowest scores. However, taking the long view of the ELA scores, by 7th grade, students in dual language surpassed students in English immersion and maintenance bilingual, and attained scores that were essentially the same as students in transitional bilingual. Results on the math test were much different. Students in all programs tended to have slower growth rates than average students in the state, and by 6th grade the scores of students in transitional bilingual were slightly higher than those in the other three programs with roughly similar scores.

In contrast with Thomas and Collier, the research by Umansky and her colleagues – in this particular school district – do not find a clear superiority of dual language education across all measures. Nonetheless, their findings do 'suggest that two-language programs generally benefit ELLs as much as or more than English immersion programs across academic, English proficiency, and reclassification outcomes by middle school' (p. 16). Another important finding is that 'the speed with which students are reclassified is not necessarily a good indicator of how well students progress linguistically or academically' (Umansky & Reardon, 2014: 908). Based on these findings, Umansky et al. (2016) urge schools and districts to (a) 'invest in high-quality two-language programs,' (b) 'choose among two-language programs based on community and stakeholder voice,' (c) 'opt for slow and steady – … ELLs can succeed in all three areas, but need time to do so,' and (d) 'take the long view' – tracking students for only a couple of years on a single outcome (e.g. reclassification rates) can paint a misleading picture (p. 16).

Umansky and Reardon (2014) acknowledge a number of limitations of their study. First program implementation can vary widely, and little is known about the pedagogy and practices in the actual classrooms. Second, there appears to be some barriers to reclassification even after English proficiency is attained, but it is unknown what these barriers are. The authors hypothesize these may be more political or programmatic than linguistic or academic (e.g. waiting until the natural end of a program to reclassify). Third, it is unknown what happens with students after they reclassify. We do not know if they excel or continue to struggle linguistically and academically. And finally, while the authors used a sophisticated statistical design and went to great lengths to control for a number of factors, they acknowledge 'this study does not provide as strong a causal warrant as would a randomized experiment or rigorous quasi-experimental design' (p. 907). Randomized experiment of this scope and magnitude are rarely feasible (see below). In addition to these author-identified limitations, another limitation is their focus on ELLs who began school in kindergarten, and most likely are mostly born in the US. Thus we do not how effective any of these programs may be for foreign-born and late-arrival ELLs, or ELLs with interrupted formal education such as refugee students. Given the limitations, the authors caution that these results may differ for other school districts and states.

One other recent study has released preliminary results, and claims to be the first to use randomized control trials in a study of the effectiveness of dual language bilingual education. RAND Education, in collaboration with the American Councils for International Education and the Portland (Oregon) Public Schools (2015) have tracked the progress of students in the district's dual language (DL) immersion programs in Spanish, Japanese, Mandarin Chinese and Russian, since 2012, across 12 schools. Because demand for the program is so high, the district uses a lottery system to allocate seats. By comparing a sample of students selected through the lottery with those students who entered the lottery but were not selected, RAND was able to claim students were randomly selected into the program. In a two-page *Year 4 Briefing Report* released in November 2015, RAND reported, 'Students randomly assigned to [DL] immersion outperformed their peers in English reading by about 7 months in grade 5 and 9 months in grade 8' (p. 2). RAND also reported that no significant statistical differences were found in students' science and social studies scores. Another finding is that, 'on average, [DL] immersion students reach intermediate levels of partner language proficiency by grade 8, with somewhat higher performance in Spanish and Chinese (intermediate mid-to-high) than in Japanese (intermediate low-to-mid) (p. 2). While these preliminary results provide the strongest evidence to date on the effectiveness of dual language programs, the two-page briefing does not include any limitations to the study. When a full report is released at the end of the study, close examinations of the details on the methods, findings and limitations will be needed.

The Effectiveness of Immersion Bilingual Education

There are four decades of research and reviews of immersion bilingual education that paint a relatively uniform picture of success. Major reviews in the 1980s include Swain and Lapkin (1982), the California State Department of Education (1984), and studies by Genesee (1983, 1984, 1987). Research and reviews in the 1990s corroborate and build on these earlier findings, including work by Arnau (1997), de Courcy (2002), Genesee (1992), Hickey (1997), C. Laurén (1994) and work by Swain her colleagues (R.K. Johnson & Swain, 1997; Swain, 1997; Swain & Johnson, 1997; Swain & Lapkin, 1991). Research on bilingual immersion continues into the 21st century (e.g. Johnstone, 2002; Nicolay & Poncelet, 2015; Swain & Lapkin, 2005, 2008; Tedick, 2014). These decades of research highlight four major outcomes of immersion bilingual education, which will now be considered.

Second Language Learning

It is easy to predict that immersion students will surpass those in mainstream (core) programs given 'drip-feed' second language lessons for 30 minutes a day. Most students in early total immersion programs approach native-like performance in the second language around 11 years old in **receptive language** skills (listening and reading). Such levels are not so well attained in the **productive** skills of speaking and writing (Swain & Johnson, 1997).

The reviews confirm that immersion students mostly succeed in gaining competence in two languages (Johnstone, 2002) although many students do not achieve native-like abilities in speaking and writing. However, as Chapter 1 revealed, bilingual ability is not the same as being functionally bilingual. One of the limitations of immersion bilingual education is that for some students, the second language can become a school phenomenon. Outside the school walls, immersion students tend not to use the second language any more than 'drip feed' students (Swain & Johnson, 1997). Such students are competent in a second language, but tend not to communicate in that language in the target community. Potential does not necessarily lead to production; skill does not ensure street speech. Lack of spontaneous or contrived second language opportunity, and a dearth of cultural occasions to actively and purposefully use the second language, may partly be the explanation (other explanations will be considered later). Ideally, immersion programs not only create bilinguals, but also widen students' cultural horizons and sensitize them to second language culture and values.

First Language Learning

If immersion education provides the route to near-native fluency in a second language, is it at the cost of attainment in the first language? Does bilingualism result in lesser achievement in the first language compared with 'mainstream' students? Like a balance, as one goes up, does the other go down?

For three or four years of early total immersion, students tend not to progress in the first language to the same extent as monolingual students in mainstream classes. This first language development relates more to school language measured by tests rather than a **vernacular** first language. Reading, spelling and punctuation, for example, are not as developed and there is a temporary lag. Since such children are usually not given first language instruction for one, two or three years after starting school, these results are to be expected. However, the initial pattern does not last. After approximately six years of schooling, early total immersion children have typically caught up with their monolingual peers in first language skills. By the end of elementary schooling, the early total immersion experience has generally not affected first language speaking and writing development. Parents of these children tend to believe the same as the attainment tests reveal.

Indeed, when occasional differences in first language achievement between immersion and mainstream children have been located by research, they tend to be in favor of immersion students (Johnstone, 2002; Swain & Lapkin, 1982, 1991). This finding links with Chapters 7 and 8 that discussed the possible cognitive advantages consequential from bilingualism. If bilingualism permits increased linguistic awareness, more flexibility in thought, more internal inspection of language, such cognitive advantages may help to explain the favorable first language progress of early immersion students.

Early partial immersion students also tend to lag behind for three or four years in their first language skills. Their performance is little different from that of total early immersion students, which is surprising since early partial immersion education has more first language content. By the end of elementary schooling, partial early immersion children typically catch up with mainstream peers in first language attainment. Unlike early total immersion students, partial immersion children do not tend to surpass mainstream comparison groups in first language achievement. Similarly, late immersion has no detrimental effect on first language skills (Genesee, 1983).

The evidence suggests that immersion children learn a second language at no cost to their first language. Rather than acting like a weighing balance, early total immersion, in particular, seems more analogous to cooking. The ingredients, when mixed and baked, react together in additive ways. The product becomes more than the sum of its parts.

Other Curriculum Areas

If immersion education results in children becoming bilingual, the question is whether this is at the cost of achievement in other curriculum areas. Compared with children in mainstream education how do immersion children progress in curriculum areas such as mathematics and science, history and geography? The reviews of research suggest that early total immersion students generally perform as well in these subjects as do mainstream children. That is, achievement in the curriculum is typically not adversely affected by early total immersion bilingual education.

The evaluations of early partial immersion education are not quite so positive. When children in early partial immersion learn mathematics and science through the medium of a second language, they tend to lag behind comparable mainstream children, at least initially. This may be because their second language skills are insufficiently developed to be able to think mathematically and scientifically in that second language.

The results for late immersion are similar. The important factor appears to be whether second language skills are sufficiently developed to cope with fairly complex curriculum material. R.K. Johnson and Swain (1994) argue that there is a gap in second language proficiency that needs bridging when students move from learning a language as a subject to learning through that second language. The more demanding the curriculum area, the higher the level of learning expected, and the later the switch to learning through a second language, the more important it is to provide 'bridging' programs. Such 'bridging programs' ease the discrepancy between second language proficiency and the language proficiency required to understand the curriculum. A 'bridging program' may require a language teacher and a content teacher (e.g. of mathematics) to operate together.

The overall results suggest that bilingual education by an immersion experience need not have negative effects on curriculum performance, particularly in early total immersion programs. Indeed, most children gain a second language without cost to their performance in the curriculum (Johnstone, 2002). However, the key factor seems to be whether their language skills have evolved sufficiently in order to work in the curriculum in their second language (see Chapter 8).

There is also some evidence to suggest that immersion programs are suitable for almost all children, including those in the lower ability ranges. de Courcy *et al.* (2002) found that, in Australia, such children were successful in immersion education (e.g. in mathematics). Indeed, in immersion classes they appear to fare better, partly due to 'the attention to language the teachers need to have' (p. 117). There is care with vocabulary, sensitivity to language form and not just to subject content. This parallels Bruck's (1978, 1982) research in Canada where 'language impaired' children were not found to suffer but gain some second language proficiency from the immersion experience. Canadian research also suggests that there are no adverse effects from immersion on below average IQ students compared with such students being in a monolingual program. Rather, some degree of bilingualism is attained (Genesee, 1992). de Courcy *et al.* (2002) found that:

> The research identified in the literature review and our own data leads us to conclude that children from diverse backgrounds should not be forced out of immersion programmes, as they would do no better in the English mainstream, but would lose the benefit of learning an additional language, at a cost to their self-esteem. (p. 125)

Attitudes and Social Adjustment

Apart from performance throughout the curriculum, evaluations of immersion education have examined whether immersion has positive or negative effects on students' motivation, attitude and study skills. The most positive results in this area have been found with early total immersion students. Parents of such students tend to express satisfaction with their offspring's learning as well as their personal and social behavior (e.g. Hickey, 1997 in Ireland). Early immersion students also tend to have more positive attitudes towards themselves, their education and in Canada, to French Canadians (in comparison, for example, with late immersion students). However, the danger here lies in attributing the positive attitudes to schooling. The cause may alternatively be parental values and beliefs, home culture and environment. This is further discussed in the next section.

Problems and Limitations

Over the years various scholars and educators have highlighted potential problems and limitations in immersion education (Dagenais, 2003; de Courcy, 2002; Hammerly, 1988; Heller, 2003; Netten & Germain, 2004; Swain & Lapkin, 2008). Some of these concerns include the following:

- Canadian immersion students do not always gain grammatical accuracy or competence in all dimensions in their French comparable to native speakers. This may be due to the limited nature of communication between students and teachers in the social environment of the classroom and a greater instructional focus on content and curriculum achievement.
- Graduates of Canadian immersion programs may not make much use of French after leaving school. This partly reflects opportunity, partly a lack of confidence in their competence in speaking French, and partly a preference for English use.
- There is difficulty in pinpointing the crucial interacting factors that create an effective immersion experience. There are, for example, intervening variables such as teacher preparation, teaching techniques, student motivation, parental attitudes, curricular choices, and classroom management. Also there are debates over what is more important – the intensity of language learning (i.e. number of hours of study per day) or length of time learning the language (i.e. number of years of language instruction).
- Immersion programs can have effects on mainstream schools such as a redistribution of classroom teachers and leaders, a change in the linguistic and ability profile of mainstream classes, and discrepancies in class size with increasing numbers of mixed aged classes.
- Canadian immersion schools provide Anglophones with the linguistic and cultural capital for increased social and economic mobility and for political power. Hence, immersion education may produce conflict with the minority Francophone community (e.g. in Ontario) rather than the harmonious unity and 'bridge building' that bilingualism aims to achieve in Canadian society.
- Research has concentrated more on the outcomes of immersion education, and less on the immersion learning processes from the students' perspectives.
- There is a danger in generalizing from the successful Canadian experience to elsewhere in the world (see Box 12.1). In Canada, immersion concerns two major high status international languages: French and English. In many countries where bilingualism is present or fostered, the situation is different. Often the context is one of a majority and a minority language (or languages) co-existing.

The more educators are aware of and acknowledge these problems and limitations, the better they can attempt to address them.

Box 12.1 Cautions in generalizing Canadian immersion education

If immersion education is thought worthy of generalizing from Canada to other countries, there are certain conditions that need to be kept in mind:

- *Conviction* – Immersion bilingual education as practiced in Canada is optional. The convictions of teachers and parents and of the children themselves affect the ethos of the school and the motivation and achievement of the children. Immersion education will work best when there is conviction and not enforced conformity.
- *Homogeneity* – Immersion education in Canada typically starts with children who are at a similar level in their language skills. Such a homogeneous grouping of children may make the language classroom more efficient. Outside of Canada adjustments may be needed when such homogeneity is not realistic or even desirable.
- *Respect* – The Canadian immersion experience ensures that there is respect for the child's home language and culture. Parents are generally seen as partners in the immersion movement and some dialogue has existed with administrators, teachers and researchers.
- *Commitment* – Immersion teachers in Canada tend to be committed to such immersion education. Research in teacher commitment is of crucial importance to bilingual education in effecting achievement in school.
- *Ideologies* – Behind Canadian immersion education is political, social and cultural ideology aimed at creating a different kind of society. By promoting bilingualism in English speakers, immersion education in Canada may support French language communities, increase the opportunities for Francophones outside Québec and help promote bilingualism in the public and private sectors. However, immersion education is seen as a Trojan horse of further English assimilation by some Francophones while giving Anglophone children with bilingual abilities an advantage in the jobs market.

The Effectiveness of Heritage Language Education

Reviews and evaluations of heritage language education programs also span four decades and multiple countries. Reviews focused on Canada include those by Cummins (1983, 1993), Cummins and Danesi (1990), the Canadian Education Association (1991) and Duff (2008). Reviews focused on heritage language programs for indigenous (e.g. American Indian, Hawaiian) and immigrant communities in the US include work by Brinton (2008), Demmert (2001), McCarty (2002, 2008, 2013, 2017), J.S. Lee and Wright (2014), Peyton *et al.* (2001) and Wiley *et al.* (2014). While these evaluations are from the northern hemisphere, there is a growing literature from the southern hemisphere (e.g. Heugh *et al.*, 2007; Heugh & Skutnabb-Kangas, 2010; Mohanty *et al.*, 2009) and literature that looks internationally (e.g. Dutcher & Tucker, 1996; Kagan *et al.*, 2017). Apart from looking at individual international educational interventions, the reviews also look at the pattern that can be found in the results of evaluations of heritage language education, thus attempting to derive international generalizations.

The results of such evaluations suggest that heritage language programs can be effective in four different ways. First, the students develop and maintain their home languages. Second, such children tend to perform as well or better academically as comparable mainstream children. Third, studies suggest that children's attitudes are particularly positive when placed in heritage language education. When the home language is used in school, there is the possibility that a child's sense of identity, self-esteem and self-concept will be enhanced. In comparison, a language minority child who is mainstreamed is vulnerable to a loss of self-esteem and status. The home language and culture may seem disparaged. The school system and the teachers may seem latently or manifestly to be rejecting the child's home language and values. This may affect the child's motivation and interest in schoolwork and thereby affect performance. A student whose skills are recognized and encouraged may feel encouraged and motivated; a student whose skills are ignored may feel discouraged and rejected. Hence, intra-family communication may improve both in terms of language, cultural identity and bonding. The fourth finding of heritage language evaluations is perhaps the most unexpected. Indeed, it tends to go against 'common sense'. Even with less instructional time devoted to English, when **testing** children's English language performance (or whatever the second language is for that child), they are likely to perform at least as well as children in mainstream education. The explanation seems to lie in self-esteem being enhanced, language and intellectual skills better promoted by education in the home language, and the transfer of such skills into second language (majority language) areas.

While evaluations of heritage language education are positive, not all Canadians are agreed on the issue. For some, **empowerment** of heritage language groups (i.e. non-English and French) is perceived as a major societal challenge – a challenge to existing power and political arrangements. Official Canadian policy has been supportive of multiculturalism, especially of the two 'solitudes' – French language and English language cultures. Extending multiculturalism to other 'heritage' languages has been more contentious. Lukewarm support for heritage language communities tends to stop short if public monies are to be used to support heritage language education. The anxieties of sections of public opinion and of government include: the disruption of mainstream schools (e.g. falling rolls), problems of staffing, minimal communication between heritage language teachers and mainstream teachers, segregation of school communities, the financial costs of the absorption of immigrants into a bilingual education system, loss of time for core curriculum subjects, social tensions, and effects on the integration and stability of Canadian society. Such anxieties have grown with the increased levels of immigration into Canadian. Owing to low birth rates and an aging population in Canada, the population has been increased by government immigration policies. Hence language diversity in Canada has increased. In Toronto and Vancouver, for example, more than half the school population comes from a non-English speaking background.

An important extra perspective comes from a World Bank report in the mid 1990s which included an economic analysis of heritage language and other forms of bilingual education (Dutcher & Tucker, 1996). The report examined international evidence from Haiti, Nigeria, the Philippines, Guatemala, Canada, New Zealand, the United States (Navajo), Fiji, the Solomon Islands, Vanuatu and Western Samoa. The report found bilingual education is not an expensive option and has similar costs to mainstream programs. However, the most important conclusion is that strong forms of bilingual education create cost savings for the education system and for society. For example, such bilingual education provides higher levels of achievement in fewer years of study. Student progress is faster, and higher achievement benefits society by less unemployment and a more skilled work force.

When there are 'weak' forms of bilingual education, or language minority children are mainstreamed, there may be costs to a national economy owing to slower rates of progress at school, lower levels of final achievement, and sometimes the need for special or compensatory education. Higher drop-out rates mean lower potential for the employment market, and the economy suffers with a lower level of skills among the work force and higher unemployment rates. In economic terms, students need to gain productive characteristics through education and early use of the native language.

For example, Dutcher (2004) describes a World Bank cost-effectiveness study on Guatemala that found that bilingual education was an economically prudent policy (see World Bank, 1997). Repetition and drop-out rates were decreased through a bilingual education intervention program, and standards of achievement rose (including in Spanish). It was estimated that education cost savings due to bilingual education were 5.6 million US dollars per year, while cost benefits were in the order of 33.8 million US dollars per year. Also, individual earnings rose by approximately 50%. In Guatemala, a strong form of bilingual education made economic sense as it produced a more skilled, highly trained and employable work force. Weak forms of bilingual education in comparison tend to have higher drop-out rates and lower levels of achievement, and thus have less chance of serving and stimulating the economy through a skilled work force.

Research Limitations

So far in this chapter, we have examined research on specific models of bilingual education (dual language, heritage language, immersion). Underneath such bilingual education, irrespective of which model is being discussed is politics. Bilingual education is, and will continue to be, a political issue. For some, pluralism, biculturalism and **multilingualism** are a desirable outcome. For others the assimilation of minority languages and the integration of minorities within the overall society are the important outputs. This suggests that a definitive statement on whether bilingual education is more or less successful than, for example, mainstream education is impossible owing to the variety of underlying values and beliefs that different interest groups have about education and the future society they envisage. 'Effective in doing what?' is the key question, with different answers by different political groups.

It may appear that the research reviews highlighted in this chapter can directly inform policy-making. In reality, there are hundreds of variables that affect program outcomes such that research cannot, by itself, directly advise policy, provision and practice. Within the complex nature of educational settings, data or 'facts' become relevant for policy purposes only in the context of a coherent theory. It is the *theory* rather than the individual research findings that permits the generation of predictions about program outcomes under different conditions (Cummins, 1999). That is, research should commence from theoretical propositions, testing, refining and sometimes refuting those propositions. When theory is firmly supported by research and if it accounts for findings from a variety of contexts, theory will explicitly inform policy-making.

However, policy makers rarely base their decisions solely on theory or research. The reason is that the researcher/policy-maker relationship is not one of 'truth speaking to power', or 'science providing evidence-based decisions'. That is too simplistic. Policy in bilingual education is shaped by myriad influences other than research and theory (e.g. political **ideology**, attractiveness to voters, pragmatism, economics, conflicting interests and varied stakeholders). When research does have an influence, it can be through 'cherry-picking' the most convenient and supportive findings for a particular viewpoint. Evidence from research and theory can inform policy and be a part of the shaping of that policy. Its effects will be partial and modest, and be part of a continuous shared search for worthwhile education.

Thus, research cannot provide evidence-based policy, only evidence-informed policy. No research on bilingual education is perfect, even totally objective. This section now provides the critical lens to assess such research.

Methodological and Theoretical Issues

In the US since the passage of NCLB in 2001, education programs are expected to be grounded in 'scientifically based research'. While there are many types of research methods and approaches used within the education field, in this context 'scientifically based research' usually suggests quantitative experimental research studies comparing groups of students who receive or do not receive some kind of treatment or intervention through valid and reliable measures and statistical analyses. The gold standard is randomized controlled trails (RCTs), meaning study participants are randomly assigned to one of two groups: the treatment group (i.e. those who receive the treatment), and control group (i.e. students who don't receive the treatment). RCTs are important in medical research studies such as drug trials to determine if a new drug is effective. In the context of an idealized bilingual education study, for example, half the students would be randomly assigned to a well-designed dual language classroom (the treatment group), and half the students would be randomly assigned to a typical English-only mainstream classroom (the control group). However, in reality, meeting this gold standard is problematic. To date only the RAND (2015) study has used RCTs, however in this case random assignment was a result of a lottery system developed by the district used to address demand for the program, and did not originate as part of the research design. The randomized students were only a small sample of the larger population of students in the program and in the control group. Even in this case, randomization only occurred among those students with highly engaged parents who actively sought enrollments for their children in the program. True randomization would be free of parental demand.

C. Baker and Lewis (2015) argue that randomized controlled trials 'are normally pragmatically unachievable and ethically undesirable in education' (p. 119). They explain:

> [RCTs only tend] to work in a laboratory setting which can be reduced to single components and controls, whereas schools and classrooms have complex multi-causality, are ever dynamic and fluid, evolving and every-changing, some unpredictable and inconsistent. The gold standard is thus not usually possible in bilingual education effectiveness research. A randomized controlled trial is still dependent on local conditions and is situated within a particular time. Students, teachers, and instructional styles cannot be reduced to isolated variables and manipulated as if they were seeds in agricultural experimental research. ... The search for the Holy Grail of a perfect piece of research on bilingual education is not elusive. It is unattainable. (p. 119)

Nevertheless, the push for 'scientifically based research' led to the establishment of the What Works Clearinghouse (WWC) in 2002 as an initiative of the Institute of Education Sciences (IES) at the US Department of Education (DOE). The goal of the WWC is to provide educators with information needed to make evidence-based decisions. The WWC prioritizes randomized control trial experiments, though quasi-experimental designs and other well-designed quantitative experimental designs may partially meet the clearinghouse's rigorous requirements of evidence of effectiveness. Over 11,000 studies have been reviewed, and not surprisingly, very few meet the WWC's high evidence standards. This is especially true of the studies included in the English language learners section. The IES and DOE now require recipients of their research and even professional development grants to include evaluation studies that (attempt to) meet these rigorous standards. These requirements have greatly narrowed the range of potential research projects and programs eligible for federal funding.

C. Baker and Lewis (2015) argue that imperfect research studies – those that don't meet the WWC standards (and even those that do) – still have important value:

> Research is valuable when it is well replicated, cumulative across time, place and person, and when the limitations of individual research are honestly and openly stated. That individual pieces of research on bilingual education are imperfect also means that reviews and overviews are essential. One piece of research can never be final, conclusive, or definite. It is the accumulation of research across time, place and person that allows trends to be located, generalizations to be attempted, and policymakers presented with a synopsis of well-replicated and evidenced-informed conclusions, even if they are temporary, transient, and to be further tested. (p. 119)

The Sample of Children

The results of one study are limited to that sample of children at the time of the study. If there is some form of probability sampling (e.g. a random sample of a defined population is chosen), then these results may generalize to that specific population. Such sampling rarely occurs in bilingual education evaluations. Instead, most studies are small-scale and utilize convenient or purposive sampling. As noted above, it is usually ethically questionable and practically impossible to allocate children randomly into experimental and control groups that contain perfect mirrors of a large population of schoolchildren (see August *et al.*, 2006 for an alternative design). Generalization of results from one group to another is rarely valid because bilingual students vary widely in terms of home languages, length of time in the target country or school, number of years learning the new language, socio-economic status, parents' level of education, prior schooling and on many other factors.

Interacting Factors

Various factors, other than the sample of children, may have a variable effect on the effectiveness of bilingual education. Parental interest (e.g. parental involvement in their children's education and parental cooperation with teachers) is one intervening factor. Another factor is likely to be the enthusiasm and commitment of teachers to the education program. The level of resource support (e.g. books, curriculum guidelines, computers, science equipment) may also produce variable outcomes. In contrast, policy makers deal in general scenarios and trends and prefer a broad-brush canvas.

There can be as much variation in outcomes inside a particular bilingual education program (e.g. achievement in different curriculum areas) as between different types of program (e.g. transitional, immersion or heritage language). The crucial point is this: the language policy and language practice in schooling are only one element among many that make a school more or less successful. A recipe for success is unlikely to result from one ingredient (e.g. the language of the classroom). A great variety of factors act and interact to determine whether bilingual education is successful or not. It makes more sense to consider the wide variety of conditions which make bilingual education more or less successful. Bilingual education, whatever the type or model, is no guarantee of effective schooling. Particular models of bilingual education interact with a host of student, teacher, curriculum and contextual variables in complex ways to influence student outcomes. Also, attempts to compare different types of program models can be difficult because programs are often not labeled accurately (e.g. a **sheltered English immersion** labeled as a 'bilingual program' simply because it serves bilingual children), and there is often great variability in how specific programs (e.g. dual language, heritage language) are actually structured and put into practice at the classroom level.

Measures of Success

In bilingual education investigations, there is a range of measurement problems that need to be addressed. The following are just four important issues to consider:

(1) Measuring something like language proficiency is more elusive than portrayed due to problems such as definition, ambiguity, **validity** and **reliability** (see Chapters 1 and 2).
(2) Measuring constructs such as academic achievement in reading and math are also plagued with problems of definitions, ambiguity, validity and reliability, particularly when testing students in a language in which they are not yet proficient.
(3) Timing of the measurement is key. If intended outcomes (e.g. English vocabulary knowledge) are measured too soon, we may draw the wrong conclusion about the effectiveness of the bilingual program. If the intended outcome is measured too late, we may wrongly attribute causality to a bilingual program after a range of other factors (e.g. parental, peer, and out-of school experiences) have entered into the equation to affect the outcome.
(4) An important question in any research study is: what tests or other sources of evidence are used to determine whether a form of bilingual education is successful? Should the sole outcomes be competence in one or two languages, or performance across the whole curriculum? Measures of success in bilingual education tend to narrowly focus on tests of language proficiency, literacy and math. What of important outcomes such as personality and identity development, social and emotional adjustment, self-esteem, integration into society, cultural and ethnic participation, moral development and employment? These are rarely included as measurements of successful outcomes. These questions suggest that there will be debates and disputes over what are the valuable outcomes of schooling. Research on the effectiveness of bilingual education has varied in the choice of measures of outcome. Such a choice reflects a particular emphasis, ideology or conviction. It is not a neutral or value-free judgment.

The Style of the Research

There is continuous debate regarding the appropriate research methods to be used when studying bilingual education. There is tension between quantitative research studies that attempt to analyze 'objective' measures such as test scores, and qualitative research that seeks a deeper understanding of a phenomenon through observations, interviews, and analysis of artifacts (e.g. policy documents, school memos, teacher lesson plans, student classwork). However, chosen methods are often ostensibly related to the research questions asked (Hult & Johnson, 2015). If the question is on the effectiveness of a particular bilingual program model in helping students gain high levels of proficiency in both English and Spanish, then English and Spanish language test scores from the beginning and end of the school year could be collected from hundreds of students in similar programs across a school, district, state, or even the nation. The researchers would not even need to visit the classrooms or meet the students to answer such a question. However, if the research question is *how* a bilingual program helps students to attain high levels of bilingualism, then a researcher needs to spend time in the classroom to observe instruction, talk to students and teachers, and review program documents, lesson plans, and curricular materials. Mixed methods studies are often used together. For example, a large-scale survey of bilingual teachers can provide a broad overview of teacher's attitudes and beliefs that can then be explored in greater depth through observations and focus group interviews with representative samples of teachers. A wide variety of both quantitative and qualitative research methods and approaches are needed to research various aspects of bilingual education to inform policy and practice.

However, as noted above, in the US context only certain experimental studies that meet the highest standards of rigor (e.g. randomized control trials) are considered acceptable for providing strong evidence of 'what works.' Such a narrow view is akin to suggesting that a play can only be judged by objective measures using an applause meter. The following illustrate some of the limitations of such experimental research:

- A new program approach to bilingual children may exaggerate its effectiveness (novelty effect).
- There may be extra enthusiasm and motivation to succeed (and better materials) in a new approach. A comparison of new and old can be unfair as the effect is temporary.
- Being in an experiment can change schools' or teachers' behavior (Hawthorne effect). Being 'under the spotlight' can make a difference (positive or negative) to customary performance in teachers and students.
- It is impossible to match teachers, so differential gains may be due to teachers rather than a particular model of bilingual education. Even when (unusually) the same teachers are used in different models, their motivation may be different in each, thus not controlling this important and influential variable.
- An intervention found to be effective through experimental research in one context (e.g. among middle-class **language majority students** in an urban French immersion class) can not necessarily be generalized to another context (e.g. a sheltered English immersion class in a low socio-economic rural community along the Arizona-Mexico border)
- An experiment measures success on a very narrow range of outcomes. It does not usually measure side-effects (e.g. less enthusiasm, less time for leisure activities). There is a distinction between program effectiveness (e.g. attaining learning outcomes) and effects (i.e. any consequence, intended or not).
- An experiment does not investigate process (e.g. how a teacher interprets and operates within a program). Fidelity of implementation of a 'treatment' can vary widely. In other words, within a given program or intervention, teachers interpret and adapt in the light of their own experience and the type of students to be instructed, so that the process can vary considerably across classrooms within the same program.
- Experimental studies are assumed to be 'objective'. Yet the decisions about what variables to include and exclude in a model (e.g. test scores, English proficiency level, parents' level of education) and decisions about where to collect data, from what types of students, and how to interpret the findings are all highly subjective decisions.

- Random assignment of students to different types of program models is unethical. Parental choice is taken away. Assigning students randomly to a known-inferior program (e.g. English submersion) deprives them of a quality education.
- An experiment is a 'black box model' of research. It can be run by researchers without ever visiting a school. They need to send pre-tests and post-tests to the school and then analyze the returned results. There is no guarantee all were administered in a standardized way. In contrast, engaging in the processes of classrooms is called a glass box model of research, whereby the detail of classroom activity is open to viewing. Experiments take snapshots. A glass box model (e.g. observation) takes a film.
- Attention is focused on program aggregation and averages. Outstanding individual schools that may be atypical are lost in an overall result. Outliers – those at the highest and lowest ends – are often removed from the sample for being 'atypical'. Yet an in-depth (qualitative) study of these outliers could potentially result in important discoveries.
- The assumption is that there is an objective scientific truth, experimentally demonstrable that allows a trustworthy prediction of outcomes. This can sometimes be linked to the desire to impose uniformity and political control. Instead, educational outcomes will always be debated and contested, being changeable across time and ideology.

The Researchers

Research on bilingual education is rarely neutral. Often the researchers have hypotheses that hide their expectations. No educational research can be totally value-free, neutral or objective. The questions asked, the methodological tools chosen, decisions in analysis and manner of reporting usually reveal ideological and political preferences. Many researchers will be supporters of bilingual education, ethnic diversity, minority language rights and **cultural pluralism**. Such supporters may be convinced of the correctness of their beliefs. This is definitely not to argue that all evaluation research on bilingual education is invalid. Rather, it cannot be assumed that results are not affected by researchers, their beliefs, opinions and preferences.

There is a fine line between research and advocacy which some attempt not to cross; others cross it very quickly. However, this is not to suggest that researchers are relieved of their responsibility to give back to the communities they research by ensuring their research is used in ways that are beneficial to these communities. Indeed, research on the effectiveness of bilingual education can and should inform practice in building effective bilingual education programs (see Box 12.2).

Conclusion

This chapter has examined the development of studies that have investigated whether bilingual education is more or less effective than monolingual education. It has also examined studies that look at the relative effectiveness of different forms of bilingual education. The initial studies examined individual programs and schools. A wide variety of different outcomes and conclusions resulted.

The evaluations of immersion bilingual education and heritage language education tend to favor 'strong' forms of bilingual education. Such studies indicate that such

---

Box 12.2 Building bilingual education systems

Peter Mehisto and Fred Genesee (2015) are co-editors of the groundbreaking book *Building Bilingual Education Systems: Forces, Mechanisms, and Counterweights*. In the concluding chapter, Mehisto (2015) has developed an overarching and relatively comprehensive overview of bilingual and multilingual education. He suggests that such language education can be globally analyzed using a conceptual prism of forces, mechanisms and counterweights.

Mehisto (2015) provides an overarching table of 35 forces, 52 mechanisms and 14 dimensions of counterweights. By addressing the needs of a variety of stakeholders (e.g. politicians, providers, practitioners, parents), the framework is extensive and far-reaching. While elements will vary across countries, contexts and creeds, the lists are nevertheless wide-ranging and quite inclusive. To give a brief flavor:

- *Forces* belong to the ideational realm, but lead to action and affect people and decisions. For example, a force can be a belief in and a commitment to bilingual education; concerns about justice and injustice, social cohesion and national unity.
- *Mechanisms*, in contrast, are material and tangible (e.g. teacher education, leadership initiatives, learning resources, budgets).
- *Counterweights* consider the inherent tensions of bilingual education and the balancing needed between the different interests of stakeholders. One such dimension is seeking stability and the status quo compared with a need for change and development. Another dimension can be the positive tension between 'top-down' implementation compared with grassroots initiatives and allowing for more local autonomy in the gradual evolution of bilingual education.

In addition, the book's Appendix provides valuable tools for planning, implementing and evaluating bilingual and multilingual education. These tools include:

- National and regional level planning considerations for bi/trilingual education. The checklist includes: identifying and working with stakeholders, key considerations for government officials, public issues, needs for learning resources, the selection and training of teachers, principals and other school staff, professional development of staff, financing, curriculum decisions, 'good pedagogy', student assessment and high-stakes assessment, extra-curricular activities, libraries, managing risks, research and working with disadvantaged students.
- A Bilingual Education Continuum provides a list of factors fostering but also undermining the meaningful learning of the curriculum, alongside a list of effective and ineffective pedagogical practices in bilingual and multilingual education (e.g. ample and detailed language scaffolding, psychologically safe environment for students to experiment with content and language, authentic materials).
- Additional Resource Tools are available on the book's website – http://tinyurl.com/zwg6utq

In particular, results-based management frameworks are offered as planning tools for establishing a bilingual program. In the book itself, over 50 outputs (short-term results) from one of these frameworks are provided in Chapter 4. The results-based management frameworks provide an overview of the investments made into establishing both an early and late bilingual education program in Estonia (regarded as one of the most systematically designed bilingual education programs in Europe and the world). The frameworks also include success indicators and a selection of program development activities.

---

bilingual education not only results in bilingualism and biliteracy but also tends to heighten achievement across the curriculum. Strong forms of bilingual education tend to raise the standards and performance of children. However, these results do not stop at individual achievement. In societal terms, there are benefits for the economy in strong forms of bilingual education.

The chapter has revealed a paradox. US research on bilingual education has clearly shown advantages for bilingual approaches and has tended to favor stronger forms with more years rather than fewer in bilingual education. Yet during periods when federal support for bilingual education is offered, it tends to mainly support weaker transitional forms that last only a few years at the most. Politics has proved stronger than research, selectively using the evidence, and marching on regardless. Bilingual education, as practiced in the United States, has tended to be more about politics than pedagogy, 'mythodology' more than effective methodology, and prejudice rather than preferable practice.

However, another conclusion is that simple questions give simplistic answers. We cannot expect a simple answer to the question of whether or not bilingual education is more (or less) effective than mainstream education. The question itself needs to be more refined. It needs to look at the conditions under which different forms of bilingual education become more or less successful. This means departing from simple studies and simple results to broad investigations that include a wide variety of conditions and situations. The scales of justice of bilingual education cannot give a simple verdict. The evidence needs to be wide-ranging and complex; witnesses have complex accounts and arguments. There is no simple right or wrong, good or bad; no simple orthodoxy of approach that can guarantee success.

The effectiveness of bilingual education needs to consider children, teachers, the community, the school itself and the type of program. One particular factor cannot be isolated from another. Children have a wide variety of characteristics which also need investigation. Children cannot be isolated from the classroom characteristics within which they work. Within the classroom there are a variety of factors that may make for effective education. Outside the classroom the different attributes of schools may, in their turn, interact with children and their classrooms to make education for language minority children more or less effective. Outside the school is the important role played by the family and the community. The social, cultural and political environment in which a school works will affect the education of language minority children at all levels.

The key issue becomes 'what are the optimal conditions for children who are either bilingual, becoming bilingual or wish to be bilingual?' The following chapters address this issue.

Key Points in This Chapter

➤ Immersion, heritage language and dual language bilingual education generally promote both first and second languages for academic purposes with no lowering of performance elsewhere in the curriculum and typically increased achievement.

➤ Research generally supports 'strong' forms of bilingual education where a student's home language is cultivated by the school. 'Weak' forms of bilingual education (where the student's minority language is quickly replaced for educational purposes by a majority language) tend to show less effectiveness.

➤ Strong forms of bilingual education can be an economically valuable policy. Repetition and dropout rates are decreased, and a more skilled, highly trained and employable work force is produced.

➤ Individual studies, meta-analyses, expert reviews and public opinion polls do not demonstrate an agreed belief in the effectiveness of bilingual education.

This is explained partly by the varying political aims of those who either support or oppose bilingual education.

➤ Experts fail to agree about the value of bilingual education because their political beliefs differ. Reliance on tested theory is one answer to differing opinions.

Suggested Further Reading

📖 August, D., & Shanahan, T. (2006). *Developing literacy in second-language learners: Report of the National Literacy Panel on Language-Minority Children and Youth.* Mahwah, NJ: Lawrence Erlbaum Associates Publishers.

📖 García, O., & Lin, A. (Eds.). (2017). *Encyclopedia of language and education, Volume 5: Bilingual Education* (3rd ed., Stephen May, General Editor). New York, NY: Springer.

📖 Genesee, F., Lindholm-Leary, K., Saunders, W. M., & Christian, D. (2006). *Educating English language learners: A synthesis of research evidence.* New York: Cambridge University Press.

📖 Hult, F., & Johnson, D. C. (Eds.). (2015). *Research methods in language policy and planning: A practical guide.* Malden, MA: Wiley-Blackwell.

📖 Mehisto, P., & Genese, F. (Eds.). (2015). *Building bilingual education systems: Forces, mechanisms, and counterweights.* Cambridge, UK: Cambridge University Press.

On the Web

🖥 What Works Clearinghouse – English Language Learners (Institute of Education Sciences)
http://ies.ed.gov/ncee/wwc/Topic.aspx?sid=6

🖥 Video – The benefits of a bi-lingual education (TedX talk by 7th grade student Madison Bonaventura)
https://youtu.be/eVg2BC038kc

🖥 What is Bilingual Education? Why Bilingual Education? Is it Effective? (National Association for Bilingual Education)
http://www.nabe.org/BilingualEducation

🖥 Building Bilingual Education Systems: Forces, Mechanisms and Counterweights (Companion Website for book edited by Peeter Mehisto and Fred Genesee)
http://tinyurl.com/zwg6utq

🖥 Video – Are Bilingual Education Programs Effective and How do We Know? (Interview with Peeter Mehisto and Fred Genesee)
https://youtu.be/emzegJOxlCw

Discussion Questions

(1) Why is it difficult to conduct research comparing English only and various types of bilingual education programs to determine which is the most effective? And why must we be careful generalizing the findings of a single study conducted in a school or district to other schools and districts across the state, nation, or around the world?

(2) Scientifically based research using experimental randomized control trials (RCTs) are considered the 'gold standard' in research. Many scholars, however, argue that use of RCTs in bilingual education effectiveness research (and in education in general) is impractical and unethical. Do you agree? Why or why not?

(3) Despite the political debates surrounding bilingual education and the lack of 'perfect' research studies, what have been the consistent overall findings of four decades of research about the effectiveness of bilingual education? Why do you think that, despite this evidence, debates over bilingual education continue?

Study Activities

(1) Locate and review a recent research article on the effectiveness of a particular bilingual education program. Identify the strengths and limitations of the study, and the extent to which findings can be generalized to other contexts.

(2) Design a research proposal for comparing two or more program types (e.g. sheltered English immersion and dual language immersion) at a local school to determine which program is most effective. Determine what data you will collect, how you will collect it, and how you will analyze it. Discuss the challenges and limitations you may have in conducting this study.

(3) Interview teachers of various bilingual (and non-bilingual) program types. Ask the teachers, 'Is your program effective?' 'How do you know?'

CHAPTER 13

Effective Schools and Classrooms for Bilingual Students

Effective Schools and Classrooms for Bilingual Students

Introduction

The aim of this chapter is to outline some of the foundational elements of effective and successful bilingual schools and classrooms for their students. When a school adopts a particular model (e.g. **submersion**/mainstreaming, bilingual immersion, **dual language bilingual education, heritage language**), there is an implementation that entails interpretation, adjustments and compromises to meet local traditions and realities. The idealized model is translated from academic and administrative concepts into the intricate actualities of local school and classroom life.

Schools and classrooms are highly complex organizations. They are sites where there are a multitude of actions and reactions, inputs and processes, variable and changing environments, and differing local, regional and national expected learning outcomes, targets and outputs. The formula for success is never simple, partly as success is diversely defined and understood, and partly as perceived effectiveness varies across person, administration, region and time. Also, the mixture of factors affecting effectiveness is so complex that simple recipes are impossible. Effectiveness inevitably goes far beyond language medium and language outcomes to embrace the full education of a student. Ultimately, effectiveness concerns what is deemed best for the child and society, and not just for the future of a language. However, there is sufficient international research, grounded wisdom and accumulated expertise to make it possible to suggest key factors that need discussion and interpretation in effective bilingual schools and classrooms. This chapter attempts to provide a menu for that dialogue.

Two introductory points: first, it is important to repeat the distinction between teaching a language and teaching through a language. Language acquisition in bilingual immersion, heritage and dual language bilingual programs is mostly through a second language being used as a medium of instruction (see Chapter 11). In the US, this is sometimes called **content-based instruction**. In Europe, it is increasingly referred to as **CLIL** (**content and language integrated learning**). This chapter is about such an approach, and not about teaching a language for its own sake, as in second language lessons.

Second, close to the idea of two or more languages being used for instruction is the concept of **language across the curriculum**. In all content areas, students learn skills, knowledge, understanding, concepts and attitudes mostly through language. Thus, every curriculum area develops **language competence**. All subject areas, from music to mathematics, science to sport, contribute to the growth of a child's language or languages. At the same time, achievement in a particular curriculum area is partly dependent on proficiency in the language of that area. Obtaining fluency in the language of chemistry, psychology or mathematics, for example, is important to understanding that subject. The chapter now proceeds to consider those classroom **contexts** where the home language of students is developed.

First Language Development at School

For **language minority** bilingual children, the school is usually an essential agent in developing the home language. When a child enters kindergarten or elementary school, first language development needs to be formally addressed, irrespective of whether or not that child has age-appropriate competency in the home language (Menyuk & Brisk, 2005). While first language development throughout schooling is important for majority and minority language children, the minority context gives extra reasons for careful nurturance of a minority language, otherwise the majority language may become dominant even to the detriment of the minority language. (The immersion approach for majority language children is considered later).

Two quotes from a historically influential report by UNESCO (1953) entitled *The Use of Vernacular Languages in Education* provide the basis for the development of the home language in school:

> It is axiomatic that the best medium for teaching a child is his mother tongue. Psychologically, it is the system of meaningful signs that in his mind works automatically for expression and understanding. Sociologically, it is a means of identification among the members of the community to which he belongs. Educationally, he learns more quickly through it than through an unfamiliar linguistic medium. (p. 11)

> It is important that every effort should be made to provide education in the mother tongue … On educational grounds we recommend that the use of the mother tongue be extended to as late a stage in education as possible. In particular, pupils should begin their schooling through the medium of the mother tongue, because they understand it best and because to begin their school life in the mother tongue will make the break between home and school as small as possible. (pp. 47–48)

Millions of school-age children of lesser-used languages live in non-industrialized countries of the world. Many never go to school. Others drop out early. The remainders are often struggling to learn through a majority language they hardly understand. As described in UNESCO's (2007) *Advocacy Kit for Promoting Multilingual Education*:

> The true panorama of languages found in a nation's population is rarely reflected in their educational systems, and large numbers of learners are confronted with either a foreign medium of instruction or a language that is different from their mother tongue. … It is an obvious yet not generally recognized truism that learning in a new language that is not one's own provides a double set of challenges: not only of learning a new language but also of learning new knowledge contained in that language (p. iii).

Dutcher (2004) has observed, 'When the mother tongue is not used, they are made to feel backward, inferior, and stupid. Their culture is denigrated, and the children are

---

Box 13.1 If you don't understand, how can you learn?

In recognition of International Mother Tongue Day (February 21), UNESCO (2016) issued a Global Education Monitoring Report entitled *If You Don't Understand, How Can You Learn?* The report notes that 'as much as 40% of the global population does not have access to education in a language they speak or understand' (p. 1). The following are UNESCO's recommendations for policy and program changes to ensure the needs of linguistic minority students are being met (p. 9):

1. *Teach children in a language they understand.* At least six years of mother tongue education should be provided in ethnically diverse communities to ensure those speaking a different language from the medium of instruction do not fall behind. Bilingual or multilingual education programs should be offered to ease the transition to the teaching of the official languages.
2. *Train teachers to teach in more than one language.* To fully support the implementation of mother tongue based bilingual/multilingual education programs, teachers should receive pre-service and ongoing teacher education to teach in more than one language.
3. *Recruit diverse teachers.* Policy-makers need to focus their attention on hiring and training teachers from linguistic and ethnic minorities, to serve in the schools of their own communities.
4. *Provide inclusive teaching materials.* Curricula need to address issues of inclusion to enhance the chances of students from marginalized backgrounds to learn effectively. Textbooks should be provided in a language children understand. Classroom-based assessment tools can help teachers identify, monitor and support learners at risk of low achievement.
5. *Provide culturally appropriate school-readiness programs.* Locally recruited bilingual teaching assistants can support ethnic minority children from isolated communities as they make the transition into primary school, including by providing additional instruction to them after they have enrolled.

---

scared, confused, and traumatized. This can have long-term effects' (p. 19). Therefore, use of the **mother tongue** in education is important for children's transition from home to school, achievement, self-esteem, and not least for learning the majority language (see Box 13.1 and Chapter 8).

When some minority language children start school, teachers do not always believe they are fluent in their mother tongue. For example, a teacher may consider that the child has a dialect that needs developing into a more standard variety. Or a US teacher may hear the child speak a 'limited' or a 'non-standard' variety of English, and therefore wrongly deduce that a child's home language is under-developed. In such cases, securing the minority (and majority) language can become a valuable classroom aim.

Securing the Minority Language

Special attention needs to be paid to the continuous evolution and progression of the minority language in heritage language bilingual education and dual language bilingual schools. This is due to the typically lower status of the minority language, the Anglophone nature of much mass media, and the dominance of 'common denominator' majority languages outside the school. Such bilingual schools can considerably develop the minority language learnt at home so that it has more uses and potentially can be used in more domains (e.g. reading, writing, preparation for employment). The home language is raised to a much higher level of complexity, communication, competence and confidence. The school will widen vocabulary, deepen meanings, teach conventional **syntax**, and help with the standardization of the minority language (e.g. new **terminology** in information technology). The school also gives the minority language status, esteem and market value to its students.

To preserve and reproduce the minority language in the young, a strong form of bilingual education needs to include a 'first language' program with explicit language development aims and goals. Such a program may involve lessons devoted to that language (e.g. Spanish language arts in the US). It may also valuably involve a strategy for first language development across the curriculum through content-based language approaches. Where children take lessons (e.g. social studies, science) through the medium of their home language, language development in those curriculum areas can be overtly planned and fostered. A child's home language develops when it is cultivated, encouraged and promoted in a purposeful way in many or all curriculum areas (e.g. humanities, sciences, mathematics). Such content areas shape the language that is learnt, although **language proficiency** may constrain or liberate the content that can be learnt.

The learning methodologies and teaching strategies used to support language minority children in school are also important. Mainstream classrooms often assume a homogeneous student population, with similar linguistic and cultural characteristics, delivering a standardized 'transmission' or 'banking' curriculum with individual competitiveness symbolized in regular standardized tests.

In contrast, language minority students may thrive in an atmosphere where linguistic and cultural diversity is assumed, sharing a **bicultural** or **multicultural** curriculum with multiple perspectives and linguistic equality of opportunity. Supportive and non-threatening cooperative learning techniques that stress teamwork, interdependence, social interaction and partnership have been successfully used with culturally and linguistically diverse students (Echevarría *et al.*, 2016). For example, small groups of around four students work together to complete a given task, especially in classes that are numerically large. Active learning, the amalgamation of language and content, and the integration of linguistically diverse students can be engineered in such cooperative learning (Ovando & Combs, 2017).

For such children, Cummins (2000a) argues for a 'transformative pedagogy' that sees knowledge as fluid and not fixed, collaboratively constructed rather than memorized, where the sharing of experiences affirms students' **identity**, but essentially also involves critical enquiry to understand power, inequality, justice, and local social and economic realities (see the critical literacy approach, Chapter 14).

The benefits inherent in a well-developed home (minority) **language spread** to the learning of an additional language(s). As Swain and Lapkin (2008) found, those students literate in their heritage language progressed significantly more in written and oral second language French than those without such skills. First language literacy, in particular, enables relative ease of learning (and learning through) a second language by the transfer of knowledge, language abilities (e.g. literacy strategies, communication skills) and learning processes (see Chapters 8, 11, 12 and 14).

Codeswitching in the Classroom

As discussed in Chapter 5, there is a possible overlap between the terms **codeswitching** and **translanguaging**, with the former seen by some as part of the latter. However for others there is a strict differentiation (see Box 13.2). Since there has been an empirical research tradition on codeswitching in the classroom, this will be considered first. Then, the recent exploration of translanguaging will be discussed.

Codeswitching is a common phenomenon in many bilingual classrooms (Barnard & McClellan, 2014). G. Ferguson (2003) suggests that codeswitching:

is not only very prevalent across a wide range of educational settings but also seems to arise naturally, perhaps inevitably, as a pragmatic response to the difficulties of teaching content in a language medium over which pupils have imperfect control. Moreover, because teaching is an adrenalin-fuelled activity, making numerous competing demands on one's attentional resources, much switching takes place below the level of consciousness. Teachers are often simply not aware of when they switch languages, or indeed if they switch at all. (p. 46)

Lin (2006) has shown that the patterns of codeswitching in Hong Kong classrooms are highly ordered and patterned (e.g. using Cantonese to explain or interpret English key terms) and also have pedagogic and social functions (e.g. increased communication of meaning, decreasing distance, saving face, emphasis). In countries such as Malawi in Africa, codeswitching is a resource particularly when there are multiple languages (16 in Malawi). It allows a child to understand areas such as mathematics in their home language while learning the national language of Chichewa (Chitera, 2009).

Martin-Jones (2000) surveyed three decades of research on such interactions between students, and between students and teachers. They observe that bilingual classroom talk is best understood within the context and traditions of that school and class. Such situations provided clues and cues for expected and allowable patterns of talk. For example, codeswitching by the teacher may be used to signal the start of a lesson or a transition in the lesson, to specify an interaction with a particular student, or to move from teaching content to classroom management. Such codeswitching may occur simultaneously with body communication such as gestures and eye contact. Children also initiate codeswitching in the classroom, and have an influence on a teacher's use of two or more languages, and particularly the languages used in small group work and conversations with other students.

Choice by a student of 'which language to use and when' tends to be reasonably regular and patterned and will reflect (a) the teacher 's declared preference and management of languages, (b) a student's proficiency or choice or (c) a negotiation between teacher and child. A teacher's language choice tends to be more child-centered in the early years of schooling, for example when explanations, clarifications and checks on understanding are needed with young children (e.g. language minority children in mainstream, language majority classes).

Facilitating understanding by moving between two or more languages tends to underlie much classroom codeswitching (and this has recently become part of 'translanguaging' considerations – see the next section). Such codeswitching in classrooms varies among teachers, schools and countries in terms of its prohibition, discouragement, allowance or encouragement (Martin-Jones, 2000). For example, the Education Department of Hong Kong (1997) decreed that 'mixed-code teaching should not be used in [secondary] schools' (p. 2). Even when there is discouragement, students may privately move from the teacher's language to their own preferred language, for example to help each other understand. Thus, there is often a difference between formal policy and the informal practice of codeswitching, with 'center stage' and 'back stage' choices (Chan, 2016).

Research has examined the patterns of language choice and codeswitching in classrooms (e.g. Barnard & McClellan, 2014). Behind such patterns are often traditions and histories of dual or multiple language use, latent and stated pedagogies from different models of bilingual education (e.g. immersion, dual language), and the pressures of regional or national politics. There is also the typical preference of a teacher to do whatever it takes to help students learn, which includes codeswitching and trans-languaging even when it is discouraged by policy makers or administrators.

The use of two languages in the classroom is also about which language is relatively valued or privileged, how use of two languages is synchronized and sequenced, negotiated and changed, and how meanings and understandings are constructed. Such bilingual talk occurs in the classroom, yet can often *only* be understood and explained beyond the school through the lens of community, economic, historic and especially political contexts.

For example, there is a tendency in classrooms for minority language children, even when very young, to move towards the majority high status language. The research of D.K. Oller and Eilers (2002) in Miami found that regardless of school type (e.g. dual language education), and regardless of age, students from Spanish-language homes spoke predominantly in English. Even in the first semester of kindergarten, the Miami Spanish-speaking children seemed to be aware that English was the prestigious language and used English for conversations. Jaffe (2007) has shown that the distribution of Corsican and French in the bilingual classrooms in Corsica aims to achieve balance in parity between the two languages, yet Corsican is privileged as the language of discovery and learning. Thus codeswitching in the classroom has to be understood within a particular political context, the history of two languages within a region, values, expectations and intentions. It is this wider contextual consideration that has become one major strand of considerations about translanguaging, and this is now discussed.

Translanguaging and Transliteracy

Imagine a lesson that uses two languages. The teacher introduces a topic in English, making some remarks in Spanish. Handouts and worksheets are in English. Class activities (e.g. teamwork) are carried out in the students' preferred language or they use both their languages, and even three or more languages. The teacher interacts with the small groups and individual students in a mixture of Spanish and English, but mostly in English as the principal desires. The students complete the worksheet in English. English thus dominates. This type of situation is unlikely to develop students' literacy in Spanish. The languages have an unequal status and use. To allow students to make progress in both languages, there needs to be more strategic classroom **language planning**.

Cen Williams (1994, 1996) was among the first researchers to suggest that there are pedagogical strategies that develop both languages successfully and also result in effective content learning. In particular he found 'translanguaging' to work well in high schools in Wales. Since 1994, the concept of translanguaging has been gaining ground, capturing the imagination of those who believe that teachers and particularly students naturally use both (or all) their languages to maximize learning. We have recently become emancipated from strict language separation ideas to concepts about **bilingualism** that are holistic rather than fractional (see Chapter 1), less compartmentalized than **diglossia** with separate functions for two languages (see Chapter 4), with codeswitching in early childhood language acquisition more customary than strict OPOL type strategies (see Chapter 5), and less concerned with language separation in the classroom than strategic language integration (C. Baker, 2010b).

Separating languages in the classroom by subject or topic, teacher, or time (half days, whole days) has hitherto been fashionable but is beginning to move to considerations of the use of two or more languages in the same lesson (C. Baker, 2010b; O. García & Li Wei, 2015). This reflects the idea that children pragmatically use both of their languages in order to maximize understanding and performance in any lesson. Translanguaging is the process of making meaning, shaping experiences, understandings and knowledge through the use of two languages. Both languages are used in an integrated and coherent way to organize and mediate mental processes in learning (O. García, Johnson & Seltzer, 2016).

Cen Williams created the term 'translanguaging' for the planned and systematic use of two languages inside the same lesson. It originated as a Welsh word 'trawsiethu' and was coined by him and a colleague (Dafydd Whittall) during an in-service course for Deputy Principals in Llandudno (North Wales, UK) in the early 1980s. In English, it was initially called 'translinguifying' but then changed to 'translanguaging'. It has remained a developing and important concept in Welsh bilingual education ever since, and has now been adopted as a key modern concept in bilingual classrooms and communities (O. García, 2009a, 2009b; O. García *et al.*, 2016; O. García & Li Wei, 2015) although with ambiguity (e.g. Joneitz, 2003).

In Cen Williams' (1994, 1996) pedagogical use of 'translanguaging', the input (reading and/or listening) tends to be in one language, and the output (speaking and/or writing) in the other language, and this is systematically varied. For instance, a science worksheet in English is read by students. The teacher then initiates a discussion on the subject matter in Spanish, switching to English to highlight particular science terms. The students then complete their written work in Spanish. In the next lesson, the roles of the languages are reversed. In this example, the students need to understand the work to use the information successfully in another language.

Ofelia García (2009a) suggests that translanguaging is a very typical way in which bilinguals engage their bilingual worlds not only inside school but throughout their everyday life. It is not just codeswitching but more about hybrid language use that is systematic, strategic and sense-making for speaker and listener. 'Bilinguals translanguage to include and facilitate communication with others, but also to construct deeper understandings and make sense of their bilingual worlds' (p. 45). It expresses the idea that there are no clear-cut boundaries between the languages of bilinguals, but functional integration. It is dynamic bilingualism with the interconnected use of the two languages being used to negotiate meaning and situations (Creese & Blackledge, 2010b). Teachers can maximize learning by encouraging children to use both of their languages, for example in collaborative writing, task-based conversations with other children, use of resources, and not least when working electronically (e.g. on the internet) (O. García & Li Wei, 2015).

Ofelia García (2009a) also suggests that bilingual children regularly use both their languages for learning, even when this is surreptitious. She suggests that linguistically integrated group work is increasingly prevalent in many bilingual classrooms. This suggests a movement away from the compartmentalization of languages and requiring clear boundaries of language use towards strategic translanguaging that maximizes students' language repertoires, preferences and practices. 'Translanguaging is indeed a powerful mechanism to construct understandings, to include others, and to mediate understandings across language groups' (p. 307).

Translanguaging and transliteracy (C. Baker, 2003) has four potential advantages. First, it may promote a deeper and fuller understanding of the subject matter. Given that (a) pre-existing knowledge is a foundation for further learning and (b) there is ease of crosslinguistic transfer as two languages are inter-dependent (Cummins, 2017b),

> **Box 13.2** What is the difference between codeswitching and translanguaging?
>
> The acceptance and usage of the term translanguaging is growing rapidly. However, this has led to some confusion, including how exactly it differs from codeswitching. There are also questions as to the rationale for introducing a new term when many decades of research on language contact and codeswitching have laid an important foundation for understanding the phenomenon. When asked these questions in an interview with Francois Grosjean (2016), Ofelia García responded as follows:
>
> > There is an epistemological difference between the theoretical position on language contact that has led to the constructs of borrowing, codeswitching, calques, language interference, etc. and the concept of translanguaging. Language contact studies start with named languages as categories, and then look across these named categories. Linguists often refer to the behavior of bilinguals when they go across these named language categories as codeswitching. It is an external view of language. But translanguaging takes the internal perspective of speakers whose own mental grammar has been developed in social interaction with others. For these bilingual speakers, their language features are simply their own. Translanguaging is more than going across languages; it is going beyond named languages and taking the internal view of the speaker's language use. (p. 1)
>
> In the interview, García acknowledged that from an external social perspective, the behavior of codeswitching and translanguaging may look the same, 'but seen from the internal perspective of the bilingual speaker, translanguaging behavior is clearly different' because it 'legitimizes the fluid language practices with which bilinguals operate' and also 'posits that bilinguals have a much more complex and expanded repertoire than monolinguals' (p. 1).

then translanguaging builds understanding in a most efficient way. It is possible, in a **monolingual** teaching situation, for students to answer questions or write an essay about a subject without fully understanding it. Processing for meaning may not have occurred. Whole sentences or paragraphs can be copied or adapted out of a textbook, from the internet or from dictation by the teacher without real understanding. It is less easy to do this with 'translanguaging'. To read and discuss a topic in one language, and then to write about it in another language, means that the subject matter has to be processed and 'digested'.

This fits into a sociocultural theory of learning (Lantolf, 2011; Swain *et al.*, 2015). Sociocultural theory provides reasons why a classroom should not operate solely through a second language, even in an immersion situation. A child who is speaking and writing is not just involved in language development. Speaking and writing mediate learning. Speaking and writing, irrespective of using a first, second or third language, is how we learn. When a student cannot cope with processing in their second or third language (e.g. early on in an immersion classroom), then they naturally turn to their first language for thinking, to find answers and to be cognitively successful. In this sense, telling children to work through a second language on a problem they cannot cope with in that language is asking the child to fail.

The first language is often the best resource that the child has in order to respond to a classroom task, including in private speech and retrieving from the memory. Requiring such a child to *only* work in a second or third language is reducing their thinking power. When curriculum content is cognitively very demanding, then using the first language (as well as a second language) may both achieve success and enhance second language development. This includes developing strategies to manage a task, **scaffolding**, externalizing in speech, and working through a task with others (Gibbons, 2015).

Language occurs in social situations within a cultural context. The social, political and cultural context shapes what somebody says. As Bakhtin (1994) maintained, a word in language is half someone else's. It is derived from previous social exchanges and then is used in future exchanges. Thus sociocultural theory is relevant to the bilingual classroom, in that the teacher can allow a student to use both languages, but in a planned, developmental and strategic manner, to maximize a student's linguistic and cognitive capability, and to reflect that language is sociocultural both in context and process.

Second, 'translanguaging' may help students develop oral communication and literacy in their weaker language. Students might otherwise attempt the main part of the work in their stronger language and then undertake less challenging, related tasks in their weaker language. 'Translanguaging' attempts to develop academic language skills in both languages leading to a fuller bilingualism and biliteracy. Third, the dual use of languages can facilitate home–school cooperation. If a child can communicate to a minority language parent in their usual medium, the parent can support the child in their schoolwork.

This overlaps with one complaint from some parents when their children are operating bilingually in school. Such a complaint is that the child is being educated in one language that the parent does not understand. The claim is then made that the parent cannot help the child with their homework or discuss their schoolwork with them in a language that they do not understand. The idea of translanguaging is that movement from one language to another involves much more than translation of words. The reprocessing of content may lead to deeper understanding and learning. If so, what the child has learned through one language in school can be expanded, extended and intensified through discussion with the parent in the other language. What appears to be a potential weakness between school and home may become a strength in learning.

Fourth, the integration of fluent English speakers and English learners (e.g. in US schools) of various levels of attainment is helped by 'translanguaging'. If English learners are integrated with first language English speakers, and if sensitive and strategic use is made of both languages in class, then learners can develop their second language ability concurrently with content learning. In Cen Williams' (1994, 1996) original conceptualization, translanguaging is important, strongly developing a student's minority language, whether it be their first or second language.

There are potential problems in the complexity of managing, allocating and organizing such a use of two languages. A threatened language, for example, may need protected space and dedicated time in the classroom. Otherwise, the higher status majority language will increasingly dominate. Thus in the strategic allocation of language in learning in the classroom as directed by the teacher, translanguaging needs care and consideration. However, even in those spaces reserved for a minority language, translanguaging may still be used by a child in making meaning and in speaking and writing.

For some minority language educators, translanguaging may not be seen as valuable in a classroom when a child is in the early stages of learning a language. For input and output to occur in both languages requires both languages to be reasonably well-developed or emerging strongly. This will vary according to different curriculum areas, with some areas requiring less technical and complex language and therefore being more suitable for translanguaging at an earlier time. For example, translanguaging in an area of the curriculum where there is more jargon, more abstract language and greater complexity may not be appropriate, particularly for those who are still beginning to develop their second language. For other educators, however, using a child's perspective, translanguaging may have a valuable different role in early learning. It may help them scaffold. The teacher then needs to understand that the active use of the child's entire language repertoire in learning means that they will increasingly integrate the developing language into this own holistic repertoire. With those students further along the bilingual continuum, translanguaging is potentially more transforming in learning, and not just a scaffold.

Another issue is that while the teacher may favor translanguaging, students may prefer using their stronger language or the one which has the higher status. In dual language bilingual programs, for example, students may mirror language prestige by moving from Spanish to English even in Spanish-medium lessons (Henderson & Palmer, 2015). Thus, translanguaging may be naturally used by children; it may be engineered by the teacher (DePalma, 2010). Yet sometimes students may prefer one language rather than two.

One value of the idea is that each teacher plans the strategic use of two languages, thinks consciously about the allocation of two languages in the classroom, reflects and reviews what is happening, and attempts to cognitively stimulate students by a 'language provocative' and 'language diversified' lesson. This is in contrast to 'two solitudes' or the 'monolingualism principle' where languages are kept apart (as in dual language education) in the teaching of a second language (Cummins, 2014). In **communicative language teaching**, the first language is often ignored, even forbidden. Indeed, almost all 20th century language teaching methods either banned or minimized the use of the first language in teaching a second language.

It is often more efficient to use the first language in a second language classroom, to convey content, explain grammar, provide a shortcut for giving instructions and explanations, to build on rather than denying existing understanding, to interlink L1 and L2, increase learning, and create more authentic and natural situations that reflect the world outside the classroom (Cook, 2001; Wright, 2015). This suggests that the separation of L1 and L2 belongs to the 20th century, while the 21st century will see the deliberate and systematic use of both languages in the classroom. For example, a PowerPoint slide may present both languages on the screen, using the same content but using a different font or different color, arranged systematically so that students can easily understand using one language or both (Welsh Language Board, 2001). Translanguaging in a mainstream classroom with deaf students occurs when deaf students follow a talk through sign and others through hearing, and when a video presentation allows some students to listen and others to read the subtitles.

Cultural Awareness

Developing cross-cultural competence and appropriate cross-cultural attitudes and behaviors has increasingly become a part of bilingual education. 'Strong' forms of bilingual education generally have this as an outcome, although occasionally **heritage language education** can concentrate on the minority language culture. Thus it is possible to become bilingual and not develop cross-cultural or multicultural competence. While developing heritage cultural awareness alongside first language teaching is an important element in minority language education, developing intercultural competence is also important (Valdiviezo & Nieto, 2015).

Classroom activities to foster minority language cultural awareness can include: enacting social conventions; cultural rituals and traditions using authentic visual and written materials; discussing cultural variations (e.g. the colorful kaleidoscope of Latin American dances, festivals, customs and traditions); identifying the varying experiences and perspectives of the particular language variety (e.g. of French Canadians, of the French majority in France, of bilinguals in France [e.g. Bretons, Provencal]); classroom visits by native speakers of the language for 'question and answer' sessions. It is important for bilingual classrooms to go beyond the surface level features of cultures (e.g. food, holidays, dance, traditional costumes, etc.) to deeper understandings of how culture frames one's understanding of and interactions with the world, how culture is dynamic, and the complex and ever-shifting relationships between language, identity and culture – especially as experienced by bilingual students (Valdiviezo & Nieto, 2015).

In Wales, developing a cultural awareness about Wales is contained in a central curriculum concept called the '*Curriculum Cymreig*' (Welsh Cultural Curriculum) that endeavors to reflect the whole range of historical, social, economic, cultural, political, communication, technical and environmental influences that have shaped contemporary Wales. This involves giving students a sense of place, distinctiveness and heritage, of belonging to the local and wider community with its own traditions, a strong Welsh identity, access to the literature of Wales, differences and traditions in the use of the Welsh and English languages in Wales, and the distinctive nature of Welsh music, arts, crafts, technology, religious beliefs and practices (ESTYN, 2001). Such activity is directly related to students' experiences, contexts and interests, and is therefore seen as important and relevant. Homework can involve active discovery and personal research. Fieldwork, visits and extra-curricular activities may be integral to such an approach. It uses teachers' local knowledge, enabling teachers to be creative and original, hopefully firing their enthusiasm.

There can also be an emphasis on developing heritage cultural awareness in mathematics, science and technology and not just in humanities and aesthetic areas. For example, in Wales, students study the Welsh mathematician William Jones (1675–1749) who first used the 'pi' (p) symbol and Robert Recorde (16th century) who devised the 'equals' (=) symbol. In science, children discuss local soil samples and how they connect with local farming and agriculture, the coal and slate mining that have been important to the Welsh economy, local small industries, local environmentalism and sustainability, and working from home via computer and communication networks. Some of this involves cross-curricular activity. In San Antonio, Texas, Al-Gasem (2015) describes an ethnomathematics curriculum which raised interest in mathematics among at-risk Latina youth and instilled in them cultural pride as they studied the way the ancient Mayans and Aztecs understood and made use of math in their daily lives.

It is sometimes argued that a minority language must be fostered to preserve the attendant culture. The opposite is also possible. The attendant culture must be fostered in the classroom to preserve the minority language. While separation of culture and language is false, minority language culture can be weakly or strongly represented in the classroom and in the whole ethos of the school. Such culture may be incidentally taught with little intent or rationale. Alternatively, such culture may be consciously included in language teaching and the overall physical and psychological environment of the school. This is particularly valuable in encouraging participation by children in their heritage language culture. Language skills in the minority language are no guarantee of continued use of that language into teens and adulthood. **Enculturation** therefore becomes essential if that language is to be useful and used.

Not all language minority children are allowed to develop their home language at school. Many such students are mainstreamed, where all content teaching is through the majority language. The chapter now considers this context.

Monolingual Schools and Classes

Majority Language Development in Monolingual Schools

When language minority children are placed in mainstream schools, the emphasis is on securing proficiency in the second (majority) language (e.g. English in the US). This section examines the issue of how long this takes, and then how 'scaffolding' is important to ensure a sensitive and sympathetic transition into the second language.

If a student is required to work through a second language in school, a deep level of language proficiency is required and this has to be developed throughout schooling. It is difficult for second language students to develop proficiency levels in their second language to compete with native speakers. One reason is that native speakers are not static and waiting for non-native speakers to catch up. During the school years, native speakers' first language development continues at a rapid rate, such that the goal of proficiency equal to a native speaker is a moving target for the language learner. Thomas and Collier (2002a) found that such students in mainstreaming or transitional forms of education 'must make fifteen months of progress for each ten months of progress that the native-English speaker is making each year of school, and they must do this for six consecutive years to eventually reach the 50th percentile – a dramatic accomplishment!' (pp. 19–20).

In the US, estimates vary on how quickly ELLs (**English language learners**) can reach a level of English proficiency to work successfully in a mainstream classroom. A review of research by Genesee *et al.* (2006) suggests that such a level of oral English proficiency is reached within three to five years. Progress at the beginning is rapid, but is slower from middle to higher levels of oral language proficiency. As higher levels of oral proficiency develop, reading achievement and academic uses of language both increase (August & Shanahan, 2008). ELL students with well-developed English oral skills achieve greater success in English literacy than those with less well developed skills. However, if a student has literacy skills in their first language, these transfer relatively easily to reading in English (see Chapter 14). The review by Genesee *et al.* (2006) also indicates that oral proficiency increases with: (a) use of English outside school (which increases with proficiency), (b) friendships with fluent or native English speakers (which also increase with proficiency), and (c) paired work with native or fluent speakers, so long as the task is well designed.

Collier's (1995) longitudinal studies suggest that, in US schools where all the instruction is given through the second language (mainstream schooling), second language speakers of English with no schooling in their first language take between seven and 10 years or more to reach the language proficiency of native English speaking peers. Some never reach native levels of language proficiency. Where students have had two or three years of first language schooling in their home country before emigrating to the United States, they take between five and seven years to reach native speaker performance. Collier found this pattern among different home language groups, different ethnic groups and different socioeconomic groups of students.

In a longitudinal study by Umansky *et al.* (2016) on ELLs who began schooling in the US in kindergarten, over 80% were considered to be proficient in English by Grade 5, and more than 90% were proficient by Grade 7. This is consistent with prior estimates of 5 to 7 years to attain English proficiency (Crawford & Krashen, 2007).

Decisions about when students are ready for mainstream instruction in the majority language are also highly political. In Arizona, for example, state education leaders have resisted federal pressures to increase school funding for ELLs (S.C.K. Moore, 2014). Within this context, Arizona made changes to the way ELLs were identified, and also lowered the cut scores on tests used to reclassify ELLs as proficient in English. These changes resulted in far fewer ELLs being identified, and also exited large numbers of students from ELL programs more quickly. In 2015 research by WestEd raised concerns when it found that over 90% of the Arizona's ELLs were reclassified as proficient in English within six school years (Haas *et al.*, 2015). WestEd also found that only 18% of ELL high school students graduated within four years – the lowest in the nation. Upon investigation, the US Office of Civil Rights (of the Department of Education) and the US Department of Justice found that Arizona's practices were in violation of ELL students' civil rights resulting in both under-identification and pre-mature exiting of tens of thousands of ELLs from language assistance programs (Mitchell, 2016). Resolution agreements between Arizona and the federal government signed in 2016 require the state to provide or restore language-support services for the affected ELLs students.

The most significant variable in becoming proficient in the second language is often the amount of formal schooling students have received in their first language. Those students who are schooled solely in their second language, particularly from the 4th grade onwards, when the academic and cognitive demands of the curriculum increase rapidly, tend to progress relatively slowly and show less academic achievement. Thus an essential feature in students acquiring **academic language proficiency** is that there is strong development through the first language of academic-cognitive thinking skills. Thinking abilities, literacy development, concept formation, subject knowledge and learning strategies developed in the first language transfer to the second language. As students expand their vocabulary and literacy skills in their first language, they can increasingly demonstrate the knowledge that they have gained in the second language.

Teachers and Bilingual Support Assistants

In many mainstream schools where there are bilingual students, there is a frequent shortfall of teachers who are either trained to work with such children, or who come from the same language communities, or both of these. This is a worldwide experience. In the US following the No Child Left Behind Act of 2001, it was estimated that between 2 and 3.5 million new teachers were required for bilingual and ESL education (Menken & Barron, 2002). This shortage is far from rectified. For example, the state of Indiana only began serious efforts in 2016 to require teachers of ELLs to obtain additional training and licensure in 'teaching English as an Additional Language' (Morita-Mullaney, 2016).

One solution to a lack of suitable bilingual teachers has been to hire bilingual teaching assistants who work, especially in the early grades, under the guidance of the mainstream teacher and typically can speak the home language of some, most or all of the bilingual students. In the UK, such support workers help the very young, newly arrived and slower learners, often working with small groups (European Commission,

2015). They may translate, interpret, create classroom materials (e.g. dual language texts), sometimes also assisting the mainstream teacher in **assessment**. The assistant may also be the link between teacher and home, enabling parents to collaborate in their children's education.

At its best, this creates a bilingual resource that enables the student to learn in their home and stronger language while they are acquiring a majority language such as English. This discussion will be extended in terms of 'scaffolding' (see the next section). In the UK and US experience, however, there are a few challenges to using bilingual teaching assistants properly. One danger is that the bilingual assistant uses English rather than the home language because English is the dominant and prestige language of a mainstream school. Another is that the mother tongue is used by the bilingual assistant mainly for discipline and control, sending the wrong message about language use and functions. Conversely, in teacher-centered and lecture-dominant classrooms, the bilingual assistant may not be able to provide much help beyond looking over the students' shoulders, pointing to things in their books and on their worksheets, and occasionally whispering a bit to the students in their home language so as not to interrupt the teacher or disturb the rest of the class. The asymmetry of power between a qualified monolingual teacher and a lower paid bilingual assistant, and allowances for only short, discrete and quiet uses of the home language may also send the wrong language status message to students.

Scaffolding Language

Many bilingual children are required to attend mainstream schools and learn to operate as quickly as possible in a second language (e.g. ELL students in the United States). They are expected to learn a new language, engage in subject learning, and develop thinking skills at the same time. Content instruction will be in that new language and will increasingly become more complex, abstract and require a different **register** from informal conversation. Within a short period, such students are expected to have developed a second language so that they can operate in the subject curriculum and show success (e.g. on tests, grade transfer).

Taking the US as an example, it is unlikely that such students will learn English solely through content instruction. Their level of understanding of English is often too rudimentary to comprehend mathematics or social studies. Irrespective of whether a 'transmission of knowledge' (pouring nuggets of knowledge into empty heads) approach or a progressive 'discovery learning' approach is taken by the teacher, the language level of the child may be insufficient to assimilate content and engage in the process of learning.

Hence, such students need two types of language support if they are to succeed in the classroom (Wright, 2015). First they need direct and systematic instruction in the new language. In the US this may be called **English as a second language** (ESL), English for speakers of other languages (ESOL), English as an additional language (EAL), English as a new language (ENL) or **English language development** (ELD). Second, students need content-area instruction in the second language that is made comprehensible and which supports their English language development. In the US this is typically called **sheltered instruction, or specially designed academic instruction in English** (SDAIE) (see Box 13.3). Within these classrooms teacher-student cooperation appears to be very important for students. In such a social collaboration, the teacher supports the student by a careful pitching of comprehensible language. This is termed

Box 13.3 The Sheltered Instruction Observation Protocol (SIOP) Model

A challenge in both bilingual and non-bilingual forms of education is making language and content-area instruction in the second language comprehensible and effective. Sheltered instruction, or specially designed academic instruction in English (SDAIE) has long been used to address this challenge. Out of concern that the field lacked a clear model for providing effective sheltered instruction, in the early 1990s Echevarría *et al.* (2016) developed the Sheltered Instruction Observation Protocol (SIOP) Model. The SIOP Model has been widely adopted by schools in the US and is beginning to gain an international footing. The SIOP consists of 30 observable strategies and techniques organized into three major sections (preparation, instruction and assessment) and six subsections under instruction. These items are used to plan, deliver and evaluate sheltered instruction. When used for evaluation purposes, each of the 30 items are scored on a scale of 0 (not evident) to 4 (highly evident). Thus, the higher the total SIOP score, the more effective the lesson for second language learners. For example, in an effective lesson, the following features would be highly evident during instruction:

- *Building Background* – Concepts are linked to students' background experiences and previous lessons. Key vocabulary is emphasized.
- *Comprehensible Input* – Teachers modify their speech as appropriate to their students' levels, provide clear explanations of academic tasks, and use a variety of techniques to make content concepts clear (e.g. modeling, visuals, hands-on activities).
- *Strategies* – Students are given opportunities to learn and use strategies, teachers use scaffolding techniques consistently throughout the lesson, and use a variety of question types to promote higher-order thinking skills.
- *Interaction* – Teachers provide frequent opportunities for student interaction, use a variety of grouping configurations (e.g. whole class, small groups, pairs), allow for wait time, and clarify key concepts in the home language.
- *Practice/Application* – Teachers engage students in hands-on activities and tasks that enable them to integrate the four language domains (listening, speaking, reading, and writing) and apply content and language knowledge.
- *Lesson Delivery* – Language and content objectives are fully supported by the lesson delivery, the pacing of the lesson is appropriate to the students' levels, and students are engaged 90% to 100% of the time.

The model has been criticized by some as behavioristic and representing an eclectic set of strategies that lack a strong unifying theoretical grounding (Crawford & Reyes, 2015). Another concern is that teachers are often given a few days of SIOP training without developing a sufficient understanding of foundational knowledge about language, second language development, and bilingualism (Wright, 2015). Nonetheless, many of the individual items in the SIOP represent tried-and-true strategies, in practice the SIOP is used for lesson planning and instruction in flexible ways, scores on the SIOP are used more as a starting point for self-reflection and professional constructive feedback and dialogue, and the SIOP is often a gateway for teachers into ELL teaching and can lead to teachers pursuing additional training and certification. Some research evidence demonstrates higher academic achievement among second language learners in SIOP classes than in non-SIOP classrooms (Guarino *et al.*, 2001).

'scaffolding' (Gibbons, 2015) and originates from the Russian psychologist, Lev Vygotsky (1986) and American psychologist Jerome Bruner (1983). Vygotsky argued that student learning occurs when the present level of understanding of a child is moved to a further level that is within the child's capability.

During the decade 1924–1934, Vygotsky outlined the ways that teachers can intervene and arrange effective learning by challenging and extending the child's current level of understanding (Walqui & van Lier, 2010). This is achieved by the teacher moving from the present level of understanding of a child to a further level that is within the child's capability. This 'stretching' of the child is by locating the **zone of proximal development (ZPD)**. Vygotsky (1986) saw this ZPD as the distance between a student's level of current understanding as revealed when problem solving without adult help, and the level of potential development as determined by a student problem solving in collaboration with peers or teachers. The ZPD is where new understandings are possible through collaborative interaction and inquiry. Scaffolding can only occur within the ZPD.

Lessons learned from the US (August, 2002) and the UK (Breen, 2002) suggest that when bilingual children are not in 'strong' forms of bilingual education (e.g. transitional, **sheltered English immersion**, mainstream), the following school attributes are important:

- Teachers build on the prior knowledge and experience of children that has often been built through the minority language, and not just concentrate on developing the majority language.
- Peer support systems are used in the classroom for language shepherding and support.
- Student linguistic and cultural diversity is valued and elaborated.
- High expectations are communicated to language minority students.
- The curriculum is carefully paced so that children comprehend, but is ever challenging and enriching.
- Linguistic competence and conceptual understanding are not confused. For example, a student's proficiency in second language English is not a measure of the quality of their thinking.
- Language and content is comprehensible to the student.
- Literacy and oral language development is integrated.
- Translanguaging enables meaning-making when instruction is not in the language of the child.
- Higher order thinking skills are developed (e.g. in a literacy program).
- Assessment needs to be fair and valid especially when not conducted in a child's stronger language, and avoid using monolinguals for unfavorable comparisons.
- Local language minority communities and parents are seen as partners.
- Teachers are carefully selected, trained and consistently developed to teach language minority students.
- Schools are advocates of children and their families.

One danger faced by some bilingual students is that teachers present less challenging content to them compared with monolinguals. This is because some teachers perceive that bilingual children, especially emergent bilinguals, do not have the appropriate levels of language proficiency to cope with complex material. Rather than over-simplifying a task, the teacher can provide 'scaffolding' so that the student is working within their 'zone of proximal development'. Scaffolding is thus a temporary device to enable understanding of content. When learning is successful, that support is removed as the child can then complete the same task independently.

Gibbons (2015) and Walqui and van Lier (2010) provide a wealth of illustrations for the scaffolding of listening, speaking, reading and writing. This includes use of gestures, visual aids, repeating something in a different way, recasting what a child has said, using concrete examples, and summaries. The provision of **primary language support** and use of translanguaging pedagogies is also a form of scaffolding (Wright, 2015). Scaffolding can be both designed before a lesson and more spontaneous to fit a child's immediate need and the occasion. Thus scaffolding is both a supportive structure and also social collaboration between teacher and student. It is not just support around the building, but building work as well; not just about structure but also about the process by which learning is handed over to a more independent student.

As an example, consider the scaffolding that may be provided as students are learning to write in their second language. Scaffolding occurs when a teacher ensures: (a) that a student has enough prior experience or prior knowledge to make a task understandable and personally relevant; (b) that the student is made familiar with the purpose, structure and linguistic features of the kind of text that they will write; (c) that the teacher and the student write the text together, with advice on the process, content and form; and (d) that students should then be able to write their own text with the scaffold being removed, often gradually. They have moved from the familiar to being stretched, from guidance to independence. Such scaffolding can be provided by strategies other than teacher mediated support (Santamaría *et al.*, 2002). Task scaffolds may give directions (e.g. on cue cards) as to steps through a task. Materials scaffolds are 'advance organizers' or prompts for students (e.g. story maps) regarding content.

Box 13.4 The transition of refugee and immigrant children into a new classroom

Coelho (2012) provides advice regarding the transition of immigrant and refugee children into the classroom. A few of her wealth of ideas are listed below:

- Create welcome signs in the children's languages.
- Use an interpreter where possible, to facilitate transition. Interview parents with the interpreter present, to provide basic information and begin a relationship with parents in a friendly and facilitative manner.
- Provide children with a welcome booklet of basic school information, in their own language. Include the day-to-day life, special events, role of parents.
- Encourage the home use of the first language and explain to the parents that first language development will help the child in acquisition of the majority language.
- Appoint friendly and sensitive children as official student ambassadors or student friends, to nurture newcomers and help them adjust.
- Introduce newcomers positively, showing the country of origin with the aid of a world map, ensuring that all children learn to pronounce and spell new names. Make it clear the new child speaks a different language at home and is learning the majority language, avoiding the negative 'So-and-so doesn't speak English.' Display photographs of all the children to show they all belong equally to the classroom. Provide a resource corner for newcomers and ensure they understand via translation or paralinguistic language the daily activities and announcements. Communicate positive attitudes about the linguistic and cultural diversity of the classroom.
- A second (host) language program for adult learners, that encourages immigrant parents to attend, helps both parents and children. Such a program in the school can also provide information about the area and about survival and success in the new culture and employment system.
- Announce events in the different school languages, to spread information and raise the status of heritage languages.
- Select classroom and library materials with a multicultural and multiracial approach, as well as books in heritage languages.

Language Teaching and Learning in Bilingual Immersion Classrooms

Immersion is a strong form of bilingual education, but begins with the formidable task of teaching **language majority students** through the minority language. This section considers the approach to language learning often taken in bilingual immersion education programs, and recently in CLIL (see Chapter 11).

Main Classroom Features of Bilingual Immersion Classrooms

What are the main classroom features of successful **bilingual immersion programs** in Canada, Finland, Australia, the Basque Country, Catalonia and Wales and elsewhere? The following are eight general features, challenges, and issues in providing successful immersion programs (Fortune & Tedick, 2008; Genesee, 2013).

First, the minimum time the second language needs to be used as a medium to ensure customary achievement levels is four to six years. Around the end of elementary schooling, immersion students show equal or higher performance in the curriculum compared with their mainstream peers. Second, the curriculum tends to be the same for immersion children as for their mainstream peers. While immersion attempts to cultivate empathy for a student's second language culture, the immersion curriculum has hitherto tended not to have major distinctive components to develop such empathy and participation. For example in Canada, a known challenge is that French becomes the language of school, and English the language of the playground, street and vocational success. The anglophone North American cultural influence is often so strong and persuasive that French immersion children are in danger of becoming passive rather than active bilinguals outside the school gates. The same occurs in immersion schools in many other countries, where the minority language is a language of the classroom, but the majority language is the peer 'prestige' language in the schoolyard and on the streets. Engineering formal language use inside an immersion classroom is possible; what happens outside the classroom walls is very difficult to influence.

Third, it has often been thought preferable to separate languages in instruction rather than to mix them arbitrarily during a single lesson. Sustained periods of monolingual instruction will require students to attend to the language of instruction, thereby both improving their language competence and confidence, and acquiring subject matter simultaneously. However, if mathematics, science, technology and computing are taught in English, will the hidden message be that English is of more value for scientific communication, for industrial and scientific vocations? Will English latently receive a special, reserved status? If the minority or second language is used for humanities, social studies, sport and art, is the hidden message that minority languages are only of value in such human and aesthetic pursuits? The choice of language medium for particular subjects may relegate or promote both the use and the status of minority languages. Also, the recent ideas about translanguaging suggest that translanguaging may initially be used by the student as scaffolding. As languages develop, it becomes a way the bilingual student thinks and works in the classroom. This can operate through a teachers' strategic use of two or more languages, or, much more frequently, latently and spontaneously in thinking and collaborating.

Fourth, how much time should be devoted to the two languages? Typically a minimum of 50% of instruction is in the second language. Thus, in French immersion in Canada, French-medium instruction may occur from 50% to 100% of the school week. The amount of instruction in English may increase as children become older. One factor in such a decision can be the amount of exposure to English a child receives outside school. Where a child's environment, home and street, media and community are English medium, for example, such saturation may imply that a relatively smaller proportion of time needs to be spent on English in the school. At the same time, the public will usually require bilingual schools to show that children's majority language competences, particularly literacy, are monitored and promoted, and not affected by bilingual education. Bilingual schools need to ensure that, through school instruction and school learning experiences, majority language proficiency and literacy is monitored and promoted.

Fifth, immersion education has historically enjoyed the synergy of teacher enthusiasm and strong parental commitment. Immersion parents have tended to be middle class, involved in teacher-parent committees, and taken a sustained interest in their children's progress. Immersion teachers tend to have native or native-like proficiency in both languages, are fully able to understand children speaking their home language, but speak to the children almost entirely in the immersion language. Teachers are thus important language models through their status and power role, identifying the immersion language with something of value and importance. Immersion teachers also provide the child with a model of pronunciation and style in the immersion language. They are typically enthusiastic about bilingualism in society, acting as bicultural and multicultural crusaders. The enthusiasm and commitment of teachers, administrators and staff in an immersion education school is an important and often underestimated factor in success.

Sixth, the immersion approach implies a relatively homogeneous language classroom. For example, in Canada or Finland early total immersion, all children are beginners without second language proficiency. This makes the task of the teacher less complex than in other types of bilingual classes where there is a mixture of first and second language speakers. However, an increasing number of French immersion students are immigrant students who have some degree of bilingualism in their home language and English, and are adding French as a third language. And in immersion programs in other countries (e.g. Irish immersion) there is sometimes a wide range of proficiency in the classroom language. The Irish and Welsh experiences tend to suggest that most children whose home language is English will cope successfully in minority language immersion classrooms. The danger is that the majority language of English, being the common denominator, will be the language used between students in the classroom, on the playground and certainly out of school (Hickey *et al.*, 2013). It is unclear as to what may be the optimal classroom composition of majority and minority language students in successful bilingual education. A balance towards a greater proportion of minority language speakers may help to ensure that the 'common denominator' majority language does not always dominate in informal classroom and playground talk.

Seventh, immersion provides an additive bilingual environment. Students acquire a second language at no cost to their home language and culture. Such enrichment may be contrasted to subtractive bilingual environments where the home language is replaced by the second language. For example, where the home language is Spanish and the submersion approach is to replace Spanish by English, negative rather than positive effects may occur in school performance and self-esteem. French must not develop at the expense of the home language, irrespective of that home language(s), otherwise the school becomes a subtractive environment. This underlines that the term immersion education is best reserved for additive rather than subtractive environments.

Finally, most immersion teachers have to 'wear two hats': promoting achievement throughout the curriculum and ensuring second language proficiency. Such a dual task requires immersion teacher training at the pre-service and in-service levels. This has tended to be a weakness in some countries. Immersion teaching (and teacher training) methods are still evolving.

Language Strategies in Immersion Classrooms

Immersion education is based on the idea that a first language is acquired relatively subconsciously. Children are unaware that they are learning a language in the home. Immersion attempts to replicate this process in the early years of schooling. The focus is on the content and not the form of the language. It is the task at hand that is central, not conscious language learning. In the early stages, there are no formal language learning classes, although simple elements of grammar such as verb endings may be taught informally.

In the latter years of elementary schooling, formal consideration may be given to the rules of the language (e.g. grammar and syntax). The early stages of immersion tend to mirror the subconscious acquisition of learning of the first language. Later a child will be made conscious of language as a system, to reinforce and promote communication. Children will initially speak their first language to each other and to their teacher without any objection or reprimand. Immersion teachers do not force children to use the immersion language until they are naturally willing to do so. Early insistence on the immersion language may inhibit children and develop negative attitudes to that language and to education in general. Over the first two years, immersion children gradually develop an understanding of the immersion language and begin to speak that language, particularly to the teacher.

In Canada, the most frequent grade in which English becomes part of the formal curriculum in early total French immersion is Grade 3. Other practices include introducing English at an earlier grade or kindergarten and at Grade 4. While initially students will lag behind mainstream students in English **language achievement**, by Grade 5 or 6 early immersion students catch up and perform as well.

In these beginning stages of early immersion, it is crucial that the teacher is comprehensible to the children. The teacher needs to be sympathetically aware of the level of a child's vocabulary and grammar, to deliver in the immersion language at a level the child can understand, and simultaneously be constantly pushing forward a child's competence in that language. The teacher will aim to push back the frontiers of a child's immersion language by ensuring that messages are both comprehensible and are slightly ahead of the learner's current level of language competence.

The language used to communicate with the child at these early stages is sometimes called **caretaker speech**. For the first year or two in immersion education, the vocabulary will be deliberately limited with a simplified presentation of grammar and syntax. The teacher may be repetitive in the words used and the ideas presented, with the same idea presented in two or more different ways. The teacher will deliberately speak slowly, giving the child more time to process the language input and understand the meaning. This tends to parallel the talk of mother to child (**motherese**) and foreigner talk (a person deliberately simplifying and slowing down so a foreigner can understand). During this caretaker stage, the teacher may be constantly questioning the child to ensure that understanding has occurred.

A teacher may also advise on the language to be used before a lesson topic is presented. When new words and new concepts are being introduced into a lesson, the teacher may spend some time in introducing the words and clarifying the concepts so that the language learner is prepared. Such teachers may also be sensitive to non-verbal feedback from students: questioning looks, losing concentration and glazed attention. Students will be encouraged to question the teacher for clarification and simplification when a misunderstanding has occurred.

Such teaching strategies thus cover two different areas: the importance of **comprehensible input** and the importance of negotiating meaning. The worst case is when neither the teacher nor the student is aware that misunderstanding (or no understanding) has taken place. A more effective classroom is when students and teachers are negotiating meaning, ensuring that mutual understanding has occurred. Not only is the negotiation of meaning important in language development and in maximizing achievement throughout the curriculum, it is also important in aiding motivation of children within the classroom. Patronizing such children and oversimplifying are two of the dangers in this process. Therefore, constantly presenting students with ever challenging and advancing learning situations is important in fostering classroom achievement.

Immersion classrooms need to have a particular view about language errors. Language errors are a usual and frequent part of the language learning process. Errors are not a symptom of failure. Errors are not permanent. They are a natural part of learning. With time and practice, they disappear. Therefore, immersion teachers are often discouraged from over-correcting children's attempts to speak the immersion language. Just as parents are more likely to correct children's factual errors than their language errors, the immersion teacher will tend to avoid constant correction of errors. Constant error correction may be self-defeating, even penalizing second language acquisition. Language accuracy tends to develop over time and with experience. Constant correction of error disrupts communication and content learning in the classroom. When a child or several children constantly make the same errors, then appropriate but positive intervention may be of value.

In the early stages of immersion, there will be a natural language use among children, including using features of their home language(s) that help them communicate meaning. A child may change the correct order in a sentence yet produce a perfectly comprehensible message. For example, different syntax may occur due to the influence of the first language on the second language. A child may put the pronoun or a preposition in the wrong order: as in 'go you and get it'. Traditionally the term **interlanguage** was used to describe such language use, suggesting a halfway stage in-between monolingualism and becoming proficient in a second language. However this term is now questioned, given the way it suggests that language learners are somehow less than whole. Regardless of the label used, such use of home language features at the beginning of the language learning process should not be seen as an 'error'. Rather it indicates the linguistic creativity of students who are using their latent understanding of their home language(s) to construct meaningful communication in the new language. Such use is intermediate, approximate and temporary. It is a worthwhile attempt to communicate and therefore needs acceptance rather than condemnation. Furthermore, students' attempts to produce **comprehensible output** in the new language facilitates the language learning process (Swain, 2000).

However, a danger of bilingual immersion is that students reach high levels in reading and listening but not in writing and speaking. Once students are able to communicate their meaning to teachers and peers, there can be a lack of incentive for achieving native-like accuracy. Therefore, at later stages, intervention in error correction and more focus on form and not just content may be valuable. Encouraging students to be more analytical of the accuracy of their speech may be important if native-like performance is targeted.

Proficiency in the first language will contribute to proficiency in the second language. Concepts already attached to words in the first language will easily be transferred into the second language. The acquisition of literacy skills in the first language tends to facilitate the acquisition of literacy skills in the second language. However, not all aspects of a language will transfer. Rules of syntax and spelling may not lend themselves to transfer. The closer a language structure is to the second language structure, the greater the transfer there is likely to be between the two languages. For example, the transferability between English and Spanish is likely to be greater than from Arabic to English owing to differences in syntax, symbols and direction of writing. However, the system of meanings, the conceptual map, and skills that a person owns may be readily transferable between languages.

The focus of bilingual immersion classrooms is typically on real, authentic communication, tasks, curriculum content and creative processes. Willingness to communicate is particularly aided when there are authentic uses for the language. There is also a place for an analytical approach to the second and the first language in the classroom. A bilingual immersion classroom will not just enable children to acquire the second language in a subconscious, almost incidental manner. Towards the end of elementary education, the experiential approach may be joined by a meaning-based focus on the form of language. A child may at this point be encouraged to analyze their vocabulary and grammar. At this later stage, some lessons may have progress in the second language as their major aim. After early sheltering with language, the development of vocabulary and grammar may be dealt with in a direct and systematic manner. However, Lyster and Mori (2008) indicate the value of 'counter balanced instruction' where students are encouraged to consider language form but in a meaning-oriented context. That is, highlighting the nature of the language, including both giving corrections and allowing translanguaging, can be achieved within a context where meaning, understanding and content are important.

Key Topics in Effective Bilingual Schools

As this and previous chapters have shown, there are a wide variety of program types for bilingual students, and numerous variations. Wright (2015) argues that regardless of program type, all effective bilingual programs contain three essential components: (a) Second language instruction for non-native speakers, (b) content-area instruction provided in the home language and through sheltered instruction, and (c) primary language support or translanguaging pedagogies. Table 13.1 provides an overview of each of these components.

Table 13.1 Essential components of effective bilingual programs

Second language instruction for non-native speakers		Content-area instruction		Primary language support/ translanguaging pedagogies
Pull-out instruction	In-class instruction	Home language instruction	Sheltered instruction	
A trained specialist teacher pulls students out of regular classroom for second language instruction.	The classroom teacher is trained and certified to provide second language instruction within the classroom.	One or more content areas are taught in students' home languages.	One or more content areas are taught in the second language using sheltered instruction strategies and techniques.	The classroom teacher employs a variety of strategies and techniques involving the effective use of students' home languages and translanguaging pedagogies to increase their comprehension of second language and sheltered content instruction.

Note. Modified from Wright (2015: 90)

However, bilingual schools must deliver highly effective education for students, not just on language dimensions but also on other areas where varied stakeholders want success (Mehisto, 2012). There is no justification for bilingual education solely from a language perspective. Even if the school is excellent at **language maintenance** and **language revitalization**, its justification for students, parents, public and politicians ultimately derives from it being a form of holistically effective education. While social equity and justice can be a colorful flag to wave for bilingual schools, their success in developing each child academically as well as linguistically, cognitively and as citizens, as contributors to the economy as well as to a community, requires a bilingual school to deliver the multiple and complex agenda of education and schooling. While this section concentrates on language issues, all the attributes of effective schooling are relevant to bilingual schools.

There are elements that make all types and models of bilingual education more or less effective (Mehisto, 2012; Mehisto & Genesee, 2015). While dual language policies, provision and practices are a keystone of such schools, effectiveness reaches far beyond language (Baetens Beardsmore in O. García, 2009a). For a bilingual school to become a shining success, the following themes may need addressing, albeit not in separation but as an entity, and as part of a process of continuous enhancement and school development.

Intake of Students and Language Balance

The ingredients of bilingual schooling commence with the students. Their life history (e.g. as immigrants or refugees), identity, community background (e.g. isolation or saturation in their community of their home language), proficiency in languages on entry to the school, cultural knowledge, language aptitude, motivation and self-esteem all affect the process of classroom interaction and learning outcomes. A key issue has been the balance of majority and minority language students in a school so that the majority language does not increasingly dominate. This has been an issue both in US dual language bilingual schools and in Irish heritage language schools called 'Gaelscoileanna' (Hickey, 2007; W.G. Lewis, 2004). Where the balance is weighted too much to majority language speakers, informal classroom language may turn to the majority language. What is officially about minority language development can become unofficial immersion in the majority language.

Particularly in rural language minority areas, bilingual classrooms may have a mixture of majority language speakers who are learning through the minority language (e.g. Irish) and native speakers of that minority language. This can mean two different language agendas: minority language children speedily acquiring the majority language; majority language children being applauded for acquiring the minority language.

In Ireland, Hickey (2001) found that in pre-school mixed language classes, Irish first language speakers may not be achieving sufficient enrichment in their language development as the emphasis is on second language learners of Irish. Teachers tended to tailor their language to accommodate second language learners, asking fewer questions, giving less feedback and more repetition for understanding by L2 children. Even at the pre-school level, children appear aware of the different status, power and intergroup relationship between the two languages (Hickey, 2001). Their language preference can thus be affected by the saturation of majority language speakers and also newcomer immigrants in a mixed language classroom (Hickey & Ó Cainín, 2001; Little *et al.*, 2014).

The language of teachers is likely to be affected by the balance of native speakers and learners in mixed language classrooms. One concern is that teachers may ask fewer questions in mixed language groups compared with more homogeneous language groups. Teachers may also use more simplified language to accommodate the second language learners. Native speakers may thus not be receiving the native language enrichment they need. What is a language opportunity is also a language challenge for the teacher. Conversely, the teacher may tend to gear instruction to the more proficient and native speakers of the target language, and thus deprive the lower-level second language learners of the modified linguistic input they need to comprehend and succeed. Thus, a major challenge in such mixed language classrooms is striking an acceptable balance, and learning to differentiate instruction appropriate to students' level of language proficiency and academic understanding.

While native speakers of a minority language provide a language role model for second language speakers in speaking that minority language, the danger is that second language speakers overly influence minority language speakers (W.G. Lewis, 2004). Hickey (2001) aptly asked, when beginners and native speakers are mixed in minority language immersion, 'who is immersing whom?' Researching in Ireland, she found that in such mixed home language classrooms, children from minority language homes tended to switch to English. Such children had less language effect on majority language speakers than those English-only speakers had on Irish speakers. Even at pre-school level, the majority language was pervasive and was eroding the minority language. Majority language students immerse native speakers in the majority language. Similar concerns arise in in US dual immersion classrooms (Henderson & Palmer, 2015; K.A. Hinton, 2015).

This suggests that the numerical balance of native speakers and learners of a minority language is important, possibly tilted to a predominance of minority language speakers. Also, supporting and enriching the first language competences of native speakers of a minority language is crucial in such schools. This implies the possible separation of children of different language abilities for 'language lesson' sessions while avoiding language group separation and discrimination. Small-group composition of students needs care and consideration by teachers. Such teachers need training to become aware of cross-language influence, and of the need to raise the status and increase the use of the minority language in the classroom by well-designed activities and reward systems. It is important that language minority students are empowered by having positions of responsibility in the class and school, and are actively involved in school activities (e.g. sports teams, societies).

Muller and Baetens Beardsmore (2004) provide illustrations of teacher accommodation from the European School experience of mixed language students in European Hours sessions (see Chapter 11). Discrimination, exclusion, ghettoization and separation of languages are avoided by rewarding the plurality of (majority) languages and language use. Translanguaging is used strategically by the teacher, and accepted, so as to integrate languages and their native speakers. Bilingualism is celebrated.

Shared Vision, Mission and Goals among Staff

A consensus in the goals of the school is needed among staff, with consistency across staff in the treatment of language minority students, and effective collaboration across staff. Value and status should be given to the language minority students' language and culture. Native language skills need to be celebrated and encouraged inside and outside the formal curriculum and flagged as an advantage rather than a liability. While clear and agreed aims, goals and mission are important, an effective bilingual school will have a system for constant improvement and development, and will be always seeking to increase its effectiveness.

Staffing

Without teachers, administrators, and other staff members, no bilingual school can commence, continue or succeed. With untrained or poor quality staff, the best bilingual program will fail, whatever the model. Highly skilled teachers, excellent teacher training and constantly developing teacher effectiveness are a foundation of the sustainability and success of any bilingual program (Brisk, 2008). Thus a foundational ingredient into a bilingual school is the characteristics and language proficiency of the teachers and other support staff, their own biculturalism or multiculturalism, attitudes to minority languages and minority students, and their professional and personal identity (de Mejía & Hélot, 2015). Mehisto (2012) suggests that the attributes of effective teachers in bilingual education include: high levels of language proficiency, knowledge of students' languages, cooperation with other teachers in delivering the language curriculum, and dedication to student learning.

It is important that teachers are positive towards students' language and cultural backgrounds, are sensitive to their home and community contexts, respond to children's language and cultural needs, celebrate diversity and recognize the talents of such children (O. García, 2008a; Téllez & Varghese, 2013). Teachers in bilingual classrooms may sometimes find barriers to success in large and overcrowded classes of undernourished students, inadequate teacher training, a lack of teaching resources, poor pay and promotion prospects, the stigma of working with lowly regarded bilinguals, and limited funding (Benson, 2004).

As Benson (2004) reminds us in the context of developing countries, bilingual teaching is often more challenging than monolingual teaching, frequently occurring in contexts with inequality between urban and rural areas, between elite and subordinate power and status divisions, between language/ethnic groups, and between genders. Teachers are expected to address such inequalities, provide cultural and linguistic capital, meet high-stakes test standards of student achievement in literacy and numeracy, bridge the home and school gap, become respected members of the community, and advocate for educational reform and innovation. The roles include: 'pedagogue, linguist, innovator, intercultural communicator, community member, and even advocate of bilingual programmes' (pp. 207–208).

Teaching in such bilingual contexts therefore requires much professionalism, enthusiasm, commitment and support. School staff need to be committed to the **empowerment** of language minority students through education. Such commitment is not just realized in the classroom but also in staff involvement in extra-curricular activities, participation in community events, interest in developing their pedagogic skills, and even cooperation in the political process of improving the lot of language minority students.

Teacher Professional Development and Training

Teacher professional development can be designed to help all staff members effectively serve all students. For example, professional development programs can sensitize teachers to students' language and cultural backgrounds, increase their knowledge of second language acquisition and help develop effective curriculum approaches in teaching language minority students (de Mejia & Hélot, 2015). All teachers can be trained to recognize themselves as teachers of language irrespective of their subject area. The mentoring of new teachers by more expert and experienced teachers can be valuable.

Such initial and in-service staff development may include an individual person, community and wider societal awareness program, models and curriculum approaches to bilingual education, cultural diversity, and the politics that surround local and regional implementation of education for bilinguals (Cabellero, 2014). Fillmore and Snow (2000) indicate particular teacher competencies that bilingual (and all) teachers need, based on their multiple roles as classroom communicators, educators, evaluators, citizens and socializers. They suggest that teachers need to know the basics of language form (e.g. phonemes, morphemes, regularity, **lexicon**, structure, dialects, academic English, spelling) and not just language functions and uses.

B.B. Flores *et al.* (2011) note that despite a strong theoretical knowledge base, 'there is minimal empirical evidence regarding the nature of bilingual education teacher preparation models and their impact on teacher quality and effectiveness' (p. xiv). They argue that it is thus important to understand the elements of bilingual teacher preparation as a whole, and to examine its various components. Taking a sociocultural perspective, B.B. Flores *et al.* propose their own model of bilingual teacher preparation – *Educar Para Transformar (Educate for Transformation)* – with two overarching interdependent, complementary frameworks: *transformación (transformation)* and *revolución* (revolution), with three interconnecting dimensions – *iluminación (illumination)*, praxis and *concientización (awareness)*, directing programmatic content (p. xiv). Téllez and Varghese (2013), argue that it is also essential to provide professional development for bilingual teachers to build their 'capacity to promote policies and practices to empower language minorities and help bilingual education survive in a hostile political climate' (p. 129).

Leadership

The leadership of the school is a crucial factor, and ideally the principal, for example, has an excellent knowledge of curriculum approaches to language minority children and communicates this to all the staff (Scanlan & López, 2015). Strong leadership, the willingness to hire bilingual teachers and high expectations of bilingual students tend to be part of the repertoire of effective leaders (E. Hamayan & Field, 2012). Effectiveness research tends to suggest that such leaders should demonstrate a strength of purpose and proactive management while engaging the professionalism of teachers and empowering all staff in decision-making processes (Mehisto, 2012). Not only do they inspire, motivate, support and communicate well with staff, they also identify, secure and mobilize human, financial and material resources. Open to change and innovation, they are not only politically informed but also developing themselves as educationalists and leaders. Excellent leaders also project their leadership beyond the school into the neighborhood, and liaise with homes and families. Such leaders are likely to be well known, highly respected and easily accessible in their communities. They are likely to work in partnership with community leaders. The crucial nature and influence of leadership is well illustrated in studies by Potowski (2007) of a dual immersion school in Chicago, and by Menken and Solarza (2015) of principals in New York City.

Curriculum

The curriculum of a bilingual program needs to provide intellectually challenging, active and meaningful lessons that have coherence, balance, breadth, relevance, progression and continuity. This entails a focus on basic skills but crucially also on developing higher-order thinking skills. Effective curriculum planning also tends to include: language and literacy development across the curriculum; smooth language transitions between grades; systematic, equitable and authentic assessment integrated with learning goals; a bilingual and bi/multicultural hidden curriculum and ethos throughout the school; a safe and orderly school environment and a supportive, constructive classroom atmosphere.

Supportive Ethos and Environment

The student may experience prejudice and discrimination, the subordinate status of their language minority group and **assimilation** influences. Such external influences may affect internal psychological workings such as self-esteem, anxiety, integration with peers and achievement in school. A socioculturally supportive environment for language minority students is therefore important. What is also vital is a safe and orderly school and classroom environment where students feel they belong, are cared for as well as educated, and that values linguistic, cultural, ethnic and racial diversity.

UNICEF (2012) has developed a framework for promoting such educational environments called 'Child Friendly Schools.' Within this framework:

- The school is a significant personal and social environment in the lives of its students. A child-friendly school ensures every child an environment that is physically safe, emotionally secure and psychologically enabling.
- Teachers are the single most important factor in creating an effective and inclusive classroom.
- Children are natural learners, but this capacity to learn can be undermined and sometimes destroyed. A child-friendly school recognizes, encourages and supports children's growing capacities as learners by providing a school culture, teaching behaviors and curriculum content that are focused on learning and the learner.
- The ability of a school to be and to call itself child-friendly is directly linked to the support, participation and collaboration it receives from families.
- Child-friendly schools aim to develop a learning environment in which children are motivated and able to learn. Staff members are friendly and welcoming to children and attend to all their health and safety needs. (p. 1)

High Expectations

High expectations among teachers and peers are important for all students, but no more so than for 'at risk' minority students (N. Gold, 2006). When bilingual students come from materially impoverished homes, with low aspirations present in the family and community, then low expectations may too easily and implicitly be embedded in a school's ethos. Instead, a positive 'can do' atmosphere for the 'have nots' will attempt to reverse a self-perpetuating pattern of low expectation and consequent failure. High expectations need to be clearly communicated to such students, with the school responsive to a student's individual needs and to varying community profiles (e.g.

culture, newcomers). High expectations are conveyed, for example, by providing opportunities for student-directed activities, involving students in decisions and building their competences, trust and self-esteem, with positive and regular feedback based on careful monitoring.

Individualization

Apart from strategies to motivate students and recognize their achievement, the provision of individualized support for language minority students is often needed. The provision of counseling, cooperation with parents and the hiring of language minority staff in leadership positions to act as role models are some of the ploys used to raise expectations of success at school.

Parents

Plenty of parental involvement, with home–school collaboration that is reciprocal is typically a major dimension of school effectiveness (Arias, 2015). Bilingual programs recognize that parental involvement may vary as driven by cultural factors and parents' prior experiences (or lack thereof) with schooling, and that parents may be actively involved in their children's education in ways that are less visible. Nonetheless bilingual education opens the doors for active minority language parent involvement simply by overcoming traditional language and cultural barriers between families and the school. Parents of language minority children can be encouraged to become actively engaged in their children's education, including in governance. This includes participation in parents meetings, contact with teachers and counselors, telephone contact and neighborhood meetings. Parents and their children can be perceived as stakeholders, customers and partners whose satisfaction levels are valued and with whom there is regular two-way communication (see Chapter 14).

Conclusion

In schools and classrooms, there are myriad decisions to make daily, hourly, second by second. Bilingual classrooms and schools add a language dimension to such decision-making. The allocation of languages and support for growing languages mixes with decisions about grouping, curriculum materials, styles of learning and use of support assistants and parents. The relationship between language, culture and literacies interacts with overall curriculum decisions about intake, ethos and expectations.

In such complexity, teacher training and continuous professional development of the teachers, administrators, and other staff is crucial. Without teachers there can be no bilingual school or classroom provision. With effective leadership and well-trained staff, the effectiveness of any bilingual school is greatly enhanced.

Key Points in This Chapter

➢ Heritage language classrooms integrate minority language maintenance, majority language development, biliteracy and cultural awareness.

➢ Minority language bilinguals in mainstream classrooms often take seven or more years to reach the language proficiency in the majority language.

➢ Mainstream classrooms sometimes use bilingual support assistants to help the teacher with minority language students in a transition phase.

➢ Language scaffolding is often needed to support minority language students in the early stages of using the majority language in a mainstream classroom.

➢ 'Translanguaging' involves using both languages to maximize learning, for example, by varying the language of input and output in a lesson.

➢ Bilingual school effectiveness includes attention to: intake of students, staffing and professional development, vision, aims and goals, leadership, a challenging curriculum, supportive ethos, high expectations and home–school collaboration.

➢ Immersion methodology attempts to ensure high levels of academic proficient language development in both languages, empathy for two or more cultures, and thus an additive experience.

➢ Teacher enthusiasm and parental commitment are important ingredients in effective immersion approaches.

➢ Policies for when to introduce formal attention to the home language, comprehensible communication in the immersion language, plentiful feedback, attitude to language errors and interlanguage are needed in effective immersion classrooms.

Suggested Further Reading

📖 Baker, C. (2014). *A parents' and teachers' guide to bilingualism* (4th ed.). Bristol, UK: Multilingual Matters.

📖 Barnard, R., & McClellan, J. (Eds.). (2014). *Codeswitching in university English-medium classes: Asian perspectives*. Bristol, UK: Multilingual Matters.

📖 García, O., Johnson, S. I., & Seltzer, K. (2016). *Translanguaging classrooms: Leveraging student bilingualism for learning*. Philadelphia, PA: Caslon Publishing.

📖 Gibbons, P. (2015). *Scaffolding language, scaffolding learning: Teaching English language learners in the mainstream classroom* (2nd ed.). Portsmouth, NH: Heinemann.

📖 Hamayan, E., & Field, R. F. (Eds.). (2012). *English language learners at school: A guide for administrators* (2nd ed.). Philadelphia: Caslon Publishing.

📖 Wright, W. E. (2015). *Foundations for teaching English language learners: Research, theory, policy and practice* (2nd ed.). Philadelphia, PA: Caslon.

On the Web

- Video – Languages Matter! (Produced by UNESCO for International Mother Tongue Day)
  https://youtu.be/Q-XozG0RSCo
- UNESCO: Mother Tongue Multilingual Education (Information and Advocacy Kit for Promoting Multilingual Education)
  http://www.unesco.org/new/en/education/themes/strengthening-education-systems/languages-in-education/multilingual-education/
- What is Translanguaging? An Interview with Ofelia García (Francois Grosjean's Life as a Bilingual Blog on Psychology Today)
  https://www.psychologytoday.com/blog/life-bilingual/201603/what-is-translanguaging

Discussion Questions

(1) Why is it important to teach children in a language they understand? What is needed for schools to be able to do so effectively?
(2) Many bilingual education programs insist on the strict separation of the languages. Why is this strict separation difficult to maintain? What is more recent research suggesting?
(3) The effectiveness of bilingual education inevitably goes far beyond language of instruction and language outcomes. What other factors are essential to consider?

Study Activities

(1) Make a list of 'classroom effectiveness factors' from your reading. Following observation in one or more bilingual classrooms, consider the effectiveness of these classrooms against this list. What factors seem, as the result of your classroom observation, to be more and less important?
(2) Observe a bilingual education classroom paying attention to the nature of language use by the students, teacher, and any bilingual support assistants. Is there an attempt for strict separation of languages? When the focus is on one of the languages, do students or teachers ever use the other language, or engage in translanguaging? Does such language use appear to hinder or support the learning objectives of the lesson or activity?
(3) Conduct an interview with a current bilingual teacher focused on the key topics in effective bilingual schools as outlined in this chapter. How does the teacher view each of these factors, and how much importance is placed on each?

Literacy, Biliteracy and Multiliteracies for Bilinguals

Literacy, Biliteracy and Multiliteracies for Bilinguals

Introduction

Different bilingual classrooms and schools, different languages and **cultures**, tend to have different views about the purposes of reading and writing for bilingual children. Politicians and parents often vary in their viewpoints; educationalists passionately debate methods and strategies. Some think that, for immigrant bilinguals and multilinguals, literacy should be about **enculturation** and **assimilation** into a new language and culture. For indigenous and minority language bilinguals, literacy may be aimed at reading and writing fluently in two or more languages. In some 'prestigious bilingual' **contexts**, biliteracy is about promoting a wider rationality, critical thinking, balanced and detached awareness, empathy and sensitivity to varied cultures. Some scholars define basic skills in learning to read such as phonemic awareness, phonics, fluency, vocabulary and comprehension (National Reading Panel, 2000). Other academics, such as those from the New Literacy Studies camp (Street, 2017), talk about multilingual literacies and multiliteracies among bilingual and multilingual children.

Thus the nature of being a bilingual (e.g. immigrant, indigenous, elite) interacts with the type of literacy that is offered and experienced. It is not just the school that delivers this. For some **language minority** parents, literacy is about memorization, transmission of life stories revealing their heritage, values and morality. In some religions, literacy concerns the transmission of rules of religious and moral behavior. A Muslim for example, will be expected to read aloud from the Qur'an but will not necessarily be expected to understand what they read, this being provided in their **mother tongue**. In some cultures, the mother is expected to read to her children and help them develop literacy skills, but she is not expected to read national newspapers or complete bureaucratic forms herself. Older siblings may also be expected to help develop the skills of reading and writing in younger siblings. So while school is important in developing literacy, a bilingual also develops literacies in the family, community and religion, for example.

Where language minority members are labeled as immigrants, under-achievers or as a potentially dissident minority, literacy can be variously regarded as a key to economic self-advancement, personal **empowerment** or as social control. Such literacy may be encouraged at school only in the majority language and not in two or more languages (e.g. English language literacy in the US; English in parts of Africa as an 'official' or international language). In the US, access to English literacy is essential for higher education, employment and vocational mobility. 'The pinnacle of young children's educational development is the acquisition of literacy. Literacy is the ticket

Box 14.1 The Seal of Biliteracy

In 2011 California became the first state in the US to pass legislation creating a 'Seal of Biliteracy'. The concept was originally developed by Californians Together, and is now promoted nationally in collaboration with the National Association for Bilingual Education, the American Council of Foreign Language Teachers, and Velásquez Press. As of 2016, 23 states had adopted the Seal, and another 7 were in various stages of consideration for adoption. As explained on the group's website (http://sealofbiliteracy.org/):

- The Seal of Biliteracy is an award given by a school, district, or county office of education in recognition of students who have studied and attained proficiency in two or more languages by high school graduation.
- The Seal of Biliteracy encourages students to pursue biliteracy, honors the skills our students attain, and can be evidence of skills that are attractive to future employers and college admission officers.

The Seal is typically awarded to graduating seniors affixed to their high school diplomas or awarded as a separate certificate or medal. This recognition marks a significant turn after many years of policies that have devalued bilingual education. However a state's adoption of the Seal is no guarantee the schools will adopt the types of strong bilingual programs that will enable students to develop biliteracy skills and properly earn the Seal. Some have expressed concerns about how this proficiency is to be demonstrated, and fear that the Seal may lead to greater recognition and benefits for proficient English speakers who attain a modicum of proficiency in a second language (e.g. Native English speakers in advanced placement foreign language classes), and less benefits and recognitions for emergent bilinguals who enter school as English language learners and who attain a high-degree of proficiency in their second language – English. Criteria and implementation vary across states.

of entry into our society, it is the currency by which social and economic positions are waged, and it is the central purpose of schooling' (Bialystok, 2001a: 152). Thus, while US students need English language literacy, many have tended to exit with 'survival' levels of English literacy that channels them into low paid jobs. With a growing number of US states adopting the Seal of Biliteracy (see Box 14.1), it may be possible to begin to track the percentage of students who graduate from high school with well-developed literacy in more than language. In 2015 it was estimated around 32,000 graduating seniors earned the Seal – an impressive number, yet is only represents about one percent of high school graduates that school year (Mitchell, 2015).

In contrast, where language minorities have access to 'strong' forms of bilingual education, literacy may be introduced in the home/minority language. Whether language minority children should first become literate in the majority language or in their minority language will be discussed later. Before engaging in such discussions, it is important to explore the kind of literacy that language minority students may be given. We start by considering contrasting viewpoints on literacy. This provides an instant flavor of the debate about the nature and value of different kinds of literacy for bilingual and particularly language minority students (Street, 2002, 2013; Wiley, 2005).

Differing Viewpoints on Literacy for Minority Language Students

The Skills Approach

The US No Child Left Behind Act (NCLB) of 2001 mandated that literacy in English from Kindergarten to the 3rd grade should contain explicit instruction in phonemic awareness, phonics, vocabulary development, reading fluency (including oral reading skills) and reading comprehension strategies (Section 1208 (3) of Title 1). NCLB has been replaced by the Every Student Succeeds Act (ESSA) of 2015, and these skills remain as a key part of 'comprehensive literacy instruction' for all students (Subpart 2, Section 2221(b)(1)(B)). A narrow focus on these skills alone represents a skills (or bottom-up) approach to literacy. It assumes that literacy is the ability to decode symbols on a page into sounds, followed by making meaning from those sounds. Reading is about saying the words on the page. Writing is about being able to spell correctly, and writing in correct grammatical sentences. This approach is also found in the National Curriculum and the National Literacy Strategy in the UK (Street, 2002).

The US research backing for the skills-based approach derives from the National Reading Panel (2000) with their evidence-based assessment of the scientific research literature on reading and its implications for reading instruction. The report declares that the key to literacy is developing skills in phonemic awareness, phonics, fluency, vocabulary, text comprehension and oracy. For many teachers, these skills are an essential foundation for learning to read and write, and do not preclude other approaches that are considered below. Closing the achievement gap for language minority students may require such foundations, but may also need approaches to literacy that are much more than just skill acquisition. Indeed, a comprehensive review of the academic literature on the literacy development of second language made clear that typical literacy instruction for English proficient students is not sufficient for second language learners (August & Shanahan, 2006). It is essential that second language learners receive **English language development**, including a focus on oral language skills, and also that literacy instruction is differentiated, sheltered and scaffolded as needed commensurate with students' current language and literacy levels. Strategic use of the home language is also found to be beneficial for English literacy development (August & Shanahan, 2006).

The **assessment** of success in a skills approach is measured by standardized tests of reading and writing. Such tests tend to assess decomposed and decontextualized language skills, eliciting skills comprehension rather than deeper language thinking and understanding. These tests tend to be used as templates for instruction. Measurement-led instruction promotes 'teaching to the test' and possibly decreases the importance of developing higher order language and thinking skills. However, others in the US argue that, for **English language learners**, an over-emphasis on literacy skills in the early grades will fail to incorporate students' language and cultural backgrounds. This will limit their ability to construct meaning.

While there is unlikely to be a simple formula or universal 'best bet' to acquiring reading and writing skills, a review by Genesee *et al.* (2006) of literacy approaches for ELLs (English language learners) in the US suggests that explicit instruction of reading and writing skills and interactive instruction (e.g. interaction with teachers and competent readers and writers) are both effective approaches, as is a combination of the two. In contrast, solely using process approaches that emphasize authentic uses and de-emphasize skills, is less effective. It appears insufficient just to expose students to literacy-rich environments for reading and writing skills to evolve. A balanced approach is needed. However, there are differences in defining 'effectiveness', as the remainder of this chapter demonstrates.

The Construction of Meaning Approach

In contrast to the skills approach, there is a 'constructivist' view of literacy that is particularly relevant to classrooms where there are bilinguals and multilinguals. It emphasizes that readers bring their own meanings to text, and therefore that reading and writing is essentially a construction and reconstruction of meaning. This implies that the meaning individuals give to a text depends on their language(s), culture, personal experiences and histories, personal understandings of the themes and tone of text, and the particular social context where reading occurs.

Within Vygotskian theory, students are viewed as active constructors of meaning from text. Learning is mediated by the social interaction between the child and an experienced teacher or parent, for example, or peer modeling and coaching, **scaffolding**, and instruction that is directed toward the child's 'zone of proximal development' (Vygotsky, 1986; see Chapter 13).

Teachers using a meaning construction approach will typically attempt to help language learners bridge any cultural mismatch through explicitly teaching them the culture, understandings and values of the dominant culture, as well as by providing them with the vocabulary and strategies needed to construct meaning. For language minority students, initial understandings will partly or mainly derive from their minority language culture. Different students of varying backgrounds will make different interpretations of the text. When there is a mismatch between the reader's knowledge and that which is assumed by the school, the construction of meaning will be affected. Language minority children, in particular, can be trapped in this situation. Trying to make sense out of texts from a different culture, with different cultural assumptions, makes predicting the storyline and understanding the text more difficult. One role for teachers therefore is to mediate in the construction of meaning, helping students to construct meaning from text.

The Sociocultural Literacy Approach

A related view to that of 'construction of meaning' is found in the ideas of sociocultural literacy. This allows for the possibility that different language minority communities attach a different value to different types of literacies or multiliteracies. The social nature of literacy encourages many authors to use the term 'literacies' and 'multiliteracies' (Martin-Jones & Jones, 2000). The use of the plural 'literacies' suggests that reading and writing is not autonomous or independent.

> Literacies are social practices: ways of reading and writing and using written texts that are bound up in social processes which locate individual action within social and cultural processes … Focusing on the plurality of literacies means recognizing the diversity of reading and writing practices and the different genres, styles and types of texts associated with various activities, domains or social identities. (Martin-Jones & Jones, 2000: 4–5)

Sociocultural literacy approaches use the idea of 'Discourses' that do not just include reading and writing but also different ways of talking, listening, interacting, believing, valuing and feeling, and which cannot be explicitly taught (Gee, 2012). Many language minority children enter school with **discourses** that differ from the dominant school discourse, leading to difficulties in students achieving well. Sociocultural literacy is the ability to construct appropriate cultural meaning when reading. In theory, a person can be functionally literate but culturally illiterate (e.g. reading without meaning). In reading and writing, we bring not only previous experience, but also our values and beliefs enabling us to create cultural meaning from what we read and insert cultural understanding into what we write.

For some people, such cultural literacy may lead to the assimilation of language minority immigrants (e.g. accepting the values and norms embedded in English language classics). **Assimilationists** may argue for a common literacy, transmitting the majority language culture to ensure assimilation of language minority groups within the wider society. In contrast, a cultural pluralist viewpoint will argue that national unity is not sacrificed by cultural literacy in the minority language or by **multicultural** literacy. Multicultural literacy is likely to give a wider view of the world, more windows on the world, a more colorful and diverse view of human history and customs, and a less narrow view of science and society.

Where there is much variety of language and cultures within a region, issues about 'local literacies' arise (Lin, 2015). Street (2002) regards local literacies as literacy practices identified with local and regional cultures (as different from national culture). Such local literacies may be forgotten by international and national literacy campaigns or there may be tensions between local and national/international literacy practice. Local literacies avoid the impoverishment of uniformity in literacy that is created by the dominance of English, for example. They make literacy relevant to people's lives, their local culture and local community relationships (Hornberger, 2006).

The Critical Literacy Approach

The critical literacy approach is 'a sociocultural orientation to literacy that takes seriously the relationship between meaning making and power' (Janks, 2013: 1). Literacy can work to maintain the status quo, to ensure that those with power and dominance in society influence, even control, what language minorities read and think. Propaganda, political pamphlets, newspapers and books can all be used to attempt to control the thinking and minds of the masses. Literacy can be conceived as an attempt through schooling and other formal and informal means of education to socialize citizens and produce hegemony in society. Thus, those in power maintain control over those who could be subversive to social order, or democratically challenge their power base. Literacy can be used to instill centrally preferred attitudes, beliefs and thoughts. Similarly, some religious traditions have deliberately used literacy to ensure that their members were, at the least, influenced by writings, at the worst, brainwashed. Careful selection by religious leaders and parents over what their children read is an attempt to use literacy to control and contain the mind.

Those with power and dominance in society also maintain their position by their view of what is 'correct language'. Language minorities with little political and economic power are often taught that their patterns of speech and writing are inferior and deficient, and such language varieties are connected with their economic social and cultural deprivation. Such groups are expected to adopt standard majority language use (e.g. to speak 'proper' or 'correct' or 'standard' English).

A philosophical basis of critical literacy is that all cultures are attempts to discover meanings and understandings. No one culture (including the umbrella idea of Western culture) has the monopoly of understanding, knowledge or wisdom. The Postmodernist view is that there is little or no transcendent truth, no ultimate reality or wisdom outside of culture, no unalterable or fundamental qualities of women, ethnic groups or language minorities. All meaning is socially constructed. In Postmodernism, all meanings are unstable, and none are neutral, but change through continuous negotiation and reconstruction. There is value in the meanings of people in a subordinate position (e.g. language minorities) just as there is in those of language majorities.

The voices of the poor are as meaningful as the privileged; the understandings of the oppressed become as valid as those of the oppressor.

Literacy can be a tool of oppression; it can also be a liberator for language minorities. It can be a bar to opportunity, or a means of opening a door to empowerment. One way of attempting to empower people is through critical literacy. Freire (1993) and Freire and Macedo (1987) argued for a literacy that makes oppressed communities socially and politically conscious about their subservient role and lowly status in society. The argument is that literacy must go well beyond the skills of reading and writing. It must make people aware of their sociocultural context and their political environment (Wink, 2010). This may occur through mother tongue literacy and local/national/international multiliteracies (discussed later).

For language minority speakers, literacy for empowerment can be about stimulating language activism, the demand for language rights, self-determination and an equitable share of power. Freire's literacy education in Brazil's peasant communities (and with other oppressed groups around the world) assumes that when people become conscious about their subordinate role and inferior position in their community and society, they then become empowered to change their own lives, situations and communities (Freire, 1993).

What alternative is posed by the critical literacy movement? At school level, the critical literacy approach is that language minority students should not just be invited to retell a story. They should be encouraged to offer their own interpretation and evaluation of text. Who is the writer? What is their perspective and **bias**? What kind of moral interpretation is made? What alternative interpretations and viewpoints are

---

Box 14.2 Alma Flor Ada's creative reading or creative dialogue methodology

Alma Flor Ada presents a critical literacy approach for bilingual students based on Paulo Freire's work. She describes four phases in the creative reading or creative dialogue act that can facilitate the process in any subject matter:

1. Descriptive Phase
Recognize or investigate the existing knowledge. The teacher is mainly responsible for presenting this information, but students can also participate in researching information, according to their age and preparation.

2. Personal/Interpretive Phase
Students are encouraged to express:
a. Their personal feelings and emotions as related to the information presented. It is important that the teacher also shares, although always mindful of not supplanting the students' voices.
b. Their previous knowledge about the topic. Does the new information support (enrich, contradict) what they knew or had experienced? How can their experiences and the new knowledge be reconciled? This personal interaction with the information is essential for true learning to take place.

3. Critical/Reflective/Multicultural/Anti-Bias Phase
Students and teachers should address the important questions: How has this knowledge been generated? Who supports it? Whose interests does it serve? Who benefits from it? Is this information inclusive? Who has not been included, considered, or respected? Were all possible alternatives considered? Which other alternatives are possible? What would be the consequences of each of the alternatives?

4. Transformative Action Phase
Learning should provide the possibility to act better in the future, not only to be well informed but to consider the consequences of our choices.

Source: (Interview with Alma Flor Ada by P.C. Ramirez, 2013: 126)

possible? Children will be encouraged not just to seek answers to such questions, but to look critically and take on multiple viewpoints (see Box 14.2). Multicultural and multi-lingual children may be given diverse pieces of writing that reflect different cultural knowledge and attitudes. Differences in interpretation, and differences in experience and knowledge children bring to the text can be contrasted and compared. Diversity of understanding can be celebrated.

To conclude this section, Table 14.1 lists some of the practical contrasting charac-teristics of the functional/transmission and critical literacy classrooms.

Table 14.1 Functional/transmission vs. critical literacy classrooms

Functional literacy/transmission classrooms	Critical literacy classrooms
• Literacy is decoding words, sometimes without understanding their meaning. • Literacy is spelling words correctly, and writing in correct grammar. • Literacy is getting the correct answers on worksheets, filling in blanks, circling appropriate answers. • Literacy is answering closed questions having read a story. • Literacy is reading aloud to the teacher and the rest of the class, being perfect in pronunciation, intonation and accent. • Literacy is mechanically going through exercises, practicing skills, and giving correct answers on tests. • Literacy is learning to do but not necessarily to think.	• Literacy is seeing oneself as an active reader and writer. • Literacy involves enjoying reading, developing independent thoughts and judgments about reading and writing. • Literacy is sharing ideas, reflections, experiences and reactions with others in the classroom, both peers and teachers. • Literacy is gaining insights into oneself, one's life in the family and the community, into social and political control, the use of print and other mass media to inform, persuade and influence so as to maintain the status quo. • Literacy is about understanding the power relationships that lie behind reading and writing. • Literacy is about constructing and reconstructing meaning, critically examining the range of meanings in the story and outside the story. • Literacy is active writing for various purposes and audiences, often to influence and assert. • Literacy is about developing consciousness, increased self-reflection, increased reflection about status, power, wealth and privilege in society. • Literacy is about developing critical thinking habits, creative imagination, and posing alternatives, some of which may be radical. • Literacy is about learning and interpreting the world, explaining, analyzing, arguing about and acting upon the world in which a person lives.

Biliteracy

This section examines biliteracy and strategies that promote biliteracy and trans-literacy (C. Baker, 2003) in the home and classroom. The notion of biliteracy adopted in this chapter is that of 'any or all instances in which communication occurs in two (or more) languages in or around writing, where these instances may be events, actors, interactions, practices, activities, classrooms, programs, situations, societies, sites, or worlds' (Hornberger, 2013: 1). Literacy in two or more languages is advantageous at the individual and societal levels. For individuals, biliteracy reinforces and develops both oral languages in terms of, for example, vocabulary, automatic decoding, fluency and positive attitudes. In her psychological review of the acquisition of literacy in bilingual children, Bialystok (2007) concludes that

> children who have learned skills in one language can potentially benefit from that mastery by applying them to the other ... the differences between monolinguals and bilinguals that occur are invariably to the benefit of the bilinguals. Knowing more has never been a disadvantage when compared to knowing less. (p. 71)

There are also reasons why biliteracy is societally important. In **language revitalization,** for example (see Chapters 3 and 4), a minority language has higher status and a greater chance of survival when bureaucracy and books, newspapers and magazines, adverts and signposts are in that language. Literacy in the minority language enables the attendant traditions and the culture to be accessed, reproduced and renewed. Reading in the minority language may be both for education and recreation, for instruction and for enjoyment. Whether minority language literature is regarded as aiding moral or religious teaching, of value as an art form, or as a form of vicarious experience, literacy is both an emancipator and an educator. Literacy in the minority language is of value because it recreates the past in the present. It may both reinforce and extend the oral transmission of a minority culture. Literacy facilitates the development of oral language proficiency. Minority language oracy without literacy can disempower the student. Literacy in the minority language not only provides a greater chance of survival at an individual and group level for that language. It also may encourage rootedness, self-esteem, the vision and worldview of one's heritage culture, self-identity and intellectual empathy.

Literacy enables access to language minority practices that help make sense of the world and hence affect the structure of human cognition. Biliteracy gives access to different and varied social and cultural worlds and is a strong source of cognitive and curriculum advantage for bilinguals (see Chapter 7). In the US, research has found that children's reading proficiency in their native language is a strong predictor of their English reading performance (Slavin & Cheung, 2005) as is their oral proficiency in English (August & Shanahan, 2006; Bialystok, 2007). That is, children who have gained more rather than less reading proficiency in their home language are more likely to learn to read in English with success. Thus biliteracy is strongly preferable to 'weak' approaches to bilingual education that stress literacy in the majority language (e.g. English in the US). In their extensive synthesis of the academic research literature on literacy development for second language learners in the US, August and Shanahan (2006) conclude:

> Research indicates that instructional programs work when they provide opportunities for students to develop proficiency in their first language. Studies that compare bilingual instruction with English-only instruction demonstrate that language-minority students instructed in their native language as well as in English perform better, on average, on measures of English reading proficiency than language-minority students instructed only in English. This is the case at both the elementary and secondary levels. (p. 5)

Mother tongue literacy, while often culturally advantageous, is sometimes not without practical problems nor protests. Some languages lack a writing system, have few educational materials for teaching purposes, and/or a shortage of bilingual teachers and teacher training. Political objections include native language literacy being an impediment to national unity and immigrant assimilation, and the cost of maintaining a variety of indigenous and 'immigrant' languages in a region. The supply of well-trained teachers who can support mother tongue literacy is problematic in many regions. These issues, however, are not insurmountable. For example, Cambodia, with support from UNICEF and Care International has developed bilingual education programs in six indigenous languages that previously had no writing system. Orthographies were developed based on the national Khmer script – a political move that was specifically designed to facilitate rapid transition to literacy in the national language (Gregerson, 2009). Books and other curricular materials were then developed in those languages, which then made it possible to recruit local speakers and provide intensive bilingual teacher training (Wright & Boun, 2015, 2016). As a result, thousands of ethnic minority indigenous students previously excluded from public education now have access to schooling and are developing their biliteracy skills through effective bilingual education programs (S. Lee *et al.*, 2015).

The Development of Biliteracy

Given that literacy empowers, emancipates, enculturates, educates and can be an inherently enjoyable activity, there seems to be a strong argument for biliteracy. Pragmatically, most students from a minority language need to function in the minority and majority language society. This requires biliteracy rather than literacy only in the minority language.

Beeman and Urow (2012) explain that 'biliteracy instruction includes the broad range of teaching and learning activities involving reading and writing that occurs in Spanish [or other home languages] and English across the curriculum' (p. 1). It allows students to 'use all of the languages in their linguistic repertoire to develop literacy' (p. 5), and embraces a holistic, multilingual perspective on teaching, learning and assessment that is embraced by translanguaging (see Chapter 13) and transliteracy. Beeman and Urow (2012) use the metaphor of a bridge to emphasize the benefits of teaching for biliteracy:

> The Bridge occurs once students have learned new concepts in one language. It is the instructional moment when teachers bring the two languages together to encourage students to explore the similarities and differences in the phonology (sound system), morphology (word formation), syntax and grammar, and pragmatics (language use) between the two languages, that is, to undertake contrastive analysis and transfer what they have learned from one language to the other. The Bridge is also the instructional moment when teachers help students connect the content-area knowledge and skills they have learned in one language to the other language. The Bridge is a simple but powerful concept: with strategic planning, the Bridge allows students who are learning in two languages to strengthen their knowledge of both languages. The Bridge is a tool for developing metalinguistic awareness, the understanding of how language works and how it changes and adapts in different circumstances. An important aspect of the Bridge is that it is two-way. ... It recognizes that because bilinguals transfer what they have learned in one language to the other, they do not have to learn content in both languages. (p. 4)

While the bridge is a helpful metaphor, translanguaging suggests there is integration and merging rather than a separation of languages beneath the surface.

Key reviews of the research in biliteracy provide strong evidence of positive linguistic transfer (Bialystok, 2007, 2013; V. Edwards, 2015; Krashen, 2002, 2004b). Bialystok (2013) has shown that children who learn to read in two languages early on have an initial advantage over their monolingual peers. A commonly used test in her studies is the 'moving word' task. She shows 4 to 5 year old monolingual and bilingual children two pictures: a picture of a dog and a separate picture of a tree. She then shows children a card with the word 'tree' written on it. She first places that word 'tree' under the picture of the tree. This is seen to be correct. Then, when the children are distracted, she moves the word 'tree' to underneath the picture of the dog. The children are asked what the card said with the word on it. She consistently finds that most of the bilingual children know the word still refers to the tree, while most monolingual children say that the word 'tree' referred to the picture of the dog.

Bialystok (2001b) suggests that children who are familiar with print and story books in two languages (e.g. French and English, or English and Chinese), more quickly develop an understanding that words are symbols that correspond to specific meanings. When bilingual children are shown a picture accompanied by a word, they understand early on that the word contains the meaning as well as the picture.

> Across all the studies, the bilingual children outperformed the monolingual children by a large margin, often revealing more than a year advantage in understanding this principle. On average, the monolinguals were correct about 40% of the time and the bilinguals, about 80% … Just being exposed to two writing systems, or two kinds of storybooks, enabled bilingual children to appreciate that the written forms are the symbolic system from which the story emerges. (Bialystok, 2001b: 22)

Research has also suggested that many academic and linguistic skills in a minority language transfer relatively easily to the second language. Simply stated, a child who learns to read in Spanish at home or in school does not have to start from the beginning when learning to read in English (August, 2012; August & Shanahan, 2008; Beeman & Urow, 2012). An example is that, once a student has learnt that there is a correspondence between letters and sounds in the first language, they use this understanding immediately when learning to read in the second language. While some of the sounds and letters may be different in the second language, they do not have to be re-taught that such a relationship exists. Such metalinguistic awareness of the relationship between sound and meaning is important in learning to read, and bilinguals gain advantages in understanding such insights.

Thus, when biliteracy is encouraged in minority language children, many literacy skills and strategies from the first language appear to transfer to the second language. The degree to which there is transfer may depend somewhat on how similar are the writing systems (Bialystok, 2013). For example, one may expect more transfer between languages such as English, French, German and Spanish which share a common alphabet and less between languages such as English, Chinese, Khmer, Russian and Arabic which have different writing systems. Nonetheless, despite differences in orthography, vocabulary and grammar, generalizable skills in decoding and reading strategies may transfer from first language literacy to second language literacy (Bialystok, 2013; Koda & Zehler, 2008). Concepts and strategies easily transfer from first to second language literacy such as scanning, skimming, contextual guessing of words, skipping unknown words, tolerating ambiguity, reading for meaning, making inferences, monitoring, recognizing the structure of text, using previous learning, using background knowledge about the text. For example, Pu (2008) followed the reading development of a group of Chinese American students in both their regular mainstream English classrooms in the public schools and in their Chinese **heritage language** classes on the weekend. She found that despite the significant differences in the Chinese and English writing systems, there was positive transfer from their Chinese literacy skills to their English literacy skills, and vice-versa.

Having self-confidence as a reader of one language tends to lead to being confident in reading in two languages. Bilinguals will use both of their languages to make sense of meaning when reading in a second language, for example by translating, and looking for **cognates**. They will compensate for gaps when reading in a second language by drawing on the corresponding skills and knowledge from their first language. While the decoding of words has a separation in learning to read in each language, the higher cognitive abilities and strategies required in making meaning from text are common to both languages. Overall, reading competence in two languages does not operate separately (Bialystok, 2013).

Transfer from first language to second language literacy is not unconditional and is likely to be contingent on the context of learning and the characteristics of the learner. The following factors may play an intervening role: (a) differences in the facilitating nature of the school, home and community environment; (b) individual differences in **language ability**, language aptitude and language learning strategies; (c) individual differences in the analysis of their language (i.e. metalinguistic abilities); and (d) the inter-relationship between pairs of languages (e.g. Portuguese and Spanish compared with English and Chinese). Reading ability in a second language is also strongly related to the degree of proficiency in that second language (August & Shanahan, 2008). Children literate in their first language still need to acquire the differences found in the second language (e.g. different sounds, vocabulary, grammatical structures), and these may need explicit instruction.

In contrast, Kenner (2004a) proposes that some bilingual children acquire literacy in two languages (biliteracy) simultaneously and not as the separate entities that a 'transfer' idea may suggest. Kenner and Gregory (2012) provide evidence that young children are able to differentiate two or more script systems, are able to begin to distinguish the principles on which these are based. Kenner (2004a) found in her study that 6-year-olds in London learning to write in Chinese, Arabic or Spanish as well as English sought connections between different writing systems. In drawing on experiences from different social and linguistic worlds, these children combined, integrated creatively and synthesized imaginatively. Such children may learn to understand the diverse perspectives of people from different cultures and languages, including beyond their own, in a synchronized manner.

This 'transfer' rather than 'separation' viewpoint has implications for the teaching of reading among language minority students. A 'separation' view is that reading in the second language (e.g. English for language minority students in the US) depends on the level of proficiency in the second language and not on first language reading ability. According to this view, students should be swiftly moved to education through the second language; maximal exposure to literacy is needed in the second (majority) language. The belief is that time spent reading in the minority language is time lost in learning to read in the majority language. In contrast, a 'transfer' view argues for an initial mastery of literacy in the minority language so that the cognitive skills and strategies needed for reading can be fully developed. Once well developed, these literacy skills and strategies transfer easily and readily to the second language. It is this latter view that receives research support (August & Shanahan, 2006). Alternatively, literacy may be developed simultaneously in both languages (see below).

Classroom Contexts

An important intermediate factor is the classroom context in which such language and literacy acquisition occurs. Strategies and advice for developing biliteracy are not universal, but context bound. In Canadian immersion programs, for example, the context is additive. That is, the child's home language of English is not being replaced but is being added to by the acquisition of French. Literacy in French is acquired at no cost to literacy in English. In contrast, in a subtractive environment (e.g. English-only programs in the US for ELLs) the transfer of literacy skills between the two languages may be impeded. In such subtractive situations, literacy tends to be developed through the second language (e.g. English in the US).

However, research shows that literacy may more efficiently be acquired through the home, heritage, minority language (Goldenberg, 2008). When literacy is attempted through the second, majority language in the US, the child's oracy skills in English may be insufficiently developed for such literacy acquisition to occur effectively (Genesee *et al.*, 2006). 'If feasible, children should be taught reading in their primary language. Primary language reading instruction a) develops first language skills, and b) promotes reading in English, and c) can be carried out as children are also learning to read, and learning other academic content, in English' (Goldenberg, 2008: 42).

For teachers, this leaves the question of when to encourage biliteracy, given that there is some degree of literacy in one language. One model will be the simultaneous acquisition of biliteracy as well as **bilingualism**. This tends to be the approach in the 50:50 dual language model (see Chapter 11) where both minority and majority language children remain integrated all day. A second approach is when children learn to read in their second language before they learn to read in their first (majority) language. An example is immersion education in Canada, where children learn to read in French before learning to read in English. This approach tends to result in successful biliteracy, but note that it takes place in an additive language context. The first language, a majority language, is not threatened, and literacy in both languages will follow. The third approach is where children acquire literacy in their first language, a minority language, and then later develop literacy skills in the majority language. In the 90:10 dual language model (see Chapter 11) and **heritage language education** all children typically receive literacy instruction in the minority language first.

Krashen (2002) neatly sums up the argument for language minority children developing literacy in their first language early in order to facilitate strong literacy development in English:

> There is very good reason to believe that learning to read in the primary language is a shortcut to reading in the second language. The argument in favor of this consists of three stages:
>
> 1. We learn to read by reading, by understanding what is on the page.
> 2. It is easier to understand text in a language you already know.
> 3. Once you can read, you can read; reading ability transfers across languages. (p. 143)

Simple answers about when to promote literacy in the second language are made difficult by other factors such as the educational and societal context, but also the age and ability of the child. Contrast the six-year-old just beginning to acquire pre-reading and pre-writing skills in the first language with an 18-year-old student, fluent in a first language. In the first case, biliteracy may be delayed. In the latter case, oracy and literacy in the second language may be mutually reinforcing. Contexts will vary. When a language minority child is constantly bombarded with majority language written material, from adverts to comics, computers to supermarkets, basic biliteracy may occur relatively easily. The accent in school can be on minority language literacy, but not exclusively. The preference with younger children may be to ensure first language literacy is relatively well established before introducing literacy in a second language.

Literacy Squared

Escamilla *et al.* (2013) have developed a comprehensive model that emphasizes the development of biliteracy from the start of **emergent bilingual** children's education in kindergarten. In other words, rather than in some traditional bilingual approaches where students are first taught to read in their home language, and then transitioned into English literacy, 'paired literacy' provides simultaneous development of literacy in both languages. Also, rather than aiming for eventual transition to all English instruction, Literacy Squared calls for home language literacy and literacy-based English language development instruction through the 5th grade. Other key features include the explicit teaching of cross-language connections, and assessments that account for biliteracy development. For example, the Literacy Squared writing rubric provides a single tool to evaluate students' writing development in both languages. The rubric includes quantitative measures of the content, structural elements and spelling in each language, and also enables qualitative analysis of students' bilingual strategies at the discourse, sentence/phrase, word, and phonics levels. This enables teachers to evaluate student writing for such features as literal translations, **codeswitching**, use of loan words, and approximate spellings using phonics rules from one language in the other.

Escamilla *et al.* (2013) have also developed templates to help teachers create holistic biliteracy lesson plans and units, as well as a comprehensive Literacy Squared Observation Protocol. These include space for planning and observing literacy instruction in both languages on the same lesson plan template and protocol, including sections for planning and evaluating cross-language connections. On the observation protocol, these cross-language connections include:

(1) Connections between literacy environments (e.g. theme, genre, standards)
(2) Visual side-by-side analysis of languages (e.g. cognates, anchor posters)
(3) Metalanguage
(4) Strategic translations
(5) Teachers use languages strategically to enhance student learning
(6) Teacher flexibly responds to student's language alternations. (pp. 187–188)

Escamilla and her colleagues (2013) argue that this model, (a) 'shifts the debate in the field from a narrow focus on the language of instruction to include the qualities of instruction,' (b) that their instructional framework 'provides guidance to teachers, in the form of pedagogical methods, about how to maximize the bidirectional transfer of students' knowledge and skills', and (c) that their assessment procedures 'foster the development of biliteracy' and enable 'teachers and schools to monitor student progress via the interpretation of trajectories towards biliteracy' (p. 4).

The Continua of Biliteracy

The literacy that is developed in classrooms varies considerably, and escapes neat classification into transmission, construction of meaning, sociocultural and critical literacy orientations. Such classification is best achieved by reference to Hornberger (2008) who provides a comprehensive set of dimensions to understand, elaborate and situate the nature of biliteracy in the contexts of research, classroom practice and language policy in multilingual settings. Hornberger's Continua of Biliteracy (Figure 14.1) has four nested and intersecting components (each of which has three sub-dimensions). From this framework, Hornberger (2013) argues that for multilingual learners:

> the development of biliteracy occurs along intersecting first language–second language, receptive–productive, and oral–written language skills continua; through the medium of two (or more) languages and literacies whose linguistic structures vary from similar to dissimilar, whose scripts range from convergent to divergent, and to which the developing biliterate individual's exposure varies from simultaneous to successive; in contexts that encompass micro to macro levels and are characterized by varying mixes along the monolingual–bilingual and oral–literate continua; and with content that ranges from majority to minority perspectives and experiences, literary to vernacular styles and genres, and decontextualized to contextualized language texts. (p. 1)

This framework suggests the need to 'contest traditional top-down power weightings in education toward compartmentalized, monolingual, written, decontextualized language and literacy practices, by intentionally opening up implementational and ideological spaces for fluid, multilingual, oral, contextualized practices and voices at the local level' (Hornberger, 2013: 1).

Contexts of Biliteracy

Micro	⟷	Macro
Oral	⟷	Literate
Bilingual	⟷	Monolingual

Development of Biliteracy

Reception	⟷	Production
Oral	⟷	Written
First language	⟷	Second language

Content of Biliteracy

Minority	⟷	Majority
Vernacular	⟷	Literacy
Contextualized	⟷	Decontexualized

Media of Biliteracy

Simultaneous exposure	⟷	Successive exposure
Dissimilar structures	⟷	Similar structures
Divergent scripts	⟷	Convergent scripts

Figure 14.1 Continua of Biliteracy (Hornberger, 2008)

Hornberger (2013) further explains:

The continua model posits that what (content) biliterate learners and users read and write is as important as how (development), where and when (context), or by what means (media) they do so. Whereas schooling traditionally privileges majority, literary, and decontextualized contents, the continua model argues for greater curricular attention to minority, vernacular, and contextualized whole-language texts. Minority texts include those by minority authors, written from minority perspectives; vernacular ways of reading and writing include notes, poems, plays, and stories written at home or in other everyday non-school contexts; contextualized whole-language texts are those read and written in the context of biliteracy events, interactions, practices, and activities of biliterate learners' everyday lives.

Multiliteracies in the Classroom

In the mid-1960s, a group of 10 scholars met together and formed the New London Group (1996). They proposed a pedagogy of multiliteracies to broaden literacy to include visual, audio, gestural and spatial modes of literacy, plus the importance of cultural and linguistic diversity evidenced in migration and globalization. Recently, information literacy, emotional literacy, scientific literacy, financial literacy, and technology and digital literacy have all been added to a much expanded view of literacy.

From this 1990s movement derive the contemporary concepts of multilingual literacies and multiliteracies. Two original members of the New London Group, Kalantzis and Cope (2013), explain that multiliteracies refers to two major aspects of communication and representation:

> The first is the variability of conventions of meaning in different cultural, social or domain-specific situations. … The sociolinguistic conditions of our everyday lives increasingly require that we develop a capacity to move between one social setting and another where the conventions of communication may be very different. Such differences are the consequence of any number of factors, including, for instance, culture, gender, life experience, subject matter, discipline domain, area of employment, or specialist expertise.
>
> The second aspect … is multimodality … a significant issue today in part as a result of the characteristics of the new information and communications media. The asynchronous meanings across distance that were once the main preserve of the written word are now made in conditions where written linguistic modes of meaning interface with recordings and transmissions of oral, visual, audio, gestural, tactile, and spatial patterns of meaning. (p. 1)

Multiliteracies also refers to different languages, different varieties of a particular language, and different regional uses of a language. Since literacy is formed in varied social, cultural and religious contexts, there are diverse reading and writing practices. For example, a person may speak Sylheti (a regional language of Bangladesh), read and write in Bengali (the standard language of Bangladesh) as well as English, be fluent in English but also use a local variety of East London English. Such a person may exhibit multiple literacies that have varied and different: specific uses, levels of expertise, degrees of prestige, which contain different symbols of social and linguistic **identity**, have different opportunities for use (e.g. according to the speaker's gender), which change over time with experience and opportunity, and are often not used separately but in combinations with innovative blending (syncretism). Such multilingual children do not remain in separate language and literacy worlds but acquire their **multilingualism** and multiliteracies simultaneously (Kenner & Gregory, 2012).

This is not just an academic point, but it has implications for literacy in the classroom. Kalantzis and Cope (2013) argue, 'it is no longer sufficient for literacy teaching to focus, as it did in the past, primarily on the formal rules and literary canon of a single, standard form of the national language' (p. 1). They also note the need to supplement traditional reading and writing with multimodal representations, particularly those typical of digital media. Teachers have choices about what to develop and how. For example, should a classroom concentrate on literacy in 'standard English' or include local regional varieties of English? Is just majority language literacy developed or are multilingual literacies developed as well? Are students only taught traditional school-based genres like the five-paragraph essay? Or do teachers also recognize the multiliteracies students engage in via multimodal e-mails, text messages, social media postings, and in digital storytelling? What value does the teacher give to literacy practices outside the school, including in the early stages of reading and writing? Are such home and community multiliteracies incorporated in the school and classroom, for example by help from parents, grandparents and siblings (V. Edwards, 2009)? Research suggests that teachers may not be aware of home and community literacies, resulting in much potential loss of a valuable resource for classroom learning (Pu, 2008).

Multiliteracies also open up possibilities for what some scholars call translingual literacy or practices. Canagarajah (2013) explains: 'the term translingual enables a consideration of **communicative competence** not restricted to predefined meanings of individual languages, but the ability to merge different language resources in situated interactions for new meaning constructions' (p. 2). This goes beyond simple codeswitching in writing; bilingual and multilingual writers are often able to 'mesh their resources for creating new forms and meanings' (p. 2). The term 'codemeshing' is also used to described such translingual literacy practices (Milson-Whyte, 2013).

School Resources

Where multilingual classes exist, then learning, motivation and self-esteem may be raised by celebrating multiliteracies. For example, Kenner (2004b) recommends displays in a classroom that celebrate the different scripts of children (e.g. photos of the children with text about their languages and literacies; text on community and religious schools attended to learn to read other languages). In whole class or school events, children reading in their heritage language may give them both recognition and pride, and also be educative for other children.

Culturally relevant books for children are valuable to engage and excite. Such books will be more understandable (and supportively predictable) as they connect with the children's personal histories, cultural backgrounds and communities. Motivation to read, and to read independently and enjoyably, will be enhanced when the student meets text that has a friendly cultural meaning. This can be achieved by (a) characterizations that are similar to the student's family and language community, (b) themes and contexts that are comprehensible within their life experiences, and (c) language and discourse that are familiar to the student (Y.S. Freeman et al., 2003).

As computers, smartphones and other mobile internet devices increasingly become a part of children's lives, representing their varied language worlds and multiliteracies on screen builds status and use for multilingualism. Devices once limited to English or other languages using the Latin alphabet are now capable of displaying and receiving input in a wide variety of orthographies. Such electronic literacies build international (e.g. with a 'heritage' country) as well as local networks of multilinguals. Such literacies then become more multimodal: scripts, pictures, moving images and sounds. Children (and parents) telling stories about their homes and family lives which value their home and community culture, can be stored and relayed to other children beyond the classroom via the internet.

As far as possible, the language resources of the classroom need to be multilingual partly to reflect the mother tongues of the children in the classroom, but also for the multilingual awareness of all children. Sometimes it is difficult to find the quantity, quality and variety of reading materials in the mother tongues of children in bilingual classrooms. There are often problems importing books from other countries and problems in purchasing expensive books. Yet some schools do manage to collect excellent libraries of books in different languages (and multicultural books) via the internet and help from language communities, parents of children in the school and using minority language organizations who have contacts and a commitment to literacy development in children's mother tongues. Partnership with parents in literacy events is important, especially in multilingual classrooms.

Resources include not just materials and literacy strategies but also people. Apart from parents, teacher support staff may be able to help literacy development in another language. Similarly, peer teaching and peer support can be utilized to introduce different scripts, listen to someone reading in a language the teacher does not understand, comparing the script that is used predominantly in the classroom (e.g. directionality, accents), and sometimes providing a model to emulate.

Literacy strategies typically include combinations of whole classwork, individual tasks, partner activity, small group discussion, use of technology, and individual self-directed learning (Wright, 2015). In contexts where bilingual students come from language minorities, cooperative learning can effectively increase intergroup friendships

---

Box 14.3 Dual language books

Dual language books contain a story, folk tale, myth or information in two languages. Such languages may have a similar script (as in French and English, or Spanish and English) or different scripts (for example Chinese and English, Urdu and English, Bengali and English). Often the two languages are on the same page or on opposite sides of the page, sharing the same pictures (V. Edwards, 2009).

Some dual language books are professionally produced and published. However, teachers may work with students (and their parents) to produce their own bilingual books (Cummins et al., 2005). For example, students from the Thornwood Public Schools near Toronto, Canada have produced bilingual books in 28 languages with help from their families.

Such books help children, both bilinguals and monolinguals become aware that other languages have value and functions. Blackledge (2000) suggests 'The best dual-text books are often written from the perspective of the home culture and translated into English, rather than vice-versa, making them more culturally relevant than books written from an Anglo-centric perspective and translated into the community language' (p. 86).

For children whose first language is not the majority language of the country, dual language books may serve as a bridge to literacy in English. Such children will read the story in Greek or Korean, Russian or Spanish first of all. Subsequently, they may read the other language (e.g. English version) and, having already understood the storyline, be able to make sense of English words.

Dual language books act as an important bridge between parents and children, and between the home and the school. Parents and other members of the extended family may be able to read to their children in their home language (Wright, 2015). Such books can enable small groups or pairs of students to work collaboratively on the book. If one child can read in Arabic and the other in English, they can work together, discuss the story and complete activities set by the teacher around that story.

Dual language books are not without controversy. Firstly, some teachers and parents argue that children only read one language in the book, and ignore the other. Having understood the story in one language, it may be tiresome and pointless reading the story in another language. Children may thus concentrate on just one half of the book. Secondly, teachers and children sometimes observe that the presence of the majority language such as English tends to remove the desire to read in the home, minority language. The different status of the two languages may mean that the child will only wish to read in the higher status language. The positioning and quality of the minority text can also send subtle messages. For example, a clear bold English text in a large font on top followed by a Vietnamese translation written in a plain, smaller, and harder-to-read font underneath makes clear which is the privileged language.

and increase the achievement of such students, raising their motivation, self-esteem and empathy for others (see Chapter 12). Multiliteracy strategies and activities utilize the child's experience in both private and interactive social activity: for example discussing experiences of the home as well as the 'home country', of trips and television, religion and family rituals, anecdotes and achievements, imaginations and shared incidents. Teachers, older siblings, grandparents, aunts and uncles and parents can help provide multilingual classroom displays (and video recordings of multiliteracies, for example in community or religious language classes) celebrating a diversity of script (e.g. Arabic, Chinese, Cyrillic, Greek, Urdu, Hebrew as well as English).

Such a multilingual approach also means avoiding assessment solely by narrow standardized tests that only reflect a skills approach to **dominant language** literacy. Classroom-based assessment needs to go much further than tests of inauthentic, de-contextualized language skills (see Chapter 2). Student portfolios, for example, are one important way that a teacher may gather information about the performance of their bilingual children in a classroom; they may give a much fuller understanding of the strengths and weaknesses of, and therefore the diagnostic attention needed to improve and develop, a child's literacies (see Chapters 2 and 15).

Community Relationships

The social and cultural context of literacy importantly includes the relationship between an ethnic community and literacy acquisition (O. García, Zakharia & Otcu, 2013). What constitutes 'reading' differs between cultures, sub-cultures and ethnic groups. The purposes of reading, the resources provided by the home, and the process of parents helping their children to read may differ from the purposes, resources and processes for literacy in the school (Ma & Li, 2016). The school may teach reading for recreation and enjoyment; a language minority group wants literacy for utilitarian purposes (e.g. avoiding unemployment and poverty, for trading and business trans-actions). The school literacy policy may aim for a child-centered, individualized approach, with the teacher as facilitator, partner and guide, allowing a wide choice of colorful attractive books. An ethnic group may, in contrast, provide literacy classes in Saturday schools, at the mosque or temple, sometimes with large numbers being tutored in the same class.

In such out-of-school classes, the teacher may act as an authority and director. Learning the will of Allah, for example, may be the valued outcome. A treasured Bible, the Qur'an or other holy or highly valued book may be the focus of reading. At its best, the biliterate child comes to appreciate and understand different cultures, differing traditions and viewpoints, leading to greater cultural sensitivity and inter-group tolerance.

Gregory (2008) further compares the style of literacy teaching in the community and the school. In the schools she researched, the child was socialized gently into the 'literary club' via 'playing' with books in a relaxed atmosphere with little correction of mistakes. In ethnic Saturday schools children tended to learn by rote, repeating letters, syllables and phrases until perfect. There is continuous practice, **testing** and correction of mistakes in a fairly strict and disciplined regime. Children may be given books only after they have proved their reading skills are worthy of such esteemed treasures.

The difference between school and ethnic group literacy expectations and practices may be challenging for the child. The child is exposed to two literacy worlds, two versions of appropriate literacy behavior. The school, in particular, has a responsibility to defuse tension, create a fusion and a harmony between the differences, such that both approaches are respected, prized and celebrated. If this is achieved, the bilingual student becomes not just biliterate but more deeply **bicultural**, with an expanded vision of literacy practices, even more tolerant of difference and variety. Too often, schools take little or no account of the community literacies that children bring to school. This will be discussed in the next section.

Alternatively, some schools disparage such ethnic group literacies and infer that parents and their children are illiterate if they do not function in English, and exclude parents as literacy partners. When children come from economically poor, minority language culture homes, there is a tendency to assume they derive from less effective language and literacy environments than those from middle-class majority language backgrounds (Blackledge, 2000). Literacy is not a separate cultural event, but mirrors in its form and function general socialization practices. For particular cultural and ethnic groups, this may make the transition from home to school a relatively more challenging and strange experience.

Home and School Relationships

Many multilingual children often move seamlessly between different literacies. For example, Arabic may be used for reading the Qur'an, Urdu for family talk, and English for classroom activities. Such biliteracy practices facilitate creating deep links with the extended family and local networks, the child's heritage and cultural identity, and broadening the curriculum of the school. Parents and siblings are typically important in a student's multiliteracy development. They often provide a literacy 'ecosystem' where there is mutual support (e.g. the children help with the parents' English writing), adaptability, and linguistic survival and spread. Different languages may mean differing roles. For example, older siblings may help with school homework, father may help with a religious literacy, with mother listening to her younger children reading story books in one or more languages.

The literacy practices of the school are often different from that of the home. Parents may be educated by the school about 'good reading habits' in their children, mirroring school literacy practices and school culture. This assumes a deficit in family literacy practices that may be unwarranted. Parents are seen as failing to provide school-style literacy experiences and therefore contributing to underachievement in their children. In reality, no home is without literacy, yet multilingual literacy knowledge tends to be invisible in English-dominant neighborhoods. Teachers visiting such homes may find no classroom-type storybooks, but miss the newspapers, religious texts, shopping lists, calendars, flashcards, videos and internet use that provide a different but rich literacy background. Children themselves engage in much hidden self-initiated literacy activity. When children commence elementary school, their literacy worlds may be ignored, with an accent on one literacy only (e.g. school English).

Arias (2015) traces 50 years of US history of parental involvement from culturally and linguistically diverse families. She observes that traditional models of parental in-volvement focused on activities such as (a) assisting parents with childrearing skills and creating home environments conducive to learning, (b) communicating with families about schools programs and student progress, (c) recruiting parent volunteers for classrooms and school activities, (d) getting parents to assist with homework and other curricular activities, and (e) getting parents to participate in parent councils and organizations to assist with school decision-making. However, she argues this represents an 'Anglo-centric model,' serving as 'a vehicle for getting parental support for school activities and for getting parents to be teachers of children in the home with little recognition of the meaning that these activities held for immigrant parents' (p. 295). She also argues these traditional models cast parents and their culture in a deficit mode, questioning their support for their children's education.

As an alternative, Arias (2015) argues for non-traditional models of parental engagement that include the following features:

(1) Develops reciprocal understanding of schools and families.
(2) Situates cultural strengths of family and community within the school curriculum.
(3) Provides parental education that includes family literacy and understanding school community.
(4) Promotes parental advocacy that informs and teaches parents how to advocate for their children.
(5) Instills parental empowerment through parent-initiated efforts at the school and community level.
(6) Implements culturally and linguistically appropriate practices in all aspects of communication. (p. 289)

Arias describes a successful non-traditional parental involvement model originally developed in San Diego, California called Parents Involved in Quality Education (PIQE). The PIQE model seeks to create a full partnership between parents and schools and develop networks of communication and coordination between parents, administrators and teachers to benefit children, and to respond to issues of change and empowerment. PIQE had reached over 400,000 parents, demonstrating that 'most immigrant and minority parents not only want to be involved, but they will make significant sacrifices for their children' (p. 290). Evaluation studies credit PIQE with substantially increasing levels of parent engagement, and with high graduation rates and college attendance among participating Latino students (Vidano & Sahafi, 2004). Another successful non-traditional parental involvement program described by Arias (2015) is the *Padres Comprometidos* [Committed Parents] program developed by the National Council of La Raza. In this community-based organization partnership program with schools, local chapters of La Raza work to develop the parental involvement skills of Latino parents to effectively engage with the schools and help their children prepare for college. Arias notes, 'An important aspect of this program is that it addresses language and culture as assets – rather than obstacles – upon which skills, confidence, and empowerment are built' (p. 295).

An important explication of processes in teacher–parent relationships is given by Moll (2001) and his colleagues (N. González *et al.*, 2005). They used ethnographic studies to identify skills, knowledge, expertise and interests that Mexican households possess that can be used for the benefit of all in the classroom. Moll shows how Latino parents and other community members have much to offer children in classrooms through their **funds of knowledge**. Funds of knowledge broadly means any knowledge that derives from outside of school, not just in the home, and concerns how such knowledge is constructed, revised, maintained and shared (Moje, 2017). Funds of knowledge provides another avenue for non-traditional parental involvement. For example, schools may tap into the knowledge of parents who have experience and expertise with things such as flowers, plants and trees, seeds, agriculture, water distribution and management, animal care and veterinary medicine, ranch economy, car and bike mechanics, carpentry, masonry, electrical wiring and appliances, fencing, folk remedies, herbal cures and natural medicines, midwifery, archaeology, biology and mathematics. The literacy skills and practices in the home and community are also an important knowledge source that may be drawn upon. The concept of 'funds of knowledge' also serves 'to debunk the prevalent idea of working-class households as devoid of intellect or of worthwhile resources' (Moll, 2001). The 'funds of knowledge' framework is equally applicable to other linguistic minorities communities around the world (see, e.g. Martin-Jones & Saxena, 2003).

Barriers to active parental engagement for linguistic minority parents include language barriers, low levels of education, lack of familiarity with the school system, cultural differences in views of appropriate parent-school relationships, feelings of intimidation by the high status of the school, fear of showing disrespect, the lack of transportation and childcare, lack of time due to work schedules and often the need to work multiple low-wage jobs, and negative experiences with the school including condescending attitudes from administrators, teachers, and/or staff members (Arias, 2015; Zhou & Logan, 2003). However, many of these barriers are most easily overcome in schools with strong bilingual education programs. Simply having teachers and other school personnel who are bilingual, who are familiar with the home cultures, who recognize and know how to tap into the funds of knowledge available in the homes, and who understand the challenges faced by families, can go a long way in breaking down communication barriers and opening opportunities for mutual dialogue to find solutions (e.g. holding parent meetings at convenient times, providing interpreters and child care for parent meetings and teacher conferences, sending home notes, books, and instructional materials in the home languages, etc.).

It is also important to remember that many bilingual programs are the direct result of parent grassroots efforts. In some cases parents have turned to the courts to ensure their local schools adequately fund and deliver high quality programs that meet their children's language and academic needs. The landmark *Lau v. Nichols* case was brought by Chinese parents in the San Francisco area leading to the 1974 ruling by the US Supreme Court that schools must address the unique language and academic needs of ELLs. In New York a group of Puerto Rican parents filed suit against the New York City Board of Education, leading to the 1974 ASPIRA Consent Decree that subsequently guided policy for providing bilingual education for over 30 years. A group of Latino parents in Los Angeles under the name of Comité Padres de Familia brought a suit against the state of California in 1987 for failing to monitor district bilingual, ESL and other ELL programs for compliance with state and federal laws to ensure students were receiving appropriate language and academic programs. In the decades since, 'Comite' monitoring 'became a major force in propelling stronger programs for ELLs' (Olsen, 2015: 6). These are just a few of many examples of the power of highly engaged linguistic minority parents in effecting positive school changes.

Conclusion

This chapter has revealed that different approaches to literacy have different expectations about bilingual children that pervade national and school literacy policies, curriculum provision and classroom practices. One recent contrast is literacy only in a majority language (e.g. English) compared with an accent on local, regional literacies perhaps leading to 'multiple literacies' with different uses of literacy in different contexts.

Schools are a powerful provider of literacy and help dictate what counts as proper language, correct ideas and appropriate knowledge to be transmitted though literacy practices. Superior forms of literacy, and the kinds of literacy required for success in education are school transmitted; other literacies are often devalued (except religious literacies). Therefore, the self-esteem and identity of language minority children may be affected by which literacies are legitimated by the school, and which are ignored or despised.

One expectation of education is that children acquire literacy skills so they can function as 'good citizens' in a stable society. A contrasting expectation is that children should become empowered, even politically activated, by becoming literate. Language minority children should be able to read, for example, to understand propaganda, and write to defend their community's interests or protest about injustice, discrimination and racism. They need to read the world and not just the word (Freire & Macedo, 1987).

The importance of different literacy and multiliteracy approaches lies in their varying proposals for the role, status and self-enhancement of bilingual children and adults. Does literacy produce cogs who aid the smooth running of a well-oiled wheel? Does literacy produce bilingual students who are activated into asserting their rights to equality of power, purse and opportunity? A fundamental issue of literacy, biliteracy and multiliteracy is thus political. When clarity is achieved in defining the intended uses of literacy for bilingual students, educational considerations such as approaches, methods and strategies become more rational.

This chapter has suggested the importance of literacy and biliteracy in the empowerment of bilingual students and their communities. Classroom practicalities are not divorced from educational and political policies; education provision cannot be separated from issues of power that affect the lives of bilinguals.

Key Points in This Chapter

➢ Literacy has many uses in bilingual, multicultural societies: for learning, citizenship, pleasure and employment for example.

➢ Cultures, sub-cultures and localities differ in their uses of literacy (e.g. religious groups, transmission of heritage values and beliefs).

➢ Approaches to literacy include: the skills approach (functional literacy), construction of meaning, sociocultural literacy and critical literacy.

➢ A transmission style to classroom literacy is contrasted to a critical approach where issues of power, status, equity and justice are addressed through a language minority perspective.

➢ Strategies in the classroom to promote biliteracy require cross-curriculum, collaborative and personalized approaches.

➢ When biliteracy is encouraged in minority language children, specific skills and strategies from the first language transfer to the second language.

➢ Some bilingual children simultaneously learn to read and write in both languages. Other children will learn to read in their first language before they learn to read in their second (majority) language. In immersion education this order is reversed. Both these approaches will tend to result in successful biliteracy. Contexts become important in the decision.

➢ Multiliteracies broadens literacy to include visual, audio, gestural, spatial, and digital modes of literacy, plus the importance of cultural and linguistic diversity including different languages, different varieties of a particular language, and different regional uses of languages

➢ Translingual literacy practices refer to the abilities of bilinguals and multi-linguals to draw upon and mesh together their linguistic resources in creative ways to create new forms and meanings in their writing.

➢ Parents as partners in biliteracy development is important, including when local and family 'funds of knowledge' are utilized.

Suggested Further Reading

📖 Beeman, K. & Urow, C. (2012). *Teaching for biliteracy: Strengthening bridges between languages.* Philadelphia, PA: Caslon Publishing.

📖 Canagarajah, A. S. (Ed.) (2013). *Literacy as translingual practice: Between communities and class-rooms.* New York, NY: Routledge.

📖 Escamilla, K., Hopewell, S., & Butvilofsky, S. (2013). *Biliteracy from the start: Literacy squared in action.* Philadelphia, PA: Caslon Publishing.

📖 Palfreyman, D. M., & van der Walt, C. (Eds.). (2017). *Academic biliteracies: Multilingual repertoires in higher education.* Bristol, UK: Multilingual Matters.

📖 Rodríguez, D., Carrasquillo, A., & Lee, K. S. (2014). *The bilingual advantage: Promoting academic development, biliteracy, and native language in the classroom.* New York, NY: Teachers College Press.

On the Web

💻 Biliteracy: Teaching Bilingual Children to Read and Write in More Than One Alphabet (Blog post on Multilingual Living)
http://www.multilingualliving.com/2011/07/25/biliteracy-teaching-bilingual-children-read-write-alphabet/

💻 Funds of Knowledge and Home Visits Toolkit (Washington Office of the Superintendent of Public Instruction)
http://www.k12.wa.us/MigrantBilingual/HomeVisitsToolkit/default.aspx

💻 Seal of Biliteracy (official website)
http://sealofbiliteracy.org/

💻 ChalkBeat: We asked a Denver student what graduating with a seal of biliteracy means to her. Here's what she said. (Web Article and Video)
http://tinyurl.com/z6m77at

💻 Literacy Squared®: Valuing Bilingualism (YouTube video of Presentation by authors Kathy Escamilla, Lucinda Soltero-González, and Susan Hopewell)
https://youtu.be/c_511EXuv_s

Discussion Questions

(1) In biliteracy development, what are the various views on when and in what order literacy in each language should be introduced? Which approach do you feel would be most successful?
(2) Discuss the meanings of the terms critical literacy, multiliteracies, translingual literacy, and code-meshing. Give examples of what these may look like in the classroom, and describe how these differ from traditional views of functional literacy in transmission classrooms.
(3) Examine some commercial and/or student-made dual language books. How can the reading and creation of such books support biliteracy development? What are some of the pros and cons of such books? Analyze the positioning and quality of the texts in the two languages and what messages these may send to readers.

Study Activities

(1) Visit a classroom where there is some attention to biliteracy. Discuss with the teacher the aims of such biliteracy. Report on the reading materials and instruction in the classroom and discuss how effective these practices appear to be in facilitating students' biliteracy development.
(2) Work with bilingual and multilingual students and their families from a particular classroom to create bilingual and multilingual books in their home languages and the dominant societal language.
(3) Choose two or three states in the US that have adopted the Seal of Biliteracy. Compare the criteria for earning the Seal, the processes for evaluating students' biliteracy skills, and how and in what forms the Seals are awarded. Analyze these policies and procedures in terms of the extent to which the biliteracy skills of both language minority and language majority students may be recognized and awarded.

Support and Assessment of Special Needs and Exceptional Bilingual Students

CHAPTER 15

Support and Assessment of Special Needs and Exceptional Bilingual Students

Introduction

This chapter considers those bilingual and multilingual children needing special educational support, as well as those who qualify for gifted and talented education programs. We will consider the value of bilingual **special education** or inclusive education, and bilingual **gifted and talented education** programs. We will take a close look at the role of **assessment** in the identification and placement – and the misidentification and misplacement – of bilingual students in such programs. Finally, we will discuss the challenges of assessing and accommodating such bilingual students on tests of English language proficiency and academic achievement.

Special or additional needs have many different acceptable and less acceptable terms: disability, handicap, impairment, difficulties and disorders for example. Such terms refer to problems that are individual and suggest a deficit rather than problems lying outside the individual, for example in an unjust society or deprived community. These terms center on the person rather than on sociocultural factors; on the person rather than their context; on disabilities rather than potential capabilities. Some prefer the term (dis)ability to emphasize that those classified as 'disabled' actual have much ability. Preferred terms vary across time. What is acceptable in one decade typically becomes unacceptable in the next decade as undesirable or negative associations develop.

Also such terms vary across countries. For example, in the US, the current term is 'exceptional children', used to refer to both students with disabilities and gifted and talented students. Some US schools use the term 'twice exceptional' to refer to gifted students with disabilities. In Wales the preferred terms have been children with 'Additional Learning Needs' and children with 'Additional Educational Needs'. In contrast, Scotland uses the term 'children and young people with additional support needs', while England has preferred 'children with special educational needs and disability'.

Special needs that are perceived to affect language vary in definition from country to country but are likely to include the following areas: communication, learning (e.g. dyslexia and developmental aphasia), illiteracy, a low level of cognitive development, behavioral and emotional problems. There is a distinction between special needs that can be assessed by objective criteria (e.g. visual impairment and deafness) and those where a more subjective, value judgment is required (e.g. emotional and behavioral difficulties). The risk of an assessment **bias** against those who are refugees, immigrants, live in material poverty and speak a minority language at home tends to be greater in the latter category. For example, the placement of immigrants into special education may increase where there is a subjective judgment about their perceived language deficit.

Certainly, some bilingual and multilingual children do have special needs, and this includes children from 'elite' bilingual families (e.g. English-German) as well as from language minorities. However, none of these is caused by bilingualism. **Bilingualism** does not cause speech or language impairment, autism, dyslexia, developmental aphasia, severe subnormality in cognitive development, serious emotional disturbance or behavioral problems (e.g. see Peer & Reid, 2016 on dyslexia in bilinguals). Being a member of a **language minority** may co-exist with such conditions, but is not a cause, as will be illustrated later. Bilinguals with such special needs will equally experience these problems if they are raised as a **monolingual**. However, a bilingual special needs child may have increased needs for support (e.g. if working in school in their second language).

Gifted and Talented Bilingual Children

Exceptional students include those with gifted abilities (e.g. high IQ, very creative, outstanding musical or mathematical talent, artistic, and students who excel in leadership or in specific performance areas such as sports). Such gifted multilinguals and bilinguals are rarely discussed in the literature, and often much under-represented in acceleration programs for the gifted (Beam-Conroy & McHatton, 2015). It is valuable to recognize that many bilinguals are high-achievers, and research on immersion students (see Chapter 11) suggests that bilingualism has been linked with enhanced achievement. Similarly, Chapters 7 and 8 have portrayed the cognitive giftedness that many bilinguals share (e.g. metalinguistic abilities, creative thinking). Such examples suggest a distinction between those who share language gifts due to their **multilingualism** or bilingualism, and those whose academic, artistic, scientific or musical gifts are less related to their bilingualism, although not necessarily irrelevant to their success.

Research by Valdés (2003) portrays a particular language giftedness of many bilingual students who act as interpreters, especially in immigrant families (see Chapter 5). A review by Beam-Conroy and McHatton (2015) examines the identification, assessment and classroom education of gifted bilinguals in the US. Kharkhurin (2015) proposes a bilingual creative education program that fully taps into the creative talents of bilingual students. Such recent attention to gifted multilinguals and bilinguals helps to reconstruct the negative 'remedial' and 'deficit' labels that have surrounded bilinguals in past decades.

Asperger's syndrome and other disorders at the higher end of the autism spectrum typically involve a combination of giftedness and challenges. Albert Einstein, composers Mozart and Bela Bartok and pianist Glenn Gould, all had Asperger's syndrome. Temple Grandin is a well-known animal expert who has autism. These individuals and many others exemplify the fact that people on the spectrum are often highly intelligent and artistically gifted. However, such people often lack an understanding of expected appropriate social behavior and of how to interpret emotions. Bilingualism can be blamed by teachers and other professionals for the early signs of Asperger's syndrome or autism, and a move to monolingualism has been frequently regarded as a solution. This is unlikely to be helpful and will have minimal or no effect on Asperger's syndrome or autism.

There is very little research on autism or Asperger's syndrome and bilingualism. Marinova-Todd and Mirenda (2016) provide a comprehensive review of the limited research on autism and bilingualism. Their reviews suggests that bilingual families should continue to use both languages at home with their children, and also that language specialists provide interventions in both languages.

A book-length study by Rubinyi (2006) of her son who has Asperger's syndrome also provides initial insights. Her son, Ben, became bilingual in English and French using the one parent-one language approach (OPOL). Rubinyi sees definite advantages for a child who has such challenges, with bilingualism increasing flexibility in thinking and understanding different perspectives. That there are two different ways to describe the same object or concept when using two languages enlarges the perception of the possible. Using two languages encourages the child to view alternative ways of approaching multiple areas of life (food, sports, transport). Rubinyi suggests that, because of bilingualism, Ben's brain had a chance to partly rewire itself even before Asperger's syndrome became obvious. Also, the intense focus of Asperger's syndrome meant that Ben absorbed vocabulary at a very fast rate with almost perfect native speaker intonation. Thus, bilingual students, special education students, and gifted and talented students are not mutually-exclusive categories. Indeed a student may be in all three categories.

Some states and school districts in the US recognize this and follow procedures to ensure that bilingual ELL students are considered for gifted and talented (GT) programs. For example, the Northside School District in San Antonio and other districts throughout Texas use Spanish-language tests as part of the identification process for potential Spanish-speaking ELL students in GT programs. Texas is just one of seven states that require students be assessed for GT programs in either their home language or tested non-verbally (Beam-Conroy & McHatton, 2015). Even rarer are GT programs targeting bilingual students. For example, the Milwaukee Public Schools has a dedicated bilingual gifted and talented program at one of its elementary schools – the only one of its kind in Wisconsin. However, such designations do not necessarily need to be official. For example, one 4th grade bilingual Spanish teacher at in inner-city elementary school in Southern California simply self-declared her students to be gifted and talented, and provided a rich curriculum for her students that paralleled if not exceeded the curriculum provided for English-proficient students in the school's official GT classrooms.

The Frequency of Special Needs in Bilingual Children

In the US, around 13% of students are in programs serving students with disabilities (National Center for Education Statistics, 2016). Of these, 21% were identified as having a speech or language impairment. There is evidence that bilingual children in the US are both over-represented and under-represented in special education (Sullivan, 2011; Sullivan & Bal, 2013). For example, Mercer's (1973) pioneering study found that Mexican-Americans were 10 times more likely to be in special education than White Americans. However, as shown in Figure 15.1, in 2014 only 12% of Hispanic students were in special education compared to 13% of White students. Black (15%) and American Indian/Alaska native students (17%) had the highest percentages in special education, suggesting over-representation.

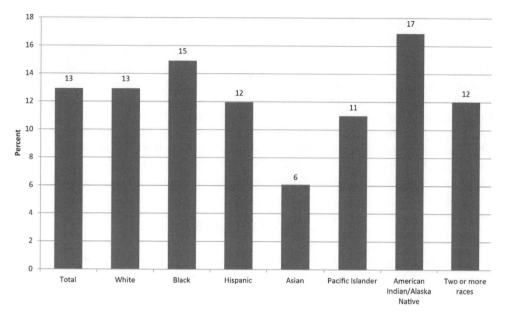

Figure 15.1 Percentage of US students receiving special education services, 2014

Source: National Center for Educational Statistics: Children and Youth with Disabilities (2016). https://nces.ed.gov/programs/coe/indicator_cgg.asp

Nonetheless, there have been great variations across and within US states. Sullivan (2011) notes extremes in the past with states reporting from 0 to 17.3% of ELLs receiving special education services. Her own detailed study of one state revealed that over an eight-year period, ELLs were increasingly likely to be identified as students with disabilities.

Over-representation, however, is not the only scenario. Under-representation also occurs over fears of misdiagnosis, and particularly in states and districts where language minority students are a relatively small percentage of the population (Artiles, 2003). In the UK, Cline and Frederickson (1999) reported that the identification of dyslexics who are also bilingual is often overlooked. If bilinguals are ignored or unobserved by teachers, for example, then they may not be allocated the usual assessment or treatment process.

This raises questions as to why language minority children may need special education. Does bilingualism in some students lead to language and communication disorders? One incorrect assumption is that bilingualism leads to language delay. Research does not attribute such challenges to bilingualism (Li Wei, Miller & Dodd, 1997), as will be discussed below. The communicative differences of bilingual children must be distinguished from communicative disorders. The failure to make this important distinction partly occurs because basic mistakes in assessment and categorization are sometimes made. For example, a bilingual child is often assessed in their weaker, second language. Hence, both language development and general cognitive development are measured inaccurately. In the US and the UK, immigrant children are often assessed through the medium of English and on their English proficiency. Their level of language and cognitive competence in Spanish, Vietnamese, Hmong, Korean, Cantonese, Turkish, Tagalog, Bengali or Panjabi, for example, is ignored.

As a result, such children can be classed as having a 'language disability' and perhaps, by an unfair implication, as having a 'learning disability'. Instead of being seen as developing or emergent bilinguals, they may be falsely viewed as having general difficulties with learning. Their below-average test scores in the second language (e.g. English) are wrongly defined as a 'deficit' or 'disability' that can be remedied by some form of special education. One current US issue is how to distinguish between English language learners (ELLs) who are struggling to learn to read and write in English because of their limited abilities in English, and ELLs who have additional learning needs or 'learning disabilities' (Klingner et al., 2008).

Language Delay

A particular pathology in children – language delay – is often erroneously attributed to bilingualism. Language delay occurs when a child is very late in beginning to talk, or lags well behind peers in language development. Estimates of young children experiencing language delay vary across research studies from 1 in 20 to 1 in 5 of the child population. Such varying estimates partly reflect that some delays are brief and hardly noticeable, while others are more longer-lasting.

Language delay has a variety of causes (e.g. autism, severe subnormality, cerebral palsy, physical problems such as cleft palate, psychological disturbance, and emotional difficulties). However, in approximately two-thirds of all cases, the precise reason for language delay is not known (Li Wei et al., 1997). Children who are medically fit, with no hearing loss, of normal IQ and memory, who are not socially deprived or emotionally disturbed, can be delayed in starting to speak, slow in development or have problems in expressing themselves well. In such cases, specialist, professional help is best sought. Speech therapists, clinical psychologists, educational psychologists, counselors or doctors may be able to give an expert diagnosis and suggest possible treatment of the problem. It is vital that such professionals have an understanding of the nature of bilingualism in the clients they advise and treat.

For the teacher, psychologist, speech therapist, counselor and parent, a decision needs to be made in respect of severely language delayed bilingual children. Will the removal of one language improve, worsen or have no effect on such a child's language development? Given that the cause of the problem may be partially unknown, intuition and guesswork rather than 'science' often occurs. Research in this area is still developing.

Let us assume the professional advice is to move from bilingualism to monolingualism. One issue immediately becomes which language to concentrate on if there is major diagnosed language delay. The danger is that parents, teachers and other professionals will want to emphasize the perceived importance of the majority language. In the US, the advice is often that the child should have a solid diet of English (at home and particularly at school). The perceived language of school and success, employment and opportunity is the majority language. The advice often given is that the home, minority language should be replaced by the majority language. Even when professionals accept that bilingualism is not the cause of a child's problem, moving from bilingualism to monolingualism is seen by some as a way to help improve the problem. The reasoning is usually that the 'extra demands' of bilingualism, if removed, will lighten the burden for the child. For example, if the child has an emotional problem or a language delay condition, for whatever cause, simplifying the language demands on the child may be seen as one way of solving or reducing the problem. The apparent complexity of a two-language life is relieved by monolingualism. Is this the rational and suitable solution?

There are many occasions when changing from bilingualism to monolingualism will have no effect on language delay. For example, if the child seems slow to speak without an obvious cause, or seems low in self-esteem, dropping one language is unlikely to have any effect. On the contrary, the sudden change in schooling or family life may exacerbate the problem. The child may be further confused, even upset, if there is a dramatic change in the language of the school or family. If someone who has loved, cared for, or educated the child in one language (e.g. a minority language) suddenly only uses another language (e.g. the majority language), the emotional well-being of the child may well be negatively affected. Simultaneously, and by association, the child may feel that the love and care has changed. Such an overnight switch may well have painful outcomes for the language-delayed child. The mother tongue is denied, the language of the family is implicitly derided, and the communicative medium of the community is disparaged. The solution in itself may exacerbate the problem.

An alternative is that the home language is retained if pragmatically possible. Even if the child is slow in developing in that language, with progress delayed, it is the vehicle best known to the child. Being forced to switch to the majority language will not make the journey faster or less problematic. Thus, in most cases, it is inappropriate to move from bilingualism to monolingualism. However, it is dangerous to make this suggestion absolute and unequivocal. When there is language delay, there may be a few situations where maximal experience in one language is preferable. For example, where one language of a child is much securer and more well developed than another, it may be sensible to concentrate on developing the stronger language.

This does not mean that the chance of bilingualism is lost forever. If, or when, language delay disappears, the other language can be reintroduced. If a child with language delay really dislikes using (or even being spoken to) in a particular language, then as part of a solution the family may sensibly decide to accede to the child's preference. Again, once behavioral and language problems have been resolved, the 'dropped' language can be reintroduced, so long as it is immediately and consistently associated with pleasurable experiences.

Any temporary move from bilingualism to monolingualism need not be seen as the only solution needed. A focus on such a language change as the sole remedy to the child's problem is naive and dangerous. For example, emotional problems causing language delay may require other rearrangements in the school or family's pattern of behavior. Language delay may require visits to a speech therapist for advice about language interaction between the child and significant adults. Temporary monolingualism is one component in a package of attempted changes to solve the child's language problem. However, it is important to reiterate that, in the majority of cases, language delay will not be affected by retaining a bilingual approach.

As Ardila and Ramos (2007) conclude generally with regard to bilingual children with language impairments:

> As expected, the children showed difficulties in both languages, but their difficulties were comparable to those shown by monolingual speakers of each language who also have specific language impairment. Apparently, in this population, learning a second

language did not present an extra burden, and while these children may never become completely proficient in both languages (just as monolingual speakers with specific language impairment may never become completely proficient in their one language), they are likely to enjoy many of the benefits of being bilingual in their community. (p. 207)

Similarly, Martin (2009), using a sociocultural approach to language disabilities, argues that 'bilingualism does not cause speech and language difficulties. Although there are early publications that link multilingualism with speech pathology, more recent research shows that dual language development is a positive experience for bilingual children with language learning difficulties' (pp. 69–70). Bilingual speech therapy may be more effective than traditional monolingual therapy in the majority language (Marinova-Todd & Mirenda, 2016).

Bilingual Special Education

Special education bilingual children can be served by a variety of institutional arrangements. These include: Special education schools (resident and non-resident), special education units attached to mainstream schools, specially resourced classes in mainstream schools, withdrawal and pull-out programs (e.g. for extra speech and language help, behavioral management) and special help given by teachers, para-professionals or support staff in 'regular' classes. A common preference is to integrate such children into mainstream or 'inclusive' education. In the US this is called **full inclusion**. The guiding principle is to place students in the **least restrictive environment**, that is students with disabilities should be given the opportunity to learn alongside non-disabled students in a regular classroom as much as possible. The extent to which such provision will be bilingual or monolingual will vary within and across countries, regions and institutions. Such bilingual or monolingual provision will depend on the availability of provision (material, human and financial), the type and degree of special education need or condition, the degree of proficiency in both languages, learning capacity, age, social and emotional maturity, degree of success in any previous education placements, and the wishes of the parents and child.

When bilingual or language minority children have been assessed as having special needs, some educators argue that education is needed solely in the dominant, majority language. In the US, the advice given is sometimes that Latino and other language minority children with special needs should be educated in monolingual English language special schools. The argument is that such children are going to live in an English speaking society.

Many special needs bilingual children will benefit from bilingual provision rather than monolingual education, where this is practicable. One example is the recently arrived (immigrant) special needs child. Placing such a child in a class where he or she doesn't speak the language of the classroom (e.g. English in the US) may only increase failure and lower self-esteem. To be educated, the child preferably needs initial instruction mostly in the first language, with the chance of becoming as bilingual as possible.

Many children with special needs are capable of developing in two languages, including children with Down's Syndrome (see Kay-Raining Bird, 2007; Kay-Raining Bird *et al.*, 2005) autism (Marinova-Todd & Mirenda, 2016), and Asperger's syndrome (Rubinyi, 2006). Such children may not reach levels of proficiency in either language compared with their peers in mainstream classrooms. Nevertheless, they can reach functional levels of proficiency in two languages according to their abilities. As the above authors testify, becoming bilingual does not detract from achievement in the curriculum (e.g. mathematics and the creative arts).

Early Canadian research showed that less able bilingual children share some of the cognitive and curriculum advantages of bilingualism (Bruck, 1978, 1982). J. Paradis *et al.* (2003) found that eight French–English bilingual children with specific language impairment (SLI) were successful in learning two languages at least in terms of grammatical **morphology**. 'Instead of demonstrating that bilingualism impedes language acquisition under conditions of impairment, the children in this study showed that they had the ability to learn two languages despite their impairment' (p. 125).

Just as their mathematical ability, literacy and scientific development may occur at a slower pace, so the two languages will develop with less speed. The size of vocabulary and accuracy of syntax may be less in both languages than for the average bilingual child. Nevertheless, when such children acquire two languages early, they typically communicate in both languages as well as a comparable monolingual communicates in one language.

This suggests that bilingualism and multilingualism are possible despite children with language and cognitive challenges often being recommended by well-meaning professionals to become monolingual. When such children live in a bilingual or multilingual environment, such a recommendation can isolate children from social and cultural activities in the community. If their parents naturally use two or more languages, then natural patterns of communication in the home may not occur. As Kay-Raining Bird *et al.* (2005) conclude: 'rather than restricting input to one language, it seems important for speech-language pathologists to provide appropriate supports in both languages to bilingual children so as to ensure that they acquire each language to the best of their ability' (p. 197).

The school or class placement of a bilingual student often occurs after a professional assessment suggesting that the child's needs cannot be met by inclusion in a regular classroom. If children are placed in special education classes, it is important that they gain the advantages of those in other forms of bilingual education: dual language competence, increased achievement and thinking benefits, and other educational, cultural, self-identity and self-esteem benefits. These benefits have been discussed previously in this book.

However, full inclusion has increasingly been regarded as preferable to the stigmatization of segregation (Frederickson & Cline, 2015). Segregation can restrict access to educational opportunities. In the UK, children who failed an English language screening test were sometimes cut off from a mainstream school environment, with a restricted subject curriculum, and subsequent stereotyping as failures and outcasts. Inclusion tries to combat any intolerance of language and cultural difference and the perpetuating of inequalities by severance from mainstream education. Thus UNESCO (1994) adopted the 'principle of inclusive education, enrolling all children in regular schools unless there are compelling reasons for doing otherwise' (p. 44). Such inclusion means special needs bilinguals attending a mainstream classroom and fully participating in the curriculum. Special needs teachers, paraprofessionals and teacher assistants will typically work with such children in that school and surrounded by an inclusive education philosophy. Apart from locational integration of bilingual special needs students, inclusion attempts social (peer) integration and curriculum integration. Social inclusion and matching the mainstream curriculum to the special needs of the child require well-trained teachers, high quality material support, parental involvement and constant monitoring (Frederickson & Cline, 2015).

The concept of inclusion is an important comparison to the historical view of bilingual special needs children. The belief has been that such students have a 'problem' that needs to be 'cured' by 'treatment' (Martin, 2009). The inclusion movement holds that all children can learn successfully within integrated education that is adapted to their particular needs. Inclusive education may increase positive expectations of special needs students by their teachers, peers and themselves. In contrast, the current account-ability ideology and high-stakes testing systems tend to exclude or negatively label culturally and linguistically diverse students in a mainstream system. Menken (2008) argues that it is often automatically assumed with high-stakes testing that Latinos and Spanish speakers will under-achieve, and that their language and cultural difference is the major explanation.

One example not discussed so far is when children fail in a mainstream school due to their language proficiency not being sufficient to operate in the curriculum. For example, in the US, most Spanish-speaking children are in mainstream schools (a 'submersion' experience) and, although of normal ability, fail in the system (e.g. drop-out of school, repeat grades, leave high school without a diploma) because their English proficiency is insufficiently developed to comprehend the increasingly complex curriculum.

This situation creates an apparent dilemma. By being placed in some form of special education class, the child is possibly stigmatized as having a 'deficiency' and a 'language deficit'. Such classes may not foster bilingualism. Often, they will emphasize children becoming competent in the majority language (e.g. English in the US). Such segregation may allow more attention to the second language but result in ghettoization of language minorities. While giving some sanctuary from sinking in second language submersion in a mainstream school, special education classes can be a retreat, marginalizing the child. Will such children in special education realize their potential across the curriculum? Will they have increased access to employment? Will the perception of failure be increased because they are associated with a remedial institution? Will there be decreased opportunities for success in school achievement, employment and self-enhancement?

The ideal for children in this dilemma may be education that allows them to start and continue learning in their first language. The second language (e.g. English) is nurtured as well, so as to ensure the development of bilinguals who can operate in mainstream society. In such schools, both languages are developed and used in the curriculum. Such schools avoid the 'remedial' or 'compensatory' or deficit associations of special education. Such schools celebrate the cultural and linguistic diversity of their students.

Yet such mainstream bilingual education is sometimes in danger of being seen as a form of special education. Even when the 'second language delayed' are separated from those who are in the early stages of learning the majority language (e.g. English in the US), the danger is that the latter will still be assessed as in need of compensatory, remedial special education.

It is also the case that bilingual students with special needs are most often placed in monolingual special education classes owing to no bilingual special education provision being viable. Where particular language minority special needs students are geographically isolated or unique, then pragmatism predominates.

Alternative Causes of Special Needs and Learning Difficulties in Children

Six examples of causes of special needs and learning difficulties outside the child and his or her bilingualism follow. This list, though not exhaustive nor comprehensive, will indicate that bilingualism has nothing directly to do with many learning problems, either as a secondary or a primary cause.

(1) Poverty and deprivation, child neglect and abuse, feelings of pessimism, helplessness and desperation in the home, extended family and community may create personality, attitudinal and learning conditions that make the assessment of learning difficulties more probable. Sometimes, such assessment will reflect prejudice, misjudgments and misperceptions about the child's home experiences. The learning problem may thus be in a mismatch between the culture, attitudes, expectations about education and values of the home and school. Different beliefs, culture, knowledge and cognitive approaches may be devalued with the child immediately labeled as of inferior intelligence, academically incompetent and of low potential.

(2) The problem may be in the standard of education. A child may be struggling in the classroom because of poor instruction methods, a non-motivating, culturally alien classroom environment, a dearth of suitable teaching materials, or relationship issues with the teacher.

(3) The school may be inhibiting or obstructing learning progress. If a child is being taught in a second language and the home language is ignored, then failure and perceived learning difficulties may result (e.g. Spanish-speaking ELLs placed in mainstream English-only classes and left to 'sink or swim') By being assessed in their weaker second language (e.g. English) rather than in their stronger home language (e.g. Spanish), such children are labeled as in need of special or remedial education. Thus the monolingual school system may itself be responsible for learning failure. A school that promoted bilingualism would more probably ensure learning success for the same child.

(4) Emotional causes of learning difficulties include a lack of self-confidence, low self-esteem, a fear of failure and high anxiety in the classroom.

(5) Failure may be caused partly by interactions among children in the classroom. For example, where a group of children encourage each other to misbehave, have a low motivation to succeed, or where there is bullying, prejudice, hostility, racism, social division, rather than cohesion among children in a classroom, the learning ethos may hinder the child's development.

(6) There may be a mismatch between the gradient of learning expected and the ability level of the child. Some children learn to read more slowly than others, still learning to read well, but over a longer period of time. Less able children can learn two languages within the (unknowable) limits of their ability.

Appropriate Placement of Exceptional Bilingual Children

Bilingual children are often over-represented in special needs education, and this is frequently due to assessment practices. This over-representation can result from both cultural and linguistic bias in the testing and the tester, in referral practices, poorly trained school psychologists and other professionals, or use of untrained interpreters.

When bilingual children are assessed, it is important to keep distinct three different aspects of their development: (a) first language proficiency; (b) second language proficiency; and (c) the existence (or not) of a physical, learning or behavioral difficulty. This three-fold distinction enables a more accurate and fair assessment to be made with regard to special education.

The student's level of functioning in a second language must not be seen as representing the child's level of language development. The child's development in the first language needs to be assessed (e.g. by observations, interviews, tests) so as to paint a picture of proficiency rather than deficiency, of potential rather than deficit. The child's language proficiency is different from potential problems in an individual's capacities that require specialist treatment (e.g. hearing impairment). Neither the language and culture of the home, nor socioeconomic and ethnic differences, should be considered as handicapping conditions in themselves. Social, cultural, family, educational and personal information needs to be collected to make a valid and reliable assessment and to make an accurate placement of the child in mainstream or special education (Burr et al., 2015). This is considered separately in the following section on the assessment of exceptional bilingual children.

A key element of assessment with language minority children is that there needs to be early identification, assessment and intervention (Artiles & Ortiz, 2002). Yet assessment systems often wait until the child fails before there is assessment and intervention. The 'wait to fail before action' approach means that effective early supports are missing, and later support may have decreased effectiveness. This problem is exacerbated when students come from disadvantaged communities and attend poorly resourced schools. Early screening is therefore important where disadvantaged language minority children exist.

The Example of the United States

The frequent misdiagnosis of bilingual students and placement in special education in the US led to court cases that revealed how bilingual students were wrongly assessed as in need of special education. For example, the 1970 California case of *Diana v. The California State Board of Education* was based on nine Mexican-American parents who protested that their children (who were dominant in Spanish) were given an English language IQ test. The IQ test revealed 'normal' non-verbal IQ scores, but very low verbal IQ scores (as low as 30 for one child). As a result of using this linguistically and culturally inappropriate IQ test, the Mexican-American children were placed in classes for the 'mentally retarded'. In a preliminary settlement, it was established that testing should be conducted in a child's native language (and in English), and that non-verbal IQ tests were usually a fairer measurement of IQ than verbal tests. As a result of this case, the collection of broader data on language minority children was required (rather than simple test data) to justify placement of such children in Special Education.

In 1975, Public Law 94–142, the Education for All Handicapped Children Act, guaranteed a 'free appropriate public education' to all children with disabilities. This law was replaced in 1990 with the Individuals With Disabilities Act (IDEA), which added the requirement for eligible students to have their education planned and monitored with an individualized education program (IEP). IDEA was reauthorized in 2004 with an emphasis on IEPs containing measurable annual goals and plans for meeting those goals. The 2004 reauthorization acknowledges problems of misdiagnosis and over-representation of students from non-English language backgrounds in special education, and thus calls for students to be assessed in the 'language and form most likely to yield accurate information on what the child knows and can do academically, developmentally, and functionally, unless it is not feasible to so provide or administer' (Section 614[a](e)[ii]). All testing and assessment procedures should also be non-discriminatory, by using tests that are culturally and linguistically appropriate. Such testing procedures are to be carried out by trained members of a multidisciplinary team (see below). Apart from tests, factors such as teacher recommendations, observations of the child and other relevant information should create a multi-source file (portfolio) of evidence.

Multidisciplinary teams are not always pragmatically possible, but remain a most effective practice. Such a team may be drawn from a school/educational psychologist, a speech pathologist/ therapist, a social worker, a bilingual or ESL specialist, and the student's teacher(s). The involvement, and not exclusion, of parents in such a team process is important, as is collecting evidence other than test scores about the student's family and home, learning history and community/cultural lifestyle.

Such US litigation and law has shown the importance of separating bilinguals with real learning difficulties from those bilinguals whose English proficiency is below 'native' average. The latter group should not be assessed as having learning difficulties and therefore in need of special education. The litigation also showed the potential injustices to bilingual students: misidentification, misplacement, misuse of tests and resulting failure when allocated to special education.

The fear of litigation by school districts can lead to both over-referral and under-referral of bilingual students with a real need of special education. In the early 1980s, the trend in California, for example, was to assume that too many language minority students were in need of special education. When students did not appear to be benefiting from instruction in 'regular' classrooms, special education classes became the answer. Or, if teachers were unsure how to deal with a bilingual with a behavioral or learning problem, a transfer to special education provision became a favored solution.

Towards the end of the 1980s, this was reversed. The tendency moved to under-estimating the special needs of language minority children. Wrongful placement of children in special education (over-referral) made various administrators cautious of special education placement. A fear of legal action by parents, and a realization that assessment devices often had low validity, led administrators to be hesitant to place bilingual children in special education.

The seesaw between over- and under-referral to special education makes accurate assessment a key focus, and schools in the US are thus in need of expert guidance (see Box 15.1). However, accurate assessment and placement in different schools is not enough. The development of effective instruction strategies and an appropriate curriculum for such students is crucial (Hoover et al., 2008). So is the need to train teachers for bilingual students in special education (Burr et al., 2015). Educating the parents of special needs bilingual children is also a high priority.

Many US schools use a Response to Intervention (RTI) model focused on a close monitoring of student progress and providing interventions in three tiers:

- Tier 1 – Universal screening and research-based instruction (all students).

Box 15.1 Identifying and supporting ELLs with disabilities

A report by researchers from WestEd (Burr *et al.*, 2015) prepared for the Institute of Educational Sciences of the US Department of Education provides guidance for US Schools in identifying and supporting ELL students with disabilities, drawing on academic research and their own study of practices in 20 states. The report notes that 'no single method has proven effective in differentiating between English learner students who have difficulty acquiring language skills and those who have learning disabilities' (p. i). However, they recommend asking the following questions to help distinguish when academic challenges are caused by learning disabilities, vs. those that are natural occurrences during the English language development process:

- Is the student receiving instruction of sufficient quality to enable him or her to make the accepted levels of academic progress?
- How does the student's progress in hearing, speaking, reading, and writing English as a second language compare with the expected rate of progress for his or her age and initial level of English proficiency?
- To what extent are behaviors that might otherwise indicate a learning disability considered to be normal for the child's cultural background or to be part of the process of US acculturation?
- How might additional factors – including socioeconomic status, previous education experience, fluency in his or her first language, attitude toward school, attitude toward learning English, and personality attributes – impact the student's academic progress? (p. i)

The report also offers five guiding principles for effective policy and practice:

1. Having a clear policy statement that additional considerations will be used in placing English learner students in special education programs.
2. Providing test accommodations for English learner students.
3. Having exit criteria for English language support programs for English learner students in special education.
4. Assessing English learner students' language and disability needs using a response to intervention approach.
5. Publishing extensive, publicly available manuals to aid educators in identifying and supporting English learner students who have learning disabilities. (p. ii)

- Tier 2 – More intensive, targeted, short-term support and supplemental instruction through small-group instruction (20–30% of students).
- Tier 3 – Intensive individualized instruction and interventions (5 – 10% of students).

The RTI model originated in special education and is used to identify students in need of special education services or placement (Tier 3). In other words, students who do not respond to 'good' instruction (Tier 1) or to more intensive targeted small-group instructional interventions (Tier 2) are referred to special education (Tier 3). However, as RTI has gone mainstream and school-wide, there are concerns about its appropriateness for bilingual students, especially those classified as English language learners (Echevarría & Vogt, 2011). First, as noted above, many of the screening and monitoring assessments used in Tier 1 and Tier 2 are inappropriate for bilingual students. Second, RTI makes the assumption that Tier 1 and Tier 2 represents high-quality effective instruction. However, this is often is not the case due to lack of materials, trained teachers, and supportive policy environments for effective ELL and bilingual program models. And third, bilingual students are blamed for not responding to (ineffective) Tier 1 and Tier 2 interventions, thus reinforcing a deficit view of students and inappropriate placement into special education (Tier 3). If more students were placed in strong bilingual education programs (Tier 1), far fewer would likely be deemed in need of Tier 2 and Tier 3 interventions.

In addition, a major problem with the RTI model is the whole notion of 'interventions'. As Wright (2015) has argued:

> ELLs don't need intervention. They need instruction. No temporary 'intervention' is going to quickly make them proficient in English. Rather, ELLs need consistent, high-quality language and content-area instruction appropriate to their educational background and level of English proficiency over a period of several years across grade levels. (p. 16)

In recognition of the shortcomings of RTI, Beam-Conroy and McHatton (2015) have proposed an RTI Model for Exceptional ELLs. Unlike traditional RTI models, their model is 'predicated on linguistically and culturally responsive practice whether ELLs need special education and/or gifted services' (p. 384).

The Assessment and Testing of Exceptional Bilingual Children

The allocation of bilinguals to special education or to gifted and talented education programs usually depends on some form of assessment. It is essential for any psychological and educational assessment of bilingual children to be fair, accurate and broad. Assessment is varied including tests, observation, interviews, portfolios of work and professional judgment (Gottlieb, 2016). Thus tests are just one form of assessment. Tests are frequently predetermined and highly structured, obtain a very small sample of behavior under standardized conditions, have rules of scoring, and result in a numerical outcome.

Tests given to bilingual children often serve to suggest their 'disabilities', supposed 'deficits' or lack of proficiency in a second language. Such students may come to be stigmatized by such tests, for example, because tests locate apparent weaknesses in the majority language and use monolingual scores (norms) as points of comparison. Such practices tend to lead to over-identification of bilingual students for special education and under-identification of bilingual students for gifted and talented education.

Despite advice in legislation, discussions in academic literature and findings from research, bilinguals tend in many countries to be discriminated against in testing and assessment (Shohamy & Menken, 2015). Chapter 2 provides a detailed discussion on the general challenges of the assessment of bilingual students. Below we review several important overlapping and interacting issues that must be considered in the assessment of exceptional bilingual children.

(1) *Language(s) of assessment.* Children should be assessed in their strongest language. Bilingual assessments may also be appropriate, allowing students to draw more broadly from their linguistic repertoire to demonstrate what they know and can do (Shohamy & Menken, 2015). To be valid, testing instruments in other languages must be developed in parallel and cannot simply be translations (e.g. from English to Spanish). Such translation may produce inappropriate, stilted language; differences in vocabulary and grammar may affect the item difficulty. Also consideration must be given to when bilingual students speak a different variety of the native language than the standard variety used on the test (e.g. Puerto Rican Spanish, Chicano Spanish, Castilian Spanish). The language used must be authentic, capturing the quality of a child's communication abilities across school and home contexts.

(2) *Normal second language development vs. learning disabilities.* The temporary difficulties faced by bilinguals in the natural second language development process must be distinguished from actual learning disabilities.

(3) *Teacher observations.* It is important to use the understanding of a child's teachers who have observed that child in a variety of learning environments over time. What do the child's teachers think is the root problem? What solutions and interventions do teachers suggest?

(4) *Multidisciplinary assessment teams.* A multidisciplinary team of teachers and specialists (e.g. classroom teacher, ESL/bilingual teachers, special education teachers, counselors, psychologists, speech therapists, parents, etc.) meeting regularly to discuss children's developmental and academic strengths and challenges is a valuable first attempt to assess and develop an instructional or interventional plan for the child. Such a team should be the school decision-maker for referral to special education, gifted and talented education, or other services (Hamayan *et al.*, 2013).

(5) *Qualified assessors.* Assessors must be trained and qualified to administer the assessments, and be proficient in the languages used in the assessments. The degree to which the assessors are perceived to be from the same ethnic or language group as the child (or not), may affect the child's performance (and possibly the diagnosis).

(6) *Qualified interpreters.* If a valid version of a test or assessment device is not available in the child's stronger language, interpreters are sometimes necessary and have a valuable function. If trained in the linguistic, professional and rapport-making competences needed, they can make assessment more fair and accurate. Interpreters, however, can also bring a possible bias ('noise') into the assessment (i.e. 'heightening' or 'lowering' the assessment results through the interpretation they provide), or provide unintended (or intended) hints that invalidate test results.

(7) *Multiple measures.* Important diagnostic, identification, or placement decisions should not be based on the results of a single test. Multiple measures including both formal and informal assessment instruments and procedures, given over an extended period of time, will provide a more valid language, academic, and behavior profile of bilingual students.

(8) *Test scores.* On educational and psychometric tests, test scores tend to be like latitude and longitude. They provide points of reference on a map of human characteristics. As a standard measurement usable on all maps, they provide initial, rapid and instantly comparable information. But imagine the most beautiful place you know (e.g. a flower-enfolded, azure-colored lake set amid tall, green-sloped, ice-capped mountains). Does the expression of the latitude and longitude of that scene do justice to characterizing the beauty and distinctiveness of that location? The attempted precision of the sextant needs to be joined by the full exploration and evaluation of the character and qualities of the exceptional student.

(9) *Sociocultural context.* Assessment typically focuses solely on the child. The assumption is that the 'problem' lies within the child. A sociocultural focus is needed to consider causes outside the child. Is the problem in the school? Is the school failing the child by denying abilities in the first language and focusing on failure in the second (school) language? Is the school system denying a child's culture and ethnic character, thereby affecting the child's academic success and self-esteem? Is the curriculum delivered at a level that is beyond the child's comprehension or is culturally foreign to the child? The remedy may be in a change in the school and not to the child.

(10) *Students' best interest.* Assessment should work in the best, long-term interests of the bilingual child. 'Best interests' does not only mean short-term educational remedies, but also long-term educational and employment opportunities. Assessments that separate children from powerful, dominant, mainstream groups in society, may lead to children becoming disempowered. The assessment may lead to categorization in an inferior group of society and to marginalization.

Testing Accommodations for Bilingual Students with Disabilities

In the US the 'No Child Left Behind Act' (NCLB) of 2001 halted the exclusion of English language learners (ELLs) and students with disabilities from large-scale assessments and mandated their inclusion in statewide testing. This policy and practice continues with the Every Student Succeeds Act (ESSA) of 2015, though with some leeway in terms of how and when ELL test scores are reported and used in school-wide achievement calculations (see Chapter 9). As before with NCLB, under ESSA the performance of different subgroups must be tracked separately, including ELLs and students with disabilities. However, ESSA includes a new requirement to separately track and report the progress of ELLs with disabilities. Such data has been seriously lacking. For example, Lazarus *et al.* (2016) reported that in 2014 'Only 4 states reported both participation and performance for ELLs with disabilities for the general [state] assessment' (p. iii).

ESSA requires that ELL students be 'assessed in a valid and reliable manner' and 'provided with appropriate accommodations' on assessments. Accommodations are also required for students with disabilities. This includes bilingual and ELL students with disabilities, and accommodations must be provided on both state-level language and content-area academic achievement tests.

When English language learners are tested in English in the US, support or 'accommodations' are often given. The aim of accommodations is to try to produce fairness (a level playing field) for ELLs and students with disabilities (Abedi, 2017). Accommodations originally derived from testing children with additional learning needs. For example, Braille is used for blind children, computerized assessment for students with physical difficulties, extended time is often given to dyslexic students, and longer or multiple test time breaks are given for various reasons. Examples of accommodations are: simpler English in the instructions without changing the content, use of a bilingual dictionary and glossary, small group or individual administration, extra time to complete, oral administration (reading items aloud), oral response and directions in the student's language. The test may be explained to students in an easier form of language and they may be given longer to complete, so that use of a second language becomes less of an influence and performance is more accurate. Ideally, this produces a more level playing field for ELLs. A translation into the student's home language may not always help as the instruction and hence 'curriculum language' will have been in English.

The use of accommodations is a much debated topic (Abedi, 2017). How can we be sure that accommodations, or which accommodations, have the desired outcome? Research is only just beginning on this area. A comprehensive report commissioned by the US Department of Education designed to provide guidance to states and schools on the use of accommodations acknowledges that research is thin, and that 'None of the accommodations examined has leveled the playing field for ELLs (Francis *et al.*, 2006: 29).

One accommodation that shows some potential for reducing the performance gap between ELLs and non-ELLs is linguistic simplification of test directions and test items (Abedi, 2017). When such linguistic complexity is reduced, then the student is assessed more on content than on a lack of English. Measurement error or 'noise' is then reduced. For example, changes can be made to: unfamiliar words, long and complex questions with many relative clauses, an abstract rather than concrete presentation, use of the passive voice and confusing negatives. Of course, such linguistic simplification is not appropriate when the assessment construct is ability to process and comprehend complex texts, such as on an English language proficiency test or an English language arts reading comprehension exam.

On the ACCESS 2.0 English language proficiency exam – in use in over half the states in the US belonging to the WIDA Consortium – some accommodations are built into the computer-based exam. For examples, students can use a highlighter tool to emphasize parts of a question, can use a line guide to focus their reading line-by-line, and use a magnifying glass to zoom in on text or images. The English Language Proficiency Assessment for the 21st century (ELPA21) includes comprehensive guidelines, procedures, alternative forms (e.g. paper-and-pencil forms, enlarged text and braille), and supplemental materials (e.g. real objects (realia), manipulatives and other hands-on items) for assessing ELLs with hearing and vision loss, speech and language disorders, physical disabilities, and cognitive impairments.

For bilingual and other students with severe cognitive disabilities, an alternative form or procedure may be used in lieu of a state's regular English language arts (ELA) or mathematics exams. ESSA caps the allowance for alternative forms to 1% of all students, which roughly equals about 10% of special education students. This number is arbitrary; it is not grounded in any research suggesting the number or percentage of students who would benefit from the alternative form.

In the US there are two state consortiums that have developed shared alternative forms. The National Center and State Collaborative (NCSC) includes 24 state education agencies at various levels of adoption (as of 2016, see http://www.ncscpartners.org/). The NCSC provides singular summative assessments for ELA and math in a form that member states believe are more appropriate for students with disabilities. The Dynamic Learning Maps (DLM) Alternative Assessment System consortium, with 17 member states (as of 2016), takes a very different approach. Rather than a single summative selected-response assessment form, the DLM Alternative Assessment System integrates assessment with instruction throughout the school year. As described on the consortium's website:

> Think of a dynamic learning map model as a common road map. Although students may share the same destination, they all begin their journeys from different starting points on the map. ... A map shows where a student is starting from, as well as the main route, which is the shortest, most direct way to reach the destination. ... It also shows several alternate routes in case the main route cannot be taken. Finally, the map shows all the places students must travel through to get to their destinations. Learning map models developed by the Dynamic Learning Maps Alternate Assessment System help us see beyond where students are today to show us how they can get to where they need to go.
>
> We call the map models dynamic because they show a learning landscape in which multiple skills are related to many other skills. They also show the relationships among skills and offer multiple learning pathways. ... Nodes in the maps represent specific knowledge, skills, and understandings in English language arts and mathematics, as

well as important foundational skills that provide an understructure for the academic skills. The maps go beyond traditional learning progressions to include multiple and alternate pathways by which students may develop content knowledge. (http://dynamiclearningmaps.org/about/model)

The DLM model in particular seems to have the potential for opening up new ways for accommodating ELLs. However, for both the NCSC and the DLM alternative assessments, it is unclear how the specific and unique needs of ELLs with disabilities are currently being addressed.

There are many remaining questions about the influence of accommodations on the validity of the test result, which students are eligible for accommodations and on what criteria, plus the amount of advantage (even unfair advantage) resulting from different accommodations (Abedi, 2017; Wright, 2015).

Assessment Solutions and Conclusions

An alternative approach to testing exceptional bilingual children is more authentic curriculum-based assessment and portfolio type assessment, and greater cultural and linguistic awareness (Hamayan et al., 2013). Authentic assessment that is developmental and which has width – linguistically and contextually – is particularly important (Hoover et al., 2008). Such assessment is a collection over time of a portfolio of a child's unique growth (e.g. in both their languages). A student's portfolio will reveal advancing accomplishments in the form of authentic activities (possibly with staff observations included). A sense of ownership of the portfolio by the student is important to raise awareness of evolving accomplishments and a personal possession of progress. Frederickson and Cline (2015) argue for the child's perspective to be part of this assessment (e.g. self-perceptions of the school, special needs, friends, home, feelings and the future). Parents' and family collaboration and viewpoints add a further important dimension to assessment and to solutions (S.B. García, 2002). An extension of this is the gathering of information not just about the student but also about teaching, program design, family dynamics, parental involvement, previous schooling, cross-cultural expectations and available human and material resources (Hamayan et al., 2013).

An ecological approach to assessment assumes that an exceptional bilingual student is part of a complex social system, and that their behavior cannot be understood except within its context. Thus assessment has to sample students' communication in a variety of contexts and environments, including outside the classroom. This also means collecting information about the expectations of family, friends and teachers for a child's communication. This is exemplified in the RIOT assessment procedure that Reviews all available information, Interviews teachers, friends and family, Observes a student in multiple contexts and Tests school and home languages (Martin, 2009).

Another recent approach to assessment of exceptional children is dynamic assessment. 'Dynamic' means that assessment is a process rather than an outcome. It explores mediation between a teacher and student by examining their co-construction of learning and mutual understanding of what is occurring. The emphasis is not just on a student's current level of functioning, but also on assessing the best means to facilitate further learning. It goes beyond assessing how much language the child has already learnt to examining what new language is needed. It assesses how **scaffolding** can best take place, thus informing planning by the teacher and her intervention with individual students. It works best with expert teachers who have sufficient professional knowledge both to prevent bias in assessment and to have the insights to inform future lessons.

A radical solution to testing places change in assessment within (and not separate from) a change in expectations about the nature and behavior of exceptional bilingual students. This entails a shift in the politics and policy dimensions of the assessment of bilinguals. Merely changing tests may alleviate the symptoms of a problem, but not change the root cause. The root cause tends to be a bias against language minorities that is endemic in many societies and is substantiated by unfair tests (Shohamy & Menken, 2015). By being biased against bilinguals in a cultural and linguistic form, and by a failure to incorporate an understanding of the cognitive constitution of bilinguals, assessment confirms and perpetuates various discriminatory perceptions about language minority children.

Assessment thus sometimes serves by its nature and purpose, its form, use and outcomes to provide the evidence for discrimination and prejudice against language minorities (e.g. in the US and UK) to be perpetuated. Assessment results can serve to marginalize and demotivate, to reveal underachievement and lower performance in language minority children. Hence, there is both the over- and under-representation of exceptional bilingual children in special education and in gifted and talented education programs.

Assessment must not in itself be blamed. It is a conveyer and not a root cause of language minority discrimination and bias. Until there is authentic and genuine acceptance of language pluralism in a region, a minimizing of racism and prejudice against ethnic minorities, assessments will likely continue to confirm the 'lower status' and perceived 'deficiencies' of exceptional bilingual and multilingual children.

Key Points in This Chapter

➢ Bilingual children are often over-represented in special education, being seen as having a language deficit. Paradoxically, they can also be under-represented when there is a fear of legal action for wrongful placement.

➢ Bilingual children are often under-represented in gifted and talented education programs.

➢ Bilingualism has been associated with language and communication disorders (e.g. language delay). This is not supported by research.

➢ Special education bilingual children are served by a variety of institutional arrangements including special education schools, special education units attached to mainstream schools, specially resourced classes in mainstream schools, withdrawal and pull-out programs and special help given by teachers, paraprofessionals or support staff in 'regular' classes.

➢ Most bilingual special needs children will benefit from bilingual special education rather than monolingual special education.

> ➤ Assessment of exceptional bilingual children is enhanced when there is not just testing but also observation (in and out of the classroom), curriculum based assessment, a cultural and linguistic awareness of bilinguals, the use of appropriately trained assessors who seek to empower such children, and the use of multidisciplinary teams of teachers and specialists, and parents.

Suggested Further Reading

📖 Burr, E., Haas, E., & Ferriere, K. (2015). *Identifying and supporting English learner students with learning disabilities: Key issues in the literature and state practice.* Washington, DC: Institute for Educational Sciences, US Department of Education.

📖 Echevarria, J., & Vogt, M. (2011). *Response to Intervention (RTI) and English learners: Making it happen.* Boston, MA: Pearson.

📖 Frederickson, N., & Cline, T. (2015). *Special educational needs, inclusion, and diversity* (3rd ed.). Buckingham, UK: Open University Press.

📖 Mueller Gathercole, V.C. (Ed.) (2013). *Solutions for the assessment of bilinguals.* Bristol, UK: Multilingual Matters.

📖 Shohamy, E. & May, S. (2017). *Language testing and assessment* (Vol. 7 of the *Encyclopedia of Language and Education*, Stephen May, Editor). Heidelberg, Germany: Springer.

On the Web

💻 Colorín Colorado! – Special Education and English Language Learners
http://www.colorincolorado.org/school-support/special-education-and-english-language-learners

💻 Special Education and English Learners (Illinois Department of Education)
http://www.isbe.net/bilingual/htmls/bilsp.htm

💻 YouTube Video – Celebrating Bilingual Special Education – P.S. 112 Jose Celso Barbosa Elementary School
https://youtu.be/UqOOgAHrAWs

💻 YouTube Video – Bilingual Gifted and Talented Education program at Hollinger Elementary School in Tucson Unified School District
https://youtu.be/AcnnxWclFAU?t=1m13s

💻 Gifted, But Still Learning English, Many Bright Students Get Overlooked (National Public Radio)
http://www.npr.org/sections/ed/2016/04/11/467653193/gifted-but-still-learning-english-overlooked-underserved

Discussion Questions

(1) Why are exceptional bilingual students often over- or under-represented in special education and gifted and talented programs?

(2) Is it possible for a student to be bilingual/multilingual, disabled, and gifted and talented? Give some examples, and discuss how schools could best serve these students.

(3) What are some of the considerations educators must address when using assessment tools and procedures to identify exceptional bilingual students for special education and/or gifted and talented education programs?

Study Activities

(1) Conduct interviews with parents or teachers of a bilingual student who has special needs. Define the exact nature of those special needs. Document the history of that student's education. Ask the parents or teachers what their preferences are for the use of languages in school and if they want their children to be bilingual as a result of schooling. Inquire about the value and use they see in languages for special needs children.
(2) Conduct a case study of an exceptional bilingual student in a special education and/or gifted and talented education program. How was the student identified and placed in the program? How does the program address, ignore, build upon, or suppress the student's home language(s)?
(3) Conduct an analysis of the identification and assessment process used in a local school or district for special education and gifted and talented programs. How are the needs of exceptional bilingual students addressed in this process? Analyze the assessment instruments used to identify students to determine the degree to which they are appropriate to different populations of bilingual students.

Deaf People, Bilingualism and Bilingual Education

Deaf People, Bilingualism and Bilingual Education

Introduction

The chapter concerns bilinguals who form their own **language minority**: deaf people. Often a neglected language minority, it will be demonstrated that many of the attributes of hearing bilinguals are shared by deaf bilinguals. Different views about deaf bilinguals are presented, followed by the debate about which kind of bilingual education is valuable for deaf students. The recent rise in self-confidence of deaf people, increasing understanding in society of their needs and importance, and the value of sign language in deaf children's education has been derived, in small part, from the identification of deaf people with bilinguals and multilinguals throughout the world. Their **bilingualism**, in turn, has added to the diversity of understanding of bilingualism and bilingual education.

Deaf People

Most deaf people are bilingual, but many deaf people do not consider themselves as bilingual (Grosjean, 2010). For example, a deaf person may use sign language and a written language, or a sign language and a spoken language such as English or Spanish, including in school. Some deaf children experience bilingual education, but with many different arrangements across districts and countries.

There are many similarities between the bilingualism of deaf people and issues already considered in this book. For example, deaf people often use their languages for different purposes, in different **contexts**, and with different people. Such similarity also extends to: variability in the definition of a 'deaf bilingual', changes in the **dominant language** across time and place, **simultaneous** and **sequential bilingualism, additive** and **subtractive bilingualism,** language as a problem/right/resource, **assimilation** and integration, and two languages in the brain. In addition, language similarities extend to socio-political areas such as language rights, **identity** and **culture** which are discussed in later chapters of this book.

In writings about deaf people, the word 'deaf' is sometimes spelt with a lower case 'd'; other times with a capital 'D'. As James and Woll (2004) state: 'To be deaf is to have a hearing loss; to be Deaf is to belong to a community with its own language and culture' (p. 125). This is a contentious area (see Monaghan *et al.*, 2003) but the spelling distinction is retained in this chapter. There may be times and places where having the identity of a deaf person and belonging to the Deaf community is valued and enjoyed. However, a deaf person may not always want to identify (see later) as 'Deaf'. On some occasions, that same person may want her identity to be about gender, ethnicity, teenage culture and friendships, but not about her deafness (see Chapter 18). Also, the term 'deaf' has increasingly been used to cover mild, moderate, severe and profound deafness, leaving some ambiguity, for example, when talking about classroom teaching and learning styles.

After centuries of deaf people being required to operate in a majority language (spoken and written), since the late 1970s (e.g. in Scandinavia) there have been major changes. There has been a call for deaf people to become bilingual (also termed 'bimodal bilinguals' – see later) for example through learning to sign, followed by literacy in the language of the non-deaf and/or in a spoken language (e.g. English in the United States). This has recently grown into an interest in deaf children **translanguaging** (Swanwick, 2017). This entails using all their language resources for maximizing learning by flexibly varying their mode of communication to suit the context. Another major change is deaf people being helped by recent social media: text messaging, chat rooms, emailing, blogs and vlogs, wireless text pagers, videophone, Skype, and video relay services. Progress in hearing technologies is changing communication among deaf people including combining different modes of communication.

Who are Deaf Bilinguals?

About two to three in every 1,000 children are born with varying degrees of deafness. Around 95% of deaf children are born to hearing parents, and approximately 90% of children born to deaf parents have no deafness. However, such estimates vary across different research studies and in different countries. There are many different sub groups of deaf people, and such sub groups are varied within themselves by, for example, language group affiliation (e.g. Native American, Basque), age (e.g. newborn, elderly), age when became deaf, cochlear implantation surgery, and use of hearing technologies.

Hagemeyer (1992) suggested that there are nine overlapping sub-populations among deaf people in the United States, although later discussion in this chapter will extend and complexify this:

(1) Those who use sign language (e.g. American Sign Language – often represented as ASL) as their primary language.
(2) Those who can communicate both in ASL and English.
(3) Those mostly from the hearing impaired group who can communicate primarily through speech.
(4) Adults who became deaf later in life, who were not born deaf and may have acquired speech before deafness. Such people have the experience of hearing normally for a shorter or a longer period and may have had speech patterns relatively well embedded before deafness occurred.
(5) The elderly who became hearing impaired or deaf later in life as the result of the aging process.
(6) Those who do not know either ASL or English, but communicate through gestures, mime and their own signing system. Such people may have been denied access to a Deaf culture, to ASL and to education at an early age.

(7) Those who have residual hearing, perhaps describing themselves as hard of hearing, and who can hear with the use of various aids.
(8) Those people who are deaf and blind. An example is Helen Keller (1880–1968).
(9) Those people who have normal hearing, but because their parents, children, or other members of the family are deaf, they understand signing, or are fully conversant with Deaf culture and integrate with the Deaf community.

Such sub-dimensions refer to Deaf language(s) and culture and not to whether a person is also a member of Hispanic, Native American, Asian or any other ethnic group that exists alongside being deaf. For example, bilingual education for a child born profoundly deaf to a Spanish-speaking family in the US will be different from a child who loses his/her hearing at 9 or 10 years old and has grown up speaking Swedish in Finland. The educational options for children who undergo cochlear implantation surgery as infants will look different from children who do not. Thus the nine sub-populations are valuable for indicting variety among deaf people, but do not include many other dimensions of bilingualism that give deaf people even more variety and vitality, individuality and identity.

One classification for the degree of hearing loss is the system based on Clark (1981) used by the American Speech-Language-Hearing Association, as shown in Table 16.1.

Table 16.1 A United States classification of degree of hearing loss

Degree of hearing	Hearing loss range in decibels (dB)
Normal	-10 to 15
Slight loss	16 to 25
Mild loss	26 to 40
Moderate loss	41 to 55
Moderately severe loss	56 to 70
Severe loss	71 to 90
Profound loss	91+

There are many forms of bilingualism among deaf people, for example, those who learn to speak from hearing parents, followed by learning to sign. Others learn to sign and speak in parallel, while some learn to communicate by all available means, by signs, gestures, speaking and writing. Some people become deaf later in life, including as part of the aging process, and have acquired speech before deafness.

Some deaf people sign when in face-to-face communication, and use a written form (e.g. English) to communicate with members of the Deaf community via channels such as text messaging, textphone and email. The term 'bimodal bilingualism' has become a recent way of referring to deaf people using two or more modalities (sign, text, speech) and two or more languages (e.g. ASL and English). What routes and choices are preferable is debated, varies across countries, and is a live issue with relatively little research evidence (Knoors et al., 2014).

Deaf people may be **bicultural** as well as bilingual. Some deaf people belong to their own language community (e.g. Deaf social clubs, social networking across the internet) and identify with a Deaf cultural community. On other occasions, they have been required to attempt, or have themselves chosen, to integrate into the hearing community. Those with a hearing loss (severe, moderate, mild) vary in their identification, sometimes identifying with profoundly deaf people, at other times with hearing people, and sometimes with both groups, with many possible variations (Leigh, 2009). Hence, audiological levels of deafness and deaf identity are two different concepts and vary in their relationship. Deaf people are quite varied in the way they construe their deafness, identity and their cultural preferences (Monaghan *et al.*, 2003).

Like many hearing bilinguals, deaf people who are bilingual may use their two languages for different functions and purposes (see Chapter 3). For example, signing may be used to communicate with the Deaf community, while a spoken language or literacy is used to communicate with the hearing community. However, there is also a looseness and flexibility in language use among many deaf people, for example, in translanguaging between combinations of sign, speaking, gesturing, lip-reading, finger-spelling and writing.

Such flexibility is partly due to circumstances and changing technology, as Swanwick (2010: 155) suggests:

> The last decade has seen immensely successful changes in terms of early intervention and audiological support. Newborn babies in the UK are now all screened for deafness within the first few weeks of life, allowing for early detection and intervention, and the audiological aspects of this intervention have become increasingly sophisticated over the last 10 years. ... More than half of the profoundly deaf population now have a cochlear implant when they start school. Technology is changing the potential of these deaf children to use their hearing and this is changing their learning needs. One evident outcome of this is the increasing numbers of pupils in inclusive settings rather than special schools for the deaf.

Newborn hearing screening, cochlear implants (including in the first year of life), middle ear implants, bone anchored hearing aids, digital hearing aid technology, and brainstem implants have increased recently, improving the potential for spoken language development. Thus J. Mayer and Leigh (2010) report that in Canada, fewer parents are choosing the sign bilingual education option, and there is a renewed emphasis on the development of spoken language. There is a growing preference among US hearing parents for their children to have cochlear implants (Cerney, 2007). While cochlear implants have become more sophisticated and enable many children to develop speech communication skills, their effectiveness varies by individual due to suitability and preference. The most sophisticated hearing technologies typically do not fully replace normal hearing.

There are other dimensions that affect deaf people as bilinguals and multilinguals, and the future demographics of deaf students (Compton, 2014). For example in the US, deaf children can come from language minority communities where a minority language is transmitted. Recent US immigrants may change the demographics of deaf children's schooling, and there are many other sign languages apart from American Sign Language (ASL) that parents and children may desire (Compton, 2014). Thus deaf bilingualism and **multilingualism** has considerable variety, is in a period of change, and adds a distinct diversity to the study of bilinguals and multilinguals.

However, positive views about deaf people as bilinguals are quite recent. Therefore, a historical perspective is needed to understand recent changes in perceptions, policies and practices about deaf children's bilingualism and bilingual education.

Two Viewpoints About Deaf People

Medical Viewpoint

The first viewpoint is the medical (or pathological) view of deafness. Here deafness is defined as a defect or a handicap that distinguishes 'abnormal' deaf people from 'normal' hearing persons. Deafness is seen as a condition that needs to be remedied or cured as far as possible. Viewed as a physiological disability, cochlear implants, hearing aids and other devices that enhance hearing or the understanding of speech are recommended. Deaf people are expected to become as 'normal' as possible by avoiding purely visual methods of communication such as sign language, and by learning spoken language (as much as is viable) to integrate into mainstream society. In this 'deficit' viewpoint, the education of deaf children frequently focuses on lip-reading skills (better termed 'speech reading skills' as this includes all forms of non-verbal communication) and speech in a majority language and not sign language. Such children are regarded as best integrated into mainstream society through speaking and literacy in the language of hearing children.

One historical conception of deaf people is that they live in a silent and therefore deprived world. The following poem from William Wordsworth (1770–1850) extracted from *The Excursion*, Book VII sums up how hearing people have often conceived of deafness: A world that is silent, tragic and empty, unable to experience the stimulating and wonderful sounds of nature.

> … there, beneath
> A plain blue stone, a gentle Dalesman lies,
> From whom, in early childhood, was withdrawn
> The precious gift of hearing. He grew up
> From year to year in loneliness of soul;
> And this deep mountain-valley was to him
> Soundless, with all its streams. The bird of dawn
> Did never rouse this Cottager from sleep
> With startling summons; not for his delight
> The vernal cuckoo shouted; not for him
> Murmured the labouring bee.

A historical negative view of deaf people was not just about individuals and sound. It also had social dimensions. For example, Alexander Graham Bell, the inventor of the telephone, had controversial views on deaf people. Bell opposed the marriage of deaf people to other deaf people. He feared the 'contamination' of civilization by the spread of deaf people, (even though now we know that about 95% of deaf children are born to hearing parents). Bell, in his 1883 paper *Memoir Upon the Formation of a Deaf Variety of the Human Race* to the National Academy of Science stated:

> Those who believe as I do, that the production of a defective race of human beings would be a great calamity to the world, will examine carefully the causes that will lead to the intermarriage of the deaf with the object of applying a remedy.

Even today, some well-intentioned educators, professionals and policy-makers see themselves as helping deaf people to overcome their 'handicap' and to live and marry in the hearing world.

Wordsworth's view that deaf people inhabit a world that is silent and hollow is not a view shared by deaf people themselves. Nor do they believe Alexander Bell's view that they have 'defects'. Sound, or the lack of sound, is not an issue for deaf people unless they are told by hearing people that it is a problem. Sign language provides a natural form of communication (discussed later). To some people, sign language may seem primitive, rudimentary, and just a simple picture language, whereas the spoken language is seen as the natural language for all in the community, including deaf people.

A central aim of education for deaf students deriving from this viewpoint therefore becomes a mastery of spoken and written language. Such education, and social pressures within the community, aim for the integration or assimilation of deaf people with hearing people. What is not entertained as wholesome or desirable is deaf people existing, at least in part, in Deaf communities, signing to each other or having a Deaf culture.

Sociocultural Viewpoint

A second viewpoint is more in line with that increasingly expressed about hearing bilinguals: one that emphasizes the advantages of **additive bilingualism**, vitality in a linguistic and cultural minority community, and the need for an enriching bilingual education. This view is often called the 'sociocultural approach' to deaf people. It seeks to understand them in a multidimensional manner and not purely as having an auditory handicap. Like many language minorities, deaf individuals are 'members of other non-dominant (and often oppressed) cultural and linguistic groups ... lead us to efforts that focus on issues of civil rights and to assist the Deaf to function fully, *as deaf people*, in the dominant culture' (Reagan, 2015: 392).

Such a sociocultural viewpoint commences with the belief that deaf people can do everything except hear. For deaf children, a key question from a sociocultural position is: which languages (and language modalities) can the child access? This has significant implications for the child's cognitive, social and linguistic development. While there are differences between deaf and hearing people, these are cultural differences, not deviations from a hearing norm.

Thus, in this second viewpoint, deafness is regarded as a difference, a characteristic that distinguishes 'normal' deaf people from 'normal' hearing people. A sign language is a full language in itself, grammatically complex and capable of expressing as much as any spoken language. Deaf people are regarded as a linguistic and cultural minority that needs preservation, enrichment and celebration. By signing, they add diversity and much color to the languages of the world

Instead of highlighting the deficiencies of deaf people, their abilities are emphasized in the sociocultural approach. Rather than focusing on a loss of hearing, the gaining of sign language is emphasized. A strong emphasis is placed on the use of vision as a positive, efficient and full communicative alternative to audible speaking and hearing. Sign language is thus seen as not only equal to spoken language, but also the most natural language for people who are born deaf.

In deaf children's education, the sociocultural approach focus has been on language development through signing, and sooner or later on bilingualism through literacy and oracy in the majority language. It is felt important that maximal language development occurs early on through signing. Early signing enables a focus on learning elements of the curriculum (rather than learning to speak a majority language – see later). While there tends to be a lack of teachers fluent in sign, the importance of signing in deaf children's education, including when deaf students are mainstreamed, has become largely accepted, with variations in views about timing, balance with speaking, and curriculum distribution. However, research is notably lacking on such topics.

In this second viewpoint, deaf people are encouraged to engage, where possible, with a cultural community of their own and acquire Deaf identity. Deaf people have a common language in signing, a Deaf culture (see Ladd, 2003) and a set of needs that are distinct from those of the hearing community. Deaf communities typically share the same sign language as well as their own artistic tradition, shared identity with distinctive cultural norms and values, shared expectations and perspectives, and their own forms of socialization into that community. As Hoffmeister (2008):

> Deaf people have developed their own rules of behavior that are different from Hearing people. Cultural norms, attitudes, and perspectives are based on a world that is visual as opposed to auditory. Deaf and hearing differences in cultural norms, attitudes, perspectives, and ways of analyzing the world are numerous. (p. 74)

A Deaf community may include Deaf social clubs, but increasingly it is about social interaction by recent technological advances: text messaging, email, blogs and vlogs, wireless text pagers, videophone, Skype, and video relay services. Sign language has entered computers and cyberspace, and deaf people have their own chat rooms. Such modern deaf adults can provide important role models for deaf children, either as teachers or in the community. Thus, this second viewpoint supports bilingualism, a Deaf culture and some form of bilingual education for deaf students.

However, deaf people do not usually live apart from hearing people, and are rarely isolated in schools and communities. Like most bilinguals, they typically operate in two or more different language communities and cultures. Since some 95% of deaf children have hearing parents, and about 90% of deaf parents have hearing children, so integration into the hearing world is typical. Deaf people therefore tend to be bicultural as well as bilingual, sometimes multilingual, and may operate in Deaf, majority and minority language communities simultaneously. However, deaf people are not a single group, and therefore viewpoints have to adjust for differences between sub-groupings.

The sociocultural viewpoint is a crucial counterweight to the medical viewpoint and valuably accents the many positive aspects of deaf individuals, their education and lifestyle. However, hearing loss for many people still has adverse associations (e.g. underachievement at school, reduced employment opportunities).

Deaf People and Sign Language

There are over 200 sign languages in the world, almost all with no official status or recognition. To name but a few: American Sign Language (ASL), British Sign Language (BSL), Chinese Sign Language, Danish Sign Language, French Sign Language, Russian Sign Language and Thai Sign Language (Pfau et al., 2012; Woll et al., 2001).

Sign language may seem primitive, rudimentary, and just a simple picture language. Not so. Sign language is not gesturing. Gesturing tends to convey a relatively small number of expressions (e.g. pointing to something that is wanted). We all use gestures to add emphasis to our speech but not as speech by itself. In contrast, signing is a very extensive, structurally complex, rule-bound means of communication. Sign languages are full and complete languages in themselves, grammatically complex and capable of expressing as much as any spoken language.

Sign languages have allowed deaf people to match the skills and abilities of hearing people: in communication, **cognition** and having an empowering Deaf community. Because sign language is a fully developed and authentic language, it allows its users to communicate the same, complete meaning as a spoken language. Sign language can perform the same range of functions as a spoken language. As will be discussed later, sign language can be used to teach any aspect of the curriculum.

The varied modalities that many US bilingual deaf children and adults use are portrayed in the table below (see also Grosjean, 2010; Nover *et al.*, 1998) although more complex, flexible and simultaneous patterns also exist, including where minority languages are used (Compton, 2014; C. Mayer, 2015).

Table 16.2 Languages, abilities and modalities of US bilingual deaf people

	Sign language (e.g. ASL)	Other	English literacy	English oracy
Receptive Mode	Viewing Sign Language	Finger-reading, Lip-reading	Reading	Listening
Productive Mode	Signing	Finger-spelling, Typing	Writing	Speaking

Many deaf children learn a sign language as a second language, as their families initially use a spoken language (e.g. English). Other children will learn to speak and sign simultaneously. Blending, and the flexible mixing of spoken language and signing, may occur both when addressing those who sign, and those who do not, (just as hearing people are often bimodal by gesturing when speaking). Thus, many deaf children translanguage in a pragmatic way according to whom they are communicating with, and according to the context, with changes over time, perceived language status and prestige, identity, language development, **language competence** and language preferences (Menéndez, 2010).

However, many deaf people do not use sign language. This is a global phenomenon. In the US, for example, some children have not learned ASL because their parents are hearing people. Other children have been to schools that taught them oralist (e.g. speaking plus lip-reading; speaking, use of residual hearing) approaches. Other deaf people prefer to use speech rather than sign language in their communities.

There are continuing differences of opinion about the development of language(s) among deaf children from birth onwards, and differences about the education of deaf students and their integration into mainstream speaking society. Deaf students may or

---

Box 16.1 The cognitive development of sign language

The recent neurolinguistic research of Laura-Ann Petitto supports early signing and bilingualism through findings on language acquisition in the brain. It had hitherto been believed that the auditory cortex tissue in the brain was exclusively for sound processing, and this was important tissue for language development. She has shown that sign language development uses the same brain tissue, and that the brain does not discriminate between tongue and hands in language development. This is because the brain is concerned with the organization of language patterns which can derive from sound or sign.

Source: www.gallaudet.edu/petitto.html

may not use sign language in their education. The education of deaf students is variable across localities, states and countries. Such education tends to center around four overlapping possibilities: auditory-oral, auditory-verbal, Total Communication (TC), and some form of bilingual education (C. Mayer, 2015). However, C. Mayer (2015) adds a warning that classroom practice is less tidy and more intricate compared with theory:

> The options continue to be framed in the same terms that have always been used – auditory-oral, auditory-verbal, TC, and bilingual. While it is possible to find definitions of each of these approaches that appear to be quite 'tidy', the reality is that each is far messier in practice than in theory. (p. 40)

Such possibilities in the education for deaf students will now be briefly considered.

The Education of Deaf Students

There are a variety of overlapping styles and approaches to the education of deaf students. Some are about institutional placement (e.g. inclusive classrooms, separate units, special schools), some about preferred language(s) in the curriculum (e.g. use of sign language), and some are based on particular pedagogical and political philosophies (e.g. Total Communication). These options range from minimal support to specially designed programs. Some of the overlapping and interacting different approaches are considered below, but there is much diversity inside each approach.

Mainstreaming and Inclusion

An auditory-oral approach has a relatively long tradition of emphasizing access to a spoken language (e.g. English) but not to sign language. It emphasizes speech reading and spoken language development (plus literacy). Located mainly in mainstream schools, it emphasizes inclusion and assimilation.

In many countries, inclusion policies have increasingly sought to integrate special needs children into mainstream schools and regular classrooms. This tends to be the current practice in most countries. For example, the Consortium for Research into Deaf Education (CRIDE) 2015 survey in the UK found that among deaf children 85% are in mainstream provision, 3% are in special schools for deaf children, and 12% are in other special schools (see: http://www.batod.org.uk/content/resources/survey/CRIDEUK2015.pdf).

Where such children are given support by classroom assistants (e.g. especially those who can sign), such integration is often preferred by policy makers and politicians. The benefits for inclusive education for deaf students are often claimed as: improved communication skills and self-esteem, enriched social relationships and integration with all kinds of children, fuller access to the curriculum and raised academic achievement related to higher expectations, improved societal integration and respect for differences, better employment prospects, preferred by families, and a more effective and cost-efficient use of educational resources.

While there tends to be a lack of teachers fluent in sign, the importance of signing in many deaf children's education (including when mainstreamed) has become largely accepted, with variations in views about timing (early as possible or later), balance with speaking (e.g. English), and curriculum distribution (e.g. mathematics).

However, there can also be occasions when mainstreaming may seem like inclusion, but potentially results in isolation, loneliness and disempowerment for some deaf students, such that academic, social and emotional under-development may occur. Attempting to work through a spoken language (e.g. English) may result in the opposite of intended inclusion: separation and distance from understanding curriculum content; creating social and achievement distance from their hearing peers. This will link with Chapter 18 where assimilation is discussed, and is somewhat parallel to the historical integration of minority language speakers into majority language classrooms (e.g. Welsh speakers into English-language classrooms). Nevertheless, inclusion in regular schooling has become more rather than less frequent, and sensitive and effective policies to avoid such issues (see above) have grown.

Total Communication

An approach developed since the 1970s is based on the philosophy of Total Communication where all modes of communication are regarded as appropriate for those who are deaf or partially hearing (C. Mayer, 2015). All modalities (e.g. speech, sign, print) alone or in combination allow communication and the development of language. The use of hearing technologies such as hearing aids was encouraged when this commenced in the 1970s.

Increasing emphasis on speaking the majority language has often been prevalent. Hence, a Total Communication philosophy can be **assimilationist** or transitional, aiming to enable deaf people to communicate with hearing people, but without evidence to show its effectiveness in the education of deaf students, including in increasing literacy levels. However, under this heading goes different practices such that its realization in classrooms has been diverse (C. Mayer, 2015). Total Communication differs from translanguaging as the former is a philosophy and style of classroom teaching, while translanguaging is a regular, everyday (mostly subconscious) occurrence used by deaf people to scaffold understanding and engage in effective communication (Swanwick, 2015).

Bilingual/Bicultural Approach

A different approach concerns bilingualism for deaf children through sign bilingual education, also termed a Bilingual/Bicultural approach (Swanwick, 2010). This may occur in special schools or units, although it is increasingly occurring in more inclusive, mainstream settings (Swanwick *et al.*, 2014). However, bilingual education for deaf students is an ambiguous concept. There is no standard model or agreed 'best practices' partly due to the scarcity of effectiveness research on the education of deaf students.

Bilingual education for deaf children was developed in Scandinavia, the US and the UK in the 1980s. Under a general heading of 'Bilingual Education for Deaf Students' is the following diversity: sequential bilingual education which develops sign language first and then written and /or spoken language; simultaneous (parallel) bilingual education where sign language and a spoken language are used concurrently in the curriculum; residential and special schools/units where sign language predominates; and mainstream 'inclusive' schooling with an emphasis on the written and spoken language supported by sign language.

Recently, an argument has been made for encouraging translanguaging so as to provide 'opportunities to develop spoken and sign languages in one space, where movement across and between languages, or translanguaging, is seen as the norm and part of a life-long repertoire of language skills' (Swanwick *et al.*, 2014: 298). Translanguaging (see Chapter 13) in deaf student education may shift the focus to maximizing student learning rather than on the debate about 'which language(s) to use'.

Deaf student learning can valuably occur through using various modes at different times and occasions, singularly and in combinations, so as to encourage deep learning and collaboration in inclusive education contexts. Translanguaging among deaf students suggests that language boundaries (e.g. between signing and speaking/writing) can be loosened and crossed (Swanwick, 2017). Such students use their full language repertoire to optimize their understanding of the curriculum. Translanguaging is thus a normal and natural form of communication for deaf students who learn by a flexible, creative, adaptive, fluid and interconnected use of their different modalities. Translanguaging thus encourages the use of hearing technologies and social media by deaf students as a pragmatic and holistic approach to learning.

It has been suggested that learning to sign should occur as early as possible in schooling (Reagan, 2015). In school, early signing can enable a focus on the subject matter of the curriculum rather than learning a language. This is similar to minority language children using their minority language in **heritage language** schools for most early learning rather than a **submersion** in the majority language (see Chapters 10 and 11).

Special Schools for Deaf Children

There has recently been a declining number of special schools, classes and units for deaf students where, for example, the children are taught to learn signing, are given a full curriculum mostly through signing, and develop written and/or oral skills in the majority spoken language. This needs a historical perspective.

Compton (2014) provides the following historical US perspective (see Box 16.2). In 1817, the first American School for the Deaf was founded in Hartford, Connecticut with two pioneering teachers – Laurent Clerc from France and Thomas Gallaudet – using ASL and written English as their bilingual teaching and learning strategy. But this bilingual approach did not last as ASL was seen as leading to the non-integration of deaf people into mainstream society. For example, in 1867, the Governor of Massachusetts commissioned a review of deaf children's education that led to a ban on the use of ASL in the local School for the Deaf, and to spoken English becoming the only language of instruction.

Such historical assimilationist approaches to deaf people (see Chapter 18) have a modern trend in the education inclusion and mainstreaming of deaf children. The US Individuals with Disabilities Education Act (initially passed in 1975 and reauthorized in 2004) emphasized an inclusion philosophy for the education of deaf students. Compton (2014) reports that over the last three decades, almost a third of US schools for deaf students have closed as mainstreaming and inclusive education has become the dominant expectation. She suggests that there is also a growing US trend for 'cluster campuses', with 'districts designating particular campuses to serve deaf and hard-of-hearing students from across the school district. In effect, these cluster campuses could be considered mini schools of the deaf' (p. 279).

To conclude, there is much discussion and debate surrounding the education of deaf students. There is no agreement as to 'best practice': for example, is it best to use a bilingual approach of signing plus literacy in the spoken language; or sign

---

Box 16.2 The education of deaf students in the United States

- From the 1950s to the late 1970s, approximately 85% of deaf students attended residential schools.
- In 1975, Public Law 94–142 (The Education for All Handicap Children Act of 1975) mandated public schools to provide appropriate education for deaf students and all students with 'disabilities'.
- Between 1975 and 1985, residential schools experienced a 65% drop in enrolment, with many deaf students being mainstreamed or partly mainstreamed.
- By the mid-1990s, approximately 90% of deaf students were being educated in some kind of schooling in their locality.
- Statistics from the Gallaudet Research Institute (2011) indicate that 24.3% of deaf students are instructed in a special or center school; 57.1% attend a regular school setting with hearing students; 22.7% are located in a self-contained classroom in a regular school setting; 11.9% are educated in a resource room; 3.1% are educated at home; and 3.9% are in 'other education'.
- Across the United States, there is considerable variety in the kind of support given to deaf students, for example, the use of interpreters, note takers, and itinerant deaf teachers. Resources and equipment vary from state to state.
- Approximately one in five teachers of deaf students are deaf themselves.
- Some teachers of deaf children act as consultants to the school and its teachers, while others collaborate with the teacher, for example in a team teaching role.

Language of Instruction of Deaf Students

- Speech only (typically spoken English) = 53.0%
- Sign supported spoken language and Speech = 12.1%
- Sign language only = 27.4%
- Spoken language with cues = 5.0%
- Other = 2.5%

Sources: Gallaudet Research Institute (2008); Scheetz (2012)

---

language along with early development of a spoken language; or a Total Communication approach; or Sign Supported English or Signed Exact English or Fingerspelling or Cued Speech or Visual Phonics; how to develop oral and/or written skills in the spoken majority language including in a minority language context; whether to separate languages or to encourage multimodal translanguaging; whether full integration and inclusion with hearing children is preferable for all deaf students?

As Swanwick (2016) concludes in her state-of-the-art article, 'empirical evidence demonstrating the success of any one approach over another cannot be found' (p. 18). Knoors *et al.* (2014) similarly conclude in their overview that 'The history of deaf education, however, is marked with adopting and abandoning approaches without sufficient evidence, sometimes giving the impression that it is fashion more than reason that controls developments in the field – often to the detriment of deaf children' (p. 15).

Hence, there are few answers to these questions above as 'effectiveness research' is relatively rare and has mainly concentrated on deaf students' literacy development. The research that does exist is summarized in Swanwick (2016) and Knoors *et al.* (2014). The education of deaf students is a topic of continuing debate, and much-needed research evidence.

Parallels with Spoken Language Minority Education

There are parallels between language minority education (see Chapters 10–14) and the education of deaf students. Ideas and issues that are at least partly paralleled in language minority education/bilingual education are illustrated below. These are partly posed as questions to illustrate that there is much debate and discussion as to how to achieve optimum effectiveness for deaf students.

(1) Is sign language the preferable language main modality in the education for many deaf children? The parallel is with language minority children and the arguments for **heritage language education** (see Chapter 11).
(2) How is it possible to avoid or minimize language delay in deaf children, particularly to help optimal curriculum achievement? The parallel is partly with language minority children who are in a majority language assimilationist environment (see Chapter 18).
(3) Should sign language be used to teach all curriculum subjects such as science, humanities, social studies and mathematics, where appropriate? This parallels debates in language minority education, for example, about whether to teach mathematics and science through the minority or the majority language.
(4) Can bilingual education for deaf students be partly based on the arguments (as exemplified below) for an enrichment form of bilingual education for hearing children?
    - If the curriculum is transmitted in a student's weaker language, are students being expected to learn the content of the curriculum using a level of language not yet acquired? 'Strong' bilingual education typically builds on a child's existing linguistic and intellectual resources.
    - The relevance of Cummins' Linguistic Interdependence Theory (see Chapter 18) to sign languages (as these do not have a written form) needs testing (Knoors *et al.*, 2014). This is currently being researched among deaf students, as the extent and nature of transfer between sign and a second language/literacy needs defining. Sign languages have no written form, so the transfer between two 'literacy' languages is not the same. Also, 'deaf children are usually unable to approach the learning of L2 literacy with established and fluent L1 sign language skills. Deaf children are thus not able to approach the learning of literacy as an L2 or an L1 experience' (Swanwick, 2016: 11). This illustrates that the generalization of bilingual education models and strategies to the education of deaf students is not simple or straightforward. Also, instead of 'interdependence' the notion of translanguaging has a different emphasis, with languages in the latter being more fluidly inter-connected, with 'soft assembly' that helps classroom learning and communication.
    - Cognitive skills, concepts and knowledge developed in the first **language transfer** to the second language such as when learning to read (Hermans *et al.*, 2010).
    - Use of a child's heritage language gives pride and confidence in their culture and community.
    - A child's self-esteem and self-identity are boosted and not threatened by use of their heritage language.
    - School performance and curriculum attainment are raised when the heritage language is celebrated rather than devalued.
    - The lower achievement of many minority language students (especially in literacy) can to be addressed by enrichment forms (or 'strong forms') of bilingual education. We 'have not resolved the general issue of under-achievement in deaf education. The proportion of deaf pupils who do not reach national goals is still disquieting.... even after many educational reforms, a gap in attainments

that exists between deaf pupils and their hearing counterparts' (Knoors *et al.*, 2014: 299).

- If literacy development is highly important for deaf students, (e.g. for everyday living, employment, leisure and inclusion), and is a current weakness in much education for deaf students, when and how should literacy education be introduced (see Chapter 14 for comparisons with hearing bilinguals)?
- If bimodal bilingual deaf students are flexible in their blending of languages, should **assessment** in school *not* separately assess (and assess through) languages but celebrate that 'translanguaging' (see Chapter 15)? This relates to fractional and holistic (multicompetence) views of bilinguals (see Chapter 1).
- A growing number of deaf students come from homes where minority languages are used (immigrants especially but also indigenous language speakers). As Compton (2014) indicates: 'Historically, the language debate in deaf education in the United States has focused on ASL and English to the exclusion of other spoken and signed languages. However, today there are almost as many deaf and hard-of-hearing students from homes in which minority spoken languages are used (47%) as from **monolingual** English-speaking ones' (p. 280).
- In such language minority contexts, what bimodal bilingualism exists? What role do sign language(s) play, or not? What role do majority and minority spoken languages play? What use is made of minority languages and their associated sign language (e.g. Vietnamese and Vietnamese Sign Language), including in education? Is there increasing multilingualism among deaf children from language minority communities and families?

Teachers and Families in the Education of Deaf Students

Teachers

Since there has been a decrease in special schools and units for deaf children with increasing inclusion in the mainstream, it makes the topic of teacher selection, training and teaching styles highly important. Native sign language teachers may be employed in schools, where available, to teach and to act as language role models. But the supply of trained personnel in deaf students' education, staff pre-service education programs, in-service education and certification and funding are often current challenges. These are practical problems to be overcome rather than problems of principle that are insurmountable.

One part-solution has been team teaching or 'paired teaching'. A teacher (or teacher's assistant) who can sign works with a hearing teacher. Ideally, both teachers should be bilingual models, being able to communicate in both sign language and the 'hearing' language. Also, both teachers in the team should have a knowledge of Deaf culture and differences among deaf students. However, not all agree with this strategy. Is this going back to the days of one language, one person, and one language at a time? How does this fit with contemporary plural language contexts in deaf education and translanguaging?

Families

The relationship between a deaf student's teachers and family is also important. In order for cognitive, linguistic, social and emotional development to occur among deaf children, there needs to be a partnership between school and parents, and between school and community. Such parents often ask for a voice in their children's education. Also, parents of deaf children sometimes need much social and emotional support, information and guidance, inclusion and **empowerment** to help their children become bilingual.

Conclusion

This chapter has shown that there are many similarities between hearing and deaf students. Many of the justifications for developing a child's minority language (and for a 'strong' form of bilingual education for such children) also hold for deaf children. However, there are also differences between deaf students in their deafness, socialization, identity and culture. For example, deaf students can also be a minority group within a language minority. When deaf people come from language minority communities they form a minority of a minority. The examples of a Latino deaf person in the US, a deaf Turk in Germany, and a deaf Bengali in England all represent individuals who are a minority within a minority. Where a deaf person is also a member of a language minority, low status and low self-esteem may be compounded. Diagnosis may be difficult, delayed or distrusted. If many groups of bilinguals from language minorities are underprivileged, even more so can be deaf students who come from such a language minority.

Key Points in This Chapter

➤ Deaf people are frequently bilinguals, with sign language plus literacy (and/or oracy) in another 'hearing' language. The order in which these languages are learnt varies among deaf students.

➤ There is a growing preference for seeing the languages of the deaf in a more integrated and fluid manner as in 'multimodality' and 'translanguaging'.

➤ Bilingual education for deaf students has many parallels with discussions about language minority education and bilingual education.

➤ The balance between sign language and speaking and literacy varies in different forms of education for deaf students. This ranges from sign language plus literacy in a second language, to all forms of communication being utilized (the philosophy of Total Communication), and recently towards deaf children's typical translanguaging with a more refined understanding of how deaf students learn effectively through utilizing all their language resources.

Suggested Readings

📖 Compton, S. E. (2014). American Sign Language as a heritage language. In T. G. Wiley, J. K. Peyton, D. Christian, S. C. K. Moore & N. Liu (Eds), *Handbook of heritage, community, and Native American languages in the United States*. New York, NY & Washington, DC: Routledge and Center for Applied Linguistics.

📖 Marschark, M., Tang, G. & Knoors, H. (Eds) (2014). *Bilingualism and bilingual deaf education*. New York, NY: Oxford University Press.

📖 Reagan, T. (2015). Bilingual deaf education. In W. E. Wright, S. Boun, & O. García (Eds.), *The handbook of bilingual and multilingual education* (pp. 391–408). Malden, MA: Wiley-Blackwell.

📖 Scheetz, N. A. (2012). *Deaf education in the 21st Century: Topics and trends*. Boston, MA: Pearson

📖 Swanwick, R. (2017). *Languages and languaging in deaf education*. New York, NY: Oxford University Press.

On the Web

🖥 Deaf Education – Educational Enhancement for the Field of Deaf Education
http://www.deafed.net/

🖥 Laurent Clerc National Deaf Education Center
http://www.gallaudet.edu/clerc-center.html

🖥 Gallaudet University
http://www.gallaudet.edu/

🖥 Indiana School for the Deaf
http://www.deafhoosiers.com/

🖥 Language Diversity and Plurality in Deaf Education
http://deafed.leeds.ac.uk/

Discussion Questions

(1) Do you support the integration of deaf students into mainstream schools? What are the benefits and issues?

(2) View the YouTube video – *Two Deaf Women Show us Bilingualism at its Finest* (https://youtu.be/M5vPEhAuLWQ). How is bilingualism defined here? And how and why did these two women resist monolingual norms? How do they benefit from their bilingualism?

(3) Examine the William Wordsworth (1770–1850) poem on p. 356. What experiences does it consider 'normal' and essential, and what characterization of deaf people does it make? What does the following poem 'My Sign' by Kate Wheat convey in contrast? How does this viewpoint differ from Wordsworth's?

My Sign
The silent hand moves slowly with grace
then bursts with excitement and quickens the pace
Images drawn with precision in air
with energetic passion, beauty and flair
Saying so much more than the spoken word
A language of generations, never to be heard
The magnet just drew me, it all seemed to fit
Sparking powerful emotions – the flame had been lit
Just like the return to a well loved home
no longer on the outside feeling alone
No more incomprehension, struggling to see
What people are saying – I've now found the key

I've unlocked the door and found what I'd lost
I'm staying right here whatever the cost!
A new freedom of speech to express what I feel
With meaning and depth, in a language that's real
This is what matters, now I feel I can shine
As I show to the world my language, my sign ...

This poem is by Kate Wheat from *Between a Rock and a Hard Place* (2003) edited and published by the Deaf EX-Mainstreamers' Group, Wakefield, West Yorkshire, WF5 9JN, UK. (http://www.dex.org.uk/). Reprinted with the kind permission of Kate Wheat and the Deaf EX-Mainstreamers' Group.

See also the poem in Cerney (2007: 182) which includes:

You live in a box, where
voices are shut out,
and relationships are unreachable.
Do you know you are not alone?
You are a part of a rich culture of people.
Smart, Funny, and Talented
You are not alone.

Study Activities

(1) Visit a family with a deaf student and/or a school where there are deaf students. What are the goals in language development? What form of bilingualism exists? What are the attitudes and aspirations of the student and parents/teachers regarding language?
(2) Read the following brief article about the groundbreaking work of Dr Laura-Ann Petitto on bilingualism and the brain (http://oes.gallaudet.edu/bl2/). Then explore the web page of Dr Petitto's Visual Language and Visual Learning (VL2) Lab at Gallaudet University (www.gallaudet.edu/petitto.html). In what ways is her research challenging prior beliefs and what are the implications for deaf people and deaf education?
(3) Select a few schools from this list of Residential Schools for the Deaf in the United States (http://www.deafed.net/PageText.asp?hdnPageId=105), or search the internet for Deaf children's schools in other countries. Explore the school websites to compare and contrast each school's philosophy in relation to language, bilingualism, and the types of programs and approaches used in education programs.

Bilingualism and Bilingual Education as a Problem, Right and Resource

Bilingualism and Bilingual Education as a Problem, Right and Resource

Introduction

Bilingualism is not only studied linguistically, psychologically and sociologically, it is also studied in relationship to power and political systems in society. The basis of this and the next chapter is that bilingualism and bilingual education, whatever form they take, cannot be properly understood unless connected to ideologies and politics in society. The activity of a bilingual classroom, and decisions about how to teach minority language children, are not based purely on educational preferences. Rather, calls for and against bilingual education are surrounded and underpinned by basic beliefs about minority languages and **cultures**, linguistic and cultural diversity, immigration and immigrants, equality of opportunity and equality of outcomes, **empowerment**, affirmative action, the rights of individuals and the rights of **language minority** groups, **assimilation** and integration, desegregation and discrimination, pluralism and multiculturalism, diversity and discord, equality of recognition for minority groups, social division and social cohesion.

In the view of some people, bilingual education will facilitate national cohesion and cultural integration, and enable different language communities inside a country to communicate with each other (e.g. Singapore). In the view of other people, bilingual education will create language factions, national disunity, and cultural, economic and political disintegration. Education has thus been conceived as both part of the solution and part of the problem of achieving national unity, achieving diversity or unity in diversity.

Teachers and education administrators are not only affected by political decisions and processes, they also deliver and implement those decisions and processes. Teachers are language planners and policymakers (Menken & García, 2010). As such, teachers are part of language paradoxes that are daily enacted and temporarily resolved in the classroom: ensuring equality of opportunity for all while celebrating distinctiveness and difference; ensuring that diversity does not become discord; encouraging students to share a common purpose while encouraging colorful variety; developing the dignity of ethnicity while aiding national stability. In multilingual classrooms, teachers have overt and covert beliefs about languages ranging from prohibition to tolerance, limited permission to promotion. Teachers and students are often unwitting actors in the drama of language and politics.

Three Perspectives on Languages

We begin by considering different assumptions and varying perspectives that are at the root of the politics of bilingualism and bilingual education. In a now classic article, Richard Ruiz (1984) proposed three basic orientations or perspectives about language around which governments, groups and individuals vary: language as a problem, language as a right and language as a resource. These three different orientations may be conscious but they are also embedded in the subconscious assumptions of teachers, planners and politicians. Such orientations are regarded as fundamental and related to a basic philosophy or **ideology** held by an individual or group. Ruiz's framework has been widely adopted, expanded upon (Lo Bianco, 2001, 2016), critiqued (Ricento, 2009), defended (Ruiz, 2010), and continues to have great influence (de Jong, Li, Zafar & Wu, 2016; Hornberger, 2017; Wright & Boun, 2016), as will be evident in the discussion below.

Language as a Problem

Public discussions of bilingual education and languages in society often commence with the idea of language as causing complications and difficulties. This is well illustrated in the historical debates about the supposed cognitive problems of operating in two languages (see Chapters 7 and 8). Perceived problems are not limited to thinking. Personality and social problems such as split-identity, cultural dislocation, a poor self-image, low self-esteem, alienation, emotional vulnerability and anomie (normlessness) have also sometimes been attributed to bilinguals (Pavlenko, 2014). Bilinguals sometimes have a language anxiety ('schizoglossia') because they feel their language does not compare well with the supposed **monolingual** standard, and in extreme cases this has led to psychoanalysis and therapy (Pavlenko, 2005).

The positioning of bilingual women has been connected to a deficit framework (Mills, 2006). For example, women have been posed as less bilingual than men and also more connected to a minority language: 'in many language contact communities, the **dominant language**, perceived as a power code, is associated with masculinity, and the minority language with domestic values and femininity' (Pavlenko, 2001: 128). This serves as an important reminder that gender and languages interact in ways that make bilingualism have different meanings to different groups, including more of a problem for one, more of a benefit for another (Mills, 2006). For example, in some communities, women may be given less access to a second, prestigious language (e.g. English), restricting their bilingualism, access to education, employment or economic advancement. The opposite can also occur. 'Where bilingualism is associated with inequality and social disadvantage, ideologies of language and gender may conspire to put more pressure to be bilingual on the less powerful group, often women' (Pavlenko, 2001: 131).

At a group rather than an individual level, bilingualism is sometimes connected with the potential for national or regional disunity and inter-group conflict. Language is thus viewed by some people as a political problem. Part of the 'language-as-problem' orientation is that perpetuating language minorities and language diversity may cause less integration, less cohesiveness, more antagonism and more conflict in society. It is sometimes claimed that immigrant language minorities threaten national unity and political stability by building self-segregated enclaves and establishing regular connections back to their country of origin, called 'immigrant transnationalism' (Patten & Kymlicka, 2003). This is to be solved by assimilation into the majority language (see Chapter 18). Such an argument holds that the majority language (e.g. English) unifies the diversity. The ability of every citizen to communicate with ease in the nation's majority language is regarded as the common leveler. Unity within a nation is seen as synonymous with uniformity and similarity. The opposing argument is that it is possible to have national unity without uniformity. Diversity of languages and national unity can co-exist (e.g. Singapore, Luxembourg, Switzerland, Wales, Ireland).

The co-existence of two or more languages is rarely a cause in itself of tension, disunity, conflict or strife. Rather, the history of war suggests that economic, political and religious differences are typically the causes. Language, in and by itself, is seldom the cause of conflict. Religious crusades and jihads, rivalries between different religions, rivalries between different political parties and economic aggression tend to be the instigators of conflict. Where there is language conflict, language is often the symbol but not the underlying issue. The underlying issue is often more about economic advantage and disadvantage, contests of power and status, religion and nationalism, military power and imperialism, of which language can be an outward marker but not the inner issue. Research by Sallabank (2013) in Europe suggests that minority language policy sometimes serves ends other than language, and includes the desire for political autonomy, economic equality or advantage, and group empowerment.

In an internationally comparative research study on causes of civil strife, Fishman (1989) found that language was not a cause of such civil discord. His analysis involved 130 countries with one outcome (dependent) variable, namely civil strife (defined as the frequency, duration and intensity of conspiracy, internal war and turmoil). Predictor variables concerned measures of linguistic homogeneity/heterogeneity, social-cultural, economic, demographic, geographic, historical and political measures. 'The widespread journalistic and popular political wisdom that linguistic heterogeneity per se is necessarily conducive to civil strife, has been shown, by our analysis, to be more myth than reality ' (Fishman, 1989: 622). Rather, the causes of strife were found to be deprivation, authoritarian regimes and modernization. Romaine (2000) thus concludes:

> Because languages and dialects are often potent symbols of class, gender, ethnic and other kinds of differentiation, it is easy to think that language underlies conflict. Yet disputes involving language are really not about language, but instead about fundamental inequalities between groups who happen to speak different languages. (p. 14)

However, Lo Bianco (2016), in his on-the-ground work with peacebuilding efforts in Southeast Asia, concludes, 'some aspect of language is present in many conflicts, some kinds of conflicts involve many aspects of language, and some conflicts are only about language' (p. 2). He also found 'that disputes around language problems often represent a positive opening as well, sometimes the means whereby entry to solutions can be explored using an engaged and democratic language planning practice' (p. 3).

In the United States, 'becoming American' has historically been symbolized by being English-speaking. That means English-speaking monolingualism and not bilingualism. Bilingualism is seen as a characteristic of the poor, the disadvantaged, the foreigner, and the unassimilated immigrant. Speaking English is valued for its perceived link with liberty, freedom, status, justice and wealth. In consequence, other languages in the US are sometimes seen as linked to terror, injustice, poverty and other societal problems.

American ideals and dreams are learnt through English. A belief of some is that other languages teach non-American ideas, and therefore must be discouraged in schools (Valdés *et al.*, 2006). Bilingualism, in this US 'problem' viewpoint, will lower the GNP, increase civil strife, foster political and social unrest, and endanger US stability.

A minority language is often connected with the problems of poverty, economic disadvantage, underachievement in school, political marginalization, less social and vocational mobility and with a lack of integration into the majority culture. Menken (2013) uses the term '(dis)citizenship', meaning 'citizenship minus' 'or 'disabling citizenship', to suggest that many US immigrant students are implicitly restricted by the dominant monolingual 'English only' idea of citizenship in the US (see Ramanathan, 2013 for more on (dis)citzenship). This is especially due to schools where the curriculum is only through English, and due to high-stakes testing and the current school accountability ideology. 'Dis-citizenship' disables students from fully accessing and participating in society, limiting their future economic opportunities. Thus such students are often seen as having a language problem.

In this 'language as a problem' perspective, the minority language is perceived as a partial cause of social, economic and educational problems rather than an effect of such problems. This 'language is an obstacle' attitude is illustrated in the phrase, 'If only they would speak English, their problems would be solved'. The minority language is thus seen as a handicap to be overcome by the school system.

One resolution of the problem is regarded as the increased teaching of a majority language (e.g. English) at the expense of the home language. Thus, mainstreaming, **English as a second language, sheltered English immersion** and **transitional bilingual education** aim to develop competent English **language skills** in minority language children as quickly as possible so they are on a par with English first language speakers in the mainstream classroom. In the US, the rise of **high-stakes testing** has suggested that language is a problem since Spanish-speakers have relatively lower test scores. The group label (e.g. Latinos, Hispanics, Spanish speakers) becomes the named cause such that, for example, Latinos are immediately associated with lower test performance. The home language is wrongly attributed as the origin of under-achievement rather than, for example, the relatively poor economic conditions that surround many such bilinguals and the poor-quality of instruction.

A language problem is sometimes perceived as caused by 'strong' forms of bilingual education. Such education, it is sometimes argued, will cause social unrest or disintegration in society. Fostering the minority language and ethnic differences might provoke conflict and disharmony, political and social unrest. The response is generally that 'strong' forms of bilingual education do not create a language problem, but rather, lead to better integration, harmony and social peace. The evidence suggests that developing bilingualism and biliteracy within 'strong' bilingual education leads to higher achievement across the curriculum and therefore a better usage of human resources in a country's economy and less wastage of talent. Fostering self-esteem, self-identity and a more positive attitude to schooling through such bilingual education may also relate to increased social harmony and contentment.

Within this 'problem' orientation, there not only exists the desire to remove differences between groups to achieve a common culture. There can be the positive desire for intervention to improve the position of language minorities. 'Whether the orientation is represented by malicious attitudes resolving to eradicate, invalidate, quarantine or inoculate, or comparatively benign ones concerned with remediation and "improvement," the central activity remains that of problem-solving' (Ruiz, 1984: 21).

Language as a Right

A different orientation from that of 'language as a problem' is thinking of language as a basic human right. Just as there are often individual rights in choice of religion, so, it is argued, there should be an individual right to choice of language, and to bilingual education. Just as there are attempts to eradicate discrimination based on color and creed, so people within this orientation will argue that language prejudice and discrimination need to be eradicated in a democratic society by establishing language rights (May, 2011; Skutnabb-Kangas, 2000, 2015).

At one level, language rights concern protection from discrimination. Many language minorities (e.g. Māori, Native Americans) have suffered considerable discrimination. Skutnabb-Kangas (2000) vividly portrays the oppression of the Kurdish language by torture, imprisonment, confiscation of books, dismissal from jobs, even execution. Ngugi wa Thiong'o (2005) depicts the discrimination that African people have suffered economically, politically, culturally and linguistically from a European colonialist attitude and Americanization. For Ngugi wa Thiong'o, African language rights concern self-regulation and self-determination, and not just non-discrimination. Ngugi wa Thiong'o spoke Gĩkũyũ as a child, in the fields, in the home, and in the community. However, he was sent to a colonial school that taught solely through the medium of English. The language of education was at variance with the language of his culture. Gĩkũyũ was suppressed, as he vividly recalls:

> In Kenya, English became much more than a language: it was the language, and all others had to bow before it in deference. Thus one of the most humiliating experiences was to be caught speaking Gĩkũyũ in the vicinity of the school. The culprit was given corporal punishment – three to five strokes of the cane on bare buttocks – or was made to carry a metal plate around the neck with the inscription: I AM STUPID or I AM A DONKEY. Sometimes the culprits were fined money they could hardly afford' (Thiong'o, 2005: 149).

Such discrimination continues today. In Arizona, in the **context** of the state's enforcement of **Proposition 203** to restrict bilingual education (see Chapter 9), some educators believed (and were led to believe) that the proposition prohibited any use of Spanish or other languages in the classroom. One principal attempted to ban the use of Spanish school-wide, even in the cafeteria and out on the playground. At another Arizona school, a teacher was fired for hitting students speaking Spanish in her classroom. When asked to comment on the case, the state's Superintendent of Public Instruction essentially praised the teacher for enforcing English-only rules in her classroom, but noted it was wrong for her to hit the students (Wright, 2005b).

Kloss (1998) makes a distinction between tolerance-oriented rights and promotion-oriented rights (see also Wiley, 2015). At a promotion-oriented level, language rights are more positive and constructive, asserting the right to use a minority language freely, including in all official contexts. Such rights flourish particularly where there is relatively greater individual and group self-determination. However, language rights can sometimes be idealistic rather than realistic. For example, if all majority and minority European languages were used in the European Parliament, translation and interpretation would be cost-prohibitive. In South Africa, it is costly to produce the full range of educational resources (for different ages, curriculum areas, and ability levels) for the 11 official languages. Yet to privilege one or more languages over the others will be at a cost to the speakers (e.g. less educational success) and the languages themselves (e.g. **language shift**).

A 'non-rights', laissez-faire approach to minority languages serves to strengthen the already powerful and prestigious languages. Therefore, some form of intervention on linguistic rights becomes important for the protection and preservation of minority languages, particularly in public domains. Governments typically have less power in economic activities, making rights in government-controlled areas (e.g. law, local government, education) more possible.

Such language rights may be derived from personal, human, legal and constitutional rights. Personal language rights will draw on individual liberties and the right to freedom of individual expression (May, 2011). It has also been argued that there may be language rights in group rather than individual terms. Languages are rarely spoken in solitude but in pairs, groups and networks. The rights of language groups may be expressed in terms of the importance of the preservation of **heritage language** and culture communities and expressed as 'rights to protection' and 'rights to participation'. This includes rights to some form of self-determination and social justice. May (2011) argues the case for greater ethnocultural and ethnolinguistic self-determination and democracy as nation states fragment.

Group rights are likely to be contested. What constitutes a group (or **identity** with a group) for collective linguistic human rights, and defining who is, or is not, a member of a language community is problematic. Also, nation states, and liberalism as a political ideology are both built on the notion of individual citizenship rights and not group rights (May, 2011). Such collective rights may at times clash with individual rights and freedoms (e.g. local employment when a person has the professional qualifications but not bilingual competence). C. Hoffmann (2000) cites the case of Catalonia (Spain) where 'access to white-collar jobs has become increasingly restricted to those with fluency in Catalan ... amid claims that this situation pushes disproportionately high numbers of non-Catalan speakers into low-status occupations' (p. 435).

Language rights are inclusive of users of non-standard dialects. In the US, the College Composition and Communication (CCCC) – the predecessor of the National Council of Teachers of English (NCTE) – passed the controversial *Students' Right to Their Own Language* (SRTOL) resolution in 1974. The resolution was reaffirmed and broadened by NCTE in 2003 (Scott *et al.*, 2008). The resolution primarily addressed the debates among composition teachers about requiring students to adhere to the norms of standard American English in their writing. The resolution begins, 'We affirm the students' right to their own patterns of varieties of language – the dialects of their nurture or whatever dialects in which they find their own identity and style'. A detailed statement providing background on SRTOL also affirms the importance of students learning to write in standard American English (called edited American English in the document) (Perryman-Clark *et al.*, 2014). A driving force behind SRTOL were a number of African American scholars, educators and instructors of composition, many of whom worked in programs with a predominance of African American students. However, SRTOL applies as well to minority-language speakers and writers (Scott *et al.*, 2008). Reflection and debate over the SRTOL continues (Perryman-Clark *et al.*, 2014).

A further level of language rights is international deriving mostly from the United Nations, UNESCO, the Council of Europe and the European Union. For example, the 2007 *United Nations Declaration on the Rights of Indigenous Peoples* states in Article 3 that 'Indigenous peoples have the right to self-determination. By virtue of that right they freely determine their political status and freely pursue their economic, social and cultural development.' Such peoples are also accorded the 'right to establish and control their educational systems and institutions providing education in their own languages (Article 14.1). Language rights are also affirmed for children (see Box 17.1). The European Charter for Regional or Minority Languages (Council of Europe, 1992) tends to be more about standards than rights, but it has options (e.g. use of a minority language in pre-school education) from which states can choose (Grin *et al.*, 2003). Education is one of the domains in which the Contracting States undertake to protect and promote minority languages in their territories. Such education can range from being exclusively in the minority language (**heritage language education**) to dual language education, and to other forms of bilingual education where there is a demand and sufficient numbers. However, individual countries have often ignored such international declarations or violated the agreements (Skutnabb-Kangas, 2015). Nevertheless, a struggle over language rights is important. Non-recognition of language human rights (as often occurs among immigrant language minorities) is in itself a form of oppression, **domination** and injustice (K. Hall, 2002).

Box 17.1 United Nations' Convention on the Rights of the Child

Tove Skutnabb-Kangas (2015) provides an analysis of where linguistic human rights may be found in various international and regional human rights documents. She notes that at the international level, the 1989 *United Nations' Convention on the Rights of the Child* (CRC) provides the best protections to date. The CRC addresses a wide range of basic rights associated with child welfare, and includes brief mention of language. Skutnabb-Kangas explains:

'Article 29, subparagraph (d) stipulates that education should be directed to the development of *respect for the child's parents, his or her own cultural identity, language, and values*. Article 30 provides: *In those States in which ethnic, religious or linguistic minorities or persons of indigenous origin exist, a child belonging to such a minority or who is indigenous shall not be denied the right, in community with other members of his or her own group, to enjoy his or her own culture, to profess and practice his or her own religion, **or to use his or her own language*** (emphasis added)' (p. 194).

As of 2016, the US and Somalia are the only UN member countries who have not ratified the CRC (see http://www.unicef.org/crc/index_30225.html).

The kind of rights, apart from language rights, that ethnic groups may claim include: protection, membership of their ethnic group and separate existence, non-discrimination and equal treatment, education and information in their ethnic language, the preferred script of the language, freedom to worship, freedom of belief, freedom of movement, employment, peaceful assembly and association, political representation and involvement, and administrative autonomy. Thus language rights are a component in a wider constellation of rights for minorities.

In the US, the rights of the individual are a major part of democracy. From the expert perspective of a civil rights lawyer, Del Valle (2003) analyzes how advocates of language rights in the US can take much heart from an early history of tolerance, from the absence of a history of monolingualism in the US, the growth and uses of the 14th Amendment of the US Constitution (e.g. equal protection clause), and supportive court cases (e.g. *Meyer v. Nebraska*). Del Valle shows that English-only laws tend to be 'more symbolic than restrictive' (p. 79) but that there has been a 'proliferation of English-only workplace rules enforced by employers of bilingual employees. Unlike state-wide or public English-only laws, these rules can be easily passed, explicitly, consciously, and in writing by an employer without company-wide discussion ... that may be challenged in court' (p. 118). Del Valle's wide-ranging examination of language rights in the US includes interrogation, searches, interpreters, document translation, unfairly removing bilingual jurors and commercial labeling, and serves to demonstrate that linguistic human rights goes much deeper than national and international laws and charters, as such rights are enacted at a local level, in courts, workplaces and, not least, classrooms.

In the US, language rights have a history of being tested in courtrooms. This is significantly different from European experience where language rights have rarely been tried in law. From the early 1920s to the present, there has been a continuous debate in US courts of law regarding the legal status of language minority rights (Del Valle, 2003). To gain short-term protection and a medium-term guarantee for minority languages, legal challenges have become an important part of the language rights movement in the US. The legal battles are not just couched in minority language versus majority language contests. The test cases also concern children versus schools, parents versus school boards, state versus the federal authority (Del Valle, 2003). Whereas minority language activists among the Basques in Spain and the Welsh in Britain have been taken to court by the central government for their actions (C.H. Williams, 2007), US minority language parents and activists have taken the central and regional government to court. Two connected examples will illustrate.

A crucial Supreme Court case in the US was *Brown v. Board of Education* in 1954. African American children were deliberately segregated in southern schools. The Supreme Court ruled that equality in the US educational system was denied to such African American children owing to segregation from their peers. Segregation denied equal educational opportunity through a crucial element in classroom learning: peer interaction. The Court decided that education must be made available to all children on equal terms, as guaranteed by the 14th Amendment. A segregationist doctrine of separate but equal education was inherently unequal.

A landmark in US bilingual education was a lawsuit. A court case was brought on behalf of Chinese students against the San Francisco School District in 1970. The case concerned whether or not non-English speaking students received equal educational opportunity when instructed in a language they could not understand. The failure to address the linguistic needs of the students was alleged to violate both the equal protection clause of the 14th Amendment and Title VI of the Civil Rights Act of 1964. The case, known as *Lau v. Nichols*, was rejected by the federal district court and a court of appeals, but was accepted by the Supreme Court in 1974. The verdict prohibited English **submersion** programs, and required school districts to offer programs that address the unique linguistic and academic needs of students not yet proficient in English. Soon after the US Department of Education issued 'Lau remedies'. The remedies strongly encouraged districts to adopt bilingual education programs as a means of complying with the Supreme Courts ruling in *Lau*. The remedies also helped to broaden the goals of bilingual education to include the possible maintenance of minority language and culture. The Lau remedies created some expansion in the use of minority languages in schools, although they rarely resulted in strong forms of bilingual education designed to help students develop and maintain their home languages. As time passed the *Lau Remedies* were challenged given the court did not mandate bilingual education or any other specific program. Nonetheless, for the purposes of this chapter, the *Lau* case is symbolic of the dynamic and continuing contest to establish language rights in the US particularly through testing the law in the courtroom.

Language rights are not only expressed in lawsuits. Language rights are often expressed at the grassroots level by protests and pressure groups, by local action, assertiveness and argument. For example, by such means the Kohanga Reo (language nests) movement in New Zealand provides a grass-roots-instituted immersion pre-school experience for the Māori people (May, 2011). One example of grass-roots expression of 'language as a right' is the Celtic (Ireland, Scotland and Wales) experience. In these countries, it is bottom-up (rather than top-down) 'grassroots' movements that created pre-school playgroups, 'mother and toddler' groups and adult language learning classes for heritage language preservation (I.W. Williams, 2003). Strong activism and non-violent but insistent demands led to the establishment of Welsh heritage language elementary schools, particularly in urban areas (C.H. Williams, 2014). Not without struggle, opposition and antagonistic bureaucracy, parents obtained the right for education in the indigenous tongue. Such pressure groups have contained parents who speak the indigenous language, and those who speak only English, yet wish their children to be taught in the heritage language of the area and become thoroughly bilingual (Sallabank, 2013).

In North American and British society, no formal recognition is usually made in politics or the legal system to categories or groups of people based on their culture, language or race. Rather the focus is on individual rights. The accent is on individual equality of opportunity, individual rewards based on individual merit. Policies of non-discrimination, for example, tend to be based on individual rather than group rights (Patten & Kymlicka, 2003).

Language minority groups will nevertheless argue for rewards and justice based on their existence as a definable group in society. Sometimes based on territorial rights, often based on ethnic identity, such language group rights have been regarded as a way of redressing injustices to language minorities. This may be a temporary step on the way to full individual citizenship rights as participative democracy tends to favor the equality of each individual rather than group privilege. Alternatively, language minorities may claim the right to some independent power, some measure of decision-making and some guarantee of self-determination. This is typically seen by the majority language group as a step on the road to self-determination.

When language group rights are obtained, 'even very little autonomy granted to indigenous peoples is usually viewed with a great deal of suspicion, and often with outright opposition, because it may infringe on the individual rights of majority group members' (May, 2011: 288–289). An example is when English monolinguals cannot obtain teaching or local government posts in a bilingual community, and they feel their rights to employment have been infringed.

Two notes of caution about language rights need sounding. First Bruthiaux (2009) argues that the financial implications of language rights need considering so that any implementation is reasonable and not idealistic. For example, when the number of official languages within the European Union rose from 11 in 1995 to 23 in 2007, the costs of interpretation and translation potentially became exceptionally large. In any cost-benefit analysis, the options for linguistic diversity are neither none nor infinite (Grin, 2005). Towards the 'zero' end of the dimension power is transferred to dominant languages; towards the 'infinite' end costs may become prohibitive. Also, the costs of interpretation and translation can be calculated, whereas the benefits may be less measurable but nevertheless valuable to the status of a language. Second, lofty rhetoric about individual rights can hide coercion, conformity and empty promises. When some school administrators express a 'language as right' orientation, they tend to provide

---

Box 17.2 Guidelines for communicating rights to non-native speakers of English

An international group of linguists, psychologists, lawyers, and interpreters drafted *Guidelines for Communicating Rights to Non-Native Speakers of English in Australia, England and Wales, and the USA*. In 2016 these *Guidelines* were endorsed by several national and international language and linguistic professional organizations (see http://www.aaal.org/?page=CommunicationRights). The Preamble states, in part:

> *Suspects' interview rights, referred to as Miranda Rights in the United States and as police cautions in Australia, England and Wales, are country-specific mechanisms for protecting due process in criminal investigations and trials. These rights include the right not to incriminate oneself. … The purpose of the requirement to communicate these rights/cautions to suspects is to ensure that those in criminal proceedings know their fundamental rights under the law. A failure to protect the rights of individuals during interviews risks the integrity of any investigation.*
>
> *… People who have learned another language later in life process information differently in this second language than in their native language. This processing difference compounds their linguistic and cultural difficulties in communicating in English. Even speakers who can maintain a conversation in English may not have sufficient proficiency to understand complex sentences used to communicate rights/cautions, legal terms, or English spoken at fast conversational rates. They also may not be familiar with assumptions made in the adversarial legal system. Yet, like other vulnerable populations, non-native speakers of English have the right to equal treatment. Therefore, if they do not have mastery of English, it is crucial that their rights be delivered to them in the language they can understand.*

The *Guidelines* make the following recommendations to law enforcement agencies on the wording and communicating of rights/cautions:
1. Use standardized version in plain English (clear English).
2. Develop standardized statements in other languages.
3. Inform suspects about access to an interpreter at the beginning of the interview.
4. Present each right individually.
5. Do not determine understanding by using yes or no questions.
6. Adopt an in-your-own-words requirement.
7. Videorecord the interview.

---

the legal minimum in support services for language minority students. Words do not often relate to action.

Language as a Resource

An alternative perspective to 'language as a problem' and 'language as a right' is the idea of language as a personal, community and regional resource. Bilingualism can provide an intellectual (see Chapter 7), cultural, economic (see Chapter 19), social, communication (see Chapter 19) and citizenship resource (Lo Bianco, 2001). Bilingualism is seen as an asset, both for communities and for individuals. Languages aid individual participation in public, leisure and private lives. For example, public participation is aided when a person can operate in the different languages of varying groups, fostering inclusion by being able to debate and persuade in the language of the group.

The movement in mainland Europe for increased **multilingualism** (e.g. in Spain, Scandinavia, Slovenia) fits into this orientation. Under the general heading of 'language as a resource' also come minority and lesser-used languages as a cultural and social resource. While languages may be viewed in terms of their economic bridge building potential (e.g. foreign trade), languages may also be supported for their ability to build social bridges across different groups (e.g. where there is religious conflict), and bridges for increasing intercultural understanding.

The recent trend in mainland Europe, for example, has been to attempt to expand foreign language education. In many regions of the world, English as an international language has been added to the school curriculum. Second and third language study is increasingly viewed as an important resource to promote foreign trade, world influence, even peace. The paradox is that while bilingual education to support minority languages has tended to be undervalued in the US, the current trend is to appreciate English speakers who learn a second language to ensure a continued major role for the US in world politics and the world economy (Wright, 2010). There is a tendency to value the acquisition of languages while devaluing the language minorities who own them (e.g. Spanish, Arabic, Chinese Mandarin, Hindi and Korean speakers in the US). While integration and assimilation is still the dominant ideology in US internal politics, external politics increasingly demands bilingual citizens. Dual language bilingual education programs often created by Latino activists since the 1960s have been of increasing interest to some middle class parents who see, for example, possible employment and economic gains for their children (see Chapter 11).

Ovando and Combs (2017) observe the irony of English monolinguals being encouraged to study a foreign language at great cost and with little efficiency while at the same time the linguistic gifts that children from non-English language backgrounds bring to schools are being destroyed. It is thus ironic that many US and UK students spend time in school learning some of the very languages that children of immigrants are pressurized to forget (Ricento, 2009). The politics of immigration serve to deny bilingualism; the politics of global trade serve increasingly to demand bilingualism and multilingualism. One result is that, along with the UK, the US is a 'graveyard for languages because of its historical ability to absorb immigrants by the millions and extinguish their **mother tongues** within a few generations' (Rumbaut, 2009: 64).

In the US, the idea of language as a resource not only refers to the development of a second language in monolingual speakers; it also refers to the preservation of languages other than English. For example, children whose home language is Spanish or German, Italian or Mandarin, Greek or Japanese, Hmong or French have a home language that can be utilized as a resource (see Chapter 5). One case is Spanish speakers in the US who together make the US the fifth largest Spanish-speaking country in the world. Just as water in the reservoir and oil in the oil field are preserved as basic resources and commodities, so a language such as Spanish, despite being difficult to measure and define as a resource, may be preserved for the common economic, social and cultural good. Suppression of language minorities, particularly by the school system, may be seen as economic, social and cultural wastage. Instead, such languages are a natural resource that can be exploited for cultural, spiritual and educational growth as well as for economic, commercial and political gain.

Within the 'language as a resource' orientation, there tends to be the assumption that linguistic diversity does not cause separation nor less integration in society. Rather, it is possible that national unity and linguistic diversity can co-exist. Unity and diversity are not necessarily incompatible. Tolerance and cooperation between groups may be as possible with linguistic diversity as they would be unlikely when such linguistic diversity is repressed.

A frequent debate concerns which languages are a resource? The favored languages tend to be those that are both international and particularly valuable in international trade. A lower place is given in the status rankings to minority languages that are small, regional and of less perceived value in the international marketplace. For example, in England, French was traditionally placed in schools in the first division. German, Spanish, Danish, Dutch, Modern Greek, Italian and Portuguese were the major European languages placed into the second division. Despite large numbers of mother tongue Bengali, Panjabi, Urdu, Gujarati, Hindi and Turkish speakers, the politics of English education relegates these languages, and many others, to a lowly position in the school curriculum. Thus a caste system of languages can be created.

At a minimal level, a **language-as-a-resource orientation** can open space for the use of students' home languages in schools, even in non-bilingual classrooms. Teachers who adopt this orientation recognize that students' home languages are a strength they bring into the classroom and a valuable resource upon which they can build. Providing brief explanations, previews, and reviews in the home languages, and allowing students to use their home languages to help each other in the classroom can enable students to comprehend and complete academic tasks in the majority language (Wright, 2015). A language-as-a-resource opens space for translanguaging pedagogies and practices that may lead to greater academic success (O. García & Li Wei, 2014). Views of language-as-a-resource can eventually lead to stronger forms of bilingual education.

To conclude: while the three language orientations have differences, they also share certain common aims: of national unity, of individual rights, and of fluency in the majority language (e.g. English) being important to economic opportunities. The basic difference tends to be whether monolingualism in the majority language or bilingualism should be encouraged as a means to achieving those ends. All three orientations connect language with politics, economics, society and culture. Each orientation recognizes that language is not simply a means of communication but is also connected with socialization into the local and wider society, as well as a powerful symbol of heritage and identity. Each uses liberal values such as individual freedom and equality of opportunity to advance its cause (R. Schmidt, 2009). The differences between the three orientations lie in the socialization and identity to be fostered: assimilation or pluralism, integration or separatism, monoculturalism or multiculturalism.

United States Language Orientations

That the three orientations have common aims as well as differences is illustrated in the case of the US. The US has long been a willing receptacle of peoples of many languages: German, French, Yiddish, Polish, Italian, Irish, Greek, Russian, Welsh, Arabic, Mandarin and Cantonese Chinese, Korean, Japanese and particularly Spanish to name just a few examples. 'A melting pot' ideology aimed to assimilate and unify immigrants, especially via English language hegemony (R. Schmidt, 2009). The dream became an integrated United States with shared social, political and economic ideals. Quotes from US Presidents and presidential candidates illustrate this 'melting pot' attitude. In 1917 Theodore Roosevelt declared:

> We must have but one flag. We must have but one language. That must be the language of the Declaration of Independence, of Washington's Farewell Address, of Lincoln's Gettysburg Speech and Second Inaugural. We cannot tolerate any attempt to oppose or supplant the language and culture that has come down to us from the builders of the republic with the language and culture of any European country. The greatness of this nation depends on the swift assimilation of the aliens she welcomes to her shores. Any force which attempts to retard that assimilative process is a force hostile to the highest interests of our country. (quoted in Wagner, 1981: 32)

The same year, Roosevelt urged (or warned) all immigrants to adopt the English language:

It would be not merely a misfortune but a crime to perpetuate differences of language in this country... We should provide for every immigrant by day schools for the young, and night schools for the adult, the chance to learn English; and if after say five years he has not learned English, he should be sent back to the land from whence he came. (quoted in J.M. González, 1979)

President Reagan's view in the late 1980s was that it is 'absolutely wrong and against American concepts to have a bilingual education program that is now openly, admittedly dedicated to preserving their native language and never getting them adequate in English so they can go out into the job market and participate' (quoted in Crawford, 2000: 120).

President George W. Bush had some proficiency in Spanish and used it on occasion in speeches and interviews, yet his signature education bill, No Child Left Behind, ended the **Bilingual Education Act** and represented a strong **assimilationist** perspective (see Chapter 9). President Barack Obama made positive comments about linguistic diversity and occasionally expressed concerns about immigrant students losing their native languages. Yet education priorities and policies during his administration did little to promote bilingual education or reverse the assimilationist focus of federal education policies. During the 2016 presidential campaign, three of the major Republican primary candidates were Spanish speakers – Jeb Bush, Marco Rubio and Ted Cruz; both Rubio and Cruz were the children of immigrants from Cuba, and Bush's wife was an immigrant from Mexico. None spoke openly in favor of bilingual education, though all were defensive of their bilingual skills and language diversity in general when attacked by fellow candidate Donald Trump (whose wife Melania is an immigrant from Slovenia and is reputed to speak Slovene, English, French, German, Italian and Serbo-Croation). Trump had declared, 'Well, I think that when you get right down to it, we're a nation that speaks English. I think that, while we're in this nation, we should be speaking English. ... Whether people like it or not, that's how we assimilate' (The Hollywood Reporter, 2015: 1). Trump even chastised Jeb Bush for using Spanish on the campaign trail saying 'he should really set the example by speaking English while in the United States' (p. 1). Trump, who made headlines with his frequent disparaging comments about Muslims, Mexicans and other minorities, and who pledged to build a wall between the US and Mexico, won the primary election and became the Republican Party's nominee for president in the general election. On the Democrat side, Vice Presidential candidate Tim Kaine readily showed off the Spanish speaking skills he picked up as a Catholic missionary in Honduras. Reactions to Kaine's Spanish ranged from praise, to ridicule, to charges of pandering to Hispanic voters (Flegenhiemer, 2016). Donald Trump defeated Hillary Clinton in the general election on November 8, 2016. The US now has the paradox of a monolingual President who has been critical of immigrants and bilingualism, and an immigrant First Lady who is only the second to have been born outside of the US (following Louisa Catherine Johnson Adams, wife of 6th president John Quincy Adams, born in England) and who is the first non-native English speaker and first truly multilingual First Lady in US history. The assimilationist melting pot attitude among many Americans continues.

The Advance of English in the United States

Within the US, basic differences in 'language orientation' are especially exemplified in the movement to make English the official rather than the de facto national language. The political debate over the place of English in the US illustrates how languages can be alternatively seen as a problem, right or resource.

At the federal level, there is no reference to language in either the 1776 Declaration of Independence or the 1789 United States Constitution, the two founding documents of the US. However, in the last 25 years, there have been proposals to add amendments to the Constitution that would name English as the official language. Considerable debate about Official English or English-only legislation has occurred (Dicker, 2003).

In April 1981, Senator S.I. Hayakawa, a Californian Republican, proposed an English Language Amendment to the US Constitution. This aimed at making English the official language of the US so as, he said, to develop further participative democracy and unification. The Amendment failed but it helped spawn the 'English-only' or 'official English' movement in the US. US English was founded in 1983 by Senator Hayakawa and John Tanton, who was particularly interested in restrictions on immigration and population control. While failing to pass federal legislation declaring English as the official language of the US, the movement has been more successful lobbying at the state level. By 2016 31 states had some form of legislation declaring English to be the official language of the state.

The English-only movement argues that English is the social glue that bonds diverse Americans and overcomes differences. English is therefore best learnt early (e.g. by mainstreaming) to counteract the tendency for immigrants to refuse to learn English. If heritage languages are allowed to flourish, there will be conflict, separatism and inter-group hostility.

As Barker and Giles (2002) found in one of the few empirical studies of the English-only movement, Anglo-Americans supporting the English-only position believe that Latino vitality (e.g. economic and political power and status) is growing in the US as Anglo vitality is decreasing. In this research, attachment to a traditional conceptualization of 'good Americans' was connected to an English-only position. Less contact with the Spanish language was associated with greater support for the English-only position. Those with lower levels of education were more likely to support such a position, as were those who were blue-collar or unemployed. Such groups may perceive Latinos as more of a threat to their chances of enhancement and improvement. This suggests that the roots of English-only may lie not only in personal insecurity and intolerance of difference but also in perceived threats to power, position and privilege, plus a fear of difference and competition for perceived scarce resources (Barker *et al.*, 2001).

For English-only advocates, bilingual education is seen as promoting separatist language communities, a division in US society, an indifference to English, and making English speakers strangers in their own localities (Crawford, 2003). Instead, the English language should unite and harmonize. Learning English early in school, and learning curriculum content through English, would produce, it is claimed, integrated neighborhoods. The preferred immigrant is someone who learns English quickly as well as acquiring US customs and culture, acquires skills that are useful to the economic prosperity of the country, works hard and achieves the US dream. For critics of bilingual education in the US, such education only serves to destroy rather than deliver that dream.

The movement for English as the proclaimed US national language has not been purely about English and national unity. Racism, bigotry, paranoia, xenophobia, white superiority and dominance have also been present (Crawford, 2004). A Memorandum by Dr John Tanton, when Chairman of US English, revealed the darker side: 'As Whites see their power and control over their lives declining, will they simply go quietly into the night? Or will there be an explosion?' (quoted in Crawford, 2004: 136). This Memorandum went on further to pose perceived threats from Latinos: bribery as an accepted culture, Roman Catholicism as cultivating church authority rather than national authority, the non-use of birth control and fast population growth, high drop-out rates in school and low educability. This suggests scapegoating, the displacement of fears about social, political and economic positioning onto language, and using English as a means of asserting cultural and economic superiority (Dicker, 2003).

Schmidt (2009) argues that Latinos are surrounded by English-language hegemony in the US. Such hegemony refers to the apparent consent of oppressed Latinos to their own domination by the most powerful class in society who are monolingual English language speakers. 'This hegemonic status of the English language is supported as well by the frequent conflation of race, class and language in US society' (p. 142). To some, Latino can mean a different race, an underclass of 'maids, leaf blowers, gardeners ... and a foreign identity' (García, 2009b: 153), with an inherent perceived explanation for failure by being a Latino. Spanish can then be stigmatized as a barrier to social class and economic mobility. A Spanish accent or Spanglish becomes associated with low achievement and illiteracy. Bilingual neighborhoods become equated with slum areas. 'The hegemonic status of the English language, not only in the US itself but increasingly throughout the world, renders English dominance so powerful that living one's public life through it exclusively is experienced as "common sense" for any rational person trying to advance her interests in the "real" world' (Schmidt, 2009: 147).

While the debate about integration and pluralism will be examined in the next chapter, there is agreement about certain desirable outcomes between the positions of the English-only group and the 'English-plus' pro-bilingual response in the US (e.g. both agree about children becoming fluent in English). The difference is in the route to its achievement. For the English-only group, English language skills are best acquired through English monolingual education. For the English-plus group, skills in the English language can be successfully fostered through 'strong' forms of bilingual education. Both groups appear to acknowledge that full English proficiency is important in opening doors to higher education, the economy and the occupational market. Full proficiency in the majority language is usually equated with a route to equality of educational and vocational opportunity.

However, as Crawford (2003: 7) suggests, the danger of English-plus is 'plus what?' If 'plus what' means 'the priority of bilingual education was not to teach English but to maintain other languages', it fails to capture the aspirations of children and parents, and is a red rag to the political English-only bull. The goal of bilingualism must be strongly identified as meaning high competence in English and not just in a heritage language. Strong forms of bilingual education can deliver that agenda.

As Chapter 12 shows, there is considerable evidence to support 'strong' versions of bilingual education and hence for the 'English-plus' position. Such evidence supports the use of the home minority language in the classroom at no cost to majority **language competence**. Achievement across the curriculum, achievement in subjects as diverse as science and social studies, mathematics and foreign language learning would not seem to suffer but to be enhanced by 'strong' forms of bilingual education. Research on the cognitive effects of bilingualism supports the ownership of two languages to enhance rather than impoverish intellectual functioning.

However, the dominant majority often see bilingual education as creating national disunity rather than unity, disintegration rather than integration. The frequent criticism of bilingual education is that it serves to promote differences rather than similarities, to separate rather than integrate. In the US, the expressed public viewpoint tends to be for unity, integration and assimilation of immigrant, language minority communities. Indeed, the strongest arguments for bilingual education on cognitive and educational grounds may well fail unless a strong argument can be advanced for linguistic and **cultural pluralism**.

Conclusion

Whether the surrounding community and society sees language as a problem, right or resource affects the role of languages in a school. When a 'language as a problem' attitude is dominant, bilingual education is likely to be discouraged. Language rights may give bilingual education a protected entitlement to exist. The 'language as a resource' orientation may allow bilingual education to flourish. Thus these three orientations have different outcomes for bilinguals and bilingual education.

But political debates about bilingual education go deeper into politics and personal arguments. Does bilingual education lead to greater or lesser tolerance, a common or a separate identity, a sense of anomie (normlessness) or an ability to belong to two cultures simultaneously? Are language minority children taught (rightly or wrongly) to be in conflict or at peace with the majority? Is bilingual education the arena for a power struggle between majority and minority? These questions are examined in the next chapter through the central debate on assimilation and pluralism.

Key Points in This Chapter

- ➤ Three perspectives on languages depict variations among people: language as a problem, right or resource.
- ➤ The 'language as a problem' is currently a prevalent political and mass media viewpoint in the US where the cultural assimilation of immigrants is sought, but not necessarily their economic assimilation.
- ➤ Language rights can be individual, group and international. In the US, rights are tested in law courts.
- ➤ 'Language as a resource' includes languages as a personal, community and societal resource.
- ➤ Bilingualism can provide a communication, intellectual, cultural, economic, social, and citizenship resource.
- ➤ The place of English in the US is frequently contested, with English-only groups asking for English as the sole official language and the removal of bilingual education.

Suggested Further Reading

Hornberger, N.H. (Ed.). (2007). *Honoring Richard Ruiz and his work on language planning and bilingual education*. Bristol, UK: Multilingual Matters.

Irujo, X., & Miglio, V. (Eds.). (2013). *Language rights and cultural diversity*. Reno, NV: Center for Basque Studies, University of Nevada, Reno.

📖 May, S. (2011). *Language and minority rights: Ethnicity, nationalism and the politics of language* (2nd ed.). New York, NY: Routledge.

📖 Perryman-Clark, S., Kirkland, D. E., & Jackson, A. (Eds.). (2014). *Students' rights to their own language: A critical sourcebook*. New York, NY: Bedford/St. Martin's.

📖 Pupavac, V. (2012). *Language rights: From free speech to linguistic governance*. New York, NY: Palgrave Macmillan.

On the Web

💻 English Plus vs. English Only (League of United Latin American Citizens)
http://lulac.org/advocacy/issues/english_vs_spansih/

💻 James Crawford's Language Policy Web Site and Emporium
http://www.languagepolicy.net/

💻 Language Rights – Interview with Colin Williams (video)
https://youtu.be/3x81y0yg13Y

💻 Ted Talk – Suzanne Talhouk: Don't Kill Your Language (video)
https://www.ted.com/talks/suzanne_talhouk_don_t_kill_your_language

Discussion Questions

(1) What policies, programs, or leaders in your local area appear to take a language-as-problem orientation? What impact does this orientation have on bilingual students and communities? How do such local language issues connect to topics such as immigration, racism, politics, employment and religion in your community?

(2) How can viewing language as a resource help mitigate debates between those viewing language as a problem and those viewing language as a right?

(3) How are debates over language and language policy in the US or other nations linked to larger issues of immigration and immigrants? Are the debates about language, or more about the people who happen to speak those languages? Organize a group presentation or debate in class, where each of the three subgroups takes one of the three orientations.

Study Activities

(1) Visit a local school to learn more about the programs and services for bilingual students. Determine if these programs take a language as problem, right, or resource orientation. If language as problem, what changes could be made to shift it towards a right or resource orientation?

(2) Conduct an internet search for speeches, comments, and position statements of local or national politicians or candidates running for public office as related to language. Analyze these to determine the orientation this individual takes towards language (i.e. problem, right, resource). How might you respond to either challenge or support this individual's views?

(3) Explore the website of US English (http://www.usenglish.org/). What arguments do they give for making English the official language of the United States? How might you counter some of these arguments? What recent activities has the organization been involved in, and how successful have they been? What does this reveal about language orientations in the United States?

Bilingualism and Bilingual Education: Ideology, Identity and Empowerment

CHAPTER 18

Bilingualism and Bilingual Education: Ideology, Identity and Empowerment

Introduction

Politicians, policymakers and the public have varying agendas about languages. Some wish to assimilate different language groups to a homogeneous society of **monolinguals**, others are keen to retain linguistic diversity. Some language minorities dream of self-sustainability and self-determination. Others aspire to internationalism (e.g. Europeanization) and globalism. Education for bilingual students is impacted by a range of ideologies, which in turn may impact students' identity. **Empowerment** and the healing of past language minority discrimination can enable students to develop positive bilingual identities and higher levels of academic success. We explore each of these issues below.

Ideology and Bilingualism

Bourhis (2001) proposes four ideologies related to language minorities and **bilingualism**: pluralism, civic, **assimilation** and ethnist:

(1) *Pluralist ideology* tends to assert an individual's liberty to own, learn and use two or more languages (e.g. in school, work). This right is then supported by those in power by promotion-oriented language policies (Wiley, 2015). Given that a **language minority** pays taxes, then 'it is equitable that state funds be distributed to support the cultural and linguistic activities of both the majority and the minority group' (Bourhis, 2001: 11). Schools, the judiciary and civil administration will expect to operate bilingually, where reasonable, and not in opposition to national coherence and unity. Canada's Official Languages Act (1969, 1988) and Multiculturalism Act (1988) reflect such a pluralist ideology.

(2) *Civic ideology* expects language minorities to adopt the public values of the politically dominant majority while allowing freedom in the private values of individuals (e.g. to a minority language and **culture**). But no public funding of the language minority is expected. Instead civic ideology 'is characterized by an official state policy of non-intervention and non-support of the minority languages and cultures' (Bourhis, 2001: 12). This is considered as a tolerance-oriented language policy (Wiley, 2015).

(3) *Assimilation ideology* tends to argue that there may be some areas of private values where the state has a right to intervene. Language is such an area. Immigrants are expected to abandon their **heritage language**. This may be voluntarily and gradually across generations, or speedily by state regulation in public domains (e.g. exclusion of minority languages in schools). The politically and economically dominant group often has a vested interest in preserving its privileged position by asserting that its majority language is a symbol and creator of a unified and integrated nation. In contrast, minority languages and cultures are seen as potentially divisive and conflictive, working against national loyalty and allegiance by producing factions. Many forms of restricted-oriented language policies facilitate this ideology (Wiley, 2015).

(4) *Ethnist ideology* encourages or forces language minorities to give up their language and culture and adopt those of the dominant group. It also attempts to prevent or exclude such minorities from assimilating legally or socially, even when such individuals seek cultural, linguistic and economic assimilation. The ideology is exclusive and defines who can be a rightful member of the dominant group or a legitimate citizen. For example, only certain racial groups are given full legal status as determined by 'blood', birth and kinship. Political, economic and social marginalization may result. Wiley (2015) terms this a repression-oriented language policy. As an extreme, ethnist ideology results in a policy of exclusion, expulsion, apartheid, ethnic cleansing, and even genocide.

The social and political questions surrounding bilingual education tend to revolve around two contrasting ideological positions – assimilation and pluralism. Assimilation is a belief that cultural groups should give up their heritage cultures and take on the host society's way of life. In contrast, pluralism believes that these groups should maintain their heritage cultures in combination with the host culture. In the US, for example, pluralists favor the state recognizing, supporting and promoting minority languages, while **assimilationists** push for national and state policies making English the sole official language. In the **context** of schools, de Jong (2011) distinguishes between those that reflect **assimilationist discourses** compared with **pluralistic discourses**. In schools that uphold assimilationist discourses, the home languages and cultures of bilingual students are devalued, and seen as a problem. In contrast, schools sustaining pluralist discourses recognize the home languages and cultures of bilingual students as rich resources for helping students learn academic content, and strive to help students develop high levels of proficiency and literacy in both languages (Wright, 2015).

We now consider assimilation and pluralism in more depth, along with potential policy alternatives.

Assimilation

Assimilation has been a favored response to the considerable immigration in the US and many other countries. Historically the US deal with immigrants has been: 'Come to this economically prosperous land, start a new and better life, but assimilate and become "American"'. As early as the 1890s, assimilationists (including Presidents such as Theodore Roosevelt and Woodrow Wilson) attacked 'hyphenated Americans' (e.g. German-Americans, Irish-Americans, etc.) accusing them of maintaining allegiance to a foreign country. The assimilationist expectation is giving up the native tongue and not taking on such 'hyphenated' dual identities. Thus, cultural unity and national solidarity are seen as achieved through assimilation. The pattern of a three-generation shift from a native language to English (see Chapter 4) among immigrant families delivers this, with 80% of the third generation being English-only speaking in the US (Salaberry, 2009a). The transition to English monolingualism and loss of bilingualism can be swift and successful, with recent trends for some minority groups showing shift to English by the 1.5 generation (Rumbaut, 2009).

The assimilationist viewpoint is pictured in the idea of a melting pot. Zangwill's (1909) play *The Melting Pot*, first performed in 1908 at the Columbia Theater in Washington, introduced the idea of diverse immigrant elements being merged to make a new homogenized whole. 'Into the Crucible with you all! God is making the American' (Act 1). The idea of the melting pot immediately offers two different perspectives. First, there is the idea that the final product, for example the US American, is made up by a contribution of all the cultural groups that enter the pot. The cultural groups melt together until the final product is a unique combination. No one ingredient dominates. Each cultural group makes its own contribution to the final product. However, this is not the usual view associated with the melting pot. Second, the melting pot often means cultural groups giving up their heritage culture and adopting that of the host culture. They have been melted into just one substance. The problem with this view is that white-skinned immigrants may 'melt' more easily than immigrants of color. For example, many Latino and Asian Americans born and raised in the US and who grew up only speaking English frequently face questions from fellow Americans such as 'What country are you from?' and 'How did you learn to speak English so well?' Such questions may appear as friendly conversation starters, harmless curiosities, or ignorance at best, yet to the recipient they can be 'microaggressions' that send subtle yet hurtful messages such as 'you're not a real American', 'you don't really belong here', and 'you will forever be a foreigner'.

An assimilationist perspective is partly based on equality of opportunity and a meritocracy that enables each individual to have a fair chance of economic prosperity. Such a view argues that the separate existence of different racial and cultural groups prevents such equality occurring. When the emphasis is on individuality in terms of rights, freedom, effort and affluence, the argument for assimilation is that language groups should not have separate privileges and rights from the rest of society. The advantage and disadvantage associated with language minority groups must be avoided so individual equality of opportunity can prevail.

Assimilationists also argue that bilingual education produces segregation, because language minority children are isolated from the mainstream society, thereby depriving them of economic, political and social opportunities. Such segregation is claimed to both impede their learning of English and produce physical segregation from mainstream students. Another element claimed by assimilationists is that bilingual education teaches children to have a separate sense of ethnic and national **identity**, for example, to be Latino rather than 'American'.

Measuring the extent to which assimilation has occurred is going to be difficult. Is assimilation measured by segregation and integration in terms of housing of immigrants, by their positions within the economic order, by the extent of intermarriage between different cultural groups or by the attitudes they exhibit? Assimilation is thus multidimensional and complex. Assimilation is neither easily defined nor easily quantified. Assimilationists may also have differing views. One example will illustrate. A few assimilationists may accept that school students should maintain their home language and culture. However, they would argue that this is the responsibility of the home or the local language community and not the school. This tolerance-oriented view (Wiley, 2015) opens space for acculturation, that is, immigrants may adopt the host society's language and culture without sacrificing their own. Other assimilationists, however, want the abandonment of the minority language and culture.

In a decade-long longitudinal study on the assimilation of children of immigrants, Rumbaut (2009) followed over 3,000 adolescent students in the 1.5 and later generations from age 14 (1992) to age 24 (2002) in South Florida and Southern California. Rumbaut found that for the 2.0 generation, preference for English increased from 81% in 1992 to 98% by 2002. By 2002 less than 45% of the 2.0 generation, and less than 29% of the 1.5 generation considered themselves to be fluent bilinguals. The move to English as the dominant or only language was thus apparent. Drawing from the same data Portes and Rumbaut (2006) used measures of family solidarity, intergenerational conflict, ambition and self-esteem. Their statistical analyses show that fluent bilinguals had the most positive profiles. For example, those fluent in English and their parents' native language were 8% more likely to hold higher educational aspirations. Those children who retained their native language without learning English showed high family solidarity, but had much lower self-esteem and ambition. They conclude that such second generation immigrants who do not become fluent bilinguals are deprived of key social resources at a critical time in their lives. Indeed, a complete transition to English monolingualism in the US is not the most desirable outcome. Assimilation that produces English language monolingualism has hidden costs for family relationships, personality development and adaptation.

Pluralism

With an increased accent on ethnicity since the 1960s, the assumptions of assimilation have been challenged and a 'new ethnicity' born (see Fishman, 2010). Ideologies that surround the terms 'integration', 'ethnic diversity', 'pluralism', 'superdiversity', and 'multiculturalism' challenged the assimilationist philosophy. The picture of the melting pot has been contrasted with alternative images: the patchwork quilt, the tossed salad, the linguistic mosaic and the language garden. One popular metaphor is the salad bowl, with each ingredient separate and distinguishable, but contributing in a valuable and unique way to the whole. A different 'integration' metaphor, favored in Canada, is the linguistic mosaic, with different pieces joined together in one holistic arrangement. But such pictures are essentially simplistic.

A pluralist approach assumes that different language groups can live together in the same territory in relative harmony and without the unjust **domination** of one group by another. An atmosphere of mutual understanding and tolerance is the ideal. As Schmidt (2000) explains:

> Pluralists also argue that individual bilingualism is not only possible but desirable in that it facilitates cultural enrichment and cross-cultural understanding. By combating distrust and intolerance toward linguistic diversity, pluralists hope to create a climate of acceptance that will promote greater status equality between ethnolinguistic groups and therefore a higher level of national unity. (pp. 62–63)

Assimilationists suggest that rather than promoting harmony, linguistic pluralism leads to ethnic enclaves that cause inequalities between groups and ethnic conflict. For such people, linguistic assimilation provides the social, political, and economic integration necessary for equality of opportunity and political harmony. In reality, there are often large status differences between languages in a society. Where one language is associated with power, wealth and prestige, the tendency of individuals is to choose the language of economic and social mobility. The economic dice are often so loaded against pluralism that forced assimilation is a superfluous idea.

Language Policy Alternatives

The assimilationist argument ignores the legacy of racialized ethnic injustice in the US and misconstrues the nature of relationships between individual identity, culture, the state, and equality of opportunity. But there are also obstacles to complete acceptance of the pluralist alternative. Schmidt (2000) argues that the kind of social integration envisioned by pluralism may actually perpetuate the very social inequalities between language groups that it seeks to overcome. Pluralists argue for individual choice in language and culture, but there is no equal choice if there is no equal starting point or level playing field. The context of choice for individuals is constrained by numerous unequal circumstances for which language minorities bear no responsibility. The language of power in the US is English, so individuals will typically choose English in pursuit of their own social and economic advantage. Social mobility and economic advance are pragmatically unlikely from a pluralist position, however strong the intellectual arguments. As Schmidt (2000) concludes, both views are unrealistic:

> Assimilationists are unrealistic because their ideology posits a monocultural and monolingual country that does not exist in the real world; more importantly, a consequence of its unrealistic assumptions is the continued unjust subordination of language minority groups by the privileged Anglo, European-origin majority. Pluralists too are unrealistic in that they assume that an egalitarian society of multiple cultural communities can be achieved through a combination of individualistic rights-based free choice measures and moral exhortations to Anglos to respect linguistic and cultural diversity. (p. 209)

In Québec, one political answer has been to seek to establish a separate French language community. Historically, the establishment of separate linguistic territories was common in the US as different linguistic minority groups immigrated and established isolated small towns across rural areas of the country. Tribal lands and Native American reservations also technically provided linguistic territories free from pressures to shift to English (Wiley & Wright, 2004; Wright, 2015). However, with the advent of infrastructure (e.g. rails, roads, bridges), increased trade, the growth and draw of large cities, and easy access to English-language mass media (radio, television, newspapers, movies, the internet), maintaining such linguistic isolation and avoiding contact with English speakers became increasingly impossible and impractical. Even in Puerto Rico, English is an official language alongside Spanish, even though Spanish continues to be the **dominant language** of most residents. Another alternative is an enhanced pluralist language policy in the US that aims for pluralistic integration. This alternative is supported by May (2011) who argues for language minority group rights that retain within them the protection of individual liberties.

The two positions of assimilation and pluralism differ in such fundamental ideological ways that simple compromises and resolutions are virtually impossible. When evidence for the maintenance of minority languages and cultures is produced, assimilationists are likely to argue that attitudes and behavior are still in the process of change. That is, assimilationists will argue that, over time, people will move away from minority cultural maintenance and prefer the majority language and culture. Assimilationists tend to believe that bilingualism and biculturalism are temporary and transient, and lead eventually to a preferable, unifying monolingualism. When evidence favors assimilation having taken place in society (e.g. by the second or third generation), pluralists will tend to argue in two different ways. First, that the change towards assimilation has only occurred on certain dimensions (e.g. language rather than economic assimilation). Second, that sometimes the wheel turns full circle. Revival and resurrection in future generations may occur in response to repression and renouncement by previous generations.

Any such resolution of the assimilation versus pluralism debate is strongly affected by economics. Both assimilation and pluralism can be promoted and defended by the need to earn a living and the desire to acquire or increase affluence. Assimilation may be chosen to secure a job, to be vocationally successful and to achieve affluence. The minority language and culture may be left behind in order to prosper in the majority language community. At the same time, knowledge of the minority language and culture may provide access to further economic opportunities, especially when **language planning** is used to ensure that there are jobs and promotion within the minority language community (see Chapters 3 and 19).

Resolution of assimilation versus pluralism is sometimes avoided. The dominant group in society may, at times, not prefer the assimilation of minority groups. Such minority groups may not be permitted to assimilate, thus keeping their members in poorly paid employment. Such a minority group is then exploited by the dominant group. The economic interests of the majority group can be served by 'internal co-lonialism' rather than assimilation (e.g. economically isolating or manipulating an indigenous minority language group for majority group advantage).

Despite popular tales of rags-to-riches and 'living the American Dream', proficiency in the majority language is no guarantee of economic improvement. According to 2011 data from the US Census Bureau (Macartney *et al.*, 2013), English-speaking Whites make up the greatest numbers of Americans living in poverty at 25.6 million (11.6%), in comparison, only about 9.5 million African Americans live below the poverty line, though the percentage is higher (25.8%). Even with high and increasing levels of English proficiency and English dominance, poverty rates among Native Americans (27%) and individuals of Hispanic origin (23.2%) remain high.

Two opposing views – assimilation and pluralism – have so far been discussed. Other positions are possible. It is possible to participate in mainstream society and maintain one's minority language and culture (i.e. acculturation). For many individuals, there will be both a degree of assimilation and a degree of preservation of one's heritage. Total assimilation and total isolation may be less likely than some accommodation of the majority ideology within an overall ideology of pluralism; cultural maintenance within partial assimilation. Within multiculturalism and pluralism, an aggressive, militant pluralism may be seen as a threat to the social harmony of society. Instead, a more liberal pluralistic viewpoint may allow both membership of the wider community and an identification with the heritage cultural community.

The political debate over assimilation and pluralism is fundamental to understanding language minorities and is ever-present in language debates (D.A. Friedman, 2010). But such debates need placing in their historical context, particularly where immigrants are concerned. The expectation was that refugees and immigrants into the US, Australia, Canada, Germany and the UK, for example, would be pleased to have escaped political oppression or economic disadvantage and be jubilant to embrace equality of opportunity and personal freedom. The expectation was that an individual would be pleased to give up their past identity and make a commitment to a new national identity. Yet heritage culture and cultural identity have persisted, resisted and insisted. Assimilation has not always occurred among immigrants. Is this deliberate or unintended, desired or unwelcome?

Assimilation may be sought by immigrants. Many wish to assimilate, but come to reside in segregated neighborhoods and segregated schools. Thus desired assimilation can be prevented by social and economic factors outside the wishes of the immigrants. Some groups of immigrants may wish to be categorized as US citizens, but are categorized and treated by mainstream society as different, separate and 'foreigners'. The conditions under which immigrants live may create the negative labels and social barriers that enforce non-integration. The result may be the prevention of assimilation and integration with a consequent need to embrace some form of pluralism for survival, security, status and self-enhancement.

The fact that the US is a 'language graveyard' with rapid shifts to English dominance among the 1.5 and 2.0 generation (Rumbaut, 2009), makes it clear that language minority immigrants want to learn English. Thus strong measures to assimilate immigrants or initiatives to promote English assimilation in schools are not necessarily needed. There is an intrinsic motive in many immigrants to learn English rapidly and well (Salaberry, 2009a). Immigration does not pose a threat to the dominance of English in the US or UK.

If the linguistic assimilation of immigrants occurs so easily, what happens to their identity? What is won and lost by an immigrant when assimilating? Why is pluralism not easily accepted by some language minorities and by many language majorities? To begin to answer this, the nature of identity needs exploring.

Identity

The reciprocal relationship between language and identity is complex (see Chapter 6). For someone who expresses their identity as being Basque or Catalan, speaking in Basque or Catalan language is typically an important boundary marker. Ask a Celtic person if it is essential to speak Gaelic or Irish to feel Scottish or Irish, the answer would usually be 'no'. There are other ways of establishing a Scottish or Irish identity than through language. Otherwise, for example, almost 99% of Scottish people would not identify as being Scottish as they do not speak Gaelic.

Yet language is one of the strongest symbols and boundary markers in having a group, regional, cultural or national identity. Language is a highly influential but not an essential element in a collective identity such as identifying as being Welsh or Māori or Latino. Del Valle (2009) argues that only relatively unchangeable characteristics essentially define particular groups, such as gender. Languages change in individuals across time in terms of competence, usage and attitude. Someone may not retain their Spanish language yet still express identity as a Latino.

Views about the relationship of language and identity are contested and conflicted (Blackledge et al., 2008; Block, 2014; Salaberry, 2009b). There are also recent changes in the way identity can be viewed. Our individual identity is not fixed, given or unitary. Identity is socially created and developed through language, through an intentional negotiation of meanings and understandings. We speak a language or languages and it often identifies our origins, history, membership and culture. But that identity is daily re-written, imagined, re-constructed and displayed as we interpret sociocultural experiences and take on multiple roles and identities (Norton, 2013). Our identity is conveyed in our language, in our expressions and engagements, predilections and preferences. Language is a symbol of our identity, conveying our preferred distinctiveness and allegiance (e.g. Irish). However, language does not by itself define us. It is one feature or marker among many that makes up our constructed, shifting and hybrid identity.

We do not own an identity so much as hybrid and multiple identities. The sociocultural constructions of our gender, age, ethnicity, race, dress, nationality, region (e.g. county, state), locality, group membership (e.g. religion, politics), status, socioeconomic class, for example, provide us with a host of complementary, diverse, interacting, ever-changing, negotiated identities. A girl can speak English and Spanish, be a Muslim, Democrat, see herself as American, San Francisco Californian and Mexican, with identity as a teenager and trombonist, a gifted student, and lesbian. As contexts change, so our identities are re-framed, developed, sometimes challenged, sometimes in conflict. We do not establish our identities by ourselves but through social comparison, labeling by others, dialogue within ourselves and with others, and through the experience of ever-varying dramas and arenas, plays and stages.

No one is purely their labels. To share identity as a woman, white and Welsh-speaking is just a temporary starter and is left behind as further distinctiveness, connections and complexity become apparent. Labels are sometimes fleeting as situations and contexts change. This is particularly the case with ethnic labels (or national identities) that are too general and reductionist. Being a Jew or Arab does not immediately correspond with other fixed religious, economic or personality attributes. Young people in particular re-construct their 'language' and 'culture' with new mixtures that vary across situations (Chhuon & Hudley, 2010; Ngo, 2010). Rampton (2014) noted the 'language crossing' of teenagers in London who shared expressions in each other's languages, a multiethnic form of talking. Such a friendly crossing of languages created a new set of multilingual identities. But multiple identities may involve a challenge to establishing a coherent sense of Self, which is not always achieved as inherent tensions and conflicts may remain (Block, 2014).

A context that affects how language and identity interact is immigration. Eva Hoffman (1989) recalls herself as a 13-year-old Polish immigrant to Canada:

> I wait for the spontaneous flow of inner language which used to be my night-time talk with myself ... Nothing comes. Polish, in a short time, has atrophied, shriveled from sheer uselessness. Its words don't apply to my new experiences ... In English, words have not penetrated to those layers of my psyche from which a private conversation could proceed. (p. 107)

When writing in her teenage diary, Hoffman found that her Polish is now connected with the past, so she writes in impersonal, school English, the language of the present, but not the language of the Self. However, immigrants often produce vibrant, volatile, commodified, new ethnic identities and are not easily classified into existing cultural, ethnic or linguistic groups. Young people growing up in multilingual urban settings (e.g. Utrecht, London, New York) are simplistically considered as Turkish-Dutch, Somali-British or Cuban-American. They may be seen by others as Dutch, British or American, but the self-perception of identity may be of a new, dynamic, multiple, overlapping and situationally-changing nature. Language and ethnic dimensions of identity interact with other attributes such that we have simultaneous, fluid and complex multiple classifications. Stereotyping, prejudice and distance may be reduced when we see others across multiple classifications rather than just by, for example, ethnicity or language. Reyes (2011), in her study of language, identity, and stereotype among Southeast Asian American youth, found that students often reappropriate stereotypes to reposition their own identities and others in meaningful ways. Deaf people are much more than being deaf, and vary, not only among themselves in identity, but also on different occasions in seeing themselves as Deaf people, or not.

Identity is more or less imposed, assumed and negotiated (Chhuon & Hudley, 2011). For some, being called a member of a language minority is imposed and negative since 'minority' suggests a stigma of being marginal, non-mainstream and unusual. They are 'minoritized' by the dominant group. Hence, labels such as 'linguistically diverse' try to create an identity that is more positive. Such labels can be ascribed rather than chosen. For example, an individual may not describe themselves as a 'Bengali speaker' or 'Cantonese bilingual' or a Deaf person, as these may hint at negative, unwanted differences in a homogeneous society. Instead of 'native speaker' and 'heritage language' to describe the language of a child, 'language expertise' and 'language affiliation' may be more positive. Similarly, the label 'Hispanic' for some is a derogatory term. Just as 'Negro' became 'Black person' to signal an identity based on freedom rather than slavery, and to 'African American' to signal an identity connected to geographical space instead of a skin color. So too language-based identity labels are sometimes renewed to attempt more positive associations and expectations. Hence, some have a preference for 'Latina' and 'Latino', or the gender neutral 'Latinx', instead of Hispanic. Chhuon and Hudley (2011) describe the contradictory perceptions of Cambodian American students by educators and how students must negotiate between their identities as Cambodian vs. the pan-ethnic Asian identity that is often imposed upon them by others. While identities are frequently negotiated (e.g. being American, Sudanese, and bilingual), other times not (e.g. Jews in Nazi Germany and middle class 'enemies of the people' in Stalinist Russia).

Such group labels are never static. In Europe, ethnic and linguistic identity is dynamic as mass immigration, technology (e.g. air travel, satellite, social media), religion, post-colonialism, mythologizing the past, the enlargement of the European Union, UK's exit from the EU, feminism, and intercultural marriage are just some of the many interacting modern trends that create ever changing, hybrid language identities. This is witnessed in the adaptation of English in Europe. In Germany, Germans want to sound like Germans when they speak English, not like North Americans or the British. Speaking Indian English in India is the accepted norm. Native speakers of English are outnumbered by second language speakers of English around the globe. The existence of multiple varieties of 'World Englishes' reveals that no single nation or ethnic group can claim sole ownership of English. New varieties of English emerge in multilingual communities, especially in the context of multiple identities found in youth culture (Cheshire, 2002). These differ from their family identities, and allow different strengths of membership of different networks, plus shared (not divided) loyalties.

Another debate accenting the negative, sometimes voiced by politicians and members of the public, is whether **multilingualism** leads to being caught in-between two languages, with a resulting conflict of identity, social disorientation, even isolation and split personality. This narrow monolingual view is out of touch with the reality that most people in the world are bilingual. However, if there are anxieties and struggles in identity, bilingualism is unlikely to be the cause: 'it is not language *per se* that causes the identity crisis; rather, it is often the social, economic and political conditions sur-rounding the development of bilingualism' (Li Wei, Dewaele & Housen, 2002: 4). Such conditions tend to be economic (e.g. material poverty), political oppression, racism, social exclusion, discrimination, hostility and powerlessness.

Pavlenko and Lantolf (2000) suggest that there is a process of reconstruction of identity (e.g. in children and adults following immigration). Examples include thousands of refugees entering Europe from Syria, Iraq and Afghanistan following conflict, civil war, widespread terror and mass killings. Mango (2012) portrays the difficulties of identity for Arab American women born in the US. They are often misrepresented in the mass media (e.g. as belly dancers) and stereotyped (e.g. as anti-American following 9/11). This can lead internally to frustration and annoyance, yet externally (in interactions) from remaining silent to speaking up and challenging the very negative associations often ascribed to Arab American women.

Pavlenko and Lantolf (2000) suggest that after an initial loss of linguistic identity comes a period of recovery and transformation that goes through stages of: appropria-tion of others' voices, emergence of a new voice (e.g. in writing), and reconstructing one's past and continuous growth into new understandings and subjectivities. In terms of language, there is transformation or 're-narratization' (reconstruction) rather than replacement, with an outcome that represents an identity in motion that is not exclusively anchored in one language or another (see, e.g. M. Kim, 2016). Data from Rumbaut's (2009) study suggests that even with the rapid shift to English, there is a slight increase in reported bilingualism once adolescents leave high school and enter adulthood. This may be due to less political and social pressures to 'fit in' (assimilate) in high school and the greater freedom and acceptance of diversity in college and in adult life. The growing number of foreign language courses tailored to heritage language speakers at colleges and universities demonstrate some desire on the part of many students to reclaim the language the K-12 school system attempted to eradicate (Wiley et al., 2014).

Empowerment

This chapter has suggested that bilingualism and bilingual education can only be properly understood through the lens of power, identity, ideology and politics. Relations of power are at the heart of bilingual schooling (Pai et al., 2015). This is no more so than for minority language children who often suffer devaluation of identity, added subordination and disempowerment in their schooling experience. For example, in history lessons that celebrate majority languages and cultures while devaluing minority language groups, a student's identity may be challenged and changed. When such minority languages and cultures are celebrated, the student's identity may be affirmed and accepted. Learning about local geography, reading set books including novels, and many writing assignments can influence a student's identity and empower-ment or disempowerment.

Cummins (2013) has developed a theoretical framework that directly relates to politics, policy, provision and practice with language minority students. He argues that language of instruction is just one of many pedagogical factors leading to empower-ment and affirmation of students' identities. Thus, 'bilingual education, by itself, is not a panacea for reversing underachievement if other aspects of students' experience are not focused on empowerment' (p. 2). In his framework, Cummins makes an important distinction between *coercive* and *collaborative* relations of power:

Within a societal context of unequal power relations, classroom interactions are never neutral – they are always located on a continuum ranging between the reinforcement of coercive relations of power and the promotion of collaborative relations of power. Coercive relations of power refer to the exercise of power by a dominant individual, group or country ... Collaborative relations of power, by contrast, reflect the sense of the term *power* that refers to 'being enabled,' or 'empowered' to achieve more. (p. 4)

An example of *coercive* relations of power would be the assimilationist approaches described above where schools view the home languages and culture of students as a problem to overcome and aim to replace them with the dominant language and culture.

While coercive power moves in one direction from the top down, collaborative relations of power are generated through interactions with others. Thus, power is not a fixed quantity. Cummins (2013) explains:

The more empowered one individual or group becomes, the more is generated for others to share. ... Within this context *empowerment* can be defined as the *collaborative creation of power*. Students whose schooling experiences reflect collaborative relations of power know that their voices will be heard and respected within the classroom. Schooling opens up identity options and amplifies rather than silences their power of *self*-expression. (p. 4, emphasis in original)

Cummins (2013) suggests that in strong forms of bilingual education – where the aim is to develop and maintain high levels of proficiency and literacy in both languages – the incorporation of the home language contributes to the collaborative creation of power. In contrast, monolingual programs in the dominant language and even in weak forms of bilingual education, 'are unlikely to create contexts of empowerment for bilingual students' given the aim is to move students as quickly as possible into mainstream instruction. Education and the spread of literacy are primary mechanisms for cultural and linguistic homogenization, even disempowerment of language minorities. However, Cummins suggests that even in cases where the majority language is the predominant language of instruction, empowerment can still be generated through the adoption of bilingual strategies such as encouraging writing and group discussions in the home language or other opportunities for students to showcase their multilingual talents. Empowerment also comes from developing students' higher-order thinking skills, allowing them to demonstrate their talents, and other activities that reinforce students' sense of pride in their identities. As Cummins summarizes, effective programs leading to empowerment – whether labeled bilingual or not – 'will enable bilingual students to carry out powerful intellectual work using both of their languages as cognitive and creative tools' (p. 4).

While the discussion in Box 18.1 focuses on students, these dimensions also empower or 'disable' teachers and other educators in schools, and affect their professional identity (Wu *et al.*, 2011). The four dimensions can inspire teachers to take ownership of classroom language policy, provision and practices, for the benefit of language minority students (D.C. Johnson, 2010).

Empowerment thus becomes an important concept in transforming the situations of many language minorities. Empowerment means movement for minority language students from coercive, superior–inferior (subordinate) relationships, to collaborative relationships, power sharing and power creating, where the identities of minorities are affirmed and voiced. Such empowerment is often part of a healing process for language

---

Box 18.1 School characteristics for language minority student empowerment

Cummins (2000a) suggests that minority language students are 'empowered' or 'disabled' by four major characteristics of schools:

- *The extent to which minority language students' home language and culture are incorporated into the school curriculum.* If a minority language child's home language and culture are excluded, minimized or quickly reduced in school, there is the likelihood that the child may become academically 'disabled'. Where the school incorporates, encourages and gives status to the minority language, the chances of empowerment are increased. This inclusion may also have effects on personality (e.g. self-esteem), attitudes, and social and emotional well-being.

- *The extent to which minority communities are encouraged to participate in their children's education.* Where parents are given power and status in the partial determination of their children's schooling, the empowerment of minority communities and children may result. When such communities and parents are kept relatively powerless, inferiority and lack of school progress may result. Empowerment is encouraged through home reading programs involving bilingual books, family literacy projects that value home language and literacy practices, and collaborative decision making with parents.

- *The extent to which education promotes the inner desire for children to become active seekers of knowledge and not just passive receptacles.* A transmission or 'banking' model of teaching views children as buckets into which knowledge is poured or deposited. It is disabling. In contrast, a transformative model is empowering. It requires reciprocal interaction involving genuine dialogue between student and teacher in both oral and written modalities, guidance and facilitation rather than control of student learning by the teacher, and the encouragement of student/student talk in a collaborative learning context. This model emphasizes the development of higher-level cognitive skills rather than just factual recall, and meaningful language use by students rather than the correction of surface forms. Language use and development are consciously integrated with all curricular content rather than taught as isolated subjects, and tasks are presented to students in ways that generate intrinsic rather than extrinsic motivation.

- *The extent to which the assessment of minority language students avoids locating problems in the student and seeks to find the root of the problem in the social and educational system or curriculum wherever possible.* Psychological and educational tests tend by their very nature to locate problems in the individual student (e.g. low IQ, low motivation, poor reading skills). Assessment needs to be advocacy-oriented, by critically inspecting the social and educational context in which the child operates to locate the root of the problem (e.g. devaluing of home languages and cultures, a transmission model of instruction, exclusions of parents and the community from participation in the school and in the education of their children, etc.). This may involve comments about the power and status relationships between the dominant and dominated groups, at national, community, school and classroom level.

---

minority students who have historically been marginalized, discriminated against and disempowered. Empowerment can be furthered by strong forms of bilingual education, but also needs to be realized in legal, social, cultural and particularly economic and political spheres.

Conclusion

Underneath 'weak' and 'strong' forms of bilingual education lie different views about language communities, ethnic minorities and language itself. When language is viewed as a problem, there is often a call for assimilation and integration. Such a view most often leads to monolingual or weak forms of bilingual education with a focus on moving students to mainstream instruction in the dominant language as quickly as possible. Pluralists view language as a right and/or resource. This view will often lead to stronger forms of bilingual education with high levels of bilingualism and biliteracy as the aim. The relationship between language and identity, and the identity development of bilingual students is complex, constantly negotiated, and ever changing. Coercive relations of power are at play when assimilationist policymakers impose education solely in the medium of the dominant language and instigate other policies and programs designed to encourage students to abandon their home languages and cultures. Collaborative relations of power can lead to empowerment of bilingual students and communities. Such empowerment is facilitated through strong forms of bilingual education, as well as education programs that value and allow students to use and showcase their talents and bilingual skills.

Key Points in This Chapter

➢ Four ideologies underpin discussions about languages in society and in schools: pluralist and assimilationist being the main 'opposites', but also with civic and ethnist ideologies being present.

➢ Assimilation is a belief that linguistic minority groups should give up their home languages and cultures and adopt those of the dominant group in the host society.

➢ Pluralism is a belief that linguistic minority groups should maintain their home languages and cultures in combination with those of the dominant group in the host society.

➢ The identity or hybrid identities of immigrants is a key debate, with modern views of identity suggesting social construction, constant change, negotiation and complexity.

➢ Coercive relations of power refer to the exercise of power by a dominant individual, group or country.

➢ Collaborative relations of power refer to the empowerment of individuals or groups by enabling them to achieve more. Through collaboration, power is generated and shared.

Suggested Further Reading

📖 Norton, B. (2013). *Identity and language learning: Extending the conversation* (2nd ed). Bristol, UK: Multilingual Matters.

📖 Rampton, B. (2014). *Crossing: Language and ethnicity among adolescents* (2nd ed.). New York, NY: Routledge.

📖 Salaberry, M. R. (Ed.). (2009). *Language allegiances and bilingualism in the US*. Bristol, UK: Multilingual Matters.

📖 Trudell, B. & Young, C. (Eds.). (2016). *Good answers to tough questions in mother tongue-based multilingual education*. Dallas, TX: SIL International. Available as free eBook at:https://www.sil.org/sites/default/files/files/sil_2016_good_answers_to_tough_questions_0.pdf

On the Web

- Bilingual Family Night for ELL Families
  http://www.colorincolorado.org/article/bilingual-family-night-ell-families
- Guide for Engaging ELL Families: 20 Strategies for School Leaders
  http://www.colorincolorado.org/article/introduction
- Journal of Language, Identity, and Education
  http://www.tandfonline.com/toc/hlie20/current
- Things Bilingual People Do (YouTube Video)
  https://youtu.be/ReHdQsB5rI8
- Lost in Translation: An interview with Eva Hoffman
  https://www.psychologytoday.com/blog/life-bilingual/201511/lost-in-translation

Discussion Questions

(1) What are the differences between assimilationist and pluralist ideologies? What are the limitations of each, and what alternatives are there to these views?

(2) How would you describe your identity or identities, especially in terms of your languages or bilingual abilities? How have you negotiated your identities, and how have they changed over time?

(3) How can schools and teachers promote the empowerment of bilingual students in a context where coercive relations of power often dictate standards, curriculum, and program models from an assimilationist point of view?

Study Activities

(1) Follow a political debate concerning languages in school or bilingual education or language minorities in the local or national media. Portray in words the varying political dimensions of the controversy. Identify and analyze the ideologies present in the debate. Does the controversy fit neatly into a two-way split (e.g. assimilationist vs. pluralists)? Or does the controversy have a number of overlapping or conflicting ideologies, even among those who appear to be on the same side?

(2) Conduct an interview with one or more bilingual or multilingual immigrant adults who completed at least part of their schooling in the local education system. Ask about their struggles with identity, if any, how they negotiated their identities, and how their identities have changed over time.

(3) Using a school you are familiar with, ask teachers and parents about school–home relationships. What forms of collaboration exist? What power relationships exist between teachers and parents? What part do parents play in the language and literacy development of their children?

CHAPTER 19

Bilingualism in the Modern World

Introduction

Occupational Bilingualism

Bilingualism and Tourism

Bilingualism and the Mass Media

Information Technology, the Internet and Bilingualism

Bilingualism and the Economy

Bilingualism as an Economic Advantage

The Economic Usefulness of Different Languages

Minority Languages and the Economy

Is There an Economic Advantage for Being Bilingual?

Bilingualism and Economic Inequality

Conclusion

Bilingualism in the Modern World

Introduction

This chapter takes a contemporary and future look at **bilingualism** and bilinguals. In the modern world, is a heritage (minority) language going to be an asset and/or a hindrance? Will bilinguals and multilinguals with two or more majority languages have a competitive advantage in developing global economies? Are bilingualism and **multilingualism** valuable for employment? Does developing tourism help sustain and/or dilute minority languages and their related **cultures**? Do the internet, social networking and mass media ensure that English increasingly becomes the international language for global communication, or is there an increasing place for bilingualism and multilingualism?

Forecasting the future is hazardous. The future of majority and minority languages in the world is unpredictable. Current economic, political, religious, social and cultural change is rapid (e.g. globalization), affecting all languages of the world. The flow of people (e.g. migrants, refugees, tourism), the international movement of money and fast changes in technology, the global spread of information and images, and the flow of ideas and ideologies are more rapid than ever before. Therefore, five key modern themes are highlighted – employment, tourism, mass media, information technology and the economy – to demonstrate how languages within an individual and within society are likely to be subject to fast moving tides of local and global development.

Occupational Bilingualism

The ownership of two or more languages is increasingly seen as an asset as the 'communication world' gets smaller. Globalization increases the demand for multilinguals in the workplace (Gunnarsson, 2013; Roberts, 2010). With immediate communication by phone, VOIP (Voice over Internet Protocol), emails and messaging, distant communications and negotiations across the world has become a reality, favoring bilinguals and multilinguals. As air travel has brought peoples and countries closer together, so the importance of those who can operate in two or more languages has been highlighted. As the amount of information available has dramatically increased, and the ease of delivering information round the world has quickened, many bilinguals, particularly those with 'English bilingualism and multilingualism', have become more important in the employment market. As Angouri (2014) suggests:

> The modern workplace is international and multilingual. Both white and blue collar employees are expected to be mobile, work increasingly in (virtual) teams ... in

a language that, often, is not their first language (L1). This results in a number of languages forming the ecosystem of public and private workplace settings ... the linguistic landscape of both small/medium enterprises (SMEs) and multinationals (MNCs) is rich and diverse. Employees cross professional, linguistic and national boundaries as part of their daily routine. (p. 1)

In tourism, marketing, call centers, retailing, airlines, public relations, banking, performing arts, media, information and communications technology, accountancy, business consultancy, secretarial work, hotels, law and teaching, for example, bilingual and multilingual employees may often have the competitive edge when applying for a post or for advancement. At the least, a bilingual has 'value added' by offering language competencies in employment (Alarcón & Heyman, 2013). In the growing prevalence of screen-based and information-based labor, bilinguals are often very marketable and seen as more multi-skilled. Where there is a customer interface, then interacting in the language of the customer is typically excellent for business. Porras *et al.* (2014) quote a banker in their interview research who revealed how his bilingualism and cultural competency evoked trust in his clients: 'I am not paid more for being multilingual, but as a banker, I make more money than the monolinguals because I have more clients that come to me and have faith in me. They want to invest their money with me' (p. 251).

Ever since the September 11, 2011 (9/11) terrorist attacks by al-Qaeda targeting symbolic US landmarks, intelligence-gathering, diplomacy and national security have led to an even greater need for those fluent in languages other than English. The US Defense Language Institute (DLI) in Monterey, California supplies the US military, Department of Defense, CIA and FBI with employees whose language and cultural skills are vital to their post. The DLI's mission is to 'provide culturally based foreign language education, training, evaluation and sustainment to enhance the security of the nation' (http://www.dliflc.edu/about/). The languages taught include: French, Portuguese, Spanish, German, Indonesian, Hebrew, Hindi, Persian Farsi, Russian, Serbian/Croatian, Tagalog, Turkish, Urdu, Modern Standard Arabic, Egyptian Arabic, Iraqi Arabic, Levantine Arabic, Sudanese, Chinese (Mandarin), Japanese, Korean and Pashto. Such languages are regarded as not only important in national security, but also for encouraging reform in other countries, promoting understanding, and communicating with other countries, especially for economic purposes.

A report from the British Council (2013) warned of the diplomatic and trading isolation of the UK in an era when **language skills** were increasing the employability of government staff, yet such skills were decreasing in availability among recruits and employees. Language skills within the UK government have traditionally been regarded as essential for diplomacy, national security and defense. However, the report warns that the decline in graduate language capacity in recent years endangers the UK's future capabilities and influence. Unless the current decline in language skills is reversed, the report argues that the UK will become 'lost for words' with severe consequences for diplomacy and national security:

> The radically different landscape of international engagement and security that confronts Britain today means that language skills can no longer be regarded simply as an optional adjunct to those other skills needed by government employees working in outward-facing roles. Economic, technological, geopolitical and societal shifts over the last few decades mean that language skills for diplomacy and national security are now needed across a growing number of government departments. ... How well-equipped

a society and its government are in terms of languages skills should be regarded as a key indicator of how prepared they are to operate effectively within the fast changing landscape of global engagement. (British Council, 2013: 8)

However, there is a marked contrast between bilingual professions that carry a high prestige, and professions where bilinguals are in jobs that symbolize the lower status of many **language minority** bilinguals (Roberts, 2010; Zhu, 2014). In this latter case, language minority members may speak two languages, yet be in low paid jobs, even unemployed, and be marginalized in their employment prospects and chances of sharing wealth. We will first consider bilingual professions that are prestigious.

In the tourism and travel business there are bilingual and multilingual professions that are often prestigious and prosperous: international flight attendants, instructors on ski slopes, tour guides, hotel staff, those who conduct safaris in Africa, and those who cater to sun seekers around the world. To communicate with clients, to inform those being instructed, to satisfy those seeking rest and excitement, the use of two or more languages enhances job performance.

For bilinguals and multilinguals who are skilled in two or more languages, being an interpreter or translator is often a prestigious post. When politicians meet (e.g. United Nations, European Union, on foreign visits) interpreters form the essential bridge, provide a smooth connection and maintain communication. Interpreting can also exist in a local language minority region. In the highlands and islands of Scotland, translating facilities are available for those English-only speakers who need a translation when local government officials or elected community representatives are speaking Gaelic. Translating can also exist as a large-scale enterprise (e.g. in the United Nations, NATO and the European Union) where many documents have to be translated into official languages. In the United Nations organization, the Translation Services department translate all official United Nations documents, meeting records and correspondence from and into Arabic, Chinese, English, French, Russian and Spanish. Some official documents are also translated into German. United Nations translators must have a perfect command of their first language and an excellent knowledge of at least two other official languages (see: http://www.un.org/Depts/DGACM/Translation.shtml). Translation may also occur in language minority communities where, for example, a book or an article may be translated to or from the minority language.

Another example of a relatively prestigious bilingual profession is that of local government officials. When enquiries are made about education, health, social benefit or local taxes, it is often necessary to have people who can use the language(s) of the local people. In many language minority situations, bilinguals in local government may have to work with their superiors and official documents in the majority language, but deal orally and in letters in the minority language(s) with some or many of the local population. Another example is when a local government official in Africa or India visits an indigenous ethnic group in a relatively remote part of the country. That local government official may need to talk in the dialect or local language of the people as well as talking to colleagues back in the town or city in a more widely used language.

In many developing nations, there is a need for government officials and staff to speak international languages to communicate effectively with visiting delegations, international assistance providers, and neighboring countries. In Cambodia, for example, there is a concerted effort to develop the English **language proficiency** of key personnel from the Ministry of Education, Youth, and Sport so they can represent the country at regional and international education meetings such as those associated with ASEAN and the United Nations. These skills are also needed in countries to work with international aid agencies and international consultants. Those with strong English language skills are also in high demand among local and international non-governmental organizations. In fact, it is often difficult for government ministries to recruit and retain highly bilingual staff members as they are frequently drawn to the higher-paying NGO and private-sector jobs in need of their language skills.

In the caring professions (e.g. counselors, therapists, psychologists, doctors, midwives, nurses, religious leaders), one key performance factor can be the bilingual or multilingual ability of such professionals (Martinovic & Altarriba, 2013). Take, for example, the midwife. The midwife is present at that very special moment of a mother's experience. Communication with the midwife is not only important, it is also very emotional and precious. Can the midwife assist in the moment of pain and joy in the preferred language of the mother? If not, the mother will need to switch to using her second language, or may not be able to communicate with the midwife at all.

When people visit a psychiatrist or counselor, it may be important for them to discuss and reveal the innermost depths of their being in the language of their choice. To switch to a second or third language because the professional is monolingual may be unsatisfactory for both the client and the professional. In a religious service, it can be important for a religious leader to conduct prayers or a funeral service in the language of the people. People may find praying in a second or third language unnatural, even awkward.

There are many times when the more prestigious professional (e.g. the consultant surgeon) only speaks the majority language, while the relatively less prestigious professional (e.g. the nurse on the hospital ward) is bilingual. This raises the occasional dilemma about whether it is more important to hire a monolingual who is more skilled at a profession, or a bilingual who is less skilled. (There will be many cases when bilinguals are as skilled as, or more skilled than the monolingual applicant for a post.)

This leads to the second part of this discussion about bilingual professions. In many minority language situations, those who are bilingual may be unemployed or in lower status jobs. In some immigrant situations in the United States and Europe, immigrants do not have the majority language skills for the most prestigious positions, or are simply lower graded in the employment market because they are immigrants. The more prestigious jobs are sometimes filled by monolinguals and less prestigious posts by bilinguals. The managers may be majority language speakers with high status, while the lowly-paid workers are from the local language minority. This may send a signal. Monolingualism symbolically connects with higher status employment, and bilingualism with lower status employment.

In some cases where bilingualism is needed among the employees, employers elect to try and train their existing monolingual employees from the majority group in a basic level of the target language, rather than hire and train actual bilinguals from the target language minority communities. For example, some local police departments in the US will provide beginning-level Spanish classes or even send officers to short-term immersion programs in Spanish-speaking countries rather than make efforts to recruit bilingual Latinos from the local community. Another challenge is when employers do try to hire heritage speakers of needed languages who are proficient in English, only to discover that their proficiency in the **heritage language** is limited due to the monolingual and weak forms of bilingual education they received in school.

There is sometimes a vicious cycle of poverty, powerlessness, low expectations and lower motivation leading to under-achievement at school, with unemployment and lower status jobs becoming part of this cycle. For example, in some cities in the US where there are large proportions of language minority students, most teachers are English language monolinguals. The cooks, cleaners, secretaries, teacher assistants and janitors in the school may often be bilinguals. For students in the school, such a differentiation between monolinguals and bilinguals in the roles they play may send out signals and messages to the students and parents (Wright & Boun, 2011). There is a hidden agenda in employment patterns within the school. The students may acquire the idea subconsciously that monolingual English speakers are prestigious, relatively well paid and in relatively secure jobs. Those who speak other languages as their home language tend to be allocated the lower class, more menial jobs. The role models in the school convey the message that to be bilingual is to be associated with less status and more poverty and disadvantage, less power and more subservience.

This discussion of bilingual professions has revealed the paradoxical nature of the link between bilingualism and employment. In the first case, there are those who can use their bilingualism as an advantage: to sell, to satisfy clients' needs, to succeed in providing a service. Bilingualism has an economic potential; it is an asset used by an individual for advancement. Bilingualism can become a marketable ability to bridge languages and cultures, securing trade and delivery of services. In the second case, there are those people, for example many immigrants, whose bilingual nature tends to mark them for lower status, more marginalized and precarious employment. Such bilinguals and multilinguals may be less proficient in the majority language and/or may lack the needed professional native language skills. They may be allocated the poorest paid jobs in schools and shops. Thus bilingualism is attached to low status jobs that symbolize the least powerful, the least affluent and the least prestigious sections in a society.

Bilingualism and Tourism

In recent decades, tourism has been a major growth industry. There are hundreds of millions of international travelers, and most are 'visitors from a non-English-speaking country traveling to a non-English-speaking destination,' thus highlighting 'the need for face-to-face international communication' (Graddol, 2006: 29). Increasing ease of international travel and communications, the opening of national boundaries, more leisure time, earlier retirement, longer life and a greater disposable income have meant that vacations in other countries are part of the lifestyle of an increasing proportion of the affluent population of many developed countries. When people go on vacation, some are seemingly indifferent to the indigenous language and culture of the region they are visiting, especially if it is a minority language and culture. Others are curious, charmed, even captivated by different tongues and traditions, by varied communication and cultures.

Travel and tourism involves the contact of cultures and languages. This can be an enlightening and enriching experience. However, tourism is sometimes seen as the enemy of multiculturalism and multilingualism and especially of minority languages and cultures. Language minority activists can argue that tourism ruins unspoiled areas of great beauty with large hotels, even larger blocks of flats and marinas. Tourism can negatively affect the linguistic environment as those on vacation expect services to be in their majority language. Tourists can be unaware of, and insensitive to cultural and linguistic diversity by expecting the language, food and other customs to be the same as at home.

If use is made of minority languages and cultures in tourist enterprises, this tends to follow an 'ethnic approach', focusing on history, traditions, customs and cultural artifacts in a way that may portray them as 'quaint', 'archaic' or 'strange' (Jaworski & Thurlow, 2010). Whether we are talking about Breton embroidered costumes, Scottish tartan, Welsh harp music, Amish traditional dress, Hawaiian grass skirts and hula dances, Native American rituals or Māori war dances, they may be presented as spectacles for gawking tourists rather than as part of real-life, contemporary living cultures. However, alongside such difficulties, 'ethnic' tourism can also bring money into the community, educate tourists about minorities, and enable empathy with their current language and cultural concerns (Heller, Jaworski & Thurlow, 2014; Heller, Pujolar & Duchéne, 2014).

Mass tourism has contributed to the spread of the English language and Anglo culture throughout the world. English is often the expected means of communication when tourists from different continents are abroad. However, translanguaging also exists, with those working in the tourist trade becoming fluent in a majority language such as English, while still retaining their heritage language. In Slovenia, for example, tourism appears to have led to Slovenians becoming multilingual in German, Italian and English as well as Slovene. Mass tourism can also weaken the cultural, linguistic and economic structure of a region by its tendency to provide casual, seasonal employment and also a mass influx of temporary workers from other regions. Because of all these negative implications, tourism is sometimes viewed with suspicion and concern by language minority groups.

Tourism that promotes the host language and culture has been called 'cultural tourism' (also called 'heritage tourism' and 'ethnic tourism'). With the growth of tourism throughout the world, more sophisticated and diverse strategies for boosting the tourist market have been devised. Tourism that includes different cultures and their languages have been part of this growth. For example, different languages and their attendant cultures may be present in visits to the following: archaeological and architectural sites, museums and cultural/sporting events, crafts and festivals, music and theatre, dance and drama, religious festivals and pilgrimages. The importance of cultural tourism has been increasingly recognized, and language minorities can raise their profile, create employment and find a niche economy in such cultural tourism.

Bilingualism and the Mass Media

Radio, television, newspapers, magazines, the internet and smartphones have become important vehicles of mass communication, in the form of news, information, entertainment, and social media. The majority of households in Western countries possess at least one television set, and to own a television is the ambition of many families in less economically advanced countries. Television (especially satellite television) has contributed to the creation of the global village with worldwide diffusion of important and immediate news, sport and culture. Television enables viewers to cross cultures and countries. The development of satellite and cable technology has facilitated the transmission of programs worldwide. Television can contribute to an empathy and insight into other cultures, languages and lifestyles.

However, there is another side to television. The largest television and movie industry in the world is in North America. It provides a mass of programs and films, light entertainment and news. These programs often transmit Anglo-American culture to other parts of the world. Anglo-American news broadcasts, music, cultural practices and lifestyles may be seen as prestigious and important, and, by implication, the indigenous cultures of other countries may seem outmoded and outdated. Kelly-Holmes and Milani (2011) pose the key questions: Whose voices are heard? Who are the speakers, objects and audience? What identities are constructed for the participants and how? How are expert voices constructed?

The English language is also diffused throughout the world by the mass media. The use of subtitling (cheaper than dubbing) means that the English language is experienced by audiences in many worldwide countries, though in many cases subtitles are done poorly and inaccurately, sometimes with comical results (see, for example, these English subtitles accompanying the Chinese version of *Harry Potter* – http://tinyurl.com/gonpbse). Since the advent of satellite television, even more viewers have access to English language programs.

The widespread mass media diffusion of the English language has had some beneficial effects. It has contributed to the development of bilingualism. It has provided a means for speakers of other languages to develop competence in English as a useful language of international communication. In Scandinavian countries for instance, many English language films and other programs have traditionally been broadcast with subtitles. Only children's programs are dubbed. Motivation to learn English is usually high in Scandinavian countries, and television is one aid to competence in English. This is an additive bilingual situation, where the second language does not displace the first.

However, the English language has entered, via television, into many majority languages. For example, an influx of borrowings from English into other languages via the mass media has provoked anxiety among language purists in countries such as Japan and France. The French government has therefore taken steps to reduce the quantity of non-French language broadcasting on radio and television. The Cambodian government likewise placed limitations on the amount of English, Thai, and other foreign language programming that may be broadcast on local television channels. One result of this policy has been a revitalization of the Cambodian television and film industry with a substantial increase in the quantity, quality, and variety of local programming in the national Khmer language. However, there has also been an increase in the number of English-language channels via satellite, and new developments such as the availability of Netflix now making thousands of English language television shows and movies instantly available in Cambodia presents a whole new variable.

One positive development caused by the proliferation of international satellite, cable, and streaming video channels is that there is an increasing international market for television programs. This, and the increasing use of subtitling, 'voice-overs' and dubbing, means that such programs and films can be made in many lesser used languages. The cost can then be recouped by selling them on the international market. In some rare instances such dubbing may simply be a goodwill gesture. For example, in an initiative with the Navajo National Museum to help with Navajo language revitalization and maintenance, Walt Disney Studios recruited native speakers of Navajo to professionally dub *Star Wars Episode IV: A New Hope*. The efforts were so well received the studio dubbed a second popular film: *Finding Nemo*. This version features an original song in Navajo performed by (non-native) Fall Out Boy front man Patrick Stump. The dubbed version was shown free-of-charge in selected theaters in Arizona, New Mexico and Utah. Navajo leaders see these efforts as important for connecting the younger generation to their language, and call it 'a huge leap forward in getting the awareness out there and getting kids interested' (Grinberg & Watts, 2016).

This is not to suggest that English language channels (and internet use) are totally dominant in English-speaking countries. In the UK, US, and Australia there are Arabic, Asian and many other language television channels on satellite watched by speakers of those languages. Non-English movies and television programs are often dubbed or subtitled into English and other languages. Korean soap operas (or K-dramas) are particularly popular throughout Asia and among the Asian diaspora around the world. In the US, the Spanish television network Univision, for example, has grown from small beginnings in the early 1960s to a major provider with a large Spanish-speaking audience across North America and the Caribbean, and has now achieved parity in terms of viewership with the major English language broadcasting networks. Spanish language television is now recognized for its influence on Latino voters, such that many politicians – including those who support strict immigration controls and the dismantling of bilingual education – are enthusiastic to reach and persuade voters in their heritage language. Univision even co-sponsored, with the Washington Post, one of the democratic primary debates during the 2016 presidential election.

However, when majority language mass media (e.g. English) enter minority language homes, the effect may be a subtractive bilingual situation. For example, language minority children can be exposed to the English language and Anglo-American culture on television from an early age. Minority language groups tend to be concerned about a daily diet of majority language and culture having a harmful effect on speakers of their language, especially teenagers and younger children. They are concerned that it further weakens the prestige and status of their own language and culture, further widening the gap between English (or another majority language) as the language of power, prestige, modern technology, fashion and entertainment and their own language as unfashionable, outmoded and diminishing. There is thus concern that watching majority language television may affect children's acquisition of their native language, and hasten **language shift** to the majority language.

During recent decades, there has been a concerted effort by many minority language groups to gain access to radio and particularly television. As demonstrated in the above example of *Star Wars* and *Finding Nemo* in Navajo, minority language activists have seen minority language radio, television and film as vitally important to the maintenance of their language for the following reasons:

(1) Minority language media add to the prestige and status of a language in the eyes of its speakers.
(2) Minority language media can add to a sense of unity and **identity** among its speakers.
(3) Minority language media help to keep minority language speakers, especially children and young people, from being overwhelmed by the influence of majority language and culture. They acquaint them with their own heritage and culture and give them pride in it.
(4) Minority language media can help disseminate a standard form of the language and also promote new and technical vocabulary. Mass media can help the standardization of a minority language across a variety of **registers**.
(5) Minority language media can help the fluency of minority language speakers and can also help learners acquire the language.
(6) Minority language media create well-paid, high prestige jobs for minority language speakers. The radio and television industry can help boost the economy of minority language regions.

The value of minority language media in the maintenance of minority languages and the reversal of language shift was disputed by Joshua Fishman. Fishman (1991) argued that radio and television should *not* be hailed as the rescuers of a minority language. He maintained that many minority language groups spend valuable resources in the lengthy and expensive task of establishing and maintaining minority language media, at the cost of more basic and fundamental issues such as the **intergenerational transmission** of the minority language. Fishman suggested that the impact of majority language television, particularly English language television in the UK and North America, is so immense that it cannot be countered by the much lesser influence of a minority language.

Intergenerational transmission of the minority language may be key, but needs to be supported with bilingual education and opportunities to use the language outside the home and school in ways that are meaningful and interesting to children and youth. Thus, attempting to do something to counteract majority language mass media by minority language ventures is much better than doing nothing. In such ventures there can be added prestige for a minority language, leading to the maintenance and promotion of minority languages, cultures and economies (e.g. Irish language comedy – see Moriarty, 2011). In Wales, the establishment of a Welsh language television channel (S4C) in 1982 led to the creation of various independent television companies in Wales, which have boosted the economy of the country (as has recently occurred in Scotland with the Gaelic language). Such minority language television is regarded as important in standardizing the language in a wide range of registers across a region or country. Welsh language television has also been viewed as a major force in the creation and maintenance of a sense of identity and unity among Welsh speakers.

Information Technology, the Internet and Bilingualism

On buses and trains, in lecture theatres and playgrounds, shopping malls and busy streets, smartphones, tablets and other mobile internet devices are ever present. Some people are texting, instant messaging, using translators (e.g. Google Translate) in live chat rooms or on discussion boards. Many 'surf' the World Wide Web for news, information and entertainment. Others are on email, Facebook, YouTube, Twitter, Tumblr, LinkedIn, Instagram, Snapchat, buying and selling, or blogging and Googling, and many other forms of social networking via technology. Communication for the hearing and Deaf people, for old and young, students and staff, has increasingly become electronic. What language is dominant? What languages are used by social media for social networking? Does such a rapid change lead to extra functions, status and use of majority languages such as English? Does the value and use of minority languages suffer? Has minority language use been valuably extended to electronic communication? Are bilingualism and multilingualism central or peripheral on the web?

With the rapid spread of technology and networked information has gone the rapid spread of English. The inherent danger is that minority languages, cultural diversity and therefore bilingualism come under threat. As shown in Table 19.1, over 949 million people in the world are estimated to access the internet in English (http://www. Internetworldstats.com/stats7.htm), followed by Chinese (752 million), Spanish (277 million) and Arabic (168 million). However, irrespective of the language(s) of the user, information that transfers across the internet tends relatively often to be in English, but growingly in other languages.

Table 19.1 Top 10 languages used on the internet (at June 30, 2016)

Language	Estimated number of users	% of all speakers of the language	Growth since 2000
English	949 million	67.8%	574%
Chinese	752 million	53.1%	2,228%
Spanish	277 million	61.6%	1,424%
Arabic	168 million	43.4%	6,603%
Portuguese	155 million	57.9%	1,940%
Japanese	115 million	91.0%	145%
Malay	109 million	37.8%	1,809%
Russian	103 million	70.5%	3,227%
French	102 million	25.9%	752%
German	84 million	88.3%	205%
Other Languages	797 million	33.7%	1141%

Source: Adapted from http://www.Internetworldstats.com/stats7.htm

The language of digitized encyclopedias and the multiplicity of software tend also to be in English, as does the language of gaming software. Another cyber example, Wikipedia articles per language, shows English (5.2 million) at the top, followed by German (2.0 million), Dutch (1.9 million), French (1.8 million), Italian and Russian (both 1.3 million), and Spanish and Polish (both 1.2 million). However, this virtual linguistic landscape is changing with over 250 other languages (e.g. Navajo with 2,483 articles; Khmer with 6,140; Hebrew with 191,515 and Pennsylvanian German with 1,914 articles) developing their linguistic presence (https://stats.wikimedia.org/EN/Sitemap.htm). Cyberworld is becoming increasingly multilingual in content and usage. However, Ensslin (2011) suggests differences between explicit values supporting multilingualism and implicit **pragmatics** that tend to favor a few majority languages and English in particular (e.g. Wikipedia).

It is for sure that the linguistic diversity of the world is not represented on the internet in numbers or status. What is not for sure is whether minority languages may be at risk as the status of larger languages is consolidated on the internet, or whether the online presence of smaller languages may strengthen them in terms of visibility, status, opportunities and usage.

Minority languages may seem in comparison to cyber languages to be part of heritage and history, and may fail to attain the status of modern, high-prestige and high-profile international languages used by information technology. The danger lies in the identification of advanced technological society particularly, but not exclusively, with the English language, and consequently minority languages being identified with home and history, ritual and religion. The danger is of a tiered information society: those who have the linguistic abilities to access information; and those who cannot access new forms of communication and information as they do not own a language often used in the information society.

Yet it is possible to harness technology to aid minority language education. For example, software can be displayed in or translated into the heritage language. Email, texting and tweeting and information exchange, for example, can be in that minority language. As more businesses begin to advertise using websites, regional networks have developed using local languages on the internet. As schools, colleges, universities, local government, libraries, record offices and local information agencies go online, their local pages are sometimes bilingual or multilingual.

What is also important in preserving minority languages in a technological age is to ensure that there is appropriate **terminology** in the minority language. It is necessary to extend minority language vocabulary to embrace technological and computer terms in languages other than English. Such modernization aids the symbolic status of the language, particularly among the impressionable young. Such a modernization of a language also attempts to move that language into modern domains, and ensure that information technology is a supporter and not a destroyer of bilingualism in children.

It is also possible to harness technology to aid minority language employment. The increasing speed of connections to the internet makes residence in language minority rural areas more possible. This can also enable home-based or locally-based employment through high-speed computer links to receive and deliver services and products. Thus minority languages and bi/multilingualism can potentially benefit from the current and future growth of the internet.

The internet is ever-changing and developing. It has the potential to increase bilingual and multilingual communication providing new possibilities for social networking among bilinguals: conversations across countries and continents, playing out multiple identities, a vicarious sense of belonging to other speakers of the heritage language, and a private space to be different, distinct and linguistically diverse. This includes Deaf people who can use new technologies to join Deaf communities across the world and not just in the locality. The rise of messaging (e.g. texting on phones) and VOIP (Voice over internet Protocol) services (e.g. Skype) makes communication in any language possible across a few blocks, meadows or wide oceans.

When students use communication technology, bilingual and multilingual proficiency can be enhanced. Through the internet, for example, authentic language practice is possible via purposeful and genuine activities (e.g. the use of social networking sites). There may be increased motivation to acquire a language via contact with real students in other countries and accessing authentic language sources to complete curriculum activity (e.g. a project on another country).

Email, chat rooms and messaging are a few of the well-established internet activities for language students, using both text and video, giving the feeling of the global village where barriers to communication (such as cost and the time of travel) are removed. There are increasing numbers of language servers on the internet accessible via 'sensitive maps' of sites in each country. They provide useful, relevant and topical information that is in a different language. Linguistic competence develops as a by-product of interest in such information.

By its interactive nature, the internet brings people speaking different languages into closer contact. By exchanging information with students in other countries, students can build increasing independence in language use, vary their language according to audience, and use language for real purposes. For example, the site ePals (www.epals.com) is a global community that pairs educators and students around the world in project-based learning activities for language learning practice and cultural exchange. In one project partner classrooms from different parts of the world discuss the games they like to play, while another involves students in partner classrooms exchanging information about the causes and effects of poverty, and students collaborate to develop a plan to address one aspect of global poverty.

Students can take part in conversations over the internet with native speakers, using not only written text but increasingly video and audio conferencing as well. Exchange visits can be reinforced with preparatory and follow-up internet links, and there are possibilities of virtual exchanges and 'telepresence'.

Technology also holds the future promise of conversations between speakers of different tongues, minority and majority. The dream is to combine (1) speech recognition (turning spoken words into text) followed by (2) a machine translator (converting text to other languages) and then a speech synthesizer that (3) turns translated text back into audible words in the language of the listener's choosing. This would enable conversations in two (or more) languages, and help protect minority language use and users.

The internet provides teachers and learners with ready-to-use banks of multimedia language resources: a wealth of video and audio recordings from all over the world, aural, pictorial and written information, and activities generated by many different language centers in varied countries. Providers of information and training for language teachers can use the internet to publicize events, courses, materials, services and a subscription-based, remote training, advice and information service.

Bilingualism and the Economy

Bilingualism as an Economic Advantage

In most of the great cities of the world, there is a multilingual economy. In such cities, international political (e.g. embassies) and financial (e.g. banks) institutions, multinational businesses and education establishments often employ many bilinguals and multilinguals. In cities such as New York, London, Tokyo and Seoul, many bilinguals and multilinguals own rich linguistic capital. For example, in London which is one of the world's leading financial centres for international business and commerce and is one of the 'command centres' for the global economy, P. Baker and Kim (2003) portray multilingual London as having over 10,000 language facilities and services in 444 different languages.

Bilinguals and especially multilinguals frequently have marketable language skills and intercultural knowledge. However, some minority language bilinguals are economically impoverished yet linguistically accomplished. Can such dual or triple **language competence** be an economic asset? Is there an earning bonus or differential for bilinguals? The foreign language skills of employees are sometimes rewarded by employers, showing that employers find these skills valuable (Grin, Sfreddo & Vaillancourt, 2010).

In an increasingly bilingual and multilingual world, with trade barriers falling, with new international markets growing, and with economic competition rapidly developing on a global scale, competence in languages may be increasingly important. An example is Southern Florida which has become a main center for South American business, and where Spanish language skills have become a bridge between the business cultures of the US and Latin America. The growth of multinational corporations in Southern Florida has increased with the emergence of markets in Latin America requiring Spanish, and not just English, as the language of trade. The growth of legal, financial and banking services in Miami is another example where bilinguals (Spanish and English) have distinct economic and employment advantages. Thus, Spanish language skills are in high demand in Florida's labor force to meet the needs of international business, tourism and Spanish language media enterprises, yet demand can outstrip supply.

Heller (2006) suggests that, to gain advantage in the new global economy, bilinguals will need to adopt a different concept of their identity. The old politics of identity concern maintaining a heritage language and culture, conserving and protecting traditions, and perpetuating a minority cultural identity. In contrast, Heller (2002, 2006) talks about a new pragmatic identity for language minorities, which allows them to take advantage of their multiple linguistic and cultural resources to participate in a global economy. The nature of the New World economy is an ability to cross boundaries, and many bilinguals are relatively skilled in such behavior. She suggests that it is not multilingualism or a hybrid dual language system that is valued in the new economy, but parallel monolingualism (Heller, 2002).

In such a context, language minorities can act as brokers between different monolingual economic and political zones. However, this requires bilinguals to have appropriate linguistic resources that are sufficiently well developed to operate in either language group. In a Canadian context, Heller (2006) argues that 'minorities are now in a good position to market their linguistic capital' (p. 26). To do so, they have to move away from the politics of ethnicity and tradition towards a politics based on capital, globalization and a new international political and economic order. However, language minorities are often politically and economically marginalized, with little chance of escape.

The Economic Usefulness of Different Languages

This immediately raises the question about which languages may be useful for economic advancement? In many countries of the world, it is English as a second or foreign language that has the most visible economic value. As Coulmas (1992) suggested:

> No Japanese businessman ever tries to operate on the American market without a sufficient command of English, whereas the reverse case, of American business people who expect to be able to do business in Japan without being proficient in Japanese, is not at all rare. On the one hand, this is a reflection of the arrogance of power, but on the other hand, it testifies to the fact that the opportunities for realizing the functional potential of English on the Japanese market are far better than those of realizing the functional potential of Japanese on the American market. (pp. 66–67)

However, Willy Brandt, a former Chancellor of the old Federal Republic of Germany once said: 'If I'm selling to you, I speak your language. If I'm buying, dann müssen Sie Deutsch sprechen (*then you must speak German*)'.

Alongside the English language, the French, German, Arabic, Japanese, Chinese Mandarin, Russian, Portuguese and Spanish languages have historically been regarded as important trading languages. However, in the future, this list of modern languages for marketing and trading purposes is likely to grow significantly. For example, Bahasa Melayu and Korean, Vietnamese and Cantonese, Swahili and Hausa, Bengali, Hindi and Urdu may each become increasingly valuable. Although the world is getting economically richer, the wealth created and spent by Eastern countries may proportionally increase in relation to the West, and therefore positively affect the economic attractiveness of major eastern languages, and particularly the employability of bilinguals and multilinguals. The predicted growth of newer economic superpowers in the BRICS group (Brazil, Russia, India, China and South Africa) may mean the end of five centuries of domination by Europeans and recently North Americans and thus could change the face of dominant languages. The rise of Mandarin Chinese in the coming decades is likely to make it a crucial international language for marketing and trade, politics and power. However, the future of individual economies in the world is not predictable, nor is the future of the global economy.

This scenario contains the idea of 'language skills as determinants of the economic variables such as productivity, costs and profits' (Grin *et al.*, 2010: 6). A workplace may need to take into account the language expectations of its target markets, the language profile of its suppliers, and ensure that its workforce has the multilingual skills to meet such expectations and preferences. Profitability may be enhanced by such considerations, whether the business is goods or services, and increasingly whether it is about the globalized knowledge economy (G. Williams, 2010).

In the context of Ireland, Ó Riagáin (2001) argues that profit margins lead language life. With the growth of economic prosperity in Ireland from the 1960s to 2009 came ever-widening international trade contacts, export markets, foreign investment, incorporation into international capitalism, and economic marriage with mainland Europe. English and other major European languages gained importance. However, this 'created severe problems for policies designed to maintain Irish as a minority language' (p. 206). The lower economic value of the Irish language has made it difficult to preserve that language.

In both the US and the UK, English is not enough. English is a global trading language but, in an export-wise and economically competitive world, exclusive reliance on English leaves the US and the UK vulnerable and dependent on the linguistic competence and the goodwill of others.

Box 19.1 Excerpt from *The Bilingual Advantage: Language, Literacy and the US Labor Market*

The United States has the unique opportunity to be at the forefront of a more visionary, but also more practical, language policy. The nation is host to most of the world's languages due to trends in immigration flow. In fact, the three most spoken languages in the US are also the three most spoken languages in the world: English, Spanish and Chinese. The US is home to literally hundreds of thousands of bilingual and biliterate youth.... However, the nation must actively seize the opportunity rather than squander it. The US is poised to take the lead in the global marketplace, but to do so, it must first acknowledge the tremendous, unique resource that exists in its cultural and linguistic diversity. (Callahan & Gándara, 2014: 287)

Minority Languages and the Economy

In suggesting that bilingualism can have economic advantages for individuals and organizations, the languages highlighted so far have mostly been majority languages. What is the place of local minority languages in the economy? Will bilinguals from language minorities have no economic advantage, no valuable trading language in their minority language, and no chance of getting out of the poverty trap that some bilinguals experience? Compared with a mainstream language majority, a marginalized language minority may experience relatively higher unemployment, lower pay, even poverty and powerlessness. Where language minorities live in relatively remote rural areas or in downtown inter-city areas, then often there is relative material deprivation.

The economy of many countries has recently moved from material resources and goods partly under the control of a government to an economy based on services and information under the control of multinational corporations and more global enterprises. In this new worldwide knowledge economy, can language minorities use their linguistic resources and social networks for economic and personal gain? The new knowledge economy requires the crossing of linguistic boundaries, and bilinguals and multilinguals are ahead of monolinguals in having this potential. They can become the pivotal bridge makers and go-betweens in global economy operations. Crossing borders can be geographical and linguistic for bilinguals and multilinguals. However, this may be restricted to bilinguals whose languages cross frontiers and are not only used locally or regionally.

The harsh reality for many of the world's bilinguals is that their minority language typically has minimal economic value. The pressure is on them to move into a majority language. Where there is economic value associated with an immigrant language it is frequently in sweatshops, factories, and fast food restaurants and is not connected with wealth, affluence or influence. A language is supported by businesses where factory workers, shop workers and managers work partly or mainly through their heritage language. On occasion, the migrant language is a trade language with another trading country (e.g. Spanish, Urdu, Panjabi, Hindi), with profitability and local niche economies.

Where and when there is some small economic value associated with an indigenous minority language, it is often associated with non-sustainable developments in rural areas. Such bilinguals may work in barely profitable industries in remote language heartland areas. In Europe, for example, the move from regional and state economies to a single European market policy (with interlocking business structures in different European countries encouraging mobility in businesses across European countries), may leave a distinction between core and periphery, between those in important urban business areas and those in rural peripheries (e.g. rural areas and scattered communities in Ireland, Wales and Scotland). Since many indigenous minority languages in Europe are found in regions that are relatively sparsely populated, economically underdeveloped, with poorer rural road and transport systems, there is a danger that there will be growing inequality between core and periphery.

In the economic restructuring that has occurred in recent decades, increased competition has led to the need for more efficiency to maintain profit. Industries and services have frequently had to 'automate, emigrate or evaporate'. Emigration of industries has been to countries such as India, Taiwan, Mexico, Brazil, China and Singapore, where wages, and therefore production costs, are relatively low. Such outside investment may sometimes offer work and wages to language minority members, but may also have negative wealth (low pay) consequences for language minorities. Another negative consequence is that economic investment may not reach a language minority. For example, where such minorities live in remoter rural areas, economic growth may be in the urban 'core' rather than the rural periphery. Alternatively, the higher-grade jobs may be in relatively affluent city areas, and the lower grade, poorly paid work in the more remote areas.

A different scenario is when a peripheral area attracts inward investment (e.g. factories are located in remoter areas). The tendency is for the local language minorities to provide relatively cheap workers, while the better paid (language majority) managers either operate from their far-away city headquarters or move into the periphery language community. In either cases, each language is identified with greater or lesser affluence, higher and lower status, more or less power.

The absence of community-based, ethnically-based businesses increases the risk of the emigration of more able, more skilled and more entrepreneurial people away from the area, hence leaving the language itself in peril. Also, a language community without economic activity is in danger of starving the language of one essential support mechanism. An economically wealthy language has a higher probability of being a healthy language. An economically impoverished language is placed at great risk.

There are also success stories. For example, the development of the Cuban enclave economy in Miami shows the possibility of a minority language economy developing in a region. Following the influx of Cubans into Miami in the 1960s, a Cuban-focused economy developed. Based on sufficient capital, a capable labor force, a ready market for products and a sufficient Cuban population to support Cuban-owned businesses, economic success of the enclave soon resulted.

Is There an Economic Advantage for Being Bilingual?

The potential advantages of bilingualism particularly for an individual have hitherto been broadcast as communication, cognitive, cultural, curriculum and character (C. Baker, 2014). It has also been suggested in recent decades that bilinguals have a potential economic advantage. For example, Alarcón *et al.* (2014) suggest that: 'Workers who deal with the public in a multilingual society are helped in their jobs by being able to use diverse languages. Doctors, nurses and medical assistants can understand and communicate more clearly with patients, improving health outcomes; lawyers, police officers, fire officers and government leaders gain similar benefits for public safety' (p. 132). The economic advantage could be in having a competitive advantage against monolinguals in finding employment, in opening up more job opportunities, in initial salary, with a salary premium, in promotion and/or in lifetime earnings. Such an advantage may be within a city (e.g. London, Brussels, Washington), a particular state or region (e.g. Catalonia), in some countries (e.g. Switzerland, Canada, Finland, Sweden) but not others, but also as a potential trans-national asset in times of the growth of multinational companies, a global economy and increasing international trade.

However, research on the potential economic advantage of being bilingual/multilingual shows varied outcomes, some positive, some negative. This is well illustrated in a book edited by Callahan and Gándara (2014) entitled *The Bilingual Advantage: Language, Literacy and the US Labor Market*. Research in the US reported in its chapters finds (initially) different conclusions. For example:

- When bilingual and monolingual workers' earnings are analyzed without controlling for age or gender, there is no apparent advantage for bilinguals in the labor market.
- Spanish speakers with competence in English show a 6% decrease in wages in comparison to monolingual English speakers.
- A more developed language competence of immigrants in English is related to higher wages in some research.
- There is evidence for the benefits of fluent bilingualism – and even of moderate or **balanced bilingualism** – in the labor markets and local economy of Southern California.
- Balanced bilinguals are more likely to be employed full-time compared with English dominant individuals and to earn significantly more than the monolingual English speakers (between $2,000 and $3,200 more annually).

- A Forbes Insights survey showed that managers of businesses operating internationally are increasingly multilingual. More businesses are seeing bilingualism and multilingualism as a significant advantage.
- The economic benefit to a bilingual applicant for a job may not be through increased salary but rather in the hiring process and winning the job competition.
- Bilingual females are more likely to be employed than their monolingual peers.

The problem of these mixed conclusions lies with a too-simple and 'black box' question: 'do bilinguals have an economic advantage'? The answer is never going to be straightforward as there are so many factors that can (by themselves but also in interactions and combinations) be influential. It is almost impossible to isolate bilingualism as a factor when there are so many other factors causing variations. For example, it also depends on these kind of other factors:

- What job?
  - Are there different results with different types of employment (e.g. professional, managerial, skilled, semi-skilled and unskilled)?
  - Does the job have a customer interface needing bilinguals to serve (e.g. doctor, nurse, teacher, sales person) or is the role less customer-oriented with less language requirements (e.g. software developer, chef, builder)?
- Do males and females show different results?
- Do younger workers show a different trend compared with older workers?
- What socio-economic class/ethnic group are the workers?
- What are the social class attributes and expectations of the employment?
- In which district, county, state, region, country, continent?
- In which decade (e.g. 1980s or current decade) as statistics change across time?
- Which international/regional languages does the bilingual/multilingual speak?
- How fluent and biliterate, advanced and balanced in two or more languages is the person?
- How scarce or multitudinous are the speakers of the languages (e.g. English, Chinese, Frisian, Fijian) and hence the size of the population requiring bilingual services?
- How scare or abundant are the applicants for the job with relevant language competencies?
- How well educated (drop-out, high school, college, university) is the person?
- How competent is the person in the skills needed in the job (e.g. medical, legal)?
- At which stage in the person's career (e.g. early, middle, late)?

The simple question 'do bilinguals have an economic advantage?' becomes even more complex, as the answer depends on what is used as the measure of economic success or advantage, for example:

- Winning a job – getting hired.
- Salary size.
- Salary premium for multilingual skills.
- Early or later advancement/promotion.
- Final position/status/role as an employee.
- Lifetime earnings.
- Unemployment/employment rates.
- Longer term effects (e.g. on 2nd and 3rd generation immigrants).
- Amount of local or international trade.

So with any piece of research, we have to ask (a) if any of the factors listed above could explain the findings other than (or as well as) bilingualism and (b) if the outcome (success/advantage) measure was different, would we have obtained different results? Over time, with the accumulation of many pieces of research, patterns in the findings will emerge allowing stronger conclusions. Callahan and Gándara (2014) conclude that a unifying socio-politico-linguistic theory is also something to work towards – a theory that can encapsulate the variations and factors above.

Bilingualism and Economic Inequality

Historically, antagonism towards immigrants (particularly in times of economic recession) is typically directed at newcomers who are blamed for taking away jobs from long-standing citizens. Immigrants are then blamed for economic and social ills in society. However, immigrants can have a stimulating effect on the economy by (a) opening many new businesses, and (b) keeping businesses from relocating outside the country by providing inexpensive labor, which (c) keeps down the costs of goods and services.

While there are ethnic group differences, the overall picture is of low-wage employment among language minority members, relatively fewer opportunities for promotion and upward mobility, low vocational expectations and motivation, more economically disenfranchised communities and hence a possible economic poverty trap. However, it is not an inevitable condition of language minorities that they are economically deprived or impoverished. In the US, poverty and inequality are not equally shared by all Latinos, with a difference between US Cubans and Puerto Rican, Mexican and Dominican language groups. With the Spanish-speaking population of the US increasing, and with Spanish an important trading language in Latin America and elsewhere, there is a possibility that Spanish may be of increasing economic value in the years ahead.

Conclusion

For many, but not all bilinguals, it seems increasingly economically valuable to be able to work in two, three or more languages. For some individuals, this is to gain employment and try to avoid poverty. For others, bilingualism may be of value in working locally or abroad for international and multinational corporations. For yet others, who wish to go abroad to trade or translate, teach or travel, two or more languages become important.

The concept that speaking English is all one needs, whether in Europe or the US, is naive and outdated. While English is often at the leading edge of economic modernization and technological development, selling, marketing and tailoring products and services to suit local markets require other languages.

Moving from a minority language to a majority language for perceived economic purposes does not guarantee the expected rewards. There is no assurance that those who become linguistically assimilated (e.g. speak English only) in countries like the US will gain employment. The ability to speak English does not give equal or automatic access to jobs and wealth. Linguistic **assimilation** does not mean incorporation into the economic structure of the country. If there is a growth of ethnic businesses (e.g. in urban areas), and a development of language minority businesses in peripheral,

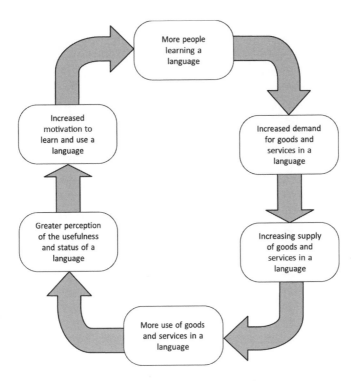

Figure 19.1 Catherine wheel cycle. Adapted from Strubell (2001)

rural areas, then bilingualism rather than English monolingualism may become more economically valuable.

The economic importance of languages, and the path to self-perpetuating change, is neatly summed up by Strubell (2001) in terms of a positive 'Catherine wheel' cycle (see Figure 19.1).

Key Points in This Chapter

➤ In a global economy and with the ease of international communications, bilinguals and multilinguals are increasingly required in many occupations.

➤ The growth of tourism has potential economic benefits for many minority languages, but is allied to the rapid spread of English and preference for historical culture rather than contemporary living culture.

➤ Minority language mass media and use in information technology are required for the status of a language but are often in competition with the dominant English language mass media.

➤ Minority language groups are often identified with relatively high unemployment, low pay, poverty and powerlessness. However, local niche economies, working from home, and community initiatives can support and sustain a language minority.

> ➤ Bilingualism can be more valuable than majority language monolingualism, giving a competitive edge for an increasing number of vocations.
>
> ➤ Research on whether bilinguals and multilinguals have an economic advantage is at an early stage of evolution. There are no easy answers as there are so many other contributing factors (e.g. age, gender, different regions and countries).
>
> ➤ What is considered as an economic advantage for bilinguals and multilinguals is varied and multiple.

Suggested Further Reading

Callahan, R. M. & Gándara, P. C. (Eds.). (2014). *The bilingual advantage: Language, literacy and the US labor market*. Bristol, UK: Multilingual Matters.

Duchéne, A., Moyer, M., & Roberts, C. (Eds.). (2013). *Language, migration and social inequalities: A critical sociolinguistic perspective on institutions and work*. Bristol, UK: Multilingual Matters.

Edwards, V. (2008). *Multilingualism in the English-speaking world: Pedigree of nations*. Oxford, UK: Blackwell.

Grin, F., Sfreddo, C., & Vaillancourt, F. (2010). *The economics of the multilingual workplace*. New York: Routledge.

Rubdy, R., & Alsagoff, L. (Eds.). (2014). *The global-local interface and hybridity: Exploring language and literacy*. Bristol, UK: Multilingual Matters.

On the Web

ePals: Connect, Communicate and Collaborate with Educators Around the World
http://www.epals.com/

Wikipedia (Explore the offerings in other languages for this online multilingual encyclopedia)
https://www.wikipedia.org/

Online Translation Tools
http://www.internetworldstats.com/links7.htm

Video: Yann Martel – How Travel Opens Your Mind and Your Language Defines Who You Are
http://bigthink.com/videos/yann-martel-breaking-down-language

Discussion Questions

(1) Is there an economic advantage to bilingualism? What factors may or may not contribute to economic advantages for bilingual individuals in your local area?

(2) Consider your own use of the internet and social media. If you are bilingual or multilingual, what language(s) do you regularly use online, and for what purposes? If you are not bilingual, do you ever encounter other languages online in your routine internet use? Have you used any translation tools with this content?

(3) Examine and discuss a selection of the dualisms or dimensions presented below. These sum up some of the debates and important dimensions of thinking in this

book. Please regard this as a 'summative' question that requires other chapters of the book to be considered and integrated:

- Linguistic compared with the sociocultural/sociolinguistic view of bilinguals.
- Individual compared with societal analysis of bilingualism.
- Language skills compared with language competences.
- Fractional compared with a holistic view of bilinguals.
- Subtractive compared with an additive view of bilinguals.
- The rights (individual and group) view compared with the empowerment view.
- Assimilationist compared with the pluralist view.
- The deprivation, remedial, problem, disabled view of bilinguals compared with the resource, beneficial, talent, diversity view of bilinguals.

(a) Briefly state what are the different viewpoints alluded to in those dualisms/dimensions you have selected.
(b) Indicate how these dualisms/dimensions relate to different views of bilingualism, bilingual education and multicultural education. What are the implications for the kind of language and cultural approach adopted in a school?

Study Activities

(1) Within your local area, make a list of newspapers, radio stations and television stations that are available in languages other than English (or other than the local/national language)? What does the presence (or absence) of these media indicate about bilingualism and multilingualism in your local area?
(2) Carry out a survey of markets, restaurants, service providers, and other businesses in your local area that cater to linguistic minority communities and/or tourists. What languages are used in these businesses? How important is it for the employees to be bilingual or multilingual?
(3) Conduct a job search via the US online job board Monster.com. Enter 'bilingual' into the search box and choose a state or city of interest. What kinds of jobs are in this area requiring bilingual skills? Do similar searches using other job board websites or local newspaper want ads in the country or region where you live or where you want to live.

Glossary

Note: Many of the terms in this glossary represent highly complex social phenomenon, and some terms and their definitions are the topic of debate. Simple and basic definitions are provided here, but fuller treatment of these terms may be found in this and other texts.

academic language proficiency. Refers to the level of language proficiency students need to successfully comprehend and perform grade-level academic tasks. The level of proficiency needed varies widely and depends on the tasks and the language demands.

acculturation. The process by which an individual or group adapt to a new culture.

acquisition planning. Part of formal language planning where interventions are made to encourage families to pass on their minority language, and schools to produce more minority language speakers.

additive bilingualism. A situation in which a second language is eventually added to a student's native language without replacing it.

ascendant bilingualism. When a second language is developing.

assessment. The process of collecting and analyzing a wide variety of data from students that provides evidence of their learning and growth over an extended period.

assimilation. The process by which a person or language group lose their own language and culture which are replaced by a different language and culture.

assimilationist. Persons who maintain the belief that cultural groups should give up their heritage languages and cultures and take on the host society's way of life.

assimilationist discourses. Discourses that devalue ELLs' home languages and cultures, seeing them as problems to overcome (also called monolingual discourses).

balanced bilingualism. Approximately equal competence in two languages.

bias. In testing, refers to the unfair advantages or disadvantages that may be given to certain students that can impact their performance. For example, a test given in English will be biased in favor of proficient English speakers and biased against students who lack proficiency in English.

bicultural. Identifying with the culture of two different language groups. To be bilingual is not necessarily the same as being bicultural.

bilingual. A term to describe an individual with command of two languages.

Bilingual Education Act. Title VII of the Elementary and Secondary Education Act of 1968, established US federal policy for bilingual education for language minority students. Reauthorized in 1994 as part of the Improving America's Schools Act, replaced in 2012 by Title III under No Child Left Behind.

bilingual immersion programs. This model typically involves the immersion of a language majority student in a classroom where the target non-dominant language is taught initially 90–100% of the time for first couple of years, and gradually to 50/50 in the target language and the dominant language. Examples include French Immersion programs in Canada and Spanish Immersion programs in the US for English speakers.

bilingualism. The ability of an individual to use two languages. The use of two languages within a community.

caretaker speech. A simplified language used by parents to children to ensure understanding, also called Motherese. Caretaker Speech usually has short sentences, is grammatically simple, has few difficult words, much repetition and with clear pronunciation.

circumstantial bilinguals. Groups of individuals who must become bilingual to operate in the majority language society that surrounds them.

codemixing. The mixing of two languages within a sentence or across sentences. Sometimes used interchangeably with codeswitching.

codeswitching. When a bilingual speaker uses more than one language inside a sentence or across sentences. Sometimes used interchangeably with codemixing.

cognition. The internal processing involved in language, memory, perception and thought.

cognates. Words that are similar in two languages because they come from the same root (e.g. education in English and educación in Spanish).

common underlying proficiency (CUP). Two languages working integratively in the thinking system. Each language serves one underlying, central thinking system.

communicative competence. The ability to use a language to communicate effectively and appropriately with other speakers of the language. Includes grammatical, discourse, sociolinguistic and strategic competence.

communicative language teaching (CLT). Language teaching approaches, methods, strategies and techniques that focus on helping students develop communicative competence.

communicative sensitivity. Sensitivity to the social nature and communicative functions of language.

comprehensible input. Oral or written language that is slightly above a second language learner's current level of proficiency in the second language and thus provides linguistic input that leads to second language acquisition.

comprehensible output. Oral or written language produced by a second language speaker that is comprehensible to the individual or individuals with whom he or she is communicating.

content and language integrated learning (CLIL). An inclusive term, particularly used in Europe, for bilingual or multilingual education in which a second or later language is used for learning subject content, and where both language learning and content learning occur simultaneously with an emphasis on their integration.

content-based ESL. Using content areas (i.e. math, language arts, science, social studies, etc.) as the basis for teaching English as a second language. In contrast with sheltered content instruction, the emphasis is on learning English more than learning the content area.

content-based instruction (CBI). An approach to second language instruction in which content area subjects and topics are used as the basis of instruction.

context. The setting in which communication occurs, and which places possibilities and constraints on what is said, and how it is said. The context can refer to the physical setting or to the language context in which a word or utterance occurs.

corpus planning. The selection, codification and expansion of norms of language.

critical period hypothesis. States that younger learners have certain cognitive advantages in learning a new language that end around a certain age. The exact age, and the degree to which a critical period or cognitive advantages exist has been the subject of much debate.

criterion-referenced test. Test designed to measure the degree to which students have mastered tested content.

culture. The set of shared meanings, beliefs, attitudes, customs, everyday behavior and social understandings of a particular group, community or society.

cultural pluralism. The ownership of two or more sets of cultural beliefs, values and attitudes. Multicultural education is often designed to encourage cultural pluralism in children.

developmental (maintenance) bilingual education. A form of bilingual education where students initially receive about 90% of content area instruction in their native language (L1) and 10% of content area instruction through sheltered instruction in the target dominate language (L2). L1 instruction decreases slowly as sheltered L2 instruction increases as students move up in grade level. Instruction continues in both languages until the end of the program, even after students attain proficiency in the L2, to ensure that students attain strong bilingual and biliteracy skills. Also referred to as maintenance late exit bilingual education.

diglossia. Two languages or language varieties existing together in a society in a stable arrangement through different uses attached to each language.

discourse/Discourse. As defined and distinguished by Gee (2012), discourse (with a lowercase d) refers to language in use or connected stretches of language that make sense, such as conversations, stories, reports, arguments, essays, and so forth. Discourse (with a capital D) is made up of distinctive ways of speaking/listening and often, too, writing/reading coupled with distinctive ways of acting, interacting, valuing, feeling, dressing, thinking and believing with other people and with various objects, tools and technologies in order to enact specific socially recognizable identities engaged in specific socially recognizable activities.

divergent thinking. Thinking that is original, imaginative and creative. A preference for open-ended, multiple answers to questions.

domains. Particular contexts where a certain language is used. For example, there is the family domain where a minority language may be used. In the work domain, the majority language may be used.

dominant language. The language which a person has greater proficiency in or uses more often.

domination. The ascendance of one group over another. The dominant group expects compliance and subservience from the subordinate group.

dual language (or Two Way) bilingual education. (See dual language programs.)

dual language books. Books printed in two languages in which one language appears above the other or the two languages are written side by side on one page or on opposite pages.

dual language programs. A variety of bilingual program models for ELL and English-proficient students designed to help them become bilingual and biliterate. In a 50/50 model, half of the students are fluent English speakers and half are ELLs, and 50% of instruction is English and 50% in the native language of the ELLs. In the 90/10 model, for the first few years, 90% of instruction is in the non-English language and 10% is in English. Instruction gradually reaches 50% in each language. Other variations exist. Also called two-way immersion.

dynamic bilingualism. This view of bilingualism focuses on the ways bilinguals draw on the range of features associated with socially constructed languages within their linguistic repertoire in complex and dynamic ways as they communicate with others and engage in collaborative tasks.

ecology of languages. The study of interactions between one or more languages and a social environment.

elite/prestigious bilingualism. Typically refers to bilingualism by choice in two (or more) elite or prestigious national and/or international languages, among the highly privileged members of a dominant society.

emergent bilingual. An alternative label for ELLs that draws attention to the other language or languages in the learners' linguistic repertoires, situates these learners in a continuum of bilingual development, and emphasizes that a fundamental goal of programs for these learners should be to help them attain high levels of proficiency in both their first language and English.

empowerment. The means by which those of low status, low influence and power are given the means to increase their chances of prosperity, power and prestige. Literacy and biliteracy are major means of empowering such individuals and groups.

enculturation. The process of adapting to a new culture.

endogenous communities. Communities that use more than one language on an everyday basis.

English as a second language (ESL). An academic subject, course, or program designed to teach English to students who are not yet proficient in the language. This term is commonly used with bilingual students, even when English may be their third or later language.

English for the Children initiatives. Referendums put to voters in four states with large ELL populations that would place severe restrictions on bilingual education programs. In 1998 California voters approved Proposition 227, in 2000 Arizona voters approved Proposition 203, and in 2002 Massachusetts voters approved Question 2. An attempt to pass a similar initiative in Colorado (Amendment 31) failed. California repealed Proposition 227 by passing Proposition 58 in 2016.

English language development (ELD). An alternative label for English as a second language (ESL) programs and instruction, commonly used at the elementary school level.

English language learners (ELLs). A label for students who are non-native speakers of English and are in the process of attaining proficiency in English. Sometimes shortened to English learner (EL).

enrichment bilingual education. A form of bilingual education that seeks to develop bilingualism, thus enriching a person's cultural, social and personal education.

executive function. A set of interrelated processes in the brain, particularly the frontal lobe. The executive function system is generally believed to consist of three components: inhibition, updating (a.k.a. working memory) and shifting (a.k.a. cognitive flexibility).

fixed mindset. A belief that one's intelligence cannot be changed.

fluent English proficient (FEP). The official designation for former ELLs who have attained sufficient English proficiency to meet their state's criteria for redesignation.

formative assessment. The use of ongoing assessments that help to identify a student's strengths and needs and thus informs subsequent instruction, building on these strengths while addressing these needs.

full inclusion. In special education, refers to placement of students with disabilities into a regular classroom as the least restrictive environment.

functional bilingualism. The ability to use bilingual skills to accomplish basic functions.

funds of knowledge. Knowledge that exists in communities and individuals outside of school that is valuable to share. Such knowledge particularly derives from heritage language and cultural minorities and is not transmitted in a majority language school curriculum.

gifted and talented education. Educational programs and classes designed for children considered to have, or potential to have, superior intellectual and/or creative abilities.

global language proficiency. Refers to an individual's overall proficiency in a second language inclusive of listening, speaker, reading and writing.

growth mindset. A belief that one's intelligence can increase with hard work and persistence.

heritage language. The language a person regards as their native, home, or ancestral language. This covers indigenous languages (e.g. Welsh in Wales) and in-migrant languages (e.g. Spanish in the United States).

heritage language education. Education programs for language minority students to develop or maintain their heritage language; includes bilingual programs for ELLs, foreign language classes targeting native speakers in K–12 and post-secondary education, and community-based after-school or weekend programs.

heteroglossic perspective. Views bilingualism as the norm and treats the languages of bilinguals as co-existing.

high-stakes testing. The use of tests to make important decisions about students (e.g. entrance or exit from special programs, grade promotion, high school graduation, etc.) and/or teachers, schools, districts, or states.

identity. The combinations and interactions between an individual's values, beliefs, views, experiences, cultures, languages, etc., that make the individual a unique person.

ideology. A set of views, beliefs, and values that influence the way an individual or group view and interpret the world surrounding them.

immersion bilingual education. Schooling where some or most subject content is taught through a second language. Pupils in immersion are usually native speakers of a majority language, and the teaching is carefully structured to their needs.

incipient bilinguals (bilingualism). The early stages of bilingualism where one language is not strongly developed. Beginning to acquire a second language.

indigenous language. A language spoken by an ethnic minority group considered to be an original inhabitant of a given land or area.

individual bilingualism. The bilingual language competencies of an individual language user.

instrumental motivation. Wanting to learn a language for utilitarian reasons (e.g. to get a better job).

integrative motivation. Wanting to learn a language to belong to a social group (e.g. make friends).

intelligence. There are many different definitions of intelligence. In general, it refers to individuals' intellectual capacity to deal with cognitive complexity, learn from experience, act purposefully, adapt effectively to the environment, and achieve goals across different environments.

intelligence quotient (IQ). A score derived from standardized tests that are designed to measure human intelligence.

intergenerational transmission. The passing on of a home language from the parents to their children.

interlanguage. An intermediate form of language used by second language learners in the process of learning a language. Interlanguage contains some transfer or borrowing from the first language, and is an approximate system with regard to grammar and communicating meaning.

language ability. An 'umbrella' term and therefore used ambiguously to describe the outcome of language learning, providing an indication of current language level.

language achievement. Normally seen as the outcome of formal language instruction. Proficiency in a language due to what has been taught or learnt in a language classroom.

language across the curriculum. A curriculum approach to language learning that accents language development across all subjects of the curriculum. Language should be developed in all content areas of the curriculum and not just as a subject in its own right. Similar approaches are taken in writing across the curriculum and reading across the curriculum.

language-as-a-problem orientation. A point of view in which the home languages of bilinguals are viewed as a problem to be overcome as students learn English and academic content through English.

language-as-a-resource orientation. A point of view in which the native languages of bilinguals are viewed as a strength to be developed and built on to help the students learn English and academic content.

language attrition. The loss of a language within a person or a language group, gradually over time.

language borrowing. A word or a phrase from one language that has become established in use in another language. When borrowing is a single word, it is often called a loan word.

language brokers. Any individual who interprets or translates between speakers or writers of two different languages. Children of immigrants often become language brokers between their parents and members of the dominant society.

language competence. A broad and general term, used particularly to describe an inner, mental representation of language, something latent rather than overt. Such competence refers usually to an underlying system inferred from language performance.

language death. Language death is said to occur when a declining language loses its last remaining speakers through their death or their shift to using another language. This language no longer exists as a medium of communication in any language domains.

language interference. Interference (or transfer) in second language learning is said to occur when vocabulary or syntax patterns transfer from a learner's first language to the second language, causing errors in second language performance. The term interference has been decreasingly used because of its negative and derogatory connotations. See: language transfer.

language loss. The process of losing the ability or use of a language within an individual or within a group. Language loss is particularly studied amongst in-migrants to a country where their mother tongue has little or no status, little economic value or use in education, and where language loss subsequently occurs.

language maintenance. The continued use of a language, particularly among language minorities (for example through bilingual education). The term is often used with reference to policies that protect and promote minority languages.

language majority students. Describes students who are native speakers of the standard language variety spoken by the dominant group of a given society.

language minority. A language community (or person) whose first language is different from the dominant language of the country. A group who speaks a language of low prestige, or low in power, or with low numbers in a society.

language minority students. Describes students who are not native speakers of the language spoken by the dominant group of a given society.

language performance. A person's production of language, particularly within a classroom or test situation. The outward evidence of language competence, but which is not necessarily an accurate measure of language competence.

language planning. The development of a deliberate policy to engineer the use of language varieties within a region or country on linguistic, political or social grounds. Language planning often involves Corpus Planning (the selection, codification and expansion of norms of language) and Status Planning (the choice of language varieties for different functions and purposes).

language proficiency. An 'umbrella' term, sometimes used synonymously with language competence; at other times as a specific, measurable outcome from language testing. Language proficiency is viewed as the product of a variety of mechanisms: formal learning, informal uncontrived language acquisition (e.g. on the street) and of individual characteristics such as 'intelligence'.

language revitalization. The process of restoring language vitality by promoting the use of a language and its range of functions within the community.

language shift. A change from the use of one language to another language within an individual or a language community. This often involves a shift from the minority language to the dominant language of the country. Usually the term means 'downward' shift (i.e. loss of a language).

language skills. Language skills are usually said to comprise: listening, speaking, reading and writing. Each of these can be divided into sub-skills. Language skills refer to highly specific, observable, clearly definable components such as writing.

language spread. An increase in the number of speakers and/or use of a language in or across geographical areas and societies.

language socialization. The process by which individuals acquire the knowledge and practices that enable them to participate effectively in a language community.

language transfer. The effect of one language on the learning of another. There can be both negative transfer, sometimes called interference, and more often positive transfer, particularly in understandings and meanings of concepts

language vitality. The extent to which a language minority vigorously maintains and extends its everyday use and range of functions. Language vitality is said to be enhanced by factors such as language status, institutional support, economic value and the number and distribution of its speakers.

least restrictive environment. In special education, the principle that students with disabilities should be given the opportunity to learn alongside non-disabled students in a regular classroom as much as possible.

lexicon. The vocabulary of a language.

limited English proficient (LEP). A label used in the US to refer to a student who is in the process of developing English language proficiency. This term has been criticized for taking a deficit view of students. English language learners, emergent bilinguals, and other terms are typically preferred.

linguistic imperialism. Typically refers to situations where an imperial, colonial or other dominant power imposes their language on speakers of other languages.

metalinguistic awareness. May loosely be defined as thinking about and reflecting upon the nature and functions of language. Metalinguistic awareness includes a collection of abilities, such as print awareness, morphological awareness, grammatical awareness and phonological awareness. They are distinct from language proficiency, but are crucial to academic achievement and the acquisition of literacy.

monocultural. Following the cultural practices associated with a single cultural or ethnic group.

monoglossic perspective. Views monolingualism as the norm and treats the languages of bilinguals as two separate distinct systems, as if students are two monolinguals in one (double monolingualism).

monolingual. A person who knows and/or uses one language.

morphology. The study of the structure of words. The central unit of study is the morpheme, the smallest unit of meaning or grammatical function.

motherese. A simplified language used by parents to children to ensure understanding. See: caretaker speech.

mother tongue. The term is used ambiguously. It variously means (a) the language learnt from the mother (b) the first language learnt, irrespective of 'from whom' (c) the stronger language at any time of life (d) the 'mother tongue' of the area or country (e.g. Irish in Ireland) (e) the language most used by a person (f) the language to which a person has the more positive attitude and affection.

multicultural. Adopting the cultural practices associated with more than one cultural or ethnic group.

multilingualism. Typically used to describe the use of three or more languages by an individual or within a society.

multiple intelligences. A theory which includes eight types of intelligences: logical-mathematical, verbal-linguistic, visual-spatial, musical-rhythmical, bodily-kinesthetic, naturalist, interpersonal and intrapersonal.

norm-referenced tests. A test designed to compare a student's score to those of other students. Test results are usually reported as percentile rankings (e.g. a student at the 71st percentile rank scored higher than 71% of the students in the test's norming population, that is, a group of students who have already taken the test).

passive bilinguals (bilingualism). Being able to understand (and sometimes read) in a second language without speaking or writing in that second language.

phonology. The study of the sound systems of languages.

pluralist discourses. Discourses that recognize ELLs' home languages and cultures as rich resources for helping them learn English and academic content and that strive to help them develop high levels of proficiency and literacy in both languages (also called multilingual discourses).

pragmatics. The study of the use of language in communication, with a particular emphasis on the contexts in which language is used.

primary language support (PLS). Using a student's native language during English as a second language (ESL) or sheltered English content area instruction to make the English instruction more comprehensible.

productive bilingualism. Speaking and writing in the first and second language (as well as listening and reading).

productive language. Speaking and writing.

Proposition 58. A voter initiative in California passed in 2016 that repealed Proposition 227 (1998) and thus removed restrictions on bilingual education programs.

Proposition 203. An English for the Children voter initiative passed in Arizona in 2000, placing restrictions on bilingual education.

Proposition 227. An English for the Children voter initiative passed in California in 1998, placing restrictions on bilingual education. It was repealed by Proposition 58 in 2016.

pull-out ESL. A program model for ELLs in which students are placed in mainstream or sheltered English immersion classrooms but are regularly pulled out of class for English as a second language (ESL) lessons taught by an ESL teacher.

Question 2. An English for the Children voter initiative passed in Massachusetts in 2002, placing restrictions on bilingual education.

receptive bilinguals (bilingualism). Understanding and reading a second language without speaking or writing in that language.

receptive language. Listening/understanding and reading.

recessive bilingualism. When proficiency in one of a bilingual's languages is decreasing due to lack of use or development.

recursive bilingualism. A view of bilingualism, especially as related to revitalization of endangered languages, to describe the ways bilinguals reach back to the bits and pieces of their ancestral language as they reconstitute it for new functions and move the language forward towards the future.

redesignation. The reclassification of a student from English language learner (ELL), or limited English proficient (LEP), to fluent English proficient (FEP), based on criteria established by a school district or state.

register. Variation in the use of language based on the context in which the language is used.

reliability. The consistency with which a test or assessment measures what it is measuring.

scaffolding. Providing support to build on a student's existing repertoire of knowledge and understanding. As the student progresses and becomes more of an independent learner, the help given by teachers can be gradually removed.

semantics. The study of the meaning of words, phrases, and sentences.

semilingual. A controversial term used to describe people whose two languages appear to be at a low level of development in comparison with the standardized varieties of those languages.

separate storage hypothesis. States that bilinguals have two independent language storage and retrieval systems in their brain.

separate underlying proficiency (SUP). The largely discredited idea that two languages exist separately and work independently in the thinking system.

sequential/consecutive bilingualism. Bilingualism achieved via learning a second language later than the first language. When a second language is learnt after the age of three, sequential bilingualism is said to occur.

shared storage hypothesis. States that the two languages are kept in a single memory store in the brain with two different language input channels and two different language output channels.

sheltered content instruction. Content (subject) classes that also include English language development. The curriculum is taught in English in the United States at a comprehensible level to minority language students. The goal of sheltered English is to help minority language students acquire proficiency in English while at the same time achieving well in content areas of the curriculum.

sheltered English. Content (subject) classes that also include English language development. The curriculum is taught in English in the United States at a comprehensible level to minority language students. The goal of sheltered English is to help minority language students acquire proficiency in English while at the same time achieving well in content areas of the curriculum.

sheltered English immersion (SEI). A program model for ELLs that combines English as a second language (ESL), sheltered content area instruction, and primary language support. Sometimes called structured English immersion.

sheltered instruction. Grade level content area instruction provided in English in a manner that makes it comprehensible to ELLs while supporting their English language development.

Sheltered Instruction Observation Protocol (SIOP). A tool for planning, implementing and evaluating sheltered English content area instruction.

simultaneous bilingualism. Bilingualism achieved via acquiring a first and a second language concurrently. When a second language is learnt before the age of three, simultaneous bilingualism is said to occur.

societal bilingualism. A broad term used to refer to the use of two (or more) languages within a given society.

sociolinguistics. The study of language in relation to social groups, social class, ethnicity and other interpersonal factors in communication.

special education. Specially designed instruction to meet the unique needs of a child with a disability, guided by regulations in the Individuals with Disabilities Education Act.

specially designed academic instruction in English (SDAIE). Another term for sheltered instruction, preferred in California and other states because it places emphasis on the fact that such instruction is academically rigorous but specially designed to match the linguistic needs of the student.

speech community. A group of people who share a common language(s) and norms and expectations for its use.

status planning. Language planning which centers on language use and prestige within a region and within particular language domains. See: language planning.

strategic competence. A speaker's ability to adapt their use of a second language to compensate for gaps in their proficiency.

structured immersion. The curriculum is taught in English in such programs in the United States at a comprehensible level to minority language students. The goal is to help minority language students acquire proficiency in English while at the same time achieving well in content areas of the curriculum.

submersion. The teaching of minority language pupils solely through the medium of a majority language, often alongside native speakers of the majority language. Minority language pupils are left to sink or swim in the mainstream curriculum.

subtractive bilingualism. A situation in which a second language eventually replaces a student's native language.

summative assessment. Assessments that provide a summary of what students know and can do. Typically given at the end of a unit or at the end of a school year.

syntax. The study of the rules governing the relationships between words and the ways they are combined to form phrases and sentences.

terminology. The creation, selection and standardization of terms for use in specific (e.g. school curriculum) or technical (e.g. science, medicine, computing) contexts. See: corpus planning/language planning.

testing. The administration of tests, singular instruments designed to systematically measure a sample of a student's ability at one particular time.

testing accommodations. In testing ELLs, refers to modifications in the testing environment or testing procedures, or modifications to the test instrument itself, that are intended to make up for a student's lack of proficiency in the language of the test (e.g. providing extra time, oral interpretation of test directions or items, native-language versions of the test).

threshold theory. A contested theory that suggest that certain cognitive advantages of bilingualism may be available only after a certain level of bilingualism has been attained.

transglossia. In contrast to models of diglossia which typically sees majority and minority languages relegated to specific domains, functions and use, transglossia considers the ways in which multiple languages are used across multiple domains and functions within a society, or the ways in which multiple languages may be used within a single domain or function.

transitional bilingual education (TBE). A program model for bilingual students. As commonly used in the United States, native language content area instruction is provided for the first few years of the program, in addition to sheltered content area instruction and English as a second language (ESL). The amount of native language instruction decreases as sheltered English immersion increases. Students are transitioned to mainstream classrooms after just a few years in the program.

translanguaging. In its original conceptualization, refers to the practice in which bilinguals receive information in one language and then use or apply it in the other language. In its expanded sense, refers to the natural and normal ways bilinguals use their languages in their everyday lives to make sense of their bilingual worlds. In teaching, refers to pedagogical practices that use bilingualism as a resource rather than ignore it or perceive it as a problem.

trilingual education. The teaching and use of three or more languages for instruction in the classroom. Typically, these would include the home language, a regional and/or national dominant language, and/or a major international language.

validity. The accuracy of a test or assessment in measuring what it purports to measure.

vernacular. An indigenous or heritage language of an individual or community. A vernacular language is used to define a native language as opposed to (1) a classical language such as Latin and Greek, (2) an internationally used language such as English and French, (3) the official or national language of a country.

zone of proximal development(ZPD). Refers to a metaphorical space between what an individual can do on his or her own, and what she or he can do with support from a teacher or other more knowledgeable person.

Bibliography

Abedi, J. (2017) Utilizing accommodations in assessment. In E.G. Shohamy and S. May (eds) *Encyclopedia of language education* (3rd ed., Vol. 7). New York, NY: Springer.

Abley, M. (2005) *Spoken here: Travels among threatened languages* (First Mariner Books ed.). Boston, MA: Houghton Mifflin.

Adesope, O.O., Lavin, T., Thompson, T. and Ungerleider, C. (2010) A systematic review and meta-analysis of the cognitive correlates of bilingualism. *Review of Educational Research, 80*(2), 207–245.

Al-Gasem, N.S. (2015) 'A nerdy adrenalie': The influence of ethnomathematics on female mathematical identity. (PhD Dissertation), University of Texas at San Antonio.

Alarcón, A., Di Paolo, A., Heyman, J. and Morales, M.C. (2014) The occupational location of Spanish-English bilinguals in the new information economy: The health and criminal justice sectors in the US borderlands with Mexico. In R. Callahan and P. Gándara (eds) *The bilingual advantage: Language, literacy and the US labor market* (pp. 110–137). Bristol, UK: Multilingual Matters.

Alarcón, A. and Heyman, J. (2013) Bilingual call centers at the US-Mexico border: Location and linguistic markers of exploitability. *Language in Society, 42*(1), 1–21.

Alim, H.S. (2005) Critical language awareness in the United States: Revisiting issues and revising pedagogies in a resegregated society. *Educational Researcher, 34*(7), 24–31. doi:10.3102/0013189X034007024

Alim, H.S. (2010) Critical language awareness. In N. Hornberger and S. McKay (eds) *Sociolinguistics and language education* (pp. 205–231). Bristol, UK: Multilingual Matters.

Amara, M., Azaiza, F., Hertz-Lazarowitz, R. and Mor-Sommerfeld, A. (2009) A bew bilingual education in the conflict-ridden Israeli reality: Language practices. *Language and Education, 23*(1), 15–35.

American Council on the Teaching of Foreign Languages (2011) *Foreign language enrollments in K–12 public schools: Are students prepared for a global society? (Executive Summary)*. Retrieved from Alexandria, VA: http://www.actfl.org/sites/default/files/pdfs/ReportSummary2011.pdf

American Education Research Association, American Psychological Association and National Council on Measurement in Education (2014) *Standards for educational and psychological testing* (2nd ed.). Washington, DC: American Education Research Association.

American Institutes for Research and WestEd (2006) *Effects of the implementation of Proposition 227 on the education of English learners, K–12: Findings from a five-year evaluation*. Retrieved from Washington, DC and San Francisco, CA: http://www.wested.org/online_pubs/227Reportb.pdf

American Psychological Association (1982) *Review of Department of Education report entitled 'Effectiveness of bilingual education: A review of the literature.' Letter to Congressional Hispanic Caucus*, April 22.

Andrews, E., Frigau, L., Voyvodic-Casabo, C., Voyvodic, J. and Wright, J. (2013) Multilingualism and fMRI: Longitudinal study of second language acquisition. *Brain Sciences, 3*(2), 849–876.

Angouri, J. (2014) Introduction: Multilingualism in the workplace: Language practices in multilingual contexts. *Multilingua, 33*(1–2), 1–9.

Ardila, A. and Ramos, E. (2007) Bilingualism and cognition: The good, the bad and the ugly of bilingualism. In A. Ardila and E. Ramos (eds) *Speech and language disorders in bilinguals* (pp. 213–234). New York, NY: Nova Science Publishers.

Arias, M.B. (2015) Parent and community involvement in bilingual and multilingual education. In W.E. Wright, S. Boun and O. García (eds) *Handbook of bilingual and multilingual education* (pp. 282–298). Madlen, MA: Wiley-Blackwell.

Arnau, J. (1997) Immersion education in Catalonia. In J. Cummins and D. Corson (eds) *Bilingual Education* (pp. 297–303). Dordrecht, NL: Kluwer.

Artigal, J.M. (1993) Catalan and Basque immersion programs. In H.B. Beardsmore (ed.) *European models of bilingual education*. Clevedon, UK: Multilingual Matters.

Artiles, A.J. (2003) Special education's changing identity: Paradoxes and dilemmas in views of culture and space. *Harvard Educational Review,* 73(2), 164–202.

Artiles, A.J. and Ortiz, A.A. (2002) English language learners with special education needs. In A. Artiles and A.A. Ortiz (eds) *English language learners with special educational needs*. Washington, DC and McHenry, IL: Center for Applied Linguistics and Delta Systems Co.

Arviso, M. and Holm, W. (2001) Tséhootsooídi Olta'gi Diné Bizaad Bíhoo'aah: A Navajo immersion program at Fort Defiance, Arizona. In L. Hinton and K. Hale (eds) *The green book of language revitalization in practice*. San Diego, CA: Academic Press.

Athanasopoulos, P. (2007) Interaction between grammatical categories and cognition in bilinguals: The role of proficiency, cultural immersion, and language of instruction. *Language and Cognitive Processes,* 22(5), 689–699.

Athanasopoulos, P. (2011) Cognitive restructuring in bilingualism. In A. Pavlenko (ed.) *Thinking and speaking in two languages*. Bristol, UK: Multilingual matters.

Atkins, J.D.C. (1887) *Annual report to the Commissioner of Indian Affairs to United States Bureau of Indian Affairs*. Washington, DC: Government Printing Office.

Atkinson, D. (ed.) (2011) *Alternative approaches to second language acquisition*. New York, NY: Routledge.

Aucamp, A.J. (1926) *Bilingual education and nationalism with special reference to South Africa*. Pretoria, South Africa: Van Schaik.

August, D. (2002) *Transitional programs for English language learners: An examination of the impact of English-only versus bilingual instruction*. Baltimore, MD: CRESPAR Publications Department, John Hopkins University.

August, D. (2012) How does first language literacy development relate to second language literacy development? In E. Hamayan and R. Freeman (eds) *English language learners at school: A guide for administrators* (2nd ed., pp. 56–57). Philadelphia, PA: Caslon Publishing.

August, D. and Hakuta, K. (1997) *Improving schooling for language-minority children: A research agenda*. Washington, DC: National Academy Press.

August, D. and Shanahan, T. (2006) *Developing literacy in second-language learners: Report of the National Literacy Panel on Language-Minority Children and Youth*. Mahwah, NJ: Lawrence Erlbaum Associates Publishers.

August, D. and Shanahan, T. (2008) *Developing reading and writing in second-language learners: Lessons from the report of the National Literacy Panel on Language-Minority Children and Youth*. New York, NY: Taylor and Francis.

August, D., Calderon, M., Carlo, M. and Eakin, M. (2006) Developing literacy in English-language learners: An examination of the impact of English-only versus bilingual instruction. In P. D. McCardle and E. Hoff (eds), *Childhood bilingualism: Research on infancy through school age* (pp. 91-106). Clevedon, UK: Multilingual Matters.

Austin, P.K. and Sallabank, J. (eds) (2015) *The Cambridge handbook of endangered languages*. Cambridge, UK: Cambridge University Press.

Avni, S. and Menken, K. (2013) Educating for Jewishness: The teaching and learning of Hebrew in day school education. In O. García, Z. Zakharia and B. Otcu (eds) *Bilingual and community multilingualism: Beyond hertiage languages in a global city* (pp. 190–203). Bristol, UK: Multilingual Matters.

Babaee, N. (2012) *Heritage language learning in Canadian public schools: Language rights challenges*. Paper presented at the 13th Annual Education Graduate Student Symposium, the University of Manitoba, Winnipeg, Manitoba, Canada.

Bachi, R. (1955) A statistical analysis of the revival of Hebrew in Israel. *Scripta Hierosolymitana, 3,* 179–247.

Bachman, L.F. and Palmer, A.S. (1996) *Language testing in practice: Designing and developing useful language tests*. Oxford, UK: Oxford University Press.

Bailey, A.L. and Carroll, P.E. (2015) Assessment of English language learners in the era of new academic content standards. *Review of Research in Education, 39,* 253–294.

Baker, C. (1992) *Attitudes and language*. Clevedon, UK: Multilingual Matters.

Baker, C. (2003) Biliteracy and transliteracy in Wales: Language planning and the Welsh national curriculum. In N.H. Hornberger (ed.) *Continua of biliteracy: An ecological framework for educational policy, research, and practice in multilingual settings*. Clevedon, UK: Multilingual Matters.

Baker, C. (2008) Postlude. 'Multilingualism and minority languages: Achievements and challenges in education'. *AILA Review, 21,* 69–86.

Baker, C. (2010a) Bilingual education. In R.B. Kaplan (ed.) *The Oxford handbook of applied linguistics*. Oxford, UK: Oxford University Press.

Baker, C. (2010b) Increasing bilingualism in bilingual education. In D. Morris (ed.) *Welsh in the 21st Century* (pp. 61–79). Cardiff, UK: University of Wales Press.

Baker, C. (2014) *A parents and teachers guide to bilingualism* (4th ed.). Bristol, UK: Multilingual Matters.

Baker, C. and Jones, M.P. (2000) Welsh language education: A strategy for revitalization. In C.H. Williams (ed.) *Language revitalization: Policy and planning in Wales* (pp. 116–137). Cardiff, UK: University of Wales Press.

Baker, C. and Jones, S.P. (1998) *Encyclopedia of bilingualism and bilingual education*. Clevedon, UK: Multilingual Matters.

Baker, C. and Lewis, G. (2015) A synthesis of research on bilingual and multilingual education. In W. E. Wright, S. Boun and O. Garcia (eds) *Handbook of bilingual and multilingual education* (pp. 109–126). Malden, MA: Wiley-Blackwell.

Baker, F.S. (2012) The role of the bilingual teaching assistant: Alternative visions for bilingual support in the primary years. *International Journal of Bilingual Education and Bilingualism, 17*(3), 255–271. do i:10.1080/13670050.2012.748013

Baker, K.A. (1987) Comment on Willig's 'A meta-analysis of selected studies in the effectiveness of bilingual education'. *Review of Educational Research, 57*(3), 351–362.

Baker, K.A. (1992) Ramirez *et al.*: Misled by bad theory. *Bilingual Research Journal, 16*(1–2), 63–90.

Baker, K.A. and de Kanter, A. (1983) *Bilingual education: A reappraisal of federal policy*. Lexington, MA: LexingtonBooks.

Baker, P. and Kim, J. (2003) *Global London: Where to find almost everything ethnic and cultural in the multilingual capital*. London, UK: Battlebridge.

Bakhtin, M.M. (1994) *The dialogic imagination: Four essays*. Austin, TX: University of Texas Press.

Bali, V.A. (2001) Sink or swim: What happened to California's bilingual students after Proposition 227? *State Politics and Policy Quarterly, 1*(3), 295–317.

Ball, P., Kelly, K. and Clegg, J. (2016) *Putting CLIL into practice*. Oxford, UK: Oxford University Press.

Barker, V. and Giles, H. (2002) Who supports the English-only movement? Evidence for misconceptions about Latino group vitality. *Journal of Multilingual and Multicultural Development, 23*(5), 353–370.

Barker, V., Giles, H., Noels, K., Duck, J., Hecht, M.L. and Clement, R. (2001) The English-only movement: A communication analysis of changing perceptions of language vitality. *Journal of Communication, 51*(1), 3–37.

Barnard, R. and McClellan, J. (eds) (2014) *Codeswitching in university English-medium classes: Asian perspectives*. Bristol, UK: Multilingual Matters.

Barron-Hauwaert, S. (2004) *Language strategies for bilingual families: The one-parent-one-language approach*. Clevedon, UK: Multilingual Matters.

Barron-Hauwaert, S. (2011) *Bilingual siblings: Language use in families*. Bristol, UK: Multilingual Matters.

Bartlett, L. and García, O. (2011) *Additive schooling in subtractive times: Dominican immigrant youth in the heights*. Nashville, TN: Vanderbilt University Press.

Barwell, R. (ed.) (2009) *Multilingualism in mathematics classrooms*. Bristol, UK: Multilingual Matters.

Bassetti, B. (2007) Bilingualism and thought: Grammatical gender and concepts of objects in Italian-German bilingual children. *International Journal of Bilingualism, 11*(3), 251–273.

Batibo, H. (2005) *Language decline and death in Africa: Causes, consequences, and challenges* (Vol. 132). Clevedon, UK: Multilingual Matters Clevedon.

Bayley, R. and Langman, J. (2011) Language socialization in multilingual and second language contexts. In E. Hinkel (ed.) *Handbook of second language learning and teaching* (Vol. 2, pp. 291–302). New York, NY: Routledge.

Beam-Conroy, T. and McHatton, P.A. (2015) Bilingual education and students with dis/abilities and ex-ceptionalities. In W.E. Wright, S. Boun and O. García (eds) *Handbook of bilingual and multilingual education* (pp. 370–383). Malden, MA: Wiley-Blackwell.

Bedore, L.M., Peña, E.D., Garcia, M. and Cortez, C. (2005) Conceptual versus monolingual scoring: When does it make a difference? *Language, Speech, and Hearing Services in Schools, 36*(3), 188–200.

Beeman, K. and Urow, C. (2012) *Teaching for biliteracy: Strengthening bridges between languages*. Phila-delphia, PA: Caslon Publishing.

Bekerman, Z. (2016) *The promise of integrated multicultural and bilingual education: Inclusive Palestinian-Arab and Jewish schools in Israel*. Oxford, UK: Oxford University Press.

Bell, A.G. (1883) *Memoir Upon the Formation of a Deaf Variety of the Human Race. Paper presented to the National Academy of Sciences (New Haven, Connecticut, 13 November 1883)*. Washington, DC: Alexander Graham Bell Association for the Deaf, Inc.

Ben-Zeev, S. (1977a) The effect of bilingualism in children from Spanish-English low economic neighbor-hoods on cognitive development and cognitive strategy. *Working Papers on Bilingualism, 14*, 83–122.

Ben-Zeev, S. (1977b) The influence of bilingualism on cognitive strategy and cognitive development. *Child Development, 48*(3), 1009–1018.

Benson, C. (2004) Do we expect too much of bilingual teachers? Bilingual teaching in developing countries. *International Journal of Bilingual Education and Bilingualism, 7*(2–3), 204–221.

Benson, C. (2009) Designing effective schooling in multilingual context: the strengths and limitations of bilingual 'models'. In A. K. Mohanty, M. Panda, R. Phillipson and T. Skutnabb-Kangas (eds) *Multilingual Education for Social Justice Globalising the Local*. New Delhi, IN: Orient Blackswan.

Berlin, D.C. (2013, 5 June) Death of a language: Last ever speaker of Livonian passes away aged 103. *The Times*. Retrieved from http://www.thetimes.co.uk/tto/news/world/europe/article3782596.ece

Bhabha, H.K. (2004) *The location of culture*. London, UK: Routledge.

Bhatia, T.K. and Ritchie, W. C. (2013) Bilingualism and multilingualism in South Asia. In T.K. Bhatia and W.C. Ritchie (eds) *Handbook of bilingualism and multilingualism* (2nd ed., pp. 843–870). Malden, MA: Wiley-Blackwell.

Bialystok, E. (1987a) Influences of bilingualism on metalinguistic development. *Second Language Research, 3*(2), 154–166.

Bialystok, E. (1987b) Words as things: Development of word concept by bilingual children. *Studies in Second Language Acquisition, 9*(02), 133–140.

Bialystok, E. (2001a) *Bilingualism in development: Language, literacy, and cognition*. Cambridge, UK: Cambridge University Press.

Bialystok, E. (2001b) Literacy: The extension of languages through other means. In R.L. Cooper, E. Shohamy and J. Walters (eds) *New perspectives and issues in educational language policy: In honour of Bernard Dov Spolsky*. Amsterdam, NE: John Benjamins Publishing.

Bialystok, E. (2001c) Metalinguistic aspects of bilingual processing. *Annual Review of Applied Linguistics, 21*, 169–181.

Bialystok, E. (2007) Acquisition of literacy in bilingual children: A framework for research. *Language Learning, 57*(1), 45–77. doi:10.1111/j.1467–9922.2007.00412.x

Bialystok, E. (2009) Bilingualism: The good, the bad, and the indifferent. *Bilingualism: Language and Cognition, 12*(01), 3–11.

Bialystok, E. (2013) The impact of bilingualism on language and literacy development. In T.K. Bhatia and W.C. Ritchie (eds) *The handbook of bilingualism and multilingualism* (2nd ed., pp. 624–648). Malden, MA: Wiley-Blackwell.

Bialystok, E. (2015) How hazy views become full pictures. *Language, Cognition and Neuroscience, Online First*. doi:10.1080/23273798.2015.1074255

Bialystok, E. and Codd, J. (1997) Cardinal limits: Evidence from language awareness and bilingualism for developing concepts of number. *Cognitive Development, 12*(1), 85–106.

Bialystok, E., Craik, F. and Luk, G. (2008) Cognitive control and lexical access in younger and older bilinguals. *Journal of Experimental Psychology: Learning, Memory, and Cognition, 34*(4), 859–873.

Bialystok, E., Craik, F.I., Binns, M.A., Ossher, L. and Freedman, M. (2014) Effects of bilingualism on the age of onset and progression of MCI and AD: Evidence from executive function tests. *Neuropsychology, 28*, 290–304.

Bialystok, E., Craik, F.I. and Freedman, M. (2007) Bilingualism as a protection against the onset of symptoms of dementia. *Neuropsychologia, 45*(2), 459–464.

Bialystok, E., Craik, F.I., Grady, C., Chau, W., Ishii, R., Gunji, A. and Pantev, C. (2005) Effect of bilingualism on cognitive control in the Simon task: Evidence from MEG. *NeuroImage, 24*(1), 40–49.

Bialystok, E., Craik, F.I., Klein, R. and Viswanathan, M. (2004) Bilingualism, aging, and cognitive control: Evidence from the Simon task. *Psychology and aging, 19*(2), 290–303.

Bialystok, E., Craik, F.I. and Luk, G. (2012) Bilingualism: consequences for mind and brain. *Trends in Cognitive Sciences, 16*(4), 240–250.

Bialystok, E. and Feng, X. (2011) Language proficiency and its implications for monolingual and bilingual children. In A. Durgunoglu and C. Goldenberg (eds) *Challenges for language learners in language and literacy development* (pp. 121–138). New York, NY: Guilford Press.

Bialystok, E., Luk, G. and Kwan, E. (2005) Bilingualism, biliteracy, and learning to read: Interactions among languages and writing systems. *Scientific Studies of Reading, 9*(1), 43–61.

Bialystok, E. and Martin, M.M. (2004) Attention and inhibition in bilingual children: Evidence from the dimensional change card sort task. *Developmental Science, 7*(3), 325–339.

Bialystok, E., Peets, K.F. and Moreno, S. (2014) Producing bilinguals through immersion education: Development of metalinguistic awareness. *Applied Psycholinguistics, 35*(1), 177–191.

Bialystok, E., Poarch, G., Luo, L. and Craik, F.I.M. (2014) Effects of bilingualism and aging on executive function and working memory. *Psychology and Aging, 29*, 696–705.

Bialystok, E. and Viswanathan, M. (2009) Components of executive control with advantages for bilingual children in two cultures. *Cognition, 113*(3), 494–500.

Birdsong, D. (2006) Age and second language acquisition and processing: A selective overview. *Language learning, 56*(1), 9–49.

Bjorklund, S. and Suni, I. (2000) The role of English as L3 in a Swedish immersion programme in Finland. In J. Cenoz and U. Jessner (eds) *English in Europe: the acquisition of a third language* (Vol. 19, pp. 198). Clevedon, UK: Multilingual Matters.

Blackledge, A. (2000) *Literacy, power and social justice.* Stoke on Trent, UK: Trentham.

Blackledge, A., Creese, A., Baraç, T., Bhatt, A., Hamid, S., Wei, L., … Yağcioğlu, D. (2008) Contesting 'language' as 'heritage': Negotiation of identities in late modernity. *Applied Linguistics, 29*(4), 533–554.

Block, D. (2014) *Second language identities* (Classics ed.). London, UK: Bloomsbury Academic.

Blommaert, J. (2013) *Ethnography, superdiversity and linguistic landscape: Chronicles of complexity.* Bristol, UK: Multilingual Matters.

Bloomfield, L. (1933) *Language.* New York, NY: Holt.

Boals, T., Kenyon, D.M., Blair, A., Cranley, M.E., Wilmes, C. and Wright, L. J. (2015) Transformation in K-12 English language proficiency assessment: Changing contexts, changing constructs. *Review of Research in Education, 39*, 122–164.

Boroditsky, L. (2001) Does language shape thought?: Mandarin and English speakers' conceptions of time. *Cognitive Psychology, 43*(1), 1–22.

Boroditsky, L., Ham, W. and Ramscar, M. (2002) *What is universal in event perception? Comparing English and Indonesian speakers.* Paper presented at the Proceedings of the 24th annual meeting of the Cognitive Science Society.

Bourdieu, P. (1991) *Language and symbolic power* (G. Raymond and M. Adamson, Trans.). Cambridge, MA: Harvard University Press.

Bourhis, R.Y. (2001) Acculturation, language maintenance, and language shift. In J. Klatter-Folmer and P. Vanavermaet (eds) *Theories on maintenance and loss of minority languages* (pp. 5–37). Münster, New York: Waxmann.

Boyle, A., August, D., Tabaku, L., Cole, S. and Simpson-Baird, A. (2015) *Dual language education programs: Current state policies and practices.* Washington, DC: American Institutes for Research.

Brecht, R.D. and Ingold, C.W. (2002) *Tapping a national resource: Heritage languages in the United States.* (ERIC Digest, EDO-FL-98–12).

Breen, M.P. (2002) Principles for the teaching of EAL/ESL children in the mainstream: Lessons from experience and professional development. In C. Leung (ed.) *Language and additional/second language issues for school education.* York, UK: NADLIC.

Brentnall, J., Cann, J. and Williams, C. (2009) *Language in multilingual Wales*: Bangor University, College of Education and Lifelong Education.

Brinton, D. (ed.) (2008) *Heritage language education: A new field emerging.* New York, NY: Routledge.

Brisk, M.E. (2006) *Bilingual education: From compensatory to quality schooling* (2nd ed.). Mahwah, NJ: Erlbaum.

Brisk, M.E. (2008) *Language, culture, and community in teacher education.* New York, NY: Routledge.

British Council. (2013) *Lost for words: The need for languages in UK diplomacy and security.* London, UK: Author. Retrieved from http://www.britac.ac.uk/policy/Lost_For_Words.cfm

Brohy, C. (2005) Trilingual education in Switzerland. *International Journal of the Sociology of Language, 171*, 133–148.

Brown, T. and Brown, J. (2015) *To advanced proficiency and beyond: Theory and method for developing superior second language ability.* Washington, DC: Georgetown University Press.

Bruck, M. (1978) The suitability of early French immersion programs for the language-disabled child. *Canadian Journal of Education/Revue canadienne de l'education, 3*(4), 51–72.

Bruck, M. (1982) Language impaired children's performance in an additive bilingual education program. *Applied Psycholinguistics, 3*(01), 45–60.

Bruner, J. (1983) *Child talk.* New York, NY: Norton.

Bruthiaux, P. (2009) Language rights in historical and contemporary perspective. *Journal of Multilingual and Multicultural Development, 30*(1), 73–85.

Buchweitz, A. and Prat, C. (2013) The bilingual brain: Flexibility and control in the human cortex. *Physics of Life Reviews, 10*(4), 428–443.

Bunch, G.C. (2014) The language of ideas and the language of display: Reconceptualizing 'academic language' in linguistically diverse classrooms. *International Multilingual Research Journal, 8*, 70–86.

Burke, A., Morita-Mullaney, T. and Singh (forthcoming) Indiana emergent bilingual student time to re-classification: A survival analysis.

Burke, G. and Sainz, A. (2016) Migrant children kept from enrolling in school. *Associated Press: The big story*. Retrieved from http://bigstory.ap.org/article/b7f933ef6e054c2ca8e32bd9b477e9ab/ap-exclusive-migrant-children-kept-enrolling-school

Burr, E., Haas, E. and Ferriere, K. (2015) *Identifying and supporting English learner students with learning disabilities: Key issues in the literature and state practice*. Washington, DC: Institute for Educational Sciences, US Department of Education.

Buttitta, I. (1972) *Lo faccio il poeta*. Milan, IT: Feltrinelli.

Byers-Heinlein, K., Burns, T. and Werker, J. (2010) The roots of bilingualism in newborns. *Psychological Science, 21*(343–348).

Bylund, E. and Athanasopoulos, P. (2014a) Language and thought in a multilingual context: The case of isiXhosa. *Bilingualism: Language and Cognition, 17*, 431–443.

Bylund, E. and Athanasopoulos, P. (2014b) Linguistic relativity in SLA: Toward a new research program. *Language Learning, 64*, 952–985. doi:10.1111/lang.12080

Bylund, E. and Athanasopoulos, P. (2015) Introduction: Cognition, motion events, and SLA. *The Modern Language Journal, 99*(1), 1–13.

Byram, M. and Parmenter, L. (eds) (2012) *The Common European Framework of Reference: The globalisation of language education policy*. Bristol, UK: Multilingual Matters.

Cabellero, A.M.S. (2014) Preparing teachers to work with heritage language learners. In T. G. Wiley, J. K. Peyton, D. Christian, S.C.K. Moore and N. Liu (eds) *Handbook of heritage, community, and Native American languaages in the United States: Research, policy, and educational practice* (pp. 359–369). New York, NY and Washington, DC: Routledge and Center for Applied Linguistics

California State Department of Education (1984) *Studies on immersion education. A collection for United States educators*. Sacramento, CA: California State Department of Education.

Callahan, R.M. and Gándara, P.C. (eds) (2014) *The bilingual advantage: Language, literacy and the US labor market*. Bristol, UK: Multilingual Matters.

Canadian Education Association (1991) *Heritage language programs in Canadian school boards*. Toronto, CA: Canadian Education Association.

Canagarajah, A.S. (2013) Introduction. In A.S. Canagarajah (ed.) Literacy as translingual practice: Between communities and classrooms (pp. 1–10). New York, NY: Routledge.

Canale, M. and Swain, M. (1980) Theoretical bases of communicative approaches to second language teaching and testing. *Applied Linguistics, 1*, 1–47.

Carder, M. (2007) *Bilingualism in international schools: A model for enriching language education*. Clevedon, UK: Multilingual Matters.

Carder, M. (2013) International school students: Developing their bilingual potential. In C. Abello-Contesse, P.M. Chandler, M.D. López-Jiménez and R. Chacón-Beltrán (eds) *Bilingual and multilingual education in the 21st Century: Building on experience* (pp. 275–298). Bristol, UK: Multilingual Matters.

Carlisle, J.F., Beeman, M., Davis, L.H. and Spharim, G. (1999) Relationship of metalinguistic capabilities and reading achievement for children who are becoming bilingual. *Applied Psycholinguistics, 20*(04), 459–478.

Carroll, L. (1872) *Through the looking glass: And what Alice found there*. London, UK: MacMillan and Co.

Cazabon, M., Lambert, W.E. and Hall, G. (1993) *Two-way bilingual education: A progress report on the Amigos Program*. Santa Cruz, CA: National Center for Research on Cultural Diversity and Second Language Learning.

Cazden, C.B. (1992) *Language minority education in the United States: Implications of the Ramirez Report*. Santa Cruz, CA: National Center for Research on Cultural Diversity and Second Language Learning.

Cenoz, J. (2003) The additive effect of bilingualism on third language acquisition: A review. *International Journal of Bilingualism, 7*(1), 71–87.

Cenoz, J. (2009) *Towards multilingual education: Basque educational research from an international perspective* (Vol. 72). Clevedon, UK: Multilingual Matters.

Cenoz, J. and Etxague, X. (2013) From bilingualism to multilingualism: Basque, Spanish and English in higher education. In C. Abello-Contesse, P.M. Chandler, M.D. López-Jiménez and R. Chacón-Beltrán (eds) *Bilingual and multilingual education in the 21st Century: Building on experience* (pp. 85–106). Bristol, UK: Multilingual Matters.

Cenoz, J. and Genesee, F. (1998) Psycholinguistic perspectives on multilingualism and multilingual education. In J. Cenoz and F. Genesee (eds) *Beyond bilingualism: Multilingualism and multilingual education*. Clevedon, UK: Multilingual Matters.

Cenoz, J., Genesee, F. and Gorter, D. (2014) Critical analysis of CLIL: Taking stock and looking forward. *Applied Linguistics, 35*(3), 243–262.

Cenoz, J. and Gorter, D. (2015) Minority languages, state languages, and English in European education. In W.E. Wright, S. Boun and O. García (eds) *Handbook of bilingual and multilingual education* (pp. 471–483). Malden, MA: Wiley-Blackwell.

Cerney, J. (2007) *Deaf education in America: Voices of children from inclusion settings.* Washington. DC: Gallaudet Univ Pr.

Chan, V. (2016) *Medium of instruction policies in higher education in Cambodia.* (PhD Dissertation), University of Texas at San Antonio.

Chang, J. (2004) *Ideologies of English teaching and learning in Taiwan.* PhD Dissertation, University of Sydney.

Chao-Jung, W. (2006) Look who's talking: Language choices and culture of learning in UK Chinese classrooms. *Language and Education, 20*(1), 62–75.

Cheatham, G.A., Santos, R.M. and Kerkutluoglu, A. (2012) Review of comparison studies investigating bilingualism and bilingual instruction for students with disabilities. *Focus on Exceptional Children, 45*(3), 1–12.

Cheshire, J. (2002) Who we are and where we're going: Language and identities in the new Europe. In P. Gubbins and M. Holt (eds) *Beyond boundaries: Language and identity in contemporary Europe* (Vol. 122). Clevedon, UK: Multilingual matters.

Chhuon, V. and Hudley, C. (2010) Asian American ethnic options: How Cambodian students negotiate ethnic identities in a U.S. urban school. *Anthropology and Education Quarterly, 41*(4), 341–359. doi:10.1111/j.1548-1492.2010.01096.x.

Chhuon, V. and Hudley, C. (2011) Ethnic and Panethnic Asian American Identities: Contradictory Perceptions of Cambodian Students in Urban Schools. *Urban Review, 43*(5), 681–701. doi:10.1007/s11256-010-0172-8

Chik, C.H. and Wright, W.E. (2017) Overcoming the obstacles: Vietnamese and Khmer heritage language programs in California. In O. Kagan, M. Carreira and C.H. Chik (eds) *A handbook of heritage language education: From innovation to program building.* New York, NY: Routledge.

Chimbutane, F. (2011) *Rethinking bilingual education in post-colonial contexts.* Bristol, UK: Multiingual Matters.

Chiswick, B.R. and Miller, P.W. (2008) A test of the critical period hypothesis for language learning. *Journal of Multilingual and Multicultural Development, 29*(1), 16–29.

Chitera, N. (2009) Code-switching in a college mathematics classroom. *International Journal of Multilingualism, 6*(4), 426–442.

Clark, J.G. (1981) Uses and abuses of hearing loss classification. *Asha, 23,* 493–500.

Cline, T. and Frederickson, N. (1999) Identification and assessment of dyslexia in bi/multilingual children. *International Journal of Bilingual Education and Bilingualism, 2*(2), 81–93.

Clyne, M., Hunt, C.R. and Isaakidis, T. (2004) Learning a community language as a third language. *International Journal of Multilingualism, 1*(1), 33–52.

Coelho, E. (2012) *Language and learning in multilingual classrooms: A practical approach.* Bristol, UK: Multilingual Matters.

Collier, V.P. and Thomas, W.P. (2009) *Education English learners for a transformed world.* Albuquerque, NM: Dual Langauge Education of New Mexico – Fuente Press.

Collier, V.P. (1995) Acquiring a second language for school. *Directions in Language and Education, 1*(4), 1–12.

Comeau, L., Genesee, F. and Lapaquette, L. (2003) The modeling hypothesis and child bilingual codemixing. *International Journal of Bilingualism, 7*(2), 113–126.

Compton, S. E. (2014) American Sign Language as a heritage language. In T.G. Wiley, J.K. Peyton, D. Christian, S.C.K. Moore and N. Liu (eds) *Handbook of heritage, community, and Native American languages in the United States.* New York, NY and Washington, DC: Routledge and Center for Applied Linguistics.

Conger, D., Hatch, M., McKinney, J., Atwell, M.S. and Lamb, A. (2012) *Time to English proficiency for English language learners in New York City and Miami-Dade County.* New York, NY: New York Univesity, Institute for Education and Social Policy.

Conklin, N. and Lourie, M. (1983) *A host of tongues.* New York, NY: The Free Press.

Cook, V. (2001) Using the first language in the classroom. *Canadian Modern Language Review/La Revue canadienne des langues vivantes, 57*(3), 402–423.

Cooper, R L. (1989) *Language planning and social change.* Cambridge, UK: Cambridge University Press.

Costa, A. (2005) Lexical access in bilingual production. In J.F. Kroll and A. De Groot (eds) *Handbook of bilingualism: Psycholinguistic approaches*. Oxford, UK: Oxford University Press.

Coulmas, F. (1992) *Language and economy*. Oxford, UK: Blackwell.

Council of Europe (1992) *European Charter for Regional or Minority Languages: Charte Europeene des Langues Regionales ou Minoritaires*. Strasbourg, FR: Council of Europe.

Coupland, N. (2013) *The handbook of language and globalization*. Malden, MA: Wiley-Blackwell.

Coyle, D. (2007) Content and language integrated learning: Towards a connected research agenda for CLIL pedagogies. *International Journal of Bilingual Education and Bilingualism, 10*(5), 543–562.

Coyle, D., Hood, P. and Marsh, D. (2010) *Content and language integrated learning*. Cambridge, UK: Cambridge University Press.

Craik, F.I.M., Bialystok, E. and Freedman, M. (2010) Delaying the onset of Alzheimer disease: Bilingualism as a form of cognitive reserve. *Neurology, 75*(19), 1726–1729.

Crawford, J. (2000) *At war with diversity: US language policy in an age of anxiety*. Clevedon, UK: Multilingual Matters.

Crawford, J. (2003) *Hard sell: Why is bilingual education so unpopular with the American public?* Tempe, AZ: Language Policy Research Unit, Education Policy Studies Laboratory, Arizona State University.

Crawford, J. (2004) *Educating English learners: Language diversity in the classroom* (5th ed.). Los Angeles, CA: Bilingual Education Services, Inc.

Crawford, J. (2008) *Advocating for English language learners: Selected essays*. Clevedon, UK: Multilingual Matters.

Crawford, J. and Krashen, S.D. (2007) *English learners in American classrooms: 101 questions, 101 answers*. New York, NY: Scholastic.

Crawford, J. and Reyes, S.A. (2015) *The Trouble with SIOP*. Portland, OR: Institute for Language and Education Policy.

Creese, A., Bhatt, A., Bhojani, N. and Martin, P. (2006) Multicultural, heritage and learner identities in complementary schools. *Language and Education, 20*(1), 23–43.

Creese, A. and Blackledge, A. (2010a) Towards a sociolinguistics of superdiversity. *Z Erziehungswiss, 13*, 549–572. doi:10.1007/s11618-010–0159-y

Creese, A. and Blackledge, A. (2010b) Translanguaging in the bilingual classroom: A pedagogy for learning and teaching? *The Modern Language Journal, 94*(1), 103–115. doi:10.1111/j.1540–4781.2009.00986.x

Creese, A. and Martin, P.W. (2008) Classroom ecologies: A case study from a Gujarati complementary school in England. In A. Creese, P.W. Martin and N.H. Hornberger (eds) *Encyclopedia of Language and Education* (Vol. 9: Ecology of Language). New York, NY: Springer.

Crystal, D. (2006) *Language and the internet* (2nd ed.). New York, NY: Cambridge University Press.

Crystal, D. (2012) *English as a global language (Canto Classics)* (2nd ed.). Cambridge, UK: Cambridge University Press.

Crystal, D. (2014) *Language death* (Canto Classics ed.). Cambridge, UK: Cambridge University Press.

Cummins, J. (1976) The influence of bilingualism on cognitive growth: A synthesis of research findings and explanatory hypotheses. *Working Papers on Bilingualism, 9*, 1–43.

Cummins, J. (1977) Cognitive factors associated with the attainment of intermediate levels of bilingual skills. *The Modern Language Journal, 61*(1–2), 3–12.

Cummins, J. (1979) Cognitive/academic language proficiency, linguistic interdependence, the optimum age question and some other matters. *Working Papers on Bilingualism*(19), 121–129.

Cummins, J. (1981) The role of primary language development in promoting educational success for language minority students. In California State Department of Education Office of Bilingual Education (ed.) *Schooling and language minority students: A theoretical framework* (pp. 3–49). Los Angeles, CA: Evaluation, Dissemination and Assessment Center, California State University, Los Angeles.

Cummins, J. (1983) *Heritage language education: A literature review*. Ontario, CA: Ministry of Education.

Cummins, J. (1984) *Bilingualism and special education: Issues in assessment and pedagogy* (Vol. 6). Clevedon, UK: Multilingual Matters.

Cummins, J. (1993) The research base for heritage language promotion. In M. Danesi, K.A. McLeod and S.V. Morris (eds) *Heritage languages and education: The Canadian experience*. Oakville, CA: Mosaic Press.

Cummins, J. (1999) Alternative paradigms in bilingual education research: Does theory have a place? *Educational Researcher, 28*(7), 26–41.

Cummins, J. (2000a) *Language, power and pedagogy: Bilingual children in the crossfire*. Clevedon, England: Multilingual Matters.

Cummins, J. (2000b) Putting language proficiency in its place: Responding to critiques of the conversational/

academic language distinction. In J. Cenoz and U. Jessner (eds) *English in Europe: The acquisition of a third language*. Clevedon, UK: Multilingual Matters.

Cummins, J. (2003) BICS and CALP: Origins and Rationale for the Distinction. In C.B. Paulston and R. Tucker (eds) *Sociolinguistics: Essential reading* (pp. 322–328). Oxford, England: Blackwell.

Cummins, J. (2013) Empowerment and bilingual education. In C.A. Chapelle (ed.) *Encyclopedia of applied linguistics*. Malden, MA: Blackwell Publishing.

Cummins, J. (2014) Rethinking pedagogical assumptions in Canadian French immersion programs. *Journal of Immersion and Content-Based Language Education, 2*(1), 3–22.

Cummins, J. (2017a) BICS and CALP: Empirical and theoretical status of the distinction. In S. May (ed.) *Encyclopedia of language and education* (3rd ed., Vol. 2: Literacy). New York, NY: Springer.

Cummins, J. (2017b) Teaching for transfer: Challenging the two solitudes assumption in bilingual education. In S. May (ed.) *Encyclopedia of language and education* (3rd ed., Vol. 5: Bilingual Education). New York, NY: Springer.

Cummins, J., Bismilla, V., Chow, P., Cohen, S., Giampapa, F., Leoni, L., ... Sastri, P. (2005) Affirming identity in multilingual classrooms. *Educational Leadership, 63*(1), 38–43.

Cummins, J. and Danesi, M. (1990) *Heritage languages: The development and denial of Canada's linguistic resources* (Vol. 5). Toronto, CA: James Lorimer and Company.

Dagenais, D. (2003) Accessing imagined communities through multilingualism and immersion education. *Journal of Language, Identity, and Education, 2*(4), 269–283.

Dannoff, M.N., Coles, G.J., McLaughlin, D.H. and Reynolds, D.J. (1978) *Evaluation of the impact of ESEA Title VII Spanish/English bilingual education programs*. Palo Alto, CA: American Institute for Research.

De Bot, K. (2008) Review article: The imaging of what in the multilingual mind? *Second Language Research, 24*(1), 111–133.

de Bruin, A., Treccani, B. and Della Sala, S. (2015) Cognitive advantage in bilingualism an example of publication bias? *Psychological Science, 26*(1), 99–107.

de Courcy, M. (2002) *Learners' experiences of immersion education: Case studies of French and Chinese* (Vol. 32). Clevedon, UK: Multilingual Matters.

de Courcy, M., Warren, J. and Burston, M. (2002) Children from diverse backgrounds in an immersion programme. *Language and Education, 16*(2), 112–127.

De Graff, R. and van Wilgenburg, O. (2015) The Netherlands: Quality control as a driving force in bilingual education. In P. Mehisto and F. Genesee (eds) *Building bilingual education systems: Forces, mechanisms and counterweights* (pp. 167–179). Cambridge, UK: Cambridge University Press.

De Houwer, A. (2003) Home languages spoken in officially monolingual Flanders: A survey. *Plurilingua, 24*, 79–96.

De Houwer, A. (2006) Bilingual development in the early years. In K. Brown (ed.) *Encyclopedia of language and linguistics*. Oxford, UK: Elsevier.

De Houwer, A. (2007) Parental language input patterns and children's bilingual use. *Applied Psycholinguistics, 28*(03), 411–424.

De Houwer, A. (2009) *Bilingual first language acquisition*. Bristol, UK: Multilingual Matters.

de Jong, E.J., Gort, M. and Cobb, C.D. (2005) Bilingual education within the context of English-only policies: Three districts' response to Question 2 in Massachusetts. *Educational Policy, 19*(4), 595–620.

de Jong, E.J., Li, Z., Zafar, A. and Wu, C.-H. (2016) Language policy in multilingual contexts: Revisiting Ruiz's language-as-resource orientation. *Bilingual Research Journal, 40*(3,4).

de Jong, E.J. (2011) *Foundations for multilingualism in education: From principles to practice*. Philadelphia, PA: Caslon Publishing.

de Jong, E.J. and Harper, C.A. (2005) Preparing mainstream teachers for English-language learners: is being a good teacher enough? *Teacher Education Quarterly, 32*(2), 101–124.

de Mejía, A.-M. (2002) *Power, prestige, and bilingualism: International perspectives on elite bilingual education* (Vol. 35). Clevedon, UK: Multilingual Matters.

de Mejia, A.-M. and Hélot, C. (2015) Teacher education and support. In W.E. Wright, S. Boun and O. Garcia (eds) *Handbook of bilingual and multilingual education* (pp. 270–281). Malden, MA: Wiley-Blackwell.

DeKeyser, R. and Larson-Hall, J. (2009) What does the critical period really mean? In J.F. Kroll and A.M.B. De Groot (eds) *Handbook of bilingualism: Psycholinguistic approaches* (pp. 88–108). Oxford, UK: Oxford University Press.

Del Valle, S. (2003) *Language rights and the law in the United States: Finding our voices*. Clevedon, UK: Multilingual Matters.

Del Valle, S. (2009) The bilingual's hoarse voice: Losing rights in two languages. In M.R. Salaberry (ed.) *Language allegiances and bilingualism in the US* (Vol. 6). Bristol, UK: Multilingual Matters.

Demmert, W.G. (2001) *Improving academic performance among Native American students: A review of the research literature*. Charleston, WV: ERIC Clearinghouse on Rural Education and Small Schools.

DePalma, R. (2010) *Language use in the two-way classroom: Lessons from a Spanish-English bilingual kindergarten*. Bristol, UK: Multilingual Matters.

Deuchar, M. and Quay, S. (2000) *Bilingual acquisition: Theoretical implications of a case study* (Vol. 2). Oxford, UK: Oxford University Press.

Dewaele, J.-M. (2000) Three years old and three first languages. *Bilingual Family Newsletter, 17*(2), 4–5.

Dewaele, J.-M. (2002) Review of M. Yamamoto (2001) Language use in interlingual families: A Japanese–English sociolinguistic study. *Applied Linguistics, 23*(4), 546–548.

Dewaele, J.-M. (2007) Still trilingual at ten: Livia's multilingual journey. *Multilingual Living Magazine*, 68–71.

Dewey, M. and Leung, C. (2010) English in English language teaching: Shifting values and assumptions in changing circumstances. *Working Papers in Educational Linguistics, 25*(1), 1–15.

Diaz, R.M. (1985) Bilingual cognitive development: Addressing three gaps in current research. *Child Development, 56*, 1376–1388.

Dicker, S. J. (2003) *Languages in America: A pluralist view* (2nd ed.). Philadelphia, PA: Multilingual Matters Ltd.

Diebold, A.R. (1964) Incipient bilingualism. In D. Hymes (ed.) *Language in culture and society*. New York, NY: Harper and Row.

Dilāns, G. and Zepa, B. (2015) Bilingual and multilingual education in the former Soviet republics: The case of Latvia. In W.E. Wright, S. Boun and O. García (eds) *Handbook of bilingual and multilingual education* (pp. 630–642). Malden, MA: John Wiley and Sons.

Dolson, D.P. and Mayer, J. (1992) Longitudinal study of three program models for language-minority students: A critical examination of reported findings. *Bilingual Research Journal, 16*(1–2), 105–158.

Dorian, N.C. (1981) *Language death: The life cycle of a Scottish Gaelic dialect*. Philadelphia, PA: University of Pennsylvania Press

Dörnyei, Z. (1994) Motivation and motivating in the foreign language classroom. *The Modern Language Journal, 78*(3), 273–284.

Dörnyei, Z. (1998) Motivation in second and foreign language learning. *Language Teaching, 31*(03), 117–135.

Dörnyei, Z., Csizér, K. and Németh, N. (2006) *Motivation, language attitudes and globalisation: A Hungarian perspective*. Clevedon, UK: Multilingual Matters.

Dörnyei, Z., MacIntrye, P.D. and Henry, A. (eds) (2015) *Motivational dynamics in language learning*. Bristol, UK: Multilingual Matters.

Duff, P.A. (2008) Heritage language education in Canada. In D. Brinton (ed.) *Heritage language education: A new field emerging*. New York, NY: Routledge.

Duff, P.A. (2010) Language socialization. In S. McKay and N.H. Hornberger (eds) *Sociolinguistics and language education* (pp. 427–455). Clevedon, UK: Multilingual Matters.

Duff, P.A. (2014) Communicative language teaching. In M. Celce-Murcia, D.M. Brinton and M.A. Snow (eds) *Teaching English as a second or foreign language* (4th ed., pp. 2–14). Independence, KY: Cengage Learning.

Dulay, H.C. and Burt, M.K. (1978) *Why bilingual education? A Summary of research findings* Francisco, CA: Bloomsbury West.

Dulay, H. C. and Burt, M. K. (1979) *Bilingual education: A close look at its effects*: Focus/ National Clearinghouse for Bilingual Education.

Dunabeitia, J.A., Hernandez, J.A., Anton, E., Macizo, P., Estevez, A., Fuentes, L. J. and Carreiras, M. (2014) The inhibitory advantage in bilingual children revisited. *Experimental Psychology, 61*, 234–251. doi:10.1027/1618–3169/a000243

Dutcher, N. (2004) *Expanding educational opportunity in linguistically diverse societies*. Washington, DC: Center for Applied Linguistics.

Dutcher, N. and Tucker, G. R. (1996) *The use of first and second languages in education: A review of international experience*. Washington, DC: East Asia and Pacific Country Dept. III, World Bank.

Dweck, C.S. (2002) Beliefs that make smart people dumb. In R.J. Sternberg (ed.) *Why smart people can be so stupid* (pp. 24–41). New Haven, CT: Yale University Press.

Dweck, C.S. (2006) *Mindset: The new psychology of success*. New York, NY: Random House.

Echevarría, J. and Graves, A.W. (2011) *Sheltered content instruction: Teaching English language learners with diverse abilities* (4th ed.). Boston, MA: Pearson Allyn and Bacon.

Echevarría, J. and Vogt, M. (2011) *Response to intervention (RTI) and English learners: Making it happen.* Boston, MA: Pearson.

Echevarría, J., Vogt, M. and Short, D. (2016) *Making content comprehensible for English learners: The SIOP model* (5th ed.). Boston: Pearson.

Economic Affairs Division (2012) *Isle of Man Census Report 2011.* Retrieved from Isle of Man, UK: http://www.gov.im/media/207882/census2011reportfinalresized_1_.pdf

Edelsky, C. (2006) *With literacy and justice for all: Rethinking the social in language and education* (3rd ed.). Mahwah, NJ: Lawrence Erlbaum Associates, Publishers.

Edelsky, C., Hudelson, S., Flores, B., Barkin, F., Altwerger, B. and Jilbert, K. (1983) Semilingualism and language deficit. *Applied Linguistics, 4*(1), 1–22.

Education Department of Hong Kong (1997) *Medium of instruction: Guidance for secondary schools.* Hong Kong: Education Department.

Edwards, J. (2012) *Multilingualism: Understanding linguistic diversity.* New York, NY: Bloomsbury Publishing.

Edwards, J. (2013) Bilingualism and multilingualism: Some central concepts. In T.K. Bhatia and W.C. Ritchie (eds) *The handbook of bilingualism and mutlilngualism* (2nd ed., pp. 5–25). Malden, MA: Blackwell.

Edwards, V. (2009) *Learning to be literate: Multilingual perspectives.* Bristol, UK: Multilingual Matters.

Edwards, V. (2015) Literacy in bilingual and and multilingual education. In W.E. Wright, S. Boun and O. Garcia (eds) *Handbook of bilingual and multilingual education* (pp. 75). Malden, MA: Wiley-Blackwell.

EngageNY. (2014) New York State Bilingual Common Core Initiative. Retrieved from https://www.engageny.org/resource/new-york-state-bilingual-common-core-initiative

Ensslin, A. (2011) 'What an un-wiki way of doing things': Wikipedia's multilingual policy and meta-linguistic practice. *Journal of Language and Politics, 10*(4), 535–561.

Errasti, M.P.S. (2003) Acquiring writing skills in a third language: The positive effects of bilingualism. *International Journal of Bilingualism, 7*(1), 27–42.

Escamilla, K., Hopewell, S., Butvilofsky, S., Sparrow, W., Soltero-González, L., Ruiz-Figueroa and Escamilla, M. (2013) *Biliteracy from the start: Literacy squared in action.* Philadelphia, PA: Caslon.

Escamilla, K., Shannon, S., Carlos, S. and Garcia, J. (2003) Breaking the code: Colorodo's defeat of the anti-bilingual education initiative (Amendment 31). *Bilingual Research Journal, 27*(3), 357–382.

ESTYN (2001) *Cwricwlwm Cymreig. The Welsh dimension of the curriculum of Wales: Good practice in teaching and learning.* Cardiff, IRL: ESTYN.

European Commission (2006) *Euromosaic III: Presence of regional and minority language groups in the new member states.* Brussels, BE: European Commission.

European Commission (2012) *Europeans and their languages. Special Eurobarometer 386.* Brussels, BE: European Commission.

European Commission (2015) *Language teaching and learning in multilingual classrooms.* Luxembourg: European Union.

Eysenck, M.W., Ellis, A.W., Hunt, E.B. and Johnson-Laird, P.N.E. (1994) *The Blackwell dictionary of cognitive psychology. Basil Blackwell.* Oxford, UK: Blackwell.

Fabbro, F. (2015) *The neurolinguistics of bilingualism: An introduction* (Reprint ed.). New York, NY: Psychology Press.

Fairclough, N. (ed.) (2013) *Critical language awareness.* New York, NY: Routledge.

Faltis, C.J. (1993) Critical issues in the use of sheltered content teaching in high school bilingual programs. *Peabody Journal of Education, 69*(1), 136–151.

Faltis, C.J. (2005) *Joinfostering: Adapting teaching strategies for the multilingual classrooms* (4th ed.). New York, NY: McMillam.

Fan, S., Liberman, Z., Keysar, B. and Kinzler, K.D. (2015) The exposure advantage: Early exposure to a multilingual environment promotes effective communication. *Psychological Science, Online First.*

Fantini, A.E. (1985) *Language acquisition of a bilingual child: A sociolinguistic perspective.* San Diego, CA: College Hill Press.

Fava, E., Hull, R. and Bortfeld, H. (2011) Linking behavioral and neurophysiological indicators of perceptual tuning to language. *Frontiers in Psychology, 2*(174), 1–14. doi:doi.org/10.3389/fpsyg.2011.00174

Fee, M., Liu, N., Duggan, J., Arias, B. and Wiley, T.G. (2014) *Investigating language policies in IB world schools: Final report.* Washington, DC: Center for Applied Linguistics.

Feng, A. (2011) *English language education across Greater China.* Bristol, UK: Multilingual Matters.

Feng, A. and Adamson, B. (2015) Contested notions of bilingualism and trilingualism in the People's Republic of China. In W.E. Wright, S. Boun and O. García (eds) *Handbook of bilingual and multilingual education* (pp. 484–494). Malden, MA: John Wiley and Sons.

Ferguson, C.A. (1959) Diglossia. *Word, 15*, 325–340.

Ferguson, C.A., Houghton, C. and Wells, M.H. (1977) Bilingual education: An international perspective. In B. Spolsky and R. Cooper (eds) *Frontiers in bilingual education* (pp. 159–174). Rowley, MA: Newbury House.

Ferguson, G. (2003) Classroom code-switching in post-colonial contexts. In S. Makoni and U.H. Meinhof (eds) *Africa and Applied Linguistics. AILA Review* (Vol. 16). Amsterdam: John Benjamins.

Fillmore, L.W. (1991) When learning a second language means losing the first. *Early Childhood Research Quarterly, 6*(3), 323–346.

Filmore, L.W. (2013) *English learners and the Common Core: A fighting chance to learn.* Paper presented at the Common Core State State Standards and English Learners (Webinar). Washington, DC: National Clearinghouse of English Language Acquisition.

Fillmore, L.W. and Snow, C.E. (2000) What teachers need to know about language. Washington, DC. Retrieved from http://www.elachieve.org/images/stories/eladocs/articles/Wong_Fillmore.pdf

Fishman, J.A. (1980) Bilingualism and biculturism as individual and as societal phenomena. *Journal of Multilingual and Multicultural Development, 1*(1), 3–15.

Fishman, J.A. (1989) *Language and ethnicity in minority sociolinguistic perspective.* Clevedon, UK: Multilingual Matters.

Fishman, J.A. (1991) *Reversing language shift: Theoretical and empirical foundations of assistance to threatened languages.* Clevedon, UK: Multilingual Matters.

Fishman, J.A. (2001) *Can threatened languages be saved? Reversing language shift, revisited: A 21st century perspective.* Clevedon, UK: Multilingual Matters.

Fishman, J.A. (2006) 300–plus years of heritage language education in the United States. In G. Valdés, J. Fishman, R. Chávez and W. Pérez (eds) *Towards the developing minority language resources.* Clevedon, UK: Multilingual Matters.

Fishman, J.A. (2010) *Handbook of language and ethnic identity* (Vol. 1). Oxford, UK: Oxford University Press.

Fishman, J.A. (2013) Language maintenance, language shift, and reversing language shift. In T.K. Bhatia and W.C. Ritchie (eds) *Handbook of bilingualism and multilingualism* (pp. 466–494). Malden, MA: Blackwell Publishing.

Fishman, J.A. (2014) Three hundred-plus years of heritage language education in the United States. In T. G. Wiley, J.K. Peyton, D. Christian, S.K.C. Moore and N. Liu (eds) *Handbook of heritage and community languages in the United States: Research, educational practice, and policy* (pp. 36–44). Washington, DC and New York, NY: Center for Applied Linguistics and Routledge.

Flegenheimer, M. (2016, 29 July) Habla Español? Tim Kaine is latest candidate to use Spanish to court voters. *The New York Times,* p. A13.

Flores, B.B., Sheets, R.H. and Clark, E.R. (eds) (2011) *Teacher preparationg for biingual student populations: Educar para transformar.* New York, NY: Routledge.

Flores, N. and Baetens Beardsmore, H. (2015) Programs and structures in bilingual and multilingual education. In W.E. Wright, S. Boun and O. García (eds) *Handbook of bilingual and multilingual education* (pp. 206–222). Malden, MA: Wiley-Blackwell.

Flores, N., Kleyn, T. and Menken, K. (2015) Looking holistically in a climate of partiality: Identities of students labeled long-term English language learners. *Journal of Language, Identity and Education, 14*(2), 113–132.

Fogle, L.W. (2013) Family language policy from the chidren's point of view: Bilingualism in time and place. In M. Schwartz and A. Verschik (eds) *Successful family language policy: Parents, children and educators in interaction* (pp. 177–200). Dordrect, The Netherlands: Springer.

Fogle, L.W. and King, K.A. (2013) Child agency and language policy in transnational families. *Issues in Applied Linguistics, 19*, 1–25.

Fortune, T.W. and Tedick, D.J. (2008) *Pathways to multilingualism: Evolving perspectives on immersion education* (Vol. 66). Clevedon, UK: Multilingual Matters.

Francis, D.J., Rivera, M., Lesaux, N., Kieffer, M. and Rivera, H. (2006) *Practical guidelines for the education of English language learners: Researched-based recommendations for the use of accommodations in large-scale assessments.* Portsmouth, NH: Center on Instruction.

Frederickson, N. and Cline, T. (2015) *Special educational needs, inclusion, and diversity* (3rd ed.). Buckingham, UK: Open University Press.

Freeman, R.D. (1998) *Bilingual education and social change.* Clevedon, UK: Multilingual Matters.

Freeman, R.D. (2004) *Building on community bilingualism: Promoting multiculturalism through schooling.* Philadelphia, PA: Caslon Publishing.

Freeman, Y.S., Freeman, A. and Freeman, D.E. (2003) Home run books: Connecting students to culturally relevant texts. *Nabe News, 26*(3), 5–12, 28.

Freire, P. (1993) *Pedagogy of the oppressed* (20th anniversary edition ed.). New York, NY: Seabury Press/ Continuum.

Freire, P. and Macedo, D. (1987) *Literacy: Reading the word and the world*. New York, NY: Routledge.

Friedman, A. (2015) America's lacking language skills. *The Atlantic*. Retrieved from http://www.theatlantic. com/education/archive/2015/05/filling-americas-language-education-potholes/392876/

Friedman, D.A. (2010) Becoming national: Classroom language socialization and political identities in the age of globalization. *Annual Review of Applied Linguistics, 30*, 193–210.

Fulcher, G. and Davidson, F. (2007) *Language testing and assessment: An advanced resource book*. London, UK: Routledge.

Fuller, J.M. (2013) *Spanish speakers in the USA*. Bristol, UK: Multilingual Matters.

Gal, S. (1979) *Language shift: Social determinants of linguistic change in bilingual Austria*. New York, NY: Academic Press.

Galambos, S.J. and Hakuta, K. (1988) Subject-specific and task-specific characteristics of metalinguistic awareness in bilingual children. *Applied Psycholinguistics, 9*(02), 141–162.

Gallagher-Brett, A. (2005) Seven hundred reasons for studying languages: Higher education academy. Retrieved from www.idiomas.idph.com.br/textos/700_reasons.pdf

Gallaudet Research Institute (2008) *Regional and national summary report of data from the 2007-08 Annual Survey of Deaf and Hard of Hearing Children and Youth*. Washington, DC: Gallaudet University Press.

Gandara, P. and Hopkins, M. (eds) (2010) *Forbidden language: English learners and restrictive language policies*. New York, NY: Teachers College Press.

Gándara, P.C., Maxwell-Jolly, J., Garcia, E., Asato, J., Gutierrez, K., Stritikus, T. and Curry, J. (2000) *The Initial Impact of Proposition 227 on the Instruction of English Learners*. University of California, Davis: UC Linguistic Minority Research Institute, Education Policy Center.

Gandhi, M. (1927) *Autobiography: The story of my experiments with truth* (1949, English translation ed.). London, UK: Cape.

García, O. (2008a) Multilingual language awareness and teacher education. In J. Cenoz and N.H. Hornberger (eds) *Encyclopedia of language and education* (Vol. 6: Knowledge about language). New York, NY: Springer.

García, O. (2008b) Teaching Spanish and Spanish in teaching in the USA: Integrating bilingual perspectives. In C. Hélot and A.-M. De Mejía (eds) *Forging multilingual spaces: Integrated perspectives on majority and minority bilingual education* (Vol. 68, p. 31). Bristol, UK: Multilingual Matters.

García, O. (2009a) *Bilingual education in the 21st Century: A global perspective*. Malden, MA: Wiley-Blackwell.

García, O. (2009b) Education, multilingualism and translanguaging in the 21st century. In A.K. Mohanty, M. Panda, R. Phillipson and T. Skutnabb-Kangas (eds) *Multilingual education for social Justice: Globalising the local*. New Delhi, IN: Orient BlackSwan.

García, O., Johnson, S.I. and Seltzer, K. (2016) *Translanguaging classrooms: Leveraging student bilingualism for learning*. Philadelphia, PA: Caslon Publishing.

García, O. and Li Wei (2014) *Translanguaging: Language, bilingualism, and education*. New York, NY: Palgrave Macmillon.

García, O. and Li Wei (2015) Translanguaging, bilingualism, and bilingual education. In W.E. Wright, S. Boun and O. García (eds) *Handbook of bilingual and multilingual education* (pp. 223–240). Malden, MA: John Wiley and Sons.

Garcia, O. and Otheguy, R. (1988) The language situation of Cuban Americans. In S. McKay and S. C. Wong (eds) *Language diversity: Problem or resource* (pp. 166–192). New York, NY: Newbury House.

García, O., Peltz, R. and Schiffman, H. (eds) (2006) *Language loyalty, continuity and change: Joshua A. Fishman's contributions to international sociolinguistics*. Clevedon, UK: Multilingual Matters.

García, O., Zakharia, Z. and Otcu, B. (eds) (2013) *Bilingual community education and multilingualism: Beyond heritage languages in a global city*. Bristol, UK: Multilingual Matters.

García, S.B. (2002) Parent–professional collaboration in culturally sensitive assessment. In A.J. Artiles and A.A. Ortiz (eds) *English language learners with special educational needs*. Washington, DC and McHenry, IL: Center for Applied Linguistics and Delta Systems Co.

García-Pentón, L., García, Y.F., Costello, B., Duñabeitia, J.A. and Carreiras, M. (2015) The neuroanatomy of bilingualism: How to turn a hazy view into the full picture. *Language, Cognition and Neuroscience, 31*(3), 303-327. doi:10.1080/23273798.2015.1068944

Garcia-Sierra, A., Rivera-Gaxiola, M., Percaccio, C.R., Conboy, B.T., Romo, H., Klarman, L., ... Kuhl, P. K. (2011) Bilingual language learning: An ERP study relating early brain responses to speech, language input ,and later word production. *Journal of Phonetics, 39,* 546–557.

Gardner, H. (2011) *Frames of mind: The theory of multiple intelligences.* New York, NY: Basic Books.

Gardner, R.C. (2008) Individual differences in second and foreign language learning. In N. Van Deusen-Scholl and N.H. Hornberger (eds) *Encyclopedia of language and education* (2nd ed., Vol. 4: Second and foreign language education). New York, NY: Springer.

Gardner, R.C. (2010) *Motivation and second language acquisition: The socio-educational model.* New York, NY: Peter Lang.

Gardner, R.C. and Lambert, W.E. (1972) *Attitudes and motivation in second language learning.* Rowley, MA: Newbury House.

Gardner-Chloros, P. (2009) *Code-switching.* Cambridge, UK: Cambridge University Press.

Garrett, P. (2010) *Attitudes to language.* Cambridge, UK: Cambridge University Press.

Gathercole, V.C.M. (ed.) (2013) *Issues in the assessment of bilinguals.* Bristol, UK: Multilingual Matters.

Gathercole, V.C.M., Thomas, E.M., Kennedy, I., Prys, C., Young, N., Vinas Guasch, N., ... Jones, L. (2014) Does language dominance affect cognitive performance in bilinguals? Lifespan evidence from preschoolers through older adults on card sorting, Simon, and meta-linguistic tasks. *Frontiers in Psychology, 5,* 1–14. doi:10.3389/fpsyg.2014.00011

Gee, J.P. (2012) *Social linguistics and literacies: Ideology in discourses* (4th ed.). New York, NY: Routledge.

General Accounting Office (1987) *Bilingual education. A new look at the research evidence.* Washington, DC: General Accounting Office.

Genesee, F. (1983) Bilingual education of majority-language children: The Immersion experiments in review. *Applied Psycholinguistics, 4*(01), 1–46.

Genesee, F. (1984) Historical and theoretical foundations of immersion education. In California State Department of Education (ed.) *California, USA.* California State Department of Education.

Genesee, F. (1987) *Learning through two languages: Studies of immersion and bilingual education* (Vol. 163). Cambridge, MA: Newbury House.

Genesee, F. (1992) Second/foreign language immersion and at-risk English-speaking children. *Foreign Language Annals, 25*(3), 199–213.

Genesee, F. (2006) Bilingual first language acquisition in perspective. In P.D. McCardle and E. Hoff (eds) *Childhood bilingualism: Research on infancy through school age.* Bristol, UK: Multilingual Matters.

Genesee, F. (2013) Insights into bilingual education from research on immersion programs in Canada. In C. Abello-Contesse, P.M. Chandler, M.D. López-Jiménez and R. Chacón-Beltrán (eds) *Bilingual and multilingual education in the 21st century: Building on experience* (pp. 24–41). Bristol, UK: Multilingual Matters.

Genesee, F. (2015) Factors that shaped the creation and development of immersion education. In P. Mehisto and F. Genesee (eds) *Building bilingual education systems: Forces, mechanisms and counterweights* (pp. 43–57). Cambridge, UK: Cambridge University Press.

Genesee, F., Boivin, I. and Nicoladis, E. (1996) Talking with strangers: A study of bilingual children's communicative competence. *Applied Psycholinguistics, 17*(04), 427–442.

Genesee, F., Lindholm-Leary, K., Saunders, W.M. and Christian, D. (2006) *Educating English language learners: A synthesis of research evidence.* New York, NY: Cambridge University Press.

Genesee, F., Tucker, G.R. and Lambert, W.E. (1975) Communication skills of bilingual children. *Child Development, 46,* 1010–1014.

Ghuman, P. (2011) *British untouchables: A study of Dalit identity and education.* Farnham, UK: Ashgate Publishing Ltd.

Gibbons, P. (2015) *Scaffolding language, scaffolding learning: Teaching English language learners in the mainstream classroom* (2nd ed.). Portsmouth, NH: Heinemann.

Gleitman, L. and Papafragou, A. (2005) New perspectives on language and thought. In K. Holyoak and R. Morrison (eds) *Cambridge handbook of thinking and reasoning.* New York, NY: Cambridge University Press.

Gold, B.T., Kim, C., Johnson, N.F., Kryscio, R.J. and Smith, C.D. (2013) Lifelong bilingualism maintains neural efficiency for cognitive control in aging. *The Journal of Neuroscience, 33*(2), 387–396.

Gold, N. (2006) *Successful bilingual schools: Six effective programs in California.* San Diego, CA: San Diego County Office of Education.

Goldenberg, C. (2008) Teaching English language learners: What the research does--and does not--say. *American Educator, Summer,* 8–44.

Goleman, D. (2006) *Emotional intelligence: Why it can matter more than IQ* (10th Anniversary ed.). New York, NY: Bantam Books.

Gollan, T.H. and Acenas, L.-A.R. (2004) What is a TOT? Cognate and translation effects on tip-of-the-tongue states in Spanish-English and Tagalog-English bilinguals. *Journal of Experimental Psychology: Learning, Memory, and Cognition, 30*(1), 246–269.

Gollan, T.H., Montoya, R.I., Cera, C. and Sandoval, T.C. (2008) More use almost always means a smaller frequency effect: Aging, bilingualism, and the weaker links hypothesis. *Journal of Memory and Language, 58*(3), 787–814.

Gómez, L., Freeman, D.E. and Freeman, Y.S. (2005) Dual language education: A promising 50–50 model. *Bilingual Research Journal, 29*(1), 145–164.

González, J.M. (1979) Coming of age in bilingual/bicultural education: A historical perspective. In H. T. Trueba and C. Barnett-Mizrahi (eds) *Bilingual multicultural education and the professional: From theory to practice.* Rowley, MA: Newbury House.

González, N., Moll, L.C. and Amanti, C. (eds) (2005) *Funds of knowledge: Theorizing practices in households, communities, and classrooms.* Mahwah, NJ: Erlbaum.

Gordon, R.A. (1997) Everyday life as an intelligence test: Effects of intelligence and intelligence context. *intelligence, 24*(1), 203–320.

Gottlieb, M. (2016) *Assessing English language learners: Bridges to educational equity: Connecting academic language proficiency to student achievement* (2nd ed.). Thousand Oaks, CA: Corwin.

Graddol, D. (2006) *English next* (Vol. 62). London, UK: British Council.

Green, D.W., Crinion, J. and Price, C.J. (2007) Exploring cross-linguistic vocabulary effects on brain structures using voxel-based morphometry. *Bilingualism: Language and Cognition, 10*(02), 189–199.

Greene, J. (1998) *A meta-analysis of the effectiveness of bilingual education.* Claremont, CA: Thomas Rivera Policy Institute.

Gregerson, M. (2009) Learning to read in Ratanakiri: A case study from northeastern Cambodia. *International Journal of Bilingual Education and Bilingualism, 12*(4), 429–447.

Gregory, E. (2008) *Learning to read in a new language.* Thousand Oaks, CA: Sage.

Grin, F. (2005) Linguistic human rights as a source of policy guidelines: A critical assessment. *Journal of Sociolinguistics, 9*(3), 448–460.

Grin, F., Hexel, D. and Schwob, I. (2003) Language diversity and language education: An introduction to the Swiss model. In P. Cuvelier, L.T. Du Plessis and L. Teck (eds) *Multilingualism, education and social integration.* Pretoria, South Africa: Van Schaik.

Grin, F., Sfreddo, C. and Vaillancourt, F. (2010) *The economics of the multilingual workplace.* New York, NY: Routledge.

Grinberg, E. and Watts, A. (2016, 18 March) 'Finding Nemo' second film to get Navajo translation, opens in theaters. *CNN.*

Grosjean, F. (2008) *Studying bilinguals.* Oxford, UK: Oxford University Press.

Grosjean, F. (2010) Bilingualism, biculturalism, and deafness. *International Journal of Bilingual Education and Bilingualism, 13*(2), 133–145.

Grosjean, F. (2012) *Bilingual: Life and reality* (Reprint ed.). Cambridge, MA: Harvard University Press.

Grosjean, F. (2016) What is translanguaging? An interview with Ofelia García. Retrieved from https://www.psychologytoday.com/blog/life-bilingual/201603/what-is-translanguaging

Grosjean, F. and Li, P. (2013) *The psycholinguistics of bilingualism.* Malden, MA: Wiley-Blackwell.

Guarino, A.J., Echevarría, J., Short, D., Schick, J.E., Forbes, S. and Rueda, R. (2001) The sheltered instruction observation protocol. *Journal of Research in Education, 11*(1), 138–140.

Gunnarsson, B.-L. (2013) Multilingualism in the workplace. *Annual Review of Applied Linguistics, 33*, 162–189.

Guo, Z. (2014) *Young children as cultural mediators: Mandarin-speaking families Chinese families in Britain.* Bristol, UK: Multilingual Matters.

Guzman, J. (2002) English: New evidence on the effectiveness of bilingual education. *Education Next, 2*(3), 58–65.

Haas, E., Tran, L., Huang, M., Yu, A. and WestEd (2015) *The achievement progress of English learner students in Arizona.* Washington, DC: US Department of Education, Institute of Education Sciences, and National Center for Education Evaluation and Regional Assistance.

Hagemeyer, A. (1992) *The red notebook.* Silver Spring, MD: National Association for the Deaf.

Hakuta, K. (1986) *The mirror of language: The debate on bilingualism.* New York, NY: Basic Books.

Hakuta, K. (2001) A critical period for second language acquisition? In D.B. Bailey Jr, J.T. Bruer, F. J. Symons and J.W. Lichtman (eds) *Critical thinking about critical periods. A series from the National Center for Early Development and Learning.* Baltimore, MD: Paul Brookes Publishing Co.

Hakuta, K., Butler, Y.G. and Witt, D. (2000) *How long does it take English learners to attain proficiency?* Retrieved from Santa Barbara, CA: University of California Linguistic Minority Research Institute.

Hakuta, K. and d'Andrea, D. (1992) Some properties of bilingual maintenance and loss in Mexican background high-school students. *Applied Linguistics, 13*(1), 72–99.

Hall, K. (2002) Asserting 'needs' and claiming 'rights': The cultural politics of community language education in England. *Journal of Language, Identity, and Education, 1*(2), 97–119.

Hall, N. and Sham, S. (2007) Language brokering as young people's work: Evidence from Chinese adolescents in England. *Language and Education, 21*(1), 16–30.

Hamayan, E.V. and Field, R.F. (eds) (2012) *English learners at school: A guide for administrators.* Philadelphia, PA: Caslon Publishing.

Hamayan, E.V., Marler, B., Lopez, C.S. and Damico, J. (2013) *Special education considerations for English language learners: Delivering a continuum of services* (2nd ed.). Philadelphia, PA: Caslon.

Hammerly, H. (1988) French Immersion (Does It Work?) and the' Development of Bilingual Proficiency' Report. *Canadian Modern Language Review, 45*(3), 567–578.

Hansen-Thomas, H. and Langman, J. (forthcoming) *Teaching through talking in secondary math classrooms: A functional language awareness approach.* Philadelphia, PA: Caslon Publishing.

Hantzopoulos, M. (2013) Going to Greek school: The politics of religion, identity and culture in community-based Greek language schools. In O. García, Z. Zakharia and B. Otcu (eds) *Bilingual and community multilingualism: Beyond heritage languages in a global city* (pp. 128–140). Bristol, UK: Multilingual Matters.

Harris, J. and Cummins, J. (2013) Issues in all-Irish education: Strengthening the case for comparitive immersion. In D.M. Singleton, J.A. Fishman, L. Aronin and M. Ó Laoire (eds) *Current multilingualism: A new linguistic dispensation* (pp. 69–98). Boston, MA: De Gruyter Mouton.

Heller, M. (2002) Globalization and the commodification of bilingualism in Canada. In D. Block and D. Cameron (eds) *Globalization and language teaching.* London, UK: Routledge.

Heller, M. (2003) *Crosswords: Language, education and ethnicity in French Ontario.* New York, NY: Walter de Gruyter.

Heller, M. (2006) *Linguistic minorities and modernity: A sociolinguistic ethnography* (2nd ed.). New York, NY: Longman.

Heller, M., Jaworski, A. and Thurlow, C. (2014) Introduction: Sociolinguistics and tourism–mobilities, markets, multilingualism. *Journal of Sociolinguistics, 18*(4), 425–458.

Heller, M., Pujolar, J. and Duchéne, A. (2014) Linguistic commodification in tourism. *Journal of Sociolinguistics, 18*(4), 539–566.

Henderson, K.I. and Palmer, D.K. (2015) Teacher and student language practices and ideologies in a third-grade two-way dual language program implementation. *International Multilingual Research Journal, 9*(2), 75–92. doi:10.1080/19313152.2015.1016827

Heredia, R.R. and Brown, J.M. (2013) Bilingual memory. In T.K. Bhatia and W.C. Ritchie (eds) *The handbook of bilingualism and multilingualism* (2nd ed., pp. 269–291). Malden, MA: John Wiley and Sons.

Hermans, D., Ormel, E. and Knoors, H. (2010) On the relation between the signing and reading skills of deaf bilinguals. *International Journal of Bilingual Education and Bilingualism, 13*(2), 187–199.

Hermanto, N., Moreno, S. and Bialystok, E. (2012) Linguistic and metalinguistic outcomes of intense immersion education: How bilingual? *International Journal of Bilingual Education and Bilingualism, 15*(2), 131–145.

Hermes, M., Bang, M. and Marin, A. (2012) Designing indigenous language revitalization. *Harvard Educational Review, 82*(3), 381–402. doi:http://dx.doi.org/10.17763/haer.82.3.q8117w861241871j

Herrera, S.G., Murry, K. G. and Cabral, R.M. (2013) *Assessment accommodations for classroom teachers of culturally and linguistically diverse students.* Boston, MA: Pearson.

Heugh, K., Benson, C., Bogale, B. and Yohannes, M.A.G. (2007) Final report: Study on medium of instruction in primary schools in Ethiopia. *Commissioned by the Ministry of Education, Ethiopia.*

Heugh, K. and Skutnabb-Kangas, T. (2010) *Multilingual education works: From the periphery to the centre.* New Delhi, IND: Orient BlackSwan.

Hibbert, L. and van der Walt, C. (eds) (2014) *Multilingual universities in South Africa: Reflecting society in higher education.* Bristol, UK: Multilingual Matters.

Hickey, T. (1997) *Early immersion education in Ireland: Na Naionrai.* Dublin, IRL: Institiuid Teangeolaiochta Eireann.

Hickey, T. (2001) Mixing beginners and native speakers in minority language immersion: Who is immersing whom? *Canadian Modern Language Review/La Revue canadienne des langues vivantes, 57*(3), 443–474.

Hickey, T. (2007) Children's language networks in minority language immersion: What goes in may not come out. *Language and Education, 21*(1), 46–65.

Hickey, T., Lewis, G. and Baker, C. (2013) How deep is your immersion? Policy and practice in Welsh-medium preschools with children from different language backgrounds. *International Journal of Bilingual Education and Bilingualism, 17*(2), 1–20.

Hickey, T. and Ó Cainín, P. (2001) First language maintenance and second language acquisition of a minority language in kindergarten. In M. Almgren, A. Barrena, M.-J. Ezeiz Abarrena, I. Idiazabal and B. MacWhinney (eds) *Research on child language acquisition: Proceedings of 8th conference for the study of child language.* Somerville, MA: Cascadilla Press.

Hilchey, M.D. and Klein, R.M. (2011) Are there bilingual advantages on nonlinguistic interference tasks? Implications for the plasticity of executive control processes. *Psychonomic Bulletin and Review, 18*(4), 625–658.

Hill, R. and May, S. (2014) Balancing the language in Māori-Medium education in Aotearoa/New Zealand. In D. Gorter, V. Zenotz, and J. Cenoz (eds) *Minority languages and multilingual education* (pp. 159–176). Dordrecht, The Netherlands: Springer.

Hinton, K.A. (2015) 'We only teach in English': An examination of bilingual-in-name-only classrooms. *Research on Preparing Inservice Teachers to Work Effectively with Emergent Bilinguals, 24*, 265–289. doi:10.1108/S1479–368720150000024012

Hinton, L. (2015) Revitalization of endangered languages. In P. K. Austin and J. Sallabank (eds) *The Cambridge handbook of endangered languages* (pp. 291–311). Cambridge, UK: Cambridge University Press.

Hinton, L. (2017) Learning and teaching endangered indigenous languages. In S. May (ed.) *Encyclopedia of language and education* (3rd ed., Vol. 4: Second and foreign language education). New York, NY: Springer.

Hinton, L. and Hale, K. (2001) *The green book of language revitalization in practice.* San Diego, CA: Academic Press.

Hoffman, E. (1989) *Lost in translation: A life in a new language.* New York, NY: Dutton.

Hoffmann, C. (2000) Balancing language planning and language rights: Catalonia's uneasy juggling act. *Journal of Multilingual and Multicultural Development, 21*(5), 425–441.

Hoffmeister, R.J. (2008) Language and the Deaf World. In M. Brisk (ed.) *Language, culture, and community in teacher education.* New York, NY: Lawrence Erlbaum Associates.

Holm, A. and Holm, W. (1990) Rock Point, a Navajo way to go to school: A valediction. *The ANNALS of the American Academy of Political and Social Science, 508*(1), 170–184.

Hong, P. and Pawan, F. (2014) *The pedagogy and practice of Western-trained Chinese English language teachers.* New York, NY: Routledge.

Hoover, J.J., Klingner, J., Baca, L. and Patton, J.M. (2008) *Methods for teaching culturally and linguistically diverse exceptional learners.* Upper Saddle River, NJ: Pearson/Merrill Prentice Hall.

Hopewell, S. and Escamilla, K. (2015) How does a holistic perspective on (bi/multi)literacy help educators to address the demands of the Common Core State Standards for English language learners/emergent bilinguals? In G. Valdés, K. Menken and M. Castro (eds) *Common Core bilingual and English language learners: A resource for educators* (pp. 39–40). Philadelphia, PA: Caslon Publishing.

Hornberger, N.H. (ed.) (2017) *Honoring Richard Ruiz and his work on language planning and bilingual education.* Bristol, UK: Multilingual Matters.

Hornberger, N.H. (2006) Voice and biliteracy in indigenous language revitalization: Contentious educational practices in Quechua, Guarani, and Māori contexts. *Journal of Language, Identity, and Education, 5*(4), 277–292.

Hornberger, N.H. (2008) Continua of biliteracy. In A. Creese, M.M. Martin and N.H. Hornberger (eds) *Encyclopedia of language and education* (Vol. 9: Ecology of language). New York, NY: Springer.

Hornberger, N.H. (2009) Multilingual education policy and practice: Ten certainties (grounded in Indigenous experience). *Language Teaching, 42*(02), 197–211.

Hornberger, N.H. (2013) Bilingual literacy. In C.A. Chapelle (ed.) The encyclopedia of applied linguistics. Malden, MA: Blackwell. doi:DOI: 10.1002/9781405198431.wbeal0095

Hornberger, N.H. and King, K.A. (2001) Reversing Quechua language shift in South America. In J. Fishman (ed.) *Can threatened languages be saved?* Clevedon, UK: Multilingual Matters.

Hornberger, N.H. and Pütz, M. (eds) (2006) *Language loyalty, language planning and language revitalization: Recent writings and reflections from Joshua A. Fishman.* Clevedon, UK: Multilingual Matters.

Horner, J.-J. (2014) *Flexible multilingual education: Putting children's needs first.* Bristol, UK: Multilingual Matters.

Housen, A. (2002) Processes and outcomes in the European schools model of multilingual education. *Bilingual Research Journal, 26*(1), 45–64.

Howard, E.R., Christian, D. and Genesee, F. (2004) *The development of bilingualism and biliteracy from grade 3 to 5: A summary of findings from the CAL/CREDE study of two-way immersion education.* University of California at Santa Cruz: CREDA (Center for Research on Education, Diversity and Excellence).

Howard, E.R., Sugarman, J. and Coburn, C. (2006) *Adapting the sheltered instruction observation protocol (SIOP) for two-way immersion education: An introduction to the TWIOP.* Washington, DC: Center for Applied Linguistics.

Huang, B.H. (2014) The effects of age on second language grammar and speech production. *Journal of Psycholinguistic Research, 43*(4), 397–420.

Huang, B.H. (2015) A synthesis of empirical research on the linguistic outcomes of early foreign language instruction. *International Journal of Multilingualism, [Online First],* 1–17. doi:10.1080/14790718.2015.1066792

Hull, R. and Vaid, J. (2007) Bilingual language lateralization: A meta-analytic tale of two hemispheres. *Neuropsychologia, 45*(9), 1987–2008.

Hult, F. (2013) Ecology and multilingual education. In C.A. Chapelle (ed.) *The encyclopedia of applied linguistics.* Malden, MA: Blackwell.

Hult, F. and Johnson, D.C. (eds) (2015) *Research methods in language policy and planning: A practical guide.* Malden, MA: Wiley-Blackwell.

Hymes, D. (1972) On communicative competence. In J.B. Pride and J. Holmes (eds) *Sociolinguistics.* Harmondsworth, UK: Penguin Books.

Ianco-Worrall, A.D. (1972) Bilingualism and cognitive development. *Child Development, 43,* 1390–1400.

Iatcu, T. (2000) Teaching English as a third language to Hungarian–Romanian bilinguals. In J. Cenoz and U. Jessner (eds) *English in Europe: the acquisition of a third language.* Clevedon, UK: Multilingual Matters.

Igboanusi, H. and Peter, L. (2015) The language-in-education politics in Nigeria. *International Journal of Bilingual Education and Bilingualism, Online First.* doi:10.1080/13670050.2015.1031633

Imai, M. and Gentner, D. (1997) A cross-linguistic study of early word meaning: Universal ontology and linguistic influence. *Cognition, 62*(2), 169–200.

International Baccalaureate Organization (2014) *Language policy: Information on the International Baccalaureate's support for languages, language courses and languages of instruction.* Genève, Switzerland: Author.

Jaffe, A. (2007) Codeswitching and stance: Issues in interpretation. *Journal of Language, Identity, and Education, 6*(1), 53–77.

James, M. and Woll, B. (2004) Black deaf or deaf black? Being black and deaf in Britain. In A. Pavlenko and A. Blackledge (eds) *Negotiation of identities in multilingual contexts.* Clevedon, UK: Multilingual Matters.

Janks, H. (2013) Critical literacy. In C.A. Chapelle (ed.) The encyclopedia of applied linguistics. Malden, MA: Blackwell. doi:DOI: 10.1002/9781405198431.wbeal0281

Jaworski, A. and Thurlow, C. (2010) Language and globalizing habitus of tourism: Toward a sociolinguistics of fleeting relationships. In N. Coupland (ed.) *Handbook of language and globalization.* Malden, MA: Wiley-Blackwell.

Jessner, U. (2006) *Linguistic awareness in multilinguals: English as a third language.* Edinburgh, UK: Edinburgh University Press.

Jessner, U. (2008) Teaching third languages: Findings, trends and challenges. *Language Teaching, 41*(01), 15–56.

Johnson, D.C. (2010) Implementational and ideological spaces in bilingual education language policy. *International Journal of Bilingual Education and Bilingualism, 13*(1), 61–79.

Johnson, R.K. and Swain, M. (1994) From core to content: Bridging the L2 proficiency gap in late immersion. *Language and Education, 8*(4), 211–229.

Johnson, R.K. and Swain, M. (1997) *Immersion education: International perspectives.* Cambridge, UK: Cambridge University Press.

Johnstone, R. (2002) *Immersion in a second or additional language at school: A review of the international research.* Scottish CILT (Center for Information on Language Teaching).

Joneitz, P.L. (2003) Trans-language learners: A new terminology for international schools. In E. Murphy (ed.) *ESL: Educating non-native speakers of English in an English-medium international school.* Woodbridge, UK: John Catt Educational Ltd.

Jones, D.V. and Martin-Jones, M. (2004) Bilingual education and language revitalization in Wales: Past achievements and current issues. In J.W. Tollefson and A.B.M. Tsui (eds) *Medium of instruction policies. Which agenda? Whose Agenda?* Mahwah, NJ: Erlbaum.

Jones, G.M. (2012) Language planning in its historical context in Brunei Darussalam. In E. Ling and A. Hashim (eds) *English in Southeast Asia* (pp. 175–188). Amsterdam, Netherlands: John Benjamins.

Jones, G.M. (2015) Bilingual and multilingual education in Brunei and Malaysia: Policies and practices. In W.E. Wright, S. Boun and O. García (eds) *Handbook of bilingual and multilingual education* (pp. 529–539). Malden, MA: Wiley-Blackwell.

Jones, W.R. (1959) *Bilingualism and intelligence.* Cardiff, UK: University of Wales Press.

Jones, W.R. (1966) *Bilingualism in Welsh education.* Cardiff, UK: University of Wales Press.

Kachru, B.B. (2005) *Asian Englishes: Beyond the canon.* Oxford, UK: Oxford University Press.

Kagan, O., Carreira, M. and Chik, C.H. (eds) (2017) *A handbook on heritage language education: From innovation to program building.* New York, NY: Routledge.

Kalantzis, M. and Cope, B. (2013) Multiliteracies in education. In C.A. Chapelle (ed.) *Encyclopedia of applied linguistics.* Malden, MA: Blackwell Publishing.

Kaminksy, J. (2014, 6 February) Last native speaker of Klallam language dies in Washington state. *Reuters.* Retrieved from http://www.reuters.com/article/2014/02/07/us-usa-klallam-death-idUSBREA1605W20140207

Kanno, Y. (2003) Imagined communities, school visions, and the education of bilingual students in Japan. *Journal of Language, Identity, and Education, 2*(4), 285–300.

Kanno, Y. and Norton, B. (2003) Imagined communities and educational possibilities: Introduction. *Journal of Language, Identity and Education, 2*(4), 241–249. doi:10.1207/S15327701JLIE0204_1

Karmani, S. and Pennycook, A. (2005) Islam, English, and 9/11. *Journal of Language, Identity, and Education, 4*(2), 157–172.

Kaushanskaya, M. and Marian, V. (2007) Bilingual language processing and interference in bilinguals: Evidence from eye tracking and picture naming. *Language Learning, 57*(1), 119–163.

Kay-Raining Bird, E. (2007) The case for bilingualism in children with Down Syndrome. In R. Paul and R. S. Chapman (eds) *Language disorders from a developmental perspective: Essays in honor of Robin S. Chapman. New directions in communication disorders research integrative approaches.* Mahwah, NJ: Lawrence Erlbaum.

Kay-Raining Bird, E., Cleave, P., Trudeau, N., Thordardottir, E., Sutton, A. and Thorpe, A. (2005) The language abilities of bilingual children with Down syndrome. *American Journal of Speech-Language Pathology, 14*(3), 187–199.

Kelly-Holmes, H. and Milani, T.M. (2011) Thematising multilingualism in the media. *Journal of Language and Politics, 10*(4), 467–489.

Kemp, C. (2009) Defining multilingualism. In L. Aronin and B. Hufeisen (eds) *Exploration of multilingualism: Development of research on L3 multilingualism and multiple language acquisition* (pp. 11–26) Amersterdam, The Netherlands: John Benjamins.

Kenner, C. (2004a) *Becoming literate: Young children learning different writing systems.* Stoke on Trent, UK: Trentham.

Kenner, C. (2004b) Living in simultaneous worlds: Difference and integration in bilingual script-learning. *International Journal of Bilingual Education and Bilingualism, 7*(1), 43–61.

Kenner, C. and Gregory, E. (2012) Becoming biliterate. In J. Larson and J. Marsh (eds) *The SAGE handbook of early childhood literacy* (pp. 364–378). Thousand Oaks, CA: Sage.

Kersten, A.W., Meissner, C.A., Lechuga, J., Schwartz, B.L., Albrechtsen, J.S. and Iglesias, A. (2010) English speakers attend more strongly than Spanish speakers to manner of motion when classifying novel objects and events. *Journal of Experimental Psychology: General, 139*, 638–653.

Kessler, C. and Quinn, M.E. (1982) Cognitive development in bilingual environments. In B. Hartfold, A. Valdman and C.R. Foster (eds) *Issues in international bilingual education. The role of the vernacular.* New York, NY: Plenum Press.

Kharkhurin, A.V. (2008) The effect of linguistic proficiency, age of second language acquisition, and length of exposure to a new cultural environment on bilinguals' divergent thinking. *Bilingualism: Language and Cognition, 11*(02), 225–243.

Kharkhurin, A.V. (2009) The role of bilingualism in creative performance on divergent thinking and Invented Alien Creatures tests. *The Journal of Creative Behavior, 43*(1), 59–71.

Kharkhurin, A.V. (2015) Bilingualism and creativity: An educational perspective. In W.E. Wright, S. Boun and O. García (eds) *Handbook of bilingual and multilingual education* (pp. 38–55). Bristol, UK: Multilingual Matters.

Kim, K.H., Relkin, N.R., Lee, K.-M. and Hirsch, J. (1997) Distinct cortical areas associated with native and second languages. *Nature, 388*(6638), 171–174.

Kim, M. (2016) A North Korean defector's journey through the identity-transformation process. *Journal of Language, Identity and Education, 16*(1), 3–16. doi:10.1080/15348458.2015.1090764

Kinzler, K.D., Dupoux, E. and Spelke, E.S. (2007) The native language of social cognition. *Proceedings of the National Academy of Sciences of the United States of America, 104*(30), 12577–12580.

Kirkpatrick, A. (ed.) (2010) *The Routledge handbook of World Englishes.* New York, NY: Routledge

Klingner, J.K., Hoover, J.J. and Baca, L.M. (2008) *Why do English language learners struggle with reading?: Distinguishing language acquisition from learning disabilities.* London, UK: SAGE.

Kloss, H. (1998) *The American bilingual tradition.* Washington, DC: Center for Applied Linguistics and Delta Systems (Original Publication, 1977).

Knoors, H., Tang, G. and Marschark, M. (2014) Bilingualism and bilingual deaf education: Time to take stock. In M. Marschark, G. Tang and H. Knoors (eds) *Bilingualism and deaf education* (pp. 1–20). New York, NY: Oxford University Press.

Koda, K. and Zehler, A.M. (2008) *Learning to read across languages: Cross-linguistic relationships in first- and second-language literacy development.* New York, NY: Routledge.

Kolers, P.A. (1963) Interlingual word associations. *Journal of Verbal Learning and Verbal Behavior, 2*(4), 291–300.

Kowalski, K. and Lo, Y.F. (2001) The influence of perceptual features, ethnic labels, and sociocultural information on the development of ethnic/racial bias in young children. *Journal of Cross-Cultural Psychology, 32*(4), 444–455.

Krashen, S.D. (1999) *Condemned without a trial: Bogus arguments against bilingual education.* Portsmouth, NH: Heinemann.

Krashen, S.D. (2002) Developing academic language: Early L1 reading and later L2 reading. *International Journal of the Sociology of Language, 155*(156), 143–151.

Krashen, S.D. (2004a) *The acquisition of academic English by children in two-way programs: What does the research say?* Paper presented at the NABE Review of Research and Practice, Albuquerque, NM.

Krashen, S.D. (2004b) *Power of reading: Insights from the research* (2nd ed.). Portsmouth, NH: Henemann.

Kroll, J.F. and Bialystok, E. (2013) Understanding the consequences of bilingualism for language processing and cognition. *Journal of Cognitive Psychology, 25*(5), 497–514.

Ladas, A.I., Carroll, D.J. and Vivas, A.B. (2015) Attentional processes in low-socioeconomic status bilingual children: Are they modulated by the amount of bilingual experience? *Child Development, 86,* 557–578. doi:10.1111/cdev.12332

Ladd, P. (2003) *Understanding deaf culture: In search of deafhood.* Clevedon, UK: Multilingual Matters.

Lambert, W.E. (1974) Culture and language as factors in learning and education. In F.E. Aboud and R.D. Meade (eds) *Cultural factors in learning and education.* Bellingham, Washington: 5th Western Washington Symposium on Learning.

Lambert, W.E. and Tucker, G.R. (1972) *Bilingual education of children: The St. Lambert experiment.* Rowley, MA: Newbury House.

Lantolf, J.P. (2011) The sociocultural approach to second language acquistion: Sociocultural theory, second language acquisition, and artificial L2 development. In D. Atkinson (ed.) *Alternative approaches to second language acquisition* (pp. 24–47). New York, NY: Routledge.

Lanza, E. (2007) Multilingualism and the family. In P. Auer and L. Wei (eds) *Handbook of multilingualism multilingual communication.* Berlin, GE: Mouton de Gruyter.

Laurén, C. (1994) Swedish immersion programs in Finland. In J. Cummins and D. Corson (eds) *Encyclopedia of language and education* (Vol. 5: Bilingual education). Dordrecht, The Netherlands: Kluwer.

Laurén, U. (1991) A creativity index for studying the free written production of bilinguals. *International Journal of Applied Linguistics, 1*(2), 198–208.

Laurie, S. S. (1890) *Lectures on language and linguistic method in the school.* Cambridge, Uk: Cambridge University Press.

Lazarus, S.S., Albus, D. and Thurlow, M.L. (2016) *2013–2014 publically reported assessment results for students with disabilities and ELLs with disabilities (NCEO Report 401).* Minneapolis, MN: University of Minnesota, National Center on Educational Outcomes.

Lee, J.S. (2014) Community support for Korean as a heritage language. In T.G. Wiley, J.K. Peyton, D. Christian, S.K.C. Moore and N. Liu (eds) *Handbook of heritage and community languages in the United States: Research, educational practice, and policy* (pp. 253–262). Washington, DC and New York, NY: Center for Applied Linguistics and Routledge.

Lee, J.S. and Wright, W.E. (2014) The rediscovery of heritage and community language education in the United States. *Review of Research in Education, 38,* 137–165. doi:10.3102/0091732X13507546

Lee, S., Watt, R. and Frawley, J. (2015) Effectiveness of bilingual education in Cambodia: A longitudinal comparative case study of ethnic minority children in bilingual and monolingual schools. *Compare: A Journal of Comparative and International Education, 45*(4), 526–544.

Lee, T.S. and McCarty, T.L. (2015) Bilingual-multilingual education and indigenous peoples. In W.E. Wright, S. Boun and O. García (eds) *Handbook of bilingual and multilingual education* (pp. 407–425). Malden, MA: Wiley-Blackwell.

Leigh, I. (2009) *A lens on deaf identities*. Oxford, UK: Oxford University Press.

Leikin, M. (2012) The effect of bilingualism on creativity: Developmental and educational perspectives. *International Journal of Bilingualism, 17*(4), 431–447.

Leonard, W.Y. (2008) When is an 'extinct language' not extinct? Miami, a formerly sleeping language. In K.A. King, N. Schilling-Estes, J.J. Lou, L. Fogle and B. Soukup (eds) *Sustaining linguistic diversity: Endangered and minority languages and language varieties* (pp. 23–34). Washington, DC: Georgetown University Press.

Leopold, W.F. (1970) *Speech development of a bilingual child: A linguist's record*. Evanston, IL: Northwestern University Press.

Lewis, E.G. (1977) Bilingualism and bilingual education: The ancient world to the rennaisane. In B. Spolsky and R.L. Cooper (eds) *Frontiers of bilingual education* (pp. 22–93). Rowley, MA: Newbury House.

Lewis, G., Jones, B. and Baker, C. (2012) Translanguaging: Developing its conceptualisation and contextualisation. *Educational Research and Evaluation, 18*(7), 655–670.

Lewis, M.P., Simons, G.F. and Fennig, C.D. (eds) (2015) *Ethnologue: Languages of the world* (18th ed.). Dallas, TX: SIL International.

Lewis, W.G. (2004) Addysg gynradd Gymraeg: Trochi a chyfoethogi disgyblion. *The University of Wales Journal of Education, 12*(2), 49–64.

Lewkowicz, D.J. and Hansen-Tift, A.M. (2012) Infants deploy selective attention to the mouth of a talking face when learning speech. *Proceedings of the National Academy of Sciences of the United States of America, 109*(5), 1431–1436.

Li, P. (2013) Cognition and the bilingual brain. In F. Grosjean and P. Li (eds) *The psycholinguistics of bilingualism* (pp. 214–228). Malden, MA: John Wiley and Sons.

Li Wei (2006) Complementary schools, past, present and future. *Language and Education, 20*(1), 76–83.

Li Wei, Dewaele, J.M. and Housen, A. (2002) Introduction: Opportunities and challenges of bilingualism. In L. Wei, J.M. Dewaele and A. Housen (eds) *Opportunities and challenges of bilingualism*. Berlin, GE: Mouton de Gruyter.

Li Wei, Miller, N. and Dodd, B. (1997) Distinguishing communicative difference from language disorder in bilingual children. *Bilingual Family Newsletter, 14*(1), 3–4.

Li Wei, Milroy, L. and Ching, P.S. (1992) A two-step sociolinguistic analysis of code-switching and language choice: The example of a bilingual Chinese community in Britain. *International Journal of Applied Linguistics, 2*(1), 63–86.

Li Wei and Moyer, M. (2009) *Blackwell guide to research methods in bilingualism and multilingualism*. Malden: Oxford: John Wiley and Sons.

Lillie, K.E. (2016) 'The ELD classes are ... too much and we need to take other classes to graduate': Arizona's restrictive language policy and the dis-citizenship of ELs. In A. Loring and V. Ramanathan (eds) *Language, immigration and naturalization: Legal and linguistic issues*. Bristol, UK: Multilingual Matters.

Lillie, K. E. and Markos, A. (2014) The four-hour block: SEI in classrooms. In S.C. Moore (ed.) *Language policy processes and consequences: Arizona case studies* (pp. 133–155). Bristol, UK: Multilingual Matters.

Lillie, K.E. and Moore, S.C.K. (2014) SEI in Arizona: Bastion for state's rights. In S.C.K. Moore (ed.) *Language policy processes and consequences: Arizona case studies* (pp. 1–27). Bristol, UK: Multilingual Matters.

Lin, A. (2006) Beyond linguistic purism in language-in-education policy and practice: Exploring bilingual pedagogies in a Hong Kong science classroom. *Language and Education, 20*(4), 287–305.

Lin, A. (2015) Egalitarian Bi/multilingualism and trans-semiotizing in a global world. In W.E. Wright, S. Boun and O. García (eds) *Handbook of bilingual and multilingual education* (pp. 19–37). Malden, MA: John Wiley and Sons.

Lindholm, K.J. (1991) Theoretical assumptions and empirical evidence for academic achievement in two languages. *Hispanic Journal of Behavioral Sciences, 13*(1), 3–17.

Lindholm, K.J. and Aclan, Z. (1991) Bilingual proficiency as a bridge to academic achievement: Results from bilingual/immersion programs. *Journal of Education, 173*(2), 99–113.

Lindholm-Leary, K.J. (1994) Promoting positive cross-cultural attitudes and perceived competence in culturally and linguistically diverse classrooms. In R.A. DeVillar, C.J. Faltis and J.P. Cummins (eds) *Cultural diversity in schools: From rhetoric to practice* (pp. 189–206). Albany, NY: State University of New York Press.

Lindholm-Leary, K.J. (2001) *Dual language education*. Clevedon, UK: Multilingual Matters.

Lindholm-Leary, K.J. and Borsato, G. (2006) Academic achievement. In F. Genesee, K. Lindholm-Leary, W.M. Saunders and D. Christian (eds) *Educating English learners: A synthesis of empirical evidence*. New York, NY: Cambridge University Press.

Lindholm-Leary, K.J. and Genesee, F. (2010) Alternative educational programs for English learners. In California State Department of Education (ed.) *Improving education for English learners: Research-based approaches*. Sacramento, CA: CDE Press.

Lindholm-Leary, K.J. and Genesee, F. (2014) Student outcomes in one-way, two-way, and indigenous language immersion education. *Journal of Immersion and Content-Based Language Education, 2*(2), 165–180. doi:10.1075/jicb.2.2.01lin

Little, D., Leung, C. and Van Avermaet, P. (eds) (2014) *Managing diversity in education: Language, policies, pedagogies*. Bristol, UK: Multilingual Matters.

Littlebear, R.E. (1996) Preface. In G. Cantoni (ed.) *Stabilizing indigenous languages*. Flagstaff, AZ: Northern Arizona University Press.

Littlebear, R.E. (1999) Some rare and radical ideas for keeping indigenous languages alive. In J.A. Reyhner, G. Cantoni, R.S. Claire and E. Pearsons Yazzie (eds) *Revitalizing indigenous languages*. Flagstaff, AZ: Northern Arizona University Press.

Lo Bianco, J. (2001) *Language and literacy policy in Scotland*. Stirling: Scottish CILT.

Lo Bianco, J. (2015) Multilingual education across Oceania. In W.E. Wright, S. Boun and O. García (eds) *Handbook of bilingual and multilingual education* (pp. 604–617). Malden, MA: Wiley-Blackwell.

Lo Bianco, J. (2016) Conflict, langauge rights, and education: Building peace by solving language problems in Southeast Asia. *Language Policy Research Network Brief, April*, 1–8.

Lucy, J.A. and Gaskins, S. (2001) Grammatical categories and the development of classification preferences: A comparative approach. In M. Bowerman and S. Levinson (eds) *Language acquisition and conceptual development* (pp. 257–283). Cambridge, UK: Cambridge University Press.

Lukes, M. (2015) *Latino immigrant youth and interrupted schooling: Dropouts, dreamers and alternative pathways to college*. Bristol, UK: Multilingual Matters.

Lüpke, F. (2015) Orthography development. In P. K. Austin and J. Sallabank (eds) *The Cambridge handbook of endangered languages* (pp. 312–336). Cambridge, UK: Cambridge University Press.

Lyster, R. and Mori, H. (2008) Instructional counterbalance in immersion pedagogy. In T. W. Fortune and D. J. Tedick (eds) *Pathways to multilingualism: Evolving perspectives on immersion education*. Clevedon, UK: Multilingual Matters.

Ma, W. and Li, G. (eds) (2016) *Chinese-heritage students in North American schools: Understanding hearts and minds beyond test scores*. New York, NY: Routledge.

Macartney, S., Bishaw, A. and Fontenot, K. (2013) *Poverty rates for selected detailed race and Hispanic groups by state and place: 2007–2011*. Washington, DC: US Census Bureau, US Department of Commerce.

MacDonald, R., Boals, T., Castro, M., Cook, H.G., Lundberg, T. and White, P.A. (2015) *Formative language assessment for English learners: A four-step process*. Portsmouth, NH: Heinemann.

Macías, R.F. (2000) The flowering of America: Linguistic diversity in the United States. In S. McKay and S.C. Wong (eds) *New immigrants in the United States*. Cambridge, UK: Cambridge University Press.

Mackey, W.F. (1970) A typology of bilingual education. *Foreign Language Annals, 3*(4), 596–606.

Mackey, W.F. (1978) The importation of bilingual education models. In J.E. Alatis (ed.) *Georgetown University roundtable: International dimensions of education*. Washington, DC: Georgetown University Press.

MacNab, G.L. (1979) Cognition and bilingualism: A reanalysis of studies. *Linguistics, 17*(3–4), 231–256.

MacSwan, J. (2000) The threshold hypothesis, semilingualism, and other contributions to a deficit view of linguistic minorities. *Hispanic Journal of Behavioral Science, 22*(1), 3–45.

MacSwan, J. (2013) Codeswitching and grammatical theory. In W.C. Ritchie and T.K. Bhatia (eds) *Handbook of bilingualism and multilingualism* (pp. 321–250). Malden, MA: Wiley-Blackwell.

MacSwan, J. (ed.) (2014) *Grammatical theory and bilingual codeswtiching*. Cambridge, MA: MIT Press.

MacSwan, J. and Rolstad, K. (2003) Linguistic diversity, schooling, and social class: Rethinking our conception of language proficiency in language minority education. In C.B. Paulston and R. Tucker (eds) *Sociolinguistics: Essential reading* (pp. 329–341). Oxford, England: Blackwell.

MacSwan, J., Rolstad, K. and Glass, G.V. (2002) Do some school-age children have no language? Some problems of construct validity in the Pre-Las Español. *Bilingual Research Journal, 26*(2), 213–238.

Mahoney, K., Thompson, M. and MacSwan, J. (2005) *The condition of English language learners in Arizona: 2005*. Retrieved from www.terpconnect.umd.edu/~macswan/EPSL-0509-110-AEPI.pdf

Makoni, S. and Makoni, B. (2015) Too many cooks spoil the broth: Tension and conflict between language institutions in South Africa In W.E. Wright, S. Boun and O. García (eds) *Handbook of bilingual and multilingual education* (pp. 552–563). Malden, MA: Wiley-Blackwell.

Makoni, S. and Pennycook, A. (2007) *Disinventing and reconstituting languages* (Vol. 62). Clevedon, UK: Multilingual Matters.

Malherbe, E.C. (1946) *The bilingual school.* London, UK: Longman.

Maneva, B. and Genesee, F. (2002) Bilingual babbling: Evidence for language differentiation in dual language acquisition. In B. Skarabela, S. Fish and A. Do (eds) *BUCLD 26: Proceedings of the 26 Annual Boston University Conference on Language Development* (Vol. 1, pp. 383–392). Somerville, MA: Cascadilla Press.

Mango, O. (2012) Arab American women negotiating identities. *International Multilingual Research Journal, 6*(2), 83–103.

Marinova-Todd, S.H., Marshall, D.B. and Snow, C.E. (2000) Three misconceptions about age and L2 learning. *TESOL Quarterly, 34*(1), 9–34.

Marinova-Todd, S.H. and Mirenda, P. (2016) Language and communication abilities of bilingual children with Austim Spectrum Disorders. In J.L. Patterson and B.L. Rodriguez (eds) *Multilingual perspectives on child language disorders* (pp. 31–48). Bristol, UK: Multilingual Matters.

Marsh, D. (2008) Language awareness and CLIL. In J. Cenoz and N.H. Hornberger (eds) *Encyclopedia of language and education* (2nd ed., Vol. 6: Knowledge about language, pp. 1986–1999). New York, NY: Springer.

Martin, D. (2009) *Language disabilities in cultural and linguistic diversity.* Bristol, UK: Multilingual Matters.

Martin-Jones, M. (2000) Bililingual classroom interaction: A review of recent research. *Language Teaching, 33*(1), 1–9.

Martin-Jones, M. and Jones, K.E. (2000) Introduction: Multilingual literacies. In M. Martin-Jones and K. Jones (eds) *Multilingual literacies: Reading and writing different worlds.* Philadelphia, PA: John Benjamins.

Martin-Jones, M. and Romaine, S. (1986) Semilingualism: A half baked theory of communicative competence. *Applied Linguistics, 7*(1), 26–38.

Martin-Jones, M. and Saxena, M. (2003) Bilingual resources and 'funds of knowledge' for teaching and learning in multi-ethnic classrooms in Britain. *International Journal of Bilingual Education and Bilingualism, 6*(3 and 4), 267–282.

Martinovic, I. and Altarriba, J. (2013) Bilingualism and emotion: Implications for mental health. In T.K. Bhatia and W.C. Ritchie (eds) *The handbook of bilingualism and multilingualism* (pp. 292–320). Malden, MA: Wiley-Blackwell.

Matthews, T. (1979) *An investigation into the effects of background characteristics and special language services on the reading achievement and English fluency of bilingual students.* Seattle, WA: Seattle Public Schools, Department of Planning.

May, S. (2011) *Language and minority rights: Ethnicity, nationalism and the politics of language* (2nd ed.). New York, NY: Routledge.

Mayer, C. (2015) Rethinking total communication: Looking back, moving forward. In M. Marschark and P. Spencer (eds) *The Oxford handbook of deaf studies: Language and language development* (pp. 32–44). New York, NY: Oxford University Press.

Mayer, J. and Leigh, G. (2010) The changing context for sign bilingual education programs: Issues in language and the development of literacy. *International Journal of Bilingual Education and Bilingualism, 13*(2), 175–186.

McBride-Chang, C., Bialystok, E., Chong, K.K. and Li, Y. (2004) Levels of phonological awareness in three cultures. *Journal of Experimental Child Psychology, 89*(2), 93–111.

McCarty, T.L. (2002) *A place to be Navajo: Rough rock and the struggle for self-determination in indigenous schooling.* Mahwah, NJ: Lawrence Erlbaum.

McCarty, T.L. (2004) Dangerous difference: A critical-historical analysis of language education policies in the United States. In J.W. Tollefson and A.B.M. Tsui (eds) *Medium of instruction policies: Which agenda? Whose agenda?* Mahwah, NJ: Erlbaum.

McCarty, T.L. (2008) Native American languages as heritage mother tongues. *Language, Culture and Curriculum, 21*(3), 201–225.

McCarty, T.L. (2013) *Language planning and policy in Native America: History, theory, praxis.* Bristol, UK: Multilingual Matters.

McCarty, T.L. (2014) Native American languages: Introduction. In T.G. Wiley, J.K. Peyton, D. Christian,

S.K.C. Moore and N. Liu (eds) *Handbook of heritage and community languages in the United States: Research, educational practice, and policy* (pp. 189–191). Washington, DC and New York, NY: Center for Applied Linguistics and Routledge.

McCarty, T.L. (2017) Bilingual education in the indigenous languages of North America. In S. May (ed.) *Encyclopedia of language and education* (3rd ed., Vol. 5: Bilingual education). New York, NY: Springer.

McConnell, B. (1980) *Effectiveness of individualized bilingual instruction for migrant students.* Washington State University, Unpublished PhD dissertation.

McField, G.P. and McField, D.R. (2014) The consistent oucome of bilingual education programs: A meta-anlysis of meta-ananyses. In G. McField (ed.) *The miseducation of English learners: A tale of three states and lessons to be learned* (pp. 267–297). Charlotte, NC: Information Age Publishing.

McGinnis, S. (2008) From mirror to compass: The Chinese heritage language education sector in the United States. In D. Brinton, O. Kagan and S. Bauckus (eds) *Heritage language education: A new field emerging.* New York, NY: Routledge.

McLeay, H. (2003) The relationship between bilingualism and the performance of spatial tasks. *International Journal of Bilingual Education and Bilingualism, 6*(6), 423–438.

McQuillan, J. and Tse, L. (1996) Does research matter? An analysis of media opinion on bilingual education, 1984–1994. *Bilingual Research Journal, 20*(1), 1–27.

Mechelli, A., Chinion, J. T., Noppeney, U., O'Doherty, J., Ashburner, J., Frackowiak, R.S. and Price, C. J. (2004) Neurolinguistics: Structural plasticity in the bilingual brain. *Nature, 431,* 757.

Mehisto, P. (2012) *Excellence in bilingual education: A guide for school principals.* Cambridge, UK: Cambridge University Press.

Mehisto, P. (2015) Conclusions: Forces, mechanisms, and counterweights and Appendix. In P. Mehisto and F. Genese (eds) *Building bilingual education systems: Forces, mechanisms, and counterweights* (Vol. 269–297). Cambridge, UK: Cambridge University Press.

Mehisto, P. and Genesee, F. (eds) (2015) *Building bilingual education systems: Forces, mechanisms, and counterweights.* Cambridge, UK: Cambridge University Press.

Menéndez, B. (2010) Cross-modal bilingualism: language contact as evidence of linguistic transfer in sign bilingual education. *International Journal of Bilingual Education and Bilingualism, 13*(2), 201–223.

Menken, K. (2008) *English learners left behind: Standardized testing as language policy.* Clevedon, UK: Multilingual Matters.

Menken, K. (2013) (Dis)citizenship or opportunity? The importance of language education policy for access and full participation of emergent bilinguals in the US. In V. Ramanathan (ed.) *Language policies and (dis)citizenship: Rights, access, pedagogies* (pp. 209–230). Bristol, UK: Multilingual Matters.

Menken, K. and Barron, V. (2002) What are the characteristics of the bilingual education and ESL shortage. *Ask NCELA* (Vol. 14). Washington, DC: National Clearinghouse for English Language Acquisition and Language Instruction Educational Programs.

Menken, K. and García, O. (2010) *Negotiating language policies in schools: Educators as policymakers.* New York, NY: Routledge.

Menken, K. and Kleyn, T. (2010) The long-term impact of subtractive schooling in the educational experiences of secondary English language learners. *International Journal of Bilingual Education and Bilingualism, 13*(4), 399–417. doi:10.1080/13670050903370143

Menken, K., Kleyn, T. and Chae, N. (2012) Spotlight on 'long-term English language learners': Characteristics and prior schooling experiences of an invisible population. *International Multilingual Research Journal, 6*(2), 121–142.

Menken, K. and Solarza, C. (2015) Principals as linchpins in bilingual education: The need for prepared school leaders. *International Journal of Bilingualism, 18*(6), 676–697.

Menyuk, P. and Brisk, M.E. (2005) *Language development and education: Children with varying language experiences.* Basingstoke, Hampshire: Palgrave Macmillan.

Mercer, J.R. (1973) *Labeling the mentally retarded.* Berkeley, CA: University of California Press.

Meyer, M.M. and Fienberg, S.E. (1992) *Assessing evaluation studies:: The case of bilingual education strategies.* Washington, DC: National Academies Press.

Michael, E.B. and Gollan, T.H. (2005) Being and becoming bilingual: Individual differences and consequences for language production. In J.F. Kroll and A. De Groot (eds) *Handbook of bilingualism: Psycholinguistic approaches.* Oxford, UK: Oxford University Press.

Mills, J. (2006) Talking about silence: Gender and the construction of multilingual identities. *International Journal of Bilingualism, 10*(1), 1–16.

Milson-Whyte, V. (2013) Pedagogical and socio-political implications of code-meshing in classrooms: Some considerations for a translingual orientation to writing. In A.S. Canagarajah (ed.) *Literacy as translingual practice: Between communities and classrooms* (pp. 115–127). New York, NY: Routledge.

Mitchell, C. (2015) Momentum building for biliteracy. *Education Week, 35*(7), 1, 12.

Mitchell, C. (2016) Arizona, Federal government settle dispute over English-language learners. Retrieved from http://blogs.edweek.org/edweek/learning-the-language/2016/05/arizona_federal_government_set.html

Miyake, A., Friedman, N.P., Emerson, M.J., Witzki, A.H., Howerter, A. and Wager, T. D. (2000) The unity and diversity of executive functions and their contributions to complex 'frontal lobe' tasks: A latent variable analysis. *Cognitive Psychology, 4*(1), 49–100.

Mohanty, A.K., Panda, M., Phillipson, R. and Skutnabb-Kangas, T. (2009) *Multilingual education for social justice globalising the local.* New Delhi, IND: Orient Blackswan.

Mohd-Asraf, R. (2005) English and Islam: A clash of civilizations? *Journal of Language, Identity, and Education, 4*(2), 103–118.

Moje, E.B. (2017) Theory and research on literacy as a tool for navigating everyday and school discourses. In S. May (ed.) *Encyclopedia of language and education* (3rd ed., Vol. 3: Discourse and education). New York, NY: Springer.

Moll, L.C. (2001) The diversity of schooling: A cultural-historical approach. In M. Reyes and J.J. Halcón (eds) *The best for our children: Critical perspectives on literacy for latino students* (Vol. 13). New York, NY: Teachers College Press.

Monaghan, L., Schmaling, C., Nakamura, K. and Turner, G.T.E. (2003) *Many ways to be deaf: International variation in deaf communities.* Washington, DC: Gallaudet University University.

Moon, C., Lagercrantz, H. and Kuhl, P.K. (2013) Language experience *in utero* affects vowel perception after birth: A two country study. *Acta Pædiatrica, 102*(2), 156–160. doi:10.1111/apa.12098

Moore, R.E., Pietikäinen, S. and Blommaert, J. (2010) Counting the losses: Numbers as the language of language endangerment. *Sociolinguistic Studies, 4*(1), 1–26. doi:10.1558/sols.v4i1.1

Moore, S.C.K. (2014) *Language policy processes and consequences: Arizona case studies* Bristol, UK: Multilingual Matters.

Moriarty, M. (2011) Minority languages and performative genres: The case of Irish language stand-up comedy. *Journal of Multilingual and Multicultural Development, 32*(6), 547–559.

Moriarty, M. (2015) New roles for endangered languages. In P.K. Austin and J. Sallabank (eds) *The Cambridge handbook of endangered languages* (pp. 446–458). Cambridge, UK: Cambridge University Press.

Morita-Mullaney, T. (2016) Borrowing legitimacy as English Learner (EL) Leaders: Indiana's 14-year history with English language proficiency standards. *Language Testing.* (Online First). doi:10.1177/0265532216653430

Morita-Mullaney, T., Gilmetdinova, A., Klassen, M. and Barry, S. (forthcoming) The language-blind, No Child Left Behind flexibility waiver for English Learners in a Midwestern, US district: A Phenomenological Case Study of school and district administrators.

Morris, D. and Jones, K. (2008) Language socialization in the home and minority language revitalization in Europe. In P.A. Duff and N.H. Hornberger (eds) *Encyclopedia of language and education* (2nd ed., Vol. 8: Socialization). New York, NY: Springer.

Moschkovich, J. (2007) Using two languages when learning mathematics. *Educational Studies in Mathematics, 64*(2), 121–144.

Moseley, C. (2010) *Atlas of the world's languages in danger* (3rd ed.). Paris, France: UNESCO.

Muller, A. and Baetens Beardsmore, H. (2004) Multilingual interaction in plurilingual classes–European school practice. *International Journal of Bilingual Education and Bilingualism, 7*(1), 24–42.

Muñoz, C. (2000) Bilingualism and trilingualism in school students in Catalonia. In J. Cenoz and U. Jessner (eds) *English in Europe: the acquisition of a third language* (pp. 157–178). Clevedon, UK: Multilingual Matters.

Muysken, P. (2000) *Bilingual speech: A typology of code-mixing* (Vol. 11). Cambridge, UK: Cambridge University Press.

Myers-Scotton, C. (1997) Code-switching. In F. Coulmas (ed.) *The handbook of sociolinguistics.* Oxford, UK: Blackwell.

Myers-Scotton, C. (2002) *Contact Linguistics.* Cambridge, UK: Cambridge University Press.

National Center for Education Statistics (2016) *Digest of education statistics, 2014 (NCES 2016-006), Chapter 2.* Washington, DC: US Department of Education.

National Clearinghouse for English Language Acquisition (2011) The growing number of limited English proficient students 2009/10. Retrieved from http://www.ncela.us/files/uploads/9/growing_EL_0910.pdf

National Clearinghouse for English Language Acquisition (2015a) *English learners and NAEP (OELA Fast Facts)* Washington, DC: Author.

National Clearinghouse for English Language Acquisition (2015b) *Languages spoken by English learners (OELA Fast Facts)* Washington, DC: Author.

National Clearinghouse for English Language Acquisition (2015c) *National- and state-level high school graduation rates for English learners (OELA Fast Facts).* Washington, DC: Author.

National Clearinghouse for English Language Acquisition (2015d) *Profiles of English learners (OELA Fast Facts)* Washington, DC: Author.

National Education Association (1966) *The invisible minority ... pero no vencibles: Report of the NEA-Tucson Survey on the Teaching of Spanish to the Spanish-Speaking.* Washington, DC: Department of Rural Education, National Education Association.

National Education Goals Panel (1999) *The National Education Goals report: Building a nation of learners.* Washington, DC: Author.

National Reading Panel (2000) *Teaching children to read: An evidenced-based assessment of the scientific research literature on reading and its implications for reading instruction. Summary report.* Washington, DC: National Institute of Child Health and Human Development

Netten, J. and Germain, C. (2004) Theoretical and research foundations of intensive French. *Canadian Modern Language Review/La Revue canadienne des langues vivantes, 60*(3), 275–294.

Nettle, D. and Romaine, S. (2000) *Vanishing voices: The extinction of the world's languages.* Oxford, UK: Oxford University Press.

New London Group (1996) A pedagogy of multiliteracies: Designing social futures. *Harvard Educational Review, 66*(1), 60–92.

Newcombe, L.P. (2007) *Social context and fluency in L2 learners: The case of Wales.* Clevedon, UK Multilingual Matters.

Ng, S. and Wicha, N.Y.Y. (2013) Meaning first: A case for language-independent access to word meaning in the bilingual brain. *Neuropsychologia, 51*(5), 850–863. doi:10.1016/j.neuropsychologia.2013.01.017

Ngo, B. (2010) *Unresolved identities: Discourse, ambivalence, and urban immigrant students.* New York: State University of New York Press.

Nicholls, C. (2005) Death by a thousand cuts: Indigenous language bilingual education programmes in the Northern Territory of Australia, 1972–1998. *International Journal of Bilingual Education and Bilingualism, 8*(2–3), 160–177.

Nicolay, A.-C. and Poncelet, M. (2015) Cognitive benefits in children enrolled in an early bilingual immersion school: A follow-up study. *Bilingualism: Language and Cognition, 18*(4), 789–795.

Norton, B. (2013) *Identity and language learning: Extending the conversation* (2nd ed.). Bristol, UK: Multilingual Matters.

Nover, S.M., Christensen, K.M. and Cheng, L.L. (1998) Development of ASL and English competence for learners who are deaf. *Topics in Language Disorders, 18*(4), 61–72.

Ó Gliasáin, M. (1996) *The language question in the Census of the population.* Dublin, IRE: Linguistics Institute of Ireland.

Ó hIfearnáin, T. (2015) Sociolinguistic vitality of Manx after extreme language shift: Authenticity without traditional native speakers. *International Journal of the Sociology of Language, 2014*(231), 45–62. doi:10.1515/ijsl-2014-0031

Ó Riagáin, P. (2001) Irish language production and reproduction 1981–1996. In J. Fishman (ed.) *Can threatened languages be saved.* Clevedon, UK: Multilingual Matters.

Okita, T. (2002) *Invisible work: Bilingualism, language choice, and childrearing in intermarried families.* Amsterdam, NL: John Benjamins.

Oller, D.K. and Eilers, R.E. (2002) *Language and literacy in bilingual children.* Clevedon, UK: Multilingual Matters.

Oller, J.W. and Perkins, K. (1980) *Research in language testing.* Rowley, MA: Newbury House.

Olsen, L. (2010) *Reparable harm: Fulfilling the unkept promise of educational opportunity for California's long term English learners.* Retrieved from Long Beach, CA: http://www.californianstogether.org/reparable-harm-fulfilling-the-unkept-promise-of-educational-opportunity-for-californias-long-term-english-learners/

Olsen, L. (2015) Bilingualism and education in California and the United States: A timeline. Retrieved from http://www.bilingualeducation.org/cabe2015/TimelineForCABE.pdf

Onysko, A. (2015) Enhanced creativity in bilinguals? Evidence from meaning interpretations of novel compounds. *International Journal of Bilingualism, 1–20.* doi:10.1177/1367006914566081

Orellana, M. (2009) *Translating childhoods: Immigrant youth, language, and culture.* New Brunswick, NJ: Rutgers University Press.

Ostler, N. (2005) *Empires of the word: A language history of the world.* New York, NY: HarperCollins Publishers.

Ovando, C.J. and Combs, M.C. (2017) *Bilingual and ESL classrooms: Teaching in multicultural contexts* (6th ed.). Lanham, MD: Rowman and Littlefield.

Ovando, C.J. (2003) Bilingual education in the United States: Historical development and current issues. *Bilingual Research Journal, 27*(1), 1–24.

Paap, K.R., Johnson, H.A. and Sawi, O. (2015a) Bilingual advantages in executive functioning either do not exist or are restricted to very specific and undetermined circumstances. *Cortex, 69,* 265–278.

Paap, K.R., Johnson, H.A. and Sawi, O. (2015b) Should the search for bilingual advantages in executive functioning continue? *Cortex, Online First.* doi:10.1016/j.cortex.2015.09.010

Pai, M., Cummins, J., Nocus, I., Salaün, M. and Vernaudon, J. (2015) Intersections of language ideology, power, and identity: Bilingual education and indigenous language revitalization in French Polynesia. In W.E. Wright, S. Boun and O. García (eds) *Handbook of bilingual and multilingual education* (pp. 145–163). Malden, MA: John Wiley and Sons.

Palmer, D.K. and Lynch, A.W. (2008) A bilingual education for a monolingual test? The pressure to prepare for TAKS and its influence on choices for language of instruction in Texas elementary bilingual classrooms. *Language Policy, 7*(3), 217–235. doi:10.1007/s10993-008-9100-0

Palmer, D.K., Martinez, R.A., Mateus, S.G. and Henderson, K. (2014) Reframing the debate on language separation: Toward a vision for translanguaging pedagogies in the dual language classroom. *Modern Language Review, 98*(3), 757–772.

Palmer, D.K., Zuñiga, C.E. and Henderson, K.I. (2015) A dual language revolution in the Untied States? On the bumpy road from compensatory to enrichment education for bilingual children in the United States. In W.E. Wright, S. Boun and O. Garcia (eds) *Handbook of bilingual and multilingual education* (pp. 449–460). Malden, MA: Wiley-Blackwell.

Panayiotou, A. (2006) Translating guilt: An endeavor of shame in the Mediterranean? In A. Pavlenko (ed.) *Bilingual minds: Emotional experience, expression and representation* (pp. 183–208). Clevedon, UK: Multilingual Matters.

Panayiotou, A. (2007) Bilingual emotions: The untranslatable self. *Sociolinguistic Studies, 5*(1), 1–19.

Panda, M. and Mohanty, A.K. (2015) Multilingual education in South Asia. In W.E. Wright, S. Boun and O. García (eds) *Handbook of bilingual and multlingual education* (pp. 542–553). Malden, MA: Wiley-Blackwell.

Paradis, J., Crago, M., Genesee, F. and Rice, M. (2003) French-English bilingual children with SLI: How do they compare with their monolingual peers? *Journal of Speech, Language, and Hearing Research, 46*(1), 113–127.

Paradis, M. (2004) *A neurolinguistic theory of bilingualism* (Vol. 18). Amsterdam, The Netherlands: John Benjamins Publishing.

Parrish, T.B., Linquanti, R., Merickel, A., Quick, H.E. and Esra, P. (2002) *Effects of the implementation of Proposition 227 on the education of English learners, K-12: Year 2 report.* Palo Alto, CA: American Institutes for Research, and San Francisco: WestEd.

Patten, A. and Kymlicka, W. (2003) Introduction: Language rights and political theory: Context, issues, and approaches. In A. Kymlicka and A. Patten (eds) *Language rights and political theory* (pp. 1–51). New York, NY: Oxford University Press.

Pavlenko, A. (2000) What's in a concept? *Bilingualism: Language and Cognition, 3*(1), 31–36.

Pavlenko, A. (2001) Bilingualism, gender, and ideology. *International Journal of Bilingualism, 5*(2), 117–151.

Pavlenko, A. (2002) Poststructuralist approaches to the study of social factors in second language learning and use. In V. Cook (ed.) *Portraits of the L2 user.* Clevedon, UK: Multilingual Matters.

Pavlenko, A. (2003a) 'I never knew I was a bilingual': Reimagining teacher identities in TESOL. *Journal of Language, Identity, and Education, 2*(4), 251–268.

Pavlenko, A. (2003b) The making of an American: Negotiation of identities at the turn of the twentieth century. In A. Pavlenko and A. Blackledge (eds) *Negotiation of identities in multilingual contexts.* Clevedon, UK: Multilingual Matters.

Pavlenko, A. (2004) 'Stop Doing That, Ia Komu Skazala!': Language Choice and Emotions in Parent–Child Communication. *Journal of Multilingual and Multicultural Development, 25*(2–3), 179–203.

Pavlenko, A. (2005) Bilingualism and thought. In J. F. Kroll and A. De Groot (eds) *Handbook of bilingualism: Psycholinguistic approaches.* Oxford, UK: Oxford University Press.

Pavlenko, A. (2011) *Thinking and speaking in two languages.* Bristol, UK: Multilingual Matters.

Pavlenko, A. (2014) *The bilingual mind and what it tells us about language and thought.* Cambridge, UK: Cambridge University Press.

Pavlenko, A. and Driagina, V. (2007) Russian emotion vocabulary in American learners' narratives. *The Modern Language Journal, 91*(2), 213–234.

Pavlenko, A. and Lantolf, J.P. (2000) Second language learning as participation and the (re)construction of selves. In J.P. Lantolf (ed.) *Sociocultural theory and second language learning*. Oxford, UK: Oxford University Press.

Pavlenko, A. and Malt, B.C. (2011) Kitchen Russian: Cross-linguistic differences and first-language object naming by Russian–English bilinguals. *Bilingualism: Language and Cognition, 14*, 19–45.

Peal, E. and Lambert, W.E. (1962) The relation of bilingualism to intelligence. *Psychological Monographs: General and Applied, 76*(27), 1–23.

Peer, L. and Reid, G. (eds) (2016) *Multilingualism, literacy and dyslexia: Breaking down barriers for education* (2nd ed.). London, UK: Routledge.

Peltz, R. and Kliger, H. (2013) Becoming Yiddish speakers in New York: Burgeoning communities of bilingual children. In O. García, Z. Zakharia and B. Otcu (eds) *Bilingual and community multilingualism: Beyond heritage languages in a global city* (pp. 190–203). Bristol, UK: Multilingual Matters.

Peng, G. and Wang, W.S.Y. (2011) Hemisphere lateralization is influenced by bilingual status and composition of words. *Neuropsychologia, 49*(7), 1981–1986.

Pennycook, A. (2013) *The cultural politics of English as an international language*. New York, NY: Routledge.

Perryman-Clark, S., Kirkland, D.E. and Jackson, A. (eds) (2014) *Students' rights to their own language: A critical sourcebook*. New York, NY: Bedford/St. Martin's.

Peyton, J.K., Ranard, D.A. and McGinnis, S. (2001) Charting a new course: Heritage language education in the United States. In J.K. Peyton, D.A. Ranard and S. McGinnis (eds) *Heritage languages in America: Blueprint for the future* (pp. 3–28). Washington, DC and McHenry, IL: Center for Applied Linguistics and Delta Systems.

Pfau, R., Steinbach, M. and Woll, B. (eds) (2012) *Sign language: An international handbook*. Berlin, Germany: de Gruyter.

Phillipson, R. and Skutnabb-Kangas, T. (2013) Linguistic imperialism and endangered languages. In T.K. Bhatia and W.C. Ritchie (eds) *Handbook of bilingualism and multilingualism* (pp. 495–516). Malden, MA: Blackwell Publishing.

Piller, I. (2001) Private language planning: The best of both worlds. *Estudios de Sociolingüística, 2*(1), 61–80.

Piller, I. (2002) *Bilingual couples talk: The discursive construction of hybridity* (Vol. 25). Amsterdam, NL: John Benjamins Publishing.

Pimienta, D., Prado, D. and Blanco, Á. (2009) *Twelve years of measuring linguistic diversity in the Internet: Balance and perspectives*. Retrieved from Paris, France: http://unesdoc.unesco.org/images/0018/001870/187016e.pdf

Pintner, R. and Arsenian, S. (1937) The relation of bilingualism to verbal intelligence and school adjustment. *The Journal of Educational Research, 31*(4), 255–263.

Pons, F., Bosch, L. and Lewkowicz, D.J. (2015) Bilingualism modulates infants' selective attention to the mouth of a talking face. *Psychological Science, 26*(4), 490–498.

Poplack, S. and Meechan, M. (1998) Introduction: How languages fit together in codeswitching. *International Journal of Bilingualism, 2*(2), 127–138.

Porras, D.A., Ee, J. and Gándara, P.C. (2014) Employer preferences: Do bilingual applicants and employees experience an advantage? In R. Callahan and P. Gándara (eds) *The bilingual advantage: Language, literacy and the US labor market* (pp. 234–260). Bristol, UK: Multilingual Matters.

Portes, A. and Rumbaut, R.G. (2006) *Immigrant America: A portrait* (3rd ed.). Berkeley, CA: University of California Press.

Potowski, K. (2007) *Language and identity in a dual immersion school*. Clevedon, UK: Multilingual Matters.

Potowski, K. and Rothman, J. (eds) (2011) *Bilingual youth: Spanish in English-speaking societies*. Amsterdam, The Netherlands: John Benjamins.

Proctor, P. (2003) *Degree of bilingualism and English reading achievement*. Paper presented at the Fourth Symposium on Bilingualism, Arizona State University.

Pu, C. (2008) *Learning Your heritage language while learning English: Chinese American children's bilingual and biliteracy development in heritage language and public schools*. (Doctoral Dissertation), University of Texas, San Antonio, San Antonio.

Purpura, J. E. (2017) Assessing communicative language ability: Models and their components. In S. May (ed.) *Encyclopedia of language and education* (3rd ed., Vol. 7: Language testing and assessment). New York, NY: Springer.

Quay, S. (2001) Managing linguistic boundaries in early trilingual development. In J. Cenoz and F. Genesee (eds) *Trends in bilingual acquisition*. Amsterdam, NL: John Benjamins.

Quay, S. (2011) Introduction: data-driven insights from trilingual children in the making. *International Journal of Multilingualism, 8*(1), 1–4.

Quezada, M.S., Wiley, T.G. and Ramirez, D.J. (1999/2000) How the reform agenda shortchanges English learners. *Educational Leadership, 57*(4), 57–61.

Rahman, T. (2005) The Muslim response to English in South Asia: With special reference to inequality, intolerance, and militancy in Pakistan. *Journal of Language, Identity, and Education, 4*(2), 119–135.

Raijman, R. (2012) Linguistic assimilation of first-generation Jewish South African immigrants in Israel. *Journal of International Migration and Integration, 14*(4), 615–636.

Ramanathan, V. (ed.) (2013) *Language policies and (dis)citizenship*. Bristol, UK: Multilingual Matters.

Ramirez, D.J., Wiley, T.G., de Klerk, G., Lee, E. and Wright, W.E. (2005) *Ebonics: The urban education debate* (2nd ed.) Clevedon, UK: Multilingual Matters.

Ramirez, J.D. (1992) Executive summary. *Bilingual Research Journal, 16*, 1–62.

Ramirez, J.D., Yuen, S.D., Ramey, D.R., Pasta, D.J. and Billings, D.K. (1991) *Final report: Longitudinal study of structured English immersion strategy, early exit and late-exit bilingual education programs for language minority children. Vol. 1 (Publication no. 300–87-0156)*. Washington, DC: US Department of Education.

Ramirez, P.C. (2013) An interview with Alma Flor Ada. *Journal of Latinos and Education, 12*(2), 121–130. doi: DOI: 10.1080/15348431.2012.745406

Rampton, B. (2014) *Crossing: Language and ethnicity among adolescents* (2nd ed.). New York, NY: Routledge.

Rampton, B. and Charalambous, C. (2012) Crossing. In M. Martin-Jones, A. Blackledge and A. Creese (eds) *Routledge handbook of multilingualism* (pp. 482–498). London, UK: Routledge.

RAND Education and American Councils for International Education and Portland Public Schools. (2015) Study of dual-language immersion in the Portland Public Schools: Year 4 briefing. Retrieved from http://res.cloudinary.com/bdy4ger4/image/upload/v1446848442/DLI_Year_4_Summary_Nov2015v3_1_jwny3e.pdf

Reagan, T. (2015) Bilingual deaf education. In W.E. Wright, S. Boun and O. García (eds) *The handbook of bilingual and multilingual education* (pp. 391–408). Malden, MA: Wiley-Blackwell.

Rebuffot, J. (1993) *Le Point sur L'immersion au Canada (The Argument for... Immersion in Canada)*. Anjou, Québec: Centre éducatif et Culturel.

Reyes, A. (2011) *Language, identity, and stereotype among Southeast Asian American youth*. New York, NY: Routledge.

Reyhner, J.A. and Eder, J.M.O. (2004) *American Indian education: A history*. Norman, OK: University of Oklahoma Press.

Ricciardelli, L.A. (1992) Creativity and bilingualism. *The Journal of Creative Behavior, 26*(4), 242–254.

Ricento, T. (2009) Problems with the 'language-as-resource' discourse in the promotion of heritage languages in the US. In M.R. Salaberry (ed.) *Language allegiances and bilingualism in the US*. Bristol, UK: Multilingual Matters.

Ricento, T. (2015) Bi/Multilingual education in Canada. In W.E. Wright, S. Boun and O. García (eds) *Handbook of bilingual and multilingual education* (pp. 461–472). Malden, MA: Wiley-Blackwell.

Richards, J.C. and Rodgers, T.S. (2014) *Approaches and methods in language teaching* (3rd ed.). Cambridge, UK: Cambridge University Press.

Rivera, C. (1984) *Language proficiency and academic achievement*. Clevedon, UK: Multilingual Matters.

Rivera, C. and Collum, E. (eds) (2006) *State assessment policy and practice for English language learners*. Mahwah, NJ: Lawrence Erlbaum Associates.

Roberts, C. (2010) Language socialization in the workplace. *Annual Review of Applied Linguistics, 30*, 211–227.

Rodriguez-Fornells, A., Van Der Lugt, A., Rotte, M., Britti, B., Heinze, H.-J. and Münte, T. F. (2005) Second language interferes with word production in fluent bilinguals: brain potential and functional imaging evidence. *Journal of Cognitive Neuroscience, 17*(3), 422–433.

Rogers, C.L., Lister, J.J., Febo, D.M., Besing, J.M. and Abrams, H.B. (2006) Effects of bilingualism, noise, and reverberation on speech perception by listeners with normal hearing. *Applied Psycholinguistics, 27*(03), 465–485.

Rolstad, K., Mahoney, K. and Glass, G. (2005a) The big picture: A meta-analysis of program effectiveness research on English language learners. *Educational Policy, 19*(4), 572–594.

Rolstad, K., Mahoney, K. and Glass, G. (2005b) Weighing the evidence: A meta-analysis of bilingual education in Arizona. *Bilingual Research Journal, 29*(1), 43–67.

Romaine, S. (2000) *Language in society: An introduction to sociolinguistics* (2nd ed.). Oxford, UK: Oxford University Press.

Romaine, S. (2013) The bilingual and multlingual community. In T.K. Bhatia and W.C. Ritchie (eds) *Handbook of bilingualism and multiliniugalism* (pp. 445–465). Malden, MA: Blackwell Publishing.

Ronjat, J. and Escudé, P. (1913) *Le développement du langage observé chez un enfant bilingue*. Paris, FR: Champion.

Rosenthal, R. (2009) Interpersonal expectations: Effects of the experimenter's hypothesis. In R. Rosenthal and R.L. Rosnow (eds) *Artifacts in behavioral research* (pp. 138–210). Oxford, UK: Oxford University Press.

Rossell, C.H. (1992) Nothing Matters?: A Critique of the Ramírez, *et al.* Longitudinal Study of Instructional Programs for Language-Minority Children. *Bilingual Research Journal, 16*(1–2), 159–186.

Rossell, C.H. and Baker, K.A. (1996) The educational effectiveness of bilingual education. *Research in the Teaching of English, 30*(1), 7–74.

Rubinyi, S. (2006) *Natural genius: The gifts of Asperger's Syndrome*. Philadelphia, PA: Jessica Kingsley Publishers.

Ruiz, R. (1984) Orientations in language planning. *NABE Journal, 8*(2), 15–34.

Ruiz, R. (2010) Reorienting language-as-resource. In J.E. Petrovic (ed.) *International perspectives on bilingual education: Policy, practice, and controversy* (pp. 155–172). Charlotte, NC: Information Age Publishing.

Rumbaut, R.G. (2009) A language graveyard? The evolution of language competencies, preferences and use among young adult children of immigrants. In T.G. Wiley, J.S. Lee and R.W. Rumberger (eds) *The education of language minority immigrants in the United States* (pp. 35–71). Bristol, UK: Multilingual Matters.

Rumberger, R. W., Callahan, R. and Gándara, P.C. (2003) Has Proposition 227 Reduced the English Learner Achievement Gap? *UC LMRI Newsletter, 13*(1), 1–2.

Ryan, C. (2013) Language use in the United States: 2011 (American Community Survey Reports). Retrieved from http://www.census.gov/prod/2013pubs/acs-22.pdf

Saer, D.J. (1923) The effect of bilingualism on intelligence. *British Journal of Psychology. General Section, 14*(1), 25–38.

Saer, D.J. (1924) *Bilingual problem*. Wrexham, UK: Hughes and Son.

Salaberry, M.R. (2009a) Bilingual education: Assimilation, segregation and integration. In M.R. Salaberry (ed.) *Language Allegiances and Bilingualism in the US*. Bristol, UK: Multilingual Matters.

Salaberry, M.R. (2009b) Language allegiances. In M.R. Salaberry (ed.) *Language allegiances and bilingualism in the US*. Bristol, UK: Multilingual Matters.

Sallabank, J. (2013) *Engandered languages: Attitudes, identities and policies*. Cambridge, UK: Cambridge University Press.

San Miguel, G. (2004) *Contested policy: The rise and fall of federal bilingual education in the United States, 1960–2001*. Denton, TX: University of North Texas Press.

Sanchez, S.V., Rodriguez, B. J., Soto-Huerta, M.E., Villarreal, F.C., Guerra, N.S. and Flores, B.B. (2013) A case for multidimensional bilingual assessment. *Language Assessment Quarterly, 10*(2), 160–177.

Santamaría, L.J., Fletcher, T.V. and Bos, C.S. (2002) Effective pedagogy for English language learners in inclusive classrooms. In A. Artiles and A.A. Ortiz (eds) *English language learners with special educational needs*. Washington, DC and McHenry, IL: Center for Applied Linguistics and Delta Systems Co.

Savignon, S.J. (2001) Communicative language teaching for the Twenty-First Century. In M. Celce-Murcia (ed.) *Teaching English as a second or foreign language* (3rd ed., pp. 13–28). Boston, MA: Heinle and Heinle.

Sayer, P. (2012) *Ambiguities and tensions in English language teaching: Portraits of EFL teachers as legitimate speakers*. New York, NY: Routledge.

Sayer, P. (2013) Translanguaging, TexMex, and bilingual pedagogy: Emergent bilinguals learning through the vernacular. *TESOL Quarterly, 47*(1), 63–88.

Scanlan, M. and López, F.A. (2015) *Leadership for culturally and linguistically responsive schools*. New York, NY: Routledge.

Scheetz, N.A. (2012) *Deaf education in the 21st Century: Topics and trends*. Boston, MA: Pearson.

Schmidt, R.S. (2009) English hegemony and the politics of ethno-linguistic justice in the US. In M.R. Salaberry (ed.) *Language allegiances and bilingualism in the United States*. Bristol, UK: Multilingual Matters.

Schmidt, R.S. (2000) *Language policy and identity politics in the United States*. Philadelphia, PA: Temple University Press.

Schroeder, S.R. and Marian, V. (2012) A bilingual advantage for episodic memory in older adults. *Journal of Cognitive Psychology, 24*(5), 591–601.

Schwartz, M. and Verschik, A. (eds) (2013) *Successful family language policy: Parents, children and educators in interaction*. Dordrecht, Netherlands: Springer.

Scott, J.C., Straker, D.Y. and Katz, L. (eds) (2008) *Affirming students' right to their own language: Bridging language policies and pedagogical practices*. New York, NY: Routledge.

Sebastián-Gallés, N., Albareda-Castellot, B., Weikum, W.M. and Werker, J.F. (2012) A bilingual advantage in visual language discrimination in infancy. *Psychological Science, 23*(9), 994–999.

Serratrice, L. (2013) The bilingual child. In T.K. Bhatia and W.C. Ritchie (eds) *The handbook of bilingualism and multilingualism* (2nd ed., pp. 87–108). Malden, MA: Wiley-Blackwell.

Shao, K., Yu, W. and Ji, Z. (2013) An exploration of Chinese EFL students' emotional intelligence and foreign language anxiety. *The Modern Language Journal, 97*(4), 917–929. doi:10.1111/j.1540–4781.2013.12042.x

Shohamy, E. (2006) *Language policy: Hidden agendas and new approaches*. London, UK: Routledge.

Shohamy, E. (2008) At what cost? Methods of language revival and protection. In K.A. King, L. Schilling-Estes, L. Fogle, J.J. Lou and B. Soukup (eds) *Sustaining linguistic diversity* (pp. 205–218). Washington, DC: Georgetown University Press.

Shohamy, E. (2011) Assessing multilingual competencies: Adopting construct valid assessment policies. *The Modern Language Journal, 9*(3), 418–429.

Shohamy, E. and Menken, K. (2015) Language assessment: Past to present misuses and future possibilities. In W.E. Wright, S. Boun and O. García (eds) *Handbook of bilingual and multilingual education* (pp. 253–269). Malden, MA: John Wiley and Sons.

Short, D. and Boyson, B. (2012) *Helping newcomer students succeed in secondary schools and beyond*. Washington, DC: Center for Applied Linguistics.

Silver, R.E. and Bokhorst-Heng, W.D. (eds) (2016) *Quadrilingual education in Singapore: Pedagogical innovation in language education*. New York, NY: Springer.

Simonton, D.K. (2008) Bilingualism and creativity. In J. Altarriba and R.R. Heredia (eds) *An introduction to bilingualism: Principles and processes* (pp. 147–166). Mahwah, NJ: Erlbaum.

Singleton, D.M. and Muñoz, C. (2011) Around and beyond the critical period hypothesis. In E. Hinkel (ed.) *Handbook of research in second language teaching and learning* (Vol. II, pp. 407–425). New York, NY: Routledge.

Singleton, D.M. and Ryan, L. (2004) *Language acquisition: The age factor* (Vol. 9). Clevedon, UK: Multilingual Matters.

Sissons, C.B. (1917) *Bi-lingual schools in Canada*. London, UK: JM Dent.

Skorton, D. and Altschuler, G. (2012) American's foreign language deficit. *Forbes*. Retrieved from http://www.forbes.com/sites/collegeprose/2012/08/27/americas-foreign-language-deficit/#3ca3d41b382f

Skutnabb-Kangas, T. (1981) *Bilingualism or not: The education of minorities*. Philadelphia, PA: Multilingual Matters.

Skutnabb-Kangas, T. (2000) *Linguistic Genocide in Education – Or Worldwide Diversity and Human Rights?* Mahwah, NJ: Lawrence Erlbaum Associates.

Skutnabb-Kangas, T. (2015) Language rights. In W.E. Wright, S. Boun and O. Garcia (eds) *Handbook of bilingual and multilingual education* (pp. 186–202). Malden, MA: Wiley-Blackwell.

Skutnabb-Kangas, T. and Heugh, K. (eds) (2013) *Multilingual education and sustainable diversity work: From periphery to center*. New York, NY: Routledge.

Slavin, R.E. and Cheung, A. (2005) A synthesis of research on language of reading instruction for English-language learners. *Review of Educational Research, 75*(2), 247–284.

Spolsky, B. (1989) Review of 'Key Issues in Bilingualism and Bilingual Education'. *Applied Linguistics, 10*(4), 449–451.

Spolsky, B. (2004) *Language policy*. New York, NY: Cambridge.

Spring, J. (2013) *Deculturalization and the struggle for equality: A brief history of the education of dominated cultures in the United States* (7th ed.). New York, NY: McGraw Hill.

Stangor, C., Lynch, L., Duan, C. and Glas, B. (1992) Categorization of individuals on the basis of multiple social features. *Journal of Personality and Social Psychology, 62*(2), 207.

Statistics Canada (2013) Study: The evolution of English-French bilingualism in Canada from 1961 to 2011. *The Daily*. Retrieved from http://www.statcan.gc.ca/daily-quotidien/130528/dq130528b-eng.htm

Statistics Canada (2015) Elementary–Secondary Education Survey for Canada, the provinces and territories, 2013/2014. *The Daily*. Retrieved from http://www.statcan.gc.ca/daily-quotidien/151119/dq151119d-eng.htm

Stavans, I. (2003) *Spanglish: The making of a new American language*. New York, NY: HarperCollins.

Stavans, I. (2014) In defense of Spanglish. *The Common Reader: A Journal of the Essay* (1 October). Retrieved from https://commonreader.wustl.edu/c/cervantes-spanglish/

Stepanova Sachs, O. and Coley, J. (2006) Envy and jealousy in Russian and English: Labeling and conceptualization of emotions by monolinguals and bilinguals. In A. Pavlenko (ed.) *Bilingual minds: Emotional experience, expression and representation*. Bristol, UK: Multilingual Matters.

Sternberg, R.J. (ed.) (2002) *Why smart people can be so stupid*. New Haven, CT: Yale University Press.

Street, B.V. (2002) Understanding literacy issues in contemporary multiethnic schooling contexts, with particular reference to EAL pupils. In C. Leung (ed.) *Language and additional/second language issues for school education*. York, UK: NADLIC.

Street, B.V. (2013) *Social literacies: Critical approaches to literacy in development, ethnography and education*. New York, NY: Routledge.

Street, B.V. (2017) New literacies, new times: Developments in literacy studies. In S. May (ed.) *Encyclopedia of language and education* (3rd ed., Vol. 2: Literacy). New York, NY: Springer.

Strubell, M. (2001) Catalan a decade later. In J. Fishman (ed.) *Can threatened languages be saved?* (pp. 260–283). Clevedon, UK: Multilingual Matters.

Sullivan, A.L. (2011) Disproportionality in special education identification and placement of English language learners. *Exceptional Children, 77*(3), 317–334.

Sullivan, A.L. and Bal, A. (2013) Disproportionality in special education: Effects of individual and school variables on disabillity risks. *Exceptional Children, 79*(4), 475–494.

Swain, M. (1997) French immersion programs in Canada. In J. Cummins and D. Corson (eds) *Encyclopedia of language and education* (Vol. Volume 5: Bilingual education). Dordrecht, The Netherlands: Kluwer.

Swain, M. (2000) The output hyptothesis and beyond: Mediating acquisition through collaborative dialogue. In J. P. Lantolf (ed.) *Sociocultural theory and second language learning*. Oxford, UK: Oxford University Press.

Swain, M. and Johnson, R.K. (1997) Immersion education: A category within bilingual education. In R. K. Johnson and M. Swain (eds) *Immersion education: International perspectives*. Cambridge, UK: Cambridge University Press.

Swain, M., Kinnear, P. and Steinman, L. (2015) *Sociocultural theory in second language education: An introduction through narratives* (2nd ed.). Bristol, UK: Multilingual Matters.

Swain, M. and Lapkin, S. (1982) *Evaluating bilingual education: A Canadian case study*. Clevedon, UK: Multilingual Matters.

Swain, M. and Lapkin, S. (1991) Additive bilingualism and French immersion education: The roles of language proficiency and literacy. In A.G. Reynolds (ed.) *Bilingualism, multiculturalism and second language learning*. Hillsdale, NJ: Lawrence Erlbaum.

Swain, M. and Lapkin, S. (2005) The evolving sociopolitical context of immersion education in Canada: some implications for program development1. *International Journal of Applied Linguistics, 15*(2), 169–186.

Swain, M. and Lapkin, S. (2008) Oh, I get it now! From production to comprehension in second language learning. In D. Brinton, O. Kagan and S. Bauckus (eds) *Heritage language education: A New field emerging* (pp. 301–320). New York, NY: Routledge.

Swanwick, R. (2010) Policy and practice in sign bilingual education: development, challenges and directions. *International Journal of Bilingual Education and Bilingualism, 13*(2), 147–158.

Swanwick, R. (2015) Scaffolding learning through classroom talk: The role of translanguaging. In P. Spencer and M. Marschark (eds) *The Oxford handbook of deaf studies: Language and language development*. New York, NY: Oxford University Press.

Swanwick, R. (2016) Deaf children's bimodal bilingualism and education. *Language Teaching, 49*, 1–34.

Swanwick, R. (2017) *Languages and languaging in deaf education*. New York, NY: Oxford University Press.

Swanwick, R., Dammeyer, J., Hendar, O., Kristoffersen, A., Salter, J. and Simonsen, E. (2014) Shifting contexts and practices in sign bilingual education in Northern Europe. In M. Marschark, H. Knoors and G. Tang (eds) *Bilingualism and bilingual deaf education* (pp. 465–494). New York, NY: Oxford University Press.

Tankersley, D. (2001) Bombs or bilingual programmes?: dual-language immersion, transformative education and community building in Macedonia. *International Journal of Bilingual Education and Bilingualism, 4*(2), 107–124.

Tannenbaum, M. and Howie, P. (2002) The association between language maintenance and family relations: Chinese immigrant children in Australia. *Journal of Multilingual and Multicultural Development, 23*(5), 408–424.

Taura, H. and Taura, A. (2012) Linguistic and narrative development in a Japanese–English bilingual's first language acquisition: A 14-year longitudinal case study. *International Journal of Bilingual Education and Bilingualism, 15*(4), 475–508.

Teachers of English to Speakers of Other Languages (TESOL) (2006) *PreK–12 English language proficiency standards*. Alexandria, VA: Author.

Tedick, D.J. (2014) Language immeresion education: A research agenda for 2015 and beyond [Special Issue]. *Journal of Immersion and Content-Based Language Education, 2*(2).

Tedick, D.J., Christian, D. and Fortune, T.W. (2011) *Immersion education: Activities, policies, possibilities*. Bristol, UK: Multilingual Matters.

Téllez, K. and Varghese, M. (2013) Teachers as intellectuals and advocates: Professional development for bilingual education teachers. *Theory into Practice, 52*(2), 128–135. doi:10.1080/00405841.2013.770330

The Hollywood Reporter (2015) Donald Trump: 'While we're in this nation, we should be speaking English'. Retrieved from http://www.hollywoodreporter.com/news/donald-trump-speak-english-spanish-820215

The Leadership Conference Education Fund. (2014) *Race and ethnicity in the 2020 Census: Improving data to capture a multiethnic America* Retrieved from Washington, DC: http://civilrightsdocs.info/pdf/reports/Census-Report-2014-WEB.pdf

Thiong'o, N.W. (2005) The language of African literature. In G. Desai and S. Nair (eds) *Postcolonialisms: An Anthology of cultural theory and criticism* (pp. 132–142). New Brunswick, NJ: Rutgers, The State University.

Thomas, W.P. (1992) An analysis of the research methodology of the Ramirez study. *Bilingual Research Journal, 16*(1–2), 213–246.

Thomas, W.P. and Collier, V.P. (2012) *Dual language education for a transformed world*. Albuquerque, NM: Dual Langauge Education of New Mexico – Fuente Press.

Thomas, W.P. and Collier, V.P. (1995) *Language minority student achievement and program effectiveness. Research summary* (Vol. 17). Fairfax, VA: George Mason University.

Thomas, W.P. and Collier, V.P. (1997) School effectiveness for language minority students. *National Clearinghouse on Bilingual Education (NCBE) Resource Collection Series, 9*, 1–96.

Thomas, W.P. and Collier, V.P. (2002a) Accelerated schooling for all students: Research findings on education in multilingual communities. In P. Shaw (ed.) *Intercultural education in European classrooms: Intercultural education partnership*. Stoke-on-Trent, UK: Trentham.

Thomas, W.P. and Collier, V.P. (2002b) *A national study of school effectiveness for language minority students' long term academic achievement*. Santa Cruz, CA: Center for Research on Education, Diversity, and Excellence.

Thomas, W.P., Collier, V.P. and Abbott, M. (1993) Academic achievement through Japanese, Spanish, or French: The first two years of partial immersion. *The Modern Language Journal, 77*(2), 170–179.

Thomason, S. G. (2015) *Endangered languages: An introduction*. Cambridge, UK: Cambridge University Press.

Thompson, M., DiCerbo, K., Mahoney, K. and MacSwan, J. (2002) Exito en California? A validity critique of language program evaluations and analysis of English learner test scores. *Education Policy Analysis Archives, 10*(7), Retrieved from http://epaa.asu.edu/ojs/article/view/286.

Tollefson, J.W. and Tsui, A.B.M. (2014) Language diversity and and language policy in educational access and equity. *Review of Research in Education, 38*(1), 189–214. doi:10.3102/0091732X13506846

Tomozawa, A. and Majima, J. (2015) Bilingual education in Japan: Slow but steady progress. In W. E. Wright, S. Boun and O. García (eds) *Handbook of bilingual and multilingual education* (pp. 493–503). Malden, MA: John Wiley and Sons.

Toribio, A.J. (2004) Spanish/English speech practices: Bringing chaos to order. *International Journal of Bilingual Education and Bilingualism, 7*(2–3), 133–154.

Torrance, E.P. (1974) *Torrance Tests of creative thinking. Directions manual and scoring guide*. Lexington, MA: Ginn.

Toukomaa, P. and Skutnabb-Kangas, T. (1977) *The intensive teaching of the mother tongue to migrant children at pre-school age. Research report No. 26*. Department of Sociology and Social Psychology, University of Tampere.

Troike, R. C. (1978) Research evidence for the effectiveness of bilingual education. *NABE Journal, 3*(1), 13–24.

Tucker, G.R. and d'Anglejan, A. (1972) *An approach to bilingual education: The St Lambert experiment*. Paper presented at the Bilingual Schooling: Some Experiences in Canada and the United States. Ontario, Canada: Ontario Institute for Studies in Education Symposium Series.

Tupas, R. (2015) *Unequal Englishes: The politics of English today*. New York, NY: Palgrave Macmillan.

Tupas, R. and Rani, R. (2015) Introduction: From world Englishes to unequal Englishes. In R. Tupas (ed.) *Unequal Englishes: The politics of English today*. New York, NY: Palgrave Macmillan.

US Census Bureau (2015a) *American Community Survey (ACS) – Why we ask: Languages spoken at home*. Retrieved from Washington, DC: http://www2.census.gov/programs-surveys/acs/about/qbyqfact/Language.pdf

US Census Bureau (2015b) *How the American Community Survey works for your community (infographic)*. Retrieved from Washington, DC: http://www.census.gov/content/dam/Census/library/infographics/how_acs_works.pdf

US Department of Education (2012) *ESEA Flexibility*. Retrieved from Washington, DC: http://www.ed.gov/esea/flexibility/documents/esea-flexibility-acc.doc

Umansky, I.M. and Reardon, S.F. (2014) Reclassification patterns among Latino English learner students in bilingual, dual immersion, and English immersion classrooms. *American Educational Research Journal, 51*(5), 879–912. doi:10.3102/0002831214545110

Umansky, I.M., Valentino, R.A. and Reardon, S.F. (2016) The promise of two-language education. *Educational Leadership, 73*(5), 10–17.

UNESCO (1953) *The use of vernacular languages in education*. Paris, FR: UNESCO.

UNESCO (1994) *The Salamanca statement and framework for action on special needs education*. Paris, FR: UNESCO.

UNESCO (2007) *Advocacy kit for promoting multilingual education: Including the excluded*. Bangkok, Thailand: UNESCO Asia and Pacific Region Bureau for Education

UNESCO (2016) *If you don't understand, how can you learn? Global Education Monitoring Report (Policy Paper 24)*. Paris, France: Author.

UNICEF (2012) Child friendly schools. Retrieved from http://www.unicef.org/lifeskills/index_7260.html

United States Department of Education (1992). *The condition of bilingual education in the nation: A Report to the Congress and the President*. Washington, DC: Department of Education.

Vaid, J. (2002) Bilingualism. In V.S. Ramachandran (ed.) *Encyclopedia of the human brain*. San Diego, CA: Academic Press.

Vaish, V. (2007) Bilingualism without diglossia: The Indian community in Singapore. *International Journal of Bilingual Education and Bilingualism, 10*(2), 171–187.

Vaish, V. (2008) *Biliteracy and globalization: English language education in India*. Clevedon, UK: Multilingual Matters.

Valdés, G. (1997) Dual-language immersion programs: A cautionary note concerning the education of language-minority students. *Harvard Educational Review, 67*(3), 391–429.

Valdés, G. (2001) *Learning and not learning English: Latino students in American schools*. New York, NY: Teachers College Press.

Valdés, G. (2003) *Expanding definitions of giftedness: The case of young interpreters from immigrant communities*. Mahwah, NJ: Lawrence Erlbaum.

Valdés, G. (2004) Between support and marginalisation: The development of academic language in linguistic minority children. *International Journal of Bilingual Education and Bilingualism, 7*(2–3), 102–132.

Valdés, G. (2006) *Developing minority language resources: The case of Spanish in California* (Vol. 58): Multilingual Matters.

Valdés, G. (2014) Heritage language students: Profiles and possibilities. In T.G. Wiley, J.K. Peyton, D. Christian, S.K.C. Moore and N. Liu (eds) *Handbook of heritage and community languages in the United States: Research, educational practice, and policy* (pp. 19–26). Washington, DC and New York, NY: Center for Applied Linguistics and Routledge.

Valdés, G. (2015) What if bilingualism/multilingualism? In G. Valdés, K. Menken and M. Castro (eds) *Common Core bilingual and English language learners: A resource for educators* (pp. 38–39). Philadelphia, PA: Caslon Publishing.

Valdés, G. and Figueroa, R.A. (1994) *Bilingualism and testing: A special case of bias*. Norwood, NJ: Ablex Publishing Corporation.

Valdés, G., Fishman, J.A., Chavez, R.M. and Perez, W. (2006) *Towards the development of minority language resources: Lessons from the case of California*. Clevedon, UK: Multilingual Matters.

Valdés, G., Poza, L. and Brooks, M.D. (2015) Language acquisition in bilingual education. In W.E. Wright, S. Boun and O. García (eds) *Handbook of bilingual and multilingual education* (pp. 56–74). Malden, MA: Wiley-Blackwell.

Valdiviezo, L.A. and Nieto, S. (2015) Culture in bilingual and multilingual education: Conflict, struggle, and power. In W.E. Wright, S. Boun and O. Garcia (eds) *Handbook of Bilingual and Multilingual Education* (pp. 92–108). Malden, MA: Wiley-Blackwell.

Valian, V. (2015) Bilingualism and cognition. *Bilingualism: Language and Cognition, 18*, 3–24.

van der Walt, C. (2013) *Multilingual higher education: Beyond English medium orientations*. Bristol, UK: Multilingual Matters.

van der Walt, C. (2015) Bi/multilingual higher education: Perspectives and practices. In W.E. Wright, S. Boun and O. García (eds) *Handbook of bilingual and multilingual education* (pp. 353–369). Malden, MA: Wiley-Blackwell.

Vandenbussche, W., Jahr, E.H. and Trudgill, P. (eds) (2014) *Language ecology for the 21st Century: Linguistic conflicts and social environments*. Oslo, Norway: Novus Press.

Vertovec, S. (2007) Super-diversity and its implications. *Ethnic and Racial Studies, 30*(6), 1024–1054.

Vidano, G. and Sahafi, M. (2004) *Parent Institute for Quality Education: Organizational special report on PIQE's performance evaluation*. San Diego, CA: San Diego State University, College of Business Adimstration, Marketing Department.

Vygotsky, L. S. (1986) *Thought and language* (A. Kozulin, Trans. Revised ed.). Cambridge, MA: MIT Press.

Wagner, S.T. (1981) The historical background of bilingualism and biculturalism in the United States. In M. Ridge (ed.) *The new bilingualism* (pp. 29–52). Los Angeles, CA: University of Southern California Press.

Walqui, A. and van Lier, L. (2010) *Scaffolding the academic success of adolescent English language learners: A pedagogy of promise*. San Francisco, CA: WestEd.

Wang, X.-L. (2008) *Growing up with three languages: Birth to eleven* (Vol. 11). Bristol, UK: Multilingual Matters.

Wang, X.-L. (2011) *Learning to read and write in the multilingual family*. Bristol, UK: Multilingual Matters.

Wang, X.-L. (2015) *Maintaining three languages: The teenage years* Bristol, UK: Multilingual Matters.

Wartenburger, I., Heekeren, H. R., Abutalebi, J., Cappa, S.F., Villringer, A. and Perani, D. (2003) Early setting of grammatical processing in the bilingual brain. *Neuron, 37*(1), 159–170.

Weber, J.-J. (2014) *Flexible multilingual education: Putting children's needs first*. Bristol, UK: Multilingual Matters.

Weber, J.-J. and Horner, K. (2012) *Introducing multilingualism: A social approach*. New York, NY: Routledge.

Welsh Language Board (2001) *A guide to bilingual design*. Cardiff, IR: Welsh Language Board.

Whorf, B.L. (1956) *Language, thought and reality*. New York, NY: Wiley.

WIDA Consortium (2012) *2012 amplification of the English language development standards: Kindergarten – grade 12*. Retrieved from Madison, WI: http://www.wida.us/get.aspx?id=540

Wiese, A.-M. and Garcia, E.E. (2001) The bilingual education act: Language minority students and US federal educational policy. *International Journal of Bilingual Education and Bilingualism, 4*(4), 229–248.

Wiley, T.G. (1998) The imposition of World War I era English-only policies and the fate of German in North America. In T. Ricento and B. Burnaby (eds) *Language and politics in the United States and Canada: Myths and realities* (pp. 211–241). Mahwah, NJ: Lawrence Erlbaum Associates, Publishers.

Wiley, T.G. (2005) *Literacy and language diversity in the United States* (2nd ed.). Washington, DC: Center for Applied Linguistics.

Wiley, T.G. (2013a) A brief history and assessment of language rights in the United States. In J.W. Tollefson (ed.) *Language policies in education: Critical issues* (pp. 61–90). London, UK: Routledge, Taylor and Francis.

Wiley, T.G. (2013b) Constructing and deconstructing 'illegal' children. *Journal of Language, Identity and Education, 12*(3), 173–178.

Wiley, T.G. (2014a) Policy considerations for promoting heritage, community, and Native American languages. In T.G. Wiley, J.K. Peyton, D. Christian, S.K.C. Moore and N. Liu (eds) *Handbook of heritage and community languages in the United States: Research, educational practice, and policy* (pp. 45–53). Washington, DC and New York, NY: Center for Applied Linguistics and Routledge.

Wiley, T.G. (2014b) The problems of defining heritage and community languages and their speakers: On the utility and limitations of definitional constructs. In T.G. Wiley, J.K. Peyton, D. Christian, S.K.C. Moore and N. Liu (eds) *Handbook of heritage and community languages in the United States: Research, educational practice, and policy* (pp. 19–26). Washington, DC and New York, NY: Center for Applied Linguistics and Routledge.

Wiley, T.G. (2015) Language policy and planning in education. In W.E. Wright, S. Boun and O. García (eds) *Handbook of bilingual and multilingual education* (pp. 164–184). Malden, MA: Wiley-Blackwell.

Wiley, T.G., Peyton, J.K., Christian, D., Moore, S.K.C. and Liu, N. (eds) (2014) *Handbook of heritage and community languages in the United States: Research, educational practice, and policy*. Washington, DC and New York, NY: Center for Applied Linguistics and Routledge.

Wiley, T.G. and Rolstad, K. (2014) The Common Core State Standards and the great divide. *International Multilingual Research Journal, 8*(1), 38–55. doi:10.1080/19313152.2014.852428

Wiley, T.G. and Wright, W.E. (2004) Against the undertow: The politics of language instruction in the United States. *Educational Policy, 18*(1), 142–168.

Williams, C. (1994) *Arfarniad o Ddulliau Dysgu ac Addysgu yng Nghyd-destun Addysg Uwchradd Ddwyieithog [An evaluation of teaching and learning methods in the context of bilingual secondary education]*. (Unpublished Doctoral Thesis), University of Wales, Bangor.

Williams, C. (1996) Secondary education: Teaching in the bilingual situation. In C.H. Williams, E.G. Lewis and C. Baker (eds) *The language policy: Taking stock* (Vol. 12, pp. 193–211). Llangefni, UK: CAI.

Williams, C.H. (2000) Restoring the language. In G.H. Jenkins and M.A. Williams (eds) *'Let's do our best for the ancient tongue': The Welsh language in the twentieth century* (pp. 657–681). Cardiff, UK: Cardiff University Press.

Williams, C.H. (2007) *Language and governance.* Cardiff, UK: University of Wales Press.

Williams, C.H. (2013) Multilingualism and minority languages. In C.A. Chapelle (ed.) *Encyclopedia of applied linguistics.* Malden, MA: Blackwell Publishing.

Williams, C.H. (2014) The lightening veil: Language revitalization in Wales. *Review of Research in Education, 38*(1), 242–272. doi:10.3102/0091732X13512983

Williams, G. (2010) *The knowledge economy, language and culture.* Bristol, UK: Multilingual Matters.

Williams, I.W. (2003) *Our children's language: The Welsh-medium schools of Wales, 1939–2000.* Talybont, UK: Y Lolfa.

Willig, A.C. (1981) The effectiveness of bilingual education: Review of a report. *NABE Journal, 6*(2–3), 1–19.

Willig, A.C. (1985) A meta-analysis of selected studies on the effectiveness of bilingual education. *Review of Educational Research, 55,* 269–317. doi:10.3102/00346543055003269

Willig, A.C. and Ramirez, D.J. (1993) The evaluation of bilingual education. In B. Arias and U. Casanova (eds) *Bilingual education: Politics, research and practice.* Berkeley, CA: McCutchan.

Wilson, D.M. (2011) Dual language programs on the rise. *Harvard Education Letter, 27*(2), 1–2.

Wilson, W.H. (2014) Hawaiian: A Native American language official for a state. In T.G. Wiley, J.K. Peyton, D. Christian, S.K.C. Moore and N. Liu (eds) *Handbook of heritage and community languages in the United States: Research, educational practice, and policy* (pp. 219–229). Washington, DC and New York, NY: Center for Applied Linguistics and Routledge.

Wink, J. (2010) *Critical pedagogy: Notes from the real world* (4th ed.). New York, NY: Pearson.

Woll, B., Sutton-Spence, R. and Elton, F. (2001) Multilingualism: The global approach to sign languages. In C. Lucas (ed.) *The sociolinguistics of sign languages* (pp. 8–32). Cambridge, UK: Cambridge University Press.

World Bank (1997) *Project Appraisal Document, Guatemala, Basic Education Reform Project.* Washington, DC: World Bank.

Wright, W.E. (2004) What English-only really means: A study of the implementation of California language policy with Cambodian American students. *International Journal of Bilingual Education and Bilingualism, 7*(1), 1–23.

Wright, W.E. (2005a) *Evolution of federal policy and implications of No Child Left Behind for language minority students* (EPSL-0501–101-LPRU). Retrieved from Tempe, AZ: http://files.eric.ed.gov/fulltext/ED508474.pdf

Wright, W.E. (2005b) The political spectacle of Arizona's Proposition 203. *Educational Policy, 19*(5), 662–700. doi:DOI: 10.1177/0895904805278066

Wright, W.E. (2008) Pull-out ESL Instruction. In J.M. Gonzalez (ed.) *Encyclopedia of Bilingual Education* (pp. 704–707). Thousand Oaks, CA: Sage Publications, Inc.

Wright, W.E. (2010) The great divide between federal education policy and our national need for bilingual citizens. Retrieved from http://www.academia.edu/3459981/Wright_W._E._2010_._The_Great_Divide_Between_Federal_Education_Policy_and_Our_National_Need_for_Bilingual_Citizens

Wright, W.E. (2014a) Khmer. In T.G. Wiley, J.K. Peyton, D. Christian, S.K.C. Moore and N. Liu (eds) *Handbook of heritage and community langauges in the United States: Research, educational practice, and policy* (pp. 284–296). Washington DC and New York, NY: Center for Applied Linguistics and Routledge.

Wright, W.E. (2014b) Teaching English language learners in Post-Proposition 203 Arizona: Structured English immersion or sink-or-swim submersion? In G.P. McField (ed.) *The miseducation of English learners: A tale of three states and lessons to be learned* (pp. 151–182). Charlotte, NC: Information Age Publishing.

Wright, W.E. (2015) *Foundations for teaching English language learners: Research, theory, policy and practice* (2nd ed.). Philadelphia, PA: Caslon.

Wright, W.E. and Baker, C. (2017) Key concepts in bilingual education. In O. García and A.M.Y. Lin (eds) *Encyclopedia of language and education, Volume 5: Bilingual education* (3rd ed.). New York, NY: Springer.

Wright, W. E. and Boun, S. (2011) Southeast Asian American education 35 years after initial resettlement: Research report and policy recommendations. Conference Report of the National Association for the Education and Advancement of Cambodian, Laotian, and Vietnamese Americans. *Journal of Southeast Asian American Education and Advancement, 6*, 1–120.

Wright, W.E. and Boun, S. (2015) Striving for education for all through bilingual education in Cambodia. In W.E. Wright, S. Boun and O. Garcia (eds) *Handbook of bilingual and multilingual education* (pp. 517–530). Malden, MA: Wiley-Blackwell.

Wright, W.E. and Boun, S. (2016) The development and expansion of multilingual education in Cambodia: An application of Ruiz's orientations in language planning. *Bilingual Review/Revista Bilingüe, 33*(3), 1–17.

Wright, W.E., Boun, S. and García, O. (eds) (2015) *Handbook of bilingual and multilingual education.* Malden, MA: John Wiley and Sons.

Wright, W.E. and Choi, D. (2006) The impact of language and high-stakes testing policies on elementary school English language learners in Arizona. *Education Policy Analysis Archives [Online], 14*(13), 1–56. Available: http://epaa.asu.edu/ojs/article/view/84.

Wright, W.E. and Pu, C. (2005) *Academic achievement of English language learners in post Proposition 203 Arizona.* Retrieved from Tempe: http://nepc.colorado.edu/publication/academic-achievement-english-language-learners-post-proposition-203-arizona

Wright, W.E. and Ricento, T. (2017) Language policy and education in the United States. In T. L. McCarty (ed.) *Encyclopedia of language and education, Volume 1: Language policy and political Issues in education* (3rd ed.). New York, NY: Springer.

Wu, H.P., Palmer, D.K. and Field, S.L. (2011) Understanding teachers' professional identity and beliefs in the Chinese heritage language school in the USA. *Language, culture and curriculum, 24*(1), 47–60.

Yamamoto, M. (2002) Language use in families with parents of different native languages: An investigation of Japanese-non-English and Japanese-English families. *Journal of Multilingual and Multicultural Development, 23*(6), 531–554.

Yow, W.Q. and Markman, E.M. (2011) Young bilingual children's heightened sensitivity to referential cues. *Journal of Cognition and Development, 12*, 12–31.

Yow, W.Q. and Markman, E.M. (2015) A bilingual advantage in how children integrate multiple cues to understand a speaker's referential intent. *Bilingualism: Language and Cognition, 18*(3), 391–399.

Ytsma, J. (2000) Trilingual primary education in Friesland. In J. Cenoz and U. Jessner (eds) *English in Europe: the acquisition of a third language* (pp. 222–235). Clevedon, UK: Multilingual Matters.

Yukawa, E. (1997) *L1 Japanese attrition and regaining: Three case studies of two early bilingual children.* Stockholm, SE: Centre for Research on Bilingualism, Stockholm University.

Zalbide, M. and Cenoz, J. (2008) Bilingual education in the Basque Autonomous Community: Achievements and challenges. *Language, Culture and Curriculum, 21*(1), 5–20.

Zangwill, I. (1909) *The melting pot: Drama in four acts.* New York, NY: Macmillan.

Zappert, L.T. and Cruz, B.R. (1977) *Bilingual education: An appraisal of empirical research.* Berkeley, CA: Bay Area Bilingual Education League.

Zhou, M. and Logan, J.R. (2003) Increasing diversity and persistent segregation: Challenges of educating minority and immigrant children in urban America. In S.J. Caldas and C.L. Bankston (eds) *The end of desegregation?* (pp. 177–194). Hauppauge, NY: Nova Science Publishers.

Zhu, H. (2014) Piecing together the 'workplace multilingualism 'jigsaw puzzle. *Multilingua, 33*(1–2), 233–242.

Zuckerman, G.A. and Monaghan, P. (2012) Revival linguistics and the new media: Talknology in the service of the Barngarla language reclamation. In T. Ka'ai, M. Ó Laoire, N. Ostler, R. Ka'ai-Mahuta, D. Mahuta and T. Smith (eds) *Language endangerment in the 21st century: Globalisation, technolgy, and new media* (pp. 119–126). Aukland, New Zealand and Bath, England: Te Ipukarea and Printsprint, AUT University and Foundation for Endangered Languages.

Index